CONSUMER GUIDE®

# 1978 CONSUMER BUYING GUIDE

# Contents

**Autos 1978** .................................................................8
*What to buy and how to buy; top models from domestic and foreign manufacturers.*
Auto Best Buys .................................................21
How to Buy an Auto ...........................................25
Auto Prices .......................................................26

**Televisions 1978** ........................................................109
*Selecting a set with the features, performance, and screen size you need.*
Television Best Buys ........................................129
Television Prices .............................................141

**Hi-Fi Components 1978** ..............................................154
*Trends and top choices in all component categories.*
Hi-Fi Component Best Buys ..............................171

**Tape Recorders 1978** .................................................179
*Selecting an appropriate tape format and machine for your recording desires.*
Tape Recorder Best Buys ..................................187

**CB Radios 1978** .........................................................193
*Highlights of the fast-moving equipment scene in radio communication devices.*
CB Radio Best Buys ..........................................195

**Food Preparation Appliances 1978** ............................200
*Factors to look for before buying anything from a can opener to a food processor.*
Food Preparation Appliance Best Buys ...............211
Food Preparation Appliance Prices .....................224

**Floor Care Appliances 1978** .......................................235
*Matching the right vacuum cleaner to the floors and other household cleaning chores.*
Floor Care Appliance Best Buys .........................239
Floor Care Appliance Prices ..............................252

**Refrigerators 1978** ....................................................256
*Evaluating size and style, energy consumption, and features.*
Refrigerator Best Buys ......................................264
Refrigerator Prices ...........................................271

---

All rights reserved under International and Pan American copyright conventions. Copyright© 1978 Publications International, Ltd. This publication may not be reproduced, or quoted in whole or in part by mimeograph or any other printed means, or for presentation on radio or television without written permission from Louis Weber, President of Publications International, Ltd. Permission is never granted for commercial purposes. Printed in USA.

**Freezers 1978** ........................................................................... 277
*Chests vs. uprights; features to look for; size and energy.*
   Freezer Best Buys ............................................................. 281
   Freezer Prices .................................................................... 285

**Washers/Dryers 1978** ............................................................. 288
*Trends in laundry appliances; deciding what you need.*
   Washer/Dryer Best Buys .................................................... 296
   Washer/Dryer Prices .......................................................... 303

**Dishwashers 1978** ................................................................... 308
*Which features to pay for; deciding on style and capacity.*
   Dishwasher Best Buys ....................................................... 312

**Garbage Disposers 1978** ....................................................... 316
*Batch-feed or continuous-capacity; features worth having.*
   Garbage Disposer Best Buys ............................................. 319

**Trash Compactors 1978** ......................................................... 322
*Convenience vs. cost; what type and features to choose.*
   Trash Compactor Best Buys .............................................. 324

**Ranges 1978** ............................................................................ 326
*Latest developments in gas and electric units.*
   Range Best Buys ............................................................... 331

**Microwave Ovens 1978** .......................................................... 339
*Simple to elaborate units; matching a microwave to personal cooking styles and needs.*
   Microwave Oven Best Buys ............................................... 346

**Air Conditioners 1978** ............................................................. 348
*What to look for in a room air conditioner; features; EER.*
   Air Conditioner Best Buys .................................................. 354

**Smoke Detectors 1978** ........................................................... 362
*Determining which type best suits your protection needs.*
   Smoke Detector Best Buys ................................................ 367

**Personal Care Appliances 1978** ............................................ 369
*Keeping up with trends in hair care devices, shavers, irons.*
   Personal Care Appliance Best Buys .................................. 375
   Personal Care Appliance Prices ......................................... 389

**Photo Equipment 1978** ........................................................... 396
*Sorting out the best in SLRs, motion picture, and other types of cameras.*
   Photo Equipment Best Buys ............................................... 401

**Video Games 1978** .................................................................. 407
*How to select a game at a price and competitive level appropriate to your needs.*

**Index** ........................................................................................ 414

# 1978 CONSUMER BUYING GUIDE

# Introduction

THERE IS a wide, wonderful world of consumer products all around, brimming with excitement, efficiency, color and sound. All beckon for a share of our attention and consideration, and we select those that we hope will serve us best.

Within the cornucopia of modern technology are so many products and so many rapidly changing models that no one person can possibly know all there is to know about every piece of equipment for a home, for personal convenience, for entertainment, or for pleasure. Yet effective buying is more than simply a matter of luck—it depends upon having the right kind of product information close at hand when you go shopping.

There probably never has been a time when good, sound consumer information was more needed than it is right now.

With this in mind, CONSUMER GUIDE Magazine designed this book to help you plan, shop, and save so that you can get more value and, hence, more satisfaction for your money. By providing realistic guidelines for the purchase of thousands of products, the following pages actually form a practical guide for better living.

CONSUMER GUIDE Magazine cares about the consumer and strives to offer a useful shopper's handbook. We have no ties to manufacturers, nor are we interested in selling products. Our only purpose is to provide people with all the information they need to decide what to buy and how to go about buying such items at the best possible price. We provide these vital data through the efforts of carefully selected consulting product experts who closely examine and critically evaluate thousands of products—from automobiles to appliances. These experts extend their authoritative advice on how to make purchases that will meet your needs at a price you can afford, and then they select name-brand products that stand above their peers in providing unmatched value for their price.

Follow these steps: first, study the section that describes the products you want. Here you will find invaluable information on trends and features, information that is crucial in getting the best value for your money. Second, check out all of CONSUMER GUIDE Magazine's "Best Buy" selections for the particular product category; you are sure to find an appropriate model for your needs, and you can rest assured that a "Best Buy" selection offers top value for its price.

Then go shopping at your local retail stores, comparing prices and models. If a dealer quotes a price close to the "Low Price" given for each Best Buy and Recommended selection, you can be sure that you are receiving first-rate value for your money. Finally, if no dealer will come close to matching our highly competitive "Low Price" on the item you want, send us one of the Special Information Service coupons (be sure to enclose 25¢ for postage and handling) in this book. We will forward your inquiry to a reputable dealer who will be happy to sell you what you want at the price you should pay. CONSUMER GUIDE Magazine has no financial connection to any retailer; we provide this service strictly to aid our price-conscious, discount-seeking readers.

# 1978 Autos

MANY FAMILIAR nameplates are back for 1978, but the cars they are attached to are vastly different from the '77s. Some names are new, but they belong to models that look very familiar; other new names belong to cars that truly are new in every way. A few of the most familiar names have disappeared.

Among the missing are the Chevrolet Chevelle and Vega, Pontiac Ventura, Plymouth Gran Fury, Dodge Royal Monaco, Ford Maverick, Mercury Comet, AMC Hornet and Volkswagen Beetle. Newcomers are the Horizon, Omni, Zephyr, Fairmont, Concord, Fiesta and Sapporo. Old names with brand-new bodies are Oldsmobile Cutlass, Pontiac Grand Prix and Buick Regal.

However, the automakers' strategy for 1978 is more than just a name game. Several engineering developments of value to the consumer are being introduced this year and are sure to find wide acceptance throughout the industry as the years go by. One of them is front-wheel drive, being offered in domestic minicars for the first time this year. Another is diesel power, available for the first time in a domestic passenger car. In addition, General Motors has taken another step in the right direction by downsizing its entire intermediate line. Automakers overseas continue to design cars that offer trend-setting technological advances.

In the midst of all these changes, there are many cars that have stayed the same. Of them, some are all right the way they are; others are gas-guzzlers just a couple of years away from extinction.

Here is a rundown of this year's offerings, followed by CONSUMER GUIDE Magazine's selection of the best automotive buys for 1978.

## AMERICAN MOTORS CORPORATION '78

**AMX,** a Hornet derivative last year, is now a model in itself. It is still based on the Hornet (now Concord) chassis and body, with pieces added to give it a performance-car appearance. The standard AMX engine is a 258 cubic-inch Six, but a 304 V8 is available. With the 258 and automatic transmission, it can be expected to provide mileage similar to that of the six-cylinder Concord: A bit over 20 miles per gallon.

**Concord** is really the AMC Hornet with new exterior styling and some improvements in ride and handling. It is AMC's entry into the luxury compact market. Concord is available in two-door sedan, four-door sedan, two-door hatchback and four-door wagon versions. A 232 cubic-inch Six is standard, but a 258 Six and a 304 V8 are available as options. Mileage for Concord with the medium-size engine and automatic transmission is about 21 miles per gallon.

**Gremlin** for '78 comes in three variations: A basic six-cylinder, a six-cylinder custom and a four-cylinder custom model. Among the few changes made for this year are a new instrument panel and other interior refinements. The deficiencies we have noted in the past—poor rear seat room, restricted luggage space and mediocre fuel economy—remain about the same. The Environmental Protection Agency has given the '78 Gremlin a rating of 26 mph with four-cylinder engine in average driving.

**Matador** is back again for 1978, virtually unchanged from the 1977 version. The interior is attractive and comfortable, and the trunk is huge. But Matador, AMC's biggest car, is underpowered with the standard 258 Six and a gas-guzzler with the optional 360 V8. In our test of the 1977 Matador with the 360 and automatic transmission, we obtained only 13.5 mpg. We expect AMC to drop the car from its lineup either in 1979 or 1980.

**Pacer** gets a new hood and grille for 1978, as well as a 304 V8 engine as an option. With the V8, the Pacer offers good performance. This, combined with good ride and handling, makes the car as satisfying as almost any other American intermediate on the road. But gas mileage is still a problem. Pacer is too heavy to be truly economical. In CONSUMER GUIDE Magazine's test of a '77 Pacer with 258 cubic-inch Six, we obtained 19 miles per gallon.

## CHRYSLER CORPORATION '78

### CHRYSLER

**Cordoba** is stuck in the big-car category for at least another 12 months. Overall dimensions are the same as they were in 1977, and this could be a handicap, because most of Cordoba's direct competitors offer better mileage. In our test of a '77 with the 318 cubic-inch V8 and automatic transmission, we obtained only 15 mpg. A new four-barrel version of that engine is available this year.

There is little doubt that Cordoba will be downsized soon to bring it into line with its competition.

**LeBaron** is difficult to label. It is smaller than a full-size or mid-size car, yet bigger than other compacts. It is little more than a Volaré with added luxury ornamentation. Few changes have been made for 1978, but a wagon has been added to the LeBaron lineup. In the Environmental Protection Agency's tests of a 1978 LeBaron, the 225 cubic-inch base sedan powerplant provided 19 mpg. A 318 and a 360 engine are also available.

**Newport** and **New Yorker** are big cars in every way. They stand almost alone as the last of the true gas gulpers. The Newport and New Yorker Brougham series each include a two-door and a four-door hardtop; the Newport four-door sedan and station wagon have been discontinued. Inside and outside changes for 1978 are almost unnoticeable. Fuel usage remains in the area of ten to 12 miles per gallon with the smaller of the big engines.

## DODGE

**Aspen** is not the small car it once was. It has not changed, but most of its competitors have been downsized. It is now the biggest car in the compact market. A new grille is the major modification for 1978. A two-door and a four-door sedan and two-seat station wagon are available. With 225 cubic-inch Six and automatic transmission, CONSUMER GUIDE Magazine obtained an average 19 miles per gallon last year from the Aspen.

**Charger** and **Magnum** are essentially the same car, although the new Magnum was styled to appeal to a "road car" audience. Both cars offer the same engine selection—318 cubic-inch V8 standard, and 360 and 400 V8s as options. CONSUMER GUIDE Magazine tested the 1977 Charger with 360 engine and automatic transmission and obtained average mileage of 15 mpg. Mileage for Magnum and Charger this year are likely to be about the same.

**Diplomat** offers two- and four-door sedans and a station wagon in the new full-size class to compete with the bigger Fords and Chevrolets. It appears to be Dodge's intermediate of the future, even though it is built on the "compact" Aspen chassis. No significant styling changes have been made in the Diplomat for 1978, but the engine selection has been expanded. Mileage for the Diplomat with the smallest 225 cubic-inch engine and automatic transmission is about 19 mpg.

**Monaco** is the biggest sedan in the Dodge lineup for 1978. Eight models are available in the Monaco and Monaco Brougham price classes. It is nearly impossible to distinguish the styling differences between the 1978 and the 1977 models, although thin-back bucket seats, standard throughout the Chrysler lineup, are new. Engine choices include the 225, 318, 360 and 400 cubic-inch sizes. With the 225 and automatic transmission, Monaco gave us 18 miles per gallon in our 1977 tests.

**Omni,** set for January introduction, is a completely new car that offers some of the most appealing small-car features to be found anywhere. Front-wheel drive, highway fuel economy in the 30s, and the fold-down rear seat cargo area available on many imports are just a few of the Omni's benefits. A four-speed transmission is standard in the five-door hatchback. Omni is about six inches longer than the two-door Chevette and five inches shorter than Ford's Pinto.

## PLYMOUTH

**Horizon,** Plymouth's version of the Dodge Omni, is the same size and shape as the Dodge, and is expected to offer the same good economy. Like the Omni, Horizon has front-wheel drive and a fold-down rear seat. One body style will be available when the car makes its debut in January—a five-door hatchback. Both of the cars are based on the Simca 1100, a car that Chrysler builds and markets successfully in France.

**Volaré** has been cut to one basic series for 1978, but continues to offer a two-door coupe, four-door sedan and a station wagon. Other Volaré models have been replaced by the LeBaron/Diplomat line. Thin-back bucket seats are the major styling change for 1978. Volaré is beginning to look dated at the tender age of two, because other cars in its class are offering better economy, handling and ride. The 19 miles per gallon we obtained in our 1977 test of a Volaré with 225 Six is not outstanding.

## FORD MOTOR COMPANY '78

### FORD

**Fairmont** is leading Ford's marketing push in 1978. This all-new car, the replacement for Maverick, represents Ford's first major move in the downsizing trend. It offers many design improvements that seem to warrant all of the optimism surrounding its introduction. A two-door sedan, four-door sedan and wagon are offered—all built on the same 105.5-inch wheelbase. Base powerplant is the Four which has been used for years in the Pinto and Mustang. Optional engines are a 200 cubic-inch Six and 302 V8. The Environmental Protection Agency has estimated mileage of 22 mpg for the Six and 19 mpg for the V8.

**Granada** is bound to feel the effects of Ford's Fairmont. The two cars overlap in some price and market areas, but the Granada is no match for the Fairmont in a direct comparison. Little has been changed from 1977. In size, it is closest to the downsized intermediates from General Motors, but it offers poorer economy than the new GM products. The Environmental Protection Agency has estimated an average of 21 miles per gallon for the Granada with 250 cubic-inch engine.

**LTD,** the car that made Ford the home of the whopper in 1977, is unchanged for 1978. It continues to offer a "boulevard" ride, but it also continues to slurp up many gallons of gas. Base engine is the 302 cubic-inch V8. Options are the 351, 400 and 460 cubic-inch mills. With the 400 engine, the LTD gave the Environmental Protection Agency an average of only 15 miles per gallon. LTD cannot match the General Motors full-size cars in mileage, handling or maneuverability.

**LTD II** is another big car from Ford, offered in two body styles this year. The station wagon has been dropped, and that is about the only change in the line for '78. Three engines are offered—all V8s. The 302 cubic-inch size is standard, with a 351 and a 400 available as options. Mileage is not good. With the 302, the Environmental Protection Agency obtained 17 mpg; with the 400, mileage dropped to 15 mpg.

**Mustang II** gets new options for 1978, but few other changes. The hardtop, Ghia and Mach I are continued, with three engines available. The smallest engine, a 140-cubic-inch Four, provides the best economy—mileage in the high 20s or low 30s. With the largest engine, a 302 cubic-inch V8, we obtained about 18 miles per gallon in our 1977 tests. A completely new Mustang is expected to be introduced in 1979. It should be smaller and more efficient than the current model.

**Pinto,** aging but still active at eight, faces what could be its toughest year. New competition from Ford's own Fiesta, Chevrolet's five-door Chevette and the new front-wheel-drive duo from Chrysler could seriously hurt Pinto sales. It enters the fray with few meaningful changes. One series, the base Pinto, is offered, but styling options are available to dress it up. A Four, a Six and an Eight are available in the Pinto. Mileage is in the range of 25 mpg with the smallest engine, about 20 with the Six.

**Thunderbird** was trimmed of some of its excess plumage in 1977, and sales soared. But, the car has been carried over with only minimal changes for '78 and seems to be in for a rough flight. A Diamond Jubilee Edition, basic Thunderbird and Thunderbird Landau are offered this year. Three V8 engines are available, offering mileage from 15 to 18 miles per gallon, according to EPA tests. Increasing competition from the downsized GM cars and newer Ford products could hurt Thunderbird in 1978.

## LINCOLN

**Continental,** one of the most inefficient cars in America, continues to sell well. The 1978 version is a duplicate of the '77, and that means mileage will be about the same. Based on CONSUMER GUIDE Magazine's tests of the '77, most drivers will obtain about 14 miles per gallon on the average. Continental is scheduled for a redesign in a couple of years that should bring it down in size and up in efficiency.

**Continental Mark V,** the other member of Lincoln's heavyweight duo, is an expensive car to own and to operate. For 1978, more luxury items are available, but little has been done to improve the car's fuel economy. City drivers are unlikely to obtain better than 13 miles per gallon. A 400 cubic-inch V8 and a 460 V8 are available. Engines that big are necessary to pull around a car of the Mark V's bulk.

**Versailles,** introduced amid great hoopla last April, has failed to make the impact on the luxury compact market that its makers had hoped it would. One model, a four-door sedan with 302 cubic-inch V8, is offered in 1978. It is a thinly disguised adaptation of the Granada. Our opinion of the car is that it is overpriced, overstuffed and overdone. Mileage, however, is not bad: it is in the range of 20 miles per gallon on the highway.

## MERCURY

**Bobcat** is available in two series for 1978—the three-door sedan and wagon and the Bobcat Villager wagon. The present body is basically a design introduced eight years ago, and is overdue for a major change. However, it offers a ride that is quieter and smoother than some of the newer cars in its class. Mileage with the smallest engine, a Four, is about 25 mpg. Bobcat's greatest competition in '78 may come from another Mercury product, Zephyr.

**Cougar** continues into 1978 with almost no changes, and faces tough competition from the downsized General Motors intermediates. Two-door and four-door sedan styles are available, and the high-line XR-7 continues as a two-door model. The station wagons have been dropped. Three engines are available: a 302 V8 is standard, and a 351 and 400 are options. With the 351, CONSUMER GUIDE Magazine obtained average mileage of 15 mpg last year.

**Marquis** enjoyed a resurgence in popularity during 1977, and Mercury is hoping it will continue through 1978, even though there is little new in the latest version of the line. A major downsizing of the Marquis is planned for 1979 or 1980. The idea is to make the car more efficient, and that will come none too soon: in our tests last year of a Marquis with the largest 460 cubic-inch engine, we obtained average mileage of only 12.2 mpg.

**Monarch** moves into 1978 with only a few cosmetic changes. The engine lineup is a direct carryover from 1977, with a 250-cubic-inch Six as the standard powerplant and a 302 V8 as the only option. Monarch is called a compact by Mercury, but it does not fare well in direct comparison with compacts from other makers or with the new Mercury Zephyr. Mileage is not outstanding. We obtained 17 mpg in our test last year of the V8 Monarch.

**Zephyr** is the only really new car from Mercury for 1978. Zephyr replaces the Comet, and does that well. The car's design is boxy and comfortable, the large glass areas provide excellent visibility and mileage is good. Three engines are available. The Four offers mileage in the range of 26 mpg; the smallest Six delivers about 22, and the largest Six delivers about 19 according to the Environmental Protection Agency. Two- and four-door sedans and four-door station wagons are available.

## GENERAL MOTORS CORPORATION '78

### BUICK

**Century,** a totally restyled intermediate, features a fastback look. The exterior appearance may keep some people away; but inside, everything seems just about right. Front legroom and headroom are excellent and back-seat room is almost as good. The interior dimensions of the 1978s are better than those of the '77s, even though Century is smaller this year. The downsizing has improved economy: the EPA estimates mileage of 19 mpg with the 301 engine and up to 23 mpg with the 196.

**LeSabre and Electra,** downsized a year ago, move into '78 with almost no changes. Two-door coupes, four-door sedans and wagons are available, with engines from 231 to 400 cubic inches. The cars are quiet, comfortable and roomy. A LeSabre with the 231 received a rating of 20 mpg average from the EPA this year. With the 350 engine in the Electra, CONSUMER GUIDE Magazine obtained average mileage of 16 mpg last year.

**Regal** has been turned loose from the rest of the Century line in 1978 and has been totally restyled and downsized. Even though it is smaller on the outside than the '77 Century Regal, it is roomier inside. Ride and interior quietness are good, and so is handling. Five engines are available, including a new turbocharged V6 with either two or four-barrel carburetion. The Environmental Protection Agency has given the medium-size 231 Six a rating of 22 mpg in average driving.

**Riviera** was downsized last year, with good results. This year's car is essentially the same as the '77 version. A 350 cubic-inch V8 is standard, but a 403 is available. With the 350, CONSUMER GUIDE Magazine obtained average mileage of 15.5 miles per gallon last year. The EPA estimates mileage of 16 mpg with the 403. While we are not impressed with the car's economy, we rate it highly for visibility, handling, ride and interior room.

**Skyhawk,** a Vega-based subcompact, is very short on back seat room because of its rakish, impractical hatchback roofline. One engine, a 231 V6, is offered. In Environmental Protection Agency tests, Skyhawk delivered 22 miles per gallon. In the opinion of CONSUMER GUIDE Magazine's test staff, better economy and more comfort are available with one of the other Vega-based GM subcompact coupes.

**Skylark** is the same this year as it was last year and for years before that. The Nova-based compact is an old-school design that looks even older when compared directly to the newly downsized GM intermediates. Coupe, sedan and hatchback styles are offered, with a choice of 231 Six or 305 V8. Last year, CONSUMER GUIDE Magazine obtained average mileage of 18 mpg with the 231. Next year, the Skylark story will be different, because the car is set for downsizing.

## CADILLAC

**DeVille** and **Brougham** retain their downsized proportions for 1978. A slightly revised grille and other minor cosmetic modifications are the only changes this year. One engine, the 425 V8, is offered. That engine provided the Environmental Protection Agency with estimated mileage of 15 mpg in this year's tests.

**Eldorado**, and its companion car, the Oldsmobile Toronado, are standouts for two reasons: their front-wheel drive and their great size. One engine, the 425 V8, is offered in the Eldorado. In our tests of a 1977 Eldorado, CONSUMER GUIDE Magazine obtained only 9.5 miles per gallon. The present design is far too overweight and big. Both of the cars are set for downsizing in 1979.

**Seville** has been highly successful since its introduction, so no styling changes have been made for 1978. However, one engineering modification is said to increase mileage by about one mile per gallon. It is the Electronic Spark Selection Control. We have criticized the car for its meager rear legroom and knee room, but that is about all we can say in a negative way. We obtained 16.5 miles per gallon last year with the Seville's only engine, a 350 V8.

## CHEVROLET

**Camaro** continues to enjoy great popularity among styling-conscious buyers, even though its design leaves much to be desired in the areas of efficiency and utility. Poor trunk room and awful rear seat accommodations result from its fastback styling. Three engines—a Six and two V8s—are available. The car's weight restricts mileage to between 16 and 19 miles per gallon. New for this year are body-colored front and rear bumpers.

**Caprice** and **Impala**, entering their second year in their new slimmed-down bodies, get only minor changes. The full-size Chevrolets are more efficient and agile than their bigger '76 versions were. Three engines are offered: a 250 Six, a 305 V8 and a 350 V8. In our tests of a 1977 Caprice equipped with the 350, we obtained mileage of 16 mpg. The smaller engines do better.

**Chevette** gets stretched this year, to make room for two more doors. The five-door Chevette is three inches longer than the original two-door hatchback. The poky 1.4-liter base engine has been dropped for all models, and the "high output" 1.6 liter mill replaces it. Mileage is good, at about 31 mpg, but the Chevette faces tough competition from Ford's Fiesta and two new subcompacts from Chrysler—all with front-wheel drive.

**Corvette** has no domestic competition. It is America's only true sports car and sells faster than Chevrolet can build it. For 1978 the major change is a new rear window called a "glassback." Power comes from a 350 V8. Corvette cannot make any claims of good gas mileage, adequate trunk space or comfortable interior accommodations, but those factors do not seem to have any effect on Corvette buyers.

**Malibu** is the name of the newly downsized intermediate from Chevrolet, replacing Chevelle. It offers a smooth ride, excellent handling and better economy than the intermediates of old. A 200 cubic-inch V6 is standard, with a 305 V8 available as an option. Mileage for Malibu this year is estimated at 20 to 21 mpg by the Environmental Protection Agency. The three-seat Chevelle wagon has been dropped, but Malibu is available in two-door coupe, four-door sedan and two-seat wagon variations.

**Monte Carlo**, like the Malibu on which it is based, is totally new for 1978. The new Monte Carlo comes in only one two-door coupe body style, with the 231 V6 engine standard and a 305 V8 available as an option. Despite its smaller outside dimensions, interior room is as good or better in most ways than that of last year's model. Economy is also better: the EPA has estimated mileage of 20 mpg for the Monte Carlo equipped with the 305. Trunk space also has been improved.

**Monza,** another of the GM subcompacts based on the Vega design, is available in coupe, hatchback and wagon versions for 1978. Engine choices are a 151 cubic-inch Four, a 196 Six and a 305 V8. The notorious 140 cubic-inch aluminum engine that did the Vega in has been dropped. Mileage with the V8 is poor, but the EPA has estimated economy of 28 mpg for the Monza equipped with the smallest engine.

**Nova,** when displayed next to the newly downsized intermediates from Chevrolet, is bound to suffer. The design is old. Nova is now heavier and bigger than the mid-size models. This overlapping, and increased competition from Ford's Fairmont and Zephyr, will make this a rough year for the aging Chevy. Things will change next year when Nova is restyled. Two engines are available—a 250 Six and a 305 V8. Concours has been replaced by the Nova Custom. Mileage is in the high teens.

## OLDSMOBILE

**Cutlass,** like the other GM intermediates, has benefitted greatly from downsizing. The new Cutlass rides better, handles better and gets better mileage than last year's version. However, Cutlass shares strange fastback rear styling with the Buick Century, and this could keep some buyers away. Engines are the 231 V6, 260 V8 and 305 V8. According to the EPA, mileage of about 22 mpg can be expected with the 260 cubic-inch engine.

**Delta 88** and **98** for 1978 are virtually indistinguishable from the 1977 editions. They come in two-door coupe and four-door sedan versions. Biggest news for 1978 is the Olds diesel engine, available as an option in both the 88 and 98. In our tests of last year's 98 with 350 cubic-inch V8, we obtained average mileage of only 16.2 mpg. The diesel 350 is expected to provide 25 percent better mileage than the gasoline 350.

**Omega** will struggle for another 12 months, then get a complete overhaul. It is another of the Nova-based GM compacts, and, like the others, suffers from a design that has not aged well. The mileage we obtained last year from an Omega equipped with a 231 cubic-inch V6 was 19 mpg. The trimmer mid-size Oldsmobile Cutlass for 1978 is expected to get better mileage than that. In addition to the 231, a 305 cubic-inch V8 is available.

**Starfire** is a car designed for people who are willing to make sacrifices in comfort for the sake of styling. With its most efficient engine, Starfire does not perform like a sports car; with its performance engine, it is too wasteful to be considered an economy car. Furthermore, the teardrop shape makes the back seat virtually useless for adult passengers. With the medium-size 231 engine, we obtained mileage of 25 mpg.

**Toronado** features front-wheel drive, the coming thing in domestic automobile design. However, everything else about the car is left over from the fuel-wasteful past. It is unchanged from 1977, which means that it is still a gas guzzler. With the 403 cubic-inch engine, the only one available, we obtained mileage last year of nine mpg. A new downsized Toronado is due next year.

## PONTIAC

**Bonneville** and **Catalina** for 1978 are basically the same as they were in '77, but that is not bad. Two-door coupes, four-door sedans and wagons are available, with a V6 and three V8s to choose from Mileage is not outstanding, but it is better than it was for the Bonnevilles and Catalinas prior to the downsizing. We obtained 16.5 mpg in our test last year of a Bonneville with the 350 cubic-inch engine.

**Firebird** offers racy styling but little practicality. However, it sells so well that few changes have been made in several years. Next year's version is expected to be much smaller and more efficient. Until then, the Pontiac "muscle car" will be incapable of more than 18 miles per gallon and will continue to inconvenience passengers because of its meager rear seat and trunk space. A V6 and three V8s are available.

**Grand Prix** may have shrunk in size, but its driving character has changed for the better. The new Grand Prix is more agile and economical and just about as roomy as the previous model. It makes Thunderbird and Cordoba seem outdated by comparison. A 231 cubic-inch V6 is standard, and two versions of the 301 V8 are available. The Environmental Protection Agency estimates mileage of about 22 mpg for the Grand Prix equipped with the 231.

**LeMans** has been substantially downsized, reengineered and restyled for 1978, and is a vastly better car as a result. Interior room is better, while outside dimensions have been decreased to provide better handling and increased mileage. With the standard 231 engine, the Environmental Protection Agency obtained an estimate of 22 mpg. A 301 V8 is available. Two-door coupes, four-door sedans and a wagon are offered.

**Phoenix,** introduced last year as a luxury version of the Ventura, has now replaced Ventura altogether. It is a Nova-based car that is essentially the same as the other GM compacts under the skin. Two-door coupe, four-door sedan and two-door hatchback versions are available, with a 151 cubic-inch Four, a 231 V6 and a 301 V8 supplying the power. The EPA gave the Phoenix with 231 a mileage rating of 20 mpg.

**Sunbird** is the only Vega-based subcompact offered by Pontiac for 1978 now that Astre has been dropped. Grilles have been revised, and the awful aluminum Vega engine has been tossed out. Other than that, there are few changes in the line for '78. A 151 cubic-inch Four is standard for Sunbird, and a 231 V6 is available as an option. With the larger engine and manual transmission, the EPA obtained a mileage estimate of 19 mpg.

## IMPORTS

**Alfa Romeo** introduced its '78 version of the Spider Veloce sports car this fall with little changed from 1977. The sleek GT fastback is also basically the same as it was last year. A new Sport Sedan is set for introduction later this year.

**Arrow,** imported by Plymouth from Japan, includes a new model for 1978. Called the Sapporo, it is Plymouth's version of the Dodge Colt Challenger. Like the Dodge, it is a standout because of its racy styling. The smaller Arrow coupe remains pretty much as it was in 1977.

**Audi** has set its sights on the luxury-import market and has introduced the 5000, a car with a five-cylinder engine and a $10,000-plus price. The Audi Fox continues in two-door coupe, four-door sedan and wagon form with few changes.

**BMW** has been building on its reputation of producing some of the world's best-handling road cars. A new, larger sedan, probably to be called the 733i, is due in January. It is intended to compete directly with the Mercedes-Benz 450SEL.

**British Leyland,** maker of MG, Jaguar and Triumph automobiles, moves into 1978 with few changes in its lineup. The out-of-date MGs and Spitfire, intriguing Triumph TR7 and luxurious Jaguars are essentially the same as they were in 1977.

**Capri II** is a product of Ford in Germany. The newest version of the car is better but more expensive than its forerunners. It is overpriced, partly because of the German economy. A Capri III, to be made in the U.S., will replace the current Capri in a couple of years.

**Datsun** has revived the 510 for 1978. The original was discontinued in 1972. It is available in two-door and four-door versions. The 710 has been dropped, and the 810 sedan and wagon introduced last winter remain the same. The F-10 coupe and wagon, plus the sporty 280-Z are unaltered.

**Colt,** imported from Japan by Dodge, gets a new model for 1978. Called the Challenger, it is a standout because of its sleek styling. The Silent Shaft engine provides smooth performance, and a long list of equipment is standard. The Colt line also includes a new wagon. The Mileage Maker models are unchanged from 1977.

**Fiat** continues to offer the aging 128, the 131 and the 124 Spider roadster series in 1978 with almost no changes from 1977. Fiat's Lancia division continues to offer a line of expensive touring models, also unchanged from last year's models.

**Fiesta,** Ford's new minicar from Germany, is an impressive little machine. It features front-wheel drive, styling along the lines of the Volkswagen Rabbit and mileage of about 38 mpg according to the Environmental Protection Agency. One body style, a three-door hatchback, is offered. However, four different levels of trim are available.

**Honda** has some minor styling changes for the Civic series and a more luxurious Accord LX ready for U.S. introduction. Both cars feature front-wheel drive and mileage in the range of 35 mpg. The Accord offers several advantages over the Civic, but carries a higher price.

**Mazda** introduced the GLC last year and is happy with its success. The Chevette-shaped, piston-powered subcompact is virtually unchanged for this year, but a five-door hatchback version has been added to the line. The piston-engine Mizer and other Mazda offerings also are basically the same for '78.

**Mercedes-Benz** continues to expand its lineup. The newest of 11 models sold in the U.S. this year is a pair of coupes that replace the 280C coupe. Next year, a station wagon is to be added to the line. The rest of the line of luxurious and well-made cars continues with no significant changes in engineering or styling.

**Opel,** imported from Japan by Buick, will be offered in four models for '78: base Coupe, Deluxe Coupe, Deluxe Sedan and new Sport Coupe. A 1.8-liter engine provides about 27 mpg in average driving, according to the Environmental Protection Agency.

**Peugeot's** newest model is the 604, introduced last summer. The car, a top-of-the-line model, is available only as a four-door sedan. It offers room for five adults and excellent handling at a price of $11,000. A 604 diesel may be introduced later in the year. The rest of the line is the same.

**Porsche** is readying a V8-powered 928 model for U.S. introduction in January. Until then, there is little new to report from this German maker of high-priced sports cars.

**Renault** changed the name of the R5 to Le Car a while back and has enjoyed a sales spurt as a result. The front-drive minicar is doing well, and that could encourage the French maker to finally introduce its R30 luxury car. Le Car is capable of about 36 miles per gallon on the average.

**Saab** is preparing to unveil a turbocharged version of its already fast 99 EMS model. The Swedish maker's 99 GLE luxury package is available with a five-door hatchback model for the first time this year. Other changes are minimal.

**Subaru,** maker of economical front-wheel-drive subcompact coupes, sedans and wagons, has slightly revamped its lineup for '78. New is a minipickup version of the four-wheel-drive wagon, called BRAT. All of the Subaru models are powered by an efficient four-cylinder engine.

**Toyota** has an all new Celica in three variations and a replacement for the Mark II series in store for '78. Improved ride and handling, better styling and more standard features are incorporated into the new Celica line. The Corona hardtop and SR5 hardtop have been discontinued. The rest of the line is basically unchanged from 1977.

**Volkswagen** has been making news with its new diesel-powered Rabbit. The car gave the EPA an average mileage of 45 mpg. The rest of the line—Scirocco and Dasher—are virtually unchanged. Perhaps the biggest news from VW is the discontinuation of the Beetle after decades of great success around the world.

**Volvo** has added a limited-edition, ultraluxurious coupe to the top of its line for 1978. Also new for this year is the sports-oriented 242GT two-door sedan. Other changes include new front styling for the Swedish maker's sedans and wagons.

# 1978 Best Buys: Autos

CONSUMER GUIDE Magazine's staff of automotive experts has carefully examined the 1978 cars. The new models have been rated on many factors, including fuel economy, safety, driver visibility, handling, steering and braking, comfort, roominess and instrumentation. Based on extensive inspections and road tests of the 1978 models, we have chosen "Best Buys" in each of the nine categories listed here.

## SUBCOMPACTS

**Horizon, Omni, Rabbit** and **Accord** are standouts in the subcompact class for 1978. All four offer good economy, surprising roominess and the excellent handling provided by front-wheel drive.

The Dodge Omni and Plymouth Horizon are essentially the same car. Both are based on the Simca 1100, which Chrysler builds and markets successfully in Europe. They closely resemble the Volkswagen Rabbit in exterior styling, although they are bigger than the Rabbit. The larger dimensions mean slightly lower gas mileage, but Horizon/Omni should still be capable of economy in the range of 30-plus mpg.

Based on value delivered for the price, Honda's sleek Accord stands head and shoulders above most of its competitors. Its price of $4500 is high by subcompact standards, but there is a waiting list of people who have recognized that its convenience and luxury features are worth the wait and the expense.

Rabbit has been one of our favorite cars right from the start. It remains a top choice in its class, even though changes in the German money market have raised its price considerably. Driver visibility is a big plus, and its cargo capacity is very good. A 1978 diesel Rabbit is available for about $170 more than the gasoline-powered version. Mileage of about 45 mpg is claimed for the diesel.

Ford's Fiesta missed being selected as a "Best Buy" in this category primarily because of Ford's plan to replace the German-built Fiesta with a domestic minicar in a couple of years.

## IMPORTED SPORTS CARS

**Volkswagen's Scirocco** delivers excellent fuel economy, with no sacrifice in performance. The driving position of the Scirocco is another point in its favor. The driver sits up where he can see the roadway ahead and easily control the steering wheel. In comparison to other sports cars that force the driver into an almost under-dash position, visibility in the Scirocco is outstanding. Front-wheel drive makes the Scirocco agile.

While fuel economy may not have been a major factor in the selection of "Best Buy" in the imported sports car class in previous years, it is becoming increasingly important to drivers of all types of cars. Scirocco's average mileage of about 34 mpg is one more plus in a long list of appealing features.

## SPORTS CARS

**Chevrolet Corvette** is at the top of its class because it is the only car in its class. It is rated as the best sports car built in America because it is the only true sports car built here. There is no other domestic two-seater to compete with the Corvette. Of the foreign automobiles that could be considered competitors, most cost thousands of dollars more than the Chevrolet.

If Corvette did not exist, the **Pontiac Firebird Trans Am** and the **Chevrolet Camaro Z28** would take top honors in this class. They might not truly fit the definition of a traditional sports car, but they come closer than anything else made on a mass-production basis in the United States.

## COMPACTS

**Fairmont**, a totally new car from Ford, takes the top spot in the compact class for 1978. In terms of interior space, fuel economy, steering and handling, Fairmont is superior to the other cars in the compact category. The high-line luxury seats are recommended because they provide what Ford calls a "command" seating position. We like them better than the standard seats which are too close to the floor. We also recommend the six-cylinder engine. The Four seems to struggle at slower speeds, although it does provide the better economy of the two powerplants.

Fairmont has thus bumped Plymouth's Volaré and Chevrolet's Nova out of the "Best Buy" spot in 1978. Nova, which has not been significantly restyled or re-engineered in many years, appears old-fashioned. Volaré, although not as old, is beginning to look outdated at the age of two.

## INTERMEDIATES

**Buick Century, Chevrolet Malibu, Oldsmobile Cutlass** and **Pontiac LeMans** take the "Best Buy" title in the mid-size class for 1978. General Motors' newly downsized intermediates are advanced so far beyond the competition from Ford, Chrysler and AMC that there is no contest. Carefully designed to offer good fuel economy, maneuverability and passenger comfort, the GM intermediates represent what the downsizing program is all about.

Mileage for the new intermediates has been improved by about three miles per gallon over the 1977 versions. However, interior room and comfort have not been sacrificed in the downsizing process. Legroom and headroom measurements of the '78s are equal to or better than those of the 1977 models.

Also worth mentioning in this category is the new **Audi 5000.** It has a five-cylinder engine to provide excellent smoothness while keeping economy high. The 5000 is worthy of consideration if you do not mind spending a few thousand dollars above the cost of a domestic intermediate for a mid-size car that looks and rides like a Mercedes-Benz.

## STANDARDS

**Chevrolet Caprice** is the best of the outstanding GM models, and wins the "Best Buy" rating for 1978. The other GM standards—the **Pontiac Bonneville, Buick LeSabre** and **Oldsmobile Delta 88**—are almost as good as the Caprice. The only competition for these cars comes from the Ford and Mercury full-size lines, which are unchanged for 1978. Two other competitors from last year, the Plymouth Gran Fury and Dodge Royal Monaco, have been discontinued.

We picked the Caprice over the other three GM intermediates because of its price, service availability and resale value. However, a car to watch in 1978 is the new Olds Delta 88 with a diesel engine. It offers outstanding fuel economy, but at a high price premium over the 88 with conventional gasoline engine.

## MEDIUM STANDARDS

**Oldsmobile's 98** with diesel engine gets the nod as "Best Buy" in 1978. This model combines the traditional ride and luxury of the higher-priced full-size lines with the economy and long life of the diesel engine, and without sacrificing much in the way of performance. The diesel costs about $850 more than the gasoline engine, and diesel fuel can be difficult to find in some areas. For those reasons, we think the diesel would be a real dollars-and-cents benefit only to people who drive as much as 20,000 miles a year.

The category of medium standards has changed because of changes in the standard and luxury classes. There seems to be little to gain anymore in selecting a medium standard over a model from one of those categories. It might have been appropriate for us to avoid choosing a "Best Buy" in the medium standard class. However, the diesel engine truly makes the Olds 98 a standout.

## LUXURY

**Cadillac Fleetwood, Cadillac Seville** and **Mercedes-Benz 300D** lead the field of luxury models in 1978.

If you are strictly an American-car buyer, there is no question that Cadillac is the "Best Buy." Both the Fleetwood and the Seville have well-earned reputations for top quality, high resale value and reliability. Compared to the overblown Lincoln Continental, the Fleetwood is easier to drive, more efficient and offers nearly the same interior space. Compared to the Lincoln Versailles, the Cadillac Seville is the better buy despite its higher price.

For buyers of luxury imports, the diesel-powered Mercedes 300D has it all—prestige, quality and excellent fuel economy. If its price were several thousand dollars lower, we would have to rank it as one of the very best cars on the market in any class.

## PERSONAL LUXURY

**Buick's Regal** is first among equals in the selection of "Best Buy" in the personal luxury class. We also must include the **Chevrolet Monte Carlo, Oldsmobile Cutlass Supreme** and **Pontiac Grand Prix.** The cars, all newly downsized for 1978, are built on the same 108-inch wheelbase and are virtually identical in major features.

Regal heads the list because of a feature that the others will not have for at least a year: a turbocharged V6 engine that provides the economy of a Six with the performance of a V8.

The competition—including the Lincoln Continental Mark V, Oldsmobile Toronado, Chrysler Cordoba and Ford Thunderbird—all suffer from serious fuel usage problems and are no match for the four "Best Buys" in terms of economy.

# 1978 Auto Prices

**B**EFORE YOU SIT DOWN to talk business with an automobile salesman, it is important to have a very good idea of what you want and how much you should pay for it. There are a few steps that you can take in the comfort and quietude of your home before you step into the hustle and bustle of a car dealer's showroom, and this forethought can prevent headaches later on. Here are our suggestions:

1. Read the brief descriptions of each car included in this book to get a general feeling of what is available. Find out as much as you can about each of the models to determine which of them may suit you best. Be sure to check our "Best Buy" selections.

2. Once you have decided on a particular make and model, make a list of the equipment you want. Check your list against the manufacturer's lists to find out which of the items are standard and which ones are extra-cost options.

3. Refer to CONSUMER GUIDE Magazine's exclusive price listings on the following pages for the car of your choice. Total the low price of your car and all of the options you want. Then add freight costs (listed as "F.O.B." on the car's window sticker), dealer preparation costs, and state and local taxes. The total figure is the best deal you can make on the model and options you have chosen.

4. With that low price as your goal, you are ready to bargain. If the dealer comes within $50 of your low price, he is offering you a good deal. If he does not offer you the car at a low enough price, shop around.

As you will notice when you read through the prices listed here, no imported cars are included. The reason is that most importers do not set their prices by this time each year. Some of the imports will not be available until January 1978. Furthermore, discounts on imports are difficult to obtain because of limited competition between dealers. Many foreign car manufacturers instruct their U.S. retailers to sell their cars at full price, and most of them can do so.

# AMERICAN MOTORS CORPORATION

|  | Retail Price | Dealer Cost | Low Price |
|---|---|---|---|
| **AMX** | | | |
| 2-Door Hatchback | $ 4599 | $ 4049 | $ 4349 |
| **AMX ACCESSORIES** | | | |
| 304 CID, V-8 Engine | $233 | $193 | $195 |
| California Emission System & Factory Testing | 74 | 61 | 62 |
| High Altitude Emission Package | 23 | 19 | 20 |
| Transmissions | | | |
| Automatic, Floor-Shift | 320 | 266 | 269 |
| Twin-Grip Differential | 55 | 46 | 47 |
| Power Steering | 147 | 122 | 124 |
| Front Power Disc Brakes | 64 | 53 | 54 |
| Exterior Color | 49 | 41 | 42 |
| "Levi's" Denim Fabric Trim Bucket Seat | 49 | 41 | 42 |
| Unique AMX Decal Package | 49 | 41 | 42 |
| Radio Equipment | | | |
| AM Push-Button | 80 | 66 | 67 |
| AM/FM Push-Button Stereo W/4 Speakers | 224 | 186 | 188 |
| AM/CB Push-Button Radio, 40-Channel | 199 | 165 | 167 |
| AM/FM/CB Push-Button Stereo W/4 Speakers | 299 | 248 | 251 |
| Rear Speaker W/AM Radio Only | 22 | 18 | 19 |
| Air Conditioning System | 478 | 397 | 401 |
| Air Conditioning Package W/A/C System, Tinted Glass & Power Steering | 679 | 564 | 570 |
| Tinted Glass, All Windows | 55 | 46 | 47 |
| Electronic Cruise Control | 99 | 82 | 83 |

*Prices are accurate at time of printing; subject to manufacturer's change.*

|  | Retail Price | Dealer Cost | Low Price |
|---|---|---|---|
| Dual Horns | $ 12 | $ 10 | $ 11 |
| Hidden Compartment | 31 | 26 | 27 |
| Electric Rear Window Defroster | 81 | 67 | 67 |
| 4 Styled Road Wheels | 71 | 59 | 60 |
| 4 Aluminum Styled Wheels | 171 | 142 | 144 |
| Extra-Quiet Insulation Package | 45 | 37 | 38 |
| Protective Inner Coating | 95 | 79 | 80 |
| Locking Gas Cap | 7 | 6 | 7 |
| Heavy-Duty Engine Cooling System | 37 | 31 | 32 |
| 70-AMP Heavy-Duty Battery | 17 | 14 | 15 |
| Heavy-Duty Suspension | 31 | 26 | 27 |
| Engine Block Heater | 19 | 16 | 17 |

## CONCORD

|  | Retail Price | Dealer Cost | Low Price |
|---|---|---|---|
| 2-Door Hatchback | $3799 | $3349 | $3549 |
| 2-Door Sedan | 3699 | 3262 | 3462 |
| 4-Door Sedan | 3799 | 3349 | 3549 |
| 4-Door Wagon | 3999 | 3524 | 3774 |

## CONCORD ACCESSORIES

|  | Retail Price | Dealer Cost | Low Price |
|---|---|---|---|
| **Engines** | | | |
| 258 CID, 6-Cyl. | $120 | $100 | $101 |
| 304 CID, V-8 Cyl. | 233 | 193 | 195 |
| California Emission System & Factory Testing | 74 | 61 | 62 |
| High Altitude Emission Package | 23 | 19 | 20 |
| **Transmissions** | | | |
| 4-Speed Manual, Floor Shift | 111 | 92 | 93 |
| Automatic, Column Shift | 296 | 246 | 249 |
| Automatic, Floor Shift | 320 | 266 | 269 |
| Twin-Grip Differential | 55 | 46 | 47 |
| Power Steering | 147 | 122 | 124 |
| Front Power Disc Brakes | 64 | 53 | 54 |
| Two-Tone Color | 75 | 62 | 63 |
| Special Color Combinations | 24 | 20 | 21 |
| Vinyl Roof | 105 | 87 | 88 |
| Vinyl Bucket Seats | 69 | 57 | 58 |
| D/L Package | 200 | 170 | 172 |
| W/Wood-Grain | (75) | (62) | (63) |
| **Sport Package** | | | |
| 2-Door Hatchback | 289 | 240 | 243 |
| All Other | 379 | 315 | 319 |
| **Radio Equipment** | | | |
| AM Push-Button | 80 | 66 | 67 |
| AM/FM Push-Button Stereo Radio W/4 Speakers | 224 | 186 | 188 |
| AM/CB Push-Button, 40-Channel | 199 | 165 | 167 |

*Prices are accurate at time of printing; subject to manufacturer's change.*

|  | Retail Price | Dealer Cost | Low Price |
|---|---|---|---|
| AM/FM/CB Push-Button Stereo W/4 Speakers | $299 | $248 | $251 |
| Rear Speaker W/AM Only | 22 | 18 | 19 |
| Air Conditioning System | 478 | 397 | 401 |
| Air Conditioning Package W/A/C System, Tinted Glass & Power Steering | 679 | 564 | 570 |
| Tinted Glass, All Windows | 55 | 46 | 47 |
| Electronic Cruise Control | 99 | 82 | 83 |
| Tilt Steering Wheel | 64 | 53 | 54 |
| Gauge Package | 99 | 82 | 83 |
| Interior Decor/Convenience Group | | | |
| All Models W/o Deluxe Pkg | 79 | 66 | 67 |
| 2- & 4-Door Sedan & Wagon W/Deluxe Pkg | 54 | 45 | 46 |
| Digital Electric Clock | 25 | 21 | 22 |
| Visibility Group | 71 | 59 | 60 |
| Left Remote-Control Mirror | 16 | 13 | 14 |
| Intermittent Wiper System | 30 | 25 | 26 |
| Light Group | 30 | 25 | 26 |
| Dual Horns | 12 | 10 | 11 |
| Center Console | 29 | 24 | 25 |
| Hidden Compartment | 31 | 26 | 27 |
| Stowage/Litter Containers | 10 | 8 | 9 |
| Electric Rear Window Defroster | 81 | 67 | 68 |
| Roof Rack, Wagon | 85 | 70 | 71 |
| Space-Saver Spare Tire | 18 | 15 | 16 |
| Sports Steering Wheel | 20 | 17 | 18 |
| Soft Feel Sports Steering Wheel | 31 | 26 | 27 |
| W/Sport Pkg. or Hatchback | 11 | 9 | 10 |
| 4 Custom Wheel Covers | 23 | 19 | 20 |
| 4 Styled Road Wheels | 136 | 113 | 115 |
| W/Sport Pkg. | 71 | 59 | 60 |
| 4 Aluminum Styled Wheels | 236 | 196 | 198 |
| W/Sport Pkg. | 171 | 142 | 144 |
| Extra-Quiet Insulation Package | 45 | 37 | 38 |
| Protective Inner Coating | 95 | 79 | 80 |
| Protection Group | 27 | 22 | 23 |
| Front & Rear Bumper Nerfing Strips | 34 | 28 | 29 |
| Front Bumper Guards | 19 | 16 | 17 |
| Front Bumper Guards & Front & Rear Bumper Nerfing Strips | 53 | 44 | 45 |
| Locking Gas Cap | 7 | 6 | 7 |
| Heavy-Duty Engine Cooling System | 37 | 31 | 32 |
| 70-AMP Heavy-Duty Battery | 17 | 14 | 15 |
| Heavy-Duty Suspension | 31 | 26 | 27 |
| Engine Block Heater | 19 | 16 | 17 |

## GREMLIN

| | | | |
|---|---|---|---|
| 2-Door Sedan, Base | $3299 | $2912 | $3112 |

*Prices are accurate at time of printing; subject to manufacturer's change.*

|  | Retail Price | Dealer Cost | Low Price |
|---|---|---|---|
| 2-Door Sedan, 2-Liter Custom | $3549 | $3130 | $3330 |
| 2-Door Sedan, Custom | 3549 | 3130 | 3330 |

## GREMLIN ACCESSORIES

|  | Retail Price | Dealer Cost | Low Price |
|---|---|---|---|
| 258 CID, Six Engine | $120 | $100 | $101 |
| California Emission System & Factory Testing | 74 | 61 | 62 |
| High Altitude Emission Package | 23 | 19 | 20 |
| Transmissions |  |  |  |
|    4-Speed Manual, Floor Shift | 111 | 92 | 93 |
|    Automatic, Column Shift | 270 | 224 | 227 |
|    Automatic, Floor Shift | 294 | 244 | 247 |
|    Twin-Grip Differential | 55 | 46 | 47 |
| Power Steering | 141 | 117 | 119 |
| Front Power Disc Brakes | 64 | 53 | 54 |
| Radio Equipment |  |  |  |
|    AM Push-Button | 80 | 66 | 67 |
|    AM/FM Push-Button Stereo W/4 Speakers | 224 | 186 | 188 |
|    AM/CB Push-Button, 40-Channel | 199 | 165 | 167 |
|    Rear Speaker W/AM Radio Only | 22 | 18 | 19 |
| Air Conditioning System | 478 | 397 | 401 |
| Air Conditioning Package W/A/C System, Tinted Glass & Power Steering | 669 | 555 | 561 |
| Tinted Glass, All Windows | 52 | 43 | 44 |
| Electronic Cruise Control | 99 | 82 | 83 |
| Gauge Package | 75 | 62 | 63 |
| Tachometer | 49 | 41 | 42 |
| Interior Decor/Convenience Group | 69 | 57 | 58 |
| Digital Electric Clock | 25 | 21 | 22 |
| Special Exterior Color Combinations | 24 | 20 | 21 |
| Vinyl Bucket Seats | 49 | 41 | 42 |
| Rally Side Stripes | 43 | 36 | 37 |
| Gremlin "X" Package | 249 | 212 | 215 |
| Visibility Group | 71 | 59 | 60 |
| Left-Remote Control Mirror | 16 | 13 | 14 |
| Intermittent Wiper System | 30 | 25 | 26 |
| Dual Horns | 12 | 10 | 11 |
| Center Console | 29 | 24 | 25 |
| Stowage/Litter Containers | 10 | 8 | 9 |
| Electric Rear Window Defroster | 81 | 67 | 68 |
| Tailgate Air Deflector | 24 | 20 | 21 |
| Roof Rack | 59 | 49 | 50 |
| Space-Saver Spare Tire | 18 | 15 | 16 |
| Sports Steering Wheel | 20 | 17 | 18 |
| Soft Feel Sports Steering Wheel | 31 | 26 | 27 |
| W/Gremlin "X" Package | 11 | 9 | 11 |
| 4 Wheel Covers | 36 | 30 | 31 |

*Prices are accurate at time of printing; subject to manufacturer's change.*

|  | Retail Price | Dealer Cost | Low Price |
|---|---|---|---|
| 4 Custom Wheel Covers | $ 23 | $ 19 | $ 20 |
| 4 Styled Road Wheels | 136 | 113 | 115 |
| W/Gremlin "X" Package | 71 | 59 | 60 |
| 4 Aluminum Wheels | 236 | 196 | 198 |
| W/Gremlin "X" Package | 171 | 142 | 144 |
| Extra Quiet Insulation Package | 45 | 37 | 38 |
| Protective Inner Coating | 95 | 79 | 80 |
| Protection Group | 42 | 35 | 36 |
| Inside Hood Release | 16 | 13 | 14 |
| Side Scuff Moldings | 29 | 24 | 25 |
| Front Bumper Guards | 19 | 16 | 17 |
| Locking Gas Cap | 7 | 6 | 7 |
| Heavy Duty Engine Cooling System | 37 | 31 | 32 |
| 70-AMP Heavy-Duty Battery | 17 | 14 | 15 |
| Heavy-Duty Suspension | 31 | 26 | 27 |
| Front Sway Bar | 18 | 15 | 16 |
| Engine Block Heater | 19 | 16 | 17 |

## MATADOR

|  | Retail Price | Dealer Cost | Low Price |
|---|---|---|---|
| 2-Door Coupe | $4799 | $4032 | $4332 |
| 4-Door Sedan | 4849 | 4074 | 4374 |
| 4-Door V-8 Wagon | 5299 | 4450 | 4750 |

## MATADOR ACCESSORIES

|  | Retail Price | Dealer Cost | Low Price |
|---|---|---|---|
| 360 CID, V-8 Engine | $190 | $150 | $152 |
| California Emission System & Factory Testing | 74 | 59 | 60 |
| High Altitude Emission Package | 23 | 18 | 19 |
| Transmissions |  |  |  |
| Automatic, Floor Shift & Console | 70 | 55 | 56 |
| Twin-Grip Differential | 59 | 47 | 48 |
| Power Window, Tailgate, Wagon | 47 | 37 | 38 |
| Power Windows, Side | 155 | 122 | 124 |
| Power Windows, Side & Tailgate | 202 | 160 | 162 |
| Two-Tone Exterior Color | 48 | 38 | 39 |
| Special Exterior Color Combinations | 24 | 19 | 20 |
| Vinyl Roof | 118 | 93 | 94 |
| Rally Side Stripes | 46 | 36 | 38 |
| Barcelona Package |  |  |  |
| Coupe | 849 | 671 | 678 |
| Sedan | 699 | 552 | 558 |
| W/Wood-Grain | 133 | 105 | 107 |
| W/o Two-Tone | (100) | (79) |  |
| Radio Equipment |  |  |  |
| AM Push-Button | 81 | 64 | 65 |
| AM/FM Push-Button Stereo W/4 Speakers | 224 | 177 | 179 |

*Prices are accurate at time of printing; subject to manufacturer's change.*

|  | Retail Price | Dealer Cost | Low Price |
|---|---|---|---|
| AM/FM/Tape Stereo W/4 Speakers | $336 | $265 | $268 |
| AM/CB Push-Button, 40-Channel | 199 | 157 | 159 |
| AM/FM/CB Push-Button Stereo W/4 Speakers | 299 | 236 | 239 |
| Rear Speaker W/AM Radio Only | 23 | 18 | 19 |
| Air Conditioning Package | 590 | 466 | 571 |
| Tinted Glass, All Windows | 64 | 51 | 52 |
| Electronic Cruise Control | 99 | 78 | 79 |
| Tilt Steering Wheel | 67 | 53 | 54 |
| Interior Decor/Convenience Group | 59 | 47 | 48 |
| Visibility Group | 81 | 64 | 65 |
| Left Remote-Control Mirror | 17 | 13 | 14 |
| Intermittent Wiper System | 32 | 25 | 26 |
| Third Seat, Wagon, W/2 Seat Belts & Power Tailgate Window | 143 | 113 | 115 |
| Stowage/Litter Containers | 10 | 8 | 9 |
| Electric Rear Window Defroster | 88 | 70 | 71 |
| Tailgate Air Deflector, Wagon | 27 | 21 | 22 |
| Roof Rack, Wagon | 84 | 66 | 67 |
| Sports Steering Wheel | 20 | 16 | 17 |
| Soft Feel Sports Steering Wheel | 31 | 25 | 26 |
| 4 Custom Wheel Covers | 23 | 18 | 19 |
| 4 Styled Road Wheels | 136 | 107 | 109 |
| 4 Aluminum Wheels | 236 | 186 | 188 |
| Protective Inner Coating | 106 | 84 | 85 |
| Door Edge Guards | 11 | 9 | 10 |
| Heavy-Duty Engine Cooling System | 29 | 23 | 24 |
| Maximum Cooling System | 48 | 38 | 39 |
| W/AC | 19 | 15 | 16 |
| 70-AMP Heavy-Duty Battery | 19 | 15 | 16 |
| Heavy-Duty Suspension | 36 | 28 | 29 |
| Rear Sway Bar | 18 | 14 | 15 |
| Rear Air-Adjustable Shock Absorbers | 48 | 38 | 39 |
| W/Heavy-Duty Suspension | 44 | 35 | 36 |
| Auxiliary Auto./Trans. Oil Cooler | 34 | 27 | 28 |
| Engine Block Heater | 20 | 16 | 17 |

## PACER

|  | Retail Price | Dealer Cost | Low Price |
|---|---|---|---|
| 2-Door Hatchback | $3998 | $3523 | $3773 |
| 2-Door Wagon | 4143 | 3650 | 3900 |

### PACER ACCESSORIES

| Engines |  |  |  |
|---|---|---|---|
| 258 CID, Six | $120 | $100 | $101 |
| 305 CID, V-8 | 233 | 193 | 195 |
| California Emission System & Factory Testing | 74 | 61 | 62 |

*Prices are accurate at time of printing; subject to manufacturer's change.*

|  | Retail Price | Dealer Cost | Low Price |
|---|---|---|---|
| High Altitude Emission Package | $ 23 | $ 19 | $ 20 |
| **Transmissions** | | | |
|    4-Speed Manual, Floor Shift | 111 | 92 | 93 |
|    Automatic, Column Shift | 296 | 246 | 249 |
|    Automatic, Floor Shift | 320 | 266 | 269 |
|    Twin-Grip Differential | 55 | 47 | 48 |
| Power Steering | 147 | 122 | 124 |
| Front Power Disc Brakes | 64 | 53 | 54 |
| Power Door Locks | 69 | 57 | 58 |
| Two-Tone Exterior Color | 84 | 70 | 71 |
| Special Exterior Color Combination | 24 | 20 | 21 |
| Vinyl Roof | 118 | 98 | 99 |
| Sport Package | 165 | 137 | 139 |
|    W/Wood-Grain | 111 | 92 | 93 |
| **Radio Equipment** | | | |
|    AM Push-Button | 80 | 66 | 67 |
|    AM/FM Push-Button Stereo W/4 Speakers | 224 | 186 | 188 |
|    AM/FM/Tape Stereo W/4 Speakers | 336 | 279 | 282 |
|    AM/CB Push-Button, 40-Channel | 199 | 165 | 167 |
|    AM/FM/CB Push-Button Stereo W/4 Speakers | 299 | 248 | 251 |
|    Rear Speaker W/AM Radio Only | 22 | 18 | 19 |
| Air Conditioning System | 478 | 397 | 401 |
| Air Conditioning Package W/A/C System, Tinted Glass & Power Steering | 679 | 564 | 570 |
| Tinted Glass, All Windows | 58 | 48 | 49 |
| Electronic Cruise Control | 99 | 82 | 83 |
| Tilt Steering Wheel | 64 | 53 | 54 |
| Gauge Package | 99 | 82 | 83 |
| Interior Decor/Convenience Group | 59 | 49 | 50 |
| Visibility Group | 61 | 51 | 52 |
| Left Remote Control Mirror | 16 | 13 | 14 |
| Intermittent Wiper System | 30 | 25 | 26 |
| Center Console | 29 | 24 | 25 |
| Hidden Compartment | 35 | 29 | 30 |
| Stowage/Litter Containers | 10 | 8 | 9 |
| Rear Window Washer/Wiper | 59 | 49 | 50 |
| Electric Rear Window Defroster | 81 | 67 | 68 |
| Roof Rack | 59 | 49 | 50 |
| Door Vent Windows | 34 | 28 | 29 |
| Sports Steering Wheel | 20 | 17 | 18 |
| Soft Feel Sports Steering Wheel | 31 | 26 | 27 |
|    W/Sport Package | 11 | 9 | 10 |
| 4 Custom Wheel Covers | 23 | 19 | 20 |
| 4 Styled Road Wheels | 136 | 113 | 115 |
| 4 Aluminum Styled Wheels | 236 | 196 | 198 |
|    W/Sport Package | 171 | 142 | 144 |
| Protective Inner Coating | 95 | 79 | 80 |

*Prices are accurate at time of printing; subject to manufacturer's change.*

|  | Retail Price | Dealer Cost | Low Price |
|---|---|---|---|
| Front & Rear Bumper Guards | $38 | $32 | $33 |
| Locking Gas Cap | 7 | 6 | 7 |
| Heavy-Duty Engine Cooling System | 29 | 24 | 25 |
| 70-AMP Heavy-Duty Battery | 17 | 14 | 15 |
| Heavy-Duty Suspension | 36 | 30 | 31 |
| Front Sway Bar | 18 | 15 | 16 |
| Engine Block Heater | 19 | 16 | 17 |

# CHRYSLER CORPORATION

# CHRYSLER

**CORDOBA**

| | Retail Price | Dealer Cost | Low Price |
|---|---|---|---|
| 2-Door Specialty Hardtop, V8 | $5750 | $4804 | $5104 |
| 2-Door Specialty Hardtop, 'S' | 5550 | 4637 | 4937 |

### CORDOBA ACCESSORIES

| | Retail Price | Dealer Cost | Low Price |
|---|---|---|---|
| **Engines** | | | |
| 400 CID 8 Cyl. 4-BBL, Heavy Duty | $128 | $102 | $104 |
| 360 CID 8 Cyl. 4-BBL, Heavy Duty | 102 | 82 | 83 |
| **Vinyl Roofs** | | | |
| Full, W/o Basic Group | 121 | 92 | 93 |
| Full, W/Basic Group | 5 | 4 | 5 |
| Landau | 117 | 89 | 90 |
| "Crown" Landau, W/o Basic Group | 785 | 596 | 602 |
| "Crown" Landau, W/Basic Group | 668 | 507 | 513 |
| Vinyl Side Moulding | 44 | 33 | 34 |
| **Tape Stripes** | | | |
| Body Side | 45 | 34 | 35 |
| Deck Lid | 23 | 17 | 18 |
| **Interior Trims** | | | |
| Vinyl Bench Seat W/Center Folding Arm Rest | 31 | 23 | 24 |

*Prices are accurate at time of printing; subject to manufacturer's change.*

| | Retail Price | Dealer Cost | Low Price |
|---|---|---|---|
| Velour & Vinyl 60/40 Bench Seat W/Center Arm Rest & Passenger Recliner | $140 | $106 | $108 |
| Velour & Vinyl Bucket Seats W/Center Seat Cushion W/Folding Center Arm Rest, Dual Recliners | 70 | 53 | 54 |
| Leather Bucket Seats W/Center Seat Cushion W/Folding Center Arm Rest, Dual Recliners | 220 | 168 | 170 |
| Light Pkg. | 28 | 21 | 22 |
| Basic Group | 1051 | 799 | 807 |
| Heavy Duty Package | 181 | 138 | 140 |
| Air Conditioning | 563 | 428 | 433 |
| Sure Grip Differential Axle | 60 | 46 | 47 |
| 500 AMP Long Life Battery | 33 | 25 | 26 |
| Protective Rub Strips, Front & Rear | 34 | 26 | 27 |
| Electronic Digital Clock | 50 | 38 | 39 |
| Console | 59 | 45 | 46 |
| Rear Window Defroster, Electric | 91 | 69 | 70 |
| Emission Control System & Testing | 78 | 59 | 60 |
| High Altitude Emission Control System | 25 | 19 | 20 |
| Locking Gas Cap | 7 | 5 | 6 |
| Tinted Glass | | | |
| All Windows | 64 | 49 | 50 |
| Windshield Only | 43 | 33 | 34 |
| Door Edge Protectors | 9 | 7 | 8 |
| Pedal Dress-Up | 10 | 7 | 8 |
| Power Assists | | | |
| Power Bench/Bucket or 60/40 Split Bench Seat, Left | 159 | 121 | 123 |
| Power Windows | 127 | 96 | 97 |
| Power Door Locks | 82 | 63 | 64 |
| Power Deck Lid Release | 22 | 17 | 18 |
| Radios & Speakers | | | |
| AM | 80 | 61 | 62 |
| AM W/40 Channel CB Transceiver & Power Tri-Band Antenna | | | |
| W/o Basic Group | 405 | 307 | 310 |
| W/Basic Group | 324 | 246 | 249 |
| AM/FM | | | |
| W/o Basic Group | 158 | 120 | 122 |
| W/Basic Group | 78 | 59 | 60 |
| W/8 Track Stereo Tape, 2 Front & 2 Rear Speakers | | | |
| W/o Basic Group | 229 | 174 | 176 |
| W/Basic Group | 149 | 113 | 115 |
| AM/FM Stereo, 2 Front & 2 Rear Speakers | | | |
| W/o Basic Group | 248 | 189 | 191 |
| W/Basic Group | 168 | 128 | 130 |

*Prices are accurate at time of printing; subject to manufacturer's change.*

|  | Retail Price | Dealer Cost | Low Price |
|---|---|---|---|
| AM/FM Stereo W/8 Track Stereo Tape, 2 Front & 2 Rear Speakers | | | |
|   W/o Basic Group | $352 | $268 | $271 |
|   W/Basic Group | 272 | 207 | 210 |
| AM/FM Stereo W/Electronic Search Tune, 2 Front & 2 Rear Speakers | | | |
|   W/o Basic Group | 379 | 288 | 291 |
|   W/Basic Group | 299 | 227 | 230 |
| Rear Speakers Single, Radio | 26 | 19 | 20 |
| Power Antenna | 46 | 35 | 36 |
| Seat Belts | 15 | 12 | 13 |
| Automatic Speed Control | 96 | 73 | 74 |
| Station Wagon Items | | | |
|   Air Deflectors | 29 | 22 | 23 |
|   Luggage Rack | 79 | 60 | 61 |
| Steering Wheels | | | |
|   Luxury | 19 | 14 | 15 |
|   Tilt | 63 | 48 | 49 |

## NEWPORT

| | | | |
|---|---|---|---|
| 2-Door Hardtop | $5727 | $4614 | $4914 |
| 4-Door Hardtop | 5802 | 4675 | 4975 |

## NEW YORKER BROUGHAM

| | | | |
|---|---|---|---|
| 2-Door Hardtop | 7591 | 5963 | 6313 |
| 4-Door Hardtop | 7715 | 6061 | 6561 |

## NEWPORT & NEW YORKER BROUGHAM ACCESSORIES

| | Retail | Dealer | Low |
|---|---|---|---|
| 440 CID 4-BBL Engine | $207 | $155 | $157 |
| Vinyl Roof | 149 | 112 | 114 |
| St. Regis Package, 2-Door Only | | | |
|   W/o Basic Group | 636 | 477 | 482 |
|   W/Basic Group | 482 | 362 | 366 |
| Vinyl Side Moulding | 51 | 38 | 39 |
| Bodyside Tape Upper Stripe | 46 | 34 | 35 |
| Deluxe Wiper/Washer Pkg. | 41 | 31 | 32 |
| Basic Group | 1237 | 927 | 937 |
| Heavy Duty Pkg. | 184 | 138 | 140 |
| Deluxe Sound Insulation Pkg. | 46 | 34 | 35 |
| Air Conditioners | | | |
|   Manual Control | 602 | 451 | 456 |
|   Automatic Temperature Control | | | |
|     W/o Basic Group | 693 | 520 | 526 |
|     W/Basic Group | 90 | 68 | 69 |
| Sure Grip Differential | 65 | 48 | 49 |

*Prices are accurate at time of printing; subject to manufacturer's change.*

|  | Retail Price | Dealer Cost | Low Price |
|---|---|---|---|
| 500 AMP Long Life Battery | $34 | $25 | $26 |
| Electric Clock | 23 | 18 | 19 |
| Electronic Digital Clock | 51 | 38 | 40 |
| Rear Window Electric Defroster | 92 | 69 | 70 |
| Emission Control System & Testing | 79 | 59 | 60 |
| High Altitude Emission Control System | 25 | 19 | 20 |
| Locking Gas Cap | 8 | 6 | 7 |
| Tinted Glass, All Windows | 80 | 60 | 61 |
| Manual Vent Windows, 4-Door Models | 46 | 34 | 35 |
| Engine Block Heater | 19 | 14 | 15 |
| Cornering Lights | 49 | 37 | 38 |
| Accessory Floor Mats | 21 | 16 | 17 |
| Power Assists | | | |
|   Power Bench or 50/50 Seat, Left 6-Way | 161 | 121 | 123 |
|   50/50 Seat, 6-Way, Left & Right | 322 | 241 | 144 |
|   Windows | 197 | 148 | 149 |
|   Door Locks | | | |
|     2-Door | 84 | 63 | 64 |
|     4-Door | 115 | 86 | 87 |
|   Deck Lid Release | 22 | 17 | 18 |
| Radios | | | |
|   AM | 103 | 77 | 78 |
|   AM W/CB Transceiver & Power Tri-Band Antenna | | | |
|     W/o Basic Group | 440 | 330 | 334 |
|     W/Basic Group | 337 | 253 | 256 |
|   AM/FM W/o Basic Group | 173 | 130 | 132 |
|   AM/FM W/Basic Group | 70 | 52 | 53 |
|   AM/FM Stereo W/CB Transceiver & 2 Front, 2 Rear Speakers | | | |
|     W/o Basic Group | 587 | 440 | 445 |
|     W/Basic Group | 484 | 363 | 367 |
|   AM/FM Stereo W/8 Track Tape & 2 Front, 2 Rear Speakers | | | |
|     W/o Basic Group | 353 | 265 | 268 |
|     W/Basic Group | 250 | 188 | 190 |
|   AM/FM Stereo W/Electronic Search Tune, & 2 Front, 2 Rear Speakers | | | |
|     W/o Basic Group | 369 | 277 | 280 |
|     W/Basic Group | 266 | 200 | 203 |
| Rear Speaker, Single | 26 | 19 | 20 |
| Power Antenna | 47 | 35 | 36 |
| Seat Belts | 17 | 13 | 14 |
| Automatic Speed Control | 99 | 74 | 75 |
| Steering Wheels | | | |
|   Tilt & Telescope | | | |
|     Newport | 119 | 89 | 90 |
|     New Yorker Brougham | 100 | 75 | 76 |

*Prices are accurate at time of printing; subject to manufacturer's change.*

|  | Retail Price | Dealer Cost | Low Price |
|---|---:|---:|---:|
| AM/FM Stereo W/40 Channel CB Transceiver & Power Tri-Band Antenna, 2 Front & 2 Rear Speakers | | | |
|    W/o Basic Group | $572 | $435 | $440 |
|    W/Basic Group | 492 | 374 | 378 |
| AM/FM Stereo W/8 Track Stereo Tape, 2 Front & 2 Rear Speakers | | | |
|    W/o Basic Group | 352 | 268 | 271 |
|    W/Basic Group | 272 | 207 | 210 |
| AM/FM Stereo W/Search Tune, 2 Front & 2 Rear Speakers | | | |
|    W/o Basic Group | 379 | 288 | 291 |
|    W/Basic Group | 299 | 227 | 230 |
|    Rear Speaker, Single | 26 | 19 | 20 |
|    Power Antenna | 46 | 35 | 36 |
| Seat Belts | 15 | 12 | 13 |
| Automatic Speed Control | 96 | 73 | 74 |
| Steering Wheels | | | |
|    Tilt | 63 | 48 | 49 |

## LE BARON

|  | Retail Price | Dealer Cost | Low Price |
|---|---:|---:|---:|
| 2-Door Coupe | $5114 | $4273 | $4573 |
| 4-Door Sedan | 5270 | 4403 | 4703 |
| Town & Country Wagon, 2 Seat | 5672 | 4739 | 5039 |
| **LE BARON MEDALLION** | | | |
| 2-Door Coupe | 5484 | 4582 | 4882 |
| 4-Door Sedan | 5640 | 4712 | 5012 |

### LE BARON ACCESSORIES

|  | Retail Price | Dealer Cost | Low Price |
|---|---:|---:|---:|
| Engines | | | |
|    318 CID 8 Cyl. 2-BBL | $176 | $141 | $143 |
|    360 CID 8 Cyl. 2-BBL | 285 | 228 | 231 |
|    360 CID 8 Cyl. 2-BBL, Heavy Duty | 345 | 276 | 279 |
|    360 CID 8 Cyl. 4-BBL | 330 | 264 | 267 |
|    360 CID 8 Cyl. 4-BBL, Heavy Duty | 481 | 385 | 389 |
|    318 CID 8 Cyl. 4-BBL | 221 | 177 | 179 |
| Vinyl Roofs | 137 | 104 | 106 |
| Vinyl Body Side Moulding | 44 | 33 | 34 |
| Rear Deck Tape Stripe | 23 | 17 | 18 |
| Interior Trim | | | |
|    Bench Seat, Vinyl, Split Back W/Center Arm Rest | 48 | 36 | 37 |
|    Leather 60/40 Split Bench Seat | | | |
|       Le Baron Madallion | 220 | 168 | 170 |
|       Town & Country Wagon | 376 | 285 | 288 |
|    Cloth 60/40 Split Bench Seat, Town & Country Wagon | 155 | 118 | 120 |
| Torqueflite Transmission | 158 | 120 | 122 |

*Prices are accurate at time of printing; subject to manufacturer's change.*

|  | Retail Price | Dealer Cost | Low Price |
|---|---|---|---|
| **Light Package** | | | |
| Le Baron | $80 | $61 | $62 |
| Le Medallion | 69 | 53 | 54 |
| Deluxe Wiper/Washer Pkg. | 41 | 31 | 32 |
| **Basic Group** | | | |
| Le Baron 2-Door Coupe | 1211 | 920 | 930 |
| Le Baron 4-Door Sedan, Town & Country Wagon | 1072 | 814 | 823 |
| Le Baron Medallion 2-Door Coupe | 1184 | 899 | 908 |
| Le Baron Medallion 4-Door Sedan | 1044 | 793 | 801 |
| Air Conditioning | 563 | 428 | 433 |
| Suregrip Differential Axle | 60 | 46 | 47 |
| 500 AMP Long Life Battery | 33 | 25 | 26 |
| Front Bumper Guards | 21 | 16 | 17 |
| Electronic Digital Clock | 50 | 38 | 39 |
| Rear Window Defroster, Electric | 91 | 69 | 70 |
| Emission Control System & Testing | 78 | 59 | 60 |
| High Altitude Emission Control System | 25 | 19 | 20 |
| Locking Gas Cap | 7 | 5 | 6 |
| Tinted Glass, All Windows | 64 | 49 | 50 |
| Cornering Lights | 48 | 37 | 38 |
| Accessory Floor Mats | 19 | 14 | 15 |
| **Power Assists** | | | |
| Power Bench Seat or 60/40 Split Bench Seat, Left | 159 | 121 | 123 |
| Power Windows | | | |
| 2-Door Models | 127 | 96 | 97 |
| 4-Door Models | 175 | 133 | 135 |
| Power Door Locks | | | |
| 2-Door Models | 82 | 63 | 64 |
| 4-Door Models | 114 | 86 | 87 |
| Power Deck Lid/Tailgate Release | | | |
| All Models Except Wagons | 22 | 17 | 18 |
| Wagons | 23 | 18 | 19 |
| **Radios & Speakers** | | | |
| AM | 80 | 61 | 62 |
| AM W/40 Channel CB Transceiver & Power Tri-Band Antenna | | | |
| W/o Basic Group | 405 | 307 | 311 |
| W/Basic Group | 324 | 246 | 249 |
| AM/FM | | | |
| W/o Basic Group | 158 | 120 | 122 |
| W/Basic Group | 78 | 59 | 60 |
| AM/FM Stereo, 2 Front & 2 Rear Speakers | | | |
| W/o Basic Group | 248 | 189 | 191 |
| W/Basic Group | 168 | 128 | 130 |
| AM/FM Stereo W/40 Channel CB Transceiver & Power Tri-Band Antenna, 2 Front & 2 Rear Speakers | | | |
| W/o Basic Group | 572 | 435 | 440 |

*Prices are accurate at time of printing; subject to manufacturer's change.*

# DODGE

| ASPEN | Retail Price | Dealer Cost | Low Price |
|---|---|---|---|
| 2-Door Sport Coupe | $3747 | $3280 | $3480 |
| 4-Door Sedan | 3865 | 3383 | 3583 |
| **ASPEN** | | | |
| 2-Seat Wagon | 4207 | 3682 | 3932 |

## ASPEN ACCESSORIES

| | Retail Price | Dealer Cost | Low Price |
|---|---|---|---|
| **Engines** | | | |
| 225 CID 6-Cyl. 2 BBL | $41 | $34 | $35 |
| 318 CID 8-Cyl. 2 BBL E.L.B. | | | |
|   Except Wagons | 123 | 102 | 104 |
|   Wagons | 82 | 68 | 69 |
| 360 CID 8-Cyl. 2 BBL H.D. E.L.B. | | | |
|   Except Wagons | 239 | 199 | 201 |
|   Wagons | 199 | 165 | 167 |
| 360 CID 8-Cyl. 2 BBL E.L.B. | | | |
|   Except Wagons | 178 | 148 | 150 |
|   Wagons | 138 | 114 | 116 |
| 360 CID 8-Cyl. 4 BBL E.L.B. | | | |
|   W/o R/T Pkg. | 378 | 314 | 318 |
|   W/ R/T Pkg. | 354 | 294 | 297 |
| 360 CID 8-Cyl. 4 BBL | | | |
|   W/o R/T Pkg. or Heavy Duty Pkg. | 378 | 314 | 318 |
|   W/R/T Pkg. or Heavy Duty Pkg. | 354 | 294 | 297 |
|   Wagons | 313 | 260 | 263 |
| 318 CID 8-Cyl. 4 BBL E.L.B. | | | |
|   Except Wagons | 168 | 140 | 142 |
|   Wagons | 128 | 106 | 108 |
| **Vinyl Roof** | | | |
| Full | 98 | 81 | 82 |
| **Interior Trim** | | | |
| Bucket Seat — Vinyl W/Cent. Cushion & C.A.R. | 102 | 85 | 86 |
| Bucket Seat — Cloth & Vinyl W/Cent. Cushion & C.A.R. | 160 | 133 | 135 |
| **Transmissions** | | | |
| Torqueflite | 286 | 238 | 241 |
| 4-Speed Manual Floor Shift O/Drive | 142 | 118 | 120 |
| Air Conditioning | 494 | 410 | 415 |
| Arm Rest Rear W/AshTray | 11 | 10 | 11 |

*Prices are accurate at time of printing; subject to manufacturer's change.*

|  | Retail Price | Dealer Cost | Low Price |
|---|---|---|---|
| Optional Axle Ratio | $15 | $13 | $14 |
| Sure Grip Differential Axle | 55 | 46 | 47 |
| 500 Amp — Long Life Battery | 30 | 25 | 26 |
| **Bumper Protection** | | | |
| Bumper Guards-Front & Rear | 39 | 32 | 33 |
| Protective Rub Strips-Front & Rear | 31 | 26 | 27 |
| Cigarette Lighter | 6 | 5 | 6 |
| Electronic Digital Clock | 46 | 38 | 39 |
| Console | 54 | 45 | 46 |
| **Rear Window Defogger** | | | |
| Blower Type | 48 | 40 | 41 |
| Electrically Heated | 83 | 69 | 70 |
| California Emission Control System | 71 | 59 | 60 |
| Emission Control System — Hi Altitude | 23 | 19 | 20 |
| Locking Gas Cap | 6 | 5 | 6 |
| **Tinted Glass** | | | |
| All Windows | 55 | 45 | 46 |
| Windshield Only | 39 | 33 | 34 |
| Inside Hood Release | 12 | 10 | 11 |
| Dual Horns | 6 | 5 | 6 |
| Glove Box Lock | 5 | 4 | 5 |
| Accessory Floor Mats | 17 | 14 | 15 |
| **Power Assists** | | | |
| Power Steering | 148 | 123 | 125 |
| Power Disc Brakes — Front | 62 | 52 | 53 |
| Power Seat — Left W/Bucket or 60/40 Split Bench Seat | 145 | 121 | 123 |
| **Power Door Locks** | | | |
| 2-Door Models | 75 | 63 | 64 |
| 4-Door Models | 104 | 86 | 87 |
| **Power Windows** | | | |
| 2-Door Models | 116 | 96 | 97 |
| 4-Door Models | 160 | 133 | 135 |
| **Radios & Speakers** | | | |
| AM | 74 | 61 | 62 |
| **AM W/40 Channel CB Trans. & Pwr. Tri-Band Antenna** | | | |
| W/o Basic Group | 370 | 307 | 311 |
| W/Basic Group | 297 | 246 | 249 |
| **AM/FM** | | | |
| W/o Basic Group | 145 | 120 | 122 |
| W/Basic Group | 71 | 59 | 60 |
| **AM W/8 Track Stereo Tape W/2 Front, 2 Rear Speakers** | | | |
| W/o Basic Group | 210 | 174 | 176 |
| W/Basic Group | 137 | 113 | 115 |

*Prices are accurate at time of printing; subject to manufacturer's change.*

|  | Retail Price | Dealer Cost | Low Price |
|---|---|---|---|
| AM/FM Stereo W/2 Front, 2 Rear Speakers | | | |
| W/o Basic Group | $227 | $189 | $191 |
| W/Basic Group | 154 | 128 | 130 |
| AM/FM Stereo W/40 Channel CB Trans. & Pwr. Tri-Band Antenna | | | |
| W/o Basic Group | 524 | 435 | 440 |
| W/Basic Group | 450 | 374 | 378 |
| Am/FM Stereo W/8 Track Stereo Tape W/2 Front, 2 Rear Speakers | | | |
| W/o Basic Group | 323 | 268 | 271 |
| W/Basic Group | 249 | 207 | 210 |
| Single Rear Speaker | 23 | 19 | 20 |
| Seat Belts | 14 | 12 | 13 |
| Automatic Speed Control | 88 | 73 | 74 |
| Station Wagon Items | | | |
| Air Deflectors | 27 | 22 | 23 |
| Car Compartment Carpet & Storage Bin | 50 | 42 | 43 |
| Luggage Rack | 72 | 60 | 61 |
| Pwr. Tailgate Release | 21 | 18 | 19 |
| Steering Wheels | | | |
| Luxury | 29 | 24 | 25 |
| "Tuff" | 37 | 31 | 32 |
| Tilt | 58 | 48 | 49 |

## CHARGER SPECIAL EDITION

|  | Retail Price | Dealer Cost | Low Price |
|---|---|---|---|
| 2-Door Specialty Hardtop | $5307 | $4434 | $4734 |

### CHARGER SPECIAL EDITION ACCESSORIES

|  | Retail Price | Dealer Cost | Low Price |
|---|---|---|---|
| Engines | | | |
| 360 CID 8-Cyl. 2 BBL — E.L.B. | $61 | $46 | $47 |
| 400 CID 8-Cyl. 4 BBL — E.L.B. | 165 | 125 | 127 |
| 400 CID 8-Cyl. 4 BBL — H.D. — E.L.B. | 308 | 234 | 237 |
| 360 CID 8-Cyl. 4 BBL | 111 | 84 | 85 |
| 318 CID 8-Cyl. 4 BBL — E.L.B. | 50 | 38 | 39 |
| 360 CID 8-Cyl. 4 BBL H.D. | 279 | 212 | 215 |
| Vinyl Roofs | | | |
| Full — W/o Basic Group | 124 | 94 | 95 |
| Full — W/Basic Group | 5 | 4 | 5 |
| Landau | 119 | 90 | 91 |
| Vinyl Side Moulding | 45 | 34 | 35 |
| Interior Trims | | | |
| Vinyl Bucket Seats W/Ctr. Cushion, Arm Rest | 187 | 142 | 144 |
| Light Pkg. | 28 | 21 | 22 |
| Basic Group | 1028 | 781 | 789 |
| Heavy Duty Pkg. | 181 | 138 | 140 |

*Prices are accurate at time of printing; subject to manufacturer's change.*

| | Retail Price | Dealer Cost | Low Price |
|---|---|---|---|
| Air Conditioning | $563 | $428 | $433 |
| Sure Grip Differential Axle | 60 | 46 | 47 |
| 500 Amp Long Life Battery | 33 | 25 | 26 |
| Electronic Digital Clock | 50 | 38 | 39 |
| Console | 59 | 45 | 46 |
| Electric Rear Window Defroster | 91 | 69 | 70 |
| Emission Control System & Testing | 78 | 59 | 60 |
| Emission Control System — Hi Altitude | 25 | 19 | 20 |
| Locking Gas Cap | 7 | 5 | 6 |
| **Tinted Glass** | | | |
| All Windows | 64 | 49 | 50 |
| Windshield Only | 43 | 33 | 34 |
| Accessory Floor Mats | 19 | 14 | 15 |
| Pedal Dress-Up | 10 | 7 | 8 |
| **Power Assists** | | | |
| Pwr. Bench or Bucket Seat—Left | 159 | 121 | 123 |
| Pwr. Windows | 127 | 96 | 97 |
| Pwr. Door Locks | 82 | 63 | 64 |
| Pwr. Deck Lid Release | 22 | 17 | 18 |
| **Radios & Speakers** | | | |
| AM | 80 | 61 | 62 |
| AM W/40 Channel CB Trans. & Pwr. Tri-Band Ant. | | | |
| W/o Basic Group | 405 | 307 | 311 |
| W/Basic Group | 324 | 246 | 249 |
| AM/FM | | | |
| W/o Basic Group | 158 | 120 | 122 |
| W/Basic Group | 78 | 59 | 60 |
| AM W/8 Track Stereo Tape | | | |
| W/o Basic Group | 229 | 174 | 176 |
| W/Basic Group | 149 | 113 | 115 |
| AM/FM Stereo, 2 Front & 2 Rear Spkrs. | | | |
| W/o Basic Group | 248 | 189 | 191 |
| W/Basic Group | 168 | 128 | 130 |
| AM/FM Stereo W/40 Channel CB Trans. & Pwr. Tri-Band Ant., 2 Front & 2 Rear Spkrs. | | | |
| W/o Basic Group | 572 | 435 | 440 |
| W/Basic Group | 492 | 374 | 378 |
| AM/FM Stereo W/8 Track Stereo Tape, 2 Front & 2 Rear Speakers | | | |
| W/o Basic Group | 352 | 268 | 271 |
| W/Basic Group | 272 | 207 | 210 |
| AM/FM Stereo W/Search Tune, 2 Front & 2 Rear Speakers | | | |
| W/o Basic Group | 379 | 288 | 291 |
| W/Basic Group | 299 | 227 | 230 |
| Single Rear Speaker | 26 | 19 | 20 |
| Pwr. Antenna | 46 | 35 | 36 |

*Prices are accurate at time of printing; subject to manufacturer's change.*

|  | Retail Price | Dealer Cost | Low Price |
|---|---|---|---|
| Seat Belts | $15 | $12 | $13 |
| Automatic Speed Control | 96 | 73 | 74 |
| **Steering Wheels** | | | |
| Luxury | 19 | 14 | 15 |
| Tilt | 63 | 48 | 49 |

## DIPLOMAT

|  | Retail Price | Dealer Cost | Low Price |
|---|---|---|---|
| 2-Door Coupe | $4991 | $4170 | $4470 |
| 4-Door Sedan | 5147 | 4301 | 4601 |
| 2-Seat Wagon | 5486 | 4584 | 4884 |
| **DIPLOMAT MEDALLION** | | | |
| 2-Door Coupe | 5361 | 4479 | 4779 |
| 4-Door Sedan | 5517 | 4610 | 4910 |

## DIPLOMAT ACCESSORIES

|  | Retail Price | Dealer Cost | Low Price |
|---|---|---|---|
| **Engines** | | | |
| 318 CID 8-Cyl. 2 BBL. E.L.B. | $127 | $102 | $104 |
| 360 CID 8-Cyl. 2 BBL. E.L.B. | 185 | 148 | 150 |
| 360 CID 8-Cyl. 2 BBL. Heavy Duty, E.L.B. | 248 | 199 | 201 |
| 360 CID 8-Cyl. 4 BBL. | 232 | 186 | 188 |
| 318 CID 8-Cyl. 4 BBL. E.L.B. | 175 | 140 | 142 |
| 360 CID 8-Cyl. 4 BBL, Heavy Duty | 392 | 314 | 318 |
| Torqueflite Transmission | 158 | 120 | 122 |
| Vinyl Roof-Landau | 140 | 106 | 108 |
| Vinyl Body Side Moulding | 45 | 34 | 35 |
| Hood Tape Stripe | 23 | 17 | 18 |
| Deluxe Wiper/Washer Package | 41 | 31 | 32 |
| **Basic Group** | | | |
| Diplomat 2-Door Coupe | 1211 | 920 | 1020 |
| Diplomat 4-Door Sedan & 2-Seat Wagon | 1072 | 814 | 913 |
| Diplomat Medallion 2-Door Coupe | 1184 | 899 | 908 |
| Diplomat Medallion 4-Door Sedan | 1044 | 793 | 801 |
| Heavy Duty Package | 153 | 116 | 118 |
| Air Conditioning | 563 | 428 | 433 |
| Suregrip Differential Axle | 60 | 46 | 47 |
| 500 AMP Long Life Battery | 33 | 25 | 26 |
| Front Bumper Guards | 21 | 16 | 17 |
| Electronic Digital Clock | 50 | 38 | 39 |
| Rear Window Electrically Heated Defroster | 91 | 69 | 70 |
| California Emission Control System | 78 | 59 | 60 |
| High Altitude Emission Control System | 25 | 19 | 20 |
| Locking Gas Cap | 7 | 5 | 6 |
| Tinted Glass, All Windows | 64 | 49 | 50 |
| Cornering Lights | 48 | 37 | 38 |
| Accessory Floor Mats | 19 | 14 | 15 |
| Power Bench Seat or 60/40 Split Bench Seat, Left | 159 | 121 | 123 |

*Prices are accurate at time of printing; subject to manufacturer's change.*

|  | Retail Price | Dealer Cost | Low Price |
|---|---|---|---|
| **Power Windows** | | | |
| 2-Door Models | $127 | $96 | $97 |
| 4-Door Models | 175 | 133 | 135 |
| **Power Door Locks** | | | |
| 2-Door Models | 82 | 63 | 64 |
| 4-Door Models | 114 | 86 | 87 |
| **Power Deck Lid/Tailgate Release** | | | |
| Models Except Wagons | 22 | 17 | 18 |
| Wagons Only | 23 | 18 | 19 |
| **Radio Equipment** | | | |
| AM | 80 | 61 | 62 |
| **AM W/40 Channel CB Trans. & Power Tri-Band Ant.** | | | |
| W/o Basic Group | 405 | 307 | 310 |
| W/Basic Group | 324 | 246 | 249 |
| **AM/FM** | | | |
| W/o Basic Group | 158 | 120 | 122 |
| W/Basic Group | 78 | 59 | 60 |
| **AM/FM Stereo W/2 Front & 2 Rear Speakers** | | | |
| W/o Basic Group | 248 | 189 | 191 |
| W/Basic Group | 168 | 128 | 130 |
| **AM/FM Stereo W/40 Channel CB Tran. & Power Tri-Band Ant. W/2 Front & 2 Rear Speakers** | | | |
| W/o Basic Group | 572 | 435 | 440 |
| W/Basic Group | 492 | 374 | 378 |
| **AM/FM Stereo W/8 Track Stereo Tape** | | | |
| W/o Basic Group | 352 | 268 | 271 |
| W/Basic Group | 272 | 207 | 210 |
| **AM/FM Stereo W/Electronic Search Tune, W/2 Front & 2 Rear Speakers** | | | |
| W/o Basic Group | 379 | 288 | 291 |
| W/Basic Group | 299 | 227 | 230 |
| Single Rear Speakers | 26 | 19 | 20 |
| Power Antenna | 46 | 35 | 36 |
| Color-Keyed Seat Belts | 15 | 12 | 13 |
| Automatic Speed Control | 96 | 73 | 74 |
| Air Deflectors, Station Wagon Only | 29 | 22 | 23 |
| Luggage Rack, Station Wagon Only | 79 | 60 | 61 |
| **Steering Wheels** | | | |
| Luxury | 19 | 14 | 15 |
| Tilt | 63 | 48 | 49 |
| Leather Covered, 2-Spoke | 19 | 14 | 15 |
| Leather Covered, 3-Spoke | 56 | 43 | 44 |

## MAGNUM XE

| | | | |
|---|---|---|---|
| 2-Door Specialty Hardtop | $5448 | $4552 | $4852 |

*Prices are accurate at time of printing; subject to manufacturer's change.*

|  | Retail Price | Dealer Cost | Low Price |
|---|---|---|---|
| **MAGNUM XE ACCESSORIES** | | | |
| **Engines** | | | |
| 360 CID 8-Cyl. 2 BBL — E.L.B. | $61 | $46 | $47 |
| 400 CID 8-Cyl. 4 BBL — E.L.B. | 165 | 125 | 127 |
| 400 CID 8-Cyl. 4 BBL H.D. — E.L.B. | 308 | 234 | 237 |
| 360 CID 8-Cyl. 4 BBL — Single Exhaust | 111 | 84 | 85 |
| 318 CID 8-Cyl. 4 BBL — Single Exhaust | 50 | 38 | 39 |
| 360 CID 8-Cyl. 4 BBL H.D. — Single Exhaust | 279 | 212 | 215 |
| Light Package | 28 | 21 | 22 |
| Basic Group | 984 | 748 | 756 |
| Heavy Duty Pkg. | 181 | 138 | 140 |
| Air Conditioning | 563 | 428 | 433 |
| Sure Grip Differential Axle | 60 | 46 | 47 |
| 500 Amp Long Life Battery | 33 | 25 | 26 |
| Front & Rear Protective Rub Strips | 34 | 26 | 27 |
| Electronic Digital Clock | 50 | 38 | 39 |
| **Tinted Glass** | | | |
| All Windows | 64 | 49 | 50 |
| Windshield Only | 43 | 33 | 34 |
| Accessory Floor Mats | 19 | 14 | 15 |
| **Power Assists** | | | |
| Pwr. Bucket or 60/40 Split Bench Seat-Left | 159 | 121 | 123 |
| Pwr. Windows | 127 | 96 | 97 |
| Pwr. Door Locks | 82 | 63 | 64 |
| Pwr. Deck Lid Release | 22 | 17 | 18 |
| **Radios Speakers** | | | |
| AM | 80 | 61 | 62 |
| AM W/40 Ch. CB Trans. & Pwr. Tri-Band Antenna | | | |
| W/o Basic Group | 405 | 307 | 311 |
| W/Basic Group | 324 | 246 | 249 |
| AM/FM | | | |
| W/o Basic Group | 158 | 120 | 122 |
| W/Basic Group | 78 | 59 | 60 |
| AM W/8 Track Stereo Tape & 2 Front & 2 Rear Spkrs. | | | |
| W/o Basic Group | 229 | 174 | 176 |
| W/Basic Group | 149 | 113 | 115 |
| AM/FM Stereo W/2 Front & 2 Rear Spkrs. | | | |
| W/o Basic Group | 248 | 189 | 191 |
| W/Basic Group | 168 | 128 | 130 |
| AM/FM Stereo W/40 Ch. CB Trans. & Pwr. Tri-Band Antenna, 2 Front & 2 Rear Spkrs. | | | |
| W/o Basic Group | 572 | 435 | 440 |
| W/Basic Group | 492 | 374 | 378 |
| AM/FM Stereo W/8 Track Stereo Tape, 2 Front & 2 Rear Spkrs. | | | |
| W/o Basic Group | 352 | 268 | 271 |
| W/Basic Group | 272 | 207 | 210 |

*Prices are accurate at time of printing; subject to manufacturer's change.*

|  | Retail Price | Dealer Cost | Low Price |
|---|---|---|---|
| AM/FM Stereo W/Search Tune, 2 Front & 2 Rear Spkrs. | | | |
| W/o Basic Group | $379 | $288 | $291 |
| W/Basic Group | 299 | 227 | 230 |
| Single Rear Speaker | 26 | 19 | 20 |
| Power Antenna | 46 | 35 | 36 |
| Seat Belts | 15 | 12 | 13 |
| Automatic Speed Control | 96 | 73 | 74 |
| Steering Wheels | | | |
| Luxury | 19 | 14 | 18 |
| Tilt | 63 | 48 | 49 |

## DODGE MONACO

### MONACO
| | | | |
|---|---|---|---|
| 2-Door Hardtop | $4230 | $3535 | $3785 |
| 4-Door Sedan | 4301 | 3602 | 3852 |

### MONACO BROUGHAM
| | | | |
|---|---|---|---|
| 2-Door Hardtop | 4476 | 3740 | 3990 |
| 4-Door Sedan | 4525 | 3783 | 4033 |

### MONACO WAGON
| | | | |
|---|---|---|---|
| 2-Seat Wagon | 5043 | 4214 | 4514 |
| 3-Seat Wagon | 5186 | 4333 | 4633 |

### MONACO CRESTWOOD WAGON
| | | | |
|---|---|---|---|
| 2-Seat Wagon | 5486 | 4584 | 4884 |
| 3-Seat Wagon | 5629 | 4703 | 5003 |

## MONACO ACCESSORIES

| | Retail | Dealer | Low |
|---|---|---|---|
| Engines | | | |
| 318 CID 8-Cyl. 2 BBL E.L.B. | | | |
| Sedans & Hardtops | $127 | $102 | $104 |
| 360 CID 8-Cyl. 2 BBL E.L.B. | | | |
| Sedans & Hardtops | 185 | 148 | 150 |
| 400 CID 8-Cyl. 4 BBL E.L.B. | | | |
| Sedans & Hardtops | 284 | 227 | 230 |
| Wagons | 99 | 79 | 80 |
| 400 CID 8-Cyl. 4 BBL H.D., E.L.B. | | | |
| Sedans & Hardtops | 419 | 335 | 339 |
| Wagons | 234 | 188 | 190 |
| 360 CID 8-Cyl. 4 BBL | | | |
| Sedans & Hardtops | 232 | 186 | 188 |
| Wagons | 47 | 38 | 39 |
| 318 CID 8-Cyl. 4 BBL E.L.B. | 175 | 140 | 142 |
| 360 CID 8-Cyl. 4 BBL H.D. | 392 | 314 | 318 |
| Torqueflite Transmission | 313 | 238 | 241 |
| Vinyl Roofs | | | |
| Full, Halo or Canopy W/Opera Window | 124 | 94 | 95 |
| Canopy | 100 | 76 | 77 |

*Prices are accurate at time of printing; subject to manufacturer's change.*

|  | Retail Price | Dealer Cost | Low Price |
|---|---|---|---|
| Air Conditioning | $563 | $428 | $433 |
| Sure Grip Differential Axle | 60 | 46 | 47 |
| 500 Amp Long Life Battery | 33 | 25 | 26 |
| Bumper Protection | | | |
|     Protective Rub Strips, Front | 17 | 13 | 14 |
|     Protective Rub Strips, Front & Rear | 34 | 26 | 27 |
| Electric Clock | 22 | 17 | 18 |
| Console | 58 | 45 | 46 |
| Rear Window Defroster | 91 | 69 | 70 |
| Emission Control System & Testing | 78 | 59 | 60 |
| Emission Control System, Hi Altitude | 25 | 19 | 20 |
| Locking Gas Cap | 7 | 5 | 6 |
| Tinted Glass | | | |
|     All Windows | 64 | 49 | 50 |
|     Windshield Only | 43 | 33 | 34 |
| Inside Hood Release | 13 | 10 | 11 |
| Dual Horns | 7 | 5 | 6 |
| Accessory Floor Mats | 19 | 14 | 15 |
| Power Assists | | | |
|     Power Steering | 162 | 123 | 125 |
|     Power Bucket or 60/40 Split Bench Seat, L. | 159 | 121 | 123 |
|     Power Windows | | | |
|         2-Door Models | 127 | 96 | 97 |
|         4-Door Models | 175 | 133 | 135 |
|     Power Door Locks | | | |
|         2-Door Models | 82 | 63 | 64 |
|         4-Door Models | 114 | 86 | 87 |
| Radio & Speakers | | | |
|     AM | 80 | 61 | 62 |
|     AM W/40 Ch. CB Trans. & Pwr. Tri-Band Ant. | | | |
|         W/o Basic Group | 405 | 307 | 311 |
|         W/Basic Group | 324 | 246 | 249 |
|     AM/FM | | | |
|         W/o Basic Group | 158 | 120 | 122 |
|         W/Basic Group | 78 | 59 | 60 |
|     AM W/8 Track Stereo Tape & 2 Front & 2 Rear Speakers | | | |
|         W/o Basic Group | 229 | 174 | 176 |
|         W/Basic Group | 149 | 113 | 115 |
|     AM/FM Stereo & 2 Front & 2 Rear Spkrs. | | | |
|         W/o Basic Group | 248 | 189 | 191 |
|         W/Basic Group | 168 | 128 | 130 |
|     AM/FM Stereo W/40 Ch. CB Trans. & Pwr. Tri-Band Ant. & 2 Front & 2 Rear Spkrs. | | | |
|         W/o Basic Group | 572 | 435 | 440 |
|         W/Basic Group | 492 | 374 | 378 |
|     AM/FM Stereo W/8 Track Stereo Tape & 2 Front & 2 | | | |

*Prices are accurate at time of printing; subject to manufacturer's change.*

|  | Retail Price | Dealer Cost | Low Price |
|---|---|---|---|
| Rear Speakers | | | |
|   W/o Basic Group | $352 | $268 | $271 |
|   W/Basic Group | 272 | 207 | 210 |
| Single Rear Speaker | 26 | 19 | 20 |
| Seat Belts, Color Keyed | 15 | 12 | 13 |
| Automatic Speed Control | 96 | 73 | 74 |
| Station Wagon Items | | | |
|   Air Deflector | 29 | 22 | 23 |
|   Auto. Lock Tailgate | 39 | 30 | 31 |
|   Luggage Rack | 79 | 60 | 61 |
|   Pwr. Tailgate Window | 46 | 35 | 36 |
| Steering Wheels | | | |
|   Luxury | 19 | 14 | 15 |
|   Tilt | 63 | 48 | 49 |

# PLYMOUTH

| | Retail Price | Dealer Cost | Low Price |
|---|---|---|---|
| **FURY** | | | |
| 2-Door Hardtop | $4212 | $3520 | $3770 |
| 4-Door Sedan | 4292 | 3587 | 3837 |
| **FURY SPORT** | | | |
| 2-Door Hardtop | 4452 | 3720 | 3970 |
| **FURY SALON** | | | |
| 4-Door Sedan | 4527 | 3783 | 4033 |
| **FURY SUBURBAN** | | | |
| 2-Seat Wagon | 5024 | 4198 | 4498 |
| 3-Seat Wagon | 5167 | 4317 | 4617 |
| **FURY SPORT SUBURBAN** | | | |
| 2-Seat Wagon | 5482 | 4580 | 4880 |
| 3-Seat Wagon | 5625 | 4700 | 5000 |
| **FURY ACCESSORIES** | | | |
| Engines | | | |
|   318 CID 8-Cyl. 2 BBL E.L.B. | $176 | $141 | $143 |
|   360 CID 8-Cyl. 2 BBL E.L.B. | 285 | 228 | 231 |
|   400 CID 8-Cyl. 4 BBL E.L.B. | | | |
|     Hardtops & Sedans | 379 | 303 | 307 |
|     All Wagons | 94 | 75 | 76 |
|   400 CID 8-Cyl. 4 BBL H.D. E.L.B. | | | |
|     Hardtops & Sedans | 507 | 405 | 410 |
|     All Wagons | 222 | 177 | 179 |
|   360 CID 8-Cyl. 4 BBL | | | |
|     Hardtops & Sedans | 330 | 264 | 267 |

*Prices are accurate at time of printing; subject to manufacturer's change.*

|  | Retail Price | Dealer Cost | Low Price |
|---|---|---|---|
| All Wagons | $ 45 | $ 36 | $ 37 |
| 318 CID 8-Cyl. 4 BBL E.L.B. | 221 | 177 | 179 |
| 360 CID 8-Cyl. 4 BBL H.D. Pkg. | 481 | 385 | 389 |
| **Vinyl Roofs** | | | |
| Full | 121 | 92 | 93 |
| Halo | 121 | 92 | 93 |
| Canopy | 100 | 76 | 77 |
| Canopy W/Opera Window | 124 | 94 | 95 |
| **Vinyl Side Moulding** | | | |
| Narrow | 45 | 34 | 35 |
| Wide | 47 | 36 | 37 |
| Torqueflite Transmission | 320 | 243 | 246 |
| Air Conditioning | 563 | 428 | 433 |
| Sure-Grip Differential Axle | 60 | 46 | 47 |
| 500 Amp Long Life Battery | 33 | 25 | 26 |
| Electric Clock | 22 | 17 | 18 |
| Console | 59 | 45 | 46 |
| Rear Window Defroster | 91 | 69 | 70 |
| **Tinted Glass** | | | |
| All Windows | 64 | 49 | 50 |
| Windshield Only | 43 | 33 | 34 |
| **Power Assists** | | | |
| Power Steering | 159 | 121 | 123 |
| Power Bucket or 60/40 Split Bench Seat, Left | 155 | 118 | 120 |
| **Power Windows** | | | |
| 2-Door Models | 129 | 98 | 99 |
| 4-Door Models | 179 | 136 | 138 |
| **Power Door Locks** | | | |
| 2-Door Models | 83 | 63 | 64 |
| 4-Door Models | 116 | 88 | 89 |
| **Radios & Speakers** | | | |
| AM | 81 | 61 | 62 |
| **AM W/40 Channel CB Transceiver** | | | |
| W/o Basic Group | 414 | 314 | 318 |
| W/Basic Group | 333 | 253 | 256 |
| **AM/FM** | | | |
| W/o Basic Group | 161 | 122 | 124 |
| W/Basic Group | 81 | 61 | 62 |
| **AM W/8-Track Stereo Tape & 2 Front & 2 Rear Speakers** | | | |
| W/o Basic Group | 237 | 180 | 182 |
| W/Basic Group | 157 | 119 | 121 |
| **AM/FM Stereo, 2-Front & 2 Rear Speakers** | | | |
| W/o Basic Group | 237 | 180 | 182 |
| W/Basic Group | 157 | 119 | 121 |
| AM/FM Stereo W/40 Channel CB Transceiver W/2 | | | |

*Prices are accurate at time of printing; subject to manufacturer's change.*

|  | Retail Price | Dealer Cost | Low Price |
|---|---|---|---|
| Front & 2-Rear Speakers | | | |
| W/o Basic Group | $570 | $433 | $438 |
| W/Basic Group | 490 | 372 | 376 |
| AM/FM Stereo W/8-Track Stereo Tape & 2 Front & 2 Rear Speakers | | | |
| W/o Basic Group | 336 | 256 | 259 |
| W/Basic Group | 256 | 194 | 196 |
| Single Rear Speaker | 26 | 19 | 20 |
| Seat Belts | 15 | 12 | 13 |
| Automatic Speed Control | 94 | 71 | 72 |
| Station Wagon Items | | | |
| Air Deflector | 29 | 22 | 23 |
| Auto. Lock Tailgate | 39 | 30 | 31 |
| Luggage Rack | 79 | 60 | 61 |
| Power Tailgate Window | 46 | 35 | 36 |
| Steering Wheels | | | |
| Luxury | 19 | 14 | 15 |
| Tilt | 63 | 48 | 49 |

## VOLARÉ

|  | Retail Price | Dealer Cost | Low Price |
|---|---|---|---|
| 2-Door Sport Coupe | $3735 | $3269 | $3469 |
| 4-Door Sedan | 3853 | 3372 | 3572 |

## VOLARÉ

|  | Retail Price | Dealer Cost | Low Price |
|---|---|---|---|
| 2-Seat Wagon | 4195 | 3672 | 3922 |

## VOLARÉ ACCESSORIES

|  | Retail Price | Dealer Cost | Low Price |
|---|---|---|---|
| Engines | | | |
| 225 CID 6 Cyl. 2-BBL | $41 | $34 | $35 |
| 318 CID 8 Cyl. 2-BBL | | | |
| Except Wagons | 170 | 141 | 143 |
| Wagons | 129 | 107 | 109 |
| 360 CID 8 Cyl. 2-BBL | | | |
| Except Wagons | 332 | 276 | 279 |
| Wagons | 292 | 242 | 245 |
| 360 CID 8 Cyl. 2-BBL | | | |
| Except Wagons | 275 | 228 | 231 |
| Wagons | 234 | 194 | 196 |
| 360 CID 8 Cyl. 4-BBL | | | |
| W/o Road Runner Pkg. or Heavy Duty Pkg. | 463 | 385 | 389 |
| W/Road Runner Pkg. or Heavy Duty Pkg. | 439 | 365 | 369 |
| Wagons | 399 | 331 | 335 |
| 318 CID 8 Cyl. 4-BBL | | | |
| Except Wagons | 213 | 177 | 179 |
| Wagons | 172 | 143 | 145 |
| Transmissions | | | |
| Torqueflite | 293 | 243 | 246 |
| Light Package | 44 | 36 | 37 |

*Prices are accurate at time of printing; subject to manufacturer's change.*

| | Retail Price | Dealer Cost | Low Price |
|---|---|---|---|
| 4-Speed Manual Floor Shift O/Drive | $42 | $118 | $120 |
| Air Conditioning | 484 | 401 | 406 |
| Rear Arm Rest W/Ash Tray | 11 | 10 | 11 |
| Axle Ratio, Optional | 15 | 13 | 14 |
| Sure Grip Differential Axle | 55 | 46 | 47 |
| 500 AMP Long Life Battery | 30 | 25 | 26 |
| Front & Rear Bumper Guards | 39 | 32 | 33 |
| Front & Rear Protective Rub Strips | 31 | 26 | 27 |
| Cigarette Lighter | 6 | 5 | 6 |
| Electronic Digital Clock | 46 | 38 | 39 |
| Console | 54 | 45 | 46 |
| Rear Window Defogger | 48 | 40 | 41 |
| Rear Window Defroster | 83 | 69 | 70 |
| Glass | | | |
|    Tinted, All Windows | 55 | 45 | 46 |
|    Tinted, Windshield Only | 39 | 33 | 34 |
| Power Assists | | | |
|    Power Steering | 145 | 121 | 123 |
|    Power Disc Brakes, Front | 66 | 55 | 56 |
|    Power Seat, Left W/Bucket or 60/40 Split Bench Seat | 142 | 121 | 123 |
|    Power Door Locks | | | |
|       2-Door Models | 71 | 59 | 60 |
|       4-Door Models | 98 | 82 | 83 |
|    Power Windows | | | |
|       2-Door Models | 113 | 94 | 95 |
|       4-Door Models | 157 | 130 | 132 |
| Radio & Speakers | | | |
|    AM | 74 | 61 | 62 |
|    AM W/40 Channel CB Transceiver & Power Tri-Band Antenna | | | |
|       W/o Basic Group | 370 | 307 | 311 |
|       W/Basic Group | 297 | 246 | 249 |
|    AM/FM | | | |
|       W/o Basic Group | 145 | 120 | 122 |
|       W/Basic Group | 71 | 59 | 60 |
|    AM W/8 Track Stereo Tape, 2 Front & 2 Rear Speakers | | | |
|       W/o Basic Group | 210 | 174 | 176 |
|       W/Basic Group | 137 | 113 | 115 |
|    AM/FM Stereo, 2 Front & 2 Rear Speakers | | | |
|       W/o Basic Group | 227 | 189 | 191 |
|       W/Basic Group | 154 | 128 | 130 |
|    AM/FM Stereo W/40 Channel CB Transceiver & Power Tri-Ban Antenna, 2 Front & 2 Rear Speakers | | | |
|       W/o Basic Group | 524 | 435 | 440 |
|       W/Basic Group | 450 | 374 | 378 |

*Prices are accurate at time of printing; subject to manufacturer's change.*

|  | Retail Price | Dealer Cost | Low Price |
|---|---|---|---|
| AM/FM Stereo W/8 Track Stereo Tape, 2 Front & 2 Rear Speakers | | | |
|    W/o Basic Group | $323 | $268 | $271 |
|    W/Basic Group | 249 | 207 | 210 |
| Rear Speaker, Single, Radio Code | 23 | 19 | 20 |
| Seat Belts | 14 | 12 | 13 |
| Automatic Speed Control | 88 | 73 | 74 |
| Station Wagon Items | | | |
|    Air Deflectors | 27 | 22 | 23 |
|    Cargo Compartment Carpet & Stowage Bin | 50 | 42 | 43 |
|    Luggage Rack | 72 | 60 | 61 |
|    Power Tailgate Release | 21 | 18 | 19 |
| Steering Wheels | | | |
|    Luxury | 29 | 24 | 25 |
|    "Tuff" | 37 | 31 | 32 |
|    Tilt Steering Wheel | 58 | 48 | 49 |
| Vinyl Roof | | | |
|    Full | 93 | 77 | 78 |
|    Halo | | | |
|       W/o Road Runner Decor Group, Custom Exterior Pkg. or Premium Exterior Pkg. | 109 | 90 | 91 |
|       W/Road Runner Decor Group, Custom Exterior Pkg. or Premium Exterior Pkg. | 93 | 77 | 78 |
|    Landau | 164 | 136 | 138 |

# FORD MOTOR COMPANY

# FORD

**FAIRMONT**

|  | | | |
|---|---|---|---|
| 2-Door Sedan | $3589 | $3124 | $3324 |
| 4-Door Sedan | 3663 | 3188 | 3388 |
| 4-Door Station Wagon | 4031 | 3508 | 3758 |

### FAIRMONT ACCESSORIES

| Engines | | | |
|---|---|---|---|
|    3.3 Litre (200 CID) IV 6-Cylinder | $120 | $102 | $104 |

*Prices are accurate at time of printing; subject to manufacturer's change.*

|  | Retail Price | Dealer Cost | Low Price |
|---|---|---|---|
| 5.0 Litre (302 CID) 2V 8-Cylinder | $319 | $271 | $274 |
| 5.0 Litre (302 CID) VV 8-Cylinder | 319 | 271 | 274 |
| Selectshift Cruise-O-Matic Transmissions | | | |
|    Sedan Models | 368 | 313 | 317 |
|    Station Wagon Models | 281 | 239 | 242 |
| Exterior Accent Group | 77 | 66 | 67 |
| Interior Accent Group | 82 | 70 | 71 |
| Selectaire Air Conditioner | 465 | 395 | 399 |
| Heavy-Duty Battery | 17 | 14 | 15 |
| Power Front Disc Brakes | 63 | 53 | 54 |
| Rear Window Defogger | 47 | 40 | 41 |
| Rear Window Electric Defroster | 84 | 72 | 73 |
| E. S. Option | 255 | 217 | 220 |
| California Emission Equipment | 67 | 57 | 58 |
| Floor Shift | 30 | 26 | 27 |
| Tinted Glass, Complete | 51 | 43 | 44 |
| Liftgate Washer/Wiper W/Lockable Side Stowage Box | 76 | 65 | 66 |
| Light Group | 39 | 33 | 34 |
| Luggage Rack | 71 | 60 | 61 |
| Radio | | | |
|    AM | 72 | 61 | 62 |
|    W/8-Track Stereo Tape, AM | 192 | 163 | 165 |
|    AM/FM Monaural | 120 | 102 | 104 |
|    AM/FM Stereo | 176 | 150 | 152 |
|    W/Cassette Tape Player, AM/FM Stereo | 243 | 207 | 210 |
|    W/8-Track Stereo Tape, AM/FM Stereo | 243 | 207 | 210 |
| Vinyl Roof | 89 | 76 | 77 |
| Bench Seat | (72) | (61) | (62) |
| Bucket Seats (Non-Reclining) | 72 | 61 | 62 |
| Squire Option | 369 | 313 | 317 |
| Power Steering | 140 | 119 | 121 |
| Lockable Side Storage Box | 19 | 16 | 17 |
| Handling Suspension | 30 | 26 | 27 |
| Sports Steering Wheel | 19 | 16 | 17 |
| Trim | | | |
|    Base Level Cloth Seat | 19 | 16 | 17 |
|    Accent Level Cloth Seat | 39 | 33 | 34 |
|    Decor Level Vinyl Seat | 22 | 18 | 19 |
| Trim Rings/Hub Caps | | | |
|    Station Wagon W/Sq. Option | | | |
|       or W/Ext. Accent | 6 | 5 | 6 |
|    All Other Models | 39 | 33 | 34 |

## GRANADA

|  | Retail Price | Dealer Cost | Low Price |
|---|---|---|---|
| 2-Door Sedan | $4264 | $3626 | $3876 |
| 4-Door Sedan | 4342 | 3693 | 3943 |

*Prices are accurate at time of printing; subject to manufacturer's change.*

|  | Retail Price | Dealer Cost | Low Price |
|---|---|---|---|
| **GRANADA GHIA** | | | |
| 2-Door Sedan | $4649 | $3954 | $4204 |
| 4-Door Sedan | 4728 | 4020 | 4320 |
| **GRANADA ESS** | | | |
| 2-Door Sedan | 4836 | 4112 | 4412 |
| 4-Door Sedan | 4914 | 4179 | 4479 |

## GRANADA ACCESSORIES

|  | Retail Price | Dealer Cost | Low Price |
|---|---|---|---|
| **Engines** | | | |
| 5.0 Litre (302 CID) 2V 8-Cylinder | $181 | $154 | $156 |
| 5.0 Litre (302 CID) VV 8-Cylinder | 181 | 154 | 156 |
| Selectshift Cruise-O-Matic Transmission | 193 | 164 | 166 |
| **Selectaire, Air Conditioner** | | | |
| W/Manual Temperature Control | 494 | 420 | 425 |
| W/Automatic Temperature Control | 535 | 455 | 460 |
| Deluxe Color Keyed Belts | 19 | 16 | 17 |
| 4-Wheel Power Disc. Brakes | 300 | 255 | 258 |
| Power Front Disc Brakes | 63 | 53 | 54 |
| Deluxe Bumper Group | 70 | 59 | 60 |
| Digital Clock | 42 | 36 | 37 |
| **Cold Weather Group** | | | |
| W/4.1 Litre (250 CID) IV or 5.0 Litre (302 CID) Engine W/Air & Elec. Defroster | 37 | 32 | 33 |
| All Other Models | 54 | 46 | 47 |
| Console | 75 | 64 | 65 |
| Front Cornering Lamps | 42 | 36 | 37 |
| Electric Power Decklid Release | 18 | 15 | 16 |
| Interior Decor Group | 182 | 155 | 157 |
| Rear Window Defogger | 46 | 39 | 40 |
| California Emission Equipment | 67 | 57 | 58 |
| Floor Shift | 30 | 26 | 27 |
| Tinted Glass, Complete | 54 | 46 | 47 |
| Illuminated Entry System | 49 | 42 | 43 |
| Luxury Interior Group | 434 | 369 | 373 |
| **Light Group** | | | |
| 4-Door Sedan | 42 | 36 | 37 |
| 4-Door Ghia & ESS W/Luxury Interior Group | 27 | 23 | 24 |
| All Other Models | 37 | 32 | 33 |
| **Electric Power Door Locks** | | | |
| 2-Door Models | 70 | 59 | 60 |
| 4-Door Models | 99 | 84 | 85 |
| Pass. Side Illum. Visor Vanity Mirror | 45 | 38 | 39 |
| **Dual Sport Mirrors** | | | |
| Sedan Models | 49 | 42 | 43 |
| Ghia Models | 36 | 31 | 32 |
| **Radios** | | | |
| AM | 72 | 61 | 62 |

*Prices are accurate at time of printing; subject to manufacturer's change.*

|  | Retail Price | Dealer Cost | Low Price |
|---|---|---|---|
| AM/FM Monaural | $135 | $115 | $117 |
| AM/FM Stereo | 176 | 150 | 152 |
| AM/FM Stereo Search | 319 | 271 | 274 |
| W/8-Track Tape Player, AM/FM Stereo | 243 | 207 | 210 |
| Citizens Band | 270 | 229 | 232 |
| W/Stereo Tape Player, AM | 192 | 163 | 165 |
| W/Cassette Tape Player, AM/FM Stereo | 243 | 207 | 210 |
| W/Quadrasonic Tape Player, AM/FM Stereo | 365 | 310 | 314 |
| Full Vinyl Roof | 102 | 87 | 88 |
| Half Vinyl Roof | 102 | 87 | 88 |
| Seats | | | |
|   4-Way Manual Driver's Bucket | 33 | 28 | 29 |
|   4-Way Power | 140 | 119 | 121 |
|   Reclining Individual | 67 | 57 | 58 |
| Fingertip Speed Control | | | |
|   ESS Models | 55 | 47 | 48 |
|   4-Door Ghia W/Luxury Interior Group | 90 | 77 | 78 |
|   All Other Models | 102 | 87 | 88 |
| Tilt Steering Wheel | 58 | 49 | 50 |
| Power Steering | 148 | 126 | 128 |
| Bodyside/Decklid Paint Stripes | 29 | 25 | 26 |
| Heavy-Duty Suspension | 27 | 23 | 24 |
| Trim | | | |
|   Cloth Flight Bench Seat | 13 | 11 | 12 |
|   Deluxe Cloth Seat/Door on Ghia & ESS Models | 99 | 84 | 85 |
|   Leather Seat | 204 | 173 | 175 |

### FORD LTD
|  | Retail Price | Dealer Cost | Low Price |
|---|---|---|---|
| 2-Door Pillared Hardtop | $5335 | $4271 | $4571 |
| 4-Door Pillared Hardtop | 5410 | 4331 | 4631 |

### FORD LTD LANDAU
|  | Retail Price | Dealer Cost | Low Price |
|---|---|---|---|
| 2-Door Pillared Hardtop | 5898 | 4722 | 5022 |
| 4-Door Pillared Hardtop | 5976 | 4781 | 5081 |

### FORD STATION WAGONS
|  | Retail Price | Dealer Cost | Low Price |
|---|---|---|---|
| LTD Station Wagon | 5797 | 4641 | 4941 |
| LTD Country Squire Wagon | 6207 | 4969 | 5269 |

### LTD ACCESSORIES
| Engines | Retail Price | Dealer Cost | Low Price |
|---|---|---|---|
| 5.8 Litre (351 CID) 2V 8-Cyl | $157 | $122 | $124 |
| 6.6 Litre (400 CID) 2V 8-Cyl | | | |
|   Hardtop Models | 283 | 221 | 224 |
|   Station Wagon Models | 126 | 99 | 100 |
| 7.5 Litre (460 CID) 4V 8-Cyl | | | |
|   Hardtop Models | 428 | 334 | 338 |

*Prices are accurate at time of printing; subject to manufacturer's change.*

|  | Retail Price | Dealer Cost | Low Price |
|---|---|---|---|
| Station Wagon Models | $271 | $211 | $214 |
| **Axles** | | | |
| Optional Ratio Axle | 16 | 12 | 13 |
| Traction-Lok Differential Axle | 61 | 47 | 48 |
| **Air Conditioner, Selectaire** | | | |
| w/Manual Temperature Control | 562 | 438 | 443 |
| w/Automatic Temperature Control | 607 | 473 | 478 |
| Heavy-Duty Battery | 18 | 14 | 15 |
| Deluxe Belts | 20 | 15 | 16 |
| 4-Wheel Power Disc Brakes | 197 | 154 | 156 |
| **Deluxe Bumper Group** | | | |
| LTD Landau Models | 49 | 38 | 39 |
| All Other Models | 70 | 54 | 55 |
| Rear Bumper Guards | 21 | 16 | 17 |
| **Digital Clock** | | | |
| LTD Landau & Country Squire Models | 28 | 22 | 23 |
| All Other Models | 49 | 38 | 39 |
| Electric Clock | 21 | 16 | 17 |
| Cornering Lamps, Front | 46 | 36 | 37 |
| Rear Window Defogger | 50 | 39 | 40 |
| Electric Rear Window Defroster | 92 | 72 | 73 |
| **California Emission Equipment (W/6.6 Litre 2V)** | | | |
| Hardtop Models | 238 | 186 | 188 |
| Station Wagon Models | 141 | 110 | 112 |
| Fender Skirts | 46 | 36 | 37 |
| Glass Tinted, Complete | 75 | 59 | 60 |
| Horn, Dual Note | 7 | 5 | 6 |
| Illuminated Entry System | 54 | 42 | 43 |
| **Electric Power Door Locks** | | | |
| 2-Door Models | 79 | 62 | 63 |
| 4-Door Hardtop & Station Wagon W/Conv. Group | 111 | 86 | 87 |
| Station Wagon Models W/o Convenience Group | 147 | 115 | 117 |
| Lockable Side Stowage Compartment | 46 | 36 | 37 |
| Luggage Rack | 80 | 63 | 64 |
| **Illuminated Visor Vanity Mirror (Pass. Side)** | | | |
| Models W/Convenience Group | 45 | 35 | 36 |
| All Other Models | 49 | 38 | 39 |
| Outside Left-Hand Remote Control Mirror | 16 | 12 | 13 |
| **Radios** | | | |
| AM | 79 | 62 | 63 |
| AM/FM Monaural | 132 | 103 | 105 |
| AM/FM Stereo | 192 | 150 | 152 |
| AM/FM Stereo Search | 349 | 272 | 275 |
| W/Quadrasonic Tape Player, AM/FM Stereo | 399 | 311 | 315 |
| W/Tape Player, AM/FM Stereo | 266 | 207 | 210 |
| Full or Half Vinyl Roof | 141 | 110 | 112 |

*Prices are accurate at time of printing; subject to manufacturer's change.*

|  | Retail Price | Dealer Cost | Low Price |
|---|---|---|---|
| **Seats** | | | |
| Power, 6-Way (Full Width or Driver Only) | $149 | $116 | $118 |
| Power, 6-Way (Driver & Passenger) | 297 | 232 | 235 |
| Dual Facing Rear | 143 | 112 | 114 |
| Split Bench W/Manual Pass. Recliner | | | |
| 2-Door W/o Convenience Group | 233 | 182 | 184 |
| 4-Door & 2-Door W/Convenience Group | 200 | 156 | 158 |
| Adjustable Level Air Shock Absorbers | 50 | 39 | 40 |
| Dual Rear Seat Speakers | 46 | 36 | 37 |
| **FORD LTD II S** | | | |
| 2-Door Hardtop | $4814 | $3998 | $4248 |
| 4-Door Pillared Hardtop | 4889 | 4060 | 4360 |
| **FORD LTD II** | | | |
| 2-Door Hardtop | 5069 | 4210 | 4510 |
| 4-Door Pillared Hardtop | 5169 | 4293 | 4593 |
| **FORD LTD II BROUGHAM** | | | |
| 2-Door Hardtop | 5405 | 4489 | 4789 |
| 4-Door Pillared Hardtop | 5505 | 4572 | 4872 |

## LTD II ACCESSORIES

|  | Retail Price | Dealer Cost | Low Price |
|---|---|---|---|
| **Engines** | | | |
| 5.8 Litre (351 CID) 2V 8-Cylinder | $157 | $122 | $124 |
| 6.6 Litre (400 CID) 2V 8-Cylinder | 283 | 221 | 224 |
| Traction-Lok Differential Axle | 59 | 46 | 47 |
| Air Conditioner, Selectaire | | | |
| W/Manual Temperature Control | 543 | 424 | 429 |
| W/Automatic Temperature Control | 588 | 459 | 464 |
| Heavy-Duty Battery | 18 | 14 | 15 |
| Deluxe Belts | 20 | 15 | 16 |
| Deluxe Bumper Group | 76 | 60 | 61 |
| Corning Lamps, Front | 46 | 36 | 37 |
| Electric Rear Window Defroster | 92 | 72 | 73 |
| California Emission Equipment | 74 | 57 | 58 |
| Tinted Glass, Complete | 61 | 47 | 48 |
| Horn, Dual Note | 7 | 5 | 6 |
| Illuminated Entry System | 54 | 42 | 43 |
| Power Lock Group | | | |
| 2-Door Models | 97 | 76 | 77 |
| 4-Door Models | 129 | 101 | 103 |
| Illuminated Visor Vanity Mirror (Pass. Side) | | | |
| Models W/Convenience Group | 45 | 35 | 36 |
| All Other Models | 49 | 38 | 39 |
| Outside Left-Hand Remote Mirror | 16 | 12 | 13 |

*Prices are accurate at time of printing; subject to manufacturer's change.*

|  | Retail Price | Dealer Cost | Low Price |
|---|---|---|---|
| Dual Sport Mirrors (W/o Convenience Group) | $ 54 | $ 42 | $ 43 |
| Radios |  |  |  |
|   AM | 79 | 62 | 63 |
|   AM/FM Monaural | 132 | 103 | 105 |
|   AM/FM Stereo | 192 | 150 | 152 |
|   AM/FM Stereo Search | 349 | 272 | 275 |
|   W/Quadrasonic Tape Player, AM/FM Stereo | 399 | 311 | 315 |
|   W/Tape Player, AM/FM Stereo | 266 | 207 | 210 |
|   40 Channel Citizens Band | 295 | 230 | 234 |
| Full or Half Vinyl Roof | 112 | 87 | 88 |
| Power 6-Way Seat (Full Width or Driver Only) | 149 | 116 | 118 |
| Bucket & Console Seats, LTD II Series 2-Door | 211 | 164 | 166 |
| Dual Rear Seat Speakers | 46 | 36 | 37 |

## MUSTANG II
**2-Door Hardtop** ... $3555 / $3094 / $3294

## MUSTANG II 2+2
**3-Door Liftback** ... 3798 / 3306 / 3506

## MUSTANG II GHIA
**2-Door Hardtop** ... 3972 / 3457 / 3657

## MUSTANG II MACH I
**3-Door Liftback** ... 4253 / 3702 / 3952

### MUSTANG II ACCESSORIES

|  | Retail Price | Dealer Cost | Low Price |
|---|---|---|---|
| Engines |  |  |  |
|   Credit for 2.3 Litre 2V Sub. From Mach I |  |  |  |
|     Base 2.8 Litre 2V (VV in State of California) | $(213) | $(181) | $(183) |
|   2.8 Litre 2V 6-Cylinder (2.8) Litre W/Vari. |  |  |  |
|     Venturi Carburetor in State of California | 213 | 181 | 183 |
|   5.0 Litre (302 CID) 2V 8-Cylinder |  |  |  |
|     Mach I Model | 148 | 126 | 128 |
|     All Other Models | 361 | 307 | 311 |
| Selectshift Cruise-O-Matic Transmission |  |  |  |
|   Models W/5.0 Litre (302 CID) Engine or |  |  |  |
|     King Cobra Option | 281 | 239 | 242 |
|   All Other Models | 281 | 239 | 242 |
| Exterior Accent Group | 245 | 207 | 210 |
| Air Conditioner, Selectaire | 459 | 390 | 394 |
| Appearance Decor Group |  |  |  |
|   Hardtop Model | 160 | 136 | 138 |
|   2+2 Model | 112 | 95 | 96 |
| Deluxe Belts | 18 | 15 | 16 |
| Power Front Disc Brakes | 60 | 51 | 52 |
| Front & Rear Bumper Guards | 37 | 32 | 33 |
| Digital Quartz Crystal Clock | 45 | 38 | 39 |
| Cobra II Package | 730 | 621 | 628 |
| Console | 80 | 68 | 69 |

*Prices are accurate at time of printing; subject to manufacturer's change.*

|  | Retail Price | Dealer Cost | Low Price |
|---|---|---|---|
| Convenience Group |  |  |  |
|   3-Door Models W/o Cobra II Pkg. or T-Roof Conv. | $69 | $58 | $59 |
|   All Other Models | 35 | 30 | 31 |
| Electric Rear Window Defroster | 73 | 62 | 63 |
| California Emission Equipment | 72 | 62 | 63 |
| Fashion Accessory Package | 228 | 194 | 196 |
| Fold Down Rear Seat | 89 | 76 | 77 |
| Ghia Sports Group | 355 | 302 | 306 |
| Tinted Glass, Complete | 52 | 44 | 45 |
| Radios |  |  |  |
|   AM | 72 | 61 | 62 |
|   W/8-Track Stereo Tape Player, AM | 192 | 163 | 165 |
|   AM/FM Monaural | 120 | 102 | 104 |
|   AM/FM Stereo | 161 | 137 | 139 |
|   W/Cassette Player, AM/FM Stereo | 229 | 195 | 197 |
|   W/8-Track Tape Player, AM/FM Stereo | 229 | 195 | 197 |
| Rallye Appearance Package | 163 | 138 | 140 |
| Rallye Package |  |  |  |
|   Mach I Model or Models W/Exterior Accent Group or Rallye Appearance Package | 37 | 32 | 33 |
|   All Other Models | 87 | 74 | 75 |
| Flip-Up Open Air Roof | 167 | 142 | 144 |
| Full Vinyl Roof | 99 | 84 | 85 |
| 4-Way Manual Driver's Seat | 33 | 28 | 29 |
| Tilt Steering Wheel | 67 | 52 | 53 |
| Power Side Windows |  |  |  |
|   2-Door Models | 121 | 94 | 95 |
|   4-Door Models | 167 | 131 | 133 |

## PINTO

|  | Retail Price | Dealer Cost | Low Price |
|---|---|---|---|
| Pony 2-Door Sedan | $2995 | $2697 | $2897 |
| 2-Door Sedan | 3336 | 2904 | 3104 |
| 3-Door Runabout | 3451 | 3004 | 3204 |
| 2-Door Station Wagon | 3791 | 3302 | 3502 |
| 2-Door Squire Wagon | 4109 | 3576 | 3826 |

## PINTO ACCESSORIES

|  | Retail Price | Dealer Cost | Low Price |
|---|---|---|---|
| 2.8 Litre 2V 6-Cylinder Engine | $273 | $232 | $235 |
| Selectshift Cruise-O-Matic Transmission | 281 | 239 | 242 |
| Optional Ratio Axle | 13 | 11 | 12 |
| Tape Stripe Option |  |  |  |
|   Models W/Exterior Decor Group | 47 | 40 | 41 |
|   All Other Models | 58 | 49 | 50 |
| Air Conditioner, Selectaire | 470 | 399 | 403 |
| Power Front Disc Brakes | 60 | 51 | 52 |

*Prices are accurate at time of printing; subject to manufacturer's change.*

|  | Retail Price | Dealer Cost | Low Price |
|---|---|---|---|
| Deluxe Bumper Group | $69 | $53 | $54 |
| Cargo Area Cover | 33 | 28 | 29 |
| Load Floor Carpet | 23 | 19 | 20 |
| Electric Rear Window Defroster | 73 | 62 | 63 |
| California Emission Equipment | 72 | 61 | 62 |
| Tinted Glass, Complete | 52 | 44 | 45 |
| Third Door Glass | 13 | 11 | 12 |
| Roof Luggage Rack | 60 | 51 | 52 |
| Dual Sport Mirrors | 49 | 42 | 43 |
| Blk. Narrow Vinyl Insert Bodyside Moldings | 40 | 34 | 35 |
| Radios |  |  |  |
| AM | 65 | 55 | 56 |
| W/Stereo Tape Player, AM | 119 | 101 | 103 |
| AM/FM Monaural | 48 | 41 | 42 |
| AM/FM Stereo | 89 | 76 | 77 |
| Rallye Appearance Package |  |  |  |
| Models W/o Calif. Emission Equipment |  |  |  |
| Sedans | 189 | 161 | 163 |
| Runabouts | 201 | 171 | 173 |
| Models W/Calif. Emission Equipment |  |  |  |
| Sedans | 158 | 134 | 136 |
| Runabouts | 171 | 145 | 147 |
| Flip-Up Open Air Roof | 167 | 142 | 144 |
| Half Vinyl Roof | 125 | 107 | 109 |
| 4-Way Manual Driver's Seat | 33 | 28 | 29 |
| Sports Rallye Package | 89 | 76 | 77 |
| Power Rack & Pinion Steering | 131 | 112 | 114 |
| Tu-Tone Paint/Tape Treatment |  |  |  |
| W/Exterior Decor Group | 5 | 4 | 5 |
| All Other Models | 54 | 46 | 47 |

## THUNDERBIRD

|  | Retail Price | Dealer Cost | Low Price |
|---|---|---|---|
| 2-Door Hardtop | $5411 | $4494 | $4794 |
| Town Landau | 8420 | 6739 | 7239 |
| Diamond Jubilee Edition | 10,106 | 8088 | 9088 |

## THUNDERBIRD ACCESSORIES

|  | Retail Price | Dealer Cost | Low Price |
|---|---|---|---|
| Engines |  |  |  |
| 5.8 Litre (351 CID) 2V 8-Cylinder | $157 | $122 | $124 |
| 6.6 Litre (400 CID) 2V 8-Cylinder | 283 | 221 | 224 |
| Traction-Lok Differential Axle | 57 | 44 | 45 |
| Air Conditioner, Selectaire |  |  |  |
| W/Manual Temperature Control | 543 | 424 | 429 |
| W/Automatic Temperature Control |  |  |  |
| 2-Door Hardtop | 588 | 459 | 464 |

*Prices are accurate at time of printing; subject to manufacturer's change.*

|  | Retail Price | Dealer Cost | Low Price |
|---|---|---|---|
| Town Landau & Diamond Jubilee Edition | $ 45 | $ 35 | $ 36 |
| Power Antenna | 45 | 35 | 36 |
| Heavy-Duty Battery | 18 | 14 | 15 |
| Color-Keyed Deluxe Belts | 20 | 15 | 16 |
| Deluxe Bumper Group | 76 | 60 | 61 |
| Clock, Day/Date | 21 | 16 | 17 |
| Convenience Group | | | |
|    Models W/Bucket Seats & Floor Shift | 93 | 73 | 74 |
|    All Other Models | 101 | 79 | 80 |
| Front Cornering Lamps | 46 | 36 | 37 |
| Exterior Decor Group | | | |
|    W/Convenience Group or Interior Luxury Group | 336 | 262 | 265 |
|    All Other Models | 391 | 305 | 309 |
| Interior Decor Group | 317 | 247 | 250 |
| Sports Decor Group | | | |
|    Models W/Convenience Group | 512 | 399 | 403 |
|    All Other Models | 566 | 441 | 446 |
| Rear Window Electric Defroster | 92 | 72 | 73 |
| California Emission Equipment | 74 | 57 | 58 |
| Tinted Glass, Complete | 64 | 50 | 51 |
| Illuminated Entry System | 54 | 42 | 43 |
| Sports Instrumentation Group | | | |
|    W/Convenience Group | 109 | 85 | 86 |
|    All Other Models | 117 | 91 | 92 |
| Luxury Sound Insulation Package | 29 | 23 | 24 |
| Light Group | 49 | 38 | 39 |
| Power Lock Group | 97 | 76 | 77 |
| Interior Luxury Group | 767 | 598 | 604 |
| Dual Sport Mirrors | | | |
|    Models W/o Convenience Group or Interior Luxury | 54 | 42 | 43 |
| Outside Left-Hand Remote Control Mirror | 16 | 12 | 13 |
| Radios | | | |
|    AM/FM Monaural | 53 | 41 | 42 |
|    AM/FM Stereo | 113 | 88 | 89 |
|    AM/FM Stereo Search | 270 | 210 | 213 |
|    40 Channel Citizens Band | 295 | 230 | 233 |
|    W/Quadrasonic Tape Player, AM/FM Stereo | | | |
|       2-Door Hardtop Model | 320 | 249 | 252 |
|       Town Landau & Diamond Jubilee Edition | 50 | 39 | 40 |
|    W/Tape Player, AM/FM Stereo | 187 | 146 | 148 |
|    Delete AM Radio | (79) | (62) | (63) |
| Two-Piece Vinyl Roof | 138 | 108 | 110 |
| Power 6-Way Seat (Full Width or Driver Only) | 149 | 116 | 118 |
| Bucket & Console Seats | | | |
|    Models W/o Interior Decor Group | 211 | 164 | 166 |
| Automatic Seatback Release | 33 | 26 | 27 |
| Dual Rear Seat Speakers | 46 | 36 | 37 |

*Prices are accurate at time of printing; subject to manufacturer's change.*

|  | Retail Price | Dealer Cost | Low Price |
|---|---|---|---|
| Tilt Steering Wheel | $ 70 | $ 54 | $ 55 |
| Power Side Windows | 126 | 99 | 100 |

# LINCOLN

### LINCOLN CONTINENTAL
| | | | |
|---|---|---|---|
| 2-Door Coupe | $9974 | $7683 | $8683 |
| 4-Door Sedan | 10,166 | 7831 | 8831 |

### LINCOLN ACCESSORIES
| | | | |
|---|---|---|---|
| 7.5 Litre (460 CID) Engine | $197 | $152 | $154 |
| Appearance Protection Group | | | |
|    2-Door Coupe | 67 | 51 | 52 |
|    4-Door Sedan | 71 | 54 | 55 |
| Higher Ratio Axle | 23 | 17 | 18 |
| Traction-Lok Differential Axle | 65 | 50 | 51 |
| 4-Wheel Disc/Sure-Track Brakes | 491 | 378 | 382 |
| Defroster Group | 113 | 87 | 88 |
| Garage Door Opener | 85 | 66 | 67 |
| Headlamp Convenience Group | 116 | 89 | 90 |
| Engine Block Heater | 21 | 16 | 17 |
| Illuminated Entry System | 60 | 46 | 47 |
| Illuminated Outside Thermometer | 28 | 22 | 23 |
| Interior Light Group | | | |
|    W/Power Moonroof | 111 | 85 | 86 |
|    W/o Power Moonroof | 127 | 98 | 99 |
| Coach Lamps | 64 | 49 | 50 |
| Dual Beam Map/Dome Light | 17 | 13 | 14 |
| Right Hand Remote Control Mirror | 33 | 26 | 27 |
| Narrow Vinyl Insert Moldings | 47 | 36 | 37 |
| Premium Bodyside Moldings | 127 | 98 | 99 |
| Fixed Glass Moonroof | 1017 | 783 | 791 |
| Power Glass Panel Moonroof | 1017 | 783 | 791 |
| Opera Windows | 93 | 72 | 73 |
| Moondust Paint | 191 | 147 | 148 |
| Custom Paint Stripes | 48 | 37 | 38 |
| Power Lock Convenience Group | | | |
|    2-Door Coupe | 100 | 77 | 78 |
|    4-Door Sedan | 131 | 101 | 103 |
| Power Vent Windows | 89 | 69 | 70 |

*Prices are accurate at time of printing; subject to manufacturer's change.*

|  | Retail Price | Dealer Cost | Low Price |
|---|---|---|---|
| Lower Bodyside Protection | $ 36 | $ 28 | $ 29 |
| **Radio Equipment** | | | |
| AM/FM Stereo | 152 | 117 | 119 |
| AM/FM Stereo Search | 304 | 234 | 237 |
| AM/FM Stereo W/8-Track Tape | 232 | 179 | 181 |
| AM/FM Stereo W/Quadrasonic 8-Track Tape | 396 | 305 | 309 |
| Citizens Band 40-Channel | 328 | 253 | 256 |
| **Roof** | | | |
| W/Town Car/Coupe | 296 | 228 | 231 |
| W/Williamsburg Limited Edition | 359 | 276 | 279 |
| Other | 548 | 422 | 427 |
| Full Vinyl Roof | 189 | 146 | 148 |
| **6-Way Power Bench Seat** | | | |
| W/o Recliner | 155 | 119 | 121 |
| W/Recliner | 239 | 184 | 186 |
| **Twin Comfort Power 6-Way/6-Way Seats W/Passenger** | | | |
| Recliner | 537 | 414 | 419 |
| Speed Control | 124 | 95 | 96 |
| Tilt Steering Wheel | 77 | 60 | 61 |
| Town Car Option | 1364 | 1050 | 1061 |
| Town Coupe Option | 1364 | 1050 | 1061 |

| **CONTINENTAL MARK V** | $12,099 | $9320 | $10,320 |
|---|---|---|---|
| Diamond Jubilee Edition | 20,099 | 15,480 | 16,480 |

## CONTINENTAL MARK V ACCESSORIES

|  | Retail Price | Dealer Cost | Low Price |
|---|---|---|---|
| 7.5 Litre (460 CID) Engine | $197 | $152 | $154 |
| Appearance Protection Group | 67 | 51 | 52 |
| Traction-Lok Differential Axle | 65 | 50 | 51 |
| Sure-Track Brakes | 297 | 229 | 232 |
| Defroster Group | 113 | 87 | 88 |
| Dual Exhausts | 75 | 58 | 59 |
| Miles to Empty Fuel Indicator | 120 | 92 | 93 |
| Garage Door Opener | 85 | 66 | 67 |
| Headlamp Convenience Group | 116 | 89 | 90 |
| Engine Block Heater | 21 | 16 | 17 |
| Illuminated Entry System | 60 | 46 | 47 |
| Illuminated Outside Thermometer | 28 | 22 | 23 |
| **Interior Light Group** | | | |
| W/Power Moonroof | 111 | 85 | 86 |
| W/o Power Moonroof | 127 | 98 | 99 |
| Dual Beam Map/Dome Light | 17 | 13 | 14 |
| Right Hand Remote Control Mirror | 33 | 26 | 27 |
| Rocker Panel Molding | 29 | 23 | 24 |

*Prices are accurate at time of printing; subject to manufacturer's change.*

|  | Retail Price | Dealer Cost | Low Price |
|---|---|---|---|
| Power Glass Panel Moonroof | $1017 | $783 | $791 |
| Moondust Paint | 191 | 147 | 149 |
| Custom Paint Stripes | 48 | 37 | 38 |
| Power Lock Convenience Group | 100 | 77 | 78 |
| Power Vent Windows | 89 | 69 | 71 |
| Lower Bodyside Protection | 36 | 28 | 29 |
| Radio Equipment | | | |
|    AM/FM Stereo | 152 | 117 | 119 |
|    AM/FM Stereo Search | 304 | 234 | 237 |
|    AM/FM Stereo W/8-Track Tape | 232 | 179 | 181 |
|    AM/FM Stereo W/Quadrasonic 8-Track Tape | 396 | 305 | 309 |
|    Citizens Band 40-Channel | 328 | 253 | 256 |
| Steel Roof (Cartier Designer Model) | (287) | (221) | (224) |
| Full Vinyl Roof | | | |
|    Designer Series | 287 | 221 | 224 |
|    All Other | 197 | 152 | 154 |
| Landau Vinyl Roof | 485 | 374 | 378 |
| Power Lumbar Seat | 107 | 82 | 83 |
| Power Passenger 6-Way Seat | 151 | 116 | 118 |
| Passenger Reclining Seat | 85 | 66 | 67 |
| Speed Control | 124 | 95 | 96 |
| Tilt Steering Wheel | 77 | 60 | 61 |

## VERSAILLES

|  | Retail Price | Dealer Cost | Low Price |
|---|---|---|---|
| 4-Door Sedan | $12,529 | $9650 | $10,650 |

## VERSAILLES ACCESSORIES

|  | Retail Price | Dealer Cost | Low Price |
|---|---|---|---|
| Floor-Mounted Transmission Selector | $36 | $28 | $29 |
| Appearance Protection Group | 71 | 54 | 55 |
| Electric Rear Window Defroster | 88 | 68 | 69 |
| Defroster Group | 113 | 87 | 88 |
| Garage Door Opener | 85 | 66 | 67 |
| Illuminated Outside Thermometer | 28 | 22 | 23 |
| Protective Bodyside Moldings | 47 | 36 | 37 |
| Power Glass Panel Moonroof | 1017 | 783 | 791 |
| Dual Shade Paint | 56 | 43 | 44 |
| Power Lock Group | 131 | 101 | 103 |
| Lower Bodyside Protection | 36 | 28 | 29 |
| Radio Equipment | | | |
|    AM/FM Stereo W/8-Track Tape | (72) | (55) | (56) |
|    AM/FM Stereo W/Quadrasonic 8-Track Tape | 92 | 71 | 72 |
|    Citizens Band 40-Channel | 328 | 253 | 256 |
| Reclining Bucket Seats | 419 | 322 | 326 |
| Tilt Steering Wheel | 77 | 60 | 61 |

*Prices are accurate at time of printing; subject to manufacturer's change.*

|  | Retail Price | Dealer Cost | Low Price |
|---|---|---|---|
| Leather Interior Trim | $ 249 | $ 192 | $ 194 |
| Wire Wheel Covers | (107) | (82) | (83) |

# MERCURY

## BOBCAT

|  | | | |
|---|---|---|---|
| Bobcat Runabout 3-door | $3537 | 3079 | 3279 |
| Bobcat 2-Door Wagon | 3878 | 3375 | 3575 |
| Bobcat Villager, 2-Door Wagon | 4010 | 3490 | 3690 |

### BOBCAT ACCESSORIES

|  | | | |
|---|---|---|---|
| 2.8 Litre V-6 Engine | $324 | $275 | $278 |
| Select-Shift Automatic Transmission | 263 | 223 | 226 |
| Manual Air Conditioning | 470 | 399 | 403 |
| Appearance Protection Group | 40 | 34 | 35 |
| Higher Ratio Axle | 14 | 12 | 13 |
| Deluxe Seat & Shoulder Belts | 17 | 14 | 15 |
| Bumper Protection Group | 65 | 55 | 56 |
| Load Floor Carpet | 24 | 20 | 21 |
| Electric Rear Window Defroster | 73 | 62 | 63 |
| All Third Door Glass | 16 | 13 | 14 |
| Tinted Glass, Complete | 49 | 42 | 43 |
| Power Disc Brakes, Front | 60 | 51 | 52 |
| Power Steering, Variable Ratio | 141 | 120 | 122 |
| Lower Bodyside Protection | 33 | 28 | 29 |
| Radios | | | |
| AM | 77 | 66 | 67 |
| AM/Digital Clock | 119 | 101 | 103 |
| AM/Stereo Tape | 204 | 173 | 175 |
| AM/FM Stereo | 171 | 145 | 147 |
| AM/FM Monaural | 128 | 109 | 111 |
| Sports Vinyl Roof | 141 | 120 | 122 |
| 4-Way Manual Bucket Seat | 34 | 29 | 30 |

## COUGAR

|  | | | |
|---|---|---|---|
| 2-Door Hardtop | $5009 | $4160 | $4460 |
| 4-Door Pillared Hardtop | 5126 | 4257 | 4557 |

*Prices are accurate at time of printing; subject to manufacturer's change.*

|  | Retail Price | Dealer Cost | Low Price |
|---|---|---|---|
| **Cougar XR-7** | | | |
| 2-Door Hardtop | $5603 | $4653 | $4953 |

## COUGAR ACCESSORIES

| | Retail Price | Dealer Cost | Low Price |
|---|---|---|---|
| **Engines** | | | |
| 5.8 Litre (351 CID) | $97 | $76 | $77 |
| 6.6 Litre (400 CID) | 220 | 171 | 173 |
| Auto. Temperature Control Air Conditioning | 591 | 461 | 466 |
| Manual Air Conditioning | 542 | 423 | 428 |
| Heavy Duty Alternator | 47 | 37 | 38 |
| **Appearance Protection Group** | | | |
| 2-Door | 45 | 35 | 36 |
| 4-Door | 53 | 41 | 42 |
| Traction-Lok Axle | 57 | 44 | 45 |
| Heavy Duty Battery | 20 | 15 | 16 |
| Deluxe Belts | 20 | 15 | 16 |
| **Brougham Option** | | | |
| 2-Door | 328 | 256 | 259 |
| 4-Door | 449 | 350 | 354 |
| Bumper Protection Group | 72 | 56 | 57 |
| Electric Rear Window Defroster | 87 | 68 | 69 |
| Tinted Glass, Complete | 61 | 47 | 48 |
| Illuminated Entry System | 54 | 42 | 43 |
| Cornering Lamps | 53 | 41 | 42 |
| Light Group | 55 | 43 | 44 |
| Luggage Compartment Trim | 37 | 29 | 30 |
| **Mirrors** | | | |
| Left-Hand Remote Control | 16 | 12 | 13 |
| Illuminated Visor Vanity | 45 | 35 | 36 |
| Dual Racing | 54 | 42 | 43 |
| **Moldings** | | | |
| Protective Bodyside | 45 | 35 | 36 |
| Rocker Panel | 28 | 22 | 23 |
| Wide Bodyside XR-7 | 54 | 42 | 43 |
| Opera Windows | 53 | 41 | 42 |
| Glamour Paint | 67 | 52 | 53 |
| Bodyside Paint Stripes | 36 | 28 | 29 |
| Power Antenna | 45 | 35 | 36 |
| **Power Lock Group** | | | |
| 2-Door | 97 | 76 | 77 |
| 4-Door | 129 | 101 | 103 |
| Power Moonroof | 991 | 773 | 781 |
| Power Seat, Bucket | 153 | 119 | 121 |
| Power Seat, Flight Bench | 153 | 119 | 121 |

*Prices are accurate at time of printing; subject to manufacturer's change.*

|  | Retail Price | Dealer Cost | Low Price |
|---|---|---|---|
| Power Seat, Twin Comfort | $153 | $119 | $121 |
| Power Side Windows, 2-Door | 121 | 94 | 95 |
| Power Side Windows, 4-Door | 167 | 130 | 132 |
| Protection, Lower Bodyside | 36 | 28 | 29 |
| Radios | | | |
| AM | 84 | 66 | 67 |
| AM/FM Monaural | 139 | 109 | 111 |
| AM/FM Stereo | 204 | 159 | 161 |
| AM/FM Stereo W/Tape | 282 | 220 | 223 |
| AM/FM Stereo Search | 370 | 288 | 291 |
| AM/FM Stereo W/Quadrasonic 8-Track Tape | 422 | 329 | 333 |
| Citizens Band 40-Channel | 300 | 234 | 237 |
| Front Vinyl Roof | 117 | 91 | 92 |
| Full Vinyl Roof, 2-Door | 117 | 91 | 92 |
| Full Vinyl Roof, 4-Door | 170 | 132 | 135 |
| Landau Vinyl Roof | 117 | 91 | 92 |
| Bucket Seats W/Console | | | |
| Cougar Models | 218 | 170 | 172 |
| Brougham Option, XR-7 Models | 149 | 116 | 118 |
| Flight Bench Seat | 70 | 54 | 55 |
| Twin Comfort Seat W/Passenger Recliner | 149 | 116 | 118 |
| Upgraded Sound Package | 29 | 23 | 24 |
| Dual Rear Speakers | 45 | 35 | 36 |

### MARQUIS
|  | Retail Price | Dealer Cost | Low Price |
|---|---|---|---|
| 2-Door Hardtop | $5764 | $4614 | $4914 |
| 4-Door Pillared Hardtop | 5806 | 4648 | 4948 |
| **MARQUIS BROUGHAM** | | | |
| 2-Door Hardtop | 6380 | 5107 | 5457 |
| 4-Door Pillared Hardtop | 6480 | 5187 | 5537 |
| **GRAND MARQUIS** | | | |
| 2-Door Hardtop | 7132 | 5708 | 6108 |
| 4-Door Pillared Hardtop | 7232 | 5788 | 6188 |
| **MARQUIS STATION WAGON** | | | |
| Marquis Station Wagon | 5958 | 4770 | 5070 |

### MARQUIS ACCESSORIES

|  | Retail Price | Dealer Cost | Low Price |
|---|---|---|---|
| 6.6 Litre (400 CID) Engine | $134 | $105 | $107 |
| 7.5 Litre (460 CID) Engine | 316 | 246 | 249 |
| Automatic Temperature Control Air Conditioning | 620 | 483 | 488 |
| Manual Air Conditioning | 579 | 452 | 457 |

*Prices are accurate at time of printing; subject to manufacturer's change.*

|  | Retail Price | Dealer Cost | Low Price |
|---|---|---|---|
| **Appearance Protection Group** | | | |
| 2-Door | $ 49 | $ 38 | $ 39 |
| 4-Door | 53 | 41 | 42 |
| Higher Ratio Axle | 22 | 17 | 18 |
| Traction-Lok Axle | 62 | 48 | 49 |
| Heavy Duty Battery (77 Amp) | 20 | 15 | 16 |
| Deluxe Seat Belts | 20 | 15 | 16 |
| Rear Bumper Guards (Station Wagons Only) | 20 | 15 | 16 |
| Bumper Protection Group | 59 | 46 | 47 |
| **Digital Clock** | | | |
| Marquis Brougham & W/Colony Park Option | 29 | 23 | 24 |
| Marquis & Marquis Wagon | 51 | 40 | 41 |
| Colony Park Option | 403 | 314 | 318 |
| Electric Rear Window Defroster | 87 | 68 | 69 |
| Fender Skirts | 46 | 36 | 37 |
| Tinted Glass Complete | 72 | 56 | 57 |
| Power Antenna | 45 | 35 | 36 |
| 6-Way Power Bench Seat | 153 | 119 | 121 |
| 6-Way Driver Side Power Seat | 153 | 119 | 121 |
| 6-Way/6-Way Power Seats | 299 | 233 | 236 |
| Power Disc Brakes, 4-Wheel | 191 | 149 | 151 |
| Power Moonroof, Glass Panel | 991 | 773 | 781 |
| Power Side Windows, 2-Door | 126 | 99 | 100 |
| Power Side Windows, 4-Door | 186 | 115 | 117 |
| Lower Bodyside Protection | 36 | 28 | 29 |
| **Radios** | | | |
| AM | 84 | 66 | 67 |
| AM/FM Stereo | 204 | 159 | 161 |
| AM/FM Stereo Search | 370 | 288 | 291 |
| AM/FM Stereo W/Tape | 282 | 220 | 223 |
| AM/FM Stereo W/Quadrasonic 8-Track Tape | 422 | 329 | 333 |
| Full Vinyl Roof | 143 | 112 | 114 |
| Landau Vinyl Roof | 143 | 112 | 114 |
| Passenger Reclining Seat | 62 | 48 | 49 |
| Removable R.R. Dual Facing Seats | 187 | 146 | 148 |
| Twin Comfort Seats, W/Passenger Recliner | 149 | 116 | 118 |
| Twin Comfort Seats, W/o Passenger Recliner | 88 | 69 | 70 |
| Dual Rear Seat Speakers | 45 | 35 | 36 |
| **Speed Control** | | | |
| Grand Marquis | 92 | 72 | 73 |
| Other Models | 114 | 89 | 90 |
| Tilt Steering Wheel | 68 | 53 | 54 |

## MONARCH

|  | Retail Price | Dealer Cost | Low Price |
|---|---|---|---|
| 2-Door Sedan, 6 Cylinder | $4330 | $3682 | $2932 |
| 4-Door Sedan, 6-Cylinder | 4409 | 3749 | 3999 |

*Prices are accurate at time of printing; subject to manufacturer's change.*

## MONARCH ACCESSORIES

|  | Retail Price | Dealer Cost | Low Price |
|---|---|---|---|
| 5.0 Litre (302 CID) Engine | $147 | $125 | $127 |
| Select-Shift Auto. Transmission | 196 | 167 | 169 |
| Floor-Mounted Selector Transmission | 33 | 28 | 29 |
| Auto. Air Conditioning | 541 | 460 | 465 |
| Manual Air Conditioning | 495 | 421 | 426 |
| Appearance Protection Group | | | |
|    Monarch, 2-Door | 36 | 31 | 32 |
|    Monarch, 4-Door | 43 | 37 | 38 |
|    Ghia Option Group | 28 | 24 | 25 |
| Deluxe Seat & Shoulder Belts | 18 | 15 | 16 |
| Bumper Protection Group | 66 | 56 | 57 |
| Digital Clock | 43 | 37 | 38 |
| Cold Weather Group | | | |
|    4.1 Litre (250 CID) or 5.01 Litre (302 CID) | 37 | 32 | 33 |
|    Other Models | 55 | 47 | 48 |
| Console | 80 | 68 | 69 |
| Decor Group | 182 | 155 | 157 |
| Rear Window Defogger | 46 | 39 | 40 |
| Electric Rear Window Defroster | 80 | 68 | 69 |
| ESS Option Group | 459 | 390 | 394 |
| Ghia Option Group | 477 | 406 | 411 |
| Tinted Glass, Complete | 54 | 46 | 47 |
| Dual Racing Mirrors | | | |
|    Monarch | 49 | 42 | 43 |
|    Monarch Ghia | 36 | 31 | 32 |
| Protective Bodyside Molding | 40 | 34 | 35 |
| Rocker Panel Molding | 22 | 18 | 19 |
| Glamour Paint | 61 | 52 | 53 |
| 4-Wheel Power Disc Brakes | 290 | 247 | 250 |
| Front Power Disc Brakes | 61 | 52 | 53 |
| Power Door Locks | | | |
|    2-Door | 70 | 59 | 60 |
|    4-Door | 99 | 84 | 85 |
| Glass Panel Power Moonroof | 907 | 771 | 779 |
| Flight Bench Power Seat | 140 | 119 | 121 |
| 4-Way Bucket Power Seat | 140 | 119 | 121 |
| Power Side Windows | | | |
|    2-Door | 111 | 94 | 95 |
|    4-Door | 153 | 130 | 132 |
| Power Steering | 146 | 124 | 126 |
| Lower Bodyside Protection | 33 | 28 | 29 |
| Radios | | | |
|    AM | 77 | 66 | 67 |
|    AM/Stereo Tape | 204 | 173 | 175 |

*Prices are accurate at time of printing; subject to manufacturer's change.*

|  | Retail Price | Dealer Cost | Low Price |
|---|---|---|---|
| AM/FM Stereo | $187 | $159 | $161 |
| AM/FM Stereo Search | 339 | 288 | 291 |
| AM/FM Stereo W/Cassette Tape | 258 | 219 | 222 |
| AM/FM Stereo W/8-Track Tape | 258 | 219 | 222 |
| AM/FM Stereo W/Quadrasonic 8-Track Tape | 387 | 329 | 333 |
| AM/FM Monaural | 143 | 122 | 124 |
| Citizens Band | 275 | 234 | 237 |
| Full Vinyl Roof | 107 | 91 | 92 |
| Landau Vinyl Roof | 107 | 91 | 92 |
| 4-Way Manual Adjustable Seat | 34 | 29 | 30 |
| Reclining Bucket Seat, Option | | | |
| Decor Group & Ghia Option Group | 67 | 57 | 58 |
| ESS Option Group | 84 | 72 | 73 |
| Speed Control | 94 | 80 | 81 |
| Tilt Steering Column | 61 | 52 | 53 |
| Heavy-Duty Suspension | 27 | 23 | 24 |

## ZEPHYR

|  | Retail Price | Dealer Cost | Low Price |
|---|---|---|---|
| 2-Door Sedan | $3742 | $3257 | $3457 |
| 4-Door Sedan | 3816 | 3321 | 3621 |
| Station Wagon | 4184 | 3641 | 3891 |

## ZEPHYR ACCESSORIES

|  | Retail Price | Dealer Cost | Low Price |
|---|---|---|---|
| 3.3 Litre (200 CID) Engine | $60 | $51 | $52 |
| 5.0 Litre (302 CID) Engine | 241 | 205 | 208 |
| Select-Shift Automatic Transmission | 273 | 232 | 235 |
| Floor-Mounted Selector Transmission | 30 | 26 | 27 |
| Interior Accent Group | 77 | 66 | 67 |
| Manual Air Conditioning | 464 | 394 | 398 |
| Appearance Protection Group | | | |
| 2-Door Models | 36 | 31 | 32 |
| 4-Door Models | 43 | 37 | 38 |
| Heavy-Duty Battery | 18 | 15 | 16 |
| Front & Rear Bumper Guards | 37 | 32 | 33 |
| Bumper Protection Group | 65 | 55 | 56 |
| Electric Analog Clock | 20 | 17 | 18 |
| Convenience Group | 36 | 31 | 32 |
| Rear Window Defogger | 46 | 39 | 40 |
| Electric Rear Window Defroster | 80 | 68 | 69 |
| Power Disc Brakes | 59 | 50 | 51 |

*Prices are accurate at time of printing; subject to manufacturer's change.*

|  | Retail Price | Dealer Cost | Low Price |
|---|---|---|---|
| Power Steering | $142 | $121 | $123 |
| Lower Bodyside Protection | 33 | 28 | 29 |
| Radios | | | |
|   AM | 77 | 66 | 67 |
|   AM/Stereo Tape | 204 | 173 | 175 |
|   AM/FM Monaural | 128 | 109 | 111 |
|   AM/FM Stereo | 187 | 159 | 161 |
|   AM/FM Stereo W/8-Track or W/Cassette Tape | 258 | 219 | 222 |
| Vinyl Roof | 90 | 77 | 78 |
| Bucket Seat | 67 | 57 | 58 |
| Sport Steering Wheel | 19 | 16 | 17 |
| Lockable Stowage Compartment | 19 | 16 | 17 |
| Handling Suspension | 30 | 26 | 27 |

# GENERAL MOTORS CORPORATION

## BUICK

| | | | |
|---|---|---|---|
| **CENTURY SPECIAL** | | | |
| 4-Door Sedan | $4486 | $3716 | $3966 |
| 2-Door Coupe | 4389 | 3635 | 3885 |
| 4-Door, 2-Seat Station Wagon | 5976 | 4122 | 4422 |
| **CENTURY CUSTOM** | | | |
| 4-Door Sedan | 4733 | 3921 | 4171 |
| 2-Door Coupe | 4633 | 3838 | 4088 |
| 4-Door, 2-Seat Station Wagon | 5276 | 4371 | 4671 |
| **CENTURY SPORT COUPE** | | | |
| 2-Door Coupe | 5019 | 4157 | 4457 |
| **CENTURY LIMITED** | | | |
| 4-Door Sedan | 5091 | 4218 | 4518 |
| 2-Door Coupe | 4991 | 4135 | 4435 |

*Prices are accurate at time of printing; subject to manufacturer's change.*

## CENTURY ACCESSORIES

| Engines | Retail Price | Dealer Cost | Low Price |
|---|---|---|---|
| 231 CID 2-BBL V6 | $ 40 | $ 31 | $ 32 |
| 305 CID 2-BBL V8 | | | |
|     Wagons | 150 | 117 | 119 |
|     Coupes & Sedans Less Sport Coupe | 210 | 163 | 165 |
|     Sport Coupe | 190 | 148 | 150 |
| 305 CID 4-BBL V8 (5.0 Litre) | | | |
|     Wagons | 200 | 156 | 158 |
|     Coupes & Sedans Less Sport Coupe | 260 | 202 | 205 |
|     Sport Coupe | 240 | 187 | 189 |
| 350 CID 4-BBL V8 (5.7 Litre) | 265 | 207 | 210 |
| **Transmissions** | | | |
| 4-Speed Manual | 125 | 98 | 99 |
| Automatic | 307 | 239 | 242 |
| Air Conditioning | 544 | 424 | 429 |
| Automatic Climate Control | 626 | 488 | 493 |
| Air Deflector | 29 | 23 | 24 |
| Positive Traction Differential Axle | 60 | 47 | 48 |
| Heavy-Duty Battery | 20 | 16 | 17 |
| **Custom Seat & Shoulder Belts** | | | |
| W/Bench, Notchback or 55/45 Seat | 20 | 16 | 17 |
| W/Bucket Seats | 16 | 12 | 13 |
| Power Brakes | 69 | 54 | 55 |
| Front & Rear Bumper Guards | 40 | 31 | 32 |
| Load Floor Area Carpet | 49 | 38 | 39 |
| Electric Dial Face Clock | 22 | 17 | 18 |
| Electric Digital Clock | 49 | 38 | 39 |
| Full Length Operating Console | 90 | 70 | 71 |
| Electric Rear Window Defogger | 92 | 72 | 73 |
| **Electric Door Locks** | | | |
| 2-Doors | 80 | 62 | 63 |
| 4-Doors | 112 | 87 | 88 |
| Soft-Ray Tinted Glass | 62 | 48 | 49 |
| Soft-Ray Tinted Windshield | 45 | 35 | 36 |
| Headlamps On Indicator | 10 | 8 | 9 |
| Trip Odometer | 12 | 9 | 10 |
| **Radio Equipment** | | | |
| AM | 83 | 65 | 66 |
| AM/FM | 154 | 120 | 122 |
| AM/FM Stereo W/Frt. & Rear Dual Speakers | 236 | 184 | 186 |
| AM/FM W/Stereo 8-Track W/Frt. & Rear Dual Speakers | 233 | 182 | 184 |
| AM/FM Stereo W/8-Track W/Frt. & Rear Dual Speakers | 341 | 266 | 269 |
| AM/FM Stereo W/Stereo Cassette W/Frt. & Rear Dual Speakers | 351 | 274 | 277 |
| Comb. AM/FM Stereo Entertainment & 40-Chan. CB Trans. W/Frt. & Rear Dual Speakers | 571 | 445 | 449 |

*Prices are accurate at time of printing; subject to manufacturer's change.*

|  | Retail Price | Dealer Cost | Low Price |
|---|---|---|---|
| **Dig. Readout AM/FM Stereo W/Frt. & Rear Dual Speakers** | $392 | $306 | $310 |
| Rear Seat Speaker | 24 | 19 | 20 |
| Rear Dual Speakers | 48 | 37 | 38 |
| Windshield Antenna | 26 | 20 | 21 |
| **Automatic Power Antenna** | | | |
| W/Radio | 45 | 35 | 36 |
| W/o Radio | 71 | 55 | 56 |
| **Triband Power Antenna** | | | |
| W/Radio | 83 | 65 | 66 |
| W/o Radio | 109 | 85 | 86 |
| Electric Sunroof | 499 | 389 | 393 |
| Electric Silver Astroroof | 699 | 545 | 551 |
| Hatch Roof | 625 | 488 | 493 |
| 6-Way Power Seat Adjuster, Driver Side | 151 | 118 | 120 |
| Reclining Passenger Seat Back | 59 | 46 | 47 |
| Sport Wagon Option | 430 | 335 | 339 |
| Power Steering | 152 | 119 | 121 |
| Custom Steering Wheel | 10 | 8 | 9 |
| Rallye Steering Wheel | 41 | 32 | 33 |
| Tilt Steering Wheel | 69 | 54 | 55 |
| Electric Trunk Release | 22 | 17 | 18 |
| **Power Windows** | | | |
| 2-Doors | 124 | 97 | 98 |
| 4-Doors | 172 | 134 | 136 |
| 2-Speed Windshield Wiper | 32 | 25 | 26 |
| **Woodgrain Vinyl Applique** | | | |
| Special Wagon | 256 | 200 | 203 |
| Custom Wagon | 235 | 183 | 185 |

## LE SABRE
| | | | |
|---|---|---|---|
| 4-Door Sedan | $5459 | $4357 | $4657 |
| 2-Door Coupe | 5384 | 4297 | 4597 |

## LE SABRE CUSTOM
| | | | |
|---|---|---|---|
| 4-Door Sedan | 5757 | 4595 | 4895 |
| 2-Door Coupe | 5657 | 4515 | 4815 |

## LE SABRE SPORT COUPE
| | | | |
|---|---|---|---|
| 2-Door Coupe | 6213 | 4958 | 5258 |

## ESTATE WAGON
| | | | |
|---|---|---|---|
| 4-Door, 2-Seat Station Wagon | 6301 | 5028 | 5378 |

## ELECTRA 225
| | | | |
|---|---|---|---|
| 4-Door Sedan | 7319 | 5697 | 6097 |
| 2-Door Coupe | 7144 | 5561 | 5961 |

## ELECTRA LIMITED
| | | | |
|---|---|---|---|
| 4-Door Sedan | 7701 | 5995 | 6395 |

*Prices are accurate at time of printing; subject to manufacturer's change.*

|  | Retail Price | Dealer Cost | Low Price |
|---|---|---|---|
| 2-Door Coupe | $7526 | $5859 | $6259 |
| **ELECTRA PARK AVENUE** | | | |
| 4-Door Sedan | 8088 | 6297 | 6797 |
| 2-Door Coupe | 7837 | 6101 | 6601 |
| **RIVIERA** | | | |
| 2-Door Coupe | 8082 | 6292 | 6792 |

## LE SABRE, ESTATE, ELECTRA & RIVIERA ACCESSORIES

|  | Retail Price | Dealer Cost | Low Price |
|---|---|---|---|
| **Engines** | | | |
| 231 CID 4 BBL V6 | $ 50 | $ 39 | $ 40 |
| 301 CID 2 BBL V8 | 198 | 152 | 154 |
| 305 CID 2 BBL V8 | 198 | 152 | 154 |
| 350 CID 4 BBL V8 | 313 | 241 | 244 |
| 403 CID 4 BBL V8 | | | |
|   LeSabre & LeSabre Cust. | 403 | 309 | 313 |
|   Electra, Riviera & Est. Wagon | 65 | 50 | 51 |
| Air Conditioner | 581 | 447 | 452 |
| Automatic Climate Control | 669 | 515 | 521 |
| Positive Traction Differential | 64 | 49 | 50 |
| Heavy-Duty Battery | 20 | 15 | 16 |
| **Custom Seat Belts** | | | |
| LeSabres & 2 Seat Est. Wagon | 20 | 15 | 16 |
| Estate Wagon, 3 Seat | 23 | 18 | 19 |
| Four Wheel Disc Brakes | 199 | 153 | 154 |
| **Bumper Guards** | | | |
| Front Only | 20 | 15 | 16 |
| Front & Rear | 40 | 31 | 32 |
| Cruise Master | 95 | 73 | 74 |
| Electric Rear Window Defogger | 94 | 72 | 73 |
| **80 AMP Delcotron** | | | |
| W/Air Conditioning or Heavy Duty Cooling | 41 | 32 | 33 |
| W/o Air Conditioning or Heavy Duty Cooling | 44 | 34 | 35 |
| **Electric Door Lock** | | | |
| 2-Doors | 82 | 63 | 64 |
| 4-Doors | 114 | 88 | 89 |
| **Automatic Electric Door Lock** | | | |
| 2-Door Electra & Riviera | 139 | 107 | 109 |
| 4-Door Electra | 167 | 129 | 131 |
| High Altitude Emission System | 33 | 25 | 26 |
| Calif. Assembly Line Emission Testing | 75 | 58 | 59 |
| Engine Block Heater | 14 | 11 | 12 |
| Estate Wagon Limited | 1568 | 1207 | 1220 |
| Soft Ray Tinted Glass | 76 | 59 | 60 |

*Prices are accurate at time of printing; subject to manufacturer's change.*

|  | Retail Price | Dealer Cost | Low Price |
|---|---|---|---|
| Soft Ray Tinted Windshield | $46 | $35 | $36 |
| Four Note Horn | 22 | 17 | 18 |
| Headlamps On Indicator | 10 | 8 | 9 |
| Low Fuel Indicator | 16 | 12 | 13 |
| Fuel Usage Light | 29 | 22 | 23 |
| Speed Alert & Trip Odometer | 22 | 17 | 18 |
| Dome Reading Light | 18 | 14 | 15 |
| Sunshade Map Light | 12 | 9 | 10 |
| Door Courtesy & Warning Lights | | | |
|     2-Doors | 35 | 27 | 28 |
|     4-Doors | 55 | 42 | 43 |
| Cornering Lights | 47 | 36 | 37 |
| Rear Compartment Courtesy Light | 15 | 12 | 13 |
| Luggage Rack W/Air Deflector | 135 | 104 | 106 |
| Front Carpet Savers | 11 | 8 | 9 |
| Carpet Savers & Handy Mats | 21 | 16 | 17 |
| Front Carpet Savers W/Inserts | 23 | 18 | 19 |
| Front & Rear Carpet Savers W/Inserts | 42 | 32 | 33 |
| L.H. Remote Control Rearview Mirror | 16 | 12 | 13 |
| R.H. Remote Control Rearview Mirror | 33 | 25 | 26 |
|     Estate Wagon | 28 | 22 | 23 |
| L.H. Remote Control Rearview Mirror W/Thermometer | | | |
|     LeSabre & Estate Wagon | 37 | 28 | 29 |
|     Electras & Estate Wagon Limited | 21 | 16 | 17 |
| L.H. & R.H. Remote Sport Mirrors | | | |
|     LeSabres | 57 | 44 | 45 |
|     Electras | 41 | 32 | 33 |
|     Estate Wagon | 52 | 40 | 41 |
|     Estate Wagon Limited | 36 | 28 | 29 |
| Right Remote Sport Mirror | 33 | 25 | 26 |
| Lighted Visor Vanity Mirror | 46 | 35 | 36 |
| Door Edge Guards | | | |
|     2-Doors | 11 | 8 | 9 |
|     4-Doors | 18 | 14 | 15 |
| Protective Body Side Molding | 42 | 32 | 33 |
| Radio Equipment | | | |
|     AM | 96 | 74 | 75 |
|     AM/FM | 165 | 127 | 129 |
|     AM/FM Stereo, Frt./Rear Dual Speakers | 239 | 184 | 186 |
|     AM W/Stereo Tape Player, Frt./Rear Dual Speakers | 250 | 193 | 195 |
|     AM/FM Stereo W/Tape Player, Frt/Rear Dual Speakers | | | |
|         Riviera | 106 | 82 | 83 |
|         All Models Exc. Riviera | 345 | 266 | 269 |
|     AM/FM Stereo W/Cassette Player, Frt./Rear Dual Speakers | | | |
|         Riviera | 116 | 89 | 90 |
|         All Models Exc. Riviera | 355 | 274 | 277 |

*Prices are accurate at time of printing; subject to manufacturer's change.*

|  | Retail Price | Dealer Cost | Low Price |
|---|---|---|---|
| Digital Readout AM/FM Stereo, Frt./Rear Dual Speakers | | | |
| LeSabre & Est. Wagon | $392 | $302 | $306 |
| Estate Wagon Limited | 342 | 263 | 269 |
| Comb. AM/FM Stereo & 40 Channel CB Trans., Frt./Rear Dual Speakers | | | |
| Riviera | 338 | 260 | 263 |
| All Models Exc. Riviera | 577 | 444 | 449 |
| AM/FM Freq. Syn. Stereo W/Tape Player, Digital Clock, Signal Seeking & Scanning, Frt./Rear Dual Speakers, Electras | 514 | 396 | 400 |
| Riviera | 275 | 212 | 215 |
| Rear Seat Speaker | 24 | 18 | 19 |
| Frt./Rear Dual Speakers | 48 | 37 | 38 |
| Windshield Antenna | 26 | 20 | 21 |
| Automatic Power Antenna | | | |
| W/Radio | 45 | 35 | 36 |
| W/o Radio | 71 | 55 | 56 |
| Triband Power Antenna | | | |
| W/Radio | 83 | 64 | 65 |
| W/o Radio | 109 | 84 | 85 |
| 6-Way Power Seat, Driver Side | 151 | 116 | 118 |
| Electra Limited & Park Ave. | 120 | 92 | 93 |
| 6-Way Power Seat, Driver & Pass. | 302 | 233 | 236 |
| Electra Limited & Park Ave. | 271 | 209 | 212 |
| Electric Seatback Recliner, Pass. Side | 113 | 87 | 88 |
| Third Seat | 186 | 143 | 145 |
| Custom Steering Wheel | 10 | 8 | 9 |
| Rallye Steering Wheel | | | |
| LeSabre | 41 | 32 | 33 |
| LeSabre Cust. & Wagon | 31 | 24 | 25 |
| Tilt Steering Column | 70 | 54 | 55 |
| Tilt & Telescoping Steering Column | | | |
| LeSabre | 126 | 97 | 98 |
| LeSabre Cust. & Electra, Estate Wagon | 116 | 89 | 90 |
| Riviera | 85 | 66 | 67 |
| Estate Wagon Limited | 46 | 35 | 36 |
| Electric Trunk Release | 22 | 17 | 18 |
| Power Windows | | | |
| 2-Doors | 130 | 100 | 101 |
| 4-Doors | 190 | 146 | 148 |
| 3-Speed Windshield Wiper | 32 | 23 | 24 |
| Woodgrain Vinyl Applique | 235 | 181 | 183 |

## REGAL

| | Retail Price | Dealer Cost | Low Price |
|---|---|---|---|
| 2-Door Coupe | $4852 | $4018 | $4318 |

*Prices are accurate at time of printing; subject to manufacturer's change.*

|  | Retail Price | Dealer Cost | Low Price |
|---|---|---|---|
| **REGAL SPORT COUPE** | | | |
| 2-Door Coupe | $5853 | $4849 | $5149 |
| **REGAL LIMITED** | | | |
| 2-Door Coupe | 5233 | 4334 | 4634 |

## REGAL ACCESSORIES

|  | Retail Price | Dealer Cost | Low Price |
|---|---|---|---|
| Engines | | | |
| 231 CID 2-BBL V6 | $40 | $31 | $32 |
| 231 CID 4-BBL Turbocharged V6 | 50 | 39 | 40 |
| 305 CID 2-BBL V8 | 190 | 148 | 150 |
| 305 CID 4-BBL V8 | 240 | 187 | 189 |
| Transmissions | | | |
| 4-Speed Manual | 125 | 98 | 99 |
| Automatic | 307 | 239 | 243 |
| Air Conditioner | 544 | 424 | 429 |
| Automatic Climate Control | 626 | 488 | 493 |
| Positive Traction Differential Rear Axle | 60 | 47 | 48 |
| Heavy-Duty Battery | 20 | 16 | 17 |
| Custom Seat & Shoulder Belts | | | |
| W/Notchback or 55/45 Front Seat | 20 | 16 | 17 |
| W/Bucket Seats | 16 | 12 | 13 |
| Power Brakes | 69 | 54 | 55 |
| Front & Rear Bumper Guards | 40 | 31 | 32 |
| Electric Dial Face Clock | 22 | 17 | 18 |
| Electric Digital Clock | 49 | 38 | 39 |
| Full Length Operating Console | 90 | 70 | 71 |
| Cruise Master | 90 | 70 | 71 |
| Electric Rear Window Defogger | 92 | 72 | 73 |
| Electric Door Locks | 80 | 62 | 63 |
| High Altitude Emission System | 33 | 26 | 27 |
| California Assembly Line Emission Test | 75 | 59 | 60 |
| Engine Block Heater | 14 | 11 | 12 |
| Soft Ray Tinted Glass | 62 | 48 | 49 |
| Soft Ray Tinted Windshield | 45 | 35 | 36 |
| Radio Equipment | | | |
| AM | 83 | 65 | 66 |
| AM/FM | 154 | 120 | 122 |
| AM/FM Stereo W/Frt./Rear Dual Speakers | 236 | 184 | 186 |
| AM W/Stereo 8-Track W/Frt./Rear Dual Speakers | 233 | 182 | 184 |
| AM/FM Stereo W/8-Track W/Frt./Rear Dual Speakers | 341 | 266 | 269 |
| AM/FM Stereo W/Cassette W/Frt./Rear Dual Speakers | 351 | 274 | 277 |
| Comb. AM/FM Stereo Entertainment W/40-Chan. CB Trans. W/Frt./Rear Dual Speakers | 571 | 445 | 451 |

*Prices are accurate at time of printing; subject to manufacturer's change.*

|  | Retail Price | Dealer Cost | Low Price |
|---|---|---|---|
| Dig. Readout AM/FM Stereo W/Frt./Rear Dual Speakers | $392 | $306 | $310 |
| Single Rear Seat Speaker | 24 | 19 | 20 |
| Rear Dual Speakers | 48 | 37 | 38 |
| Windshield Antenna | 26 | 20 | 21 |
| Automatic Power Antenna | | | |
| W/Radio | 45 | 35 | 36 |
| W/o Radio | 71 | 55 | 56 |
| Triband Power Antenna | | | |
| W/Radio | 83 | 65 | 66 |
| W/o Radio | 109 | 85 | 86 |
| Electric Sunroof | 499 | 389 | 393 |
| Electric Silver Astroroof | 699 | 545 | 551 |
| Hatch Roof | 625 | 488 | 493 |
| 6-Way Power Seat Adjuster, Driver Side | 151 | 118 | 120 |
| Reclining Passenger Seat Back, Manual | 59 | 46 | 47 |
| Power Steering | 152 | 119 | 120 |
| Rallye Steering Wheel | 31 | 24 | 25 |
| Sport Steering Wheel | 31 | 24 | 25 |
| Tilt Steering Column | 69 | 54 | 55 |
| Landau Vinyl Top | | | |
| Regal & Regal Sport Coupe | 155 | 121 | 123 |
| Regal Limited | 140 | 109 | 111 |
| Heavily Padded Landau Vinyl Top | | | |
| Regal & Regal Sport Coupe | 216 | 168 | 170 |
| Regal Limited | 168 | 131 | 133 |
| Long Vinyl Top | 116 | 90 | 91 |
| Bucket Seats | 40 | 31 | 32 |
| Electric Trunk Release | 22 | 17 | 18 |
| Power Windows | 124 | 97 | 98 |
| 2-Speed Windshield Wiper | 32 | 25 | 26 |

### SKYHAWKS

|  | Retail Price | Dealer Cost | Low Price |
|---|---|---|---|
| 2 Door Hatchback Coupe | $4103 | $3562 | $3812 |

### SKYHAWK

|  | Retail Price | Dealer Cost | Low Price |
|---|---|---|---|
| 2 Door Hatchback Coupe | 4367 | 3791 | 4041 |

### SKYHAWK ACCESSORIES

|  | Retail Price | Dealer Cost | Low Price |
|---|---|---|---|
| 5-Speed Manual Transmission | $175 | $145 | $147 |
| Automatic Transmission | 270 | 224 | 227 |
| Air Conditioner | 470 | 390 | 394 |
| Appearance Group | 73 | 61 | 62 |
| Positive Traction Differential Axle | 56 | 47 | 48 |

*Prices are accurate at time of printing; subject to manufacturer's change.*

|  | Retail Price | Dealer Cost | Low Price |
|---|---|---|---|
| Heavy-Duty Battery | $17 | $14 | $15 |
| Custom Seat Belts | 16 | 13 | 14 |
| Power Brakes, Front Disc & Rear Drum | 66 | 55 | 56 |
| Electric Clock | 19 | 16 | 17 |
| Electric Clock & Tachometer | 69 | 57 | 58 |
| Full Length Operating Console | 77 | 64 | 65 |
| Convenience Light Group | 23 | 19 | 20 |
| Electric Rear Window Defogger | 79 | 66 | 67 |
| High Altitude Emission System | 33 | 27 | 28 |
| California Assembly Line Emission Testing | 75 | 62 | 63 |
| Soft Ray Tinted Glass | 54 | 45 | 56 |
| Soft Ray Tinted Windshield | 42 | 35 | 36 |
| Door Edge Guards Moldings | 11 | 9 | 10 |
| Roof Crown Moldings | 176 | 146 | 148 |
| Protective Body Side Molding | 28 | 23 | 24 |
| W/Hawk Accent Stripe | 44 | 37 | 38 |
| W/Appearance Group & Hawk Accent Stripe | 44 | 37 | 38 |
| W/Appearance Group W/o Hawk Accent Stripe | 28 | 23 | 24 |
| W/o Appearance Group W/o Hawk Accent Stripe | 44 | 37 | 38 |
| Radio Equipment | | | |
| AM | 74 | 61 | 62 |
| AM/FM | 139 | 115 | 116 |
| AM/FM Stereo, Single Frt./Rear Speakers | 222 | 184 | 186 |
| AM W/Stereo 8-Track Tape Single Frt./Rear Speakers | 216 | 179 | 181 |
| AM/FM Stereo W/Tape Player, Single Frt./Rear Speakers | 320 | 266 | 269 |
| Rear Speaker | 23 | 19 | 20 |
| Windshield Antenna | 25 | 21 | 22 |
| Adjustable Driver's Seat Back | 19 | 16 | 17 |
| Manual Operation Glass Sunroof | 215 | 179 | 181 |
| Fixed Shadow Light Astroroof & Roof Crown Molding | 615 | 510 | 516 |
| Power Steering | 134 | 111 | 113 |
| Rallye Steering Wheel | 41 | 34 | 35 |
| Tilt Steering Column | 62 | 51 | 52 |
| Hawk Accent Stripe | 36 | 30 | 31 |

## SKYLARK S
| | | | |
|---|---|---|---|
| 2-Door Coupe | $3872 | $3359 | $3559 |

## SKYLARK
| | | | |
|---|---|---|---|
| 4-Door Sedan | 4074 | 3535 | 3785 |
| 2-Door Coupe | 3999 | 3470 | 3670 |
| 2-Door Hatchback Coupe | 4181 | 3628 | 3878 |

*Prices are accurate at time of printing; subject to manufacturer's change.*

|  | Retail Price | Dealer Cost | Low Price |
|---|---|---|---|
| **SKYLARK CUSTOM** | | | |
| 4-Door Sedan | $ 4317 | $ 3746 | $ 3996 |
| 2-Door Coupe | 4242 | 3681 | 3931 |
| 2-Door Hatchback Coupe | 4424 | 3839 | 4089 |

## SKYLARK ACCESSORIES

| | | | |
|---|---|---|---|
| Engines | | | |
|    5.0 Litre 305 CID 2 BBL V8 | $150 | $117 | $119 |
|    5.7 Litre 350 CID 4 BBL V8 | 265 | 207 | 210 |
| Automatic Transmission | 307 | 239 | 242 |
| Accessory Package | 14 | 11 | 12 |
| Acoustic Package | | | |
|    Skylark S & Skylark | 40 | 31 | 32 |
|    Skylark Custom | 27 | 21 | 22 |
| Air Conditioner | 508 | 396 | 400 |
| Positive Traction Differential Axle | 60 | 47 | 48 |
| Heavy Duty Battery | 20 | 16 | 17 |
| Custom Seat Belts | | | |
|    W/Bucket Seats | 16 | 12 | 13 |
|    W/Bench Seats | 18 | 14 | 15 |
| Rear Window Blower Defogger | 51 | 40 | 41 |
| Electric Door Locks | | | |
|    2-Doors | 74 | 58 | 59 |
|    4-Doors | 103 | 80 | 81 |
| High Altitude Emission System | 33 | 26 | 27 |
| Calif. Assembly Line Emission Testing | 75 | 59 | 60 |
| Engine Block Heater | 14 | 11 | 12 |
| Soft Ray Tinted Glass | 56 | 44 | 45 |
| Soft Ray Tinted Windshield | 44 | 34 | 35 |
| Dual Horns | 10 | 8 | 9 |
| Headlamps On Indicator | 10 | 8 | 9 |
| Front Carpet Savers | 9 | 7 | 8 |
| Carpet Savers & Handy Mats | 18 | 14 | 15 |
| L.H. Remote Control Mirror | 16 | 12 | 13 |
| L.H. Remote, R.H. Manual Sport Mirrors | 32 | 25 | 26 |
| Wheel Opening & Roof Drip Moldings | 36 | 28 | 29 |
| Rear Deck Lid | 9 | 7 | 8 |
| Rocker Panel Moldings | 17 | 13 | 14 |
| Protective Body Side Moldings | 42 | 33 | 34 |
| Radio Equipment | | | |
|    AM Radio | 79 | 62 | 63 |
|    AM/FM Radio | 149 | 116 | 118 |
|    AM/FM Stereo, Single Frt./Rear Speakers | 236 | 184 | 186 |
|    AM W/Stereo 8 Track Tape, Single Frt./Rear Speakers | 229 | 179 | 181 |

*Prices are accurate at time of printing; subject to manufacturer's change.*

|  | Retail Price | Dealer Cost | Low Price |
|---|---|---|---|
| AM/FM Stereo W/8 Track Tape, Single Frt./Rear Speakers | $341 | $266 | $269 |
| Rear Seat Speaker | 23 | 18 | 19 |
| Windshield Antenna | 26 | 20 | 21 |
| Sport Coupe or Sport Sedan | | | |
| W/Stowaway Spare Tire | 182 | 141 | 143 |
| W/Conventional Spare Tire | 200 | 155 | 157 |
| Power Steering | 152 | 119 | 121 |
| Rallye Steering Wheel | 41 | 32 | 33 |
| Tilt Steering Column | 69 | 54 | 55 |
| Body Side Stripe | 33 | 26 | 27 |
| Firm Ride & Handling | 24 | 19 | 20 |
| Rallye Ride & Handling | 46 | 36 | 37 |
| Heavy Padded Landau Vinyl Top | | | |
| Skylark S & Skylark Coupes | 184 | 144 | 146 |
| Skylark Custom Coupe | 179 | 140 | 142 |
| Heavy Padded Landau Long Vinyl Top | | | |
| Skylark S & Skylark | 102 | 80 | 81 |
| Skylark Custom | 97 | 76 | 77 |
| Interior Trim | | | |
| Vinyl Bucket | 89 | 69 | 70 |
| Cloth Bucket | 109 | 85 | 86 |
| Carpeted Door Trim W/Map Pocket & Reflector | 41 | 32 | 33 |
| Electric Trunk Release | 22 | 17 | 18 |
| Power Windows | | | |
| 2-Doors | 118 | 92 | 93 |
| 4-Doors | 164 | 128 | 130 |
| Swing Out Rear Quarter Vent Window | 54 | 42 | 43 |
| Two Speed Windshield Wiper | 32 | 25 | 26 |

# CADILLAC

### DEVILLE
| | | | |
|---|---|---|---|
| Coupe de Ville | $10,444 | $8031 | $9031 |
| Sedan de Ville | 10,668 | 8204 | 9204 |

### FLEETWOOD
| | | | |
|---|---|---|---|
| Eldorado Coupe | 11,921 | 9167 | 10,167 |
| Fleetwood Brougham | 12,292 | 9453 | 10,453 |
| Fleetwood Limousine | 19,642 | 15,111 | 16,611 |
| Fleetwood Formal Limousine | 20,363 | 15,666 | 17,166 |

### SEVILLE
| | | | |
|---|---|---|---|
| Seville Sedan | 14,267 | 10,975 | 12,475 |

*Prices are accurate at time of printing; subject to manufacturer's change.*

## CADILLAC DEVILLE, FLEETWOOD AND SEVILLE ACCESSORIES

| | Retail Price | Dealer Cost | Low Price |
|---|---|---|---|
| **Accent Molding** | | | |
| DeVille | $100 | $77 | $78 |
| DeVille W/D'Elegance & Fleetwood Brougham | 85 | 65 | 66 |
| Accent Stripes | 53 | 41 | 42 |
| Astroroof W/Full Vinyl Roof | 995 | 766 | 772 |
| Astroroof, Painted | 1106 | 852 | 861 |
| Brougham D'Elegance, Cloth | 938 | 722 | 730 |
| Brougham d'Elegance, Leather Seating Area | 1270 | 978 | 988 |
| California Emission Equip. & Testing | 75 | 58 | 59 |
| Controlled Cycle Wiper System | 32 | 25 | 26 |
| Cruise Control | 122 | 94 | 95 |
| Rear Window Grid Type Defogger | 94 | 72 | 73 |
| DeVille Cabriolet | 369 | 284 | 287 |
| DeVille Cabriolet Astroroof | 1450 | 1117 | 1129 |
| DeVille Cabriolet Sunroof | 1250 | 963 | 973 |
| DeVille d'Elegance | 689 | 531 | 537 |
| Limited Slip Differential | 67 | 52 | 53 |
| **Door Edge Guards** | | | |
| 2-Door | 11 | 8 | 9 |
| 4-Door | 18 | 14 | 15 |
| Automatic Door Locks | 114 | 88 | 89 |
| Dual Comfort Front Seats, 50/50 | 198 | 152 | 154 |
| Eldorado Cabriolet | 484 | 373 | 377 |
| Eldorado Cabriolet Astroroof | 1565 | 1205 | 1218 |
| Eldorado Cabriolet Sunroof | 1365 | 1051 | 1062 |
| Eldorado Custom Biarritz | 1865 | 1436 | 1450 |
| Eldorado Custom Biarritz Astroroof | 2946 | 2268 | 2291 |
| Eldorado Custom Biarritz Sunroof | 2746 | 2114 | 2136 |
| Electronic Fuel Injected Engine | 744 | 573 | 579 |
| Electronic Level Control | 140 | 108 | 110 |
| Engine Block Heater | 20 | 15 | 16 |
| Firemist Exterior Color | 163 | 126 | 128 |
| **Carpeted Rubber Floor Mats** | | | |
| Twin Front | 31 | 24 | 25 |
| Twin Rear | 15 | 12 | 13 |
| Front Only, One Piece | 34 | 26 | 27 |
| Rear Only, One Piece | 21 | 16 | 17 |
| Front Bumper Reinforcement | 9 | 7 | 8 |
| Fuel Monitor | 29 | 22 | 23 |
| 80 Amp. Generator | 51 | 39 | 40 |
| Guidematic Headlamp Control | 62 | 48 | 49 |
| Heavy-Duty Cooling System | 47 | 36 | 37 |
| High Altitude Package | 33 | 25 | 26 |

*Prices are accurate at time of printing; subject to manufacturer's change.*

|  | Retail Price | Dealer Cost | Low Price |
|---|---|---|---|
| Illuminated Entry System | $59 | $45 | $46 |
| **Leather Seating Area** | | | |
| DeVille | 295 | 227 | 230 |
| Fleetwood Brougham, Eldorado Coupe & SeVille Sedan | 315 | 243 | 246 |
| Two-Tone W/50/50 Dual Comfort | 556 | 428 | 433 |
| License Frame, One | 9 | 6 | 7 |
| License Frames, Two | 18 | 12 | 13 |
| Illuminated Vanity Mirror, Passenger | 50 | 39 | 40 |
| Right Side Remote Control Mirror | 34 | 26 | 27 |
| Opera Lamps | 63 | 49 | 50 |
| **Radio Equipment** | | | |
| AM/FM Stereo W/Tape Player | 106 | 82 | 83 |
| AM/FM Stereo W/Tape Player & CB | 427 | 329 | 333 |
| AM/FM Stereo Signal Seeking Scanner W/Tape Player & Digital Display | 225 | 173 | 175 |
| AM/FM Signal Seeking Scanner W/Rear Control | 203 | 156 | 158 |
| AM/FM Stereo W/Digital Display | 106 | 82 | 83 |
| AM/FM Stereo W/Citizens Band | 281 | 216 | 219 |
| **Power Seats** | | | |
| Driver's Recliner, 50/50 | 116 | 89 | 90 |
| Pass. Recliner, 50/50 | 262 | 202 | 205 |
| Seville Only | 210 | 162 | 164 |
| Notch Back Seat Pass. Recliner | 116 | 89 | 90 |
| **Padded Vinyl Roof** | | | |
| DeVille | 215 | 166 | 168 |
| Eldorado Coupe | 222 | 171 | 173 |
| **6-Way Power Pass. Seat Adjuster** | | | |
| Seville Sedan | 118 | 91 | 92 |
| DeVille, Eldorado Coupe & Fleetwood Brougham | 150 | 116 | 118 |

# CHEVROLET

## CAMARO

| | | | |
|---|---|---|---|
| Sport Coupe | $4414 | $3829 | $4079 |
| Rally Sport Coupe | 4784 | 4151 | 4451 |
| Type LT Coupe | 4814 | 4177 | 4477 |
| LT Rally Sport Coupe | 5065 | 4395 | 4695 |
| Z28 Sport Coupe | 5604 | 4863 | 5163 |

*Prices are accurate at time of printing; subject to manufacturer's change.*

## CAMARO ACCESSORIES

| | Retail Price | Dealer Cost | Low Price |
|---|---|---|---|
| **Engines** | | | |
| 305 CID V8 | $185 | $144 | $146 |
| 350 CID V8 | 300 | 234 | 237 |
| 4-Speed Manual Transmission | 125 | 98 | 99 |
| **Automatic Transmission** | | | |
| Z28 Sport Coupe | 45 | 35 | 36 |
| Sport Coupe or LT Coupe | 307 | 239 | 242 |
| Sport Cloth Bucket Seats | 21 | 16 | 17 |
| Custom Vinyl Bucket Seats | 294 | 229 | 232 |
| **Custom Cloth Bucket Seats** | | | |
| Type LT Coupe | 21 | 16 | 17 |
| Z28 Sport Coupe | 315 | 246 | 249 |
| **Custom Sport Cloth Bucket Seats** | | | |
| Type LT Coupe | 21 | 16 | 17 |
| Z28 Sport Coupe | 315 | 246 | 249 |
| Sport Vinyl Roof Cover | 102 | 80 | 81 |
| **Four Season Air Conditioning** | | | |
| W/o V8 Engine | 539 | 420 | 425 |
| W/V8 Engine | 508 | 396 | 400 |
| Power Brakes | 69 | 54 | 55 |
| Electric Clock | 20 | 16 | 17 |
| Console | 80 | 62 | 63 |
| Rear Window Defogger, Forced-Air Type | 51 | 40 | 41 |
| Power Door Lock System, Electric | 80 | 62 | 63 |
| California Emission Requirements | 75 | 59 | 60 |
| High Altitude Emission Equipment | 33 | 26 | 27 |
| Color-Keyed Floor Mats | 20 | 16 | 17 |
| Soft-Ray Tinted Glass | 56 | 43 | 44 |
| **Radio Equipment** | | | |
| AM | 79 | 63 | 64 |
| AM/FM | 149 | 116 | 118 |
| AM/FM Stereo | 229 | 179 | 181 |
| AM W/Stereo Tape System | 229 | 179 | 181 |
| AM/FM Stereo W/Stereo Tape System | 328 | 256 | 259 |
| Rear Seat Speaker | 24 | 19 | 20 |
| Windshield Antenna | 25 | 20 | 21 |
| Roof Panels | 625 | 488 | 493 |
| Adjustable Driver's Seat Back | 21 | 16 | 17 |
| Cruise-Master Speed Control | 90 | 70 | 71 |
| Rear Spoiler | 55 | 43 | 44 |
| Comfortilt Steering Wheel | 69 | 54 | 55 |
| Style Trim | 70 | 55 | 56 |
| Sport Suspension | 38 | 30 | 31 |
| Power Windows, Electric | 124 | 97 | 98 |
| Windshield Wiper Equipment, Intermittent | 32 | 25 | 26 |

*Prices are accurate at time of printing; subject to manufacturer's change.*

|  | Retail Price | Dealer Cost | Low Price |
|---|---|---|---|
| **CHEVETTE** | | | |
| Hatchback Coupe | $3354 | $2812 | $3012 |
| 4-Door Hatchback Sedan | 3464 | 3008 | 3208 |
| Scooter Hatchback Coupe | 2999 | 2693 | 2893 |

## CHEVETTE ACCESSORIES

|  | Retail Price | Dealer Cost | Low Price |
|---|---|---|---|
| 1.6 Litre 96 CID L4 Engine | $55 | $46 | $47 |
| Automatic Transmission | 270 | 224 | 227 |
| Sport Cloth Bucket Seats | | | |
|    W/o Rear Seat Deletion | 19 | 16 | 17 |
|    W/Rear Seat Deletion | 10 | 8 | 9 |
| Custom Cloth Bucket Seats | 170 | 141 | 143 |
| Custom Vinyl Bucket Seats | 151 | 125 | 127 |
| Four Season Air Conditioning | 470 | 390 | 394 |
| Performance Ratio Rear Axles | 14 | 12 | 13 |
| Heavy-Duty Battery | 17 | 14 | 15 |
| Deluxe Seat Shoulder Belts | 19 | 16 | 17 |
| Power Brakes | 66 | 55 | 56 |
| Deluxe Bumpers | 33 | 27 | 28 |
| Deluxe Guards | | | |
|    Scooter Hatchback Coupe | 71 | 59 | 60 |
|    Hatchback Coupe Sedan | 38 | 32 | 33 |
| Roof Carrier | 60 | 50 | 51 |
| Electric Clock | 18 | 15 | 16 |
| Custom Exterior | 99 | 82 | 83 |
| Rear Window Defogger, Electro-Clear | 79 | 66 | 67 |
| Soft-Ray Tinted Glass | 54 | 45 | 46 |
| Special Instrumentation | 64 | 53 | 54 |
| Cigarette Lighter | 5 | 4 | 5 |
| Day/Night Inside Rearview Mirror | 9 | 7 | 8 |
| L.H. Remote Sport Mirror | 22 | 18 | 19 |
| Twin Remote Sport Mirrors | 49 | 41 | 42 |
| Radio Equipment | | | |
|    AM | 71 | 59 | 60 |
|    AM/FM | | | |
|       Hatchback Coupe & Sedan | 68 | 56 | 67 |
|       Scooter Hatchback Coupe | 139 | 115 | 117 |
|    Rear Seat Speaker | 23 | 19 | 20 |
| Swing-Out Rear Side Windows | 51 | 42 | 43 |
| Windshield Wiper System, Intermittent | 30 | 25 | 26 |

## CORVETTE

|  | Retail Price | Dealer Cost | Low Price |
|---|---|---|---|
| Coupe | $9352 | $7284 | $8284 |

*Prices are accurate at time of printing; subject to manufacturer's change.*

## CORVETTE ACCESSORIES

| | Retail Price | Dealer Cost | Low Price |
|---|---|---|---|
| 350 CID 4 BBL V8 Engine | $525 | $404 | $409 |
| 25th Anniversary Paint | 399 | 307 | 310 |
| Four Season Air Conditioning | 605 | 466 | 471 |
| Highway Ratio Rear Axles | 15 | 12 | 13 |
| Heavy-Duty Battery | 18 | 14 | 15 |
| Trailering Chassis Equipment | 89 | 68 | 69 |
| Convenience Group | 84 | 65 | 66 |
| Rear Window Defogger, Electro-Clear | 95 | 73 | 74 |
| Power Door Lock System | 120 | 92 | 93 |
| California Emission Requirements | 75 | 58 | 59 |
| High Altitude Emission Equipment | 33 | 25 | 26 |
| L.H. Remote & R.H. Manual Sport Mirrors | 40 | 31 | 32 |
| Radio Equipment | | | |
|    AM/FM | 199 | 153 | 155 |
|    AM/FM Stereo | 286 | 220 | 223 |
|    AM/FM Stereo W/Stereo Tape System | 419 | 323 | 327 |
|    AM/FM Stereo CB Radio Power Antenna | 683 | 491 | 496 |
|    Power Antenna | 49 | 38 | 39 |
|    Dual Rear Speakers | 49 | 38 | 39 |
| Criuse-Master Speed Control | 99 | 76 | 77 |
| Tilt-Telescopic Steering Wheel | 175 | 135 | 137 |
| Gymkhana Suspension | 41 | 32 | 33 |
| Power Windows, Electric | 130 | 100 | 101 |

| **IMPALA** | | | |
|---|---|---|---|
| Coupe | $5208 | $4156 | $4456 |
| Landau Coupe | 5598 | 4468 | 4768 |
| 4-Door Sedan | 5283 | 4216 | 4516 |
| **CAPRICE CLASSIC** | | | |
| Coupe | 5526 | 4410 | 4710 |
| Landau Coupe | 5830 | 4654 | 4954 |
| 4-Door Sedan | 5626 | 4490 | 4790 |
| **IMPALA STATION WAGON** | | | |
| 4-Door Station Wagon, 2-Seat | 5777 | 4609 | 4909 |
| 4-Door Station Wagon, 3-Seat | 5904 | 4710 | 5010 |
| **CAPRICE CLASSIC STATION WAGON** | | | |
| 4-Door Station Wagon, 2-Seat | $6012 | $4797 | $5097 |
| 4-Door Station Wagon, 3-Seat | 6151 | 4908 | 5208 |

## IMPALA AND CAPRICE ACCESSORIES

| Engines | | | |
|---|---|---|---|
| 305 CID V8 | $185 | $142 | $144 |
| 350 CID V8, Coupes & Sedans | 300 | 231 | 234 |

*Prices are accurate at time of printing; subject to manufacturer's change.*

|  | Retail Price | Dealer Cost | Low Price |
|---|---|---|---|
| 350 CID V8, Wagons | $ 115 | $ 89 | $ 90 |
| Vinyl Bench Seat | 24 | 18 | 19 |
| Sport Cloth Bench Seat, Wagons | 24 | 18 | 19 |
| Knit Cloth 50/50 Seat, Coupes & Sedans | 224 | 172 | 174 |
| Vinyl 50/50 Seat, Coupes & Sedans | 248 | 191 | 193 |
| Vinyl 50/50 Seat, Wagons | 224 | 172 | 174 |
| Special Custom Cloth 50/50 Seat | 365 | 281 | 284 |
| Sport Cloth 50/50 Seat | 248 | 191 | 193 |
| Two-Tone Exterior Paint | 47 | 36 | 37 |
| Custom Two-Tone Paint | 115 | 89 | 90 |
| Vinyl Roof Cover | 142 | 109 | 111 |
| Four-Season Air Conditioning | 569 | 438 | 443 |
| Comfortron Air Conditioning | 655 | 504 | 510 |
| Performance Ratio Rear Axles | 15 | 12 | 13 |
| Positraction Rear Axles | 63 | 49 | 50 |
| Heavy-Duty Battery | 18 | 14 | 15 |
| Roof Carrier, Wagon | 110 | 85 | 86 |
| Digital Clock | | | |
| Impala | 49 | 38 | 39 |
| Caprice | 28 | 22 | 23 |
| Electric Clock | 21 | 16 | 17 |
| Litter Container | 6 | 5 | 6 |
| Rear Window Defogger | | | |
| Electro-Clear | 94 | 72 | 73 |
| Forced-Air | 51 | 39 | 40 |
| Power Door Lock System, Electric | | | |
| Coupes | 82 | 63 | 64 |
| Sedans & Wagons | 114 | 88 | 89 |
| Soft-Ray Tinted Glass | 76 | 59 | 60 |
| Dual Horns | 7 | 5 | 6 |
| Auxiliary Lighting | | | |
| Impala Coupes, Sedans & 3-Seat Wagons | 35 | 27 | 28 |
| Impala 2-Seat Wagons | 46 | 35 | 36 |
| Caprice Coupes, Sedans & 3-Seat Wagons | 32 | 25 | 26 |
| Caprice 2-Seat Wagons | 43 | 33 | 34 |
| Deluxe Luggage Compartment Trim | 44 | 34 | 35 |
| L.H. & R.H. Rearview Mirrors | 48 | 37 | 38 |
| L.H. Remote Rear View Mirror | 16 | 12 | 13 |
| Twin Remote Sport Mirrors | | | |
| W/o Landau Coupe, W/Wagons | 57 | 44 | 45 |
| W/Landau Coupe | 24 | 18 | 19 |
| L.H. Remote & R.H. Manual Sport Mirrors | 33 | 25 | 26 |
| Visor Vanity | 4 | 3 | 4 |
| Radio Equipment | | | |
| AM | 80 | 62 | 63 |
| AM/FM | 160 | 123 | 125 |
| AM/FM Stereo | 232 | 179 | 181 |

*Prices are accurate at time of printing; subject to manufacturer's change.*

|  | Retail Price | Dealer Cost | Low Price |
|---|---|---|---|
| AM W/Stereo Tape System | $250 | $193 | $195 |
| AM/FM Stereo W/Stereo Tape System | 332 | 256 | 259 |
| AM/FM CB & Power Antenna | 498 | 383 | 387 |
| Rear Seat Speaker | 24 | 18 | 19 |
| Dual Front Speakers | 20 | 15 | 16 |
| Power Antenna | 45 | 35 | 36 |
| Windshield Antenna | 25 | 19 | 20 |
| 6-Way Electric Power Seat Control | 151 | 116 | 118 |
| Power Sky Roof | 595 | 458 | 463 |
| Cruise-Master Speed Control | 95 | 73 | 74 |
| Comfortilt Steering Wheel | 70 | 54 | 55 |
| Pin Striping | 33 | 25 | 26 |
| Superlift Rear Shock Absorbers | 50 | 39 | 40 |
| Heavy-Duty Frt. & Rear Suspension | 20 | 15 | 16 |
| Sport Suspension | 38 | 29 | 30 |
| Power Tailgate Lock | 40 | 31 | 32 |
| Power Trunk Opener, Electric | 21 | 16 | 17 |
| Value Appearance Group | 73 | 56 | 57 |
| Power Windows, Electric | | | |
|   Sedans & Wagons | 190 | 146 | 148 |
|   Coupes | 130 | 100 | 101 |
| Windshield Wiper System, Intermittent | 32 | 25 | 26 |

## MALIBU

|  | Retail Price | Dealer Cost | Low Price |
|---|---|---|---|
| Sport Coupe | $4204 | $3482 | $3682 |
| Sedan | 4279 | 3544 | 3794 |

## MALIBU CLASSIC

| Sport Coupe | 4461 | 3695 | 3945 |
|---|---|---|---|
| Landau Coupe | 4684 | 3880 | 4130 |
| Sedan | 4561 | 3778 | 4028 |

## MALIBU WAGON

| 4-Door Station Wagon, 2-Seat | 4516 | 3740 | 3990 |
|---|---|---|---|

## MALIBU CLASSIC WAGON

| 4-Door Station Wagon, 2-Seat | 4714 | 3904 | 4154 |
|---|---|---|---|

### MALIBU AND MALIBU CLASSIC ACCESSORIES

| Engines | | | |
|---|---|---|---|
|   231 C.I.D. V6 | $40 | $31 | $32 |
|   305 C.I.D. V8 | 190 | 148 | 150 |
|   350 C.I.D. V8 | 305 | 238 | 241 |
| Interior Trims | | | |
|   Knit Cloth 50/50 | 164 | 128 | 130 |
|   Vinyl Bench Seat | 24 | 19 | 20 |
|   Vinyl Bucket Seats | 110 | 85 | 86 |

*Prices are accurate at time of printing; subject to manufacturer's change.*

|  | Retail Price | Dealer Cost | Low Price |
|---|---|---|---|
| Vinyl 50/50 | $ 188 | $ 147 | $ 149 |
| Vinyl Roof Cover | 116 | 90 | 91 |
| Air Conditioning | 544 | 424 | 429 |
| Rear Window Air Deflector | 28 | 22 | 23 |
| **Rear Axles** | | | |
| Performance Ratio | 15 | 12 | 13 |
| Positraction | 60 | 46 | 47 |
| Heavy-Duty Battery | 18 | 14 | 15 |
| Power Brakes | 69 | 54 | 55 |
| Roof Carrier | 85 | 66 | 67 |
| Electric Clock | 21 | 16 | 17 |
| Console | 80 | 62 | 63 |
| **Rear Window Defogger** | | | |
| Forced Air | 51 | 40 | 41 |
| Electro-Clear | 92 | 72 | 73 |
| **Electric Door Lock System** | | | |
| Coupes | 80 | 62 | 63 |
| Sedans & Wagons | 112 | 87 | 88 |
| Gage Package | 53 | 41 | 42 |
| 61-AMP Delcotron Generator | 31 | 24 | 25 |
| Soft-Ray Tinted Glass, All Windows | 62 | 48 | 49 |
| **Radio Equipment** | | | |
| AM | 79 | 62 | 63 |
| AM/FM | 149 | 116 | 118 |
| AM/FM Stereo | 229 | 179 | 181 |
| Stereo Tape System W/AM Radio | 233 | 182 | 184 |
| Stereo Tape System W/AM/FM Stereo Radio | 328 | 256 | 259 |
| Rear Seat Speaker | 24 | 19 | 20 |
| Dual Front Speakers | 20 | 16 | 17 |
| Windshield Antenna | 25 | 19 | 20 |
| Power Antenna | 45 | 35 | 36 |
| Security Pkg., Cargo Area | 35 | 27 | 28 |
| Electric Power Seat, 6-Way Control | 151 | 118 | 120 |
| Power Sky Roof | 499 | 389 | 393 |
| Cruise-Master Speed Control | 90 | 70 | 71 |
| Power Steering | 152 | 119 | 121 |
| Comfortilt Steering Wheel | 69 | 54 | 55 |
| Body Side Pin Striping | 48 | 37 | 38 |
| **Suspensions** | | | |
| Front & Rear Heavy-Duty | 20 | 16 | 17 |
| Sport | 38 | 30 | 31 |
| **Transmissions** | | | |
| 4-Speed Manual | 125 | 97 | 98 |
| Automatic | 307 | 239 | 242 |
| Power Trunk Opener | 21 | 16 | 17 |
| **Power Windows** | | | |
| Coupes | 124 | 97 | 98 |

*Prices are accurate at time of printing; subject to manufacturer's change.*

|  | Retail Price | Dealer Cost | Low Price |
|---|---|---|---|
| Sedans & Wagons | $ 172 | $ 134 | $ 36 |
| Intermittent Windshield Wiper System | 32 | 25 | 26 |

## Monte Carlo

|  | Retail Price | Dealer Cost | Low Price |
|---|---|---|---|
| Sport Coupe | $4785 | $3962 | $4212 |
| Landau Coupe | 5678 | 4704 | 5004 |

## MONTE CARLO ACCESSORIES

|  | Retail Price | Dealer Cost | Low Price |
|---|---|---|---|
| 305 C.I.D. V8 Engine | $150 | $117 | $119 |
| Interior Trim |  |  |  |
|    Vinyl Bench Seat | 24 | 19 | 20 |
|    Vinyl Bucket Seats | 110 | 86 | 87 |
|    Special Custom Cloth 55/45 Seat | 340 | 265 | 268 |
|    Special Custom Vinyl 55/45 Seat | 364 | 284 | 287 |
| Vinyl Roof Cover | 131 | 102 | 104 |
| Air Conditioning | 544 | 424 | 429 |
| Rear Axles |  |  |  |
|    Performance Ratio | 15 | 12 | 13 |
|    Positraction | 60 | 46 | 47 |
| Heavy-Duty Battery | 18 | 14 | 15 |
| Deluxe Seat & Shoulder Belts |  |  |  |
|    W/Bench Seat, 6 Seat & 2 Front Shoulder | 21 | 16 | 17 |
|    W/Bucket Seats, 5 Seat & 2 Front Shoulder | 19 | 15 | 16 |
| Power Brakes | 69 | 54 | 55 |
| Console | 80 | 62 | 63 |
| Litter Container | 6 | 4 | 5 |
| Electro-Clear Rear Window Defogger | 92 | 72 | 73 |
| Electric Power Door Lock System | 80 | 62 | 63 |
| California Emission System | 75 | 58 | 59 |
| High Altitude Emission System | 33 | 26 | 27 |
| Floor Mats, 2 Front & 2 Rear | 20 | 16 | 17 |
| Gage Package | 32 | 25 | 26 |
| 61-AMP Delcotron Generator | 31 | 24 | 25 |
| Soft-Ray Tinted Glass, All Windows | 62 | 48 | 49 |
| Radio Equipment |  |  |  |
|    AM | 79 | 62 | 63 |
|    AM/FM | 154 | 120 | 122 |
|    AM/FM Stereo | 229 | 179 | 181 |
|    Stereo Tape System W/AM Radio | 233 | 182 | 184 |
|    Stereo Tape System W/AM/FM Stereo Radio | 328 | 256 | 259 |
|    Rear Seat Speaker | 24 | 19 | 20 |
|    Dual Front Speakers | 20 | 16 | 17 |
|    Windshield Antenna | 25 | 19 | 20 |

*Prices are accurate at time of printing; subject to manufacturer's change.*

|  | Retail Price | Dealer Cost | Low Price |
|---|---|---|---|
| Power Antenna | $ 45 | $ 35 | $ 36 |
| Removable Glass Roof Panels | 625 | 487 | 492 |
| Electric Power Seat, 6-Way Control | 151 | 118 | 120 |
| Power Sky Roof | 499 | 389 | 393 |
| Cruise-Master Speed Control | 90 | 70 | 71 |
| Comfortilt Steering Wheel | 69 | 54 | 55 |
| Power Steering | 152 | 119 | 121 |
| Body Side Pin Striping | 33 | 26 | 27 |
| Front & Rear Heavy-Duty Suspension | 20 | 16 | 17 |
| Transmissions |  |  |  |
| 4-Speed Manual | 125 | 97 | 98 |
| Automatic, W/o Landau Coupe | 307 | 239 | 242 |
| Power Trunk Opener | 21 | 16 | 17 |
| Power Windows | 124 | 97 | 98 |
| Intermittent Windshield Wiper System | 32 | 25 | 26 |

## MONZA

|  | Retail Price | Dealer Cost | Low Price |
|---|---|---|---|
| Coupe | $3462 | $3005 | $3205 |
| 2+2 Hatchback Coupe | 3609 | 3133 | 3333 |
| Station Wagon | 3698 | 3209 | 3409 |
| Estate Station Wagon | 3932 | 3413 | 3613 |
| 'S' Hatchback Coupe | 3527 | 3061 | 3261 |
| Sport Coupe | 3930 | 3412 | 3612 |
| 2+2 Sport Hatchback Coupe | 4077 | 3540 | 3790 |

## MONZA ACCESSORIES

|  | Retail Price | Dealer Cost | Low Price |
|---|---|---|---|
| Engines |  |  |  |
| 3.2 Litre (196 CID) V6 | $130 | $108 | $110 |
| 231 CID V6 | 170 | 141 | 143 |
| 305 CID V8 | 320 | 266 | 269 |
| 5-Speed Manual Transmission | 175 | 145 | 147 |
| Automatic Transmission | 270 | 224 | 227 |
| Sport Cloth Bucket Seats | 19 | 16 | 17 |
| Custom Vinyl Bucket Seats |  |  |  |
| 2+2 Hatchbk. Coupe, Coupe & Station Wag. | 171 | 142 | 144 |
| 'S' Hatchback Coupe | 192 | 159 | 161 |
| Custom Sport Cloth Bucket Seats |  |  |  |
| 2+2 Sport Hatchbk. Coupe, Sport Coupe & Estate Station Wagon | 19 | 16 | 17 |
| 2+2 Hatchbk. Coupe, Coupe & Station Wag. | 190 | 158 | 160 |
| 'S' Hatchback Coupe | 211 | 175 | 177 |
| Vinyl Roof Cover | 153 | 127 | 129 |
| Four Season Air Conditioning | 470 | 390 | 394 |

*Prices are accurate at time of printing; subject to manufacturer's change.*

|  | Retail Price | Dealer Cost | Low Price |
|---|---|---|---|
| Rear Window Air Deflector | $ 26 | $ 22 | $ 23 |
| Performance Ratio Rear Axle | 14 | 12 | 13 |
| Positraction Rear Axle | 55 | 46 | 47 |
| Heavy-Duty Battery | 17 | 14 | 15 |
| Deluxe Seat & Shoulder Belts | 19 | 16 | 17 |
| Power Brakes | 66 | 55 | 56 |
| Front & Rear Bumper Guards | 38 | 32 | 33 |
| Roof Carrier | 60 | 50 | 51 |
| Digital Clock | 45 | 37 | 38 |
| Electric Clock | 18 | 15 | 16 |
| Console | 77 | 64 | 65 |
| Rear Window Defogger, Electro-Clear | 79 | 66 | 67 |
| Soft-Ray Tinted Glass | 54 | 45 | 46 |
| Special Instrumentation | | | |
|   W/Electric Clock | 82 | 68 | 29 |
|   W/Digital Clock | 64 | 53 | 54 |
| Auxiliary Lighting | | | |
|   2+2 Sport Hatchback Coupe & Sport Coupe | 17 | 14 | 15 |
|   2+2 Hatchbk. Coupe, Coupe & 'S' Hatchbk. Coupe | | | |
|     W/o Custom Interior | 22 | 18 | 19 |
|     W/Custom Interior | 17 | 14 | 15 |
|   Estate Station Wagon | 28 | 23 | 24 |
|   Station Wagon | | | |
|     W/o Custom Interior | 33 | 27 | 28 |
|     W/Custom Interior | 28 | 23 | 24 |
| Day/Night Inside Rearview Mirror | 9 | 7 | 8 |
| L.H. Remote & R.H. Manual Sport Mirrors | 31 | 26 | 27 |
| Body Side Molding | 40 | 33 | 34 |
| Door Edge Guard | 11 | 9 | 10 |
| Wheel Opening Molding | 21 | 17 | 18 |
| Quiet Sound Group | | | |
|   2+2 Hatchbk. Coupe, Coupe, Station Wag. & 'S' Hatchbk. Coupe | 34 | 28 | 29 |
|   2+2 Sport Hatchbk. Coupe & Sport Coupe | 24 | 20 | 21 |
| Heavy Duty Radiator | 29 | 24 | 25 |
| Radio Equipment | | | |
|   AM | 71 | 59 | 60 |
|   AM/FM | 139 | 116 | 118 |
|   AM/FM Stereo | 215 | 178 | 180 |
|   AM W/Stereo Tape System | 216 | 180 | 182 |
|   AM/FM Stereo W/Stereo Tape System | 308 | 256 | 259 |
|   Rear Seat Speaker | 23 | 19 | 20 |
|   Windshield Antenna | 24 | 20 | 21 |
| Adjustable Driver's Seat Back | 19 | 16 | 17 |
| Rear Folding Seat | 93 | 77 | 78 |
| Sky Roof | 215 | 178 | 180 |
| Front & Rear Spoilers | 93 | 77 | 78 |

*Prices are accurate at time of printing; subject to manufacturer's change.*

|  | Retail Price | Dealer Cost | Low Price |
|---|---|---|---|
| Spyder Appearance Package | $216 | $179 | $181 |
| Spyder Equipment | 252 | 208 | 211 |
| Power Steering | 134 | 111 | 113 |
| Comfortilt Steering Wheel | 62 | 51 | 52 |
| Sport Steering Wheel | 17 | 14 | 15 |
| Sport Suspension | 30 | 25 | 26 |
| Swing-Out Rear Side Windows | 42 | 35 | 36 |
| Windshield Wiper System, Intermittent | 30 | 25 | 26 |

### NOVA
| | | | |
|---|---|---|---|
| Hatchback Coupe | $3866 | $3354 | $3554 |
| 2-Door Coupe | 3702 | 3211 | 3411 |
| 4-Door Sedan | 3777 | 3276 | 3476 |

### NOVA CUSTOM
| | | | |
|---|---|---|---|
| 2-Door Custom Coupe | 3960 | 3436 | 3636 |
| 4-Door Custom Sedan | 4035 | 3501 | 3751 |

## NOVA & NOVA CUSTOM ACCESSORIES

| | Retail Price | Dealer Cost | Low Price |
|---|---|---|---|
| Engines | | | |
| 305 CID V8 | $185 | $144 | $146 |
| 350 CID V8 | 300 | 234 | 237 |
| 4-Speed Manual Transmission | 125 | 98 | 99 |
| Automatic Transmission | 307 | 239 | 242 |
| Sport Cloth Bench Seat | 21 | 16 | 17 |
| Custom Sport Cloth Bench Seat | 21 | 16 | 17 |
| Custom Vinyl Bucket Seats | 110 | 86 | 87 |
| Two-Tone Exterior Paint | 46 | 36 | 37 |
| Vinyl Roof Cover | 97 | 76 | 77 |
| Cabriolet Roof Cover | 179 | 140 | 142 |
| Four Season Air Conditioning | | | |
| W/o V8 Engine | 539 | 420 | 425 |
| W/V8 Engine | 508 | 396 | 400 |
| Performance Ratio Rear Axles | 15 | 12 | 13 |
| Positraction Rear Axles | 59 | 46 | 47 |
| Heavy-Duty Battery | 18 | 14 | 15 |
| Deluxe Seat & Shoulder Belts | | | |
| Coupes & Sedans W/Bench Seat | 21 | 16 | 17 |
| Coupes W/Bucket Seats | 19 | 15 | 16 |
| Power Brakes | 69 | 54 | 55 |
| Bumper Rub Strips & Guards | 73 | 57 | 58 |
| Electric Clock | 20 | 16 | 17 |
| Console | 80 | 62 | 63 |
| Rear Window Defogger, Forced-Air | 51 | 40 | 41 |

*Prices are accurate at time of printing; subject to manufacturer's change.*

|  | Retail Price | Dealer Cost | Low Price |
|---|---|---|---|
| Power Door Lock System, Electric | | | |
|    Coupe | $ 74 | $ 58 | $ 59 |
|    Sedan | 103 | 80 | 81 |
| Econominder Gage Package | 50 | 39 | 40 |
| California Emission Requirements | 75 | 59 | 60 |
| High Altitude Emission Equipment | 33 | 26 | 27 |
| Color-Keyed Floor Mats | 20 | 16 | 17 |
| Soft-Ray Tinted Glass | 56 | 44 | 46 |
| Dual Horns | 7 | 5 | 6 |
| Radio Equipment | | | |
|    AM | $ 77 | $ 60 | $ 61 |
|    AM/FM | 149 | 116 | 118 |
|    AM/FM Stereo | 229 | 179 | 181 |
|    AM W/Stereo Tape System | 229 | 179 | 181 |
|    AM/FM Stereo W/Stereo Tape System | 328 | 256 | 259 |
|    Rear Seat Speaker | 24 | 19 | 20 |
|    Windshield Antenna | 25 | 20 | 21 |
| Nova Rally Equipment | 199 | 155 | 157 |
| Cruise-Master Speed Control | 90 | 70 | 71 |
| Variable Ratio Power Steering | 152 | 119 | 121 |
| Comfortilt Steering Wheel | 69 | 54 | 55 |
| Stowaway Spare Tire | 17 | 14 | 15 |
| Body Side Pin Striping | 30 | 23 | 24 |
| Heavy-Duty Front & Rear Suspension W/o V8 Engine | | | |
|    W/o Power Steering or Steel Belted Radial Ply Tires | 33 | 26 | 27 |
|    W/Power Steering or Steel Belted Radial Ply Tires | 9 | 7 | 8 |
|    W/V8 Engine | 9 | 7 | 8 |
| Sport Suspension | 41 | 32 | 33 |
| Power Windows, Electric | | | |
|    Coupes | 118 | 92 | 93 |
|    Sedan | 164 | 128 | 130 |
| Swing-Out Rear Side Windows | 56 | 44 | 45 |
| Windshield Wiper System, Intermittent | 32 | 25 | 26 |

# OLDSMOBILE

**DELTA 88**

| | | | |
|---|---|---|---|
| Coupe | $5483 | $4376 | $4676 |

*Prices are accurate at time of printing; subject to manufacturer's change.*

|  | Retail Price | Dealer Cost | Low Price |
|---|---|---|---|
| Sedan | $ 5559 | $ 4437 | $ 4737 |
| **DELTA 88 ROYALE** | | | |
| Coupe | 5707 | 4555 | 4855 |
| Sedan | 5807 | 4635 | 4935 |
| **CUSTOM CRUISER WAGON** | 6324 | 5046 | 5396 |
| **NINETY-EIGHT LUXURY** | | | |
| Coupe | 7064 | 5498 | 5848 |
| Sedan | 7241 | 5636 | 6036 |
| **NINETY-EIGHT REGENCY** | | | |
| Coupe | 7427 | 5781 | 6181 |
| Sedan | 7611 | 5925 | 6325 |
| **TORONADO** | | | |
| Coupe | 8899 | 6929 | 7429 |

## DELTA 88, DELTA 88 ROYALE, CUSTOM CRUISER, NINETY-EIGHT LUXURY, NINETY-EIGHT REGENCY & TORONADO ACCESSORIES

| | | | |
|---|---|---|---|
| Engines | | | |
| 5.7 Litre, V8 Diesel | | | |
|   Delta 88 & Delta 88 Royale | $850 | $655 | $662 |
|   Custom Cruiser, Ninety-Eight | | | |
|     Luxury & Regency | 740 | 570 | 576 |
| 260 CID 2-BBL V8 | 100 | 77 | 78 |
| 350 CID 4-BBL V8 | 265 | 204 | 207 |
| 403 CID 4-BBL V8 | | | |
|   Delta 88 & Delta 88 Royale | 330 | 254 | 257 |
|   Custom Cruiser, Ninety-Eight | | | |
|     Luxury & Regency | 65 | 50 | 51 |
| 6-Way Power Divided Seat, Driver Side | | | |
|   Delta 88 Royale, Custom Cruiser & Toronado | 151 | 116 | 118 |
|   Ninety-Eight Luxury & Regency | 120 | 92 | 93 |
| 6-Way Power Divided Seat Pass. Side | 151 | 116 | 118 |
| Power Door Locks | | | |
|   Coupes | 82 | 63 | 64 |
|   Sedans | 114 | 88 | 89 |
|   Custom Cruiser | 149 | 115 | 116 |
| Power Door Locks & Front Seat Backrest | | | |
|   Lock Releases | 107 | 82 | 83 |
| Soft-Ray Tinted Windows | 76 | 59 | 60 |
| Soft-Ray Tinted (Fleet) Windshield | 46 | 34 | 35 |
| Power Side Windows | | | |
|   Delta 88 & Delta 88 Royale Coupes | 130 | 100 | 101 |

*Prices are accurate at time of printing; subject to manufacturer's change.*

|  | Retail Price | Dealer Cost | Low Price |
|---|---|---|---|
| Delta 88 & Delta Royale Sedans & Custom Cruiser | $190 | $146 | $148 |
| 6-Way Bench Power Seat Adjuster | | | |
|    Delta 88, Delta Royale & Custom Cruiser | 151 | 116 | 118 |
|    Ninety-Eight Luxury | 120 | 92 | 93 |
| Power Trunk-Lid Release | 21 | 16 | 17 |
| Full Vinyl Rooftop | | | |
|    Delta 88 & Delta 88 Royale | 142 | 109 | 111 |
|    Ninety-Eight Luxury, Regency Sedans & Toronado | 161 | 124 | 126 |
| Electric Rear Window Defogger | 94 | 72 | 73 |
| Four Season Air Conditioner | 581 | 447 | 452 |
| Tempmatic Air Conditioner | | | |
|    Toronado | 45 | 35 | 36 |
|    Other Models | 626 | 482 | 487 |
| L.H. Remote Rearview Mirror | 16 | 12 | 13 |
| Tilt-Away Steering Wheel | 70 | 54 | 55 |
| Tilt-And-Telescope Steering Wheel | 114 | 88 | 89 |
| High Capacity Battery | 20 | 15 | 16 |
| Twilight Sentinel | 45 | 35 | 36 |
| Cornering Lamps | 47 | 36 | 37 |
| Trip Odometer | 12 | 9 | 10 |
| Electrical Digital Clock | | | |
|    Delta 88, Delta 88 Royale & Custom Cruiser | 49 | 38 | 39 |
|    Ninety-Eight Luxury | 27 | 21 | 22 |
| Electronic Lamp Monitor | 49 | 38 | 39 |
| Radio Equipment | | | |
|    AM Pushbutton W/Stereo Tape Player | 250 | 193 | 195 |
|    AM/FM Stereo Pushbutton W/Tape Player | | | |
|       Toronado | 106 | 82 | 83 |
|       Other Models | 345 | 266 | 269 |
|    Radio Accommodation Package | 26 | 20 | 21 |
|    AM/FM Stereo Pushbutton & 40-Channel CB W/Auto. Power Front Fender Tri-Band Antenna & Two Rear Speakers | | | |
|       Toronado | 338 | 260 | 263 |
|       Other Models | 577 | 444 | 449 |
|    AM/FM Stereo Pushbutton | 239 | 184 | 186 |
|    AM Pushbutton | 96 | 74 | 75 |
|    AM/FM Pushbutton | 165 | 127 | 129 |
|    Automatic Power Antenna | | | |
|       Toronado | 45 | 35 | 36 |
|       Other Models W/Radio | 45 | 35 | 36 |
|       Other Models W/o Radio | 71 | 55 | 56 |
|    Rear Radio Speaker | 24 | 18 | 19 |
| Fuel Economy Meter | 29 | 22 | 23 |
| Rallye Cluster Instrument Panel | 52 | 40 | 41 |
| Electric Clock | 22 | 17 | 18 |

*Prices are accurate at time of printing; subject to manufacturer's change.*

|  | Retail Price | Dealer Cost | Low Price |
|---|---|---|---|
| **STARFIRE** | | | |
| Coupe | $3925 | $3408 | $3608 |
| Coupe SX | 4131 | 3585 | 3835 |
| **OMEGA** | | | |
| Hatchback Coupe | 4138 | 3590 | 3840 |
| Coupe | 3973 | 3447 | 3647 |
| Sedan | 4048 | 3512 | 3762 |
| **OMEGA BROUGHAM** | | | |
| Coupe | 4179 | 3626 | 3876 |
| Sedan | 4254 | 3691 | 3941 |
| **CUTLASS SALON** | | | |
| Coupe | 4408 | 3651 | 3901 |
| Sedan | 4508 | 3734 | 3984 |
| **CUTLASS SALON BROUGHAM** | | | |
| Coupe | 4696 | 3889 | 4139 |
| Sedan | 4796 | 3972 | 4222 |
| **CUTLASS SUPREME** | | | |
| Coupe | 4842 | 4010 | 4310 |
| **CUTLASS CALAIS** | | | |
| Coupe | 5196 | 4304 | 4604 |
| **CUTLASS SUPREME BROUGHAM** | | | |
| Coupe | 5247 | 4346 | 4646 |
| **CUTLASS CRUISER** | | | |
| Wagon | 5242 | 4343 | 4643 |

### STARFIRE, OMEGA, OMEGA BROUGHAM, CUTLASS SALON, CUTLASS SALON BROUGHAM, CUTLASS CALAIS, CUTLASS SUPREME BROUGHAM & CUTLASS CRUISER ACCESSORIES

|  | Retail Price | Dealer Cost | Low Price |
|---|---|---|---|
| Engines | | | |
| 231 CID 2-BBL V6 | $170 | $141 | $143 |
| 305 CID 2-BBL V8 | | | |
| Starfires W/o Starfire GT Pkg. | 320 | 266 | 269 |
| Starfires W/Starfire GT Pkg. | 150 | 125 | 127 |
| Omega Hatchbk. Cpe. & Cutlass Models | 150 | 117 | 119 |
| 305 CID 4-BBL V8 | 200 | 156 | 158 |
| 350 CID 4-BBL V8 | 265 | 207 | 210 |
| 260 CID 2-BBL V8 | 100 | 78 | 79 |
| Transmissions | | | |
| 4-Speed Manual | 125 | 98 | 99 |
| Automatic | | | |
| Starfire | 270 | 224 | 227 |
| Other Models | 307 | 239 | 242 |
| 5-Speed Manual | | | |
| Starfire | 175 | 145 | 147 |
| Other Models | 300 | 234 | 237 |

*Prices are accurate at time of printing; subject to manufacturer's change.*

|  | Retail Price | Dealer Cost | Low Price |
|---|---|---|---|
| 6-Way Power Bucket Seat, Driver Side | $151 | $118 | $120 |
| 6-Way Power Divided Seat, Driver Side | 151 | 118 | 120 |
| 6-Way Power Divided Seat, Passenger Side | 151 | 118 | 120 |
| Deluxe Frt. & Rear Seat Belts | | | |
|   Starfire | 17 | 14 | 15 |
|   Omega & Omega Brougham | | | |
|     W/Bench Seat | 18 | 14 | 15 |
|     W/Bucket Seats | 16 | 13 | 14 |
|   Omega Models | | | |
|     W/Bench Seat | 18 | 14 | 15 |
|     W/Bucket Seats | 17 | 13 | 14 |
| Divided Front Seat W/Dual Controls | 98 | 74 | 75 |
| Seat Back Adjuster, Driver Side | 19 | 16 | 17 |
| Manual Reclining Seat Back, Pass. Side | | | |
|   Cutlass Salon Sedan | 85 | 66 | 67 |
|   Other Cutlass Models | 59 | 46 | 47 |
| Power Door Locks | | | |
|   Omega Hatchbk. Cpe, Omega Cpe. & Omega Brougham Cpe. | 74 | 58 | 59 |
|   Omega Sedan & Omega Brougham Sedan | 103 | 80 | 81 |
|   Cutlass Coupes | 80 | 62 | 63 |
|   Cutlass Sedans & Cutlass Cruiser | 112 | 87 | 88 |
| Tailgate Window Lock Release | 23 | 18 | 19 |
| Padded Vinyl Landau Roof | | | |
|   Omega Coupe & Omega Brougham Coupe | 179 | 140 | 142 |
|   Cutlass Supreme Coupe | 183 | 143 | 145 |
|   Cutlass Calais & Cutlass Supreme Brougham | 168 | 131 | 133 |
| Full Vinyl Roof | | | |
|   W/o Omega LS Package | | | |
|     Omega & Omega Brougham | 97 | 76 | 77 |
|   W/Omega LS Package | | | |
|     Omega Brougham Sedan | 79 | 62 | 63 |
|   Cutlass Sedans & Coupes | 116 | 90 | 91 |
| Electric Rear Window Defogger | | | |
|   Starfire | 79 | 66 | 67 |
|   Cutlass | 92 | 72 | 73 |
| Forced-Air Rear Window Defogger | 51 | 40 | 41 |
| Rear Window Air Deflector | 29 | 23 | 24 |
| Four Season Air Conditioner | | | |
|   Starfire | 470 | 390 | 394 |
|   Omega & Omega Brougham | 598 | 396 | 400 |
|   Cutlass | 544 | 424 | 429 |
| Tempmatic Air Conditioner | 584 | 456 | 461 |
| Comb. Dome & Reading Lamps | 18 | 14 | 15 |
| R.H. Remote Control Rearview Mirror | | | |
|   Cutlass Salon, Cutlass Salon Brougham & Cutlass Cruiser | 32 | 25 | 26 |

*Prices are accurate at time of printing; subject to manufacturer's change.*

| | Retail Price | Dealer Cost | Low Price |
|---|---|---|---|
| Cutlass Supreme, Cutlass Calais & Cutlass Supreme Brougham | $27 | $21 | $22 |
| Litter Container | 8 | 6 | 7 |
| Inside Tilt Rearview Mirror | 8 | 7 | 6 |
| L.H. Remote Control Rearview Mirror | 16 | 12 | 13 |
| **Power Front Disc Brakes** | | | |
| Starfire | 66 | 55 | 56 |
| Omega, Omega Brougham & Cutlass | 69 | 54 | 55 |
| **Tilt-Away Steering Wheel** | | | |
| Starfire | 62 | 51 | 52 |
| Omega, Omega Brougham & Cutlass | 69 | 54 | 55 |
| **Vari-Ratio Power Steering** | | | |
| Starfire | 134 | 111 | 113 |
| Omega, Omega Brougham & Cutlass | 152 | 119 | 121 |
| **High Capacity Battery** | | | |
| Cutlass | 20 | 16 | 17 |
| Starfire | 17 | 14 | 15 |
| Cornering Lamps | 47 | 36 | 37 |
| Trip Odometer | 12 | 9 | 10 |
| Electric Digital Clock | 49 | 38 | 39 |
| **Radio Equipment** | | | |
| **AM Pushbutton W/Stereo Tape Player** | | | |
| Starfire | 216 | 179 | 181 |
| Omega & Omega Brougham | 229 | 179 | 181 |
| Cutlass | 233 | 182 | 185 |
| **AM/FM Stereo Pushbutton W/Tape Player** | | | |
| Starfire | 320 | 266 | 269 |
| W/Omega LS Package | | | |
| Omega Brougham Sedan | 105 | 82 | 83 |
| W/o Omega LS Package | | | |
| Omega, Omega Brougham & Cutlass | 341 | 266 | 269 |
| AM/FM Stereo Pushbutton W/Cassette | 351 | 274 | 277 |
| **Radio Accommodation Package** | | | |
| Starfire | 25 | 21 | 22 |
| Omega, Omega Brougham & Cutlass | 26 | 20 | 21 |
| **AM/FM Stereo Pushbutton & 40-Channel CB** | | | |
| W/Auto. Power Frt. Fender, Tri-Band Antenna & Two Rear Speakers | 571 | 445 | 450 |
| **AM/FM Stereo Pushbutton** | | | |
| Starfire | 222 | 184 | 186 |
| Omega, Omega Brougham & Cutlass | 236 | 184 | 186 |
| **AM Pushbutton** | | | |
| Starfire | 74 | 61 | 62 |
| Omega & Omega Brougham | 236 | 184 | 186 |
| Cutlass | 83 | 65 | 66 |
| **AM/FM Pushbutton** | | | |
| Starfire | 139 | 115 | 117 |
| Omega & Omega Brougham | 149 | 116 | 118 |

*Prices are accurate at time of printing; subject to manufacturer's change.*

|  | Retail Price | Dealer Cost | Low Price |
|---|---|---|---|
| Cutlass | $154 | $120 | $122 |
| Automatic Power Antenna | | | |
| W/Radio | 45 | 35 | 36 |
| W/o Radio | 71 | 55 | 56 |
| Rear Seat Speaker | | | |
| Starfire | 23 | 19 | 20 |
| Omega & Omega Brougham | 23 | 18 | 19 |
| Cutlass | 24 | 19 | 20 |
| Dual Horns | 8 | 6 | 7 |

# PONTIAC

| | Retail Price | Dealer Cost | Low Price |
|---|---|---|---|
| **CATALINA** | | | |
| Coupe | $5375 | $4290 | $4590 |
| Sedan | 5410 | 4318 | 4618 |
| **CATALINA SAFARI** | | | |
| Wagon | 5924 | 4727 | 5027 |
| **BONNEVILLE** | | | |
| Coupe | 5831 | 4654 | 4954 |
| Sedan | 5931 | 4734 | 5034 |
| **GRAND SAFARI** | | | |
| Wagon | 6227 | 4969 | 5269 |
| **BONNEVILLE BROUGHAM** | | | |
| Coupe | 6577 | 5251 | 5601 |
| Sedan | 6677 | 5331 | 5681 |

### CATALINA AND BONNEVILLE ACCESSORIES

| | Retail Price | Dealer Cost | Low Price |
|---|---|---|---|
| Engines | | | |
| 4.9 Litre 301 CID 2-BBL V8 | $150 | $116 | $118 |
| 5.7 Litre 350 CID 4-BBL V8 | 115 | 89 | 90 |
| Catalina Coupe & Sedan | 265 | 204 | 207 |
| 6.6 Litre 400 CID 4-BBL V8 | 180 | 139 | 141 |
| Catalina Coupe & Sedan | 330 | 254 | 257 |
| 6.6 Litre 403 CID 4-BBL V8 | 180 | 139 | 141 |
| Catalina Coupe & Sedan | 330 | 254 | 257 |
| Custom Air Conditioning | 581 | 447 | 452 |
| Automatic Temperature Control Air. Cond. | 626 | 482 | 487 |

*Prices are accurate at time of printing; subject to manufacturer's change.*

|  | Retail Price | Dealer Cost | Low Price |
|---|---|---|---|
| 63 AMP Heavy Duty Alternators | $31 | $24 | $25 |
| 80 AMP Heavy Duty Alternators | 49 | 38 | 39 |
| W/Electric Rear Window Defroster & Air Conditioning | 18 | 14 | 15 |
| Saf-T-Track Differential Axle | 64 | 49 | 50 |
| Heavy Duty Battery | 20 | 15 | 16 |
| Cruise Control | 95 | 73 | 74 |
| Remote Control Deck Lid Release | 21 | 16 | 17 |
| Electric Rear Window Defroster | 94 | 72 | 73 |
| California Emission Requirements | 75 | 58 | 59 |
| High Altitude Emission Requirements | 33 | 25 | 26 |
| Rally Cluster, Clock & Trip Odometer Gages | 74 | 57 | 58 |
| Bonneville Brougham | 52 | 40 | 41 |
| Rally Cluster, Fuel Econ. Gage & Trip Odometer | 81 | 62 | 63 |
| All Windows Soft-Ray Glass | 76 | 59 | 60 |
| Saf-T-Lok Power Door Locks | | | |
| 2-Doors | 82 | 63 | 64 |
| 4-Door Sedans | 114 | 88 | 89 |
| All Safaris | 146 | 112 | 113 |
| Remote Power Tailgate Lock Release | 32 | 25 | 26 |
| 6-Way Power Seat, Driver Side | 151 | 116 | 118 |
| 6-Way Power 60/40 Seat, Driver & Pass. | 302 | 233 | 236 |
| Power Windows | | | |
| 2-Doors | 130 | 100 | 101 |
| 4-Doors | 190 | 146 | 148 |
| Super-Cooling Radiator | 57 | 44 | 45 |
| W/Air Cond. W/o Trailer Group | 31 | 24 | 25 |
| Radio Equipment | | | |
| Power Antenna | 58 | 45 | 46 |
| W/Optional Radios | 40 | 31 | 32 |
| Power Antenna, AM/FM/CB Tri Band W/Optional Radios | 65 | 50 | 51 |
| AM | 96 | 74 | 75 |
| AM W/Integral 8-Track Stereo Tape | 250 | 193 | 195 |
| AM/FM | 165 | 127 | 129 |
| AM/FM/Integral 40-Channel CB | 503 | 387 | 391 |
| AM/FM Stereo | 239 | 184 | 186 |
| AM/FM Stereo W/Stereo Cassette | 355 | 273 | 276 |
| AM/FM Stereo W/Integral 8-Track Stereo Tape | 345 | 266 | 269 |
| AM/FM Stereo W/Digital Clock & Readouts | 392 | 302 | 306 |
| Bonneville Brougham | 370 | 285 | 288 |
| AM/FM Stereo W/Integral 40-Channel CB | 577 | 444 | 449 |
| Radio Accommodation Package | 21 | 20 | 21 |
| W/Power Antennas | 8 | 6 | 7 |
| Rear Seat Speaker | 24 | 18 | 19 |
| All Safaris | 28 | 22 | 23 |
| Dual Rear Speakers | 38 | 29 | 30 |

*Prices are accurate at time of printing; subject to manufacturer's change.*

|  | Retail Price | Dealer Cost | Low Price |
|---|---:|---:|---:|
| All Safaris | $ 42 | $ 32 | $ 33 |
| Full Bench Seat | 29 | 22 | 23 |
| 60/40 Notchback Seat | | | |
| Velour Lombardy Cloth or Vinyl 'Doeskin' Trim | 98 | 75 | 76 |
| Velour Valencia Cloth Trim | 165 | 127 | 129 |
| Reclining Passenger Seat | 59 | 45 | 46 |
| Third Seat | 175 | 135 | 137 |
| Custom Sport Steering Wheel | 74 | 57 | 58 |
| Bonneville Brougham | 55 | 42 | 43 |
| Luxury Cushion Steering Wheel | 19 | 15 | 16 |
| Tilt Steering Wheel | 70 | 54 | 55 |

## FIREBIRD

|  | Retail Price | Dealer Cost | Low Price |
|---|---:|---:|---:|
| Firebird | $4545 | $3943 | $4193 |
| Esprit | 4842 | 4201 | 4501 |
| Formula | 5448 | 4728 | 5028 |
| Trans Am | 5799 | 5033 | 5383 |

## FIREBIRD ACCESSORIES

|  | Retail Price | Dealer Cost | Low Price |
|---|---:|---:|---:|
| **Engines** | | | |
| 5.0 Litre 305 CID 2-BBL V8 | $150 | $117 | $119 |
| 5.7 Litre 350 CID 4-BBL V8 | | | |
| Firebird & Esprit | 265 | 207 | 210 |
| Formula | 115 | 90 | 91 |
| 6.6 Litre 400 CID 4-BBL V8 W/Auto. Transmission. | 205 | 160 | 162 |
| T/A 6.6 Litre 400 CID 4-BBL W/Auto. or 4-Speed Manual Transmission | | | |
| Formula | 280 | 218 | 221 |
| Trans Am | 75 | 59 | 60 |
| 403 CID 4-BBL V8 W/Auto. Transmission | 205 | 160 | 162 |
| 4-Speed Manual Transmission | | | |
| Firebird & Esprit | 125 | 98 | 99 |
| Formula | (182) | (142) | (144) |
| 3-Speed Automatic Transmission | 307 | 240 | 243 |
| Custom Air Conditioning | 508 | 396 | 400 |
| Heavy Duty Alternator | 31 | 24 | 25 |
| Formula Appearance Package | 137 | 107 | 109 |
| Skybird Appearance Package | | | |
| W/Velour Lombardy Cloth | 461 | 360 | 364 |
| W/Vinyl Doeskin | 426 | 332 | 336 |
| Special Edition Appearance Package | 1259 | 982 | 1002 |
| Saf-T-Track Differential Axle | 60 | 47 | 48 |
| Heavy Duty Battery | 20 | 16 | 17 |
| Custom Seat & Shoulder Belts | 21 | 16 | 17 |

*Prices are accurate at time of printing; subject to manufacturer's change.*

|  | Retail Price | Dealer Cost | Low Price |
|---|---|---|---|
| Electric Clock | $ 22 | $ 17 | $ 18 |
| Console | 80 | 62 | 63 |
| Cruise Control | 90 | 70 | 71 |
| Soft-Ray Glass, All Windows | 56 | 44 | 45 |
| Power Brakes, Front Disc, Rear Drum | 69 | 55 | 56 |
| Saf-T-Lok Power Door Locks | 80 | 62 | 63 |
| Power Windows | 124 | 97 | 98 |
| Super-Cooling Radiator | 56 | 44 | 45 |
| W/Air Conditioning | 31 | 24 | 25 |
| Radio Equipment | | | |
| AM | 83 | 65 | 66 |
| AM W/Integral 8-Track Stereo Tape | 233 | 182 | 184 |
| AM/FM | 154 | 120 | 122 |
| AM/FM W/Integral 40-Chan. Cit. Band | 436 | 340 | 344 |
| AM/FM Stereo | 236 | 184 | 186 |
| AM/FM Stereo W/Cassete Stereo Tape | 351 | 274 | 277 |
| AM/FM Stereo W/Dig. Clock & Readouts | 392 | 306 | 310 |
| AM/FM Stereo W/Integral 40-Chan. CB | 518 | 404 | 409 |
| AM/FM Stereo W/Integral 8-Track Stereo Tape | 341 | 266 | 269 |
| Radio Accommodation Package | 26 | 20 | 21 |
| Rear Seat Speaker | 24 | 19 | 20 |

**Grand Prix**

|  | Retail Price | Dealer Cost | Low Price |
|---|---|---|---|
| Grand Prix | $4880 | $4041 | $4341 |
| Grand Prix LJ | 5815 | 4817 | 5117 |
| Grand Prix SJ | 6088 | 5043 | 5393 |

## GRAND PRIX ACCESSORIES

|  | Retail Price | Dealer Cost | Low Price |
|---|---|---|---|
| Engines | | | |
| 4.9 Litre 301 CID 2-BBL V8 | $150 | $117 | $119 |
| 5.0 Litre 305 CID 2-BBL V8 | | | |
| Grand Prix | 150 | 117 | 119 |
| Grand Prix SJ | (50) | (39) | (40) |
| 4.9 Litre 301 CID 4-BBL V8 | | | |
| Grand Prix | 200 | 156 | 158 |
| Grand Prix LJ | 50 | 39 | 40 |
| Automatic Transmission | 307 | 239 | 242 |
| Custom Air Conditioning | 544 | 424 | 429 |
| Automatic Temperature Control Air Cond. | 584 | 456 | 461 |
| Heavy Duty Alternator | 31 | 24 | 25 |
| Saf-T-Track Differential Axle | 60 | 47 | 48 |
| Heavy Duty Battery | 20 | 16 | 17 |
| Power Brakes | 69 | 54 | 55 |
| Saf-T-Lok Power Door Locks | 80 | 62 | 63 |

*Prices are accurate at time of printing; subject to manufacturer's change.*

|  | Retail Price | Dealer Cost | Low Price |
|---|---|---|---|
| 6-Way Power Seat, Driver Side | $151 | $118 | $120 |
| Power Steering | 152 | 119 | 121 |
| Power Windows | 124 | 97 | 98 |
| Super-Cooling Radiator | | | |
| W/o Air Cond. or Trailer Group | 56 | 44 | 45 |
| W/Air Cond. W/o Trailer Group | 31 | 24 | 25 |
| Radio Equipment | | | |
| Power Antenna | | | |
| W/o Optional Radios | 58 | 45 | 46 |
| W/Optional Radios | 40 | 31 | 32 |
| Power Antenna, AM/FM/CB Tri Band | | | |
| W/o Optional Radios | 83 | 65 | 66 |
| W/Optional Radios | 65 | 51 | 52 |
| AM | 83 | 65 | 66 |
| AM W/Integral 8-Track Stereo | 233 | 182 | 184 |
| AM/FM | 154 | 120 | 122 |
| AM/FM/ W/Integral 40-Chan. CB | 489 | 381 | 385 |
| AM/FM Stereo | 236 | 184 | 186 |
| AM/FM Stereo W/Cassette Stereo Tape | 351 | 274 | 277 |
| AM/FM Stereo W/Integral 8-Track Stereo Tape | 341 | 266 | 269 |
| AM/FM Stereo W/Dig. Clock & Readouts | 370 | 289 | 292 |
| AM/FM Stereo W/Integral 40-Chan. CB | 571 | 445 | 450 |
| Radio Accommodation Package | 26 | 20 | 21 |
| W/ Power Antennas W/o Opt. Radios | 8 | 6 | 7 |
| Rear Seat Speaker | 24 | 19 | 20 |
| Dual Front & Rear Speakers | 48 | 37 | 38 |

## LeMANS

|  | Retail Price | Dealer Cost | Low Price |
|---|---|---|---|
| Coupe | $4405 | $3649 | $3899 |
| Sedan | 4480 | 3711 | 3961 |
| **LeMANS SAFARI** | | | |
| Wagon | 4377 | 4039 | 4339 |
| **GRAND LeMANS** | | | |
| Coupe | 4777 | 3957 | 4207 |
| Sedan | 4881 | 4044 | 4344 |
| **GRAND LeMANS SAFARI** | | | |
| Wagon | 5265 | 4362 | 4662 |
| **GRAND AM** | | | |
| Coupe | 5464 | 4526 | 4826 |
| Sedan | 5568 | 4612 | 4912 |

## LeMANS, GRAND LeMANS, AND GRAND AM ACCESSORIES

| Engines | | | |
|---|---|---|---|
| 4.9 Litre 301 CID 4-BBL V8 | $50 | $39 | $40 |

*Prices are accurate at time of printing; subject to manufacturer's change.*

| | Retail Price | Dealer Cost | Low Price |
|---|---|---|---|
| 5.0 Litre 305 CID 2-BBL V8 | $150 | $117 | $119 |
| 5.7 Litre 350 CID 4-BBL V8 | 265 | 207 | 210 |
| **Transmissions** | | | |
| 4-Speed Manual | 125 | 98 | 99 |
| Automatic | 307 | 239 | 242 |
| Custom Air Conditioning | 544 | 424 | 429 |
| Automatic Temperature Control Air Cond. | 584 | 456 | 461 |
| Electric Rear Window Defroster | 92 | 72 | 73 |
| Soft-Ray Glass, All Windows | 62 | 48 | 49 |
| Power Brakes, Front Disc & Rear Drum | 69 | 54 | 55 |
| **Saf-T-Lok Power Door Locks** | | | |
| 2-Doors | 80 | 62 | 63 |
| 4-Doors | 112 | 87 | 88 |
| Power Tailgate Lock Release | 23 | 18 | 19 |
| 6-Way Power Seat, Driver's Side | 151 | 118 | 120 |
| Power Steering | 152 | 119 | 121 |
| **Power Windows** | | | |
| Front Only | 124 | 97 | 98 |
| Rear Vent | 48 | 37 | 38 |
| **Radio Equipment** | | | |
| AM | 83 | 65 | 66 |
| AM W/Integral 8-Track Stereo Tape | 233 | 182 | 184 |
| AM/FM | 154 | 120 | 122 |
| AM/FM W/Integral 40 Chan. CB | 489 | 381 | 385 |
| AM/FM Stereo | 236 | 184 | 186 |
| AM/FM Stereo W/Cassette Stereo Tape | 351 | 274 | 277 |
| AM/FM Stereo W/Integral 8-Track Stereo Tape | 341 | 266 | 269 |
| AM/FM Stereo W/Dig. Clock & Readouts | 392 | 306 | 310 |
| AM/FM Stereo W/Integral 40-Chan. CB | 571 | 445 | 450 |
| Radio Accommodation Package | 26 | 20 | 21 |
| W/Power Antennas W/o Opt. Radios | 8 | 6 | 7 |
| Rear Seat Speaker | 24 | 19 | 20 |
| Safaris | 28 | 22 | 23 |
| Dual Front & Rear Speakers | 48 | 37 | 38 |
| Safaris | 52 | 41 | 42 |
| **Bucket Seats** | | | |
| Grand LeMans Vinyl Doeskin Trim | (30) | (23) | (24) |
| Grand Am Cloth Windsor II or Vinyl Doeskin | 70 | 55 | 56 |
| Full Bench Seats | 29 | 23 | 24 |
| Grand LeMans Notchback Seat W/Center Armrest | (100) | (78) | (79) |
| Notchback 60/40 Split W/Center Armrest | 98 | 76 | 77 |
| Reclining Passenger Seat | 59 | 46 | 47 |
| Security Package | 40 | 31 | 32 |
| W/Saf-T-Track Differential Axle | 35 | 27 | 28 |
| **Custom Sport Steering Wheel** | | | |
| LeMans, LeMans Safari & Grand Am | 73 | 57 | 58 |

*Prices are accurate at time of printing; subject to manufacturer's change.*

|  | Retail Price | Dealer Cost | Low Price |
|---|---|---|---|
| Grand LeMans & Grand LeMans Safari | $ 54 | $ 42 | $ 43 |
| Luxury Cushion Steering Wheel | 19 | 15 | 16 |
| Tilt Steering Wheel | 69 | 54 | 55 |
| Upper Accent Stripes | 43 | 34 | 35 |
| Glass Power Sunroof | 699 | 545 | 551 |
| Steel Power Sunroof | 499 | 389 | 393 |
| Automatic Level Control | 115 | 90 | 91 |
| W/Trailer Group | 63 | 49 | 50 |
| Firm Ride Option | 12 | 9 | 10 |
| Superlift Shock Absorbers | 52 | 41 | 42 |
| Full Cordova Top | 116 | 90 | 91 |

## PHOENIX

|  | Retail Price | Dealer Cost | Low Price |
|---|---|---|---|
| Hatchback | $4068 | $3528 | $3778 |
| Coupe | 3872 | 3359 | 3559 |
| Sedan | 3947 | 3424 | 3624 |
| **PHOENIX LJ** | | | |
| Coupe | 4357 | 3781 | 4031 |
| Sedan | 4432 | 3846 | 4096 |

## PHOENIX ACCESSORIES

|  | Retail Price | Dealer Cost | Low Price |
|---|---|---|---|
| **Engines** | | | |
| 2.5 Litre 2-BBL 4-Cylinder | $(170) | $(133) | $(135) |
| 5.0 Litre 305 CID 2-BBL V8 | 150 | 117 | 119 |
| 5.7 Litre 350 CID 4-BBL V8 | 265 | 207 | 210 |
| **Transmissions** | | | |
| Floor Mounted Shift Control | 33 | 26 | 27 |
| 4-Speed Manual | 125 | 98 | 99 |
| 3-Speed Automatic | 307 | 239 | 242 |
| Custom Air Conditioning | 508 | 396 | 400 |
| Heavy Duty Alternator | 31 | 24 | 25 |
| Saf-T-Track Differential Axle | 60 | 47 | 48 |
| Heavy Duty Battery | 20 | 16 | 17 |
| Custom Seat & Shoulder Belts | 21 | 16 | 17 |
| Bumper Strips & Front Guards | 53 | 41 | 42 |
| Bumper Strips, Front & Rear Guards & Body Color Front Center Pad | 83 | 65 | 66 |
| Load Floor Carpet | 25 | 20 | 21 |
| Electric Clock | 22 | 17 | 18 |
| Console | 80 | 62 | 63 |
| Cruise Control | 90 | 70 | 71 |
| Rear Window Defogger | 51 | 39 | 40 |
| Electric Rear Window Defroster | 92 | 72 | 73 |
| Power Brakes | 69 | 54 | 55 |

*Prices are accurate at time of printing; subject to manufacturer's change.*

|  | Retail Price | Dealer Cost | Low Price |
|---|---|---|---|
| Saf-T-Lok Power Door Locks | | | |
| 2-Doors | $ 74 | $ 58 | $ 59 |
| 4-Doors | 103 | 80 | 81 |
| Power Steering | 152 | 119 | 121 |
| Power Windows | | | |
| 2-Doors | 118 | 92 | 93 |
| 4-Doors | 164 | 128 | 130 |
| Radio Equipment | | | |
| AM | 79 | 62 | 63 |
| AM/FM | 149 | 116 | 118 |
| AM/FM Stereo | 236 | 184 | 186 |
| Radio Accommodation Package | 26 | 20 | 21 |
| Rear Seat Speaker | 23 | 18 | 19 |
| Full-Width Bench Seats | | | |
| Standard Seats, Vinyl | 18 | 14 | 15 |
| Custom Seats, Cloth or Vinyl | 120 | 94 | 95 |
| Bucket Seats | | | |
| Phoenix | 88 | 69 | 70 |
| Phoenix LJ | 70 | 55 | 56 |
| Luxury Cushion Steering Wheel | 19 | 15 | 16 |
| Custom Sport Steering Wheel | | | |
| Phoenix | 73 | 57 | 58 |
| Phoenix LJ | 54 | 42 | 43 |
| Tilt Steering Wheel | 69 | 54 | 55 |
| Accent Paint Stripes | 52 | 41 | 42 |
| Appearance Package | 73 | 57 | 58 |
| Full Cordova Top | 97 | 76 | 77 |
| Padded Landau Cordova Top | 179 | 140 | 142 |
| Light Trailer Group | 68 | 53 | 54 |
| W/Air Conditioning | 43 | 34 | 35 |
| Pedal Trim Package | 8 | 6 | 7 |
| Swing-Out Rear Window Vent | 54 | 42 | 43 |
| Controlled Cycle Windshield Wipers | 32 | 25 | 26 |

## SUNBIRD

|  | Retail Price | Dealer Cost | Low Price |
|---|---|---|---|
| Coupe | $3540 | $3073 | $3273 |
| Sport Coupe | 3773 | 3276 | 3476 |
| Sport Hatch | 3912 | 3396 | 3596 |
| **SUNBIRD SPORT SAFARI** | | | |
| Wagon | 3741 | 3247 | 3447 |

### SUNBIRD ACCESSORIES

|  | Retail Price | Dealer Cost | Low Price |
|---|---|---|---|
| 3.8 Litre 231 CID 2-BBL V6 Engine | $170 | $141 | $143 |
| 5-Speed Manual Transmission W/Floor Shift | 175 | 145 | 147 |

*Prices are accurate at time of printing; subject to manufacturer's change.*

|  | Retail Price | Dealer Cost | Low Price |
|---|---|---|---|
| 3-Speed Automatic Transmission | $270 | $224 | $227 |
| Custom Air Conditioning | 470 | 390 | 394 |
| 63 AMP Heavy Duty Alternator | 31 | 26 | 27 |
| Saf-T-Track Differential Axle | 56 | 46 | 47 |
| Heavy Duty Battery | 17 | 14 | 15 |
| Custom Seat & Shoulder Belts | 19 | 16 | 17 |
| Front & Rear Bumper Guards | 38 | 32 | 33 |
| Bumper Strips & Guards | | | |
|   Coupe, Sport Coupe & Sport Hatch | 71 | 59 | 60 |
|   Sport Safari | 52 | 43 | 44 |
| Electric Clock | 19 | 16 | 17 |
| Front Seat Console | 77 | 64 | 65 |
| Rear Window Deflector | 27 | 23 | 24 |
| Electric Rear Window Defroster | 79 | 66 | 67 |
| California Emission Requirements | | | |
|   W/V6 Engine | 75 | 62 | 63 |
|   W/4-Cyl. Engine | 100 | 83 | 84 |
| High Altitude Emission Requirements | 33 | 27 | 28 |
| Engine Block Heater | 13 | 11 | 12 |
| Instrument Panel W/Clock & Tachometer Gages | 82 | 68 | 69 |
| Soft-Ray Glass, All Windows | 54 | 45 | 46 |
| Roof Luggage Carrier | 60 | 50 | 51 |
| Front & Rear Floor Mats | 18 | 15 | 16 |
| Day/Night Inside Rear-view Mirror | 8 | 7 | 8 |
| L.H. Remote & R.H. Manual Sport Mirrors | 31 | 26 | 27 |
| Body Side Molding | 40 | 33 | 34 |
| Door Edge Guards | 11 | 9 | 10 |
| Rocker Panel Molding | 16 | 13 | 14 |
| Wheel Opening Molding | 21 | 17 | 18 |
| Windowsill Molding | 22 | 18 | 19 |
| Power Braks, Front Disc, Rear Drum | 66 | 55 | 56 |
| Power Steering | 134 | 111 | 113 |
| Heavy Duty Radiator | 32 | 27 | 28 |
| Radio Equipment | | | |
|   AM | 74 | 61 | 62 |
|   AM W/Integral 8-Track Stereo Tape | 216 | 179 | 181 |
|   AM/FM | 139 | 115 | 117 |
|   AM/FM Stereo | 215 | 178 | 180 |
|   AM/FM Stereo W/Integral 8-Track Stereo Tape | 308 | 256 | 259 |
|   Radio Accommodation Package | 26 | 22 | 23 |
|   Rear Seat Speaker | 23 | 19 | 20 |
| Rear Fold Down Seat | 95 | 79 | 80 |
| Rear Deck Spoiler | 48 | 40 | 41 |
| Formula Steering Wheel | 41 | 34 | 35 |
|   W/Luxury Trim Group | 23 | 19 | 20 |
| Luxury Cushion Steering Wheel | 18 | 15 | 16 |
| Tilt Steering Wheel | 62 | 51 | 52 |

*Prices are accurate at time of printing; subject to manufacturer's change.*

# 1978 Televisions

SHOPPING FOR a television set is likely to be bewildering for consumers in 1978. The reason is simple: manufacturers have taken all the doodads and gizmos previously found only on sets in the luxury or big-screen price category and scattered them throughout just about every screen size and price range.

Automatic "computerized" color-correction and channel-selection circuits are now available not only in deluxe consoles with 25-inch screens and prices above $800, but in table models with screens of 19, 17 and even 15 inches selling for less than half that price. This trend may well expand the number of options open to the would-be TV buyer, but it also poses some problems.

It is more difficult than ever to sort out the various controls and claims from manufacturers in the business. The fancy names used to describe automatic color-tuning systems such as ColorTrak, GT-Matic, VIR and Dynacolor can make the job of comparing one brand against another a complex and confusing task. In some cases, those unique trade names refer to automatic color-adjustment systems that are essentially identical; but that is not always true, and understanding the difference between one automatic color system and another can make the difference between a good and a bad purchase.

It has also become tougher for the thrifty TV shopper to buy a set that does not incorporate all the new technological wizardry which abounds in 1978 lines. Simple stripped-down models that deliver good pictures at reasonable prices are still around, but they are getting scarcer all the time. Most retail stores prefer to sell full-featured, higher-priced sets with big profit margins. Now that all those features are being made available in small-screen portables and table models, stores are not likely to spend much time promoting and advertising sets that offer them a lower profit.

**Color Tuning Advances**

AUTOMATIC and/or "one-button" color tuning is nothing new in the color television world, but several significant developments in this area for '78 are worth noting. Most important of these is the increased use of vertical integration reference circuitry, which was introduced in 1977 by General Electric. Last year, GE offered VIR in only a selected number of 19-inch and 25-inch sets. In 1978 VIR is available in an expanded range of models—sixteen 25-inch consoles and six 19-inch sets. More important is the addition of a second VIR adherent, Panasonic, which will offer a single 19-inch VIR set in 1978 and has plans for more in coming years. Montgomery Ward also is expected to offer VIR in 1978.

Why is VIR so important? The major reason is that it makes adjustments to the color picture based on a reference signal supplied by broadcasters, not on preset instructions built into the TV set itself as other automatic color systems do. VIR is a signal that is transmitted along with the picture information by most broadcasters for use by their engineers to maintain consistent color reproduction. A set using VIR receives this signal—which is broadcast 60 times a second—and automatically adjusts color intensity and tint to match broadcast levels. No automatic color-tuning feature is fail-safe, but VIR is more precise than most other systems.

Other manufacturers offer automatic color-correction systems in 1978 lines, but these differ fundamentally from VIR. Essentially, non-VIR adjustment systems "memorize" color settings, then continuously adjust the colors to match those standards. There is nothing inherently wrong with this type of color-adjustment circuitry, and after examining various one-button non-VIR systems offered by major manufacturers, CONSUMER GUIDE Magazine's testing staff found that most of them do what they are supposed to do; that is, they keep flesh tones looking natural while maintaining the purity of other colors. But it is wise to remember that corrections made by these non-VIR systems can also be made manually by viewers who are willing to take the time to adjust color, tint and other controls. With VIR, the set performs color-correction functions that cannot be made in any other way.

Non-VIR color-tuning systems go under many names, including ColorTrak, RCA; GT-Matic II, Sylvania; Color Sentry, Zenith; Color Monitor, GE on non-VIR sets; Dynacolor, Quasar; and others. In 1978 most manufacturers are offering the feature on a wider variety of sets.

Another feature being offered on many models this year along with automatic color tuning is a light sensor that automatically adjusts picture brightness and contrast to suit lighting conditions of the room; that is, if a glaring light is suddenly turned on, the set will automatically make the picture brighter. The light-level adjustment feature is not new, but this year just about all of the manufacturers—GE, Sony, Zenith, Quasar, RCA and Admiral—are offering it.

**Channel Selection**

IN KEEPING with the increased use of sophisticated technology, the television industry has taken a major step forward in the area of channel tuning also for 1978. Electronic tuning, which does away with the annoying mechanical selector that clunks its way from one channel to the next, is available in a broad range of new models under just about every major TV name.

In its simplest form the electronic tuner does not look different from a mechanical tuner, but a simple twist of the dial quickly makes the difference apparent: the electronic dial selector glides smoothly and noiselessly from one channel to another.

A step up in sophistication are the new pushbutton "random access" electronic channel tuners. They permit the viewer to switch from, say, Channel 2 to Channel 13 without going through all the channels in between. With this system the user can preset the VHF and UHF channels he or she wants (up to 18 selections on some models), then instantly tune-in the desired channel at the touch of a button. As with other forms of electronic channel tuning, this feature has spread into a broader range of consoles, table models and portables in 1978 lines. Zenith, for instance, now has random-access tuning in 48 of its 55 models available for '78. Others offering this type of electronic tuning include Panasonic, Sanyo, Sears, MGA and Sony.

In its most complex form, electronic channel tuning is now being offered by a number of leading TV makers as a dial-your-own system. Control panels for this type of tuning use keyboards with calculator-like buttons, not dials. The user simply punches in two numbers ("02" for Channel 2, "13" for Channel 13) and the set instantly switches to that channel. In some cases, the user must also punch an "enter" or "select" button after entering the channel number. Among the firms offering this feature for 1978 are Magnavox, RCA, Quasar, Sylvania, GE and Admiral.

Along with these new electronic systems, a growing number of manufacturers also are introducing a range of futuristic remote-control devices. Unlike older remote units that simply instructed a motor in the TV set to turn the selector from one channel to the next, new electronic remotes perform a whole range of volume, channel-selection and color-adjustment functions—just about anything that can be done with controls on the set itself. These sophisticated remotes have moved further down the line in 1978, and some are offered in sets with screen sizes as small as 13 inches. Two firms, Admiral and Magnavox, are even offering install-it-yourself remotes that can be added to a set at a later date.

Also new for 1978 is GE's random-access remote control, available on eight VIR sets. It uses infrared light to transmit commands rather than the ultrasonic system used by other manufacturers. Why infrared? Because, GE says, it is not susceptible to interference from other sounds, such as jangling keys, that can trick an ultrasonic remote into changing channels or making other unwanted adjustments.

**Better Picture and Sound**

MANUFACTURERS are also working to improve picture quality through new designs in picture tubes. For '78 a major development in this area is the spread of in-line tri-potential tubes that improve both color intensity and picture sharpness. Zenith has extended the tri-potential system to five 19-inch sets in its new line, and Quasar and Panasonic are offering tri-potential tubes in selected models. Also, many tubes now being introduced have a much wider deflection angle, resulting in sets with sharply reduced front-to-back measurements. Among firms offering these sets are Panasonic, Quasar, Zenith, MGA and Sony.

For years the television industry has been criticized sharply for spending so much time and effort on the improvement of picture quality, while doing so little to improve the quality of sound reproduction. This year, two manufacturers have tackled the problem. Other set makers are expected to follow suit in coming years.

Quasar is spearheading the move with its new Audio Spectrum Sound system in two 19-inch models and seven 25-inch consoles. Conventional TV sets use a single speaker to reproduce all low, mid-range and high frequencies, but Quasar uses three speakers: a 3-1/2 inch tweeter, 4-inch mid-range and 5-by-7-inch woofer. Just in case the TV viewer (or listener) does not think it makes much difference, Quasar has included a control knob that can be used to switch sound from all three speakers to the 4-inch mid-range.

Another firm, a lesser-known one, is also offering improved sound. Tatung of America, a subsidiary of a Taiwan-based firm, is now entering the U.S. market on a limited basis with sets featuring Audio-color. This system uses a high-performance audio amplifier to improve the quality of TV sound. Special audio jacks on 19-inch and 25-inch models also permit the user to hook a stereo system up to the set for enhanced sound reproduction. You may not find Tatung sets in your local appliance and TV store just yet. The company is beginning its U.S. efforts on a small scale, with initial marketing concentrated on the West Coast as new wholesale and retail accounts are lined up.

The national concern about energy conservation has affected television manufacturers, and in 1978 the shopper will find a new breed of low-power-consumption sets displayed prominently on the sales floor. RCA is probably the most active in promoting the concept, through its new XtendedLife chassis. It is designed not only to use less energy but also to run cooler, increasing a set's life expectancy. RCA says its new chassis—being offered in a wide variety of portables, table models and consoles—has an average power-consumption rate of 89 watts, compared to the 375-watt consumption of older tube sets in the firm's line and 200 watts in the solid-state sets it introduced in 1975. Other manufacturers are getting into the energy-saving act, and this approach promises to emerge as a central theme of manufacturer advertising and promotion in coming years, with the initial thrust being made in 1978.

**Built-in Games**

ANOTHER interesting new feature of some 1978 models is the built-in TV game. Magnavox remains the only firm to offer this game-TV combination, a 19-inch set introduced in 1977. At the touch of a button, the viewer can switch from Charley's Angels to Odyssey (the brand name used for TV games Magnavox sells separately).

This is a fascinating concept, but the TV shopper should approach these games with caution. Newer separate games being offered by a number of manufacturers including Fairchild, RCA, Atari and Coleco, are far more advanced than the built-in Odyssey from Magnavox. The more sophisticated versions use plug-in video tape cartridges which can be purchased to change games. Once game/TV combinations are available with plug-in cartridges—and Magnavox just may be the first to do it—the concept will make more sense.

Another twist in combination units is being offered by Zenith. It is a 25-inch color console with built-in video tape recorder cassette deck, storage space for tapes and room for camera equipment that Zenith will also market. At $2600, it is one of the most expensive TV sets available today.

While Zenith offers bigger and more expensive sets, a few companies are moving in the opposite direction—at least in terms of screen size. The tiniest set now available is a nearly pocket-size unit with 2-inch screen produced and marketed by Sinclair Radionics, a British company that previously specialized in pocket calculators. Called Microvision, this mini TV is just beginning to appear in American retail stores and is expected to be priced in the $300 range. It will play for four hours on four built-in batteries, and is equipped to receive both VHF and UHF stations almost anywhere in the world.

A step up in size is Sony's new 7.7-inch color TV portable, a companion unit to the 5-inch color set which Sony introduced earlier. The 7.7-inch set has all of the usual Sony features including Trinitron Plus picture tube, automatic fine tuning, automatic color and hue controls, and carries a price tag to match—$479.95. It operates on AC/DC or batteries (using an optional $120 battery pack), and has a glare-free screen for improved outdoor viewing.

Panasonic is also moving into smaller-screen sets. In 1978 the firm is adding a 10-inch color portable using its Quintrix II color picture tube, automatic fine tuning and one-button Q-Lock II automatic color control. Although the unit has a plastic carrying handle, this new set is designed primarily for indoor viewing using standard household current and does not come with battery options. Panasonic's suggested retail price range is about $300.

**Projection Systems**

A DRAMATIC alternative to the new tiny-screen sets is projection TV. The leading producer, Advent, is now offering systems with screens measuring up to seven feet (measured diagonally, as are other TV screens). The Advent VideoBeam projection system, with prices ranging upwards from $2495, is the best on the market. It uses a unique three-tube system. Most other projection systems—and there are now more than 50 brands on the market—use standard TV lens assemblies to form a projection system. Any TV shopper interested in a projection system should make sure to get a good demonstration under lighting conditions approximating those at home, since the picture quality varies widely from one manufacturer to the next.

For the advanced do-it-yourselfer, Heath Co., makers of the famous Heathkit audio systems, has introduced what it calls the world's first "computer TV." This little set does just about everything but whistle Dixie, and utilizes a significant device that most television manufacturers will be introducing in years to come—the programmer. The Heath programmer allows the viewer to preselect up to 32 separate times and channel numbers on two control panels, then sit back and let the computerized system do the rest. The user can preprogram nighttime shows on one panel and daytime shows on the other, or do the same with nighttime and weekend programs. Once the programs are entered into the system, the set takes over and changes channels—or turns the set off—at the preselected times. The price is $899.95.

**Recommended Features**

MANY DISCOUNT retailers are offering color TV portables and table models with screens up to 19 inches at under $300, and many of these are truly the bargains they are claimed to be. For the most part, they do not offer all the unnecessary gimmicks and geegaws which can drive the cost of a set higher without appreciably improving its performance. Nonetheless, there are a few basic features that a good color set should have. They include a solid-state chassis, matrix picture tube, automatic fine tuning and a full complement of manual tuning controls.

Fortunately, making sure a set has a solid-state chassis is far easier than it has been in past years. The last remaining "hybrid" set (part solid-state and part tubes), a 10-inch PortaColor set made by General Electric, has been replaced in the 1978 line by a totally solid-state model. Every once in a while, however, a retailer will make a good buy on some leftover hybrids and promote them at very attractive prices. Take a close look at the fine print if one of these ads catches your fancy and make sure you realize that the TV is only partially solid-state.

Solid-state chassis are important for three reasons: they are far more reliable than old sets that use vacuum tubes, resulting in fewer of those high repair bills; module circuit boards used in the overwhelming majority of solid-state sets make repairs far easier and less expensive if repairs do become necessary; and they consume less power, which can do wonders for ever-escalating electric bills.

Automatic fine tuning is another important ingredient in good color TV reception, but it should not be confused with those one-button automatic color tuning systems which go under as many different names as there are companies in the business. AFT (also called automatic frequency control, or AFC) maintains accurate fine tuning as the viewer switches from channel to channel. Most good color sets have AFT, but with the advent of one-button automatic color tuning it is not always easy to find the AFT control. Be sure and ask the salesman where it is.

Not always in plain view these days are manual color controls, again largely due to the advent of one-button automatic color systems. But such things as brightness, contrast, tint and color controls remain important, no matter how "automatic" the set may be. One problem CONSUMER GUIDE Magazine's testers have noticed is the increasing tendency to put these manual controls in what are often nearly inaccessible locations. As the other "must" features listed here, manual controls are essential to the correct operation of any color TV set. The purchaser should look around for a model with those controls mounted in a convenient spot. Once he has done that, he should play with them for a while to make sure that they are properly spaced for easy operation.

**Picture Tubes**

IN PAST YEARS, if a customer shopping for a TV set happened to ask what kind of picture tube a particular model used, he was probably told that it was either a color tube or a black-and-white tube. Those days are gone forever, because just about every producer of color TV sets has its own trade name for picture tubes. There are Dynabrites, AccuColors, Chromacolors, Trinitrons, Blackstripes, Quintrixes and more—a situation that can cause great confusion. A few basics on picture tubes may help to clear things up a bit.

Essentially, a color picture tube is a triangular glass enclosure that has three electron guns in the narrow end and phosphor coating on the inside surface of the larger, flat end. The guns fire electronic beams at the phosphors, causing them to glow in accordance with the transmitted signal. In some tubes, phosphor "dots" are used; a newer trend is the use of phosphor "stripes" (thus the name Blackstripe), said by several producers to lower manufacturing costs and improve the quality of color pictures. In selected cases, our testers have seen a difference in color purity between dot and stripe tubes, with stripe tubes delivering a more vivid, lifelike image. By no means is that always true, however, and a shopper should not avoid dot-phosphor tubes just because a salesman tells him to. The best advice is to be your own judge on picture quality, insisting only that the set have a matrix picture tube.

The TV industry has expanded its use of matrix tubes, and it is difficult these days to find a color set that uses a non-matrix design. Again, however, there could be some holdovers at the retail level. Simply stated, matrix tubes deliver brighter pictures with higher contrast than non-matrix tubes—a feature that is particularly important under bright lighting conditions.

In a matrix tube, the areas on the inside of the picture tube between the phosphor dots or stripes which make up the image are "painted" black to absorb unwanted light striking the outside surface of the tube. In a non-matrix tube, this unwanted light often manifests itself as an annoying glare or reflection. It can be counterbalanced to a certain extent through the use of tinted picture-tube glass, but this also reduces the brightness and contrast of the picture itself. The wise shopper will always pose the important question: "Is it matrix or non-matrix?"

A recent improvement over the plain matrix concept is the negative matrix tube. This means that all areas on the inside of the screen not excited by beams fired from the electron gun are covered with a light-absorbing black coating or background. Negative matrix tubes are not an essential ingredient in color sets, as plain matrix tubes are, but they are worth a close look.

## Console or Portable?

WHEN DISCUSSING color TV, there are two basic categories—consoles and table models. Many manufacturers advertise non-console sets with 19-inch screens as portables, but that is only a comparative description intended to convey the idea that they do not rest on the floor the way a console does. Many 19-inch sets—and even some 17-inch and 15-inch sets—weigh up to 45 pounds, do not have carrying handles and are simply too bulky for one person to transport. They can be moved from one room to another, but usually the chore must be done by two people or by one person using a wheeled stand. Unless the owner happens to live in an area with superb reception, each of these rooms will have to be equipped with a roof antenna or cable TV lead. The point is that 95 percent of all color TV sets are either consoles or table models and should be thought of as such. A number of manufacturers do offer small, relatively lightweight color sets with screen sizes up to 23 inches and with carrying handles. These can truly be called portables, but they generally account for only a small portion of their manufacturers' total color TV lines.

In the console category, practical considerations often fly out the window. The primary factors here involve more than just the size of the screen or the quality of the picture: most of the larger color TV console manufacturers appeal to the consumer's interest in such things as "distinctive styling," "rich cabinetry" and the like. There is nothing wrong with this approach, and obviously there is nothing wrong with buying one. But the shopper should consider several factors before deciding on a console. For one thing, the screen in a console probably will be larger than that of a table model set. Currently, the majority of consoles have 25-inch screens, although a few companies continue to offer 21- and 23-inch consoles. In table models, some 21-, 23- and 25-inch sets are available, but most are those in the 19-inch-and-under category. The bigger screen does not in any way mean improved picture quality over table models: the TV receiver in a console is of the same quality as the receiver in a portable or table set.

Translated into dollars, the shopper buying a console can generally expect to pay a certain amount for the TV receiver and an additional amount for the cabinetry. The difference between a deluxe 25-inch table model selling for $600 and a 25-inch console selling for $900 is often nothing more than the cabinet.

One area where this difference becomes particularly important is with the so-called home entertainment center, which often includes a 25-inch color set and stereo system. Prices on these all-in-one units are often stratospheric, and a closer examination usually reveals that the individual components could have been purchased for far less. Again, consoles—and even home entertainment centers—may be just what the TV shopper wants, but he should know that before venturing out into the realm of salesmen intent on making the big sale.

**Optional Features**

IN THE NEXT few years, one "extra" may become so standard that the TV purchaser will not have any choice. That extra is one-button automatic color tuning, and TV producers are moving it throughout TV lines so rapidly that nonautomatic color sets may become extinct in the near future. Before that happens, however, the shopper still has a choice.

Buying a set with one-button automatic color setting (the non-VIR type) is like buying a car with both manual and automatic transmission. Although the TV will bring in a true, vivid picture, the same job also can be accomplished by the viewer using the manual color-tuning controls. On the sales floor, the salesman might misadjust all the picture controls until the image looks like a scrambled Salvador Dali painting, then hit the automatic button and watch the picture unscramble itself right before the shopper's eyes. The point is that the viewer could do the same thing with several buttons if he wanted to. If you do not think it is worth the time or effort to tune-in a color picture, then one-button color is for you.

GE and others, however, are offering an "automatic" feature which strikes us as something of a gimmick. This is the light-sensor feature, which adjusts picture brightness and contrast to lighting conditions in the room. In our experience, lighting conditions in the average TV viewing room do not change enough to justify the expense of this doodad.

Another optional extra touted by TV salesmen is remote control. Deciding whether to buy a set with remote control—and if so, just how complex a remote system to buy—is extremely subjective, since viewing patterns differ drastically. For the sedentary viewer who watches a lot of TV and skips frequently from one channel to the next, a remote is probably worth the money. For the infrequent viewer, however, who generally turns the set on for one specific program and turns it off when the program is over, remotes have very little practical value. One thing to keep in mind about remotes: they will push up the price of a set anywhere from $40 to $150.

Set makers are adding several new controls to more deluxe models, and one of the most important is picture control. This control combines the function of brightness, contrast and color level controls in a single knob and makes it possible to manually readjust all three simultaneously to match changes in room lighting. It does the job better than most automatic light-sensor systems. Another new control is called sharpness or tone. On several sets, we found a noticeable difference in actual picture sharpness and definition after adjusting the sharpness control.

Another feature becoming commonplace in new TV lines is the lighted channel display. These large, glowing numerals can make a significant difference in both selecting and monitoring channels, particularly if the viewer is using a remote system. We find them easier to see than numbers that are merely painted on a channel-selector dial.

### Pricing

AS THE INDUSTRY introduced the 1978 models, there was some competitive price jockeying, but generally TV shoppers will not notice a major difference between 1977 and 1978 prices. In some cases, prices went up $10 to $20 on a model or two and down by about the same amount on other "promotional" models—those low-priced sets used to attract the shopper's attention.

The rapidly changing yen-to-dollar exchange rate over the past year forced many Japanese producers to increase U.S. prices just to keep even. When the exchange rate was in the neighborhood of 300 yen to a dollar, a set valued at 90,000 yen sold in the U.S. for $300. As the rate slipped to 265 yen to a dollar late in the summer, however, that same set had to be sold at $340.

Prices on Japanese sets may go even higher. Recently, after a detailed investigation by the International Trade Commission determined that imports were injuring domestic TV producers, Japanese firms agreed to a quota system that will drastically reduce the number of TV sets they will bring into the U.S. over the next three years. Since the importers can no longer bring in as many sets as they wish, the emphasis is expected to shift from low-price, high-volume models to higher-priced models that offer the importer a greater profit per set. One result of that could be the disappearance of many under-$300 19-inch color portables now available throughout the country. Once lower-priced imports begin disappearing from the market, it seems certain that domestic producers will not keep their prices lower than they have to. If a shopper's primary interest is price, then a long, hard look at 1978 offerings might be wise.

### Warranties and Where to Shop

TV WARRANTIES are not what they used to be, because most manufacturers have cut labor coverage from one year to 90 days. But new solid-state sets simply do not break down as often as old tube models did. In addition to 90 days' labor, one-year coverage on parts and two years on the picture tube constitute the standard warranty of most manufacturers today. There are some exceptions, however, with a few firms offering extended warranties of various types. If you take a look at the fine print on color TV warranties, you usually will find the word "limited" somewhere. Under new federal laws, product warranties must be designated either "full" or "limited." Standards mandate that full warranties provide for replacement of a product or a refund if there is any delay in getting the product repaired. Rather than get involved in that, the TV industry has generally opted for the limited version.

When you buy a set, many retailers may try to talk you into a special warranty extension or service contract to protect the set after the manufacturer's coverage runs out. Prices on these extensions or contracts can vary widely, so the best bet is to buy the set without the contract, then engage in a little comparison shopping between the purchase date and expiration of the manufacturer's warranty.

Selecting the right store for a TV purchase can be a dilemma, since some stores concentrate on price at the expense of service while others stress service at slightly higher prices. Generally speaking, the lowest prices can be found among discounters, catalog showrooms and mail-order specialists. At the high end are traditional independent TV or appliance/TV dealers, with department stores somewhere in between. Discounters work on the high-volume, low-profit-margin principle and that is where the lowest prices will be found. Most discounters, however, do not provide the sales help or personalized service that some independents do. Although the smaller retailers work on higher profit margins than the discounters, they are more likely to lend a sympathetic and helpful ear if things go wrong after the purchase.

Those are general guidelines, but there may be exceptions. In the area of price, the careful shopper may find the best bargain on a specific model at his neighborhood appliance/TV shop. The same shopper may discover that a given model costs more at the giant discount than it does at the local department store. This is because retailers of all kinds frequently conduct special sales, either to clear out overstocks of particular models, to closeout old lines and make way for new models, or simply to build store traffic. Anyone interested in purchasing a TV set should spend some time with the local newspaper ads before setting out on a shopping tour. Special sales always show up there first, and a thorough reading of the ads can save both time and money.

**How to Shop**

THERE IS NO easy way to shop for a color TV set, since conditions under which they are displayed and sold vary from passable to terrible. Showrooms are frequently cluttered with TV sets, blaring audio systems and other distractions. In many cases, TV antenna systems used by retailers are not adequate to produce a decent color picture. Often a sales floor is strewn with TV sets that have not even been hooked up.

Yet there are a few things the shopper can do to ensure a reasonably thorough examination of the sets he has in mind. For one thing, it is best to shop for a TV set on a weekday. The contrast between a hectic Saturday afternoon and a quiet Wednesday morning can make a significant difference in the leisure a shopper will be afforded to closely examine any set under consideration. The shopper also will find the weekday salesman far more attentive, which can be a mixed blessing in some cases.

Once a model has been selected for consideration, make sure to tune it yourself. Just because one set on a retail floor looks better than all others does not mean that it is the best set in the store. Often, it may have been tuned up for a demonstration by the salesman while the others have not been touched. No matter what excuses or claims may be made, insist on seeing the set in operation. If that is not possible, shop elsewhere.

In tuning the set in the store, start by looking for those manual controls. Make sure that they are all there, convenient to use and not scattered all over the set. To begin tuning, it is best to shut off automatic color-correction systems and turn the color control all the way off. Then use the contrast and brightness controls to tune in a good black-and-white picture. Once you have done that, bring the color up slowly to the level that pleases you, then adjust flesh tones with the tint control.

By repeating this procedure on several sets, you will begin to notice differences—both in the ease with which controls can be used and how well each set performs. This comparison of one model against another is an extremely important part of the evaluation process; the more sets you look at, the better. It is also a good idea to compare two sets side-by-side if possible, tuning in a good picture on each one and then standing back to judge which one is best.

Many newer TV sets come with sliding, swinging or swiveling panels that conceal some of the controls. Open and shut these panels a few times and adjust the controls located behind them to make sure that the controls are easy to use.

Take a close look at the channel indicator numbers. Although most new sets have lighted channel numbers, there are still some around with the hard-to-read painted numbers on the face of the channel-selector knob. This is not enough reason to reject a set, but you should be aware of it when it comes time to make a final decision.

Take along a notebook and jot things down. While you are inspecting a set, you may think you can remember all the details; but after the third or fourth set, those details may start running together in your mind. Do not make an impulse decision. Shop around, take notes and ask plenty of questions. Then go home and think about it, refreshing your memory from the notes. It may take a bit longer, but the set you buy this way is likely to be the one you will be happiest with in the long run.

**Manufacturers' Review**

**Admiral** is one of the oldest television brand names around, but the name is really the only thing that has remained unchanged. Several years ago, Admiral was purchased by Rockwell International, the giant aerospace and semiconductor firm, and the parent company has poured a large amount of time, money and sophisticated electronics technology into the Admiral TV operation. Admiral's new line has been completely revamped, with new Solarcolor and Super Solarcolor chassis in 13-, 19- and 25-inch sets. Prices are roughly the same as last year's, although some changes did show up; the lowest-priced 25-inch console is down $100 and the lowest-priced 13- and 19-inch sets are down $30 and $50 respectively.

All Admiral color TV sets this year feature negative black-matrix picture tubes; five 25-inch consoles using the Super Solarcolor chassis also feature electronic keyboard tuning, a light sensor that automatically adjusts color, brightness and contrast to room lighting conditions and an optional owner-installed remote control. The latter feature allows the consumer to purchase and install a remote unit at a later date. In the 1978 line, it has been extended to Admiral's most expensive 19-inch set at an extra cost of about $100.

Admiral is based in the U.S., but its black-and-white and 13-inch color sets, plus 19- and 25-inch subassemblies, are made in the firm's Taiwan factory.

A standard warranty covers Admiral's 25-inch console line: 90 days labor, one year on parts and two years on the picture tube. But this year, the labor warranty on color portables in the 13- and 19-inch sizes (with the exception of two models) has been extended to one year. This was done, Admiral officials say, because of the improved reliability resulting from solid-state construction. The warranty extension also may give the firm a slight competitive edge over other makers. Whatever the reason, it is more of a true consumer benefit than many of the needless features TV manufacturers are now adding to color sets.

Admiral does not operate its own servicing facilities, but maintains a nationwide network of independent franchised service dealers.

**Advent** produces giant-screen projection TV sets that use three-tube projection systems. They are superior in performance to the one-tube system marketed by other firms in the projection-TV field. Advent offers two basic home units: Model 10, with a five-foot screen at a suggested price of about $2600; and Model 750, with a six-foot screen at about $3000.

**Curtis Mathes** is a Texas-based firm that specializes in TV consoles and so-called home entertainment centers with TV and stereo-systems. The company does not have its own service operation, and locating a Curtis Mathes servicer could be a problem in some areas. The company is taking a new direction this year, and in 1978 will offer a TV/video tape recorder combination.

**General Electric** has extended its VIR broadcast-controlled automatic color tuning feature, which it introduced last year on a selected number of models, to twenty-one 19- and 25-inch sets. Once VIR is activated, the set's color intensity and tint levels are adjusted automatically to conform with the signal being sent out over the air along with the picture information.

GE has introduced another new twist this year: a remote-control system that utilizes infrared light in place of the ultrasonic waves used by most other remotes as a wireless information carrier. According to the firm, the new infrared system is far less susceptible to interference than ultrasonic units are, since it cannot be triggered by false signals, such as jangling keys. CONSUMER GUIDE Magazine's test staff believes it is a marginal improvement at best.

General Electric also did away with the industry's last remaining

TV set using a chassis with tubes, replacing its "hybrid" (part solid state, part tubes) 10-inch PortaColor chassis with an all-solid-state model. The firm now offers four 10-inch color sets.

Pricing in the GE line is sharper in some cases than it was last year, with the lowest-priced or "leader" models in several screen sizes now carrying manufacturer's suggested list prices below those of last year. Examples are three 13-inch color portables, down $20 from comparable models in the 1977 line; two 17-inch sets, down $40; and the lowest-priced 19-inch set, down $10. GE offers a standard TV warranty: 90 days labor, one year on parts and two years on the picture tube. The firm operates an extensive service operation through a nationwide network of Customer Care Service Shops.

**Hitachi** is a Japanese company that has developed a well-deserved reputation for quality products. In 1978, Hitachi is offering 11 color sets in 9- through 19-inch sizes, with a deluxe 19-inch model featuring random-access electronic channel tuning and infrared remote control. The firm also has a full lineup of 12 black-and-white portables ranging in screen size from 5 to 19 inches.

Although its parent firm in Japan is one of that country's leading TV marketers, Hitachi's U.S. operation has never experienced the wide popularity of such other Japanese brands as Sony and Panasonic. Therefore, nationwide retail distribution has been somewhat spotty in the past. Hitachi has taken a more aggressive attitude toward the market recently, and that should result in better availability throughout the U.S. Hitachi does not have its own service operation, but this program of retail expansion should also make it easier to locate servicing facilities.

One attractive feature of Hitachi is its TV warranty: one year on labor, two years on the picture tube and parts, and a full ten years on transistors.

**JVC'S** real strength is high-priced audio equipment, and video tape recording systems; however, the firm continues to offer a selected range of TV sets. This year, three color sets in 13-, 17- and 19-inch sizes, and three black-and-white portables in 3-inch and 5-inch sizes make up the JVC line.

**Magnavox** is now owned by Philips of the Netherlands. The level of technological sophistication evident in its TV products has improved significantly since the acquisition.

Magnavox was one of the first TV firms to move heavily into electronic channel tuning with its keyboard-controlled STAR Touch Tune system. In addition, the STAR system offers time-of-day and channel number displays which appear on the screen for about three seconds each time a channel is changed. If the viewer wishes to reconfirm his channel selection or see the time again, a special "recall" button can be pushed.

Although many TV manufacturers have sharply reduced the number of furniture-styled console models over the past few years,

Magnavox remains committed to the deluxe console concept. Many of the company's 25-inch consoles and home entertainment centers are attractively styled and use luxurious cabinet materials. Recently, the firm introduced a special line of "Spirit of '76 Early American" consoles, including one that houses a 25-inch color set with the STAR Touch-Tune system.

The Magnavox warranty covers color TV sets for 90 days on labor, one year on parts and two years on the picture tube. Black-and-white sets are covered for 90 days on parts and labor, and one year on the picture tube. Magnavox does not maintain its own service operation, but has a nationwide network of authorized servicing dealers.

**MGA** is the U.S. brand name of Japan's industrial giant, Mitsubishi Corp. In the past year, MGA has attempted to increase its influence in the U.S. TV market by expanding its color television line to 13 models and offering two black-and-white sets. Six color models now feature the firm's random-access electronic tuning, and several also come with remote control.

MGA has a slightly stronger warranty than most TV manufacturers: coverage on color sets extends to one year on parts and labor, two years on the picture tube. Despite the added coverage, MGA sets are still marketed on a selective basis throughout the U.S. and finding service could be difficult.

**Panasonic** is a U.S. marketing arm for Japan's Matsushita. Over the years, Panasonic has established a strong reputation in the U.S. for quality and product innovation. It is one of the few Japanese firms in the U.S. to offer not only color TV portables and table models but also 25-inch consoles.

Significant in the 1978 line is the firm's first VIR set, a 19-inch model with a suggested retail price range of about $500. The VIR system automatically adjusts color picture quality based on a signal sent out by most broadcasters. Panasonic plans to extend VIR to more models and screen sizes in the next few years. Another first for Panasonic this year is a 10-inch portable color TV set that sells for about $300. The firm also markets a wide range of black-and-white TV sets, including several models that can be operated either indoors on AC current or outdoors on self-contained rechargeable batteries.

A standard warranty applies to most color sets—90 days labor, one year on parts, and two years on the picture tube—but models in a special LTD series are covered for one year on both parts and labor. Panasonic has no service operation of its own, but it is a widely distributed national brand and service is easy to obtain.

**Philco,** once owned by Ford Motor Company, is now the property of GTE Sylvania, which produces and markets Sylvania TVs as well. The Philco color line consists of portables in the 15- and 19-inch sizes, 25-inch table models and a 25-inch home entertainment center. The line also includes a set with 21-inch screen, a size that has virtually disappeared from most color TV lines.

**Quasar** is the new name for an old TV line, Motorola. Matsushita, also parent company of Panasonic, purchased the TV division from Motorola and renamed it Quasar, Motorola's name for a line of color TV sets introduced in the late 1960s. Quasar sets were centered around the "works-in-a-drawer" concept, with circuitry for the sets contained on plug-in module boards that could easily be removed and replaced with new ones. Quasar has continued the module approach; however, its new Service Miser chassis features what the firm calls a Super Module, containing more than half of all chassis components.

Quasar's 1978 TV line is greatly redesigned from past years, and now features keyboard random-access electronic channel tuning and a new circuit that automatically turns the set off when the station tuned goes off the air. Quasar has also taken a step toward improving TV sound, introducing several models with three speakers instead of one as is found in most color receivers.

Quasar offers a standard warranty of 90 days labor, one year on parts and two years on the picture tube for all color sets with 19-inch and smaller screen sizes. Labor coverage is extended to one year with screens larger than 19 inches. The firm does not have it own factory service operation, but the brand is widely serviced by former Motorola dealers and other independents.

**RCA** and Zenith have long been locked in a fierce struggle for the number one spot in TV sales, and RCA usually comes in a very close second. It is estimated that RCA accounts for roughly 20 percent of all color TV sales in the U.S. compared to about 22 percent for Zenith, and the firm is battling hard to increase that share through a variety of feature innovations and technical improvements.

This year, major emphasis is being given to a new XtendedLife chassis that is designed to run cooler, operate more reliably and consume less energy than conventional TVs. RCA has now extended the system to 31 models in its color TV line. RCA is also continuing to advertise and promote its ColorTrak system, which consists of an automatic color tuner AccuFilter picture tube with special tinted phosphors to absorb room light that would ordinarily cause annoying reflections on the surface of the tube, and an automatic contrast/color control that adjusts color quality and brightness when the contrast level is changed.

RCA is also very active in AC/DC black-and-white TV, offering a wide range of portables that can be operated on standard household current or with optional rechargeable batteries.

RCA maintains factory service branches throughout the U.S., and RCA sets are also serviced by many independents across the country.

**Sanyo** TV sets are produced by Sanyo of Japan, one of that country's leading television manufacturers. Sanyo sets are sold in this country under the Sanyo brand name, but the firm also makes many of the color models that Sears sells under its name. Sanyo has the reputation for being a price-oriented line, and some dedicated work by the TV shopper can generally turn up a Sanyo set—particularly in the 19-inch category—at a very attractive price.

Sanyo markets color TV sets in the 13-, 15- and 19-inch sizes, and black-and-white sets in the 12-, 16- and 19-inch sizes.

**Sears** does not actually produce any of its own TV sets, but through expert marketing practices and sharp pricing, the giant catalog retailer has managed to boost its share of the U.S. TV market close to the 9 percent level. This makes Sears the third leading TV marketer after Zenith and RCA, and puts it well ahead of such prominent names as Sony, GE and Magnavox.

Sears quality is high, and the careful shopper can find a good, basic color TV set with all the essentials at an attractive price. But some caution should be used: Sears' lowest-priced 19-inch color portable and several other sets do not have black-matrix picture tubes.

Like virtually every other TV marketer, Sears now offers a range of more expensive sets with random-access electronic channel tuning and one-button automatic color tuning. Sears also offers a wide variety of black-and-white sets, including a number of models that operate with optional battery packs and/or car cigarette lighters using adapters.

Most Sears sets are covered for one year on labor, but at least one model has only a 90-day labor coverage. On all sets, parts are covered for one year and the picture tube for two years. Servicing is no problem, since Sears service centers are widespread throughout the U.S.

**Sharp** is a Japanese firm that never gained wide distribution in the U.S., but this year the firm has expanded its color and black-and-white lines in an effort to increase its share of the U.S. market. The 1978 Sharp line consists of 12 color models, including one 9-, three 13-, two 15-and six 19-inch sets. The black-and-white TV line features eight sets, including Sharp's first 7-inch AC/DC portable. Highlighted in the new color line are a low-power-consumption chassis included in 11 models, and what Sharp calls "Sigma Sonic" sound using a special speaker system for wider acoustical range.

Color TV warranties on the Sharp line are generally better than those offered by other manufacturers. All sets have two-year picture tube and one-year parts warranties and—with the exception of two models—all have one-year labor coverage. The varactor electronic channel tuner in two remote-controlled models is covered for seven years. Service could be a problem with Sharp sets, since the line is not in wide national distribution.

**Sony** is the leading Japanese TV maker doing business in the U.S., and for good reason: the firm's line of color and black-and-white sets offers the consumer high quality, outstanding performance and above-average reliability. Those factors have helped to push Sony into the number four spot in U.S. sales, despite the fact that Sony offers a relatively limited line of portables and table models. Firms holding the top three marketing positions sell full portable, table model and console lines.

Sony is not the line for a shopper interested in low price. The cheapest Sony color TV set is a tiny 5-inch model that carries a suggested retail price of about $460. Three sets in the popular 19-inch size range from about $580 to $700. Sony products are sometimes discount priced at the retail level, but the firm's prices generally run $100 and more above comparable models from other TV manufacturers.

In its 1978 line, Sony is offering color portables and table models ranging in size from five to 21 inches, plus black-and-white sets in the 5-, 7-, 8-, 11- and 13-inch sizes. Five black-and-white sets can be used either indoors or outdoors with optional battery packs. The newest products for 1978 are a 21-inch table model with electronic random-access tuning and remote control at a suggested price of about $820, and a 7.7-inch color portable which features AC/DC operation at about $480.

Unlike many other makers, Sony did not raise its prices for 1978. Sony is not as strongly affected by changes in the yen-to-dollar rate or U.S. government actions against imported TV sets as other Japanese firms are, because most products aimed for the American market are produced in the firm's California factory.

**Sylvania** is now ranked as the number eight producer of color TV sets, and the firm has been battling to improve its market share for the past several years with a new family of automatic sets that feature GT-Matic color tuning and electronic random-access channel tuning. For 1978, Sylvania has introduced a keyboard-controlled electronic channel tuner with a difference: the viewer can preselect any eight VHF or UHF channels and program them into a special favorite-channel keyboard, which is lettered "A" to "H." When the viewer presses the corresponding letter on the keyboard, that station is automatically tuned.

Sylvania has also added a room-light monitor to many sets with GT-Matic tuning. This is a feature that CONSUMER GUIDE Magazine has found to be of little practical value. Sylvania's color TV line ranges from 13-inch portables to 25-inch consoles; the black-and-white line features sets in the 9- to 22-inch sizes. Sylvania maintains its own national service company, but the line is also serviced by many independents.

**Toshiba** is another firm that has not achieved wide distribution in the U.S., despite the backing of a Japanese parent company of great size and financial resources. Toshiba's color TV sets are generally rated excellent to superior in terms of performance.

For 1978, Toshiba's color TV line includes models in the 9-, 13-, 15- and 19-inch sizes; the black-and-white line includes 9- and 12-inch portables. New in the color line is an advanced chassis with snap-in circuit modules for easier and quicker repair. The firm's Blackstripe matrix picture tube is featured in all color sets.

Servicing is primarily done by authorized independents, and Toshiba's warranty covers color TV parts and labor for one year, the picture tube for two years.

**Zenith** is the nation's leading producer and marketer of color and black-and-white TV sets. The reasons behind this preeminent position include a very sophisticated marketing and advertising program, a deep commitment to technological research and development projects, and a single-minded concentration on a single product: all other Zenith activities are peripheral to TV.

Although Zenith has come up with many product innovations in color TV, the one responsible for its current position in the market is probably the Chromacolor picture tube, the first negative matrix picture tube. Other TV manufacturers have now moved into the negative-matrix field, but this year Zenith added another improvement — extended field lens electron guns in five 19-inch sets. The EFL-gun Chromacolor tubes not only improve picture quality, but have a 100-degree deflection angle resulting in shorter front-to-back set dimensions.

Zenith perhaps best exemplifies the speed with which TV manufacturers have extended electronic channel tuning, automatic color tuning and other deluxe features throughout color TV lines. In 1978, 89 percent of all Zenith color sets have automatic one-button color tuning called Color Sentry; 87 percent have electronic tuning; 40 percent have remote control. Of the 40 percent with remote control, most also feature Zenith's Zoom. Zoom is operated by touching a special button on the remote unit, resulting in an instant close-up of two-thirds of the picture being received.

Zenith does not have its own service operation, but is widely serviced by independent dealers throughout the U.S.

# 1978 Best Buys: Televisions

IN PREPARING the following test reports, CONSUMER GUIDE Magazine selected television sets that we consider the leading models in the categories of small-screen portables, large-screen portables, color consoles and black-and-white portables. All of them represent good buys. We suggest that you base your choice of one particular model on the one-word ratings at the end of each report and the set's low price.

## SMALL-SCREEN COLOR
**Best Buy**

**The Sony KV 1512** offers no more features than many less expensive competitive sets. If there is justification for the higher price of the Sony model, it lies in its quality of materials, performance and the care taken in its assembly. Channel selectors are the conventional rotary type with lighted channel numbers. A push-pull on/off/volume control allows the user to turn the power on and off without disturbing the volume setting. A picture control combines brightness, contrast and color level into one function for convenient adjustment. The KV 1512 also has automatic fine tuning to lock-in the correct frequency for each channel and an automatic color button that narrows the range of manual controls when engaged. Two earphone jacks are provided for private listening. The picture tube is Sony's new Trinitron Plus design, a black-matrix version of the old Trinitron. The essence of Trinitron design—in-line guns, striped screen and a very square-cornered cylindrical screen—has been preserved on the KV 1512. The only difference is the addition of a light-absorbing black-matrix between the color lines to enhance contrast and allow greater brightness. Warranty coverage is the usual 90 days on labor, one year on most parts and two years on the picture tube. In the opinion of CONSUMER GUIDE Magazine's testing staff, the KV 1512 is a

*Prices are accurate at time of printing; subject to manufacturer's change.*

winner. The most striking aspect of its performance is the smooth-as-butter feel to the controls and the overall ease with which excellent tuning can be achieved. The picture control is particularly well designed. It provides the set owner with a broad range of brightness from dim to very bright, with color level and contrast automatically held in balance at each level. The picture coloration is very natural and detail is sharply defined. There is more than enough brightness for any indoor viewing environment.

**Ratings: sharpness**—excellent; **brightness**—excellent; **color accuracy**—superior; **operation of controls**—superior.

**Approximate Retail Price: $459.95**            **Low Price: $390.95**

## Also Recommended

**The Quasar WP3422PW** 12-inch color portable has a plastic cabinet with simulated walnut-grained finish, weighs 28 pounds and has a molded carrying handle. Front-mounted controls include on/off, volume, AFT, VHF and UHF channel selectors, hue, color adjustment and combined brightness and contrast control. This set uses Quasar's 100 percent solid-state Service Miser chassis which is designed both for increased reliability and easier servicing. It features a matrix in-line picture tube with an additional prefocus lens, designed to deliver a sharper image. The set's warranty offers 90-day carry-in labor warranty, one year on parts and two years on the picture tube. The Quasar is a prime example of what a good TV set can do without an automatic "one-button" color tuning circuit. The accuracy of colors tuned manually remains just about perfect from channel to channel, with only minor and simple adjustments needed from time to time. In addition, picture quality is excellent; images are sharp and bright; colors are true and vivid. This model also features a handy control which allows the viewer to adjust brightness and contrast simultaneously from "soft" to "vivid." Another good feature of this set is the uncluttered location of controls. The combined volume and push-pull on/off control is handy, since the volume level does not have to be reset every time the set is turned off and on. We found the UHF and VHF channel selectors slightly stiff, but otherwise functional and convenient to use.

**Ratings: sharpness**—excellent; **brightness**—excellent; **color accuracy**—excellent; **operation of controls**—very good.

**Approximate Retail Price: $329.95**            **Low Price: $296.96**

**The Hitachi CA560** is a 15-inch color table model that is light and compact enough to qualify as a portable, but it does not have a handle of any kind. The CA560 has conventional rotary channel selectors with unlighted numbers that are simply imprinted around each dial. All other controls are neatly arranged in a straight line down the right edge of the control panel. An automatic-tuning button activates the automatic fine tuning and several color correc-

*Prices are accurate at time of printing; subject to manufacturer's change.*

tion circuits, while narrowing the range of manual controls. The Hitachi CA560 picture tube has a black-matrix, in-line design with striped screen. The chassis is completely solid-state. Independent on/off and volume controls allow the user to turn the set on and off without having to readjust the sound. The warranty is unusually long—labor costs are covered for the entire first year, while the costs of most parts are covered for two years. Transistors are covered for ten years. The Hitachi CA560 could have scored a clean sweep of the performance category with "excellent" ratings across the board if it were not for a single design flaw. Hitachi engineers combined the automatic fine tuning control with the button that activates the color correction circuits and narrows the range of manual controls. With the button engaged, manual controls of the CA560 lack sufficient range to cope with all signal conditions and viewer preferences. In particular, color intensity is sometimes too great, even with the control set at minimum. Despite this shortcoming, the Hitachi CA560 performed especially well in our tests. Its picture is sharp, bright and—even under weak signal conditions—relatively free of snow. The colors are vivid and well balanced and controls operate smoothly, with gradual and predictable effects. In addition, the controls are clearly labeled and easy to reach.

**Ratings: sharpness**—excellent; **brightness**—excellent; **color accuracy**—very good; **operation of controls**—good.

**Approximate Retail Price: $399.95**  **Low Price: $349.95**

**Panasonic's CT-117** is a 10-inch color portable that weighs 22 pounds and has a molded carrying handle. Controls are all mounted on the front of the walnut-grained cabinet. It comes with detachable VHF dipole and UHF loop antennas. It has separate manual controls for contrast, brightness, tint and color, plus Panasonic's Q-Lock II automatic color/tint adjustment. It also comes with a separate AFT control, and click-stop UHF and VHF channel selectors. An earphone is provided for private listening. The Quintrix II picture tube is an in-line black-matrix tube, and the chassis is all solid state. Panasonic's Quick-On feature results in full picture and sound about five seconds after the set is turned on. The CT-117 warranty covers labor for 90 days, parts for one year and the picture tube for two years. As with all Panasonic sets' in the 19-inch and smaller screen sizes, repairs are made on a carry-in basis, with in-home service provided on sets above 19 inches. The CT-117 earned high marks for picture quality, with colors found to be vivid and true, images sharp. Q-Lock II performs adequately in adjusting both color and tint, but we generally preferred the quality of manual settings to the ones made by Q-Lock II. The CT-117's separate AFT and automatic color settings allow the user to reap the full benefit of automatic fine tuning while making his own individual color and tint decisions. The Model CT-117 also rates high in ease of operation. Controls are all positioned on the front of

*Prices are accurate at time of printing; subject to manufacturer's change.*

the set and are convenient to use. Contrast, brightness, tint, color and Q-Lock II controls, however, are mounted along the bottom on a panel inset slightly from the rest of the cabinet, and are somewhat unwieldy.
**Ratings: sharpness**—very good; **brightness**—excellent; **color accuracy**—excellent; **operation of controls**—very good.
**Approximate Retail Price: $309.95**             **Low Price: $260.96**

**The Magnavox 4050** is a deluxe 13-inch set with exceptionally trim cabinet dimensions. It weighs 35 pounds, which is average for a 13-inch portable. The 4050 features Magnavox's Videomatic electric eye system that is designed to automatically increase brightness, contrast and color levels. In addition, it has manual controls for these and other functions along the top edge of the cabinet back, the channel numbers are lighted, and there is a push-pull volume/on/off control that allows the user to turn the set on and off without disturbing the volume setting. An earphone is provided for private listening. A recess in the middle of the top serves as a handle. The Magnavox 4050's picture tube is the modern in-line, slotted-mask type with a black-matrix striped screen. The chassis is solid state and modular, which means low power consumption, good reliability and easy service. Warranty coverage is 90 days on labor, one year on parts, and two years on the picture tube. The 4050's picture is bright and has good color, although the bright picture highlights are not as sharp as they could be. The clearly labeled, smooth controls would have received a top rating if they had been located on the front of the set where they could be adjusted without taking your eyes off the screen. However, they are located on the back of the set. The Videomatic electric eye system is virtually useless, in our opinion.
**Ratings: sharpness**—very good; **brightness**—excellent; **color accuracy**—very good; **operation of controls**—very good.
**Approximate Retail Price: $379.95**             **Low Price: $322.96**

## LARGE-SCREEN COLOR PORTABLES
**Best Buy**

**Sony's KV 2101**, with its 21-inch screen, offers as much viewing area as do some consoles. The KV 2101 features Sony's Trinitron Plus picture tube, a black-matrix version of the tube used in earlier Sony models. This is an in-line, striped-screen tube with the area between color stripes blackened out to enhance contrast and brightness without washout. The Sony KV 2101 has a conventional rotary channel selector with lighted numbers. An automatic color tuning system narrows the range of manual controls when the auto button is depressed. A picture control permits one-knob simultaneous adjustment of color level, brightness and contrast. Automatic fine tuning locks in the proper frequency of each channel. A sharpness control allows the viewer to soften the picture focus to

*Prices are accurate at time of printing; subject to manufacturer's change.*

mask poor reception. An earphone and two jacks are provided. Convenient handholds are recessed into either side of the cabinet for secure lifting and carrying. Warranty coverage is the usual 90 days on labor, one year on most parts and two on the picture tube. The KV 2101 has brightness to spare, with no loss of sharpness. Color accuracy remains one of Sony's strongest suits. The controls are superbly smooth and their effect on the picture is always gradual and predictable.

**Ratings: sharpness**—excellent; **brightness**—excellent; **color accuracy**—superior; **operation of controls**—superior.
**Approximate Retail Price: $719.95**          **Low Price: $611.95**

## Also Recommended

**The Panasonic CT-926** is a 19-inch color table model with a "digital" channel number display. A single channel window serves for both UHF and VHF. The CT-926 features a preset tuning system that overrides manual picture controls and sets the functions they govern to levels determined at the factory. Pulling out the tint control button defeats the automatic fine tuning system, and pulling the brightness control softens the picture focus to mask reception problems. The volume control pulls out to turn the set on. The Panabrite control is a combined brightness/contrast/color intensity adjustment. An earphone is provided with the CT-926. Warranty coverage is the usual 90 days free labor, one year for most parts and two years for the picture tube. It is difficult to find anything to criticize about the performance of the Panasonic CT-926. The picture is exceptionally sharp, colors are vivid and natural, and there is brightness to spare under virtually all viewing conditions. The push-pull controls for AFT, sharpness and the preset color system, however, might be a little confusing to some users. The Panabrite brightness/color/contrast control maintains balance between the three functions it controls while providing an ample range of adjustment from dim to bright.

**Ratings: sharpness**—excellent; **brightness**—excellent; **color accuracy**—excellent; **operation of controls**—excellent.
**Approximate Retail Price: $479.95**          **Low Price: $413.96**

**GE's YC7702WD** features VIR. Manual controls allow the set to be operated and tuned in the same manner as a conventional TV receiver. Accompanying the VIR circuitry is a light sensor that automatically adjusts color intensity, contrast and brightness to match room lighting. Channel numbers on the YC7702WD are much larger than conventional lighted and unlighted numbers, and resemble those used in calculators. UHF and VHF channel controls, along with on/off and volume, are positioned at the top of the set's control panel. VIR and light-sensor controls are mounted inside a tilt-out control bin. A sharpness control is also featured.

*Prices are accurate at time of printing; subject to manufacturer's change.*

The picture tube used is a black-matrix in-line tube. The chassis is all solid state, and uses plug-in circuit modules for easier and quicker repairs. Warranty coverage is standard: 90 days labor, one year on parts and two years on the picture tube. GE's YC7702WD is an outstanding color TV set in our book, primarily due to the VIR circuitry. This model provided accurate, vivid and lifelike colors from channel to channel and station to station once the "Personal Preference" controls mounted on the rear of the set were used to fine tune the picture. We also found the picture exceptionally bright and sharp. Complaints primarily involve the light-sensor device and the positioning of some controls. The light sensor does what it is supposed to do, but it does not seem to be necessary. The only gripes we have about the controls center on the on/off knob, a push-pull affair that is easy enough to push in but difficult to pull out. We also found the VIR and light-sensor controls, located behind the tilt-out bin, somewhat cramped and difficult to use.

**Ratings: sharpness**—excellent; **brightness**—excellent; **color accuracy**—superior; **operation of controls**—very good.

**Approximate Retail Price: $449.95**                 **Low Price: $382.46**

**Panasonic's CT-977** is a deluxe 19-inch set with a feature that is virtually sweeping the color TV field—electronic pushbutton channel tuning. With this system, the viewer can preselect up to 14 VHF and UHF channels. Once these have been locked into the set, any one of them can instantly be tuned by pushing the corresponding button. This model also features electronic remote control that allows the viewer to change channels in both directions; adjust volume to low, high and mute settings; and turn the set on and off. Panasonic's Q-Lock automatic color system adjusts color, tint, contrast and brightness; it also features separate AFT, sharpness and brightness controls; plus a combined color, contrast and brightness control called Panabrite. The picture tube is an in-line black-matrix tube and the chassis is all solid-state. Warranty coverage is standard: 90 days labor, one year on parts and two years on the picture tube. The Q-Lock control worked fine, keeping colors at the same levels from one channel and from one program to the next. But we found the set performed better when we deactivated the automatic one-button control. Using manual controls, we were able to tune in a superb color picture. The electronic tuning used on the CT-977 functions very well, responding at the merest touch of any of the 14 selector buttons. Preselection of the channels is difficult, however. Remote tuning on this model was rated among the most convenient of those now on the market. We changed channels and volume settings at distances of up to 50 feet.

**Ratings: sharpness**—excellent; **brightness**—excellent; **color accuracy**—excellent; **operation of controls**—good.

**Approximate Retail Price: $579.95**                 **Low Price: $503.96**

*Prices are accurate at time of printing; subject to manufacturer's change.*

**The Toshiba C-972** color model features an updated version of the firm's all-solid-state chassis. The 19-inch set incorporates an improved Blackstripe black-matrix picture tube that uses rectangular phosphor stripes instead of conventional phosphor dots. It also features Toshiba's ABC one-button tuning system that controls color, tint, brightness and contrast. Color and tint controls on the C-972 change settings only within a limited range, but the range of each can be adjusted by inserting a screwdriver in small holes beside the controls. Both parts and labor are covered for one year; the picture tube for two years. Toshiba's Model C-972 produces vivid, accurate, bright colors. Model C-972 also has a feature we think represents a good compromise in automatic color-tuning circuits. With the ABC one-button control activated, the user can still make adjustments to both color and tint by manipulating the range controls. This makes it possible to fine-tune a picture without completely disabling the automatic circuit and doing it all manually. For convenience and location, controls on this set earn high ratings. Toshiba placed the color and tint controls on a panel that is angled outward for easy accessibility. UHF and VHF channel selectors are of the nonelectronic, mechanical type, and are a bit stiff and noisy. Back-lit channel indicator lights on both UHF and VHF are bright enough, but slightly larger ones would have been easier to read from a distance.

**Ratings: sharpness**—excellent; **brightness**—excellent; **color accuracy**—excellent; **operation of controls**—very good.

**Approximate Retail Price: $479.95**　　　　　　　　**Low Price: $413.96**

**The Zenith J1930W**, a 19-inch set, features the firm's new 100-degree EFL (extended field lens) Chromacolor in-line picture tube, which makes the set slimmer than other 19-inch Zenith sets. Chromacolor is Zenith's name for its own version of a negative matrix picture tube. The J1930W also features Zenith's Color Sentry automatic color tuning system to maintain factory-set color levels and preset contrast levels. It also includes a light sensor that adjusts picture brightness as room lighting changes. The set also comes with AFC control. It has a dipole VHF antenna, detachable bow-tie UHF antenna and a solid-state chassis with nine plug-in circuit modules. Warranty coverage is standard: 90 days on labor, one year on parts and two years on the picture tube. Picture quality was crisp, with sharp images and fine detail. A manual sharpness control enhanced picture clarity and appeared to have a wider adjustment range than most other sharpness controls. Colors were also found to be accurate, although we did notice some subtle variations in flesh tones with the Color Sentry activated. We also felt the overall vitality of colors was slightly subdued with Color Sentry on, with bright reds and blues sometimes appearing faded. A full array of manual controls is available to correct this problem, but they are tucked into a small panel on the front of the set and are awkward to manipulate. All in all, the J1930W is a very good set.

*Prices are accurate at time of printing; subject to manufacturer's change.*

**Ratings: sharpness**—excellent; **brightness**—excellent; **color accuracy**—very good; **operation of controls**—good.
**Approximate Retail Price: $519.95**　　　　　　**Low Price: $417.95**

**Sylvania's CX7164W** has gone manufacturers of one-button automatic tuning circuits one better and done away with the button. This 19-inch set features GT-Matic tuning. The door covering the panel with seven different manual controls (AFC, color, tint, picture, sharpness, brightness and "PermaTint") has no handle or knob, but a small thumbnail screw lock; only the channel selector switches, volume and on/off controls, and room-light sensor are exposed. Among the circuits incorporated into the set are color level, contrast and brightness, and sharpness controls. This set also features bright channel-indicator lights, a solid-state chassis and black-matrix in-line picture tube. Warranty coverage is standard: 90 days on labor, one year on parts and two years on the picture tube. This set has clean, uncluttered lines, a bare minimum of exposed controls and attractive if somewhat plain styling. The catch is the "locked" front panel that conceals seven controls. Despite the supposedly automatic circuit, we found it necessary, or preferable, to touch up the picture from one channel and one program to the next. The seven controls are bunched so tightly together, however, that making these minor adjustments can become a tedious and difficult chore. Picture quality is not at all bad. It did appear flat or slightly washed-out where bright, vivid colors were part of the program. With a bit of manual adjustment, we found it possible to tune reasonably accurate colors with high brightness and sharp, clear detail.
**Ratings: sharpness**—excellent; **brightness**—excellent; **color accuracy**—good; **operation of controls**—fair.
**Approximate Retail Price: $429.95**　　　　　　**Low Price: $365.46**

## COLOR CONSOLES
### Best Buy

**RCA'S GB688** color TV console features a 25-inch screen and Mediterranean design with a pecan finish over oak and other hardwoods, and simulated wood trim. Among the more important features are the new XtendedLife chassis. RCA has reduced the energy consumption of the chassis to less than that of a 100-watt light bulb. Although it does not have RCA's ColorTrak automatic color system, it does incorporate automatic color control circuitry to keep colors consistent as channels and programs change. It also features an AFT control and push-pull on/off control. The picture tube is a black-matrix type and the solid-state chassis uses eight plug-in circuit modules. Warranty coverage is 90 days on labor, one year on parts and two years on the picture tube. For any TV shopper interested in a basic, functional color TV console at a reasonable price, RCA's GB688 is highly recommended. We found

*Prices are accurate at time of printing; subject to manufacturer's change.*

color accuracy, tone and intensity to be almost perfect. Once manual color controls were set, there was an insignificant amount of variation in the picture from channel to channel and program to program. Adjusting the picture is a pleasure, since the GB688 controls are among the most functional and convenient of any we have seen. Color, tint, contrast and vertical hold controls are mounted alongside the channel selector knobs on an exposed panel, rather than hidden behind a door. Control knobs are big enough to grip easily and are spaced far enough apart to allow easy access. Similarly, push-pull bright/AFT and volume/on/off controls mounted above the main panel are easy to use and totally functional. The latter two are even color-coded to simplify use.

**Ratings: sharpness**—excellent; **brightness**—excellent; **color accuracy**—excellent; **operation of controls**—excellent.
**Approximate Retail Price: $649.95**      **Low Price: $558.90**

## Also Recommended

**The Magnavox 4656** is a 25-inch console with an attractive Mediterranean cabinet in imitation pecan. Heavy moldings mark top and bottom edges and side panels are detailed in high relief. Like most of the Magnavox consoles, the 4656 features a light sensor to measure the room light and adjust color intensity, brightness and contrast to compensate for changes. The light sensor system is activated by the preset color button, which also limits the range of manual controls. A separate switch allows automatic fine tuning to be turned on when the preset button is off. Channel numbers are lighted, the on/off switch can be operated without changing the volume setting and a door in the control panel masks most of the control knobs from view. Warranty coverage is standard: one year on parts, 90 days on labor and two years on the picture tube. Under good reception conditions, CONSUMER GUIDE Magazine's test model delivered an excellent picture in all respects. Details were sharply defined, there was more than enough brightness, and colors were faithfully reproduced. Controls on the Magnavox 4656 are clearly labeled and easy to find. We found them to be difficult to manipulate, however, because of their location in a narrow compartment. The automatic tuning system is well designed, with the flexibility to allow use of manual controls in combination with selected aspects of the automatic system. The light sensor is basically a gimmick. If you inadvertently turned it off, you would not miss it.

**Ratings: sharpness**—excellent; **brightness**—excellent; **color accuracy**—excellent; **operation of controls**—very good.
**Approximate Retail Price: $779.95**      **Low Price: $662.96**

**The Magnavox 4512**, a 25-inch color TV, is actually a combination table model and console, but is included in the console section because of its size. It comes with a black pedestal base that can be

*Prices are accurate at time of printing; subject to manufacturer's change.*

removed when the set is to be placed on a table. Manual controls are mounted on the front of the set above the UHF and VHF channel selectors, and in a compartment beneath the channel selectors. Channel selectors feature lighted indicator windows, designed to allow the user to see from a distance which channel is tuned. An automatic color-leveling circuit maintains color intensity at a constant level, despite variations in the intensity of the received signal. The picture tube is a black-matrix tube and the chassis is all solid-state with plug-in circuit modules. Warranty coverage is standard: 90 days on labor, one year on parts and two years on the picture tube. The Magnavox 4512 represents a good compromise between price and features. It is a stripped-down model, without automatic color tuning, electronic channel tuning or remote control; yet, it delivers a good picture and offers the viewer a functional easy-to-use grouping of essential manual controls. Picture quality is well above average, and tuning a near-perfect image proved remarkably easy using manual controls located on the front of the set. The only problem—and it is not a significant one—is a slightly faded quality of reds and blues when flesh tones are tuned to perfection. Generally speaking, the practice of concealing manual controls is a bad one, since those little compartments behind the doors are often tiny and controls are frequently jammed close together. With this set, however, not only are controls easily accessible once the fold-down door is opened, but the location of each is printed on the inside of the door. This means the viewer is not forced to break his back bending over the set and peering into a dark bin to make adjustments.

**Ratings: sharpness**—excellent; **brightness**—excellent; **color accuracy**—very good; **operation of controls**—very good.

**Approximate Retail Price: $669.96**          **Low Price: $569.47**

**General Electric's YM9472MP** is a 25-inch color TV console with a cabinet designed in the Early American furniture style. It features VIR. This set also features pushbutton electronic tuning; remote control using infrared instead of conventional ultrasonic beams; and a light sensor that adjusts color intensity, brightness and contrast based on the level of room lighting. It employs large, calculator-style channel numbers for both UHF and VHF display. Model YM9472MP has an all-solid-state chassis and plug-in circuit modules for easier servicing, and uses a black-matrix picture tube. Warranty coverage is standard: 90 days on labor, one year on parts and two years on the picture tube. This 25-inch console is ranked high primarily because of its VIR system. On this model, VIR effectively keeps colors true and lifelike without sacrificing vivid and bright highlights. Another good feature, for those who want electronic channel tuning, is GE's keyboard system. It does not require complicated preselection of channels as some other pushbutton electronic systems do: the user simply punches in any channel number from 2 to 83, hits the "Enter" button, and that

*Prices are accurate at time of printing; subject to manufacturer's change.*

channel instantly appears. Also featured on this model is GE's new infrared remote-control system. The remote unit functions well: changing channels, turning the set on and off, and running the volume control through the three remote levels was no problem at distances of up to 30 feet. Control convenience earned only a "good" rating, since several essential controls including VIR, color and tint are mounted on a thin slide-out panel and proved ungainly to use.

**Ratings: sharpness**—excellent; **brightness**—excellent; **color accuracy**—superior; **operation of controls**—good.
**Approximate Retail Price: $899.95**  **Low Price: $764.96**

## BLACK-AND-WHITE PORTABLES
### Best Buy

**The GE XB2461SL** is an AC/DC 12-inch black-and-white portable. It does not have built-in batteries, but a DC power cord is provided for plugging into the cigarette lighter of a car or boat. A detachable sunshield improves contrast and reduces reflections under extremely high lighting conditions. Twin rotary channel selectors are mounted to the right of the screen, with the on/off switch below them. Volume, contrast and brightness controls are below the screen and easy to reach. Hold controls, however, are on the back. The set is compact and light. A recessed carrying handle in the back of the cabinet makes it very easy to lift and move with one hand. The chassis is 100 percent solid state for reliability and low power consumption. Warranty protection covers labor for 90 days and parts for one year. The GE XB2461SL has excellent contrast. At the same time, the overall picture is bright and sharp, which is particularly important for outdoor viewing. There is a noticeable but not obtrusive amount of geometric distortion present in the set's picture. Horizontal straight lines appear bowed upward slightly in the bottom half of the picture. The volume, contrast and brightness controls are a bit rough and the knobs are small, but this does not seriously interfere with their use. All controls (except the seldom-used hold controls) are conveniently located and clearly labeled.

**Ratings: sharpness**—excellent; **brightness**—excellent; **contrast**—excellent; **operation of controls**—very good.
**Approximate Retail Price: $129.95**  **Low Price: $116.96**

### Also Recommended

**The Magnavox 5320** is a 12-inch set that can be used either as an in-home set operating on standard household current, or as a portable using an optional battery pack or adaptor cord. The cord allows the set to be plugged into a car or boat cigarette lighter for 12-volt operation. It has a detachable sun screen, and telescoping

*Prices are accurate at time of printing; subject to manufacturer's change.*

VHF and loop UHF antennas. It comes with standard 13-position VHF dial and 70-position UHF channel tuner. Channel tuner controls, plus a combination on/off and volume control, are located on the front panel; contrast and brightness controls and an earphone jack are mounted on the right side. The chassis is all solid-state, with "instant-on" picture and sound. Warranty coverage is 90 days on parts and labor, one year on the picture tube. Model 5320 delivers a sharp, clear picture with good brightness and strong contrast. An important quality of this set is the wide range built into both brightness and contrast controls. This model has contrast and brightness to spare. Unlike other sun screens, the one provided with the 5320 is molded to fit completely around the outer frame of the picture tube enclosure and around the speaker grille in the lower right corner of the set. Controls are easy to use, although side-mounted brightness and contrast are slightly unwieldy.

**Ratings: sharpness**—excellent; **brightness**—excellent; **contrast**—excellent; **operation of controls**—very good.
**Approximate Retail Price: $129.95**   **Low Price: $110.46**

**Sony's TV-116** can be used indoors or outdoors with an optional rechargeable battery pack that operates for up to four hours on one charge. It has built-in VHF telescopic antenna and removable UHF loop antenna, standard 13-position VHF and 70-position UHF channel tuners, and is housed in a black cabinet with metallic gray trim. It also features a glare-proof sun screen and comes with an earphone. The chassis is all solid-state. A car antenna connector permits the viewer to watch TV while traveling, using the car's radio antenna. The 12-inch TV-116 delivers a crisp, clear picture with a high level of contrast. The brightness control has enough built-in range to produce a very bright picture, even in a brightly lighted room. The only drawback is the permanently fixed "glare-free" sun screen, which serves to mute both contrast and brightness slightly when the set is viewed indoors. A removable screen would give the viewer wider latitude when adjusting the set for either in-home or portable use. Controls are convenient to use, with UHF and VHF channel selectors spaced far enough apart for easy access. Other controls, including brightness and contrast, are mounted on the right side of the set, and can easily be manipulated as the viewer monitors the screen. Sony's side-mounted controls are more conveniently positioned than those on most other black-and-white portables.

**Ratings: sharpness**—excellent; **brightness**—excellent; **contrast**—excellent; **operation of controls**—very good.
**Approximate Retail Price: $159.95**   **Low Price: $135.95**
*Prices are accurate at time of printing; subject to manufacturer's change.*

# Television Prices

## General Electric

### BLACK & WHITE PORTABLE MODELS

| Model | Description | Retail Price | Low Price |
|---|---|---|---|
| XB411SY /TC/VY | 12 inch. | $104.95 | $94.46 |
| XB2440SY | 12 inch. | 114.95 | 103.46 |
| XB2518WD | 12 inch. | 109.95 | 98.96 |
| XB2519WD | 12 inch. | 114.95 | 103.46 |
| XB2441BK | 12 inch, AC/DC. | 119.95 | 107.96 |
| XB2461SL | 12 inch, AC/DC. | 129.95 | 116.96 |
| XB3161BK | 15 inch. | 124.95 | 112.46 |
| XB3163VY | 15 inch. | 129.95 | 116.96 |
| XB3343WD | 15 inch. | 134.95 | 121.46 |
| XB3344CO | 15 inch. | 139.95 | 125.96 |
| XA4221RW | 19 inch. | 154.95 | 131.71 |
| XA4322WD | 19 inch. | 159.95 | 135.96 |
| XA4226WD | 19 inch. | 169.95 | 144.46 |
| XA4228WD | 19 inch. | 174.95 | 148.71 |

### COLOR PORTABLE MODELS

| Model | Description | Retail Price | Low Price |
|---|---|---|---|
| AA5322SY /TC/WH | 10 inch. | $269.95 | $229.46 |
| AA5330WD | 10 inch. | 279.95 | 237.96 |
| AA5602WH | 13 inch. | 339.95 | 288.96 |
| AA5606WD | 13 inch. | 349.95 | 297.46 |
| AA5610WD | 13 inch. | 359.95 | 305.96 |
| YA6334WD | 17 inch. | 379.95 | 322.96 |
| YA6340WD | 17 inch. | 389.95 | 331.46 |
| YA7364WD | 19 inch. | 409.95 | 348.46 |
| YA7366WD | 19 inch. | 419.95 | 356.96 |
| YA7368WD | 19 inch. | 429.95 | 365.46 |

*Prices are accurate at time of printing; subject to manufacturer's change.*

|  |  | Retail Price | Low Price |
|---|---|---|---|
| YC7530WD | 19 inch. | $449.95 | $382.46 |
| YC7702WD | 19 inch. | 449.95 | 382.46 |
| YC7704WD | 19 inch. | 449.95 | 382.46 |
| YC7706MD | 19 inch. | 449.95 | 382.46 |
| YC7720WD | 19 inch. | 629.95 | 535.46 |
| YC7726MD | 19 inch. | 629.95 | 535.46 |

### COLOR TABLE MODEL
| | | | |
|---|---|---|---|
| YM9402WD | 25 inch. | $599.95 | $509.96 |

### COLOR CONSOLE MODELS
| | | | |
|---|---|---|---|
| YM9408WD | 25 inch. | $669.95 | $569.46 |
| YM9410WD | 25 inch. | 669.96 | 569.47 |
| YM9412AP | 25 inch. | 669.95 | 569.46 |
| YM9412MP | 25 inch. | 669.96 | 569.47 |
| YM9414PN | 25 inch. | 669.95 | 569.46 |
| YM9414DS | 25 inch. | 669.95 | 569.46 |
| YM9424PC | 25 inch. | 719.95 | 611.96 |
| YM9425CO | 25 inch. | 719.95 | 611.96 |
| YM9426LP | 25 inch. | 719.95 | 611.96 |
| YM9428PN | 25 inch. | 719.95 | 611.96 |
| YM9429MO | 25 inch. | 719.95 | 611.96 |
| YM9432MP | 25 inch. | 759.95 | 645.96 |
| YM9433PC | 25 inch. | 759.95 | 645.96 |
| YM9444PN | 25 inch. | 789.95 | 671.46 |
| YM9445MD /LP | 25 inch. | 789.95 | 671.46 |
| YM9472MP | 25 inch. | 899.95 | 764.96 |
| YM9473PC | 25 inch. | 899.95 | 764.96 |
| YM9474PN | 25 inch. | 929.95 | 790.46 |
| YM9475MD | 25 inch. | 929.95 | 790.46 |
| YM9476LP | 25 inch. | 929.95 | 790.46 |
| YM9480MO | 25 inch. | 929.95 | 790.46 |

# Magnavox

### BLACK & WHITE MODELS
| | | |
|---|---|---|
| BG5220-WH | $119.95 | $101.96 |
| BH5300-BR | 109.95 | 93.46 |
| BH5310-WA | 124.95 | 106.21 |
| BG5320-WA | 129.95 | 110.46 |
| BH5145-WA | 189.95 | 161.46 |
| BH5152-WA | 199.95 | 169.96 |

*Prices are accurate at time of printing; subject to manufacturer's change.*

| COLOR PORTABLE MODELS | Retail Price | Low Price |
|---|---|---|
| BH8580-WA | $369.95 | $314.46 |
| BH4050-BL/WH | 379.95 | 322.96 |
| BH4150-WA | 399.95 | 339.96 |
| BH4310-WA | 419.95 | 356.96 |
| BH4326-WA | 439.95 | 373.96 |
| BH4332-WA | 479.95 | 407.96 |
| RH4345-WA | 649.95 | 522.46 |

| COLOR TABLE MODELS | | |
|---|---|---|
| BG4305-WA Odyssey | $479.95 | $407.96 |
| BH4307-WA Odyssey | 529.95 | 450.46 |
| BH4464-PN | 539.95 | 458.96 |
| BH4466-PE | 539.95 | 458.96 |
| RH4471-WA Star System | 779.95 | 662.96 |
| RH4475-PN Star System | 799.95 | 679.96 |
| RH4477-PE Star System | 799.95 | 679.96 |

| COLOR CONSOLE MODELS | | |
|---|---|---|
| BH4512-WA | $669.96 | $569.47 |
| BH4524-MA | 739.95 | 628.96 |
| BH4526-PE | 739.95 | 628.96 |
| BH4540-WH/PE | 749.95 | 637.46 |
| BH4544-MA | 749.95 | 637.46 |
| BH4546-PE | 749.95 | 637.46 |
| BH4574-PN | 869.95 | 739.46 |
| BH4654-MA/PN | 779.95 | 662.96 |
| BH4656-PE | 779.95 | 662.96 |
| BH4640-WA | 899.00 | 764.15 |
| BH4660-PE | 929.00 | 789.65 |
| BH4662-WA | 929.00 | 789.65 |
| BH4664-PN | 929.00 | 789.65 |
| BH4666-PE | 929.00 | 789.65 |
| BH4668-FR | 929.00 | 789.65 |
| BH4668-WT | 999.00 | 849.15 |
| BH4674-MA | 999.00 | 849.15 |
| BH4676-PE | 999.00 | 849.15 |
| BH4688-PE | 1099.00 | 934.15 |
| BH4688-WT | 1150.00 | 977.50 |
| RG9000 Remote Unit | 89.95 | 76.46 |
| RH4811-WA Star System | 995.00 | 845.75 |
| RH4841-WA Star System | 1150.00 | 977.50 |
| RH4845-MA Star System | 1150.00 | 977.50 |
| RH4847-PE Star System | 1150.00 | 977.50 |
| RH4875-PN Star System | 1395.00 | 1185.75 |
| RH4899-PE Star System | 1395.00 | 1185.75 |
| BG4926-PE Stereo Theatre | 1150.00 | 977.50 |
| RG4961-PE/WT Stereo Theatre | 1895.00 | 1610.75 |

*Prices are accurate at time of printing; subject to manufacturer's change.*

|  | Retail Price | Low Price |
|---|---|---|
| RG4967-PE Stereo Theatre | $1895.00 | $1610.75 |
| RG4997-PE Stereo Theatre | 2495.00 | 2120.75 |

## ODYSSEY MODELS

|  | Retail Price | Low Price |
|---|---|---|
| BG7500 | $39.95 | $33.96 |
| BG7516 | 49.95 | 42.46 |
| BG7520 | 64.95 | 55.21 |
| BG7508 | 49.95 | 42.46 |
| BH7510 | 39.95 | 33.96 |
| BH7511 | 59.95 | 50.96 |
| BH7530 | 99.95 | 84.96 |

## VIDEO ACCESSORIES

|  | Retail Price | Low Price |
|---|---|---|
| BH5924-PN | $49.95 | $42.46 |
| BG5926-PE | 49.95 | 42.46 |
| BG5870-WA | 44.95 | 38.21 |
| BF5855-CR | 24.95 | 21.21 |
| BG5860-WA | 34.95 | 29.71 |
| BF5865-WA | 39.95 | 33.96 |
| BG5765-BL | 19.95 | 16.96 |

# Panasonic

## SOLID-STATE COLOR PORTABLES

| Model | Size | Retail Price | Low Price |
|---|---|---|---|
| CT-117 | 10 inch | $309.95 | $260.96 |
| CT-216A | 12 inch | 319.95 | 269.96 |
| CT-316 | 13 inch | 359.95 | 305.96 |
| CT517 | 15 inch | 389.95 | 332.96 |
| CT-527 | 15 inch | 469.95 | 404.96 |
| CT-727 | 17 inch | 489.95 | 422.96 |
| CT-906 | 19 inch | — | — |
| CT-917 | 19 inch | 439.95 | 377.96 |
| CT-926 | 19 inch | 479.95 | 413.96 |
| CT-947 | 19 inch ColorPilot | 519.95 | 449.96 |
| CT-946 | 19 inch | — | — |
| CT-976 | 19 inch |  |  |
| CT-977 | 19 inch | 579.95 | 503.96 |

## SOLID-STATE COLOR CONSOLE MODELS

| Model | Size | Retail Price | Low Price |
|---|---|---|---|
| CT-2526 | 25 inch | $659.95 | $593.96 |
| CT-2536 | 25 inch | 679.95 | 611.96 |
| CT-2517 | 25 inch ColorPilot | 639.95 | 575.96 |
| CT-2527 | 25 inch ColorPilot | 659.95 | 593.96 |
| CT-2537 | 25 inch ColorPilot | 689.95 | 620.96 |

*Prices are accurate at time of printing; subject to manufacturer's change.*

|         |                            | Retail Price | Low Price |
|---------|----------------------------|-------------:|----------:|
| CT-2547 | 25 inch ColorPilot         | $689.95      | $620.96   |
| CT-2557 | 25 inch ColorPilot         | 749.95       | 674.96    |
| CT-2577 | 25 inch ColorPilot, Remote | 779.95       | 701.96    |
| CT-2587 | 25 inch ColorPilot, Remote | 799.95       | 719.96    |

### SOLID-STATE BLACK & WHITE PORTABLES

| Model    | Size     | Retail Price | Low Price |
|----------|----------|-------------:|----------:|
| TR-515S  | 5 inch   | $154.95      | $130.46   |
| TR-555   | 5 inch   | 159.95       | 134.96    |
| TR-535   | 5 inch   | 209.95       | 179.96    |
| TR-707   | 7 inch   | 159.95       | 134.96    |
| TR-749   | 9 inch   | 109.95       | 89.96     |
| TR-759   | 9 inch   | 129.95       | 107.96    |
| TR-739   | 9 inch   | 179.95       | 152.96    |
| TR-822   | 12 inch  | —            | —         |
| TR-832   | 12 inch  | 129.95       | 107.96    |
| TR-862   | 12 inch  | 129.95       | 107.96    |
| TR-882   | 12 inch  | 139.95       | 116.96    |
| TR-542U  | 12 inch  | 139.95       | 116.96    |
| TR-233   | 13 inch  | 139.95       | 116.96    |
| TR-376   | 16 inch  | 154.95       | 130.46    |
| TR-386   | 16 inch  | 154.95       | 130.46    |
| TR-659   | 19 inch  | 159.95       | 134.96    |
| TR-679   | 19 inch  | 179.95       | 152.96    |

# Quasar

### SMALL SCREEN COLOR PORTABLE MODELS

| Model     | Retail Price | Low Price |
|-----------|-------------:|----------:|
| WP3402NN  | $309.95      | $278.96   |
| WP3420PH  | 319.95       | 987.96    |
| WP3404NW  | 309.95       | 278.96    |
| WP3422PW  | 329.95       | 296.96    |
| WP3832PW  | 349.95       | 314.96    |
| WP4252PW  | 369.95       | 332.96    |

### COLOR TABLE MODEL (19")

| Model     | Retail Price | Low Price |
|-----------|-------------:|----------:|
| WT5920PZ  | $429.95      | $386.96   |
| WT5921PW  | 439.95       | 395.96    |
| WT5922PW  | 449.95       | 404.96    |
| WT5942PW  | 489.95       | 440.96    |
| WT5945PW  | 519.95       | 467.96    |
| TT5947PW  | 599.95       | 539.96    |
| WT5982PW  | 549.95       | 494.96    |
| TT5988PW  | 669.95       | 602.96    |
| WT9400PW  | 609.95       | 548.96    |

*Prices are accurate at time of printing; subject to manufacturer's change.*

| DYNACOLOR CONSOLE MODELS | Retail Price | Low Price |
|---|---|---|
| WU9410PW | $639.95 | $575.96 |
| WU9420PW | 669.95 | 602.96 |
| WU9423PK/24PS/28PP | 699.95 | 629.96 |

### DYNACOLOR CONSOLES COMPU-MATIC/AUDIO SPECTRUM

| | | |
|---|---|---|
| WL9419PP | $699.95 | $629.96 |
| WL9429PP | 749.95 | 674.96 |
| WL9469PP | 799.95 | 719.96 |
| WU9462PP/3PK/4PS/5PD/8PP | 749.95 | 674.96 |
| WL9680PW/3PK/4PS | 849.95 | 764.96 |

### REMOTE MODELS

| | | |
|---|---|---|
| TT9800PW | $719.95 | $647.96 |
| TU9820PW | 789.95 | 710.96 |
| TU9824PS/28PP | 819.95 | 737.96 |
| TL9819PP | 839.95 | 755.96 |
| TL9880PW/3PK/4PS | 925.00 | 832.50 |

# RCA

### COLOR PORTABLES

| | | | |
|---|---|---|---|
| EB353M | 15 inch XL100, Jaguar Brown | $349.95 | $306.90 |
| EB393T | 17 inch XL100, Cam Tan & Char. Bronze | 379.95 | 336.55 |
| EB395W | 17 inch XL100, Walnut & Char. Bronze | 399.95 | 349.75 |
| EB398WR | 17 inch XL100 Remote Control, Walnut & Char. Bronze | 469.95 | 408.25 |

### COLOR TABLE MODELS

| | | | |
|---|---|---|---|
| FB443M | 19 inch XL100, Brown | $409.95 | $370.70 |
| FB443W | 19 inch XL100, Walnut | 429.95 | 382.75 |
| FB450W | 19 inch XL100 Single Knob Tuning, Walnut | 459.95 | 399.75 |
| FB452F | 19 inch XL100 Single Knob Tuning, Fruitwood | 459.95 | 399.75 |
| FX466S | 19 inch Colortrak, Sandstone | 439.95 | 379.50 |
| FB485W | 19 inch Colortrak, Walnut | 459.95 | 399.75 |
| FB493W | 19 inch Colortrak Single Knob Tuning, Walnut | 529.95 | 448.50 |
| FB496F | 19 inch Colortrak Single Knob Tuning, Fruitwood | 549.95 | 458.75 |
| FB497S | 19 inch Colortrak Single Knob Tuning, Silver | 529.95 | 448.50 |
| FB497W | 19 inch Colortrak Single Knob Tuning, Walnut | 549.95 | 458.50 |
| FB488WR | 19 inch Colortrak Remote Control, Walnut | 589.95 | 517.50 |
| FB498WDA | 19 inch Colortrak Remote Control, Walnut | 729.95 | 626.75 |
| FA505W | 21 inch XL100, Walnut Vinyl | 479.95 | 445.65 |
| FB528W | 25 inch Colortrak, Walnut Vinyl | 699.95 | 619.85 |
| FB530WR | 25 inch Colortrak Remote Control, Walnut Vinyl | 779.95 | 688.85 |

*Prices are accurate at time of printing; subject to manufacturer's change.*

## COLOR CONSOLES

| | | Retail Price | Low Price |
|---|---|---|---|
| GB682W | 25 inch XL100, Walnut | $599.95 | $531.30 |
| GB684L | 25 inch XL100, Maple | 649.95 | 558.90 |
| GB688S | 25 inch XL100, Pecan | 649.95 | 558.90 |
| GB744H | 25 inch XL100, Single Knob Tuning, Pine | 699.95 | 603.75 |
| GB744L | 25 inch XL100, Single Knob Tuning, Maple | 699.95 | 603.75 |
| GB748S | 25 inch XL100, Single Knob Tuning, Pecan | 699.95 | 603.75 |
| GB702S | 25 inch Colortrak Single Knob Tuning, Pecan Vinyl | 729.95 | 646.85 |
| GB702W | 25 inch Colortrak Single Knob Tuning, Walnut Vinyl | 729.95 | 646.85 |
| GB704L | 25 inch Colortrak Single Knob Tuning, Maple | 789.95 | 684.80 |
| GB705H | 25 inch Colortrak Single Knob Tuning, Pine | 789.95 | 684.80 |
| GB708S | 25 inch Colortrak Single Knob Tuning, Pecan | 789.95 | 684.80 |
| GB730A | 25 inch Colortrack Single Knob Tuning, Rosewood | 875.00 | 752.40 |
| GB733C | 25 inch Colortrack Single Knob Tuning, Cherry | 875.00 | 752.40 |
| GB734L | 25 inch Colortrak Single Knob Tuning, Maple | 875.00 | 752.40 |
| GB735H | 25 inch Colortrak Single Knob Tuning, Pine | 875.00 | 752.40 |
| GB736P | 25 inch Colortrak Single Knob Tuning, Oak | 875.00 | 752.40 |
| GB738S | 25 inch Colortrak Single Knob Tuning, Pecan | 875.00 | 752.40 |
| GB720SR | 25 inch Remote Control Colortrak, Pecan | 879.95 | 796.80 |
| GB724LR | 25 inch Remote Control Colortrak, Maple | 879.95 | 796.80 |
| GB725HR | 25 inch Remote Control Colortrak, Pine | 879.95 | 796.80 |
| GB728SR | 25 inch Remote Control Colortrak, Pecan | 879.95 | 796.80 |
| GB830S | 25 inch Colortrak Pushbutton Tuning, Pecan | 1050.95 | 862.50 |
| GB835H | 25 inch Colortrak Pushbutton Tuning, Pine | 1050.95 | 862.50 |
| GB836S | 25 inch Colortrak Pushbutton Tuning, Pecan | 1050.95 | 862.50 |
| GB838S | 25 inch Colortrak Pushbutton Tuning, Pecan | 1050.95 | 862.50 |
| GB840P | 25 inch Colortrak Pushbutton Tuning, Pecan | 1050.95 | 862.50 |
| GB935HDA | 25 inch Colortrak Control Center, Pine | 1250.00 | 980.00 |
| GB936SDA | 25 inch Colortrak Control Center, Pecan | 1250.00 | 980.00 |
| GB938SDA | 25 inch Colortrak Control Center, Pecan | 1250.00 | 980.00 |
| GB940PDA | 25 inch Colortrak Control Center, Pecan | 1250.00 | 980.00 |
| GB940SDA | 25 inch Colortrak Control Center, Silver | 1250.00 | 980.00 |
| GB814L | 25 inch Colortrack Single Knob Tuning, Maple | 925.00 | 764.75 |
| GB815H | 25 inch Colortrack Single Knob Tuning, Pine | 925.00 | 764.75 |
| GB818S | 25 inch Colortrack Single Knob Tuning, Pecan | 925.00 | 764.75 |

## BLACK & WHITE PORTABLES

| | | | |
|---|---|---|---|
| AB095A | 9 inch AC/DC (Battery Ready) Olympic Red | $129.95 | $109.15 |
| AB095S | 9 inch AC/DC (Battery Ready) Frost Silver | 129.95 | 109.15 |
| AB095Y | 9 inch AC/DC (Battery Ready) Fog White | 129.95 | 109.15 |
| AB097A | 9 inch AC/DC (Battery Included) Olympic Red | 169.95 | 141.70 |
| AB097S | 9 inch AC/DC (Battery Included) Frost Silver | 169.95 | 141.70 |
| AB097Y | 9 inch AC/DC (Battery Included) Fog White | 169.95 | 141.70 |
| AB120S | 12 inch AC Only, Diamond Silver | 99.95 | 87.50 |

*Prices are accurate at time of printing; subject to manufacturer's change.*

|          |                                          | Retail Price | Low Price |
|----------|------------------------------------------|--------------|-----------|
| AB120W   | 12 inch AC Only, Walnut Grain            | $ 99.95      | $ 87.50   |
| AB121W   | 12 inch AC Only, Walnut Grain            | 109.95       | 94.50     |
| AB123W   | 12 inch AC Only, Walnut Grain            | 119.95       | 99.95     |
| AB124N   | 12 inch AC/DC (Battery Ready) Chrome Yellow | 149.95    | 129.75    |
| AB124S   | 12 inch AC/DC (Battery Ready) Frost Silver | 149.95     | 129.75    |
| AB124Y   | 12 inch AC/DC (Battery Ready) Fog White  | 149.95       | 129.75    |
| AB127Y   | 12 inch AC/DC (Battery Included) Fog White | 189.95     | 163.90    |
| AB161W   | 16 inch, Walnut Grain                    | 139.95       | 119.10    |
| AB162W   | 16 inch, Walnut Grain                    | 149.95       | 124.95    |
| AB191S   | 19 inch, Silver and Black                | 159.95       | 136.50    |
| AB192W   | 19 inch, Walnut Grain                    | 169.95       | 141.75    |
| AB193S   | 19 inch, Frost Silver w/Stand            | 169.95       | 142.80    |

# Sony

**MODELS**

| KV-5100  | $459.95 | $390.95 |
|----------|---------|---------|
| KV-8000  | 479.95  | 407.95  |
| KV-1204A | 399.95  | 339.95  |
| KV-1215  | 419.95  | 356.95  |
| KV-1512  | 459.95  | 390.95  |
| KV-1541R | 529.95  | 450.45  |
| KV-1711D | 519.95  | 441.95  |
| KV-1712D | 539.95  | 458.95  |
| KV-1724  | 539.95  | 458.95  |
| KV-1741R | 619.95  | 526.95  |
| KV-1910D | 579.95  | 492.95  |
| KV-1921  | 599.95  | 509.95  |
| KV-1941R | 699.95  | 594.95  |
| KV-2101  | 719.95  | 611.95  |
| KV-2141R | 819.95  | 696.95  |
| TV-520   | 139.95  | 118.95  |
| TV-780   | 144.95  | 123.20  |
| TV-770   | 154.95  | 131.70  |
| TV-970   | 149.95  | 127.45  |
| TV-116   | 159.95  | 135.95  |
| TV-131   | 159.95  | 135.95  |

# Sylvania

**COLOR PORTABLE MODELS**

| CA71118N | 13 inch, Brown Cab | $329.95 | $280.46 |
|----------|--------------------|---------|---------|

*Prices are accurate at time of printing; subject to manufacturer's change.*

| | | Retail Price | Low Price |
|---|---|---|---|
| CA7112WH | 13 inch, White Cab | $ 329.95 | $ 280.46 |
| CA7115W | 13 inch GT-Matic | 349.95 | 297.46 |
| CC7154W | 17 inch GT-Matic | 399.95 | 339.96 |
| CX7163W | 19 inch GT-Matic | 399.95 | 339.96 |
| CX7164W | 19 inch GT-Matic | 429.95 | 365.46 |
| CX7165W | 19 inch GT-Matic | 469.95 | 399.46 |
| CX7167WR | 19 inch GT-Matic | 539.95 | 458.96 |

## COLOR TABLE MODELS

| | | | |
|---|---|---|---|
| CX7172W | 19 inch Superset Walnut Cab | $499.95 | $424.96 |
| CX7174C | 19 inch Superset Cherry Cab | 499.95 | 424.96 |
| CX7176P | 19 inch Superset Pecan Cab | 499.95 | 424.96 |
| CX7178WR | 19 inch Superset | 579.95 | 492.96 |
| CL7203W | 25 inch GT-Matic | 599.95 | 509.96 |
| CL7305WR | 25 inch Superset | 699.95 | 594.96 |

## COLOR CONSOLE MODELS

| | | | |
|---|---|---|---|
| CL7271W | 25 inch Superset (Electronic Tuning), Walnut Cab | $699.95 | $594.96 |
| CL7273C | 25 inch Superset (Electronic Tuning), Cherry Cab | 699.95 | 594.96 |
| CL7273C | 25 inch Superset (Electronic Tuning), Pecan Cab | 699.95 | 594.96 |
| CL7274N | 25 inch Superset (Electronic Tuning), Pine Cab | 729.95 | 620.46 |
| CL7278P | 25 inch Superset (Electonic Tuning), Pecan Cab | 729.95 | 620.46 |
| CL7223K | 25 inch GT-Matic Maple Cab | 629.95 | 535.46 |
| CL7226P | 25 inch GT-Matic Pecan Cab | 629.95 | 535.46 |
| CL7227P | 25 inch GT-Matic | 649.95 | 552.46 |
| CL7231W | 25 inch GT-Matic Walnut Cab | 669.95 | 569.46 |
| CL7233K | 25 inch GT-Matic Maple Cab | 669.95 | 569.46 |
| CL7237P | 25 inch GT-Matic, Pecan Cab | 669.95 | 569.46 |
| CL7238P | 25 inch GT-Matic, Pecan Cab | 669.95 | 569.46 |
| CL7234N | 25 inch GT-Matic, Pine Cab | 679.95 | 577.96 |
| CL7381WR | 25 inch Superset, Walnut Cab | 779.95 | 662.96 |
| CL7383CR | 25 inch Superset, Cherry Cab | 779.95 | 662.96 |
| CL7384NR | 25 inch Superset, Pine Cab | 779.95 | 662.96 |
| CL7386PR | 25 inch Superset, Pecan Cab | 779.95 | 662.96 |
| CL7388PR | 25 inch Superset, Pecan Cab | 779.95 | 662.96 |
| CL7436P | 25 inch Superset/Dig. Tun., Pecan Cab | 799.95 | 662.96 |
| CL7434N | 25 inch Superset/Dig. Tun., Pine Cab | 819.95 | 696.96 |
| CL7437P | 25 inch Superset/Dig. Tun., Pecan Cab | 819.95 | 696.96 |
| CL7438P | 25 inch Superset/Dig. Tun., Pecan Cab | 819.95 | 696.96 |
| CL7476P | 25 inch H.E.C. | 1195.00 | 1015.78 |
| CL7586PR | 25 inch H.E.C. Superset | 1695.00 | 1440.75 |

*Prices are accurate at time of printing; subject to manufacturer's change.*

|  |  | Retail Price | Low Price |
|---|---|---|---|
| **BLACK AND WHITE PORTABLE MODELS** | | | |
| MT6026GY | 9 inch | $129.95 | $110.46 |
| MW6033WH | 12 inch | 99.95 | 84.96 |
| MW6042GN | 12 inch, Green Cab. | 104.95 | 89.21 |
| MW6043WH | 12 inch, White Cab. | 104.95 | 89.21 |
| MW6044YL | 12 inch, Yellow Cab. | 104.95 | 89.21 |
| MW7038W | 12 inch, Walnut Cab. | 109.95 | 93.46 |
| MU7062WH | 16 inch | 129.95 | 110.45 |
| MU7064W | 16 inch | 139.95 | 118.96 |
| MY7083WH | 19 inch | 149.95 | 127.46 |
| MY7088W | 19 inch | 159.95 | 135.96 |
| **BLACK AND WHITE TABLE MODELS** | | | |
| MZ6092W | 22 inch | $199.95 | $169.96 |
| **BLACK AND WHITE CONSOLE MODELS** | | | |
| MZ6095W | 22 inch | $239.95 | $203.96 |
| MZ6096K | 22 inch, Maple Cab. | 249.95 | 212.46 |
| MZ6097P | 22 inch, Pecan Cab. | 249.95 | 212.46 |

# Toshiba

|  |  | Retail Price | Low Price |
|---|---|---|---|
| **SOLID-STATE COLOR MODELS** | | | |
| C097 | 9 inch | $349.95 | $296.96 |
| C383 | 13 inch | 369.95 | 314.96 |
| C385 | 13 inch | 389.95 | 332.96 |
| C389 | 13 inch | 479.95 | 413.96 |
| C571 | 15 inch | 409.95 | 350.96 |
| C771 | 17 inch | 439.95 | 377.96 |
| C970 | 19 inch | 439.95 | 377.96 |
| C971 | 19 inch | 459.95 | 395.96 |
| C972 | 19 inch | 479.95 | 413.96 |
| C985 | 19 inch | 499.95 | 431.96 |
| C987 | 19 inch | 519.95 | 449.96 |
| C989 | 19 inch | 569.95 | 494.96 |

# Zenith

|  |  | Retail Price | Low Price |
|---|---|---|---|
| **SOLID-STATE COLOR PORTABLE MODELS** | | | |
| J1310C | 13 inch Steen | $348.88 | $316.80 |
| J1316W | 13 inch Hogarth | 379.95 | 333.30 |

*Prices are accurate at time of printing; subject to manufacturer's change.*

|  |  | Retail Price | Low Price |
|---|---|---|---|
| J1320W | 13 inch Matisse | $399.95 | $347.60 |
| J1720W | 17 inch Hals | 379.95 | 352.00 |
| J1740W | 17 inch Rubens | 429.95 | 378.40 |
| HT1782W | 17 inch Bimini | 429.95 | 378.40 |
| J1912W | 19 inch Manet | 398.88 | 363.00 |
| J1922W | 19 inch Deegan | 469.95 | 396.00 |
| J1928W | 19 inch Rowland | 479.95 | 403.70 |
| J1930W | 19 inch Prentiss | 499.95 | 418.00 |
| J1930P | 19 inch Prentiss | 499.95 | 418.00 |
| S1930W | 19 inch Allston | 519.95 | 417.95 |
| J1938P | 19 inch Bonnington | 529.95 | 437.80 |
| J1938W | 19 inch Bonnington | 529.95 | 437.80 |
| J1950W | 19 inch Ellipse III | 529.95 | 437.80 |
| HT1978W | 19 inch Sahara | 539.95 | 457.60 |

**SOLID-STATE COLOR TABLE MODELS**

|  |  |  |  |
|---|---|---|---|
| J2310W | 23 inch Monet | $598.88 | $528.00 |
| J2510W | 25 inch Romney | 679.95 | 590.95 |

**SOLID-STATE COLOR CONSOLE MODELS**

|  |  |  |  |
|---|---|---|---|
| S2316P | 23 inch Lido | $598.88 | $545.60 |
| J2320W | 23 inch Watteau | 619.95 | 545.60 |
| J2322E | 23 inch Braque | 649.95 | 572.00 |
| J2324DE | 23 inch Goya | 689.95 | 591.80 |
| J2324P | 23 inch Goya | 689.95 | 591.80 |
| J2326M | 23 inch Stuart | 699.95 | 600.60 |
| J2328PN | 23 inch Weber | 699.95 | 600.60 |
| J2330X | 23 inch Celebrity III | 725.00 | 622.00 |
| J2340P | 23 inch Veronese | 725.00 | 622.00 |
| HT2380P | 23 inch Northall | 689.95 | 589.60 |
| HT2382P | 23 inch Ravenna | 699.95 | 597.30 |
| J2518W | 25 inch Mondrian | 698.88 | 616.00 |
| J2522E | 25 inch Courbet | 749.95 | 643.50 |
| J2524M | 25 inch Trumbull | 759.95 | 652.30 |
| J2526DE | 25 inch Florentino | 759.95 | 652.30 |
| J2526P | 25 inch Florentino | 759.95 | 652.30 |
| J2528E | 25 inch Lawrence | 759.95 | 652.30 |
| J2530E | 25 inch Cezanne | 759.95 | 652.30 |
| J2534X | 25 inch Avante 300 | 799.95 | 677.60 |
| J2540X | 25 inch Panorama | 825.00 | 698.75 |
| J2542E | 25 inch Raeburn | 825.00 | 698.75 |
| J2544M | 25 inch Inness | 825.00 | 698.75 |
| J2546PN | 25 inch Abbey | 825.00 | 698.75 |
| J2548E | 25 inch Raphael | 825.00 | 698.75 |
| J2550P | 25 inch Renoir | 825.00 | 698.75 |
| HT2578E | 25 inch Ludlow | 829.95 | 694.10 |
| HT2580E | 25 inch Lockhart | 829.95 | 694.10 |
| HT2582M | 25 inch Arundel | 829.95 | 694.10 |
| HT2584P | 25 inch Livorno | 829.95 | 694.10 |

*Prices are accurate at time of printing; subject to manufacturer's change.*

|  |  | Retail Price | Low Price |
|---|---|---|---|
| **SPACE COMMAND COLOR PORTABLE MODELS** | | | |
| SJ1321W | 13 inch Kirchner | $439.95 | $392.15 |
| SJ1741W | 17 inch Holbein | 519.95 | 457.60 |
| SJ1939W | 19 inch Cole | 629.95 | 537.10 |
| SJ1951W | 19 inch Ellipse IV | 629.95 | 537.10 |
| **SPACE COMMAND COLOR TABLE MODEL** | | | |
| SJ2511W | 25 inch Lebrun | $779.95 | $680.35 |
| **SPACE COMMAND COLOR CONSOLE MODELS** | | | |
| SJ2323E | 23 inch Bonnard | $749.95 | $671.00 |
| SJ2325DE | 23 inch Murillo | 789.95 | 684.20 |
| SJ2325P | 23 inch Murillo | 789.95 | 684.20 |
| SJ2327M | 23 inch Sargent | 799.95 | 693.00 |
| SJ2331X | 23 inch Celebrity IV | 825.00 | 709.50 |
| SJ2523E | 25 inch Blake | 849.95 | 722.70 |
| SJ2525M | 25 inch Peale | 859.95 | 729.85 |
| SJ2527DE | 25 inch Vecchio | 859.95 | 729.85 |
| SJ2527P | 25 inch Vecchio | 859.95 | 729.85 |
| SJ2529E | 25 inch Rousseau | 859.95 | 729.85 |
| SJ2535X | 25 inch Avante 400 | 899.95 | 763.40 |
| SJ2541X | 25 inch Panorama VI | 925.00 | 774.15 |
| SJ2543E | 25 inch Reynolds | 925.00 | 774.15 |
| SJ2545M | 25 inch Bertram | 925.00 | 774.15 |
| SJ2549E | 25 inch Tintoretto | 925.00 | 774.15 |
| SJ2571P | 25 inch Bingham | 995.00 | 820.60 |
| SJ2575E | 25 inch El Greco | 995.00 | 820.60 |
| SHT2585P | 25 inch Segovia | 929.95 | 778.25 |
| **FM/AM STEREO-SOLID STATE SPACE COMMAND COLOR CONSOLE MODELS** | | | |
| SJ2597P | 25 inch Michelangelo | $1395.00 | $1045.00 |
| SJ2599P | 25 inch Vermeer | 1795.00 | 1375.00 |
| **SOLID-STATE BLACK & WHITE PORTABLE MODELS** | | | |
| J091L | 9 inch Sentry | $98.88 | $92.35 |
| J092V | 9 inch Jet Set II | 129.95 | 114.35 |
| J092X | 9 inch Jet Set II | 129.95 | 114.35 |
| J092Y | 9 inch Jet Set II | 129.95 | 114.35 |
| S099Y | 9 inch Rechargeable Battery Pack for Model J092 | 49.95 | 41.75 |
| J121Y | 12 inch Yeoman | 119.95 | 106.65 |
| J121F | 12 inch Yeoman | 119.95 | 106.65 |
| J121X | 12 inch Yeoman | 119.95 | 106.65 |
| J122P | 12 inch Nomad | 129.95 | 114.35 |
| J123W | 12 inch Voyager | 139.95 | 123.15 |
| J126W | 12 inch Headliner | 139.95 | 123.15 |
| JT128W | 12 inch Rambler | 129.95 | 114.35 |

*Prices are accurate at time of printing; subject to manufacturer's change.*

|         |                      | Retail Price | Low Price |
|---------|----------------------|-------------|-----------|
| J162C   | 16 inch Barrie       | 148.85      | 137.45    |
| J163W   | 16 inch Glasgow      | 159.95      | 146.25    |
| J192W   | 19 inch Dryden       | 159.95      | 146.25    |
| J193W   | 19 inch Ellison      | 159.95      | 146.25    |
| J194X   | 19 inch Linden       | 169.95      | 153.95    |
| JT198W  | 19 inch Kessler      | 169.95      | 153.95    |

### SOLID-STATE BLACK & WHITE TABLE MODEL
| J221W | 22 inch Prescott | $209.95 | $192.45 |

### SOLID-STATE BLACK & WHITE CONSOLE MODELS
| J222W | 22 inch Ridgeway   | $249.95 | $216.65 |
|-------|--------------------|---------|---------|
| J223P | 22 inch Pinoza     | 269.95  | 243.00  |
| H229M | 22 inch Georgetown | 269.95  | 243.00  |

### STANDS AND CARTS FOR BLACK & WHITE MODELS
| 2793 | 12 inch High Boy Roll About            | $16.95 | $10.95 |
|------|----------------------------------------|--------|--------|
| 2065 | 12 inch-16 inch Roll About-Full Top    | 17.95  | 10.95  |
| 2835 | 19 inch Walnut and Brass               | 17.95  | 10.95  |
| 1670 | 19 inch Walnut and Brass-Full Top      | 24.95  | 18.65  |

*Prices are accurate at time of printing; subject to manufacturer's change.*

---

# SPECIAL INFORMATION SERVICE

**A Bonus for Readers of this CONSUMER GUIDE®**

CONSUMER GUIDE® offers a special bonus to its readers who are interested in obtaining information as to where they can find the low prices on specific products listed in this guide. Simply fill out the form and mail. Include 25 cents for postage and handling.
**Please send me information on:**

Product _____ Model Number _____

Manufacturer _____

Your Name _____

Address _____

City _____ State _____ Zip Code ___

**CONSUMER GUIDE Magazine**
**3841 West Oakton, Skokie, Illinois 60076**

# 1978 Hi-Fi Components

IF YOU SHOP for high fidelity components in 1978, you will notice that prices for receivers, amplifiers, tuners or other elements of a stereo system are higher than they were in mid-1977. Many distributors of foreign-made audio products have already increased their suggested retail prices from 8 to 10 percent. Most of the increases can be blamed on the plunging value of the United States dollar abroad. In less than one year, the value of the dollar has plunged from a high of around 294 Japanese yen to around 265 yen. Since the greatest percentage of high fidelity equipment bought in the United States is now manufactured in Japan, local subsidiaries and distributors of major Japanese electronic equipment have had to raise their sales prices to audio dealers accordingly. And of course, such price increases are quickly passed on to the consumer.

There is one bright side to the stereo equipment buying picture, however. Stiffer and stiffer competition among audio dealers on the retail level has offset some of the price increases. According to the Federal Trade Commission there is no such thing as a "list price" for appliances, including stereo equipment. Dealers are perfectly free to charge "what the traffic will bear." This is governed by a variety of factors including supply and demand, local dealer competition, and availability of a product.

In the case of widely distributed stereo equipment manufactured by such firms as Pioneer, Kenwood, Sansui, Marantz, Teac and others, some dealers are willing to work on minimal margins (often as low as 5 to 10 percent). Product lines with somewhat restricted distribution are often sold at "full" dealer margins ranging from 30 percent and up.

The worst situation insofar as the discount-seeking consumer is concerned is the policy of certain stereo manufacturers to substitute a price-fixing system of their own for the now illegal fair-trade practices. These manufacturers no longer require written agreements with dealers. Instead, they exact verbal promises from merchants not to sell the products in question at discount prices. What happens to dealers who either break such promises or refuse to make them initially? These merchants then discover that the components are suddenly in "short supply," although the dealers who abide by the non-discounting promises have no difficulty in obtaining all that they can sell.

The result is that for several manufacturers "limited distribution" has become a viable alternative to fair trade. They do everything they can to limit the distribution of their goods to dealers who cooperate with their pricing policy, depriving consumers of the discounts available to smart shoppers. The consumer need not become a victim to this fair-trade system in disguise, however. We urge potential buyers of limited-distribution items to examine the situation carefully. If you plan to purchase an entire audio system, you should be able to find a dealer willing to discount a limited-distribution item as part of the total package. In such a transaction, he can cloak the discount in such a way that he will not suffer the "short supply" syndrome to which other discount dealers succumb at the hands of limited-distribution manufacturers. Of course, you can always try to substitute a discounted product of equal quality for the price-controlled component, but if you must own a limited-distribution item and you are not buying more than one piece of equipment, you will have to go to a cooperating dealer and pay the price which the manufacturer has set for his product.

One positive note with respect to pricing, though, comes about from the steady technological advances being made in audio as well as other electronic products. More and more integrated circuits are being used by manufacturers to replace discrete components and, with increased production and sales of these tiny devices, their costs have been plummeting downward. Consequently, even in the face of world-wide inflation and monetary problems in the United States, the cost of raw parts used in high fidelity equipment have either remained stable or dropped slightly.

## General Trends in High Fidelity

INTEREST ON THE part of the consumer continues to increase in so-called "high end" stereo products. These are generally manufactured by small companies (often U.S. based) whose dedication to sound reproduction perfection is often more of a governing factor than their interest in high-volume sales. As a result, the price range for components is wider than ever before. In the case of the so-called esoteric products, there can be a tremendous difference in price tags. You can buy a tuner for around $100 or you can spend more than $2000 for a tuner which uses sophisticated microprocessor devices to "program" favorite stations at the touch of a pushbutton or scan the dial electronically. Some sophisticated tuners analyze their own circuitry to pinpoint defective components.

Another important trend is the virtual disappearance of quadraphonic or four-channel sound equipment from retail audio shops around the country. Most four-channel enthusiasts have become completely disenchanted with quadraphonics. One factor which could create renewed interest in four-channel sound is the Federal Communication Commission's recent announcement that it is about to consider the question of discrete four-channel FM broadcasting. The commission has invited comments from the public and interested industry members regarding the need (or lack of it) for a four-channel broadcasting system. Almost at the same time, the FCC indicated that it plans to investigate the question of stereo AM broadcasting.

Up to now, stereo broadcasting has been possible only on the FM radio band. An industry committee has been field testing at least three systems whereby stereo could be transmitted over a single AM station with full compatibility. Listeners to mono AM sets with special circuitry and twin speakers would hear the same program stereophonically.

Now that FM radio dominates the airwaves in the United States, the AM broadcasters have shown interest in stereo AM and would, of course, like to be given this competitive edge. Of course, if a system is approved by the FCC in the near future, it will take the industry some time to produce the needed receiving equipment, both for broadcast and home reception use. While all manufacturers involved would like to "get the jump" on the rest of the industry, no one is in a position to second guess the FCC as to which of the proposed systems will get the nod. Since each system requires a different circuit, even limited production must be held in abeyance at this time.

### Add-ons Abound

WHILE MOST AUDIO enthusiasts continue to assemble a basic system consisting of a receiver (or a separate amplifier and tuner, or even a separate amplifier, preamplifier and tuner), a turntable system with cartridge, and a pair of speakers, seasoned listeners have been turning their attention to a growing assortment of signal processing devices. These devices include anything from a graphic equalizer (a more flexible tone-controlling system in which small segments of the frequency spectrum are adjusted by individual controls as opposed to the simple bass and treble controls found on most receivers or amplifiers), to dynamic range expanders (devices that make loud sounds louder and soft sounds quieter, thereby restoring more of the natural dynamic range than may have been compressed in the recording or broadcast process).

Another device which has been growing in popularity is the electronic reverberation or time-delay units (which provide a sense of spaciousness to reproduced sound). Linear compressor-expanders (or companders), which permit tape recordists to record the full dynamic range of music onto such limited storage media as cassette tapes and then allow playback of such recordings with their dynamic range intact, is still another new signal processing device. So are pop and click eliminators which actually blank out such record imperfections without altering musical content.

Many add-on devices are being manufactured in the United States, primarily by smaller companies. Apparently, the limited demand for such refinements, and the specialization required by their makers, is such that small companies can produce these innovative products more economically than the giant audio equipment manufacturers in the Orient or in Europe.

CONSUMER GUIDE Magazine suggests that for your first venture into the world of high fidelity components it is best to start out with a basic system, including electronic components (receiver or separates), a pair of speakers and a compatible turntable system. Wait to add electronic devices and accessories until after you come to understand your audio system, its fine points, and its features. Listening to music reproduced through a high quality component system helps to "educate your ears." As your listening tastes become keener, you may or may not find that one or more of the electronic accessories can add to enjoyment of your basic system.

Let's take a look at specific trends in each of the product categories which go to make up a complete system.

**Electronic Component Trends**

THE RACE TOWARDS higher and higher powered receivers continues unabated, and as a result has become something of an industry joke. Latest "winner" in the power race is Marantz, with its Model 2500 boasting 250 watts of continuous power per channel. In the opinion of CONSUMER GUIDE Magazine, the question of power in a receiver has gotten out of hand. The whole purpose of an all-in-one receiver is to provide all the electronics you need in a compact configuration. The newest high-powered units from Rotel, Marantz and others seem to have forgotten that objective. They are extremely heavy and cumbersome—hardly suitable for installation on a shelf—and contain front panel controls which take a while to understand and use.

Of course, there will always be people who will buy such units simply because they want the "most powerful" receiver available, but most users who require in excess of 200 watts per channel of audio power would probably be better off purchasing separate components. While there is theoretically no restriction on the maximum amount of power that can be provided by an all-in-one receiver unit, size and weight do become major considerations.

This is especially true when you consider that so many speaker manufacturers have turned their attention back to the production of speakers that have higher efficiency than the so-called "book shelf" designs of a few years ago. With this increase in efficiency comes less need for power. It is easier and less costly for a speaker manufacturer to double speaker efficiency than it is for a receiver or amplifier manufacturer to double available distortion-free power output; yet, the net effect of either change is the same.

What is of far greater interest is the trend exhibited by many manufacturers to provide full control flexibility even on moderately powered, moderately priced receivers. Years ago, the flexibility of a receiver was almost directly proportional to its rated power output and price. That is no longer true and it is now quite common to find a 20- or 30-watt-per-channel receiver equipped with two tape monitor circuits, variable crossover tone controls, and a full complement of low and high cut filters. In some cases, even midrange or presence tone controls are included. Indeed, these extras cost very little for the manufacturer to incorporate, yet they make the equipment more valuable, regardless of its power output level.

Yamaha seems to have come up with a new trend in specifying performance of their receiver and amplifier products. It is a procedure which CONSUMER GUIDE Magazine hopes will ultimately be emulated by the rest of the component industry. Yamaha has developed a new specification called NDCR (Noise and Distortion Clearance Range) to indicate the power range of a receiver or amplifier over which the combination of noise and distortion will remain below a given level (e.g., 0.1 percent, or -60 dB).

More important, NDCR is measured from the phono input stages all the way to the speaker output terminals, just as you would use the equipment in real life. This contrasts with the practice of providing only a distortion or a separate noise specification referenced to full output and with the volume control set at maximum (a condition rarely if ever encountered in actual use). The new specification, therefore, provides the prospective user with a more meaningful number by which to compare competing products.

More and more manufacturers of tuners and amplifiers are either incorporating the required 25 microsecond deemphasis circuits needed to properly receive Dolby FM programs or employing the complete Dolby circuitry plus the new deemphasis value. Broadcasting stations, however, have been slow to adopt the Dolby system and only a few in metropolitan regions regularly use this system. If there are no stations in your area using Dolby FM, do not pay extra to obtain this extra circuitry. You can always add it later when a station begins such broadcasts.

Important things to consider besides power when choosing your system's electronics (either in the form of a receiver or as separate components) include such things as: flexible tone control facilities, an adequate number of tape out and tape in connections (even more important, now, if you plan to add a signal processing device in addition to one or more tape decks), front panel controls that are easy to understand and use, good FM reception with high signal-to-noise specifications, and a noise-free phono section. Remember, the two most often used program sources will be FM radio and records; make certain that the electronic components you purchase can handle those signals properly.

**Turntable Trends**

MORE THAN A year ago, the industry was startled by the introduction of ADC/BSR's Accutrac 4000 turntable system. A direct-drive turntable, the 4000 comes complete with tone arm and special ADC cartridge which enables the user to "program" those bands on a given recording that he or she wishes to hear, in any preferred order and even by remote control, using a hand-held remote control box that resembles a small calculator. Audio enthusiasts predicted that it would only be a matter of time until ADC (or another firm) developed a multiple-play (record changer) machine with the same capability. Sure enough, the makers of the 4000 recently introduced Model Accutrac +6, a machine that actually can handle six records in sequence and permits the user to select (again by remote control) only chosen bands.

As far as less-dramatic turntables are concerned, the early rush to direct-drive turntable systems has been slowed down by the realization that not all direct-drive turntable systems are necessarily better than belt-driven systems. Many fine record players are now available, and determining which turntable to buy can only be resolved on the basis of performance specifications and convenience features rather than on the basis of drive method alone.

Audio equipment manufacturers currently dominating the multiple-play field are Dual (distributed by United Audio), Garrard, and BIC (British Industries Company). All companies have added worthwhile record players to excellent product lines in the past year. Garrard, which had suffered a severe setback in recent years, is making a comeback with a new line of products (such as their Model GT55) in which their older zero-tracking-error articulated tone arm has been refined, lightened in weight, and reduced in pivotal friction.

BIC's top model can now be operated by means of a remote control box which, though connected to the main system by a wire, permits cueing and all other turntable motions to be initiated from the comfort of your listening chair. Garrard is also expected to introduce its own electronic device in the near future, a device designed to eliminate annoying clicks and pops caused by scratched records. The device may even be incorporated right inside one or more models of BIC's turntables.

As far as single-play machines are concerned, Technics by Panasonic continues to dominate that field with their direct-drive models, though excellent single-play models with varying degrees of automation are available from Pioneer, Kenwood, Dual, Garrard, and many other well-known firms.

Fisher Radio, in an attempt to recapture its former top-ranked position in the audio industry, has introduced a turntable which employs a completely new type of drive system. The platter itself constitutes part of the motor and is equipped with a series of magnets which are attracted and repelled by the stationary portion of the motor below. Fisher designers claim improved uniformity of rotation and reduced wow and flutter for this approach, though Fisher's published specifications and CONSUMER GUIDE Magazine's test results indicate that this motor does not perform significantly better than more conventional record player motors.

**Cartridge Trends**

AS FAR AS CONSUMER GUIDE Magazine's audio researchers have been able to tell, there have been no major breakthroughs in cartridge designs in the past year. Instead, well-known manufacturers are pursuing painstaking refinements in cartridge designs which include efforts to reduce stylus assembly mass, stylus tracking ability at low downward tracking forces, and more uniform frequency response. Although moving magnet cartridges continue to dominate the field (and are the mainstay of such well-known firms as Shure, Pickering, Stanton, Audio-Technica, Empire, and AKG), some audiophiles have turned their attention to moving coil cartridges. These usually produce less signal output than the moving magnet types and often require a matching transformer or a pre-preamplifier before they can be connected to the ordinary phono inputs on a receiver or an integrated amplifier or preamplifier. Generally, however, the moving coil types offer lighter stylus assemblies and are able to track greater groove excursions because of the greater compliance which they exhibit.

Companies such as Stanton Magnetics have been capitalizing on recent research into stylus tip shapes (which they began during the frenzied rush to develop tips that would successfully trace the complex grooves contained in CD-4 discs). Although no new four-channel cartridges have been introduced in the past 12 months, newer stereo pickups introduced by Stanton and others owe their superior performance in part to the inclusion of more precisely ground and differently shaped tips. Next to loudspeakers, the cartridge is subject to more differences in sound quality than any other hi-fi component.

**Speaker System Trends**

AFTER YEARS OF dealing with loudspeaker system design as an

art rather than a science, speaker researchers have now set down definitive complex equations that govern the operation of a vented speaker enclosure, commonly called a bass-reflex system. In addition, manufacturers are now employing computers as a design tool for new speaker systems.

Some examples of computer-assisted speaker designs can be found in the Altec 19, produced by Altec-Lansing; Electro-Voice's series of Interface speakers (the latest being a small unit known as the Interface:B); and a series of speakers recently announced by Koss. All of these new designs employ the vented box principle and the result is greater efficiency than is usually obtained from sealed, acoustic-suspension (or air suspension) designs. Of course, traditional favorites are still selling well.

Increased interest is being shown in three-unit speaker arrays in which the two conventional speakers are augmented by a third sub-woofer unit which reproduces a mix of left and right channel lowest bass tones. Such low bass frequencies are considered to have no directionality of sound, so there is no problem when left and right bass are mixed together and reproduced through a common sub-woofer.

Small audio manufacturers are turning out such add-on sub-woofers, while larger companies such as JBL (James B. Lansing) have introduced complete three-speaker systems. JBL's Model L-212, for example, has a sub-woofer that is equipped with a self-contained power amplifier, while the side speakers of the array are driven by the regular receiver or amplifier. Because of the nondirectional nature of bass tones, the sub-woofer in the JBL system can be placed almost anywhere in the room without destroying the stereo effect. Since the sub-woofer, in the case of this particular system, handles only frequencies below 70 Hz, low-frequency demands made upon the two side-firing speaker enclosures are not as difficult to meet.

Although the JBL L-212 is hardly priced for mass consumption (it sells for around $1700 for all three speakers and the necessary sub-woofer amplifier and crossover network), CONSUMER GUIDE Magazine believes that other manufacturers will be following JBL's lead in the future.

Traditionally, American consumers have shown only mild interest in speakers designed and manufactured in Japan, though they seem quite favorably disposed to every other high fidelity component coming from that country. One Japanese company, however, seems to have overcome this problem. Technics by Panasonic recently introduced a series of phase-linear speakers in which all drivers (woofers, midrange, and tweeters) have been carefully positioned to retain proper phase relationships among sounds going from them to the listener. Whether due to this design feature (which many audio experts maintain is not significant) or because Technics has simply learned to produce the kind of sound balance that Americans prefer, the new Technics speakers are enjoying success along with the ones bearing American brand names.

Despite the fact that some manufacturers have begun to publish specifications regarding their products, speaker systems still remain the most difficult high fidelity component to judge, due to the great differences in coloration when they reproduce sound. Even auditioning of speakers at the stereo store can be deceptive, since a speaker system that sounds fine in the showroom may not prove to be satisfactory when it is in your own listening room. Some dealers will not permit you to purchase speakers on a trial basis, but there are still a few who continue to offer this service, usually offering credit towards the purchase of an alternate pair instead of a refund.

Besides making certain that a speaker's minimum power requirements and maximum power input limitations are compatible with the amplifier or receiver of your proposed system, about all you can do to select a proper speaker system pair is to listen to several types of speakers within your budget range. Audition one pair of speakers against another at equal loudness levels and choose the speakers you prefer by a process of elimination.

**Headphone Trends**

HEADPHONE LISTENING is private listening. With a headset you can listen to what you want, when you want, and as loud as you want—without disturbing anyone who might not wish to share the listening experience. By the same token, headphones block out most sounds, other than the program source, that you would normally hear. Environmental noises are minimized, although the degree to which noises are eliminated varies with the design of the headset. Some models are designed to provide a truly tight, close seal around the ears. Others do not hug the ears as snugly, and while they do block out most outside noises, they still permit the listener to hear loud or shrill sounds—such as the ringing of a telephone.

At one time, the low-frequency (bass response) capability of a typical headset was directly related to how snugly the unit fit around the ears—the closer, the more bass. Recent designs, however, provide full bass response without that closed-in ultratight feeling. The result is a more comfortable headset that can be worn for longer periods of time.

In addition to their appeal as private-listening devices, headphones can provide full fidelity stereo in situations where a pair of loudspeakers might—for reasons of space or budget—be out of the question. The modern headset plugs directly into a receptacle on the typical stereo receiver, creating a complete listening setup in a college dorm room, small den, crowded office, or anywhere else that large speaker systems would pose problems.

Beyond these advantages, headphones offer a degree of "intimacy" which pleases many enthusiasts while it displeases a good number of other serious listeners. Headphones bring the program material "closer" to the music lover, allowing certain details to be heard more definitively. At the same time, of course, the listener may hear certain deficiencies either in the program material or in the stereo system or in both. In fact, headphones have been likened to an "audio stethoscope," and many record critics and audio technicians use headsets in just that way—to focus on miniscule details that may be difficult to detect when a program source is reproduced through speakers in a normal listening room.

Headphones also highlight stereo channel separation. On the negative side, this capability makes both excessive and inadequate stereo separation far more noticeable. On the positive side, the absence of an acoustic mix (such as occurs when listening to standard loudspeakers) dramatizes whatever channel separation there is.

A headphone listener who switches from mono to stereo while wearing a headset experiences a truly dramatic sensation. Music played in the mono mode seems to be inside the listener's head. A flick of the switch to the stereo mode causes the music to spread out, taking on a broad aural panorama. The music remains inside the head, but the sound seems to be coming from far beyond the headset. This little trick effectively demonstrates the magic of stereo headphones.

Like speakers, headphones are best judged according to how they sound. Such a judgment involves an evaluation of frequency response, peaks and dips across the audio range, and distortion.

Criteria of good headphone performance include reasonably full bass with good tonal definition as well as smoothness from the midrange into the extreme highs. In essence, the careful headphone shopper listens for the same virtues in headphones as he or she would expect to hear from quality speakers. Within the response limits of a given headset, the sound should be natural, with no false emphasis on one tonal range or another. Be wary of the headset, for instance, that makes all bass tones sound like one-note thumping or, at the other extreme, makes all highs sound shrill or overly bright.

The sensitivity of a headset may also be of some importance. Generally, it takes relatively little signal energy to make a set of headphones respond, but a unit that is fairly inefficient might demand so much of the driving amplifier that an otherwise favorable signal-to-noise ratio would be significantly reduced.

In addition to the quality of the sound it provides, a headset must also be judged in terms of its wearing comfort. The weight, the fit, the sense of ease with which the unit can be worn for long durations all should be considered. Adjustable headbands are quite common, but the prospective buyer should ascertain that the particular headset can be adjusted to suit his or her personal wearing comfort. Cable lengths can also have a bearing on comfort, since the length of the cable (usually from six to 12 feet) determines just how far the listener can roam from the receiver or amplifier while wearing the headset.

**Components Vs. Compacts**

SINCE THERE ARE no federal regulations governing the use of the words "high fidelity," that term can and often has been applied to everything from inexpensive compact sets to audio components costing several thousands of dollars. After all, "high" and "fidelity" are relative terms. Fidelity is defined as faithfulness, accuracy, and exactness, but the key questions one must ask are: how faithful, how accurate, how exact?

In format, there is actually little difference between a compact and a component hi-fi system. In the case of the compact, the consumer is relieved of all component-matching decisions. The manufacturer chooses the electronic apparatus (usually an all-in-one integrated receiver), the record player, and the speakers —all of which then carry a single brand name and are sold as a package. More often than not, the record player is mounted in the same cabinet as the receiver, and frequently the receiver includes an eight-track cartridge tape player or, in some cases, a cassette tape record/play unit. A complete compact system can retail anywhere from $100 on up.

On close examination, it is easy to see how the manufacturer can supply so much equipment for so few dollars. Typically, the record player utilizes a ceramic phono pickup. Ceramic pickups operate on an electro-mechanical strain principle. The stylus (needle) is physically connected to a sliver of ceramic material which, when strained by the motion of the stylus in the record groove, develops a rather substantial output voltage. Unfortunately, the fact that the stylus assembly is attached to the fixed ceramic element means that the needle is not as flexible or free to follow the wiggles in the record groove as is the free-floating stylus assembly in a magnetic cartridge. Since the constrained stylus assembly of a ceramic cartridge is less able to follow complex groove undulations, the needle actually loses contact with the walls of the record groove during loud musical passages or when very high frequencies are to be reproduced—a condition which results in high levels of distortion and loss of treble response. The ability of the stylus to move freely is known as compliance, and the higher the pickup compliance, the less downward force is required—and that means less record wear.

To compound the problem, many of the needles found in compact system record players are sapphire rather than diamond tipped. While the sapphire is a relatively hard gem, its polished tip erodes after fewer than 100 hours of playing time, whereas a diamond tip can be expected to remain useful for 1000 hours of playing time or more.

There is, however, one redeeming feature for the ceramic cartridge—at least insofar as production economies are concerned. Because a ceramic cartridge delivers such a high output voltage, the preamplifier-equalizer section normally found in high quality component amplifiers can be omitted. This electronic circuitry is the most critical and requires the greatest care in design of any element in a high fidelity component system. Its omission from the receiver circuitry of compact systems results in great savings to manufacturers and accounts, in part, for their ability to market "complete systems" at incredibly low prices.

Minimum-performance FM circuitry also finds its way into most compact systems. With the system's power line cord functioning as an "indoor antenna" and given fairly good reception conditions, these FM circuit designs do pick up local stations quite well. The differences between this sort of circuitry and the more sophisticated designs found in component FM tuners or receivers become apparent only when you try to pick up a distant station or when you compare the compact against the component for FM fidelity, frequency response, and audible distortion.

It is in the area of audio amplification, however, that compact designers achieve their greatest savings. It is not uncommon for the amplifier circuits found in compacts to be limited to around one watt per channel of audio power or even less. In contrast, the least amount of power one can buy these days in a true hi-fi component amplifier or receiver is around 10 watts per channel.

How, then, can the compact designers get away with such miniscule power ratings for their amplifier circuitry? The basic answer is that the compact manufacturer has complete control over the speakers that will be used with the system. One watt, driving a highly efficient speaker system, can produce as much sound (or loudness) as 10 or more watts driving a low-efficiency speaker system. Often, however, the manufacturer chooses a speaker system that has a particular resonant characteristic which makes it sound louder only at certain frequencies, with the result being that flatness or uniformity of frequency response is sacrificed in favor of sheer loudness of overall sound. Needless to say, this defeats one of the primary goals of true high fidelity, which is to reproduce all tones at their correct relative intensities and with as little distortion as possible.

To the uninitiated music lover, those wooden or vinyl-clad cabinets in either a compact or a high fidelity component system seem to serve no purpose other than that of a storage box for the loudspeaker elements contained inside. The more knowledgeable audio enthusiast realizes that speaker enclosures (as such cabinets are properly called) constitute a vital link in the sound reproducing chain.

Speaker enclosure design is a complex science, and many volumes of mathematical calculations have been published on the subject. Speakers and their enclosures are integrally related, and one cannot arbitrarily mount any speaker in any box and expect to get good sound out of the combination. The dimensions of the box, the material of which it is made, cutouts and ports in its front baffle (or the absence of such ports in some enclosures which are completely air-sealed) all relate to the final quality of sound which the speaker system delivers.

Unfortunately, most (though not all) compact producers pay little attention to this important component, frequently styling the speaker enclosure so that a pair will fit neatly into the carton which houses the entire compact system. In many instances, thin wood is used to construct the enclosure, resulting in a variety of self-induced resonances; the entire box "takes off" in its own vibration patterns and contributes unwanted sounds. Backs of the enclosures, if present at all, are often constructed of thin particle board. Sometimes, holes are deliberately punched into the backs, not for any sound considerations—since bass tones escaping from the rear of the cabinet tend to cancel out front-radiated bass—but rather to make it easy to hang the speakers on the wall.

Contrast these construction techniques with those of a well-designed high fidelity speaker system and it is easy to see why, in any listening comparison between a component hi-fi system and a compact system, the true component system wins hands down.

**Systems Offered by Your Dealer**

ONE OF THE ways to buy a complete system without having to choose each component yourself is to rely upon your dealer's recommendations. If he is knowledgeable and honest, his suggested system assemblies not only will save you money (generally, a dealer will sell a complete system at a price considerably below the sum of the individual components), but also will ensure a proper match of all your components. The key here is to know your dealer and be convinced of his reliability. Dealers who are overstocked with a particular model or models often assemble systems which include improperly matched components just to get rid of the overstock. It is especially important to listen to the "special" system as a whole, and not just to individual components of that system hooked up to speakers or turntables which are not included in the bargain.

**"Best Buy" Component Systems**

CONSUMER GUIDE Magazine has selected four basic component high fidelity systems in different price categories as good examples of compatibly assembled systems. Many of the components selected for these systems have been tested and analyzed in our laboratories where their specifications were measured and confirmed. In some of these systems, alternatives are offered in certain component categories to account for the price spread. The three lower-priced systems all include a receiver, a pair of speakers and a turntable/cartridge combination, while our "super" system uses a separate tuner, preamplifier and power amplifier for its central electronic components. None of the systems includes specific recommendations for associated tape recording equipment, since virtually any modern tape deck (cassette or open-reel) will work compatibly with any one of these systems.

## The Budget System

THE BIC MODEL 940 selected for this system contains all the features of the higher priced Model 980 (see mid-priced system) except for pitch control (speed variability) and a strobe indicator. It is belt driven and programmable so that up to six records can be played with repeat play of the last record. Those preferring a single-play unit might consider the BSR 20BPX, which is rated a "Best Buy" by CONSUMER GUIDE Magazine. Its belt-drive system generates substantially less rumble and flutter than competitive record players produce.

Either Shure's M91E or Audio-Technica's AT-12E cartridge will work nicely with either the BIC or BSR turntable systems. The AT-12E is capable of playing discrete quadraphonic records, if you happen to own or plan to buy any.

JVC's JR-S300 is a knobless, newly styled receiver also rated as a "Best Buy" by CONSUMER GUIDE Magazine. Its 54-watt-per-channel power output will be more than enough to drive either of our two speaker choices. Although lower in power output at 22 watts per channel, Sony's STR-2800 receiver delivers clean sound that contains little coloration or audio inaccuracies.

The low-priced Advent/2 speakers are small enough to fit into any room, but they will handle the power applied to them. Dynaco's A-25 speakers are extremely efficient, requiring only 10 watts of amplifier power per channel, yet they furnish a clean and well-balanced output.

## Mid-Priced System

THE BIC 980 belt-driven turntable is rated as a "Best Buy" by CONSUMER GUIDE Magazine. It was designed as a top-grade unit that can play up to six records sequentially. Controls work smoothly, a single pushbutton initiating the complete pre-programming playing cycle. For those audiophiles who prefer a single-play machine, the Thorens TD-160C IsoTrack is smooth, reliable, and exemplifies nearly the best in a manual record player. It lacks automation, but this is a blessing in disguise since there is little that can go wrong with the unit.

Both the Shure V15 Type III and the Empire 2000Z cartridges were rated highly by CONSUMER GUIDE Magazine's testers for good trackability at a tracking force of 1.0 gram or less. Both units also exhibited flat frequency response when installed in either of the suggested turntable systems.

Hitachi's SR-903 receiver uses a new "Class G" circuit which makes it more efficient than similarly rated (75 watts per channel) competitive models—a point worth considering in these days of concern regarding energy conservation. The new Hitachi circuit also allowed the designers to make the unit lighter in weight and smaller in dimensions. FM plus phono performance are both equal to the quality of the amplifier section. The alternative Onkyo TX-4500, although lower in power output rating (60 watts per channel), earned CONSUMER GUIDE Magazine's "Best Buy" rating because of its excellent and flexible tone control and other switching features. The TX-4500's innovative auto-lock feature lets you tune accurately to FM stations and, when you let go of the tuning knob, locks them in perfectly—even if you have slightly mistuned. Such precision tuning guarantees reception at minimum distortion.

The BIC Venturi Formula 4 speakers are excellent sound reproducers, capable of handling the full power of either of the receivers CONSUMER GUIDE Magazine has recommended. Chances are, though, you will never have to turn up the volume loud enough to approach audible clipping even from the lower-powered Onkyo, since the BIC speakers employ a highly efficient vented enclosure design (from which the name Venturi is derived).

**High-Priced System**

DUAL's MODEL 1245 is one of the two or three finest multiple-play units on the market. The Dual reputation for craftsmanship and reliability is in full evidence from the 1245's precision tone arm to its belt-driven platter. For a no-nonsense ultra-rugged single-play unit, the Empire's new 698 model is recommended. It is the successor to Empire's earlier long-lived 598. Electronic light-sensing circuits lift the arm at end of play and touch-sense switches have been added for tone arm cueing.

For those who want one of the finest available phono pickups, CONSUMER GUIDE Magazine recommends Audio-Technica's top-of-the-line AT-20SLa. A hand-selected version of Audio-Technica's less expensive AT-15Sa, the AT-20SLa comes supplied with an individually plotted frequency response curve. In addition to its fine stereo record playing capability, the AT-20SLa represents probably the finest four-channel cartridge available. If quadraphonic sound is of no interest, you can save some money by choosing the Pickering XSV/3000—a cartridge from a well-known firm distinguished for making pickups with light stylus assembly mass, excellent compliance, and almost perfect frequency response to beyond 20,000 Hz.

Sony's STR-6800SD receiver is one of the first in its price class to include complete Dolby FM, making the unit worth about $100 more than would otherwise be the case. In addition to that important feature, the receiver has been engineered for most logical control use and features all the controls you could possibly need. Power output rating is 80 watts per channel.

As an alternate, CONSUMER GUIDE Magazine recommends Tandberg's Model TR-2075. Although much higher in price than the Sony STR-6800SD and no more powerful, the TR-2075 is an exceptionally well-crafted receiver. It features first-rate FM specifications, all of which were met or exceeded in our testing. A particularly useful feature of the TR-2075 receiver is its ability to pre-equalize (by means of tone controls) any tape output intended for transcription on associated tape recording equipment—a feature not found on other receivers and rarely included even in separates.

The Acoustic Research AR-10π is a three-way acoustic suspension speaker system that features a "woofer environmental control." Its design enables the user to select three different levels of low-frequency output to suit the speaker's position in the listening room. If you prefer smaller units, the latest version of Bose's famous direct-reflecting speakers, the Bose 901 III, is suggested for this system. Increased in efficiency by nearly four times, the Bose 901 III still features nine separate driver elements, eight of which face the rear of the unit and utilize reflected sound for what Bose believes is a more natural sound field. Although placement is somewhat critical, experimentation is well worth the effort because when properly positioned, the 901 III units deliver authentic and authoritative sound.

**Super "Dream" System**

THE ELECTRONIC sections of CONSUMER GUIDE Magazine's "dream system" consist of Yamaha's top tuner, Model CT-7000, which offers variable bandwidth on FM. When conditions permit (no station crowding on the dial) the use of the "wide band" setting offers the lowest distortion in FM that CONSUMER GUIDE Magazine has measured and delivers stereo separation that is hard to beat.

CONSUMER GUIDE Magazine recommends the Soundcraftsman Model PE2217 preamplifier because, in addition to being a flexible preamp/control center, it is one of the few units available that incorporates a full graphic equalizer section which enables you to tailor overall system frequency response to compensate for everything from mismatched components to varying acoustics of the listening room.

The BGW Systems Model 250B is one of the lowest priced, high-powered basic amplifiers we have tested. It delivers a clean and tight 90 watts per channel at less than 0.1 percent total harmonic distortion across the entire audio frequency spectrum, from 20 Hz to 20,000 Hz. Because of its protection circuitry, the unit is impervious to speaker short circuits, and it will automatically shut down instantly in the event of overload or failure, resuming operation quickly once the problem has been resolved. At mid-frequencies, the amplifier delivered rated power with an unbelievably low distortion of only 0.019 percent.

CONSUMER GUIDE Magazine selects the magnificent Bang & Olufsen Model 4002 Beogram as the top record playing mechanism. This unit has won awards for its elegant styling; but more importantly it plays records the way they were meant to be played. The tone arm travels across the record tangentially, instead of pivoting from the rear, allowing the records to be tracked just as they were cut. Furthermore, it is virtually impossible to damage a record accidentally, as all motions of the 4002 are initiated by a series of touch switches and the tone arm cannot be accidentally dropped onto a precious record. The unit comes equipped with a B&O cartridge, for which no substitutions can be made by the user.

The Altec Model 19 speakers selected for this "dream system" are heavyweights, literally and in terms of their sound quality. They sound clear, open, and smooth over their entire range. What particularly distinguishes these large floor-standing units are deeper bass, greater power handling capacity, and more expanded dynamic range than most speaker systems in this price category.

---

## SPECIAL INFORMATION SERVICE

**A Bonus for Readers of this CONSUMER GUIDE®**

CONSUMER GUIDE® offers a special bonus to its readers who are interested in obtaining information as to where they can find the low prices on specific products listed in this guide. Simply fill out the form and mail. Include 25 cents for postage and handling.

**Please send me information on:**

Product _____ Model Number _____

Manufacturer _____

Product _____ Model Number _____

Manufacturer _____

Your Name _____

Address _____

City _____ State _____ Zip Code _____

**CONSUMER GUIDE Magazine**
**3841 West Oakton, Skokie, Illinois 60076**

# 1978 Best Buys Hi-Fi Components

IN SELECTING our "Best Buys" in high fidelity equipment, CONSUMER GUIDE Magazine's audio experts tested a number of leading components and chose from among those the ones which present the hi-fi purchaser with maximum value for his or her audio dollars. Testing involves precise laboratory measurement of sound characteristics, a technical analysis of design and construction, a trial period of in-home listening, and a comparative analysis of features and performance among models in each price range.

## TUNERS
**Best Buys**

**Dynaco AF-6** is a fine value for those people willing to invest a bit of time in building a component from a kit. CONSUMER GUIDE Magazine feels, however, that in its preassembled form the AF-6's price is somewhat high in relation to other state-of-the-art tuner products currently available.
**Approximate Retail Price: $269.00**　　　　**Low Price: $201.75**

**Kenwood KT-5300** is one of the lowest-priced FM/AM tuners ever tested in CONSUMER GUIDE Magazine's audio laboratories, and it does a great deal to substantiate claims of the hi-fi industry that today's components offer better value per dollar than those of just a few years ago. The KT-5300 can outperform many tuners which sell for considerably higher prices.
**Approximate Retail Price: $140.00**　　　　**Low Price: $98.00**

## AMPLIFIER
**Best Buy**

**Kenwood KA-3500** integrated amplifier offers an extremely attractive price/performance ratio, provides adequate power for most

*Prices are accurate at time of printing; subject to manufacturer's change.*

high fidelity needs, and possesses many of the control and input features of its higher-priced and higher-powered competitors. Designed to deliver 40 watts per channel, the Kenwood KA-3500 can work well with all but the extremely low efficiency speaker systems.
**Approximate Retail Price: $170.00**          **Low Price: $119.00**

## RECEIVERS
## Best Buys

**Hitachi SR-903** receiver features Class G circuitry which greatly reduces the need for massive heat sinks and results in a component that is less bulky and lower in net weight than components possessing conventional amplifier circuitry. Moreover, Hitachi has managed to come up with a good tuner design to match the SR-903's innovative amplifier section. All in all, the SR-903 is a full-featured, high-powered, all-in-one receiver at a most attractive price.
**Approximate Retail Price: $550.00**          **Low Price: $425.00**

**JVC JR-S300** delivers its power effortlessly and, in fact, seems as though it renders greater power output than it actually does — 54 watts per channel from 20 Hz to 20 kHz. Although CONSUMER GUIDE Magazine's audio experts found the unusual layout of the S-300's front panel quite attractive, its radical departure from tradition — it has no rotary knobs — may displease some buyers.
**Approximate Retail Price: $400.00**          **Low Price: $270.00**

**Kenwood KR-7600** is rated at 80 continuous watts per channel and has a tuner section which is fully competitive with receivers in its price class. But where this Kenwood unit really excels is in the not-so-obvious extra control features and layout considerations. This receiver is a joy to operate, providing fully as much control flexibility as separate tuners and amplifiers.
**Approximate Retail Price: $530.00**          **Low Price: $361.00**

**Kenwood KR-9600** receiver delivers 160 watts per channel, placing it among the more powerful receivers available. But unlike many high-powered receivers, the KR-9600 boasts a number of features worthy of consideration. In terms of performance, it produces excellent bass response with low-efficiency speaker systems, and it possesses an exceptional ability to reproduce fast transients as well as very clean and open overall sound.
**Approximate Retail Price: $750.00**          **Low Price: $524.95**

**Onkyo TX-4500** receiver is a quality unit throughout. It offers intelligently conceived controls and input facilities, is one of the easiest receivers to tune, fits on a shelf, and looks like the first-rate component it is. Although it is rated to deliver only a moderate 50

*Prices are accurate at time of printing; subject to manufacturer's change.*

watts of audio power per channel, the TX-4500 is powerful enough for about 90 percent of all the stereo systems in existence today. FM reception is first-rate, comparable to some of the finest separate tuners available, and the quartz-locked system makes tuning as easy as possible.

**Approximate Retail Price: $469.95**      **Low Price: Not Available**

**Sony STR-2800** receiver delivers clean sound that contains little coloration or audio inaccuracies, but it must be kept within its relatively low power output bounds—22 watts per channel from 20 Hz to 20 kHz. Its tuner section is quite impressive, and its signal-to-noise ratio in phono is excellent. Budget-minded buyers should certainly consider this unit carefully.

**Approximate Retail Price: $565.00**      **Low Price: $423.75**

## MULTIPLE-PLAY TURNTABLES
### Best Buys

**BIC 940,** while lacking a great number of the special features and the attention to detail lavished on more costly turntables, cannot be faulted in terms of its overall record playing ability. One could not ask for better rumble or flutter performance in a record player priced for inclusion in relatively modest music systems. Moreover, its accurate and effective anti-skating compensation, drift-free damped cueing, noise-free mechanical operation, above-average versatility, and apparent mechanical reliability place the 940 well above its competition.

**Approximate Retail Price: $109.95**      **Low Price: $85.00**

**BIC 980** is a programmed record player, able to handle up to six records in automatic sequence or to be used as a completely manual player. CONSUMER GUIDE Magazine's audio experts know of no comparably priced automatic record changer which can surpass the 980 or even match its overall combination of versatility and performance.

**Approximate Retail Price: $199.95**      **Low Price: $137.95**

**Dual 1245** offers little that is new in features or performance (previous Dual models were quite similar), but it is to be commended for retaining at a reduced price the smoothness, quietness, and mechanical precision that have earned Dual its enviable reputation in the audio field. One special factor not to be overlooked is the almost ready-to-play condition of the 1245 when it comes out of the carton. Set-up is literally a matter of a few minutes.

**Approximate Retail Price: $229.95**      **Low Price: $151.80**

*Prices are accurate at time of printing; subject to manufacturer's change.*

## SINGLE-PLAY TURNTABLES
### Best Buys

**BSR 20BPX** is a first-rate machine, superior in performance to all comparably priced record players and better than several more expensive turntables. Its belt-driven system results in substantially less rumble and flutter than competitive units. All in all, if you are more concerned with what you hear from your records than with the technological sophistication of your turntable, then you will appreciate the qualities which the BSR 20BPX has to offer.
**Approximate Retail Price: $99.95**          **Low Price: $66.00**

**Connoisseur BD/2** is a first-rate record player. Its performance matches that of many far more expensive models on the market, and its basic simplicity suggests that long and trouble-free service can be expected. By eliminating all of the automatic features typical of modern record players, the designers of the Connoisseur BD/2 have managed to deliver an exceptional value for the dollar.
**Approximate Retail Price: $144.00**          **Low Price: Not Available**

**Dual CS-510** offers remarkable handling ease, especially insofar as its simple and effective arm indexing system is concerned. Overall, the Dual 510 is a beautifully executed record player; and it deserves the attention of anyone who plays records one at a time.
**Approximate Retail Price: $210.00**          **Low Price: $138.60**

**Miida T3115** excels in styling and handling just as it does in terms of sonic specifications. The unit can be set up with no fussing whatever, and its performance is truly first-rate. Taken as a whole, the Miida is an excellent record player and a fine value. For those people who do not mind handling the tone arm (and this one is very smooth and easy to use), the T3115 will provide listening quality equivalent to just about any record player at any price.
**Approximate Retail Price: $199.95**          **Low Price: Not Available**

**Stanton Gyropoise 8004-II** is a completely manual turntable, but it illustrates how careful design can maximize the ratio of performance to price. Sold as a complete ready-to-use unit, the Stanton Gyropoise 8004-II comes equipped with the Stanton 681 EEE, one of the finest phono cartridges on the market.
**Approximate Retail Price: $199.95**          **Low Price: $159.95**

## CARTRIDGES
### Best Buys

**Audio-Technica AT-12XE** is rated for use at tracking forces between 1.0 and 1.75 grams. Although it can be used safely at 1.0 gram with perhaps 99 percent of the records one might play,
*Prices are accurate at time of printing; subject to manufacturer's change.*

CONSUMER GUIDE Magazine's audio experts suggest operating it at an indicated setting of 1.5 grams to avoid any possibility of insufficient tracking force. The cartridge's overall sound is sweet, musical, and unstrained, and it possesses flatter frequency response and better tracking ability than most cartridges in its price range.

**Approximate Retail Price: $60.00** **Low Price: $23.50**

**Micro-Acoustics 282-e** offers all the fine listening qualities of the much more expensive Micro-Acoustics 2002-e—including the top-of-the-line unit's very low noise level. The only sacrifice in performance it entails is a few tenths of a gram higher vertical tracking force, and the 282-e's lower price certainly makes that an easily accepted compromise.

**Approximate Retail Price: $89.00** **Low Price: $64.75**

**Ortofon F15E** is clearly one of the better cartridges in its price range. CONSUMER GUIDE Magazine's audio experts listened to the cartridge critically and never found it to be less than excellent. The Ortofon F15E is ample proof that it is possible to produce quality cartridges at reasonable prices.

**Approximate Retail Price: $50.00** **Low Price: $40.00**

**Pickering UV-15/2000Q,** a cartridge designed to play discrete quadraphonic discs, compares favorably with several of the more expensive quad entries.

**Approximate Retail Price: $69.90** **Low Price: $35.00**

**Shure M24H** comes close to being the ideal cartridge for both CD-4 and stereo reproduction. Only a few of the cartridges CONSUMER GUIDE Magazine has tested can match the M24H's ability to track both stereo and CD-4 records cleanly at low forces, and all these cartridges are much more expensive than the M24H. Shure's M24H must be recommended as an excellent choice for anyone who wants a first-rate cartridge at an affordable price.

**Approximate Retail Price: $84.95** **Low Price: $36.00**

**Shure V15 Type III** produced excellent results during CONSUMER GUIDE Magazine's laboratory testing, and those measurements were confirmed by later listening tests. Highs are noteworthy for their lack of fuzziness, and there are no peaks in response. Distortion is so negligible that when heard at all, it is more likely to emanate from the recordings themselves rather than from the Shure V15 Type III cartridge.

**Approximate Retail Price: $90.00** **Low Price: $61.00**

**Stanton 681EEE** is a relatively high-priced cartridge, but it offers commensurate value in terms of ruggedness and exceptionally accurate response—within one decibel across the audio band. These attributes, plus low harmonic and IM distortion and excellent

*Prices are accurate at time of printing; subject to manufacturer's change.*

tracking performance, make the 681EEE a top performer in its price category.
**Approximate Retail Price: $90.00**            **Low Price: $49.50**

**Stanton 780/4DQ** is designed to play CD-4 and matrixed quadraphonic records as well as all stereo discs. It is no small achievement for a single cartridge to excel in playing both CD-4 and stereo records, but the Stanton 780/4DQ manages to do just that. Despite the fact that it operates at 1½ to two grams of force, the 780/4DQ should never produce excessive record wear. Stanton's Quadrahedral stylus—a specially shaped diamond—distributes the force over the groove wall in such a way that the additional force presents no problems.
**Approximate Retail Price: $125.00**            **Low Price: $85.00**

## HEADPHONES
### Best Buys

**AKG K-140** produces more than enough loudness when connected to the headphone output of a modestly powered receiver. It also produces ample loudness when used for monitoring the output directly from tape decks. The K-140 headset is easy to wear for fairly long periods with a minimum of fatigue, capable of rendering transparent and balanced response, and quite attractively priced.
**Approximate Retail Price: $39.50**            **Low Price: $26.00**

**AKG K-240** is characterized by ample bass, strong and well-defined middles and highs, and overall smoothness. The unit's fine sound, combined with its extremely light weight and excellent wearing comfort, should appeal to many people who may have shied away from headphones in the past.
**Approximate Retail Price: $69.50**            **Low Price: $55.60**

**JVC HM-200E Bina-Phones** can be used as a normal stereo headphone, as a binaural microphone, or as both headphone and microphone simultaneously. One can make live recordings with the microphones while monitoring via the headset plugged into the output of a tape system. Despite the fact that each earpiece contains a built-in microphone and penlight cell in addition to the hearing elements, the JVC HM-200E offers acceptable wearing comfort. Audio response is quite good, but it is the unit's additional capability of making live recordings that puts the HM-200E in a class by itself.
**Approximate Retail Price: $89.95**            **Low Price: $63.00**

**Koss PRO-4AA** really excels in terms of sound reproduction. Bass goes down below 30 Hz, the midrange is free of bumps and dips, and the highs are fairly flat and quite clean. This highly listenable

*Prices are accurate at time of printing; subject to manufacturer's change.*

headset also offers a high degree of wearing comfort for a standard headphone design.
**Approximate Retail Price: $65.00**　　　　　　　　**Low Price: $33.45**

**Sennheiser HD-400,** weighing just three ounces and exerting a minimum of pressure against the ears, is very comfortable to wear. Response is smooth and well-balanced across the musical range, the bass extending down to below 30 Hz and the middles and highs reproduced cleanly. The HD-400 is among the least expensive of the quality headsets.
**Approximate Retail Price: $35.95**　　　　　　　　**Low Price: $24.95**

## SPEAKERS
### Best Buys

**New Advent Loudspeaker,** with its very good sound and reasonable price, merits the consideration of buyers seeking speakers for a quality home component music system. The bass response is exemplary for a speaker in its price class, and the response upward is smooth and clean and well-balanced across the audio spectrum.
**Approximate Retail Price: $155.00 each　Low Price: Not Available**

**Avid 103** is an all-purpose bookshelf speaker which provides a transparent response to program material. Efficient enough when powered by modest amplifiers, the Avid 103 is also rugged enough to handle some of the real powerhouse amplifiers.
**Approximate Retail Price: $188.00 each　Low Price: Not Available**

**BIC Venturi Formula 4** rates among the better speaker systems CONSUMER GUIDE Magazine has tested. The F-4 can be used with many of today's low- and medium-powered receivers and amplifiers with good results.
**Approximate Retail Price: $169.95 each**　　　　**Low Price: $118.95**

**Celestion UL-6** is a fine example of how a speaker system can be created with compact dimensions, sold at a reasonable price, and still provide first-rate performance in a quality home music system. Indeed, its overall performance certainly suggests a costlier speaker, and to do better in terms of deeper bass and/or higher power capacity one would probably have to pay considerably more.
**Approximate Retail Price: $179.50 each　Low Price: Not Available**

**Dynaco A-25** furnishes a clean and well-balanced output throughout the impressive range of 35 Hz to 15 kHz. Extremely efficient, it requires only 10 watts of amplifier power per channel. The A-25's sound is clean, and its price is attractive.
**Approximate Retail Price: $99.00 each**　　　　　**Low Price: $69.30**

**Dynaco A-35** is not a rock speaker in the sense that higher-
*Prices are accurate at time of printing; subject to manufacturer's change.*

efficiency units are. It cannot long survive extremely high volume levels in large rooms. But in a relatively small listening room, the A-35 renders as much good volume as anyone could desire.
**Approximate Retail Price: $129.00 each**         **Low Price: $92.25**

**Dynaco A-50** is modest and conventional in appearance, but it provides excellent performance without resorting to any gimmicks or novel design techniques. All it offers is accurate reproduction of sound at levels suitable for high quality music systems.
**Approximate Retail Price: $249.00 each**         **Low Price: $178.00**

**EPI 100** is an air-suspension design with an eight-inch woofer and one-inch dome tweeter. Its sound is honest, well-balanced and uncolored. An accurate sound-reproducing component, the EPI 100 would do very well in a system built around low- to medium-powered amplifiers or receivers.
**Approximate Retail Price: $109.00 each**   **Low Price: Not Available**

**EPI 200** — in terms of overall frequency range, dynamic capability, smoothness of sound, and dispersion — belongs among the top speaker systems in its price range. It can do justice to all kinds of reproduced music, from hard rock to the delicate shadings of classical chamber ensembles. Similarly, its power needs are broad enough to accommodate many of the most popular amplifiers and receivers on today's market and to perform well in a relatively large spectrum of listening rooms, from small to fairly large.
**Approximate Retail Price: $225.00 each**   **Low Price: Not Available**

**EPI Microtower II** is a low-cost speaker system of modest but attractive proportions that can provide satisfying sound quality. Bass response is excellent down to about 45 Hz, while midrange and highs are good. This is not, however, the speaker to buy in cases where extremely high sonic levels are desired.
**Approximate Retail Price: $179.95 each**   **Low Price: Not Available**

**JBL L-166 Horizon** is definitely a speaker system that the classical music buff can enjoy. At the same time, though, it is no slouch in reproducing pop and rock material. It is a very honest sound reproducer, and its high efficiency and rugged construction constitute other strong points in its favor. The L-166 Horizon is the best bookshelf system JBL has yet produced, and it deserves to be ranked among the top systems in its price class.
**Approximate Retail Price: $426.00 each**         **Low Price: $340.80**

**Sony SSU-2000** is a straightforward acoustic-suspension system designed for use with a fairly broad selection of receivers and amplifiers. Overall, it is a very clean sounding speaker which should appeal to many diverse musical tastes, assuming that the listener is interested in honest sound reproduction and is not seeking to be overwhelmed by phony sonic sensationalism.
**Approximate Retail Price: $150.00 each**         **Low Price: $115.50**

*Prices are accurate at time of printing; subject to manufacturer's change.*

# 1978 Tape Recorders

ADDING A TAPE DECK to your music system offers you the opportunity to take an active part in the music reproducing process, rather than remaining a passive listener. But deciding which tape format and tape deck to buy and use can sometimes be a problem. The range of available products is greater than ever. You can buy an inexpensive home cassette deck, a more costly stereo cassette deck, or a two-channel or four-channel open-reel tape machine. Where do you begin?

To answer that, you must ask yourself other questions: What type of material do you plan to record? If you plan to copy recordings or FM broadcasts onto tape, you will probably want to consider purchasing a good cassette deck. These can range in price from as little as $100 to well over $1000. If you would like to record live music at a local concert or wherever else music is performed, you will need a portable cassette deck with battery power and one or more microphones.

The open-reel tape deck, the oldest of the current tape formats, is worth considering if you plan to do recording in a very serious, semiprofessional or professional way. In earlier times, you could buy good open-reel tape decks at prices from $200 on up. These days, the conveniences and improved performance of cassette decks have prompted open-reel tape deck manufacturers to concentrate primarily on higher-priced machines intended mostly for serious tape enthusiasts. You can be more musically creative with an open-reel tape deck because such decks are available with multichannel facilities which enable you to compose music on a channel-by-channel basis—even to play and record four different musical instruments yourself. Open-reel decks are available as two-, three-, and sometimes four-speed models. For semi-professional applications, the 15 inch-per-second speed is preferred. Good musical fidelity can be obtained on many machines at the slower speed of 7½ inches per second, while 3¾ inches per second and slower speeds are often reserved for speech recording and low-fidelity applications.

A fourth tape recording format was introduced jointly by Technics by Panasonic, Teac, and Sony more than a year ago. It promised to offer the advantages of open-reel fidelity and cassette convenience in a single system. This tape format uses a tape package known as "Elcaset," which is considerably larger than a standard cassette. "Large Cassette" was first shortened to "L-Cassette" and then given the trade name Elcaset by its originators. It uses tape that is a quarter-inch wide—the same size as the tape used in open-reel machines—and runs at a speed of 3¾ inches per second as opposed to the standard cassette tape speed of 1⅞ ips. Both of these factors allow for better frequency response and a reduction in unwanted noise. As conceived by its inventors, the tape has provision for two tracks in addition to the four usual audio tracks (two stereo pairs) which are intended to be used for cueing and synchronizing purposes.

CONSUMER GUIDE Magazine has tested only one Elcaset machine, the Sony EL-5. While its basic performance was excellent, the high-priced unit did not really avail itself of the full potential of the Elcaset format. It did not utilize those extra two control tracks, nor was it equipped with separate record and playback heads for tape monitoring.

Perhaps because standard cassette machines and the tape they use keep getting better, the initial excitement following the announcement of the Elcaset has died down. Consumer interest is now centered primarily around the newer and better standard cassette machines.

## Tape Deck Specifications

SPECIFICATIONS FOR tape decks are measured in the same way for both cassette and open-reel machines. To give you some idea of how the formats have evolved in recent years, and to provide you with some basis for choosing a deck to serve your purposes, here is a brief explanation of some of those specifications.

**Wow and Flutter.** This measurement of tape speed fluctuation is usually listed in percentages with the letters WRMS, such as "0.1 percent WRMS." The WRMS stands for Weighted Root-Mean Square, but you do not have to remember that to understand what the specification sheets say. The only thing to keep in mind is that you are looking for the smallest percentage you can get for the money you have to spend. If this measurement is quoted by a manufacturer in RMS rather than WRMS, you can expect that figure to be somewhat higher than the comparable WRMS wow and flutter figure for the same machine.

Not too long ago, a wow and flutter specification of 0.1 percent WRMS was considered a minor miracle in cassette decks because the low tape speed involved made uniformity of tape motion difficult to achieve. These days, there are decks selling for as little as $250 which do better than that, rivaling open-reel machines with readings as low as 0.08 percent or even 0.06 percent WRMS. The Tandberg TCD-330, a three-head machine with tape monitoring capability, was conservatively rated by the manufacturer as having a wow and flutter of 0.12 percent, but when measured by CONSUMER GUIDE Magazine's test staff, it actually proved to have a lower wow and flutter figure of only 0.07 percent WRMS.

Frequency Response, Distortion and Signal-to-Noise. These three important specifications are very much related to each other. Unfortunately, many manufacturers tend to emphasize frequency response because that is the specification which is most readily understood by consumers. High fidelity equipment buyers have been conditioned over the years to believe that every hi-fi component must have so-called "flat" response from 20 Hz to 20,000 Hz.

In the case of tape decks and particularly cassette tape decks, however, frequency response extending to beyond 15,000 Hz is too often achieved at the expense of other desirable capabilities. High distortion and poor signal-to-noise ratios often result. Underbiasing a given tape, for example, will result in greater output at higher frequencies, but it also increases distortion during playback. Exaggerated equalization, either during recording or playback can also increase high-frequency output, but such modifications will result in higher tape noise. Ask a professional recordist whether he or she would rather have response out to 20,000 Hz and a signal-to-noise ratio of 55 dB, or response only to 15,000 Hz and signal-to-noise of better than 60 dB. The answer will always be in favor of the better signal-to-noise ratio.

While it is true that human hearing response has been assigned the rather arbitrary limits of 20 Hz to 20,000 Hz, most of us do not hear much beyond 15,000 Hz, particularly as we get older. As proof of the fact that you do not necessarily have to have flat response to 20,000 Hz in a piece of tape equipment, consider the fact that FM broadcasts transmit frequencies up to only 15,000 Hz. Since much of what you are likely to record will come from that very source, it seems unwise to worry about frequency response beyond 15,000 Hz.

Signal-to-noise ratings for cassette decks should be a prime consideration for any purchaser. Much depends here upon the type of tape used as well as on the capabilities of the deck itself. A deck capable of delivering low noise will not live up to expectations if you use inferior "bargain" cassette tapes. Such tapes can be adequate for voice recording, providing they are mechanically sound and do not jam or break in the midst of a recording session. But for serious recording work involving high fidelity music program sources, you should select a good tape, preferably one recommended by the manufacturer of your machine.

With so many different tape formulations now available, it is important, too, that your cassette machine have the necessary bias and equalization switch positions to match the characteristics of the tape you use.

Generally, you do not have to be as particular about tape types used on open-reel machines; however, if you plan serious recording work, a name-brand tape should be used. Open-reel tape recording offers considerably greater dynamic range and improved frequency response compared to cassette units. This is especially true if you operate at the high speed of 15 inches per second used by professionals, but it even applies to the slower 7½ ips speed.

At 15 ips, and even at half that speed, you can expect frequency response to go way out beyond 20,000 Hz on better machines. The trade-off between speed and performance is one that the user must decide and is based in part upon the obvious fact that operating at the higher tape speed uses twice as much tape for a given recording time.

Many of the more expensive open-reel decks will accept 10½ inch tape reels. These generally come supplied with 3600 feet of tape, enough tape to last for something more than 45 minutes at the 15 ips speed on a side and for 1½ hours at the slower 7½ inch speed in each direction. While some manufacturers do supply 4800 foot lengths of tape on a 10½ inch reel, CONSUMER GUIDE Magazine's tape experts feel that this tape is too thin to be reliable.

Dolby noise reduction is virtually a must in any cassette recorder costing more than $150. Dolby helps to reduce tape hiss without altering overall fidelity or frequency response. Other noise reduction systems, such as the ANRS system used by JVC in some of its better cassette decks, behave similarly. JVC now reports that their ANRS system is compatible with tapes that have been recorded using the Dolby system.

Normally, Dolby noise reduction systems are not included with open-reel machines and, indeed, the need for Dolby noise reduction is not as great in the open-reel format. Some open-reel recordists do add separate Dolby units, primarily for the purpose of reducing the noise which builds up during recording from one tape machine to another and "mix-downs" from multitrack to the final finished tape. Tandberg's two 10XD open-reel models include built-in Dolby.

**Beyond Performance**

IN ADDITION TO such performance specifications as wow and flutter, frequency response, signal-to-noise ratio, and distortion, you will want to consider certain other operating features and convenience controls that are available in a growing number of cassette decks. So-called memory-rewind allows you to set the tape counter to 000 at a specific point during playback of a tape; later, if you operate the tape deck in the fast rewind mode, the rewinding will come to a halt at the predetermined point, enabling you to start play at that 000 position.

Some of JVC's decks now incorporate multiple light indicators that read peak signal levels—a worthy addition to the usual slow-moving meter pointers which cannot follow rapid changes in signal level and therefore are useless when it comes to serving as indicators to prevent over-recording. Some other manufacturers, including Teac, use a single peak-reading LED over and above the usual recording level meters. This light reacts instantly to peak signals and flashes a warning when recording peak levels are too high for satisfactory magnetization of the tape. A recently announced model from Dual (United Audio Products) features a similar LED system.

Among the newer cassette machines are a few that feature three-head operation; that is, separate erase, record, and playback heads are provided so that tape monitoring can be accomplished as the recording is being made. The cassette package, as originally conceived by Philips Company of the Netherlands, made no provision for three heads, requiring a great deal of ingenuity on the part of manufacturers to cram three heads into spaces originally intended for just two heads (erase and combination record/play).

Nakamichi, one of the first companies to solve this problem with Model 700 and more expensive Model 1000 (now improved and called Model 1000 MK II), actually uses three separate head structures; other companies, such as JVC, use a single physical head casing the size of a single head but incorporate two closely spaced coil and gap structures, each separately connected to the appropriate internal electronics. The latter approach has the advantage of playing back recorded material to be monitored with almost no time delay that would otherwise occur between separate heads physically separated by an inch or so.

Some low-priced cassette decks advertise three-head operation, but the third head is simply a monitoring head which lets you hear that recordings are taking place. It is not capable of sufficient fidelity to be employed as the final playback head. Such machines continue to use combination record/play heads plus the minimal-quality monitor head and are not true three-headed machines in the sense that we have been discussing them.

The product mix of open-reel tape decks has undergone a radical change in the last few years because of the emergence of higher-quality cassette units. Most open-reel tape decks sold today border on the professional level. Two types predominate: those which permit the user to do multichannel recording of one channel at a time for ultimate mix-down into a stereo tape, usually supplied with four-channel, four-track capability; and a number of units which have abandoned the quarter-track format of two stereo program tracks in each direction of tape travel in favor of so-called half-track tape configuration. The half-track format allows for stereo recording in one direction of tape travel only, since each track occupies half the tape width instead of one-quarter of that width. The advantages of half-track recording include better signal-to-noise ratio and greater dynamic range.

A good example of this new breed of home open-reel decks is the Panasonic Technics RS-1500US. It has a refined form of tape motion system which makes tape travel unaffected by reel tension or variation in tape wind on the supply and takeup reels. The RS-1500US comes with a four-track playback head for users who already own four-track tapes, but its own record head is of the half-track variety.

Serious recording buffs now tend to purchase both a multiple-track machine such as a Teac A-3340S, Otari MX-5050-QXH, Sony TC-388-4, or Teac 2340R plus one of the newer half-track machines from Pioneer, Teac, Tandberg, or Technics, thereby equipping themselves with the basics of a total home recording studio. Essentially, the only difference between many of these machines and the types used in recording studios lies not so much in their audio performance (which is excellent and equal to anything that can be done by the professional studio units), but in their ruggedness of construction and ability to withstand 18 to 24 hours of continuous daily use. Obviously, there is no reason to increase the cost of a home machine with super-rugged construction since the deck is not likely to take that kind of punishment.

**Cassette Decks in Cars**

ALTHOUGH DETROIT'S car makers have been promising to offer cassette tape decks as optional factory equipment in new automobiles for some years, no such option has been made available to date. As a result, many automotive audiophiles have taken to installing portable cassette decks themselves. Some of the available in-dash and under-dash units are not very good, but a few companies, notably those already involved in the manufacture of home high fidelity equipment, have come up with cassette decks and even a few combination cassette/AM-FM systems that perform admirably well.

Nakamichi teamed up with ADS (a speaker and amplifier company) to provide a package consisting of the Nakamichi 250 cassette player (which is easily removed from its mounting brackets and can be operated at home as well as on the road) and a pair of ADS-2002 speaker/amplifier systems which must be heard in a car environment to be believed. These products, in the opinion of CONSUMER GUIDE Magazine's audio experts, deserve to be called car hi-fi equipment. The 250 cassette deck does not have record capability, however, so if you hope to record your own tapes, you will have to purchase a standard home unit in addition to the car player.

**Our Advice**

CONSUMER GUIDE Magazine's audio experts suggest the following: Before you make up your mind regarding which tape format will work best for you, do some hands-on investigating. In that way, you will become familiar with the features, controls, and action of each tape format and, based upon your needs and budget, you will then be able to pick a tape deck that fills your needs and properly complements the rest of your stereo component system.

A low-cost cassette deck with a minimum of features will connect easily to even the highest-quality, highest-priced system of components. Similarly, a top-of-the-line open-reel tape deck will interconnect with even the most moderately priced components.

In CONSUMER GUIDE Magazine's view, the logical choice for the hi-fi system owner who wants to buy a tape recorder is a quality cassette deck. To be sure, the cassette format cannot provide the ultimate versatility in recording and editing options that are possible with reel-to-reel tape, but it should suffice for most home users. Many of the prerecorded cassettes sound as good as high quality disc recordings and a wide variety of material is available.

On the other hand, the buyer who is seeking the ultimate in both sonic excellence and tape-recording versatility should consider a reel-to-reel deck—bearing in mind, of course, that such a product costs more than a cassette model, occupies considerably more space, and requires more skill to operate correctly.

Unfortunately, CONSUMER GUIDE Magazine has nothing encouraging to report about recent developments or even the promise of future developments in the 8-track cartridge tape format. Indeed it would appear that this tape format (both tape and machine) lags well behind the others in terms of acoustic quality and mechanical reliability. At this time, then, it is impossible to make any recommendations regarding cartridge tape or tape players.

**Tape Deck Care**

NO MATTER what type of deck you ultimately decide to purchase, you must give it proper care if you expect it to live up to its performance potential. The following procedures are simple tasks that anyone can do to keep his or her tape deck in top shape.

Tape heads, guides, capstans, puck rollers—all the surfaces that come in contact with the moving tape—should be cleaned regularly (about every twenty playing hours) with a cotton swab dipped either in alcohol or a commercial head-cleaning solution. Even the slightest buildup of flaked-off oxide particles reduces high-frequency response considerably.

In addition, the metal surfaces that touch the tape require a second kind of cleaning—degaussing. Degaussing eliminates the gradual accumulation of magnetism to which these parts are susceptible. If unremoved, this magnetism permanently erases the high frequencies on your recorded tapes and simultaneously increases their hiss level. Inexpensive head demagnetizers are available at any audio dealer, and since degaussing takes only a few seconds, you should do it about as often as you undertake the regular head-cleaning procedure.

The proper degaussing technique is as follows: 1. Turn off your tape deck and remove all recorded tapes from the vicinity. 2. If the tip(s) of the demagnetizer is exposed and hard, cover it (them) with a layer of plastic electrical tape to prevent scratching the delicate faces of the tape heads. 3. Turn on the head degausser (some are activated automatically when you plug them in; others have a pushbutton switch) while holding it at arm's length from the recorder. 4. Slowly bring it up to each of the parts to be demagnetized, move it over the affected surfaces, and then slowly withdraw it to arm's length before turning it off. That completes the demagnetizing procedure.

The drive mechanisms of tape recorders are similar to those of turntables. At least once a year you should clean the mechanism and lubricate the motor bearings and other rotating parts sparingly and with care lest oil leak onto surfaces where it has no business. Then put the whole mechanism through its paces to check for signs of slippage in fast-forward or rewind and for faults in the braking system. Tape heads should also be inspected periodically for wear. When the passage of tape has worn a groove deep enough to catch a fingernail on, the useful life of the heads has been exhausted. Replacing heads, unfortunately, requires specialized equipment and must be handled by a competent technician.

# 1978 Best Buys: Tape Recorders

IN SELECTING THE following tape recorders as "Best Buys," CONSUMER GUIDE Magazine's audio experts weighed purchase price against each unit's overall construction and design, special features and options, and such performance characteristics as frequency response, signal-to-noise ratio, wow and flutter, and harmonic distortion relative to the signal level applied to the tape.

## OPEN-REEL RECORDERS
### Best Buys

**Pioneer RT-1020L** meets the most critical high fidelity performance standards with respect to frequency response, noise and distortion. Unlike some recorders, it has a considerable safety margin above the 0 dB meter level, which means that during recording the meters can be kept near the upper portions of their scales without risking distortion. CONSUMER GUIDE Magazine found the playback performance to be excellent with either two-channel or four-channel commercially recorded tapes. This recorder required a little more familiarization than most because of its unusual switching flexibility, but it was actually quite easy to use. The tape-transport logic system worked well, with the tape stopping from a fast speed in a fraction of a second when the "play" button was pressed. There was a pause of about five seconds before it resumed play at normal speed. This seemed interminably long, but compensating for it was the assurance that the recorder would not damage or spill a tape, no matter how carelessly it was handled. In the RT-1020L's price range, one rarely finds either four-channel playback ability or the capacity to hold 10½-inch reels. It is, therefore, a pleasant surprise to find both features in a moderately priced recorder, which also offers the construction and general quality of much more expensive units.

**Approximate Retail Price: $700.00**                  **Low Price: $490.00**

*Prices are accurate at time of printing; subject to manufacturer's change.*

**Sony/Superscope TC-377** is an excellent example of the advantages and disadvantages of a single-motor tape recorder. Its electrical properties are outstanding, and in most home-recording applications its sound could not be distinguished from that of the finest three-motor machines selling for up to three times its price. Similarly, the low distortion and noise level of this recorder are excellent. The tape transport has a flutter level about as low as we have ever seen on a single-motor recorder, and its speed accuracy is certainly good enough for any nonprofessional purpose. The disadvantages inherent in the machine concern a transport-control knob that requires appreciable effort and exasperatingly long fast-forward and rewind times. Nevertheless, the serious amateur recordist should be able to produce tapes of near professional quality, with a lower financial investment than would be required for many of the leading cassette recorders.

**Approximate Retail Price: $419.95**          **Low Price: $323.35**

**Sony/Superscope TC-388-4** might be just the machine you are looking for if you are interested in four-channel recording and have never owned a tape deck before. If you want to start up your own recording studio or business, however, you will have to opt for a somewhat better machine. If you have been considering one of the super cassette decks, which sell for a bit less than this open-reel unit but offer just about the same performance quality, please remember that they cannot record or play discrete quadraphonic sound. Only open-reel units have that capability.

**Approximate Retail Price: $679.95**          **Low Price: $530.36**

## Also Recommended

**Akai GX-230D** is a two-speed (7½ and 3¾ ips), three-motor open-reel deck for mono and stereo recording and playback. It features a built-in reverse capability for playing long programs recorded in both tape directions. Although it cannot match the performance levels of the high-priced open-reel machines, the GX-230D is satisfactory for less-than-professional tasks and would be well suited to most home music systems.

**Approximate Retail Price: $585.00**          **Low Price: $406.25**

**Pioneer RT-1011L** is a solidly engineered stereo tape recorder of reliable mechanical quality and superb audio performance. It lacks the ultimate versatility of some costlier tape decks; but it yields nothing to them in terms of performance. The RT-1011L is built to live up to its published claim of extra strength and reliability, and as such, it should be a fine stereo machine for the serious or advanced home tape enthusiast.

**Approximate Retail Price: $650.00**          **Low Price: $455.00**

*Prices are accurate at time of printing; subject to manufacturer's change.*

**Sony/Superscope TC-880-2** is truly a tape recorder worthy of consideration by the serious recordist who is interested in half-track work and who can afford such an expensive unit. Its performance in the half-track configuration is unsurpassed by any consumer-oriented tape machine, and it possesses features not normally found on home or even on semi-pro tape recorders. Whether any nonprofessional really needs such extraordinary features and performance at such an elevated price, however, is a question only the individual buyer can answer.

**Approximate Retail Price: $2495.00**     **Low Price: $2070.85**

**Tandberg 10XD** is a three-speed open-reel deck capable of handling reel sizes up to the professional (NAB hub) 10½-inch diameter. It records and plays in mono or stereo, and has facilities for adding echo effects or sound-on-sound via an ingenious switch arrangement. The unit's sophisticated Dolby noise reduction system can be used at any speed, and it has special control positions for recording Dolbyized FM off the air. Even a relatively inexperienced user can make recordings with excellent dynamic range and signal-to-noise characteristics.

**Approximate Retail Price: $1400.00**     **Low Price: $1259.00**

**Teac A-6100** is a superb tape machine, among the best open-reel recorders CONSUMER GUIDE Magazine has tested. The critical tape enthusiast could hardly ask for better fidelity than the A-6100 provides at 15 ips, and even at 7½ ips this Teac machine displays true high fidelity response. Too costly for most home sound systems, the A-6100 is as professional a piece of equipment as any consumer-oriented audio component in existence.

**Approximate Retail Price: $1300.00**     **Low Price: $905.00**

**Technics RS-1500US** is not an open-reel deck for the casual or infrequent recordist. Rather, like other advanced (and extremely expensive) machines of its type, it is intended for use by tape enthusiasts who can appreciate its enviable combination of superior audio and mechanical performance and who will use its many fine attributes to full advantage. CONSUMER GUIDE Magazine's audio experts were especially impressed by its ruggedness of construction, high quality parts, and attention to detail—all of which assure years of reliable, trouble-free service.

**Approximate Retail Price: $1500.00**     **Low Price: $1125.00**

## CASSETTE RECORDERS
### Best Buys

**Bigston BSD-300** lacks some of the frills and flourishes of the more elaborate cassette decks, but it offers many important and worthwhile features—e.g., Dolby noise reduction and the facility for adjusting the deck to handle different tape types. With its very low distortion and excellent S/N characteristics, moreover, the

*Prices are accurate at time of printing; subject to manufacturer's change.*

BSD-300 provides built-in assurance of good results, making it well suited to the beginning recordist. In terms of all that it offers in performance and features, the Bigston BSD-300 carries an almost incredibly low price tag.

**Approximate Retail Price: $169.95**         **Low Price: Not Available**

**Harman/Kardon HK-2000** is a cassette recorder capable of rendering creditable performance with standard low-noise tape. But the unit really comes into its own with chrome-dioxide ($CrO_2$) tape. In fact, when recording and playing chrome tape, the Harman/Kardon HK-2000 provides frequency response that compares favorably with the best cassette machines currently available. All in all, the HK-2000 is a most attractive cassette recorder at what must be considered a fair price.

**Approximate Retail Price: $399.95**         **Low Price: $296.95**

**JVC KD-75** can be recommended as a fine consumer-oriented cassette machine that performs as well as any of the better Dolbyized cassette decks. Mechanical operation is very good (although the transport keys require a fair amount of finger pressure), and the Super ANRS feature is worth having for what it does to the linearity of response and dynamic range of high-frequency tones recorded at stronger-than-usual signal levels. For all these virtues, the KD-75 carries a most reasonable price tag.

**Approximate Retail Price: $379.95**         **Low Price: $266.00**

**Kenwood KX-720** offers distinctly better performance than one would expect from looking at its price tag. In fact, the Kenwood KX-720 ranks right up there with the best cassette decks available in terms of overall performance and features. Mechanically, the deck runs flawlessly, and its cue and review feature functions precisely — serving as a genuine operational aid in locating the desired portion of a recorded tape with great rapidity.

**Approximate Retail Price: $275.00**         **Low Price: $192.50**

**Marantz 5420** offers so many features and options — Dolby noise reduction, switchable bias and equalization, memory rewind, peak-level indicators, built-in active mixer, etc. — that the unit must almost be placed in a class by itself. From the standpoint of audio performance, moreover, the Marantz 5420 is at least the equal of the other first-rate cassette decks in its price bracket. During CONSUMER GUIDE Magazine's tests, the 5420's speeds were accurate to within a few hundredths of a percent, and the unit proved responsive and smooth in every operating mode.

**Approximate Retail Price: $429.95**         **Low Price: $343.95**

**Nakamichi 500** is one of the best cassette recorders yet tested by CONSUMER GUIDE Magazine. It earned marks of "very good" to "excellent" in all performance areas, electrical and mechanical. It

*Prices are accurate at time of printing; subject to manufacturer's change.*

features built-in Dolby and two tape-selection switches (one for bias and the other for equalization). Each switch has three positions, making this a very sophisticated and versatile tape-selection system. Response is unquestionably excellent; the signal-to-noise ratio is very high; distortion is very low. Mechanical reliability seems certain. The circuitry permits recording at unusually high levels without incurring excessive distortion, which is the case—unfortunately—on many competitive models.
**Approximate Retail Price: $440.00      Low Price: Not Available**

**Teac A-100's** signal-to-noise ratio is remarkably good and reflects, no doubt, Teac's decision to sacrifice extreme high-end response for quieter tapes with better dynamic range over the most important segment of the audio/musical spectrum. It is hard to argue with this philosophy in view of the A-100's excellent overall performance. The recorder's extremely attractive price, moreover, makes the A-100 an outstanding value.
**Approximate Retail Price: $230.00      Low Price: $180.00**

**Technics RS-671AUS** offers excellent audio performance combined with surprisingly smooth (almost professional-feel) transport. In addition, the RS-671AUS possesses a solid selection of worthwhile features plus a no-nonsense kind of product personality that should appeal to the serious home cassette user who is not yet ready for a costlier three-head deck. In view of how much it provides in terms of features and performance, the RS-671AUS is reasonably priced.
**Approximate Retail Price: $399.95      Low Price: $299.95**

## Also Recommended

**Nakamichi 550** is capable of being powered by an internal battery pack, a 12-volt DC source via direct plug-in, or by regular AC power lines via the supplied adapter. It is a portable stereo cassette recorder that can truly be described as a high fidelity component. In fact, it yields little in the way of audio response to any cassette recorder in existence. Without question, the 550 must be ranked as the best portable cassette recorder yet tested by CONSUMER GUIDE Magazine.
**Approximate Retail Price: $570.00      Low Price: Not Available**

**Nakamichi 700** may be high-priced, but the unit is a one-of-a-kind special: a feature-laden (touch-to-operate buttons, fine-speed control, test-tone and tape monitor switches), super-performing (response within $\pm 2$ dB from 20 Hz to 20 kHz, distortion below 1.4 percent, and 0.09 percent wow and flutter) cassette recorder.
**Approximate Retail Price: $1030.00      Low Price: Not Available**
*Prices are accurate at time of printing; subject to manufacturer's change.*

**Sony/Superscope EL-5** is an Elcaset tape machine that in terms of response, signal to noise, distortion, and wow and flutter noses out many first-rate conventional cassette recorders. In fact, the EL-5 compares favorably with several good open-reel decks, although it is outclassed by the best of that format. In general, this machine can be described as occupying a level somewhere between the best cassette decks and the best open-reel decks. Despite its undisputed technical excellence, however, the future of the EL-5—like that of all Elcaset machines—is an unknown quantity.
**Approximate Retail Price: $629.95**     **Low Price: $485.00**

**Sony/Superscope TC-177SD** is a three-head deck with separate heads for erase, recording and playback. It has a Dolby system, two VU meters and a peak-level indicator. The unit performed extremely well during CONSUMER GUIDE Magazine's tests, validating everything claimed for it. While its price is high, it provides significantly better performance than many other cassette units. It is, in fact, one of the best recorders on the market.
**Approximate Retail Price: $829.95**     **Low Price: $659.95**

**Tandberg TCD-310** has neither playback-level controls nor a rewind-memory feature. However, these omissions are more than offset by the genuinely superior performance which results from a combination of excellent transport action, smooth frequency response, and low distortion and noise.
**Approximate Retail Price: $550.00**     **Low Price: $499.00**

**Tandberg TCD-330** is right up there with the best cassette recorders available, but it is also one of the costliest. Those enthusiasts who can afford it, however, will find pure joy in operating the TCD-330, listening to the tapes it makes, and listening to it play commercially recorded tapes. Few cassette decks can match the TCD-330's blend of flawless functioning and superb sound.
**Approximate Retail Price: $1000.00**     **Low Price: $899.00**

**Yamaha TC-800GL** boasts unusual styling, some unique features and very high performance; it is the kind of tape machine that should appeal to a very broad market, ranging from serious listeners to the more casual owners of stereo systems. Original recordings sound remarkably close to the source material, and prerecorded cassettes are reproduced flawlessly. Anyone who wants a reliable tape facility should investigate the Yamaha TC-800GL.
**Approximate Retail Price: $390.00**     **Low Price: Not Available**

*Prices are accurate at time of printing; subject to manufacturer's change.*

# 1978 CB Radios

**E**VER SINCE the popularity explosion of Citizens Band radio a few years ago, CB rigs have continued to grow in complexity and ability. Choosing a CB now is a matter of deciding how much sophistication you want and how much you want to pay for it. The dollar figure is probably the easier one to determine. The other figures—all of those numbers on CB specification sheets—can be perplexing.

You do not have to be an electronics expert to shop for a CB radio, but it helps to know what the specifications mean.

Radio frequency output power is the power sent through the air by the transmitter section of a CB radio. The maximum allowed by the Federal Communications Commission is four watts. Virtually every manufacturer of mobile CB radios designs its models so that they will produce this amount of power, but they may vary by a few tenths of a watt. Since you would never be able to tell the difference at the receiving end with another CB radio, you don't have to concern yourself with this specification.

Receiver sensitivity is a measure of the weakest signal from another CB that a receiver can pick up as intelligible speech. A rig with better sensitivity can pick up signals from farther away than a less sensitive unit can. The rating is listed in millionths of a volt, or microvolts. The smaller the microvolt number, the more sensitive the unit. In general, a rating below one microvolt is satisfactory.

Modulation percentage is a measure of "talk power." When a radio-frequency signal is modulated by a voice as in CB operation, the higher the modulation percentage, the greater the talk power that comes out of the speaker. The percentage is increased if the voice is louder or closer to the microphone. If 100 percent modulation should be exceeded during a peak audio period, the result will be more distortion, not greater talk power. This interference can affect communications on other rigs, so CB transceivers are required by the FCC to have built-in limiters to prevent overmodulation. Some manufacturers limit the modulation capability of a CB model to 90 percent maximum to prevent exceeding 100 percent. There is no noticeable difference between 90 percent and 100 percent modulation, so you should not be swayed by this variance. A transmitter section, however, should be able to reach about 85 percent for effective communications.

Selectivity is a major figure of merit for the receiving end of a CB. It reveals a receiver's ability to distinguish between a signal that the unit is switched to and signals on adjacent channels. Most manufacturers give this specification in terms of adjacent channel rejection. CB channels are separated from each other by 10,000 cycles per second, abbreviated 10 kHz. The measurement of sound (noise from one channel to another) is decibels, abbreviated dB. So when you look at a specification sheet for a rig, the selectivity will be listed as, for instance, -60 dB $\pm$10 kHz. The larger the number, the better: -60 is better than -40. Another measure of selectivity relates to the bandwidth of the intermediate frequency stage of a receiver, which is actually a better indicator of how good the receiver's selectivity is. It reveals the "window" that the tuned circuits see. Since an audio frequency of only about 300 Hz to 3000 kHz is required for intelligible speech, measurements are generally taken at $\pm$3 kHz, sometimes stated as 6 kHz at the effective voltage mark, which is -6 dB. This is stated in selectivity specifications as 6 kHz at -6 dB. It might be listed as 5 kHz at -6 dB, which indicates that the audio passband is narrower (to 2500 Hz, as compared to 3000 Hz). Intelligibility is impaired noticeably below 2500 Hz, but because of the narrower band, adjacent channel rejection figures are improved. There is a balance between the two.

CB transceivers can develop at least one other frequency that sneaks through disguised as the one you are tuned to. Rejection of this interfering signal is sometimes noted in manufacturer's literature as so many dBs down, such as -60 dB image rejection. The bigger the number, the better the rejection.

A squelch is a standard control on every two-way radio. The incoming signal strength range can be adjusted by the user with this control. Since a receiver cannot distinguish between noise and a signal, the control is most often used to reduce the hissing type of noise over a speaker that normally occurs when no signal is being received from another CBer. It should also be used to eliminate weaker background signals so that the user can hear the stronger signal more clearly. The range of control indicates how weak and how strong a signal can be excluded. It relates to the incoming signal strength in microvolts, the lowest signal strength naturally being the inherent sensitivity rating of the rig. For example, a squelch range might typically be from 1/2 microvolt to one millivolt.

# 1978 Best Buys: CB Radios

THE FOLLOWING reports are summaries of extensive tests conducted by CONSUMER GUIDE Magazine's CB staff. Within the classifications of high-priced, medium-priced and low-priced rigs, the models are listed in order of overall quality. The units were judged on the basis of a thorough check of their specifications, their features and their cost.

## High-Priced Models

**The SBE Key/Com 1000** is one of the most exciting-looking rigs on the road today. It is a one-package under-dash unit that features keyboard entry. The dramatic color-coded keys are illuminated, giving the user direct control over a programmable memory and the control system. Among its fingertip control functions are: memory storing and recalling of a channel; scanning of up to ten selected channels with automatic stop on reaching an active one, as well as search and stop for all 40 channels; instant Channel 9 access; a fast/slow scan speed pushbutton and up/down channel selection by pushbutton. To the right of the keyboard is a large, red light-emitting-diode channel readout plus transmit and receive indicators. Sensitivity is as good as one could hope for. Selectivity is also good, and adjacent channel rejection is very impressive. Image response of this rig is healthy, maximum modulation capability is more than enough and average "talk power" is assisted by the rig's speech processing system and limiter. Add an RF gain control, noise blanker, PA provision, adjustable noise limiter and panel illumination dimmer switch and you have an all-around winner in the Key/Com 1000. Size: 5-3/4 x 8-3/4 x 2 inches.

**Approximate Retail Price: $259.95**                      **Low Price: $189.95**
*Prices are accurate at time of printing; subject to manufacturer's change.*

**The Hy-gain 2716** is another new-style 40-channel mobile unit that utilizes the latest integrated circuit technology. It features a keyboard on the microphone. The transceiver can be hidden under a seat, on the firewall or in the trunk with an optional extension cable. The microphone features a 14-function keyboard that includes a one-channel memory, pushbutton Channel 9 recall, stepped volume, squelch, channel selection, noise blanker on/off pushbutton, PA function and standby memory switch. An hours/minutes time setting is included because there is also a built-in digital clock on the mike, as well as a channel display with LEDs. Also on the microphone are transmit and receive lights and a combination microphone/speaker element. This puts a handful of excellent controls at one's fingertips, though it does make the mike a bit unwieldly to handle if you don't have a large hand. The receiver's sensitivity is fine, the passband is wide and adjacent channel rejection is good. Image rejection is acceptable, squelch range is rated fair and modulation capability proved to be virtually 100 percent. The 2716's theft-prevention features, the controls in the microphone and its very good performance put this CB at the forefront of the luxury class. Size: 7-1/2 x 6-1/2 x 2-1/4 inches.
**Approximate Retail Price: $249.95**            **Low Price: $179.95**

**Aircommand's CB640** is one entry in the CB field by Superscope, the people who distribute Sony/Superscope tape recorders and Marantz audio products. The CB640 has an LED channel readout. Among its other features is a "beep" alert when Channel 9 transmission is received regardless of what channel you are switched to. It also has Channel 9 scan defeat. Eight LEDs provide modulation readings. The LEDs are easier to read from the driver's seat than a small meter would be. Other features include switchable noise blanker and automatic noise limiters, RF gain control and PA provision. Channels are chosen by a large selector knob at the extreme right side of the front panel. The receiver section displays fine sensitivity, good adjacent channel rejection and good image rejection. Modulation capability reaches a full 100 percent. Output is 4 watts. It offers many extra features and is especially good for safety-monitoring-team use. Size: 6-1/2 x 9 x 2-1/2 inches.
**Approximate Retail Price: $209.95**            **Low Price: $149.95**

**The Cobra 29XLR** does not feature any unique extras, but it is a solid performer. Its lineup of controls includes "DynaMike," which allows you to adjust for whatever microphone gain you wish, depending on how far away you keep your mike when talking; on-off switch/volume control; and squelch. A sturdy bar-grip-type channel selector knob and LED digital channel readout add to convenience. A hash filter reduces high-frequency noise. The rig also features PA provision and an external speaker jack. All of the Cobra's specs promise excellent performance. This is a unit for CBers who want virtually all the frills possible, good reception and

*Prices are accurate at time of printing; subject to manufacturer's change.*

great transmission punch. Size: 7-1/4 x 9-1/2 x 2-1/4 inches.
**Approximate Retail Price: $229.95**     **Low Price: $164.95**

**The Kris XL-50** features big illuminated meters, large LED digital channel readouts and a large selector knob that makes for easy gripping. Squelch, noise blanker, PA provision and high/low tone controls are included. A large illuminated readout indicates receive or transmit. Selectivity is excellent and the noise blanker incorporated into the circuitry was the best we have handled. The Kris utilizes compression amplifiers to boost average modulation, which reaches 95 percent to just about 100 percent. The speaker is mounted on the left side to enhance speech intelligibility. Audio output power is 3 watts. It is an impressive performer. Size: 9 x 9-1/2 x 3 inches.
**Approximate Retail Price: $259.95**     **Low Price: $189.95**

**Medium-Priced Models**

THESE MODELS generally lack full features or have slightly fewer performance capabilities than higher-priced models. Whatever is missing is reflected in a price that might be as much as $130 lower than the units listed above.

**The Motorola 4009,** so striking in black and white, is produced by one of the leaders in the two-way radio communications field. It boasts dual receivers so that an incoming Channel 9 emergency communication will override any channel the user is listening to. If Channel 9 monitoring is not desired, the user can simply change the crystal to receive any other single channel for break-in purposes. A Channel 9 pushbutton switch also overrides existing channels, while a lighted "Priority" appears when Channel 9 is active. An "Extend" pushbutton is actually an effective noise blanker switch to reject noise from an automobile's ignition system. Automatic noise limiting is used to minimize man-made interference, but it is not defeatable. If you should wire the CB radio to the power line incorrectly by reversing leads, damage is prevented. Also, the transmitter is protected from damage should the radio be operated with a defective antenna or even without one. Sensitivity is fine, and adjacent channel rejection is good. The unit provides excellent cross-modulation rejection, and the automatic gain control circuit holds the audio output steady in the face of wide signal levels. A built-in speech compression circuit increases the average level of a voice so that even stronger audio is received by the other party when transmitting. Output is 3-1/2 watts. This rig should satisfy most discerning CB radio users. It has a lot going for it, including nationwide professional authorized service stations. Size: 7-1/4 x 9-1/2 x 2-1/2 inches.
**Approximate Retail Price: $174.95**     **Low Price: $139.95**

*Prices are accurate at time of printing; subject to manufacturer's change.*

**The Tram D-42** transceiver is a sensitive, selective rig. It uses concentric controls, which take a bit of getting used to, but save panel space. An LED channel indicator, squelch, tone control and noise limiter are built in.

Audio output is 4 watts. Also included is an antitheft snap-bracket mounting device. In sum, this model is an all-around high-quality mobile unit. Size: 7 x 9-1/4 x 2-3/8 inches.

**Approximate Retail Price: $159.95**          **Low Price: $119.95**

**Johnson American's 4145** is also made by a long-time manufacturer of commercial two-way radios with many authorized service centers coast to coast. The 4145 features a string of LEDs to display the strength of an incoming signal and the RF output. The classy-looking mobile unit also has a switchable automatic noise limiter, public-address capability, large LED channel display, squelch control and an illumination dim switch. Receiver sensitivity is excellent and selectivity is good. A speech-compressor circuit is built in. Output power is 3 watts. Size: 6-1/4 x 9 x 2 inches.

**Approximate Retail Price: $149.95**          **Low Price: $109.95**

**The Sparkomatic 2040** is all-black — the better for would-be thieves to miss. Channel selection is accomplished by pressing one of the two rectangular bars: the top one for selecting channels forward; the bottom one for a reverse sequence. Pressing the left side of either bar indexes the channels at a rate of one per second, while fingertip pressure at the right speeds up channel movement to the rate of four channels per second. Audio power is 3 watts. Size: 7 x 8-3/4 x 2-1/4

**Approximate Retail Price: $139.99**          **Low Price: $99.95**

**The Panasonic RJ-3150** is a nice, all-around transceiver, though not quite in the class of the previous four. Its receiver performs well with good selectivity and adjacent channel rejection. Audio output is 2 watts. Its controls and other features include switchable automatic noise limiting, PA capability, volume and squelch controls and external speaker jack. The transceiver comes with an easy-release dual-position mounting bracket. Its large size may make it a space waster that cannot be accommodated in many of today's smaller-size autos. Nevertheless, its all-around performance and features are good for this price class. Size: 8 x 10-1/2 x 2-1/2 inches.

**Approximate Retail Price: $159.95**          **Low Price: $119.95**

### Low-Priced Models

TWO MODELS are listed here for CBers who wish to own a 40-channel mobile unit but want to spend as little as possible, recognizing that there will be sacrifices in performance and features.

*Prices are accurate at time of printing; subject to manufacturer's change.*

**The Realistic TRC-467** is a bare-bones model available from Radio Shack. It has a big, rotary channel-selector dial, squelch control and modulation LED indicator. An external speaker jack is also included. It can run with the best of them in the sensitivity department. Moreover, adjacent channel rejection is very good and audio output is a solid 5 watts. There is a speech-processing circuit that improves the average modulation level to near 100 percent. It is a good performer for the money. Size: 5-1/4 x 9-1/2 x 2-1/4 inches.
**Approximate Retail Price: $119.95        Low Price: Not Available**

**Courier's Rogue 40** is another nice low-cost unit with performance on a par with the Realistic model. Controls are volume and squelch with PA capability and an external speaker jack. The channel selector is also an illuminated-dial type, not LED displayed. Sensitivity is very good, selectivity is especially wide with good adjacent channel rejection. The squelch range is greater than that of most rigs. Output is 3 watts. A powerful speech-processing circuit boosts the average modulation level. This is a fine-performing space saver with neat appearance for the price. Size: 5-7/8 x 8-1/4 x 2 inches.
**Approximate Retail Price: $119.95        Low Price: $89.95**
*Prices are accurate at time of printing; subject to manufacturer's change.*

---

## SPECIAL INFORMATION SERVICE

**A Bonus for Readers of this CONSUMER GUIDE®**

CONSUMER GUIDE® offers a special bonus to its readers who are interested in obtaining information as to where they can find the low prices on specific products listed in this guide. Simply fill out the form and mail. Include 25 cents for postage and handling.
**Please send me information on:**

Product _____ Model Number _____

Manufacturer _____

Your Name _____

Address _____

City _____ State _____ Zip Code _____

**CONSUMER GUIDE Magazine**
**3841 West Oakton, Skokie, Illinois 60076**

# 1978 Food Preparation Appliances

CONSUMER GUIDE Magazine tests a wide variety of new food preparation appliances every year. The reason for this activity is simple. The buyer, no matter how cautiously he or she studies the kitchen appliance, cannot be expected to learn everything about its performance capabilities or lack of them. In-store explanations or even demonstrations can be persuasive without being particularly informative. CONSUMER GUIDE Magazine's testing of food preparation equipment is designed to examine each appliance's basic functions under test-kitchen conditions. At least two greatly varying recipes are used with each appliance so that as many different conditions and ingredients as possible are used in the tests. If an appliance claims special features or attachments, these are also tested.

The consumer has to do some careful evaluation, too. Evaluating one's needs and budget is the first step to wise shopping. How much time do you devote to preparing food? Will the appliance you are considering mean you will be spending less time preparing food, or will you have to plan more elaborate and more expensive meals to get the full benefit from the appliance?

When you evaluate your needs, consider appliances that can take care of several kitchen tasks. A versatile appliance that performs all of its functions satisfactorily is usually a better buy than a single-function appliance.

**Safety**

ONE OF THE first pieces of information to look for when purchasing an appliance is the Underwriters Laboratories' approval. They perform independent tests on many appliances and they have strict requirements. A safely constructed food preparation machine will have the UL seal of approval on the machine itself, on its cord, or mentioned somewhere in the literature included with the appliance.

Although the buyer expects an appliance to perform well, some skill, care and common sense are needed to safely operate food preparation appliances. For efficient, safe use, instructions that accompany the appliance must be followed. Safety requires that the switch be off when plugging or unplugging the appliance. Counter tops should be dry. No more than one appliance should be plugged into a wall outlet. If an extension cord is necessary, it should be a heavy-duty one with a wire size of 14 or 16. Special care should be taken when children are in the kitchen; many appliances are hot to the touch and should be off limits to youngsters.

**Performance**

KITCHEN WORK is hard and appliances must be solid and sturdy to perform well. Look for solid handles, quality materials and a design that is easy to handle, store and clean. Some units may work well yet have unwanted side-effects. The emission of odors, heat, steam or noise bothers some people and not others. Capacity is a consideration, too. An appliance that is perfect for a single person could be impractical for a family. When shopping for a kitchen appliance, take a look at the use-and-care booklet—it should indicate how much food a particular appliance can prepare.

The informed buyer should look at the whole packet of information that comes with an appliance. A high-quality appliance should have a warranty of at least one year, service cards and a list of service centers.

**Cleaning**

EASE OF CLEANING is so closely related to performance that many people view them as indistinguishable. By nature, food preparation is messy, but cleaning up afterward should not require excessive effort, time or the handling of many parts. Many appliances have chrome or stainless steel exteriors and nonstick interiors. Easy-to-clean surfaces are worth the extra cost.

Totally immersible electrical appliances are the easiest to clean. Spills, drips and splashes of food cooked onto the base of an appliance are easy to remove if the cord is detachable and the whole unit can be immersed.

**Bag Sealers**

MOST BAG sealers are housed in a rectangular metal base that can store a supply of bags. There is a difference between freezable, boilable bags, and simple plastic bags. The sealer will seal either type, and for refrigerator storage of food, or shelf storage of non-perishables, the simple variety serves the purpose economically. But, if you are preparing food for freezer storage, be sure to have the right kind of plastic bags. They are not inexpensive; some cost around 14 cents per bag, but they help food to retain its value throughout freezer storage.

## Blenders

A BLENDER is a standard appliance in most kitchens, though many cooks do not use their blenders as frequently as they might. Some blenders can handle meats, ice and coffee beans, in addition to the usual tasks of chopping, grinding and making purees.

Do not judge a blender by the number of buttons it has. A wide choice of speeds is not necessarily an advantage. Even at the lowest settings a blender is quite fast, and most functions performed in the blender are best done by turning the blender on and off in short bursts to prevent the overprocessing of foods. When the blender is turned on and off in short cycles, the blades, for the most part, will be revolving at a range of speeds from the chosen setting to the lowest setting as they coast to a stop. The control you exercise in stopping the blender is more important to the finished food than a subtle range of speeds. CONSUMER GUIDE Magazine thinks that there is no significant advantage to having more than 10 speeds. Five speeds, indeed, is probably sufficient for a full range of culinary tasks. A blender with only high and low speeds, however, will lack versatility.

Many blenders have a pulse or instant off feature for short bursts. Although the pulse feature is a handy one, the same blade action can be achieved in all the blenders tested by quickly alternating between the chosen speed button and the off button. A blender's effectiveness actually depends on its power, on the way the blades work, on the shape of the jar and on how you use it. The shape of the container and the blades should be designed to work together to force foods into a vortex and down to the blades. Foods must be drawn into the blades to be properly processed. There should be no corners or areas in the container where substantial amounts of food can accumulate without being processed. The need to stop the unit to redistribute the food should be kept to a minimum. A removable blade assembly is a feature we recommend for safe and easy cleaning.

## Burger Makers

AN APPLIANCE that promises to make a hamburger in a few minutes and claims to be easy to clean, portable and easy to store sounds like an excellent idea.

Both single-burger and double-burger units were tested by CONSUMER GUIDE Magazine. Most of the hamburger makers have a reversible tray with one or two round wells on one side for meat patties; the flip side is square or rectangular for grilled sandwiches. Most of the units tested also can be used as open grills for eggs, bacon or pancakes, though some units without heat controls were too hot for eggs. Sandwiches were flattened when using the closed grilling method. When cooking with the unit closed there obviously is no way to check on the food being prepared.

CONSUMER GUIDE Magazine thinks that an appliance that successfully does several jobs is often a better buy than the single-function appliance. The convenience of cooking one or two hamburgers quickly should be weighed against the price of the units.

**Can Openers**

EASE OF CLEANING is an important feature to look for when buying a can opener. Look for a can opener that is tall enough to open large coffee and juice cans. If a can opener is too short, you have to move it to the edge of the counter and support the can while it is being opened.

A magnet to remove the lid is a convenience, but the cutting assembly is of prime importance. The cutter may be either a rotating wheel or a cutting edge. The latter is more versatile in cutting cans in unusual shapes, but the rotary wheel is best for round cans and holds its sharp edge longer.

A knife sharpener is a nice extra that comes with some can openers, giving them a little extra versatility.

**Coffee Makers (Automatic Drip)**

IN THE PAST few years, the automatic drip coffee maker has become a standard item in many kitchens, almost replacing the electric percolator. The price of coffee seems to have made people more aware of the quality of the brew they are getting — if the price is high, the quality should be high, too. The single-pass drip coffee maker can brew a respectable cup of coffee: the design principle has many advantages.

For instance, the single-pass, drip coffee maker forces heated water from a tank at the top of the brewer through a paper or permanent filter and into a pot or carafe at the bottom. That means the coffee grounds are not boiled or perked and most of the sediment is strained out. The coffee is kept hot in its carafe on a warming plate. Most automatic drip coffee makers have filters available, so the grounds are easily removed. Some units come with permanent filters that are fairly easy to empty and clean.

There are several features to look for when buying a drip coffee maker. The coffee maker should not be excessively noisy when heating the water nor should it release an excessive amount of steam. The water tank should have clear markings to help you measure cups. The scupper hole in the bottom of the tank should open and close automatically and not simply be an open hole through which water will drip as soon as it is poured into the tank. While some drip coffee makers make coffee in a very short time by using a percolator tube to bring the hot water to the top of the filter basket, CONSUMER GUIDE Magazine has found that models with a stainless steel tank that heats all the water before releasing it over the filter basket is less noisy. CONSUMER GUIDE Magazine prefers separate brewing and warming lights and switches, rather than a simple on/off switch. The drip coffee makers usually measure in five-ounce cups, so that if the consumer uses standard eight-ounce mugs, measurements must be adjusted accordingly.

This year, several manufacturers have come out with "mini" models of their single-pass coffee makers. General Electric, Sunbeam, Regal and Farberware all offer models that make only two to four cups of coffee. As with the full-sized machines, you can use them to make instant beverages. CONSUMER GUIDE Magazine thinks a small drip coffee maker would be suitable for an office or dorm room. Some of the larger coffee makers, like Proctor-Silex Deluxe Model A-100, have a special basket or device for brewing small amounts of coffee. CONSUMER GUIDE Magazine thinks that brewing only as much coffee as you will drink is an excellent idea, given the price of coffee and the fact that fresh coffee tastes best.

One final word of caution: Underwriters Laboratories has approved short cords for these coffee makers. If you use an extension cord, be sure the cord has the right wattage load capacity.

## Coffee Makers (Percolators)

SOME PEOPLE prefer to brew their coffee in a percolator. Coffee flavor is a matter of taste; CONSUMER GUIDE Magazine's testers have enjoyed good cups of coffee from both single-pass coffee makers and percolators. Single-pass coffee makers are intended to stay out on the counter; percolators can be stored easily if counterspace is at a premium. Immersible percolators are the easiest to clean. It is essential that the pot be clean to make good coffee. The percolator handle should be easy to grip and should be attached to the pot in such a way that, when the pot is full, the weight is neither awkward nor top-heavy. The base of the percolator should be insulated so that heat will not be passed to the countertop. Select a pot size to meet your needs. Good features include clear cup markings on the inside of the pot, dials to help control the coffee's strength, and mini-baskets to brew small amounts of coffee.

## Crepe Makers

CREPE MAKERS inspire visions of gourmet dining, entertaining and luxurious living. They do make crepe cooking a little simpler, especially for beginners, but by no stretch of the imagination can they be considered essential kitchen equipment. Any small, electric or non-electric heavy-gauge skillet can be used to make crepes, and other things as well.

Most electric crepe pans are "bottom baking," which means that the rounded surface is dipped into batter, then set upright on its feet to bake. Generally, the crepes are baked on just one side. Most pans have a nonstick finish to simplify removal of the crepes. A thermostatic control is needed to maintain the proper heat for crepe baking. A signal light is considered helpful as it tells when the proper baking temperature is reached. Buying decisions should be based on size, design and maintenance of even temperature.

The buyer should be aware that some small electric fry pans are designed to handle crepes as well as a number of other dishes, thus offering more flexibility.

**Electric Knives**

WHETHER OR NOT you buy an electric knife depends largely on how often it is to be used. If you pull out the electric knife only on Thanksgiving for the annual carving job, you may decide it is not worth owning. On the other hand, if you use an electric knife for slicing freshly baked bread, cutting up vegetables, slicing cheese, and dicing fruit as well as carving meat, you will develop skill with the appliance, and it will earn a spot on the counter or wall. When it is out in view, you are more apt to remember to use it.

In use, the electric knife should not require excessive pressure or sawing motion. Do not attempt to cut through bones. Even cutting through frozen foods or cardboard will dull the blades.

**Food Processors**

ALMOST EVERY motorized small appliance manufacturer has his version of a food processor. All of them are copies of the original Cuisinart processor, a French-designed machine that established itself several years ago in the hearts of famous gourmet cooks and then in the kitchens of the well-to-do. Cuisinart now has two models, both of them expensive but both of them still the standard of quality for all the others. The home-size Cuisinart is a scaled-down version of the Robot Coupe, used in many of France's finest restaurant kitchens.

A food processor is for you if you do cook quite a lot at home, if your cooking repertoire includes an assortment of preparation methods such as chopping, slicing, dicing, shredding, mixing and the like. (A convenience-food user with minimal interest in cooking or minimal space obviously is not a potential food processor owner.) The other big "if" is money. Is a handy, dandy device that performs all these functions worth the expense?

Making the most of a processor requires a period of education and adaptation. You must learn how to use it—and this means reading every word of the instructions carefully. Then you must learn how to use it in your everyday cooking. This means a "stop and think" period before each knife-and-board cutting chore, or before you get out the hand grater, or the cheese slicer. Once you have trained yourself to remember your machine and let it work for you on every possible occasion, you are hooked. You will discover yourself feeling put upon if working in a kitchen without a processor.

Braking action is, we think, important. This action helps stop the movement of the blades more quickly and is a safety feature. Since speed is such an important part of the food processor we are afraid users may get impatient with a few extra seconds waiting for the blades to stop. Opening a machine that is still running can be very dangerous. The processor operator has to practice safety, but we think machines should do their part too, since humans are often less than reliable.

Pulse switches are features on many of the newer machines. On the Cuisinart you just turn the machine on in short bursts of power. We think the top-operated mechanism is just as easy, if not easier, than an additional switch on the base of the processor. In our tests we found that on some machines it was easy to move the switch from pulse to on—too easy, in fact, and we had the machine going when we wanted it off. A lot of "switchery" is not necessarily an advantage.

Most processors have an automatic temperature control that cuts out the motor when it gets too hot. It is important to remember to turn the operating switch off when the motor cuts out. Otherwise you might walk away from it, planning to come back soon, only to find the motor has come back on when it has cooled down. If you are not right at hand, it could be a problem.

### Fryers (Fry Pans)

FEW SMALL KITCHEN appliances have been around longer than the electric fry pan, which says something for its popularity. The fry pan really has stood the test of time. However, today's fry pan is a far cry from the original. Some current models can bake, broil, deep fat fry, roast, warm, slow-cook and thaw foods in addition to frying.

CONSUMER GUIDE Magazine advises evaluating your needs before buying a fry pan. If your range has a broiler, for example, you probably do not need a fry pan that duplicates this function. If you own a slow cooking pot, you probably do not need a fry pan that does the same thing.

But there may be occasions when you will choose the fry pan for baking even though you own a full-scale oven. The fry pan is a very efficient energy user so it is less costly to operate than the oven. For baking, a high dome is helpful; some domes are high enough to accommodate a loaf of bread.

There are several fry pan features CONSUMER GUIDE Magazine recommends. A detachable heat control is considered essential. Once it is removed, the rest of the pan can be immersed in dishwater. A nonstick finish is also a plus at cleanup time. Removable legs and handles on some models aid in maintenance, but are not essential.

Look for a wide range of temperatures on the heat control for versatility. Temperatures at the lower end of the scale may permit slow cooking and thawing; high readings up to 400°F are desirable for certain baking tasks and deep fat frying. Pan sizes vary widely. Big families, naturally, will benefit from bigger pans, but singles and twosomes may prefer the midget sizes which are among the newer offerings.

### Fryers (Small Deep Fryers)

MOST OF THE new little deep fryers can handle small loads of food well. They take up little counter space. Underwriters Laboratories continues to insist that they come with short (usually about 25- to 30-inch) cords. The short cord is, they say, a safety feature. We think another foot of cord would be an added safety feature. So few kitchens have really convenient outlets that many consumers will have to use extension cords.

Most fryers hold two cups of oil and can fry about one cup of food at a time. Most have no heat ranges. All come with some device to help you get food in and out of the hot oil. Some include a handy slotted tool that is very convenient to use, others have a wire or perforated metal basket. Some have nonstick interiors (a plus, we think), some do not. All come with a one-year warranty.

A few units have several temperature settings and thus can do more than just deep fry. They can stew, steam, simmer, fondue, boil, etc. CONSUMER GUIDE Magazine has always felt that an appliance that can do more than one job is more worthy of your dollar, and your counter or cabinet space, than an appliance that performs only one function. We think a few more dollars spent for a multi-use appliance is a wise investment.

Most of the little deep fryers have no special extras. They heat oil to somewhere between 350°F and 400°F after a preheating period of seven to 10 or 12 minutes, then they cook at temperatures around 350°F. A nonstick interior finish and a fill line mark inside are important features. Signal lights are included on some frying machines—some are accurate, some are not. Most of the fryers recovered temperature in three to four minutes, so if you can learn to wait that long between batches you will not have to worry about relying on a signal light to tell you the oil is hot enough.

### Mixers (Portable)

THERE ARE STILL cooks who need just a little help when it comes to beating a cake batter or a cookie dough and who do not want to get involved with a heavy appliance. A portable mixer is easy to move and easy to store. It has a small motor assembly with detachable beaters and often has a detachable cord. You can tuck it into a drawer or even hang it under a counter. A portable mixer is excellent for whipping cream, stirring up a cake from a mix or even making a milkshake. The only disadvantage of a portable mixer is that you must hold it all the time you are using it. Some portable mixers we tested were better than the cheap stand mixers, so do not let size or portability keep you from this category of mixers.

### Mixers (Stand Mixers)

STAND MIXERS have the motor assembly attached to a base that holds the mixer bowl. Most stand mixers have slightly larger beaters than their portable counterparts, and come with at least one, sometimes two, mixing bowls. You will need to devote about a cubic foot of counter or cupboard space to a stand mixer. If you do a lot of mixing, or if breads, cookies and cakes are regulars in your cooking repertoire, and if you try to squeeze in some other kitchen work while something is being mixed, then a stand mixer might be a better choice for you than a portable. Do remember to look for a heavy-duty stand mixer that really will be helpful. Some of the stand mixers we tested were lightweights.

### Mixers (Multipurpose)

ALL OF THESE high-quality, multipurpose machines are extremely expensive and the consumer should carefully evaluate her or his culinary needs and budget before falling under the spell of these kitchen wizards. The buyer should also be aware that many of these multipurpose kitchen appliances are imported; service and parts probably cannot be as efficient as when dealing with United States-based companies.

The differences between the food processor and multipurpose machines lie in the space each occupies, the cost and the job each can perform. Multipurpose machines have attachments which can add over $500 to the total cost of the unit but a completely equipped heavy-duty mixer can do almost any food preparation task. If space is no problem and the desire and need for the useful attachments outweigh the cost, then the multipurpose machines are the best bet.

In comparing these machines for purchase, carefully weigh the limitations and disadvantages. Look at the attachments which come with the machine, as well as the ones which can be purchased at extra cost. Weigh the necessity of all the attachments;

if you will never use something like a cream separator, maybe a simpler machine would be adequate for you.

**Ovens (Broilers and Other Countertop Ovens)**

TODAY'S COUNTERTOP oven performs a maximum number of chores in a minimum of space using a minimum amount of energy. It also serves as a second oven when special-occasion meal production is underway. And, in certain situations, it can even take the place of a conventional range.

The basic countertop oven bakes and toasts. Beyond that, there are more versatile models that broil. The newest additions to countertop ovens are slow-cooking models—the oven manufacturers' answer to the slow cooker. Rival, the originator of the Crock Pot, has a slow-cooking oven that comes with a dehydrator rack.

Your needs and cooking style should be the chief considerations when choosing a toaster/broiler oven. A small family might even substitute one of the large, all-purpose broiler ovens for a regular oven. The appliances that can substitute for ovens usually have broiler, oven, and rotisserie capabilities, as well as a continuous self-cleaning feature. A smaller, portable, self-cleaning toaster oven that broils food simultaneously on both sides and bakes a variety of breads, muffins and cookies is perfect for taking to a vacation cottage. For rapid and even cooking, the relatively new convection oven is good. It circulates air throughout the oven cavity by a fan. This method has been used in restaurant ovens for many years.

**Slow Cookers**

CONVENIENCE IS the main reason for using a slow cooker. Slow cookers are extremely easy to use—one-step, one-pot cooking. They work silently and do not heat up the kitchen on hot summer days. Slow cookers are very economical to use, saving energy and using leftovers and low-cost food items.

Recommended slow cookers have a basic heating unit with coils encircling the sides. The crockery liner (in sizes from one to eight quarts) fits inside this and is covered during cooking. Switch/control types vary, some are merely plugged in to operate, others have off/on or off/low/high controls; some even have temperature selections. Recommended models have removable crockery liners that are easy to clean and which can double as a serving dish. Some slow cooking appliances add the versatility of deep frying and fast cooking techniques, with elaborate temperature controls.

CONSUMER GUIDE Magazine recommends slow cookers that will heat foods quickly to raise the temperature of the food past the prime bacterial growth temperatures of 60°F to 140°F before dropping back to the normal slow cooking temperature. Once the slow cooker is above 140°F, most of the bacteria are killed and cooking over a long period is safer. Units with the heating element only at the bottom may not get food at the top hot enough to kill bacteria.

Be careful when washing a crockery liner; it chips easily and fast changes from hot to cold may cause it to crack. Corning glass liners can withstand quick temperature changes.

Slow cookers should be at least half full for optimum efficiency—so keep this in mind when figuring what size is right for you.

## Toasters

THE TOASTER is perhaps the most familiar of all food preparation appliances. Toasting bread is still its main work, but additional uses have appeared in the last few years. With the advent of frozen waffles and various other breakfast and dessert pastries, the toaster has acquired new value as a kitchen appliance. New toasters generally offer the consumer several toasting cycles. Toaster settings for light to dark are standard and many toasters now have separate settings for pastries. A separate pastry setting is an asset and should be included in your list of toaster requirements if you plan to eat toaster pastries. The pastry control ensures that warming without burning or drying takes place.

## Waffle Bakers

FROZEN WAFFLES do not compare to the genuine article hot out of the waffle maker. CONSUMER GUIDE Magazine suggests investing in a waffle baker that has reversible grids so you can use the appliance as a grill for sandwiches, eggs, bacon or whatever. Features to look for include a nonstick coating to aid in cleaning, an automatic signal light and a control for light, medium and dark waffles. Large, square waffle bakers are good if you plan to serve waffles at a party. Specialty waffle bakers are also available for making such items as Belgian waffles and thin, crisp Italian cookies called pizzelles.

# 1978 Best Buys: Food Preparation Appliances

CONSUMER GUIDE Magazine's food appliance experts tested many products under actual kitchen conditions and judged each on its performance, cleanability and construction. At least two different recipes were prepared. In addition, the experts examined the manufacturer's claims to see if each product lived up to its advertising. The products that met all of these criteria at a reasonable price were judged "Best Buys."

## BAG SEALERS
### Best Buy

**Oster "Touch-A-Matic" Bag Sealer** requires no preheating. The on/off switch is activated by depressing the cover. By bringing the top over the bag and bottom, it very quietly seals with a thin line. It will handle any type of plastic bag up to 12 inches long. The sealing times will vary with different plastics. A funnel fill collar is included as an aid to filling the bags without spilling over. It is very important that no food interfere with the sealing process. A well-written and informative instruction booklet has suggestions for sealing items other than foods. Also enclosed are eight assorted boilable bags. This model can be mounted on the wall or will sit compactly on the counter.

**Approximate Retail Price: $19.95**　　　　　　　　**Low Price: $11.30**

### Also Recommended

**Hamilton Beach Super Sealobag 403** features a handy recess for cord storage. The recess is a simple but helpful addition to a unit that hangs on the wall or sits on the counter. This unit comes with a 25-foot length of bagging material, longer than that in some other models.

However, the Sealobag requires a preheating period, which some of its competitors do not. Two to three minutes are needed

*Prices are accurate at time of printing; subject to manufacturer's change.*

before sealing boilable bags; five minutes for non-boilable bags, such as those used for sandwich packing. The Sealobag has a special setting for each, and an indicator light to show when it is operating.

Testers liked its cutting bar, which operates through the lid of the cabinet; cutting with the lid closed made the procedure steadier than other cutting methods.

The "Clean-Fill" collar that comes with the Sealobag goes inside the prepared bag before adding the food; a clean rim is essential for proper sealing, and the collar keeps it that way. The Hamilton Beach use-and-care leaflet provides clear instructions on how to seal and store numerous items besides food.

**Approximate Retail Price: $25.95**           **Low Price: $11.95**

## BLENDERS
### Best Buy

**Oster Dual Range 10-Speed Osterizer 888-14** receives an excellent rating in ease of operation. A quick poke at any of the four cycle-speed buttons gives a pulse action on this blender. There are also six continuous speed settings. Coming with a five-cup glass container and a two-ounce measuring cap, the 888-14 performed well when we made milkshakes and peanut butter. There was little splattering and food was evenly processed, requiring little stopping and scraping. The blade assembly comes apart for easy cleaning. Oster's *Spin Cookery Cookbook* comes with the blender.

**Approximate Retail Price: $34.95**           **Low Price: $21.95**

### Also Recommended

**Oster Dual Pulse-Matic 10-Speed Osterizer 886-31** has five, large-size speed buttons that can be set for a high or low range. Once you select the speed, you can activate the pulse button for on/off bursts. The 10 speeds also can run continuously. Besides a five-cup glass container with a two-ounce measuring cap, this model comes with a handy half-pint container that can be used for food storage as well as blending. The appliance made peanut butter with ease; we did not have to stop and scrape the sides very often. Like the other Oster blenders tested, the blade assembly comes apart for easy cleaning. Oster's *Spin Cookery Cookbook* comes with the blender. We rate this model excellent for ease and efficiency of operation.

**Approximate Retail Price: $49.95**           **Low Price: $32.95**

**Oster Pulse-Matic 10-Speed Osterizer 854-04** has a switch that allows the speed setting to remain depressed while you use the "instant off" button. While such a feature is not necessary for proper processing, it certainly did not hamper its performance. As with the other Oster blenders tested, there was little splattering and foods were readily drawn to the blades. This model comes with a five-cup glass container, a two-ounce measuring cap and a helpful cookbook. The blade assembly detaches for easy cleaning of this fine appliance.

**Approximate Retail Price: $40.95**            **Low Price: $25.95**

## BURGER MAKERS
### Best Buys

**Presto Burger 2** is a double-sized burger maker with a flippable lid that becomes a handy little grill or griddle. The Presto Burger 2 has a 4-3/4 x 9 inch cooking surface. It performed well in all our tests, preheated in five minutes and cooked quickly and evenly. When using the round cooking tray you get thin burgers (only 1/3-cup each), but you can flip the tray to cook larger (1-1/4 pound) burgers. The larger burgers take a little longer to cook.

The Presto Burger booklet has drawings to help you identify its parts and assemble them all. Although the Presto Burger 2 is not immersible, it does have openings at the hinge area where water can get into the heating element when wiping it off.

**Approximate Retail Price: $35.90**            **Low Price: $21.85**

**Presto Burger MB1,** a small, round, double-surface grill, cooks hamburgers, cheese sandwiches, minute steaks and English muffins. The time for cooking these is between one and three minutes. The hinged grill tends to compress hamburgers and sandwiches. A special, hard surface makes cleaning easy. All parts, except the top holding the heating coil, are immersible. This hamburger maker has limited use, but is handy for single servings. In addition, it is simple enough and safe enough for careful, mature gradeschoolers to use.

**Approximate Retail Price: $21.50**            **Low Price: $13.23**

### Also Recommended

**Oster Sizz'l Gril 720-01** is a rectangular model that has a reversible tray. One side of the tray has a round circle for hamburger cooking and the other side is rectangular for sandwiches, up to five hot dogs, eggs, bacon or other foods. The tray has a nonstick coating. It was a little difficult to clean the corners of this unit, but the rectangular shape makes it slightly more versatile than some square models.

A hamburger cooks medium-done in one minute and the Sizz'l Gril 720-01 did not squash sandwiches to the degree that many other hamburger makers did. The lid has a lock position to hold the cover open.

**Approximate Retail Price: $21.95**            **Low Price: $13.45**

*Prices are accurate at time of printing; subject to manufacturer's change.*

## CAN OPENERS
**Best Buy**

**Hamilton Beach Can Opener/Knife Sharpener 831G** has both a finger grip for easy handling and a recess for cord storage on the back. The cutting assembly slips in and out for quick cleanup. The swing magnet on this model makes it possible to adjust the setting of the magnet to the top of the can to facilitate lid lifting. This compact and sturdy model opened variously shaped cans with ease.

**Approximate Retail Price: $17.95**            **Low Price: $11.11**

## COFFEE MAKERS (Automatic Drip Coffee Makers)
**Best Buys**

**General Electric Coffeematic DCM10** features a see-through water tank that has clearly marked 2 to 10 cup measurements for easy filling. The hot water goes through a shower head-type water spreader, uniformly wetting the coffee grounds for optimum flavor. An off/brew/warm switch is located on the side. The coffee container has a permanent filter or it may be used with disposable paper filters that also come with it. It is relatively noiseless and lets little steam escape. This fine unit makes an excellent cup of coffee.

**Approximate Retail Price: $31.98**            **Low Price: $23.96**

**Proctor-Silex Coffee Magic A-301** is a 10-cup unit that performed particularly well when using the "Brew For Two" filter basket insert, producing small amounts of flavorful coffee.

Regular machine maintenance, including a cleaning cycle keyed to water hardness, is stressed in the accompanying instructions. Samples of a recommended cleaning tablet—and instructions to send away for more at a cost of $2.95 per 13—are also included.

Basic features include an on/off switch, a signal light, and a washable glass carafe with water measurement markings on the handle. Certain plastic parts, the carafe top and the "Brew For Two" basket are not dishwasher-safe. Twenty-five paper filters and elaborate instructions for brewing tea are included.

Coffee brewed at the rate of a cup per minute. There is some noise during the entire brewing cycle and considerable steam is vented from the reservoir at the end of the cycle. On the whole, though, this machine plays down the fuss and produces a very acceptable cup of coffee.

**Approximate Retail Price: $29.95**            **Low Price: $17.95**

### Also Recommended

**Farberware Country Coffee Maker 265** has a large 12-cup capacity, an on/off switch with a signal light, and an accurately measured

*Prices are accurate at time of printing; subject to manufacturer's change.*

and dishwasher-safe carafe. The covered filter basket fits directly onto the carafe and is quite easy to handle. Fifty standard paper filters and a comprehensive instruction booklet are also included.

This coffee maker brews quickly (approximately one cup per minute), although it is not recommended for brewing less than four cups of coffee. The hot water heater makes noises at the end of the heating cycle, but the reservoir is not vented so there is not much steam. The water heater automatically shuts off, while the warming plate stays on, when the heating cycle is finished.

**Approximate Retail Price: $29.99**          **Low Price: $23.50**

## COFFEE MAKERS (Percolators)
**Best Buys**

**Sunbeam Automatic Percolator 15-62** makes from 3 to 11 cups of coffee. For once, the strength control, which ranges from mild to strong, really does adjust the strength of the coffee. A signal light comes on when it is perking and goes out when the perking is over. Three cups of coffee take about seven minutes to brew. Water level markings are on the inside of the pot. This percolator is not immersible, but is easy to rinse out. The cord is detachable. Relatively quiet, it makes good coffee with very little sediment.

**Approximate Retail Price: $26.95**          **Low Price: $17.65**

### Also Recommended

**Corning Electro-Matic** has a 10-cup capacity. This fully automatic percolator makes good coffee and keeps it at serving temperature. The pot is made of nonporous glass-ceramic and is immersible and dishwasher-safe. It has a lock-in basket and lid. The plug receptacle is under the handle.

**Approximate Retail Price: $34.95**          **Low Price: $21.70**

## CREPE MAKERS
**Best Buys**

**Sunbeam M'sieur Crepe 30-10** is a variation on the bottom-baking design that does what it is supposed to do. It makes evenly browned, thin crepes very quickly. There is no need to flip to bake the other side.

The lightweight skillet is coated with Teflon II and rests on a sculptured electric unit. The pan is heated and then dipped into the batter and returned to the heating unit to bake crepes approximately seven inches in diameter in about one minute. The thermostat maintains evenly distributed heat—well worth the four-minute preheating time. The handle and base remain cool to the touch.

*Prices are accurate at time of printing; subject to manufacturer's change.*

Compact in size, M'sieur Crepe uses its base as a storage place for the cord when not in use.

The pan may also be used as a fry pan by using the reverse side of the crepe pan. The dial on the front of the base has settings for frying, warm, and off as well as for the crepe temperature control. We found the frying takes longer than on the top of the range. Bacon took up to nine minutes to cook. If time is not of essence, it does a satisfactory job. The 48-page color recipe book is beautifully written and illustrated, and includes 70 recipes, frying guide, menus, storage ideas and other useful information. For safety, the directions note that the unit should not be moved once it has been plugged in. This is an appliance worth considering.

**Approximate Retail Price: $29.95**                      **Low Price: $24.12**

**Nordic Ware Electric Crepe Maker 85032** made evenly browned, thin crepes about eight inches in diameter in two minutes. The handle design is good for easy, inverted dipping into the batter. The pan is made of cast aluminum with a nonstick coating on the surface for easy removal of the crepes. An indicator light on the handle showed when the pan was preheated to the correct temperature for baking. This satisfactory model comes with a large dip pan for the batter and has the basic crepe batter recipe printed on the bottom—a real convenience. Nordic's recipe booklet has easy-to-follow shaping and cutting ideas for crepes.

**Approximate Retail Price: $24.95**                      **Low Price: $17.95**

### ELECTRIC KNIVES
**Best Buy**

**Sunbeam Electric Knife Deluxe 6-71** consists of a pair of stainless steel blades that fit into a unit, with a trigger switch located in the brown and white handle. The blades are immersible but the body is not. After cleaning, the knife parts fit into a plastic storage tray that can be mounted on the wall or stored. The plastic tray takes up 6 x 13 x 5 inches of storage space. Assembled, the knife is 17-1/4 inches long.

This knife does a good job carving meats, slicing fruits and vegetables, and cutting cakes and breads. It is not to be used for cutting bones, frozen foods in solid form, other hard materials such as seeds, stones, or pits in fruit. The use-and-care booklet includes illustrated instructions for carving meats and cutting cakes. The Sunbeam knife is so responsive that the user needs to be very careful while learning the proper touch. The serrated blades are extremely sharp and a light touch on the trigger activates them. There is an "on/off" button in addition to the trigger switch to prevent an accidental start-up.

**Approximate Retail Price: $29.75**                      **Low Price: $22.51**

*Prices are accurate at time of printing; subject to manufacturer's change.*

## FOOD PROCESSORS
### Best Buy

**Sunbeam Le Chef Food Processor 14-11** is among the best we tested. It has direct drive, a braking feature, comes with four blades (slicing, shredding, metal and plastic), has a hollow pusher that is graduated so you can use it as a measuring cup, an automatic cut-off feature, a signal light and three-way switch. The signal light shows you when the unit is plugged in. It is a nice extra feature, but not a necessary one. The switch has on/off/pulse positions and, as with all processors, it will not work unless the cover is locked in place. The Sunbeam Le Chef comes with an excellent guide chart showing what blade to use on different types of food. Le Chef can handle raw and cooked meat. We particularly liked the extra big, 2-1/2 quart container that allows you to process larger loads. Le Chef did a fine job in all our tests.
**Approximate Retail Price: $119.99**   **Low Price: $78.51**

### Also Recommended

**Cuisinart Food Processor CFP-9** is a fine machine, but it is expensive. Slicing, shredding, chopping, grating, mixing and puréeing are efficiently handled by changing blades inside the Lexan mixing containers. The CFP-9 lacks a handle on the bowl and has a plastic base rather than a metal one. Four blades come with the unit: a steel blade for chopping, mixing and puréeing; a thick-slicer; a thick-shredder; and a plastic blade for sauces and similar items. A number of other blades are available for about $14 each. Of these, the thin-slicer and the thin-shredder are the most useful.
**Approximate Retail Price: $160**   **Low Price: Not Available**

## FRYERS (Fry Pans)
### Best Buy

**General Electric Deluxe Dutch Skillet 3449-106 SK 29 HRT** has a large, 5-1/2 quart capacity and high domed lid that lets you fry and bake large amounts and even "roast" a small turkey.

CONSUMER GUIDE Magazine tested the several functions the Deluxe Dutch Skillet claims to do and gives it high marks on most. It fried chicken beautifully, and a pork-rice dish from the GE recipe leaflet was delicious. Slightly less satisfactory was a cake baked on a rack inside the skillet. An identical cake was baked in a conventional oven simultaneously. The Dutch Skillet cake took nearly twice as long and did not brown as well as the cake baked conventionally. However, the Dutch Skillet did not heat up the kitchen and, on a hot day, that could justify the extra time.

*Prices are accurate at time of printing; subject to manufacturer's change.*

A signal light on the thermostat indicates when the selected temperature is reached. The Teflon finish makes cleanup easy, as does the removable thermostatic temperature control and cord. Once the temperature control and cord are removed, the entire skillet and lid can be immersed for washing.

The Dutch Skillet is an all-purpose appliance that can perform most cooking tasks.

**Approximate Retail Price: $42.98**     **Low Price: $32.10**

## Also Recommended

**Proctor-Silex PanHandler PH-1 with Corn Popper Topper CPH4,** a small, versatile fry pan, consists of a round, shallow fry pan base with a seven-inch cooking diameter and sloping sides. It has a nonstick surface. A plastic spatula, designed to prevent scratches, comes with the unit. The signal light is located in a rather hard-to-see spot on the base. Next to it is a temperature control dial. A temperature guide on the handle gives settings for commonly cooked foods, and an excellent recipe booklet also accompanies the PanHandler. There is a flat lid for recipes that require a cover.

CONSUMER GUIDE Magazine tested several recipes and found them all highly satisfactory. When making crepes side by side with a bottom-baking electric crepe pan, testers found the PanHandler as good as the crepe pan.

A Corn Popper Topper can be purchased separately, giving the PanHandler one more function. Designed to fit atop the Proctor-Silex PanHandler electric pan, the Corn Popper Topper has a three-quart capacity, which is a little smaller than some other corn poppers. The machine did a good job of popping corn. A self-buttering top and a leaflet with several recipes come with the Corn Popper Topper.

**Approximate Retail Prices:**     **Low Prices:**
**Model PH1: $29.95**     **Model PH1: $17.95**
**Model CPH4: $6.95**     **Model CPH4: $4.85**

## FRYERS (Small Deep Fryers)
## Best Buys

**Nordic Ware Multi-Fri Plus 85633,** a multipurpose fryer, consists of a cooking pot and a heating base. It can stew, slow cook, steam and blanch as well as deep fry. It performed very well in all our deep frying tests. The Multi-Fri Plus holds three cups of oil and can fry two to three cups of food. This is a little more than most fryers, making it a good-sized pot for family use. The pot comes out of the base for easy cleaning (and the nonstick finish does make cleaning easy). It heats up quickly and maintains a good frying temperature, often a little higher than the 350°F average we found on other fryers. The directions do not give a preheating time, but a signal

*Prices are accurate at time of printing; subject to manufacturer's change.*

light does let you know when the oil is ready. We found this a very satisfactory multipurpose appliance.

**Approximate Retail Price: $32.95**                          **Low Price: $21.75**

**Presto Fry Baby Deep Fryer FBD1,** the first of the new generation of small deep fryers, is also one of the best we tested. Its tall, narrow design permits only two cups of oil to do a lot of frying. You can fry one cup of food in a batch. The Fry Baby heats up in 10 minutes and recovers its frying temperature rapidly after the food is added. The temperature is a little hot for general deep frying, averaging close to 400°F. (Many foods fry better at 375°F.) However, quick frying time and quick recovery help to make up for this deficiency. The little slotted spoon that comes with the Fry Baby is great for lifting foods in and out of the fryer. We found the slotted spoon an excellent kitchen tool, too.

The Fry Baby comes with good instructions and use suggestions. It is compact in size and comes with a plastic cover so it can be stored safely on the counter when you have finished frying and when the oil has cooled down. The Fry Baby is great for single or double servings of almost every food, and quick enough for a family of four or five to enjoy fried foods without much delay.

**Approximate Retail Price: $27.95**                          **Low Price: $16.10**

**West Bend Fryette Deep Fryer 5121,** is very much like the successful Presto Fry Baby. It is a tall, black unit with a nonstick finish, a handy slotted dipper for moving foods in and out of the hot oil, and a plastic cover. The Fryette works with two cups of oil and, because of its tall cylindrical vessel, you will have 2-1/2 inches of oil for cooking.

The Fryette, like the Fry Baby, preheats in 10 minutes. The Fryette's heating element provides quick recovery of oil temperature after food has been added. After preheating and before food is added, the oil temperature is about 400°F, a little hot for many deep-frying purposes. But, after the addition of such foods as frozen French fries lowers the temperature, it quickly goes back up to 350°F to 375°F, the proper temperature for most frying purposes. The Fryette, like the Presto fryer, has a handy level indicator, so you can see when you need to add more oil.

The Fryette does just what it is supposed to do—fry a little food very quickly and very easily.

**Approximate Retail Price: $26.25**                          **Low Price: $13.95**

## MIXERS (Portable)
## Best Buys

**Hamilton Beach Portable Mixer 103** has 14 speeds, an easy-to-use beater eject button, and an easily operated switch and speed control. The cord is detachable and long enough (five feet) for almost any task. There is a clear instruction booklet with a good

*Prices are accurate at time of printing; subject to manufacturer's change.*

speed selector chart. A nice little mixer, this model did well in all our tests.
**Approximate Retail Price: $21.95**                           **Low Price: $12.50**

**General Electric Portable Mixer M22 3522** is a five-speed mixer that did a fine job in all our tests. This model has a 49-inch cord, making it extra convenient for working at the range. Especially nice features on this mixer are the handy clips at the top of the mixer head to hold the beaters for storage. As with most other GE products, the use-and-care instructions and recipes are detailed and easy to follow. GE's portable mixers have beaters without a center post, making them much easier to clean. The beaters have a slight bulge at the bottom and, as a result, do a better job of mixing than the straight up-and-down construction of other brands.
**Approximate Retail Price: $18.98**                           **Low Price: $14.36**

## MIXERS (Stand)
**Best Buys**

**Sunbeam Mixmaster 2-12** can be used as a stand or portable mixer. It comes with a 150-watt motor, a beater ejector and a built-in mixing guide. The cord is removable. The entire unit with its bowl is light and moving it for cleaning is easy.
**Approximate Retail Price: $35.75**                           **Low Price: $28.78**

### Also Recommended

**GE Heavy Duty Stand Mixer M58** has two stainless steel bowls (one small and one large), 12 speeds and a timer that turns off the mixer. This mixer has dough hooks and a special head lock to hold the mixer head in place while it kneads dough. There is a detailed use-and-care booklet, including many recipes and a good introductory section on bread and flour. The powerful (235-watt) mixer did well in all our tests. The instructions caution you not to knead dough for more than five minutes, but that is usually more than enough time for most recipes. We recommend this mixer for someone who wants to make bread and have an appliance that will handle most mixing chores, but does not want all the attachments that go with a multipurpose machine.
**Approximate Retail Price: $92.98**                           **Low Price: $69.56**

## MIXERS (Multipurpose)
**Best Buy**

**Oster Kitchen Center** is a mixer, blender, bread-maker, grinder, slicer and shredder. When doing food-processor functions such as slicing, shredding and grating, it has some advantages over the processor. You can do as much food as you like without having to

*Prices are accurate at time of printing; subject to manufacturer's change.*

stop to empty the bowl because Oster's Salad Maker attachment sends the prepared food out a chute into whatever container you choose to put under it.

The Kitchen Center does not stir up pastry dough exactly like a food processor, but it can do it. The Kitchen Center does take up more counter space and cupboard space, because each of its functions rquires a different attachment. The Kitchen Center can whip cream and beat egg whites, two things a food processor cannot do. It can also process liquid mixtures better in its blender container than a food processor can.

The newest version of the Kitchen Center is quieter than its predecessor. It also combines the mixing and dough-making functions in a single mixer head. Earlier models had two separate units. Optional accessories include an ice crusher, mini-blend containers (small jars that fit on the blender attachment), a sausage making kit and a citrus juicer.

**Approximate Retail Price: $174.95**         **Low Price: $109.83**

## Also Recommended

**KitchenAid K45** is big enough to meet almost every need. It has a 250-watt motor and a 4-1/2 quart stainless steel mixing bowl. It has six speeds and comes with a beater, a whip and a dough hook. KitchenAid's "Planetary Action" moves the beater in continuous circles inside the stationary bowl, mixing a cup of cream or eight cups of dough equally well. There is no blender, but there are a variety of optional attachments. The K45 matched and often surpassed the performance of every other mixer we tested for both everyday and heavy-duty mixing.

**Approximate Retail Price: $169.95**         **Low Price: $114.89**

## OVENS (Broiler Ovens)
### Best Buy

**General Electric Toast-R-Oven Model T26** is big enough to handle four slices of toast at a time. The toast is not as evenly done as it might be in an upright four-slice toaster, but you are able to toast bigger, thicker items than just sliced bread, such as bagels, English muffins, sweet rolls, etc. The T26 does a good job of baking and broiling, as long as you follow the guidelines set down in the very complete Use and Care Book. Oven temperatures range from 200°F to 500°F. GE has lots of good suggestions, hints and recipes in the booklet, plus a handy cooking guide and a list of the baking dish or pan sizes that will fit in the oven. This, we think, is a real benefit, because eight- or nine-inch square or round baking pans will not fit in the oven.

**Approximate Retail Price: $59.98**         **Low Price: $44.99**

*Prices are accurate at time of printing; subject to manufacturer's change.*

## OVENS (Other Countertop Ovens)
### Best Buys

**Farberware 455A,** an open-hearth broiler with a rotisserie, is easy to clean (most of the parts are removable and immersible) and gives off little heat and no smoke. Only one outlet is needed to operate it. This excellent 10 x 15 inch model can handle up to six burgers at a time.
**Approximate Retail Price: $59.99**                  **Low Price: $49.91**

**General Electric Toast-R-Oven-T104** performs simple toasting and baking jobs. It has only one rack, and it is a comparatively small 7-3/4 x 11-1/4 inches, but it will bake a satisfactory meat loaf, bake potatoes and cook other small-scale oven recipes. The unit satisfactorily toasted frozen French toast, waffles, English muffins, and regular toast.

However, this oven will not hold a pie pan. A loaf of quick bread browned too much on top. The Toast-R-Oven is better for simple tasks. There is a quick guide to baking times for a few of them on the oven panel.
**Approximate Retail Price: $46.98**                  **Low Price: $35.93**

## SLOW COOKERS
### Best Buys

**Hamilton Beach Crock Watcher 415** has a four-quart, removable crockery liner, which is an advantage for cleaning and serving. It has an automatic shift from high heat to low heat without manual resetting. The unit shifts to low automatically after the initial warm-up period of about two hours, letting the food become hot quickly, passing safely through the dangerous temperature zone for bacterial growth. The Crock Watcher can also be set at high for faster cooking, but will require stirring and watching. The liner may be used in the oven alone but not on top of the range. The low setting uses 130 watts and the high uses 260 watts. We did find that the base container was hot to the touch while cooking.
**Approximate Retail Price: $33.95**                  **Low Price: $19.54**

**West Bend Slo-Cooker Plus** has a new oblong shape to accommodate a greater variety of foods. The heating base it rests on can also be used as a mini-grill, and this model also bakes and roasts, making the Slo-Cooker Plus a multipurpose appliance.

The six-quart, slow cooker pot can be used for larger cuts of meat, poultry and roasts because of the oblong shape. It can cook quickly or cook slowly all day, depending on the temperature selected. The glass cover is handy for checking the cooking progress. The handles at the side are easy to grasp and remain cool throughout cooking.

*Prices are accurate at time of printing; subject to manufacturer's change.*

The mini-grill has a nonstick coating that fries sandwiches, pancakes, bacon and eggs all equally well. However, the center area does heat a little faster than the edges. The thermostatic control ranges from "1" to "5" and will heat two quarts of water from 95°F to 212°F. Temperature selections can be made in between the numbers for complete temperature control. The 48-page recipe book gives setting numbers to use with this 300-watt unit. The lower settings will warm and simmer foods and the medium to higher settings can bake and boil. This appliance can also be used as an oven, and a chrome-plated baking/roasting rack that can be used in a high or low position is included.

People with limited space and people looking for a multipurpose unit should consider this model. CONSUMER GUIDE Magazine thinks it is a good value.

**Approximate Retail Price: $48.75**     **Low Price: $27.65**

## TOASTERS
### Best Buys

**Proctor-Silex T202B,** a two-slice toaster, has a bread-surface sensor that causes the toast to pop up when the selected color has been reached. It also has a color adjustment control on the bottom that alters the front control to match what the individual considers light and dark. This model produced evenly browned toast. Toasting can be stopped by pushing the lever latch. There is a separate setting for pastries, but the directions suggest that frozen items be thawed before toasting. Cold toast can be reheated without being over-browned.

**Approximate Retail Price: $19.95**     **Low Price: $15.95**

**Proctor-Silex Toaster T009N** has the same features as the T202B, but it has double the capacity and is double the price. There are dual controls for preparing two different hues of toast at the same time. The color selector for each two slices is located on the front—a nice feature for families who have different preferences. It is possible to reheat cold toast without changing the color greatly. This well-built model also produced evenly browned toast.

**Approximate Retail Price: $44.95**     **Low Price: $29.95**

## WAFFLE BAKERS
### Best Buy

**Black Angus 950843,** a dual-purpose baker-griller with reversible grids, is coated with Teflon II and does an excellent job on both grilling and baking. This is a unit worth considering.

**Approximate Retail Price: $45.50**     **Low Price: $27.95**

*Prices are accurate at time of printing; subject to manufacturer's change.*

# Food Preparation Appliance Prices

## American

**BURGER COOKER**
| | | | |
|---|---|---|---|
| 6000 | Great American Burger Machine | $15.95 | $10.63 |

**FOOD PROCESSOR**
| | | | |
|---|---|---|---|
| 8000 | American Gourmet Food Processor | $119.95 | $62.50 |

**FRYER**
| | | | |
|---|---|---|---|
| 7000 | Great American Frying Machine — Mini Deep Fryer | $15.95 | $10.63 |

**SLOW COOKERS**
| | | | |
|---|---|---|---|
| 5000 B | American Gourmet Casserole | $24.95 | $15.63 |
| 5000 SP | Split Personality Slow cooker | 26.95 | 17.50 |

## Farberware

**BROILERS/ROTISSERIES/TURBO OVEN**
| | | | |
|---|---|---|---|
| 450A | "Open Hearth" Electric Broiler | $44.99 | $35.18 |
| 454A | Rotisserie Assembly Only | 26.99 | 20.79 |
| 455A | "Open Hearth" Broiler/Rotisserie Comb | 59.99 | 46.91 |
| 456 | "Open Hearth" Shish Kebab Accessory | 21.99 | 16.94 |
| 460R | Turbo Oven | 144.99 | 109.24 |

**CAN OPENERS**
| | | | |
|---|---|---|---|
| 247W/G/B | Automatic Electric Can Opener | $12.99 | $10.45 |
| 248W/G/B | Can Opener/Knife Sharpener | 16.99 | 13.67 |

*Prices are accurate at time of printing; subject to manufacturer's change.*

## COFFEEMAKERS

| | | | |
|---|---|---|---|
| 134 | 4 Cup Automatic Coffeemaker | $26.99 | $20.79 |
| 138 | 8 Cup Automatic Coffeemaker | 35.99 | 26.90 |
| 142 | 12 Cup Automatic Coffeemaker | 39.99 | 30.35 |
| 265 | 12 Cup Country Coffeemaker | 29.99 | 23.48 |
| 283 | 2 Cupper | 17.99 | 14.49 |

## CREPE MAKER

| | | | |
|---|---|---|---|
| 263 | "Batter Up" Crepe Maker | $19.99 | $15.53 |

## FOOD PROCESSOR

| | | | |
|---|---|---|---|
| 286 | Food Processor | $120.00 | $82.80 |

## GRIDDLE, FRYER & FRY PANS

| | | | |
|---|---|---|---|
| 260SP | Electric Griddle & Control | $39.99 | $30.81 |
| 300B | 10½" Round Electric Fry Pan | 39.99 | 29.89 |
| 312B | 12" Round Electric Fry Pan | 49.99 | 37.36 |
| 304 | "Come Fry With Me" Deep Fryer | 14.99 | 12.08 |

## GRILLS

| | | | |
|---|---|---|---|
| 262 | Lil Grill 2 | $24.99 | $19.54 |
| 261 | Lil Grill | 14.99 | 12.08 |

## MIXER

| | | | |
|---|---|---|---|
| 287W/G/B | Hand Mixer | $12.99 | $9.71 |

## SLOW COOKERS

| | | | |
|---|---|---|---|
| 266 | Country Crock Cooker | $29.99 | $22.41 |
| 270 | Crock Cooker | 19.99 | 15.53 |
| 282 | Crock Cooker | 29.99 | 21.28 |

# General Electric

## BAG SEALER

| | | | |
|---|---|---|---|
| BAGIT | Bag Sealer | $18.98 | $13.76 |

## CAN OPENERS

| | | | |
|---|---|---|---|
| EC32 | Can Opener | $11.98 | $9.59 |
| EC33 | Can Opener/Knife Sharpener | 17.98 | 13.49 |
| EC41 | Can Opener/Ice Crusher | 24.98 | 18.42 |

## COFFEEMAKERS & PERCOLATORS

| | | | |
|---|---|---|---|
| CM11 | 8-Cup Percolator | $18.98 | $14.76 |
| P15 | 9-Cup Percolator | 27.98 | 20.87 |
| SSP12 | 12-Cup Percolator | 42.98 | 32.12 |

*Prices are accurate at time of printing; subject to manufacturer's change.*

| | | | |
|---|---|---:|---:|
| DCM4 | Drip Coffeemaker | 25.98 | 19.80 |
| DCM10 | Drip Coffeemaker | 31.98 | 23.96 |
| DCM12 | Drip Coffeemaker | 39.98 | 29.96 |
| DCM15 | Drip Coffeemaker | 44.98 | 33.56 |
| DCM20 | Drip Coffeemaker | 46.98 | 34.76 |

## CREPE MAKER
| | | | |
|---|---|---:|---:|
| CR-1 | Dip'N Flip Electric Crepe Maker | $22.98 | $16.79 |

## FOOD PROCESSOR
| | | | |
|---|---|---:|---:|
| FP-1 | Food Processor | $89.98 | $65.99 |

## FRYER
| | | | |
|---|---|---:|---:|
| DF-1 | Fry Pot Deep Fryer | $22.98 | $16.79 |

## GRIDDLE/GRILLS/WAFFLE BAKERS
| | | | |
|---|---|---:|---:|
| HM-1 | Frank-N-Burger Grill | $17.98 | $13.79 |
| HM-2 | Super Frank-N-Burger Grill | 28.98 | 21.59 |
| EGIT | Automatic Griddle | 45.98 | 34.26 |
| G44T | Auto. Grill and Waffle baker | 36.98 | 27.56 |
| G44 | Auto. Grill and Waffle baker | 34.98 | 26.09 |
| BRG20T | Broil-R-Grill | 39.98 | 29.99 |

## KETTLE
| | | | |
|---|---|---:|---:|
| K52 | Kettle | $33.98 | $25.16 |

## KNIVES
| | | | |
|---|---|---:|---:|
| EK9 | Slicing Knife | $19.98 | $14.99 |
| EK10 | Slicing Knife | 22.98 | 17.09 |

## MIXERS
| | | | |
|---|---|---:|---:|
| M54WH | Heavy Duty Stand Mixer | $68.98 | $51.56 |
| M55 | Heavy Duty Stand Mixer | 74.98 | 56.36 |
| M58WHS | Heavy Duty Stand Mixer | 92.98 | 69.56 |
| M59CS | Heavy Duty Stand Mixer | 98.98 | 74.36 |
| M44 | All Purpose Stand Mixer | 34.98 | 26.36 |
| M46 | All Purpose Stand Mixer | 48.98 | 36.92 |
| M24 | Portable Mixer | 12.98 | 10.38 |
| M22 | Portable Mixer | 18.98 | 14.36 |
| M74 | Portable Mixer | 23.98 | 17.95 |

## PEELER
| | | | |
|---|---|---:|---:|
| EP-1 | Peeling Wand Elec. Peeler | $22.98 | $16.79 |

## SKILLETS
| | | | |
|---|---|---:|---:|
| SK26 | 12" Skillet | $31.98 | $23.96 |
| SK27AV | Skillet, Removable handle and legs | 34.98 | 26.36 |
| SK27 | Skillet, Non-Stick | 37.98 | 28.16 |
| SK29 | 12" Dutch Skillet, Non-Stick | 42.98 | 32.10 |

*Prices are accurate at time of printing; subject to manufacturer's change.*

## TOASTER OVENS/TOASTERS

| | | | |
|---|---|---|---|
| T93B | Deluxe Toast-R-Oven | $41.98 | $32.33 |
| T104 | Toast-R-Oven | 46.98 | 35.93 |
| T97 | King Size Toast-R-Oven | 53.98 | 40.19 |
| T23 | Toast'n Broil Toast-R-Oven | 46.98 | 35.93 |
| T26 | Toast'n Broil Toast-R-Oven | 59.98 | 44.99 |
| T17 | 2 Slice Toaster | 18.98 | 14.36 |
| T86 | 2 Slice Toaster | 22.98 | 17.12 |
| T146 | 2 Slice Toaster | 26.98 | 20.39 |
| T124 | 4 Slice Toaster | 32.98 | 24.90 |
| T128 | 4 Slice Toaster | 40.98 | 30.56 |

# Hamilton Beach

## BACONER
| | | | |
|---|---|---|---|
| 474C | Baconer Grill | $33.95 | $18.96 |

## BLENDERS
| | | | |
|---|---|---|---|
| 612A/G | 7-Speed Blender | $29.95 | $16.09 |
| 653A/G | 14-Speed Blender | 33.95 | 18.39 |
| 658G | Insta-Blend 16-Speed Blender | 41.95 | 24.14 |
| 691G | Insta-Blend 14-Speed Blender | 36.95 | 21.26 |

## CORN POPPERS
| | | | |
|---|---|---|---|
| 507 | Self-Buttering Corn Popper | $17.95 | $10.34 |
| 500G | Butter Up Corn Popper | 20.95 | 12.06 |

## DONUT MAKER
| | | | |
|---|---|---|---|
| 200 | Donut Maker | $28.95 | $17.24 |

## ELECTRIC KNIVES
| | | | |
|---|---|---|---|
| 275A | Hole-in-the-Handle Electric Knife | $22.95 | $12.06 |
| 297A | Switchable Electric Knife | 29.95 | 17.24 |

## FAST COOKERS
| | | | |
|---|---|---|---|
| 489 | Fast Frank | $14.95 | $9.19 |
| 493 | Double Mac Fast Cooker | 39.95 | 20.11 |
| 2108 | Little Mac Fast Cooker | 25.95 | 12.64 |

## FRYER/COOKER
| | | | |
|---|---|---|---|
| 2121 | "Fry All" Fryer/Cooker | $27.95 | $16.09 |

## GOURMET CENTER & ATTACHMENTS
| | | | |
|---|---|---|---|
| 168W | Meat Grinder/Gourmet Center | $58.95 | $33.91 |
| 553 | Salad Maker Attachment | 31.95 | 18.39 |

*Prices are accurate at time of printing; subject to manufacturer's change.*

## MIXERS

| | | | |
|---|---|---:|---:|
| 40C | Chrome Stand Mixer | $69.95 | $43.13 |
| 44G | Dough Hook Stand Mixer | 64.95 | 39.09 |
| 60G | 10-Speed Stand Mixer W/Dough Hook | 98.95 | 59.23 |
| 110A/G | 5-Speed Hand Mixer | 21.95 | 12.64 |
| 34KG | 9-Position Speed Control Stand Mixer | 47.95 | 25.29 |

## ROASTER OVEN

| | | | |
|---|---|---:|---:|
| 527 | Automatic Roaster/Oven | $89.95 | $51.74 |

## SLOW COOKERS

| | | | |
|---|---|---:|---:|
| 415HD | 4-Qt. Crock Watcher | $33.95 | $19.54 |
| 417HD | 6-Qt. Crock Watcher | 39.95 | 25.29 |

## STEAMER

| | | | |
|---|---|---:|---:|
| 430 | Fresh Cooker/Steamer | $39.95 | $22.99 |

## TABLE RANGES

| | | | |
|---|---|---:|---:|
| 387 | 2 Burner Buffet Range | $39.95 | $22.99 |
| 812 | Fifth Burner | 16.95 | 9.76 |

## TOASTERS

| | | | |
|---|---|---:|---:|
| 306 | 2-Slice Pop-Up Toaster | $22.95 | $13.21 |
| 307 | 4-Slice Toaster | 33.95 | 19.54 |

# KitchenAid

## COFFEE MILL

| | | | |
|---|---|---:|---:|
| KCMW | KitchenAid Electric Coffee Mill | $39.95 | $27.03 |

## FOOD MIXERS

| | | | |
|---|---|---:|---:|
| K45A/G/W | KitchenAid Food Mixer | $169.95 | $114.89 |
| K5A | KitchenAid Heavy Duty Food Preparer/Mixer | 229.95 | 155.48 |
| FG | Grinder Attachment | 24.95 | 17.08 |
| RVS | Slicer/Shredder Attachment | 23.95 | 16.39 |

# Norelco

## COFFEEMAKER

| | | | |
|---|---|---:|---:|
| HB5170 | 12 Cup Dial-A-Brew | $48.95 | $32.18 |

*Prices are accurate at time of printing; subject to manufacturer's change.*

**BROILER/OVEN**
T04400   Toast-R-Range.......................  $59.98   $41.38

# Oster

**BAG SEALER**
75504   Continuous Roll Bag Sealer .............   $24.95   $15.87

**BURGER COOKER**
72001   Hamburger/Sandwich Maker............   $21.95   $13.77

**CAN OPENER**
55714/15/18   Can Opener.......................   $19.95   $12.43

**COOKER/POACHER**
57901   Egg Cooker/Poacher ..................   $24.95   $15.87

**FOOD GRINDER**
99008   Heavy Duty Food Grinder .............   $59.95   $37.95

**CREPE MAKER**
74203   Electric Crepe Maker ..................   $22.95   $14.55

**FONDUE**
68104/7   Electric Fondue......................   $34.95   $21.74

**FRYER**
73203   Li'l Fritter Deep Fryer .................   $30.95   $19.52

**ICE CRUSHERS**
55101   Snoflake Ice Crusher ..................   $29.95   $18.63
43504/5   Oster Ice Crusher Attachment ...........   15.95   9.72

**JUICE EXTRACTORS**
36204   Automatic Pulp Ejector/Juice Extractor .....   $85.00   $54.05
36804   Automatic Citrus Juicer ................   21.95   13.69

**KITCHEN CENTER FOOD PREPARATION**
97914/5   Kitchen Center .....................   $174.95   $109.83

**SLICER/SHREDDER/SALAD MAKER**
34114   FoodCrafter Processor ................   $49.95   $31.63

*Prices are accurate at time of printing; subject to manufacturer's change.*

# Presto

### BROILER OVEN
| | | | |
|---|---|---|---|
| BOC1 | Continuous Clean Broiler Oven Plus | $73.90 | $43.70 |

### CORN POPPER
| | | | |
|---|---|---|---|
| CPB4H/F | Automatic Buttering Corn Popper | $22.90 | $14.38 |

### EGG COOKER
| | | | |
|---|---|---|---|
| LD06 | Egg Cooker | $16.50 | $10.35 |

### FAST COOKERS
| | | | |
|---|---|---|---|
| HOTD | Hot Dogger | $11.95 | $6.90 |
| HOTD1 | Submersible Hot Dogger | 15.00 | 10.35 |
| MB1 | Presto Burger | 21.50 | 13.23 |
| PB1 | Presto Burger/1 | 25.95 | 14.95 |
| PB2 | Presto Burger/2 | 35.90 | 21.85 |

### FRYERS
| | | | |
|---|---|---|---|
| FBD1 | FryBaby Electric Deep Fryer | $27.95 | $16.10 |
| FDF1 | FryDaddy Electric Deep Fryer | 33.98 | 20.70 |

### SKILLET & OVEN
| | | | |
|---|---|---|---|
| WFS1 | WeeFry Skillet | $37.90 | $21.85 |
| WB1 | WeeBakerie Oven | 29.98 | 18.40 |

### TOASTERS
| | | | |
|---|---|---|---|
| TO2 | 2 Slice Toaster | $23.00 | $13.80 |
| TO4 | 4 Slice Toaster | 33.90 | 19.55 |

# Rival

### CAN OPENERS & KNIFE SHARPENERS
| | | | |
|---|---|---|---|
| 739H/W | Tall Can Opener | $16.95 | $9.14 |
| 791A/H | Can-O-Matic Can Opener | 26.95 | 14.51 |
| 752RA/RH | Click 'N Clean Can Opener | 16.75 | 8.73 |
| 753RA | Click 'N Clean Can Opener | 15.45 | 7.58 |

### CROCK POT SLOW COOKERS
| | | | |
|---|---|---|---|
| 2001 | Crock-Pot Cookbook | $6.95 | $3.16 |
| 3150 | 3½ Qt. Removable Crock | 32.95 | 16.68 |
| 3200 | Crock-Ette | 16.95 | 9.14 |
| 3100A/F | Crock Pot | 21.95 | 11.33 |

*Prices are accurate at time of printing; subject to manufacturer's change.*

| | | | |
|---|---|---|---|
| 3350A/H | 5 Qt. Removable Crock Pot | 42.00 | 20.64 |
| 3900H | Crock Plate | 62.95 | 34.44 |

**FOOD GRINDER/SALAD MAKERS**

| | | | |
|---|---|---|---|
| 2700 | Food Grinder/Salad Maker | $79.95 | $43.56 |
| 303A/H | Grind-O-Matic | 16.95 | 9.18 |

**FOOD SLICERS**

| | | | |
|---|---|---|---|
| 1030V | Protect-O-Matic Food Slicer | $83.95 | $44.84 |
| 1037A | Slice Crafter Elec. Slicer | 70.95 | 37.94 |
| 1101E | Electric Food Slicer | 60.95 | 33.87 |

**ICE CRUSHER**

| | | | |
|---|---|---|---|
| TW347A | Ice-O-Matic | $16.95 | $9.18 |

# Salton

**COFFEE GRINDER**

| | | | |
|---|---|---|---|
| GC4C | Coffee Grinder | $12.95 | $8.91 |

**FOOD WARMERS**

| | | | |
|---|---|---|---|
| 100 | Coffee Warmer Tray | $10.95 | $6.30 |
| BH2 | Hot Basket | 17.50 | 10.06 |
| 110 | Elite Hotray | 16.95 | 9.75 |
| 121 | Gourmet Hotray | 23.95 | 13.78 |
| 127 | Riviera Hotray | 31.50 | 18.11 |
| 132 | Dinnermate Hotray | 39.95 | 22.98 |
| 134 | Terrace Master Hotray | 47.95 | 27.58 |
| 140 | Epicure Hotray | 49.95 | 28.73 |
| WB21/22 | Electric Bun Warmer | 13.50 | 7.76 |

# Sunbeam

**BAG SEALER**

| | | | |
|---|---|---|---|
| 34-11 | Food Saver Bag Sealer | $18.95 | $15.26 |

**BLENDERS**

| | | | |
|---|---|---|---|
| 4-61 | 10-Speed Touch-Blend Blender | $36.75 | $29.59 |
| 4-71 | Deluxe 20-Speed Burst of Power | 46.95 | 37.80 |

**CAN OPENERS/KNIFE SHARPENERS**

| | | | |
|---|---|---|---|
| 5-12 | Total Clean Power Opener/Sharpener | $16.50 | $13.28 |
| 5-91 | Deluxe Total Clean Opener/Sharpener | 23.50 | 18.92 |
| 5-103 | Deluxe Total Clean w/Ice Crusher | 26.25 | 21.14 |

*Prices are accurate at time of printing; subject to manufacturer's change.*

## COFFEEMAKERS

| | | | |
|---|---|---|---|
| 15-30 | Auto. Percolator, 12-Cup | $41.95 | $33.78 |
| 15-62 | Auto. Percolator, 11-Cup | 26.95 | 21.70 |
| 15-213 | Auto. Drip Coffeemaker | 41.95 | 33.78 |
| 15-238 | Deluxe Drip Coffeemaster | 56.95 | 45.85 |
| 15-241 | Auto. Drip Coffeemaker | 43.95 | 35.39 |
| 16-13 | Party Percolator, 30-Cup | 28.95 | 23.31 |
| 17-13 | Hot Shot Hot Beverage Maker | 21.95 | 17.68 |
| 17-33 | Hot Shot Hot Beverage Maker | 26.95 | 21.70 |

## CORN POPPER

| | | | |
|---|---|---|---|
| 18-90 | The Great American Popcorn Machine | $26.95 | $21.70 |

## CREPEMAKER

| | | | |
|---|---|---|---|
| 30-10 | M'sieur Crepe Crepemaker | $29.95 | $24.12 |

## EGG COOKER

| | | | |
|---|---|---|---|
| 23-10 | Auto. Egg Cooker w/Poacher Att. | $26.50 | $21.33 |

## FRYPANS

| | | | |
|---|---|---|---|
| 7-22 | Cook & Clean Multi-Cooker Frypan | $39.95 | $32.17 |
| 7-30 | Multi-Cooker Frypan, Stainless | 46.25 | 37.24 |
| 7-210 | Deluxe Alum. Multi-Cooker Frypan | 30.50 | 24.55 |
| 7-100 | Broiler Cover Frypan | 45.95 | 37.00 |
| 94-10 | Broiler Cover, Large Size | 23.75 | 19.12 |
| 7-152 | Deluxe Cook & Clean Multi-Cooker | 52.50 | 42.26 |
| 7-313 | Multi-Cooker Frypan | 52.50 | 42.49 |
| 9-12 | 5 Qt. Cooker & Deep Fryer | 52.50 | 42.26 |
| 9-20 | 5 Qt. Cooker & Deep Fryer | 43.95 | 35.41 |
| 9-42 | Auto. Cooker & Deep Fryer | 48.75 | 39.25 |
| 9-69 | Pint Size Fast Fryer | 27.95 | 22.51 |

## GRIDDLE & WAFFLE BAKER

| | | | |
|---|---|---|---|
| 21-10 | Auto. Griddle, Teflon II | $44.50 | $35.82 |
| 22-30 | Waffle Baker & Grill | 50.75 | 40.86 |
| 22-13 | Deluxe Waffle Baker & Grill | 50.75 | 40.86 |

## HAMBURGER COOKER

| | | | |
|---|---|---|---|
| 8-19 | 1 'R 2 Burger Grill | $27.95 | $22.51 |

## JUICER

| | | | |
|---|---|---|---|
| 33-13 | Auto. Citrus Juicer | $21.95 | $17.68 |

## MIXERS & ATTACHMENTS

| | | | |
|---|---|---|---|
| 1-71 | Deluxe Mixmaster Mixer | $87.75 | $70.64 |
| 1-80 | Deluxe Mixmaster Mixer | 115.50 | 92.98 |

*Prices are accurate at time of printing; subject to manufacturer's change.*

| | | | |
|---|---|---|---|
| 94-20 | Meat Grinder | 18.50 | 14.89 |
| 94-30 | Power Unit | 18.50 | 14.89 |
| 94-70 | Juicer Attachment | 8.95 | 7.21 |
| 94-170 | Stainless Steel Set w/Covers | 18.50 | 14.89 |
| 94-190 | Set of Two Dough Hooks | 7.25 | 5.84 |
| 14-11 | Food Processor | 119.99 | 78.51 |
| 2-12 | Mixmaster Mixer, 12-Position | 35.75 | 28.78 |
| 2-51 | Mixmaster Mixer, 12-Position | 46.95 | 37.80 |
| 3-51 | 5-Speed Mixmaster Hand Mixer | 18.95 | 15.26 |
| 3-71 | Deluxe 5-Speed Mixmaster, Hand | 24.99 | 16.36 |
| 3-171 | Deluxe 5-Speed Mixmaster, Hand | 25.75 | 20.73 |
| 3-121 | Deluxe Mixmaster Hand, 12-Position | 27.25 | 21.94 |

### SLICING KNIVES
| | | | |
|---|---|---|---|
| 6-53 | Elec. Slicing Knife | $24.75 | $19.93 |
| 6-71 | Deluxe Slicing Knife | 27.95 | 22.51 |
| 6-21 | Deluxe Solid State 2-Speed | 29.95 | 24.12 |

### SLOW COOKERS
| | | | |
|---|---|---|---|
| 25-23 | 5 Qt. Slow Cooker | $19.95 | $16.05 |

### TOASTERS
| | | | |
|---|---|---|---|
| 20-540 | 4-Slice Toaster Oven | $56.75 | $45.69 |
| 20-20 | Deluxe 2-Slice Chrome Toaster | 24.25 | 19.53 |
| 20-30 | Deluxe Radiant Self-Lowering | 45.25 | 36.43 |
| 20-510 | Deluxe 4-Slice Chrome Toaster | 31.95 | 25.73 |

# Toastmaster

### HAMBURGER COOKER
| | | | |
|---|---|---|---|
| 888 | Hamburger Cooker | $29.75 | $18.34 |

### OVENS & BROILERS
| | | | |
|---|---|---|---|
| 5233 | Flip-Over Oven/Broiler | $40.75 | $25.28 |
| 5242 | Cont. Clean Tabletop Oven/Broiler | 60.95 | 37.73 |
| 5247 | Pushbutton Tabletop Oven | 53.95 | 33.47 |
| 7006 | System III Broiler/Oven | 86.50 | 53.59 |
| 7008 | Deluxe Sys. III Broiler | 104.95 | 65.26 |

### TOASTERS
| | | | |
|---|---|---|---|
| D114 | 4-Slice Food Toaster | $47.25 | $29.21 |
| B152WH | 2-Slice Food Toaster | 31.45 | 19.44 |
| D154WH | Decorated 4-Slice Food Toaster | 49.25 | 30.42 |

### WAFFLE BAKERS & GRILLS
| | | | |
|---|---|---|---|
| 269 | Waffle baker/Grill | $48.25 | $29.89 |
| W252 | Round Waffle Baker | 25.25 | 15.59 |

*Prices are accurate at time of printing; subject to manufacturer's change.*

# West Bend

### BAG SEALER
| | | | |
|---|---|---|---|
| 5137 | Bag Maker/Sealer | $19.95 | $23.94 |

### COFFEEMAKERS
| | | | |
|---|---|---|---|
| 9466 | 9 Cup Anytime Perk | $16.50 | $9.36 |
| 9450/1 | 9 Cup Flavo-Matic Perk | 16.50 | 9.36 |
| 5938 | 9 Cup Dec. Polypropylene Perk | 16.95 | 9.61 |
| 9471/2 | 9 Cup Dec. Minit Cup Perk | 21.95 | 12.44 |
| 3253 | 6 Cup Hot Pot — Hot Pepper | 20.50 | 11.63 |
| 3255 | 6 Cup Hot Pot — Butterscotch | 18.25 | 10.34 |
| 5922 | 20 Cup Decorated Polypropylene Perk | 20.95 | 11.88 |
| 33525/35 | 30 Cup Insulated Party Perk | 30.95 | 17.56 |
| 11838 | 30 Cup Polished Aluminum Perk | 21.95 | 12.48 |
| 11868/69 | 30 Cup Aluminum Perk | 22.95 | 13.02 |
| 43536 | 36 Cup Automatic Perk | 34.95 | 19.82 |
| 13500 | 55 Cup Automatic Perk | 65.95 | 37.39 |
| 33600 | 100 Cup Automatic Perk | 76.95 | 43.63 |
| 5942 | 16 Cup Executive Auto. Drip Coffeemaker | 69.95 | 39.66 |
| 5970/1/2 | 10 Cup Big Dripper Auto. Drip Coffeemaker | 49.95 | 28.32 |
| 5914 | 10 Cup Take Ten Coffee/Beverage Server | 13.95 | 7.91 |

### CORN POPPERS
| | | | |
|---|---|---|---|
| 25467 | 4 Qt. Butter-Matic, Auto. | $18.95 | $10.75 |
| 5469 | 4 Qt. Self-Buttering | 16.50 | 9.36 |

### SKILLETS & GRIDDLES
| | | | |
|---|---|---|---|
| 3371 | Skillet/Casserole/Oven | $45.50 | $25.80 |
| 1429/30 | 11" Buffet Skillet | 38.25 | 21.68 |
| 3951 | Cast Aluminum Griddle | 50.95 | 28.90 |
| 13543 | Slimline Griddle | 41.95 | 23.78 |

### SLOW COOKERS
| | | | |
|---|---|---|---|
| 3299 | Beans 'N Stuff 2 Qt. Slow Cooker | $18.95 | $10.75 |
| 5402 | Colonial 2 Qt. Slow Cooker | 21.95 | 12.44 |
| 4400 | 4 Qt. Automatic Slow Cooker | 27.50 | 15.60 |
| 5276 | Slo-Cooker Plus 6 Qt. Slow Cooker | 48.75 | 27.65 |
| 5225 | Lazy Day 6 Qt. Slow Cooker | 38.95 | 22.09 |

### WOK
| | | | |
|---|---|---|---|
| 5109 | 5½ Qt. Electric Wok | $44.50 | $25.18 |

*Prices are accurate at time of printing; subject to manufacturer's change.*

# 1978 Floor Care Appliances

Although a vacuum cleaner probably exists for every kind of cleaning problem—from pet hairs on shag rugs to sand in the family automobile—no single vacuum cleaner model can satisfactorily accomplish all cleaning chores. Therefore, you must carefully evaluate your home's major cleaning problems. For instance, you should determine how many kinds of rug and carpeting piles you have; your answer will tell you how many rug pile settings you should look for on the vacuum's nozzle. Do you have lots of bare floors? Do you have drapes that need an above-floor unit with an adjustment for less suction? Do you want a model that can clean a workshop or garage as well as the house? Your answers should direct you to the type of vacuum cleaner most appropriate for your home.

Be sure to test vacuum cleaners for yourself before buying. While examining various models, ask the following questions.

- How easily does the vacuum pick up dirt and threads?
- Will the machine remove hard-to-get-at pet hairs on drapes, upholstery and curtains?
- Will the machine pick up granular materials such as sand, salt or sugar?
- Does the machine move easily across rugs and carpeting?
- Does it have a carrying handle?
- Will it clean next to baseboards? Under low furniture?
- Can the dust bag be easily emptied or replaced?
- Is the unit noisy in a small room?
- Does it have a good warranty?
- Can it be serviced easily?

## Vacuum Ratings

MOST VACUUM cleaner manufacturers still rate their canister models on the basis of peak horsepower. Such a rating may be misleading because peak horsepower performance is not based on the constant power level you can expect for home usage but on the best the motor can do under laboratory conditions. The Vacuum Cleaner Manufacturers Association (VCMA) developed a more realistic horsepower rating system that reflects in-house usage, but this rating—about half the peak horsepower rating—is usually printed in small type, if it is given at all.

While the VCMA horsepower ratings may serve to keep the peak horsepower claims honest, such ratings do not tell you much about the overall performance of a vacuum. The sealed-suction water-lift test is misleading, too. Some vacuums with low sealed-suction ratings are as efficient as vacuums with high sealed-suction ratings.

Until the FTC comes up with an adequate rating system, you will have to rely on your own common-sense tests. Most sales departments will let you try out the vacuums they sell. You can test the suction of a canister by cupping your hand over the end of the hose and then pulling your hand away. The way a vacuum cleaner picks up cigarette butts will probably give you a better idea of its efficiency than any rating system.

## Canister Vacs

A CANISTER pulls dirt through an interlocking hose and extension wand into the dust bag. Most units have a valve (usually on the hose or wand) that can be opened to lessen the suction for drapery and furniture cleaning. Since they are usually easy to maneuver, canisters are good for cleaning stairs.

The consumer should inspect a canister vacuum to determine whether or not all interlocking connections hold firmly and are air-tight. The wands should fit together easily and not come apart under the stress of cleaning. The motor must have a filter. The dust bag should be large enough to maintain suction as it fills up.

The canister vacuum should be easy to pull with little effort, even over high-pile or shag rugs. The machine should have a handle for carrying it around from room to room or up a flight of stairs. It should be light enough to be carried without fatigue.

## Uprights

COMBINING SUCTION and the agitating action of a beater bar-brush, upright vacuum cleaners generally excel at carpet cleaning. The dirt is pulled into a dust bag attached to the handle. Some uprights house their dust bags in rigid containers while others have large, soft bag enclosures. Either type should allow bags to be replaced or emptied easily.

The upright's nozzle should be at least 11 inches across (to speed cleaning), and should have bumpers to protect the furniture. The brushes ought to be thick and extend to both ends of the rotating bar. Check to be sure the connection between the dust bag and the nozzle is tight.

Some uprights can be adjusted for different carpet heights, and some beater-bar brushes can be adjusted or replaced when worn. Although the manufacturers of most uprights offer above-the-floor attachments, such devices are cumbersome and do not provide the same cleaning performance as canister vacs. Check to see that the cleaner remains stable no matter which way the handle is positioned. The handle should lock in an upright position for storage.

**Combination Vacs**

COMBINATION VACS are double-duty units with two motors — one in the canister for suction power and the other in the nozzle for agitation. A power cord extends from the canister to the power nozzle and in some cases is molded into the hose itself.

A combination vac can be used without the powered nozzle for above-floor cleaning. Most units have a variety of accessories that can be used without the powered head. Before purchase, you should check to see if the powered nozzle is easy to attach. You should also check to see that the wands and hose will stay together tightly under considerable stress and pull.

The powered nozzle should be stable when the handle is adjusted and should have easy-to-operate controls. In addition, the powered nozzle should adjust to different rug piles and should have a low profile to clean under furniture.

Combination vacuums are not as easy to move from room to room as uprights, although they are highly maneuverable within a room. They require more storage room, however, than most canisters or uprights. Be sure to test a combination vacuum without its powered nozzle — versatility is supposed to be its advantage.

**Vacuum Brooms and Portables**

VACUUM BROOMS (also called "stick brooms") are designed for quick clean-up jobs. Because they have limited power and nozzle areas, they pick up only surface dirt. Their dust bags are generally smaller than those of uprights and they rely on suction alone to pick up dirt. Their chief advantages are light weight and ease of storage.

A good vacuum broom should have a fairly generous nozzle opening, a flat nozzle silhouette for cleaning under low furniture and should be relatively quiet in operation.

The latest trend in vacuum brooms is a powered nozzle that compares with full-sized uprights. These models are capable of cleaning an apartment or small house.

Portable vacuums are mini-cleaners that can handle quick cleaning chores around the house and can be used to clean automobiles. Most of the portables tested have shoulder straps for carrying. If you plan to buy a portable vac primarily to clean your car, remember that they operate on 115/120 volts and an electrical outlet must be handy. Portables are more powerful than auto vacs that use battery power.

**Heavy-Duty Vacs**

HEAVY-DUTY VACS feature heavy-duty tank canisters and large hoses and wands. Many of them are also designed to pick up water, something for which a regular vacuum should never be used. The wet-dry vac is insulated from electrical shock. Tank capacity runs from 3-1/2 gallons to 12 gallons.

Today, there are a few manufacturers who are designing their units to be used in the house as well as in the shop or garage. Soft colors and streamlined design are used in this effort. The consumer should look closely at the heavy-duty vacuum and consider its use indoors as well as in the shop. Some heavy-duty vacs are too bulky to maneuver indoors; others are so powerful they pick up the carpet along with the dust.

Some heavy-duty vacs have filter cartridges for dirt and debris; all of them have a filter for protecting the motor from damage. Dirt, debris and water are deposited into the tank itself for easy removal.

# 1978 Best Buys: Floor Care Appliances

"**B**est Buy" vacuum cleaners are those models that offer you the best performances in relation to their prices. Vacuum cleaners were tested on all types of carpets and surfaces—from louvered shades and delicate drapes to thick-piled rugs and shags. Adequacy of suction for picking up pet hairs, grit, threads and just plain dirt was rated. Ease of handling, maneuverability, operating noise, attachments, special features, construction and design were all considered during testing.

## UPRIGHT VACUUMS
### Best Buys

**Eureka Upright Model 2250** is a pleasure to push around, even on heavy, thick carpeting. Assembling the unit is relatively easy, with clear directions to follow. The vacuum moves in various directions with little physical effort. The range of cleaning surfaces goes from shag to low pile carpeting, allowing for the most efficient cleaning. It is powerful enough to pick up fine pet fur as well as food crumbs embedded in carpeting. The edge cleaner is a nice feature for cleaning close to carpet edges. Though not necessary, a very bright floor light helps when cleaning in dark corners and under furniture. An adjustable handle lowers enough to clean under most pieces of furniture. The on/off switch is mounted on the handle. The disposable dust bag is contained in a soft vinyl cover with zipper that offers better closure than snap designs.

**Approximate Retail Price: Not Available**     **Low Price: $95.00**

**Hoover Convertible U4103** is an excellent performer on all types of carpets except small throw rugs; it tends to push the rug around. Its four-position pile height adjustment works smoothly at the touch of a toe. The large-capacity bag is easy to change. The cleaner is equipped with a headlight and has a convenient on/off switch just below the grip on the underside of the handle. We were impressed with its ability to pick up pet hairs and ground-in dirt

*Prices are accurate at time of printing; subject to manufacturer's change.*

with equal ease. It also has an edge cleaner.
**Approximate Retail Price: $109.95**                          **Low Price: $74.70**

**Hoover Automatic Power-Drive Dial-A-Matic U6039-030** performed well on extended tests over a variety of floor coverings and even bare floors. Its Power-Drive feature makes it easy to operate for extended periods of time. Its three-position handle allowed it to clean under furniture with ease. The motor is exceptionally quiet for such a powerful machine. The nozzle edges are designed to provide full suction for cleaning close to baseboards. The U6039-030 may be converted to a canister-type vacuum, complete with six attachments. However, when used as a canister vac, the U6039-030 is rather cumbersome and may be fatiguing for the average user.
**Approximate Retail Price: $229.95**                   **Low Price: $152.99**

## Also Tested

**Douglas 6693** is a virtual twin of the Premier P4U5. Even the instruction book is identical except for the model name.
**Approximate Retail Price: $89.95**                           **Low Price: $76.45**

**Eureka 1416-B** is excellent for cleaning carpets; is not recommended, however, for use with attachments. The 12-inch beater-bar/brush roll effectively beats and sweeps up imbedded dirt. A four-way dial adjusts from low to normal to high to shag according to the height of the carpet pile. A basic upright vac without many frills, it includes the Edge Kleener feature and a foot-controlled on/off switch.
**Approximate Retail Price: $74.95**                           **Low Price: $60.00**

**Eureka 2325-A** has a one-speed motor and Eureka's patented "Dial-A-Nap" front end adjustment for different carpet heights. A good cleaning unit, the 2325 has a powerful motor and what the firm calls its "Vibra-Groomer," an hourglass-shaped power brush roll. The streamlined hood contains a headlight that is remarkably bright. The dirt is collected in a disposable paper bag within the vinyl dust bag cover. It did an excellent job on pile carpeting, shag rugs and indoor/outdoor carpeting. It also performed well on bare floors, due to the Dial-A-Nap device. Power is applied through a rocker-type switch on the handle. The 19-1/2 foot cord provided a tolerable working radius. The 2325 is equipped to take a set of six optional accessories.
**Approximate Retail Price: $109.95**                         **Low Price: $93.60**

**Premier P9U7** has some good features and some drawbacks. Among its advantages is an 18-foot rectractable cord housed in a closed compartment over the motor and played out through a device on the cleaner handle. A little switch on the device enables the user to stop the cord at any point she wishes, and we found it

*Prices are accurate at time of printing; subject to manufacturer's change.*

works admirably. The high/low suction settings, changed by foot, are also useful when cleaning small scatter rugs. Its cleaning ability, tested on low pile, high pile and shag, was uniformly good. The pile height adjustment switch, on the left of the motor housing, was less satisfactory because it must be moved by hand and the settings must be memorized, as the four markings are not actually labeled. Instead they are indicated by lettering on the side of the motor housing, with lines leading to the settings. The cleaner has a headlight. Bags are easy to change.

**Approximate Retail Price: $119.95**                  **Low Price: $99.95**

**Premier P4U5** is very much like P9U7 but lacks the retractable cord, two-speed motor, and on/off switch on the handle. The switch is on the motor housing instead, in the form of a toggle switch. This model weighs three pounds less than the more expensive P9U7 and also has the difficult-to-work pile height adjustment switch.

**Approximate Retail Price: $89.95**                  **Low Price: $79.99**

**Sears Powerease 3899** performs satisfactorily for all types of rug and floor cleaning. The edge-cleaner feature does a fine job close to the baseboards. The power pushbuttons are on top and the speed controls are on the lower back of the rigid bag enclosure. Its handle readily adjusts to three positions, and the unit has a retractable cord. This model features three traveling speeds, which can be turned off to maneuver in tight corners. You can buy a full range of attachments for cleaning above the floor. The owner's handbook clearly explains the features of this highly maneuverable upright.

**Approximate Retail Price: $199.00**        **Low Price: Not Available**

## CANISTER VACUUMS
### Best Buys

**The Douglas D6674** is a powerful canister that weighs only 7-1/2 pounds. By using a second handle directly below the hose connector hole, the user can carry it along while cleaning stairs. The same handle may be used to store the unit on end in a closet. The accessories are stored piggyback fashion on top of the machine. Extra-large wheels permit the unit to be towed along with little or no effort. Carpets, rugs, shags and indoor/outdoor floor coverings were cleaned very efficiently with the D6674. The instruction booklet was excellent.

**Approximate Retail Price: $65.95**                  **Low Price: $56.05**

**Eureka 3560-A** is one of the quieter machines tested. It is also one of the most attractively styled. Its hose has a "no kink" feature that CONSUMER GUIDE Magazine found most desirable. The 3560 did an excellent job in cleaning rugs and carpeting, including shags, with just the right amount of suction. With its above-floor attach-

*Prices are accurate at time of printing; subject to manufacturer's change.*

ments and its suction adjusting ring on the handle, the unit performs well on drapes and furniture upholstery, even removing stubborn pet hairs. The "touch-bar" activating switch on the front responds easily to the lightest touch of the foot. Accessories are stored piggyback fashion on posts that are specifically marked for each cleaning tool, and the unit can be stored on end in a closet.

**Approximate Retail Price: $89.95**          **Low Price: $75.60**

**Hoover S3033** has a lightweight and fairly powerful motor, making it a most useful cleaning machine for the average household. The 18-pound, handle-on-top canister can be used for cleaning stairs with remarkable ease. CONSUMER GUIDE Magazine found it to be especially effective in removing pet hairs from an upholstered chair. The five attachments are easily stored inside the machine when not in use. The entire unit can be stored in a closet without taking up much room. The "tip-toe" switch was easier to operate when the machine was standing on end, rather than when it was flat. The telescoping wands, a regular feature of many of Hoover's vacuums, are an ingenious innovation that makes assembly and disassembly foolproof. The combination nozzle features a retractable brush that adapts the tool to either rug or floor with the flick of a lever. Its king-sized disposable bag can hold a remarkable amount of dirt and debris. This is definitely a machine worth considering.

**Approximate Retail Price: $64.95**          **Low Price: $47.09**

## Also Tested

**Eureka Model 3240-B** is a light-duty canister vacuum with a small, quiet motor that performs best on short pile carpeting and flat surfaces. A shag attachment lifts shag yarns and offers some cleaning power at the same time. The machine is easy to maneuver and can be carried by the handle. Cleaning tools are self-storing on top of the canister. This is a no-frills vacuum with one speed for efficient cleaning purposes.

**Approximate Retail Price: $59.95**          **Low Price: $50.60**

**Hoover Celebrity Deluxe Vacuum Cleaner Model S3003-030** is powerful enough to do a good job of cleaning on various carpet heights and thicknesses. It rolls about easily and is well balanced. The lightweight wands snap together and lock tightly. Cleaning tools snap on tightly as well. The lever on the combination rug-and-floor nozzle is controlled by pushing the foot to select the proper surface. Passages at the sides of the nozzle clean carpet edges near baseboards and solid furniture. This canister is designed to be placed sideways on stairs, with the unit one stair above the one you are cleaning. The owner's manual is a thorough source of instructions on care and operation.

**Approximate Retail Price: $109.95**          **Low Price: $75.43**

*Prices are accurate at time of printing; subject to manufacturer's change.*

**Hoover Portable S3013,** at 24 pounds, is easy to maneuver on stairs. The S3013 does an adequate job on deep-pile shag carpeting, although it does not fluff the nap. It performs satisfactorily on bare floors and above the floor. Like Hoover's smaller Portapower, the S3013 has a rug nozzle that tilts when you try to clean under furniture. Since storage is obviously no problem, it would be suitable for small or medium-size apartments—anywhere your cleaning problems are not enormous.
**Approximate Retail Price: $74.95**          **Low Price: $52.89**

**Hoover Celebrity S3005-030** glides along the floor on a cushion of exhaust air with no wheels or runners. This model has a ten-quart dustbag and comes with a floor/rug nozzle that is satisfactory for medium-size general cleaning jobs. The S3005-030 also performs well on bare floors and its dust brush has been recently upgraded.
**Approximate Retail Price: $54.95**          **Low Price: $39.24**

**Premier Model P3018,** an all-steel canister vacuum, is designed for light cleaning jobs. It performs best on low pile surfaces. The 360-degree swivel top is handy for maneuvering the cleaning hose in any direction in an instant. The canister moves easily on flat surfaces but does tip over on heavier carpeting. Instructions are given for using the blower to get rid of moths, a helpful idea. Features include a suction selector for various cleaning jobs, a power selector, bag indicator and automatic cord release. A tray for tools attaches to the canister. The unit can be carried by a flexible handle, but it does not stand properly for stair cleaning.
**Approximate Retail Price: $99.95**          **Low Price: $74.95**

**Premier Swivel Model P1C28** works best on average cleaning tasks. It is a basic vacuum without a lot of extras. Attachments for various cleaning jobs include a wire tool to lift carpet nap or short shag. A lightweight unit to handle, it is easy to carry from room to room. The lightness is a disadvantage when pulling the canister in different directions because it tends to fall over.
**Approximate Retail Price: $59.45**          **Low Price: $49.95**

**Sunbeam 40-58** is quiet in operation and the suction was more than adequate on rugs, thick-pile carpets, indoor/outdoor carpets and shags. An air-adjustment feature on the hose allows it to be used on drapes without having to force the nozzle up and down on the fabric. The disposable paper filter is very easy to replace and the foot-activated switch on top of the unit is sensitive to the slightest touch. The seven attachments included are easily stored on top of the machine, piggyback fashion. Storage is relatively easy because the machine can be stood on end to fit in a closet. The instruction book is very clear and precise. The tilting feature of the wand makes cleaning under low furniture particularly easy.
**Approximate Retail Price: $83.99**          **Low Price: $67.61**

*Prices are accurate at time of printing; subject to manufacturer's change.*

**Sunbeam 40-118** delivers more than adequate suction power, and also comes complete with a number of deluxe features. The eight-piece attachment set includes a shag brush, and all accessories—in addition to wands and hose—are stored and carried piggyback. A 25-foot cord, full-bag indicator and five suction controls are standard. Exclusive features of this Sunbeam canister vac include a stair-lock wheel base and "wheelbarrow" transportation, with the wand serving as a handle. The unit stores compactly and total weight is less than 20 pounds.

**Approximate Retail Price: $129.99**        **Low Price: $104.64**

## COMBINATION VACUUMS
### Best Buys

**Eureka Power Team 1275** is a two-motor, one-speed vacuum that performs well on various carpet heights and thicknesses. It does a good job of lifting shag yarns as it cleans. The 1275 is quiet, yet the Vibra Groomer, a motorized beater bar-brush roll, is powerful enough to pull embedded dirt to the surface. The Edge Kleener is designed to clean close to baseboards. Larger openings for greater suction would help efficiency. The Vibra Groomer and flexible nozzle handle easily on thick carpeting. The canister can be carried by hand or pulled with little effort. This model works very well on stairs but does have a tendency to tip over when the hose is shifted. All parts attach tightly and resist stress. Dust is collected by an easy-to-install disposable dust bag and motor filter. Other features include a self-storing cord and a nine-piece tool set that self-stores on top of the canister.

**Approximate Retail Price: Not Available**        **Low Price: $149.95**

**Sunbeam 40-188** features a powerful 1-1/2 horsepower motor and a motorized nozzle, plus facilities for storing accessories on top of the unit. The 40-188 is a commendable machine for all-around house cleaning. Its more-than-adequate suction power proved itself on regular rugs, shags, high-pile, indoor/outdoor floor coverings and under furniture. It was a bit awkward on stairs, in spite of its extra long wands and hose, but it did an excellent job. The light on the power nozzle is a convenience, but is not necessary. The wiper blade on the nozzle made the 40-188 quite adaptable for cleaning bare floors. The locking mechanism that holds the wands upright made storage easy.

**Approximate Retail Price: $159.99**        **Low Price: $128.79**

### Also Tested

**Douglas Model C6675** is easily handled, relatively quiet, and has plenty of floor power in its motorized rug nozzle. The electric cord is incorporated into the hose. It cleaned right up to the baseboards

*Prices are accurate at time of printing; subject to manufacturer's change.*

in our test. Both metal and styrene plastic wands come with the C6675; we found the styrene plastic's light weight a bonus in above-the-floor cleaning. Above-floor cleaning tools, also of styrene plastic, fit snugly. The cleaner has good balance, large wheels, a large dustbag and a suction control on the handle. The extra handle is useful on stairs and for carrying. The one disadvantage we noted is the inconvenient and hard-to-reach toe-operated on/off switch. Tools are stored on top.

**Approximate Retail Price: $119.95**     **Low Price: $101.95**

**Eureka Power Team Model 1289,** a combination vacuum, is a heavy-duty machine that can satisfactorily perform a variety of jobs. The machine conforms to the cleaning job with a push of a button. Although the canister is very heavy to lift and carry, it does glide well on most carpeting. It balances nicely for stair cleaning. The flexible nozzle in the power head is very adaptable to stair rounds and chair and table legs, and also changes directions and positions instantly. Deluxe features include a bag-guard to indicate degree of fullness, two-speed cord release and return, power selector for various cleaning jobs and speed selector for high or normal. Accessories and extension wands lock together tightly, so pulling or yanking the hose will not loosen any of the equipment.

**Approximate Retail Price: Not Available**     **Low Price: $239.95**

**Filter Queen** has not changed its basic design for several years, though it increased the static suction of its hose inlet in 1973. The new models are available with a powered nozzle. Filter Queen vacuums are expensive and are sold only door to door. The Filter Queen does an excellent job on all cleaning problems, with or without the powered nozzle. It weighs 25 pounds and is too cumbersome to use on stairs, though it comes with a six-inch stair nozzle. The reusable filter covers have to be emptied—a messier system than disposable bags. If you are thinking of investing in a high-priced combination vacuum, test the Filter Queen. A test will be worth your time because the Filter Queen will set the standard of high-quality performance for any other vacuums you consider.

**Approximate Retail Price: $499.00**     **Low Price: Not Available**

**Hoover Elite S3061-030** is the most expensive model in Hoover's Celebrity line of combination vacs. The S3061 has an automatic cord rewind, on/off switch, pushbutton suction selectors and bag level indicator.

The three suction-regulator buttons stuck in our tests, and then loosened as the testing progressed. The maximum suction setting on this vacuum was stronger than on the Estate, the Elite's medium suction setting being equivalent to the highest suction setting on the Estate model.

The powered nozzle is basically the same for all vacuums in Hoover's Celebrity line. The only difference is that the Elite's nozzle

*Prices are accurate at time of printing; subject to manufacturer's change.*

has a headlight that prevents it from going under low furniture.

The powered nozzle presents some drawbacks in construction and performance. It is awkward to assemble. The latches on the wand are too close to the nozzle, and the connecting plugs are hard to fit into the recessed receptacles. The cord to the nozzle is on the same side as the handle-adjustment lever, and it is not easy to press the handle-adjustment lever without becoming entangled in the cord. Moreover, the powered nozzle tips over when you press the handle adjuster. There is another awkward foot lever to bring down the powered nozzle's floor brush, and it is a major operation to change from the powered nozzle to the above-the-floor attachments.

**Approximate Retail Price: $199.95**     **Low Price: $134.56**

**Hoover Estate S3059-030** is the mid-priced model in Hoover's Celebrity line. The 28-pound Estate has the same attachments as the Elite and the same tool caddy on top of its round canister. It rolls on three casters and is not as maneuverable as the Elite. It has a retractable cord, but its on/off switch is awkwardly located under the rubber rim bumper. Although the Estate has the same horsepower as the Elite, its maximum suction is not as strong as the Elite. The suction regulator on the Estate is located on the hose.

Like the other Celebrity models, the Estate has a powered nozzle that is awkward to assemble and operate. It does not have a headlight, a nonessential feature. Nevertheless, the powered nozzle cleans carpets of various pile depths satisfactorily, and the unit's above-floor performance is excellent.

**Approximate Retail Price: $179.95**     **Low Price: $121.85**

**Premier Shetland 1750** is a well-made, all steel, powerful unit that is adequate for all cleaning jobs around the largest home. It is the highest priced member of Premier's "360° Swivel-Top" line. The power head has a "hi-low" adjustment for rugs, floors, shags, high-pile carpeting and draperies, and is fairly quiet while in operation. A convenient clip-on tray allows accessories to be carried around while cleaning and for easy storing. The power cord is molded into the hose, a welcome feature. The 1750 did a good job cleaning close to baseboards and in hard-to-reach corners.

**Approximate Retail Price: $199.95**     **Low Price: $159.95**

**Sears Powermate 2899** performs superbly on every surface—bare floors, shag rugs, cut-pile rugs, louvered doors, walls and sheer drapes. It has an adjustment for every problem and even picks up pet hairs easily. Its suction control is located on the handle, and the on/off switch is a foot pedal. The Sears Powermate comes with an automatic cord rewind and headlight, and it stores the accessories inside the canister. It is extremely easy to handle; the rug edge feature can be dialed to pick up dirt in corners.

**Approximate Retail Price: $249.00**     **Low Price: Not Available**

*Prices are accurate at time of printing; subject to manufacturer's change.*

**Sunbeam "Challenger II" 40-178** has an extremely powerful suction that will clean any type of floor covering found in a home. The power head is equipped with a headlight for cleaning in corners or in closets without lights. This is a feature that is convenient, but not essential. Suction is controlled by means of a shutter-type mechanism that adjusts for shag, rug, floor, dusting, drapes and delicate fabrics. On the last two settings, the machine was rather noisy, but, until a better way is found to vent excess air, the concept will have to do for reducing or increasing suction. The 40-178 was especially effective for cleaning indoor/outdoor carpeting, perhaps one of the most difficult floor coverings to clean. The surprisingly light power head and the 25-foot retractable cord made cleaning stairs fairly easy. The toe-activated switch worked well with a minimum of pressure. The unit is equipped with an indicator light that warns when the bag is full or when the hose is clogged with dirt and/or debris. The seven attachments are easily stored, piggyback fashion, on posts on top of the machine. The 40-178 is a good machine that may be trusted to handle any cleaning situation.
**Approximate Retail Price: $214.99**    **Low Price: $173.08**

## HEAVY-DUTY VACUUMS
### Best Buys

**Douglas Wet-Dry Vac Model C6683** is a powerful unit made of high-impact styrene plastic that is rustproof. The unit sits on a four-wheeled dolly that really is tip-proof. The Douglas model handles wet or dry pickup, indoors and out. It has enough power and suction to absorb a large pan of water in a matter of seconds. It works just as well with dry materials. CONSUMER GUIDE Magazine tested this model in a garage where leaves, wood chips and floor dirt were picked up easily. The large drum-type container holds five gallons of dry material and three gallons of liquid. A float shuts off suction when the liquid capacity is reached. An assortment of tools comes with this model. All tools, hoses and wands lock into place and stay together, even under stress. The long cord is an advantage when electric outlets are not close together.
**Approximate Retail Price: $66.95**    **Low Price: $56.90**

### Also Tested

**Shop-Vac Dual Deluxe Aqua Vac 640** is designed primarily for cleaning garages, workshops and patios. However, a long line of accessories for in-house cleaning is available. CONSUMER GUIDE Magazine found it to be too powerful for cleaning some indoor carpeting and area rugs, although a 1-1/2 inch hose-wand combination is included for in-house cleaning. The 640 did an amazing job in cleaning a messy garage, using the 2-1/2 inch hose and wands. During tests, CONSUMER GUIDE Magazine experienced some difficulty in keeping the two 2-1/2 inch wands together, a

*Prices are accurate at time of printing; subject to manufacturer's change.*

problem that the manufacturer should fix. Aside from the slipping wands, the 640 proved to be a powerful, efficient unit, well-equipped to handle the heavy and difficult chores of cleaning a garage or messy workshop. The combination paper and foam filters worked well during the tests. When using the unit for removing water from floors, the manufacturer recommends removing the paper filter. Shop-Vac's 640 is an efficient and adequately powered machine.

**Approximate Retail Price: $84.95**                    **Low Price: $69.95**

**Shop Vac Dry Pick-Up Model 120-01-4** is designed for dry use only, indoors and outdoors. It works well in heavy-duty cleaning situations such as garage sweeping, workshop cleanup, or sand removal. This model is a five-gallon drum canister equipped with a six-foot flexible hose, master nozzle and dirt collection bag that is large enough to eliminate constant replacing. It can be pulled along the floor. The canister could be better balanced to eliminate tipping over. The nozzle and hose should fit more tightly. A heavy-duty cord and plug are too short to reach any distance. A long extension cord is needed to extend the cleaning area. The short hose and lightweight nozzle require hand guiding. Operating instructions are clear and easy to follow.

**Approximate Retail Price: $49.95**                    **Low Price: $39.95**

**Shop Vac 612** is the company's deluxe model with ten-gallon capacity and the ability to pick up dry material or water. It is designed for big jobs, with wide (14-inch) nozzles and large (1-1/4 inches in diameter) hose and wands. Its steel tank rolls on a four-wheeled dolly and is easy to handle, although somewhat cumbersome when emptying, despite handles on both sides of the tank. An automatic shutoff operates when the tank is full. The cord is 18 feet long. Accessories include a master nozzle for most dry jobs, a squeegee shoe for wet jobs and a rug nozzle. It converts to a blower if desired.

**Approximate Retail Price: $89.95**                    **Low Price: $69.95**

**Sunbeam Wet-Dry Vac 42-61** is designed to clean indoors and outdoors. It will clean patios, garages, shops and swimming pool decks with the same ease as it cleans the living room rug. It is not as maneuverable as a strictly indoor vacuum. The one-horsepower motor readily pulls dirt, debris and even water into its five-gallon tank through its amazingly light hose and wand. A unique feature of this unit is its pleated filter that can be cleaned and used over and over. The 42-61 is not as quiet as an upright or canister; the noise is created when it discharges air through an outlet on the top, completing its air motion cycle. Assembly instructions were clear, but in the model sent to CONSUMER GUIDE Magazine for testing, the casters would not snap into place without extreme exertion. The 42-61 performed admirably in a garage and easily picked up

*Prices are accurate at time of printing; subject to manufacturer's change.*

water through its squeegee attachment. By switching the hose from one intake outlet to the exhaust outlet, the machine blew a powerful blast of air, sufficient to dry up remaining moisture on the cement floor. Five attachments are included with the machine: a 1-1/2 inch hose, two plastic wands, a ten-inch floor nozzle and a squeegee plate. All in all, it is a good machine.

**Approximate Retail Price: $74.99**             **Low Price: $60.36**

## VACUUM BROOMS AND PORTABLES
### Best Buys

**Hoover S2029** is similar to the 2037 but lacks the power agitator. It also is lighter in weight (nine pounds), and has two speeds. This is a fine quick cleaner, and while it isn't nearly as powerful as an upright, it did an excellent job on bare floors and a very good job on carpets and rugs, including scatter rugs which it cleans without trying to pick them up. It also has a paper bag in a cassette. A dial on the nozzle has three settings, for regular cleaning and for right and left edge-cleaning. The on/off switch is on the tank rather than on the handle.

**Approximate Retail Price: $41.95**             **Low Price: $27.59**

**Hoover Handivac II S1021** is a versatile machine that comes with seven attachments for a variety of cleaning purposes. A handsomely-styled vacuum, it weighs less than five pounds. The carrying strap should be used if you have a lengthy cleaning chore. An easily activated toggle switch is conveniently located on the rear of the machine. Although it lacked the power of a larger upright, the versatility and portability of the S1021 made it a good unit for cleaning the upholstery, rugs and mats of an automobile.

**Approximate Retail Price: $36.95**             **Low Price: $24.30**

### Also Tested

**Bissell Sweep Master Deluxe Lite-Vac 3044-1** is easy to handle and adequately performs the simple surface cleaning chores for which it is intended. Like most other lightweight vacuum broom cleaners, it is inadequate for major rug and carpet cleaning. The Lite-Vac's main disadvantage is its open-end bag and tank assembly unit that dumps loose dirt when you empty the bag—an extremely messy system.

**Approximate Retail Price: $39.95**             **Low Price: $19.95**

**Hoover Quik-Broom S2037** is outstanding in its group. A separate agitator motor helps give extra cleaning power in a small, relatively lightweight (15-pound) machine. Its carpet setting, which adjusts automatically, gave excellent results when tested on both low-pile and shag rugs; it also has a bare-floor setting that did a fine job on vinyl. The edge-cleaner is efficient and the cassette bag changer is

*Prices are accurate at time of printing; subject to manufacturer's change.*

easy to handle. The cleaner is somewhat noisy. It reaches well under low furniture and hangs or stores in a small space. The optional cleaning tools were not tested.
**Approximate Retail Price: $79.95**                  **Low Price: $51.16**

**Premier Electric Portable Cleaner Model P4MV2** is a rectangular unit designed for light surface cleaning in home, car or workshop. It can be carried by a top-mounted handle or shoulder-strap attachment. The on/off switch below the handle is easily operated with a flick of the thumb. Long attachment wands can reach high places, and the four cleaning tools cover everything from lamp shades to trouser cuffs, floors and walls. This cleaner may be used to clear hose obstructions and as a blower for difficult areas that suction cannot reach. The reusable paper filter bag is easy to attach and remove. The unit is slim enough to store on a shelf, upright on the floor or on a wall peg or hook.
**Approximate Retail Price: $39.95**                  **Low Price: $34.95**

**Shop-Vac Hippo Vac 999-02-9** is a one-speed, hand-held unit for quick cleaning jobs in the home, garage, shop or patio. The Hippo-Vac's master nozzle did an efficient job on floors and the type of indoor/outdoor carpeting found on patios and swimming pool decks. The shoulder strap included should be used, as holding the machine by hand proved fatiguing after a length of time. The 18-foot cord was an asset when using the machine in the garage and workshop. Although the unit is designed to be used as a blower, CONSUMER GUIDE Magazine discovered that the blast of exhaust air from the vents on the rear of the unit scattered papers and light objects behind the tester when the Hippo-Vac was used as a vacuum. A way to muzzle the unwanted blast should be found. Two sizes of hose, 2-1/2 inch and 1-1/2 inch, are included for use in the house. The Hippo Vac did an excellent job of cleaning an automobile. A rug cleaning attachment is available.
**Approximate Retail Price: $69.95**                  **Low Price: $59.95**

**Sunbeam 43-53 Vacuum Broom** handles easily and cleans bare floors well. Though it quickly cleans surface dirt from low-pile carpets, it picks up pet hairs only from bare floors. It is not constructed for extensive or difficult cleaning jobs. The three-position rug nozzle is controlled by a flimsy plastic lever, and the suction is not good when the disposable bag is full.

Supposedly, the Sunbeam Power 43-53 can clean deep pile rugs, but CONSUMER GUIDE Magazine's tests showed that the shag and deep-pile settings on the nozzle did not work effectively. The Power 43-53, moreover, is clumsy to use on stairs. Overall, Sunbeam's stick vacuum broom has weak plastic construction and performs only a few cleaning tasks.
**Approximate Retail Price: $37.99**                  **Low Price: $30.58**

*Prices are accurate at time of printing; subject to manufacturer's change.*

**Sunbeam 43-98 Power-4** features a two-speed motor, a three-position floor nozzle and a detachable shag rake. The 43-98 proved to be a lightweight, efficient cleaning machine, but in CONSUMER GUIDE Magazine's opinion, the discharged air from vents in the top of the unit were annoying. However, the shag rake worked well on shag and high-pile floor coverings. The unit also did a fine job on indoor-outdoor floor covering, due to the retractable brush on the nozzle. Channels built into the sides of the nozzle made cleaning along baseboards fairly easy. The two-speed motor, plus a 20-foot-cord, make the 43-98 efficient for many quick cleaning jobs around the home.

**Approximate Retail Price: $48.99**                 **Low Price: $39.43**

**Osrow CV-1500,** 12-volt auto vac is designed for quick cleaning chores on auto upholstery and rugs or mats. It operates by plugging the unit into the cigarette lighter receptacle, and its 15-foot cord allows it to be used in every part of even the largest automobile. CONSUMER GUIDE Magazine thinks that the motor was not powerful enough to thoroughly clean a car. However, the unit is adequate for fast touch-up jobs on upholstery and rubber floor mats. The toggle switch on the handle operated easily, and the unit's light weight did prevent fatigue, even after prolonged use. Dirt and debris are collected in the cup container which is easy to remove. A disposable paper filter protects the motor; the user should be careful not to throw away the filter in the belief that it is part of the dirt container. Two accessories, a rug nozzle and crevice tool, are included.

**Approximate Retail Price: $19.95**                 **Low Price: $14.95**

*Prices are accurate at time of printing; subject to manufacturer's change.*

# Floor Care Appliance Prices

## Eureka

### UPRIGHT VACUUM CLEANERS

| Model | Description | Retail Price | Low Price |
|---|---|---|---|
| 1406-A | Dial-A-Nap, 2 Adjustments | $64.95 | $55.20 |
| 1416-B | Dial-A-Nap, 4 Adjustments | 74.95 | 60.00 |
| 1424-B | Dial-A-Nap, 6 Adjustments, Light | 89.95 | 72.00 |
| 1446-A | New Large Hood, 6 Adjustments | 89.95 | 69.60 |
| 1454-A | New Large Hood w Light, 6 Adjustments | 99.95 | 78.00 |
| 2315-A | Dial-A-Nap, 6 Adj. Vibra-Groomer | 99.95 | 85.20 |
| 2325-A | Dial-A-Nap, 6 Adj. Vibra-Groomer, Light | 109.95 | 93.60 |
| 2375-A | Rugulator, 2-Speed, Vibra-Groomer, Light | 129.95 | 104.40 |
| 2385-A | Rugulator, 2-Speed, Vibra-Groomer, Light, Cordaway | 179.95 | 134.40 |

### ATTACHMENTS

| Model | Description | Retail Price | Low Price |
|---|---|---|---|
| 60-A | Standard 6 piece | $19.95 | $14.40 |
| 2677-A | Custom 9 piece w/caddy | 24.95 | 19.20 |

### CANISTERS

| Model | Description | Retail Price | Low Price |
|---|---|---|---|
| 3220-B | 1-1/8 HP. Promotional, 8 pc. attachments | $49.95 | $43.70 |
| 3240-B | 1-1/8 HP. 10 pc. Attachment Tool-Pak | 59.95 | 50.60 |
| 3440-A | 1-1/8 HP. Cordaway Snap-On Tool-Pak | 69.95 | 58.65 |
| 3460-A | 2 HP. 10 pc. Attachment Tool-Pak | 79.95 | 60.95 |
| 3560-A | 2 HP. 2 Stage Cordaway | 89.95 | 75.60 |

### LIGHTWEIGHTS

| Model | Description | Retail Price | Low Price |
|---|---|---|---|
| 93-A | Promotional | $39.95 | $29.90 |
| 123-A | Super w/Handle | 49.95 | 40.25 |
| 155-A | Deluxe | 39.95 | 34.50 |
| 155-AT | Deluxe w/Tools | 49.95 | 40.25 |

*Prices are accurate at time of printing; subject to manufacturer's change.*

| | | Retail Price | Low Price |
|---|---|---|---|
| **POWER TEAMS (Two Motors)** | | | |
| 1248-A | 1-1/8 HP. Promotional w/Tool-Pak | $99.95 | $86.25 |
| 1255-B | 1.6 HP. Tool-Pak Free Standing | 139.95 | 119.60 |
| 1261-A | 2-1/3 HP. 2-Stage Free Standing | 169.95 | 144.00 |
| 1266-B | 2-1/3 HP. 2-Stage Cordaway, Light | 209.95 | 174.00 |
| 1288-A | 3.3 HP. 2-Speed, Cordaway, Light, Air-Matic Console | 279.95 | 231.25 |
| **COMMERCIAL** | | | |
| C-2035-D | Standard Commercial | $140.00 | $114.00 |
| C-2045-B | Deluxe Vibra-Groomer | 160.00 | 131.25 |
| C-2063-A | Vibra-Groomer w/Light | 190.00 | 149.50 |
| 405-F | Commercial Canister on Dolly | 220.00 | 169.00 |

# Hoover

| | | Retail Price | Low Price |
|---|---|---|---|
| **HAND CLEANERS** | | | |
| S1021 | Handivac II, Goldtone/White | $36.95 | $24.30 |
| S1019 | Handivac I, Red/White | 31.95 | 22.13 |
| **CANISTER VACUUM CLEANERS** | | | |
| S3061 | Celebrity II, Power Nozzle | $199.95 | $134.56 |
| S3059 | Celebrity II, Power Nozzle | 179.95 | 121.85 |
| S3079 | Celebrity II, Power Nozzle | 159.95 | 109.01 |
| S30803 | Celebrity II, Power Nozzle | 129.95 | 89.51 |
| S3093 | Celebrity II, Power Nozzle | 119.95 | 77.65 |
| S3001 | Celebrity Custom | 119.95 | 82.34 |
| S3003 | Celebrity Deluxe | 109.95 | 75.43 |
| S3073 | Celebrity w/Casters | 89.95 | 59.50 |
| S3015 | Portable, Tools, Cord Reel, Wheels | 79.95 | 57.59 |
| S3013 | Portable, Tools, Cord Reel, Wheels | 74.95 | 52.89 |
| 2120 | Portable, Tools, | 69.95 | 51.09 |
| S3033 | Slimline Model | 64.95 | 47.09 |
| S3005 | Celebrity Air-Ride | 54.95 | 39.24 |
| S1015 | Portapower | 49.95 | 38.88 |
| **UPRIGHT VACUUM CLEANERS** | | | |
| U6039 | Dial-A-Matic w/Headlight | $229.95 | $152.99 |
| U6041 | Dial-A-Matic, Power Drive | 214.95 | 142.90 |
| U5015 | Dial-A-Matic | 129.95 | 88.75 |
| U4103 | Convertible w/Headlight | 109.95 | 74.70 |
| U4101 | Convertible | 89.95 | 62.79 |
| U4057 | Convertible | 89.95 | 61.11 |

*Prices are accurate at time of printing; subject to manufacturer's change.*

| | | Retail Price | Low Price |
|---|---|---|---|
| **CLEANING TOOLS** | | | |
| U5909 | For Dial-A-Matic, 4 Pc. Set | $24.95 | $18.74 |
| U4903 | For Convertible, Deluxe 9 Pc. Set | 24.95 | 18.74 |
| U4901 | For Convertible, Standard 5 Pc. Set | 14.95 | 10.20 |
| 2921 | For Quik-Broom, 6 Pc. Set | 14.95 | 10.11 |
| **POLISHERS/SHAMPOOERS** | | | |
| 3614 | Floor-A-Matic w/Water Pick-Up | $89.95 | $56.76 |
| 5488 | Deluxe Shampoo-Polisher | 49.95 | 33.14 |
| 5308 | Deluxe Rug Shampooer | 44.95 | 30.05 |
| 5168 | Shampoo-Polisher | 42.95 | 28.70 |
| **STICK CLEANERS** | | | |
| S2037 | Quik-Broom w/Power Nozzle | $79.95 | $51.16 |
| S2029 | Quik-Broom, 2-Speed | 41.95 | 27.59 |
| S2031 | Quik-Broom, Single Speed | 37.95 | 25.28 |
| S2033 | Quik-Broom, Single Speed | 34.95 | 22.99 |
| S2015 | Quik-Broom, Custom, Single Speed | 29.95 | 20.68 |

# Regina

| | | | |
|---|---|---|---|
| **RUG SHAMPOOER/FLOOR POLISHERS** | | | |
| 707 | | $99.95 | $69.97 |
| 794 | 3-Speed | 79.95 | 49.97 |
| **ELECTRIKBROOMS** | | | |
| 4649 | 3-Speed | $74.95 | $38.90 |
| 8610 | Powerhead, 2-Speed | 89.99 | 56.97 |
| RB5528 | 2-Speed | 52.95 | 29.97 |
| RB5538 | 3-Speed | 59.95 | 33.90 |

# Sanyo

| | | | |
|---|---|---|---|
| **VACUUMS** | | | |
| SC-2650 | Tank Vacuum Cleaner | $59.95 | $42.56 |
| SC-1500 N | Deluxe Electric Vacuum | 69.95 | 48.16 |
| SC-2005 N | Extra Powerful Tank Vacuum Cleaner | 79.95 | 53.76 |

# Sunbeam

| | | | |
|---|---|---|---|
| **VACUUM CLEANER COMBINATIONS** | | | |
| 40-178 | Challenger II Vacuum Cleaner | $214.99 | $173.08 |
| 40-188 | Dual Deluxe Canister w/Power Drive | 159.99 | 128.79 |

*Prices are accurate at time of printing; subject to manufacturer's change.*

|  |  | Retail Price | Low Price |
|---|---|---|---|
| 40-198 | Dual Deluxe Economy Canister | $139.99 | $112.69 |

**CANISTER VACUUM CLEANERS**

| 40-18 | Special Value Canister | $56.99 | $45.87 |
|---|---|---|---|
| 40-58 | Round Canister Cleaner | 83.99 | 67.61 |

**CHALLENGER VACUUM CLEANER**

| 40-118 | Challenger 2.3 H.P. w/Stair Lock | $129.99 | $104.64 |
|---|---|---|---|

**OUTDOOR/INDOOR HEAVY DUTY VACUUM CLEANERS**

| 42-57 | Deluxe Outdoor/Indoor Vacuum | $61.99 | $49.90 |
|---|---|---|---|
| 42-61 | Deluxe Wet/Dry Outdoor/Indoor | 74.99 | 60.36 |

**VACUUM BROOMS**

| 43-53 | Power 4 Vacuum Broom, Heavy Duty | $37.99 | $30.58 |
|---|---|---|---|
| 43-98 | Power 4 + Deluxe 2-Speed Broom | 48.99 | 39.43 |

*Prices are accurate at time of printing; subject to manufacturer's change.*

---

# SPECIAL INFORMATION SERVICE

**A Bonus for Readers of this CONSUMER GUIDE®**

CONSUMER GUIDE® offers a special bonus to its readers who are interested in obtaining information as to where they can find the low prices on specific products listed in this guide. Simply fill out the form and mail. Include 25 cents for postage and handling.

**Please send me information on:**

Product _____ Model Number _____

Manufacturer _____

Product _____ Model Number _____

Manufacturer _____

Product _____ Model Number _____

Manufacturer _____

Your Name _____

Address _____

City _____ State _____ Zip Code _____

**CONSUMER GUIDE Magazine**
**3841 West Oakton, Skokie, Illinois 60076**

# 1978 Refrigerators

EVEN BEFORE the recent energy crisis, the bill-paying members of the family knew that misuse of the refrigerator meant high electricity payments. The fact is, after space heating and cooling, and after water heating, refrigeration is the third major energy consumer in the home. Thinking of the refrigerator as the biggest energy user in the kitchen means thinking in terms of long-range cost. The cost of energy during a refrigerator's lifetime may be more than double the initial price tag.

**Energy and Life Cycles**

CONSUMER GUIDE Magazine strongly recommends a life-cycle cost approach to buying a refrigerator. Refrigerators last an average of 15.2 years and initial prices range from about $200 to more than $1000. In the life-cycle approach, you look at the cost of the unit over its expected life, including its initial price, the cost of maintenance, and the cost of energy.

For instance, compare two refrigerators of the same size, both 17 cubic feet with automatic defrost. One is a high-efficiency type with a price tag of $500; it uses 100 kilowatt-hours of electricity a month. The other has an initial price of $350; it uses 160 kilowatt-hours a month. Assume each unit requires $100 in repairs and maintenance over its life. With the high-efficiency unit, your 15-year life cycle cost (with energy at 4¢ per kilowatt-hour) would be $1320. The other unit would cost you $1602. You would save $282 during the high-efficiency unit's life as compared to the other refrigerator. So, the higher priced refrigerator turns out to be $132 cheaper than the other model. The saving increases as the cost of energy increases. If your electricity is 8¢ a kilowatt-hour (as it is now for some consumers), your lifetime savings would be $714, which would be more than you paid for the unit.

The lesson to be learned from the life-cycle approach is: buy the highest efficiency model you can afford. In fact, stretch your budget for the better model if you can—it will save money in the long run.

### The Government Energy Program

THE FEDERAL Government has had a major appliance energy program underway for about two years. This voluntary program seeks to reduce energy consumption by having refrigerator makers demonstrate a specified percent of improvement across their entire refrigerator lines by 1980, compared to the base year of 1972. A manufacturer need not improve every model as long as he can show that his product sales, as a whole, represent the required target goal improvement—47 percent.

However, at this writing, a bill is pending in Congress that would change this approach significantly. The legislation, part of President Carter's National Energy Policy Program, would require that all refrigerators sold after a specified date meet minimum energy efficiency standards. In other words, a refrigerator manufacturer would have to improve every model that did not meet the minimum standard.

### Energy Saving Improvements

WHILE SPECULATION on the "minimum" energy efficiency level that will be set for refrigerators is impossible, a look at what manufacturers will do to improve efficiency is possible. Many of these steps have been (or are being) taken by the industry.

• Door heater switches have become almost standard equipment on refrigerators that have door heaters. Door heaters prevent condensation, or sweating, on the outside of the door in humid environments. With their switches set at the lowest position ("off," "low," or "dry," depending on how manufacturers refer to the settings), as much as 10 percent of the unit's energy consumption can be saved.

• Post-condenser loops or coils are used by some manufacturers in place of door heaters. In essence, hot refrigerant gas is piped around the door to prevent sweating. People who live in high-humidity climates and do not have air conditioning may save energy with the post-condenser method. Bigger savings are possible with the door heater switches for consumers that have air conditioned homes.

• Improved or increased insulation is available on several models. Many manufacturers will replace fiberglass insulation (about

40 percent of the units sold in 1975 had fiberglass insulation) with polyurethane, foamed-in-place insulation. Combined with plastic liners, this can cut down on energy usage. Some manufacturers, notably Amana, have increased the amount of insulation to produce significant energy reductions.

- Improved compressor motors can yield added savings of seven to ten percent. Many manufacturers have already made some improvements in this area.
- Other areas for improvement include better evaporator heat transfer, better condenser heat transfer, better door seals, improved cabinet designs, and demand defrost. These "hidden" changes will result in higher prices.

**Defrost Systems and Energy**

REFRIGERATOR defrost systems are frequently a central point in discussions about saving energy. Why not just eliminate automatic defrost, it is often asked. There are several reasons. Perhaps the most important reason is that consumers are buying this feature in ever-increasing percentages: 74 percent of the units sold in 1975 had automatic defrost; 76 percent had it in 1976.

Automatic defrost is popular, no doubt, because it makes a refrigerator almost carefree, though cleaning and maintenance (as specified in the owner's manual) is a must for proper function and optimum energy performance. Manual defrost uses less energy if the refrigerator is defrosted on a regular basis. Most people procrastinate. Frost buildup reduces efficiency. In addition, the hot water most people use to aid defrosting represents energy consumption. Also, the freezer compartment heats up during the defrosting process and requires more energy to be cooled back down. However, the inconvenience of manual defrost does not discount the fact that automatic defrost does use energy, about 15 to 20 percent of the refrigerator's total energy consumption.

Automatic defrost systems currently use timers to initiate the defrost cycle, which means that regular intervals generally exist between defrosts. For years, defrost-on-demand (only when there is a need to defrost) has been discussed by the manufacturers. It now appears that one such defrost-on-demand system may be coming soon. One controls supplier is selling such a device to a couple of refrigerator makers. A five to ten percent energy improvement should be possible with demand-defrost systems compared to regular, timer-defrost systems.

**Recommendations on Energy**

THE RESULT of all the government and industry work to improve energy efficiency will be higher prices, probably between ten and 30 percent higher. But remember, there will be a payback in savings on energy. And we all know what is happening to the cost of energy.

Do not buy fancy features, especially energy using ones such as icemakers, without careful thought. The extras cost you and may not return enough added convenience.

Do not buy too big a unit. If your unit is empty most of the time, you are paying to cool unnecessary space.

Do consider the Recommended Buys CONSUMER GUIDE Magazine has selected. Special attention has been paid to energy-saving features in these units. We have also considered price, features, general reliability, frequency-of-repair data where available, and convenience of design. Generally, our Recommended Buys are among the more efficient in their size class.

**Additional Trends**

LARGE-CAPACITY units are still popular, but as family size shrinks the trend may revert to medium and smaller models.

Inside and out, styling continues to receive attention by both manufacturers and consumers. Woodgrains are still popular. Multiple color combinations exist. Textured steel doors are available on more models as manufacturers respond to consumer interest. The latest color fad is called almond; it is really nothing but beige with an appealing name.

Side-by-side refrigerators are the favorites of consumers seeking large freezer capacities. There also are units with top-mounted freezers that have a larger capacity than before. Both types of products answer the need for freezer space, a need brought on in part by the continued and growing use of prepared frozen foods.

The bottom-mounted freezer/refrigerator appears to be making a comeback. Whirlpool recently reintroduced such a model. Amana has kept a unit of this type in its line. In many respects, a refrigerator with a bottom-mounted freezer is more convenient; there is little or no bending to reach items in the refrigerator section.

**Types of Refrigerator-Freezers**

THE TYPE OF refrigerator-freezer you buy should depend on your lifestyle. If you are a plan-ahead, shop-ahead person, adequate freezer space will be more important than if you shop frequently and rarely freeze food.

**Single-Door.** Refrigerators with a single door usually have a small freezer compartment inside with a small access door. These models are inexpensive to buy and operate. Selection is limited and normally these units require defrosting.

**Two-Door, Top-Mount.** These units have two horizontal doors, one for the fresh food section and one for the freezer mounted on the top. These units are the most popular and come in a wide variety of sizes. Most of the units available in the larger sizes have automatic defrost. About one fourth to one third of the unit's total capacity is in the freezer. Dollar for dollar, these units represent the best values.

**Two-Door, Bottom-Mount.** Units with a freezer on the bottom are apparently coming back. There are two such models available, one from Amana and one from Whirlpool. The freezer section slides out for easy access.

**Two-Door, Side-By-Side.** Two full-sized vertical doors distinguish side-by-sides. The freezer side normally represents between one third and one half of the unit's total capacity. These units are not quite as efficient as the top-mounted freezer refrigerators and are a little more expensive to purchase. Most models have 19 or more cubic feet of space.

**Three-Door, Side-By-Side.** On these models, there are two doors to the freezer section. A small freezer door allows access to frequently used items. The third door adds to the initial price of the unit.

**Compact.** Primarily novelty or luxury items, compacts are single-door units with less than ten cubic feet of capacity. Normally used in offices, bars, and school dormitory rooms, the units are not very efficient. CONSUMER GUIDE Magazine does not believe they represent good buys from an energy point of view. We have listed two units as Suggested Buys, but you should remember that they normally represent extra energy consumption since they are used mostly as additional or second units.

### Don't Waste Energy, Get the Right Size

EVERY FAMILY has slightly different needs in terms of a refrigerator, but there are some general guidelines to buying the right size. CONSUMER GUIDE Magazine recommends at least eight or ten cubic feet of fresh food space for a family of two. Add one cubic foot to this for each additional family member. In the freezer section, about three cubic feet of space should be adequate for a family of two. Add one cubic foot for each additional family member.

You should adjust these guidelines to coincide with your living habits. If you shop frequently, you may not need quite as much space. If you entertain a lot, or prepare meals in advance, you may want to consider more space.

The kitchen space available for a refrigerator may limit your selection to some extent. Some refrigerators vent to the front and do not require extra depth or an air circulation area above the unit. Others require this air circulation space at the sides and the top. There is also the question of which way the door should open. Do you want it to open to the left or to the right? Your best bet is to measure the space available and take this information with you when you shop. It also is a good idea to check doorways and entrances just to make sure the unit will fit into the kitchen (difficulty could occur with some large-capacity models in older homes).

## Refrigerator Features – A Wide Choice

CONSUMER GUIDE Magazine favors certain features because they add convenience. Among features that we recommend are automatic defrost, door heater switches (or post-condenser loops), adjustable cantilever shelves, dual controls, removable bins and crispers, shelves in the freezer section, removable ice bins, and rollers.

**Defrost.** Manual defrost units are the most economical. With them, you must defrost the entire unit periodically. Partial defrost systems, also called cycle defrost, require freezer defrosting, but the refrigerator section defrosts automatically. Automatic defrost systems, also called no-frost, frost-free and other names, completely defrost both the freezer and fresh food sections. Automatic defrost adds to the cost of the unit and to your operating costs, but CONSUMER GUIDE Magazine believes you will still find this the best approach, unless you are the rare kind of person who can regularly defrost the refrigerator before the frost builds up.

**Power Savers.** Door heater switches are recommended for consumers with air conditioning, as well as those who live in low-humidity areas. Post-condenser loops are best for high-humidity areas and for homes in warm climates without air conditioning.

**Controls.** A single control for both the refrigerator and freezer sections is not as convenient as a unit with dual controls. Separate controls for meat keepers are also available on some models.

**Refrigerator Shelves.** Fully adjustable, cantilever shelves are the most convenient. Units with fixed shelves and shelves that are adjustable in only one or two positions may limit your storage. Shelf materials vary from tempered glass (pretty and they clean easily, but they also break), to plastic (a good all-around shelf material), to wire (easy to see through, but food items may drip or spill onto the shelf below).

**Liners.** The refrigerator liner may be plastic or metal. The metal (steel) liners may be on the way out as manufacturers search for better insulation methods with foam and plastic liners. Plastic liners can be scratched and damaged if not properly cleaned.

**Bins and Crispers.** Steel bins are more durable than the more common plastic types. The plastic types are light and easy to clean. Either way, check for stops to keep the bins from being pulled out unintentionally.

**Refrigerator Door Shelves.** Fixed plastic shelves with a butter compartment (and sometimes a cheese compartment) and egg holder are the most common. A few models have cantilever shelves in the door or adjustable pick-off bins.

**Freezer Shelf.** A wire shelf in the freezer helps you organize frozen items more efficiently.

**Freezer Door Shelves.** Side-by-sides have several door shelves in the freezer section (some also have a bin for bulk items).

## Energy Cost Ranges for Combination Refrigerator/Freezers

| Rated Total Refrigerated Volume In Cubic Feet | Ranges of Cost of Energy In Dollars Per Month At a Rate of 4 Cents Per Kilowatt-Hour For Models With | | | |
|---|---|---|---|---|
| | Partial Automatic Defrost | | Automatic Defrost | |
| | Min. | Max. | Min. | Max. |
| Less than 10.5 | $ 2.40 | $ 2.40 | $ — | $ — |
| 10.5 to less than 11.5 | 2.40 | 4.20 | 4.60 | 4.60 |
| 11.5 to less than 12.5 | 2.90 | 4.40 | 4.60 | 5.30 |
| 12.5 to less than 13.5 | 2.90 | 4.40 | 3.80 | 5.80 |
| 13.5 to less than 14.5 | 3.20 | 4.40 | 3.80 | 6.30 |
| 14.5 to less than 15.5 | 2.00 | 4.10 | 3.40 | 6.30 |
| 15.5 to less than 16.5 | 2.00 | 3.20 | 3.40 | 6.80 |
| 16.5 to less than 17.5 | 2.00 | 3.20 | 3.40 | 6.80 |
| 17.5 to less than 18.5 | 3.20 | 3.20 | 3.60 | 8.20 |
| 18.5 to less than 19.5 | | | 3.60 | 8.20 |
| 19.5 to less than 20.5 | | | 4.00 | 8.20 |
| 20.5 to less than 21.5 | | | 4.60 | 8.40 |
| 21.5 to less than 22.5 | | | 4.60 | 8.40 |
| 22.5 to less than 23.5 | | | 4.90 | 8.40 |
| 23.5 to less than 24.5 | | | 4.90 | 9.10 |
| 24.5 to less than 25.5 | | | 5.50 | 9.10 |
| 25.5 to less than 26.5 | | | 6.50 | 9.10 |
| 26.5 to less than 27.5 | | | 7.40 | 7.40 |
| 27.5 to less than 28.5 | | | 7.40 | 7.40 |
| 28.5 to less than 29.5 | | | 7.40 | 7.40 |
| 29.5 and over | | | — | — |

This table can help you determine the energy ranking of a model if you know how much it will cost to operate it for a month (based on 4¢ per kilowatt-hour). Information is from the Association of Home Appliance Manufacturers.

Top-mounts may have one or two door shelves. Most units have a shelf or rack for juice cans in the freezer door.

**Icemakers.** Icemakers are a luxury that usually do not deliver benefits comparable to their cost. However, if you think you may have need for one later, look at units prewired and plumbed for an add-on icemaker. One feature that does add convenience is a removable ice bin.

**Rollers.** Rollers are standard on many refrigerators, and available as an option on others. They help you move the unit during cleaning. They are a recommended feature.

**Colors.** The standard appliance colors are available; white (the most popular) and at a slight extra cost (usually about $10) harvest gold, avocado, and coppertone. General Electric led the field with new colors that are a cross between the body color and edge shading currently found on most appliances. These colors have new names—snow (white), harvest wheat (similar to gold), fresh avocado (similar to avocado), and coffee (similar to coppertone), and this season's favorite, almond (beige). Poppy red is another color available from several manufacturers. In addition, most manufacturers offer decorator kits for special-effect fronts.

# 1978 Best Buys: Refrigerators

CONSUMER GUIDE Magazine examined the major brands of refrigerators on the basis of design, convenience, reliability, features, efficiency and price. Those models offering the best combinations of these elements were rated by our experts as Recommended Buys.

## SINGLE-DOOR REFRIGERATORS

**Admiral C-1073,** a 10-cubic-foot refrigerator, consumes 59 kilowatt-hours of electricity per month. It has a manual defrost system and 1.21 cubic feet of freezer space. The unit has one temperature control and a large chiller drawer below the freezer. A full-width crisper is at the bottom of the refrigerator section. Its glide-out shelves are not adjustable. The door has a butter compartment, shelves for packages and bottles, and two egg shelves.
**SPECIFICATIONS: Height,** 56-3/4''; **Width,** 24''; **Depth,** 28-1/2''; **Shelf Capacity** (square feet), 13.8; **Warranty,** one year on parts and labor, with an additional four years on the compressor system (parts).
**Approximate Retail Price: $224.00**          **Low Price: $204.00**

**White-Westinghouse RC131T** is a 12.5-cubic-foot unit that consumes 52 kilowatt-hours of electricity per month. It offers 1.74 cubic feet of freezer space and 10.77 cubic feet of fresh food storage space. The features include a vegetable crisper at the bottom of the refrigerator section and a single temperature control. The door has three shelves and a butter compartment, as well as two egg shelves. One of its two refrigerator section shelves can be adjusted to two positions. This manual defrost unit has a chiller tray beneath the freezer.
**SPECIFICATIONS: Height,** 60-1/4''; **Width,** 30''; **Depth,** 26-5/8''; **Shelf Capacity** (square feet), 17.0; **Warranty,** one year on parts and labor, with an additional four years on the compressor system (parts).
**Approximate Retail Price: Not Available**      **Low Price: $300.84**
*Prices are accurate at time of printing; subject to manufacturer's change.*

## TOP-MOUNT REFRIGERATORS

**Gibson RT-12F3SJ,** a 12-cubic-foot model, consumes 115 kilowatt-hours of electricity per month. It has automatic defrost and offers 2.6 cubic feet of freezer space. The freezer does not have a shelf, while the fresh food section has two shelves that can be adjusted to fixed positions. This model features slide-out crispers at the bottom of the refrigerator section, plastic liners, and reversible doors. The refrigerator door has two shelves, an egg shelf and a butter compartment.
**SPECIFICATIONS: Height,** 56-3/16"; **Width,** 28"; **Depth,** 26-29/32"; **Shelf Capacity** (square feet), 13.7; **Warranty,** one year on parts and labor, with an additional four years on the compressor system (parts).
**Approximate Retail Price: $405.00**       **Low Price: $329.00**

**Admiral T-1274** is a 12.2-cubic-foot model with partial defrost that consumes 95 kilowatt-hours per month. This unit offers 1.69 cubic feet of freezer space. The refrigerator section door has two shelves plus a butter compartment and an egg shelf. The refrigerator section has two glide-out wire shelves that are not adjustable. There is also a glass shelf over the full-width crisper. The freezer section does not have a shelf and there is one door shelf.
**SPECIFICATIONS: Height,** 61-1/4"; **Width,** 28"; **Depth,** 28"; **Shelf Capacity** (square feet), 15.0; **Warranty,** one year on parts and labor, with an additional four years on the compressor system (parts).
**Approximate Retail Price: Not Available**       **Low Price: $275.00**

**Hotpoint CTF-14EV,** a 14.2-cubic-foot model with automatic defrost, consumes 94 kilowatt-hours of electricity per month when the power-saver door heater switch is set on low. The unit offers 4.58 cubic feet of freezer space and includes a shelf in the freezer section. The fresh food section has two adjustable cantilever shelves, a meat keeper, and two crispers at the bottom. Its refrigerator door contains three shelves, a butter compartment and an egg tray. This model comes with rollers and requires four inches of top clearance.
**SPECIFICATIONS: Height,** 61"; **Width,** 28"; **Depth,** 29-3/16"; **Shelf Capacity** (square feet), 20.5; **Warranty,** one year on parts and labor, with an additional four years on the compressor system (parts).
**Approximate Retail Price: $499.95**       **Low Price $350.00**

**Amana ESRF-16W,** a 16-cubic-foot model with automatic defrost, consumes 84 kilowatt-hours of electricity per month with the door heater switch set on low. The unit contains 3.46 cubic feet of freezer space and features dual temperature controls, reversible doors and door stops. The refrigerator section has four half-width adjustable cantilever shelves and a meat keeper with its own temperature control. Twin crispers, two door shelves, a butter
*Prices are accurate at time of printing; subject to manufacturer's change.*

compartment and a removable egg tray are included. This model is one of the most efficient refrigerators available, although Amana's service policies are less than good.
**SPECIFICATIONS: Height,** 63"; **Width,** 32"; **Depth,** 29-1/4"; **Shelf Capacity** (square feet), 23.6; **Warranty,** five years on parts and labor.

**Approximate Retail Price: $669.95**            **Low Price: $561.20**

**Kenmore (Sears) 7677710** is a 17-cubic-foot refrigerator with automatic defrost that consumes 94 kilowatt-hours of electricity per month with the door heater switch set on low. The model offers 4.77 cubic feet of freezer space. It has porcelain-on-steel liners, dual controls and reversible doors. The fresh food section contains three full-width shelves, twin crispers, two deep-door shelves, a butter compartment and an egg rack. The freezer door has a shelf and a juice-can rack, but there is no interior shelf. The price tag is slightly higher than other refrigerators in its class because of the model's excellent energy performance.
**SPECIFICATIONS: Height,** 65-1/2"; **Width,** 32-3/4"; **Depth,** 29"; **Shelf Capacity** (square feet), 22.8; **Warranty,** one year on parts and labor, with four years more on the compressor system (parts).

**Approximate Retail Price: $459.95**            **Low Price: Not Available**

**Gibson RT-17F6,** a 17-cubic-foot unit with automatic defrost, consumes 128 kilowatt-hours of electricity per month. The freezer section offers 4.6 cubic feet of space. The fresh food section has three adjustable cantilever shelves, twin crispers, a meat keeper with a temperature control, two egg racks, a butter compartment, and two deep-door shelves. The freezer section has a full-width shelf and two door shelves. This model features plastic liners, dual controls, rollers, door stops, and reversible doors.
**SPECIFICATIONS: Height,** 62-29/32"; **Width,** 31"; **Depth,** 29-1/16"; **Shelf Capacity** (square feet), 24.3; **Warranty,** one year on parts and labor, with an additional four years on the compressor system (parts).

**Approximate Retail Price: $540.00**            **Low Price: $429.95**

**Whirlpool EET-171HK,** a 17.2-cubic-foot model with automatic defrost, consumes 94 kilowatt-hours of electricity per month with the door heater switch set on low. The unit has 4.75 cubic feet of freezer space. Rollers and reversible doors are two of its features. The fresh food section has four adjustable cantilever shelves, twin crispers, a meat pan, removable egg bin, porcelain-on-steel liners, two door shelves plus butter and cheese compartments. The freezer section contains an interior shelf and two door shelves. The unit has dual controls.
**SPECIFICATIONS: Height,** 65-7/8"; **Width,** 32-3/4"; **Depth,** 29"; **Shelf Capacity** (square feet), 24.7; **Warranty,** one year on parts and
*Prices are accurate at time of printing; subject to manufacturer's change.*

labor, with an additional four years on the compressor system (parts).
**Approximate Retail Price: $519.00**         **Low Price: $482.40**

**Hotpoint CTF-18HV** is a 17.6-cubic-foot model with automatic defrost. Consuming 89 kilowatt-hours of electricity per month with the door heater switch set on low, this is an energy-efficient model. The model has 4.69 cubic feet of freezer space. Door stops, rollers and dual controls are three of the features. The freezer section contains an ice bucket, interior shelf and two door shelves. You will find a meat keeper, twin crispers, butter and cheese bins, removable egg trays, three adjustable cantilever shelves, and three door shelves in the fresh food section.
**SPECIFICATIONS: Height,** 66''; **Width,** 30-1/2''; **Depth,** 30-7/16''; **Shelf Capacity** (square feet), 25.3; **Warranty,** one year on parts and labor, with an additional four years on the compressor system (parts).
**Approximate Retail Price: $599.95**         **Low Price: $410.00**

**White-Westinghouse RT 184T,** an 18.2-cubic-foot model with automatic defrost, consumes 119 kilowatt-hours of electricity with the door heater switch set on low. The model has 4.81 cubic feet of freezer space. In the freezer you will find a full-width interior shelf, one door shelf, and a juice-can holder. The fresh food section has three adjustable cantilever shelves, twin crispers, three door shelves, plus butter, cheese and egg servers. This model features rollers, reversible doors, and dual controls.
**SPECIFICATIONS: Height,** 64-3/4''; **Width,** 30''; **Depth,** 27-1/2''; **Shelf Capacity** (square feet), 23.5; **Warranty,** one year on parts and labor, with an additional four years on the compressor system (parts).
**Approximate Retail Price: Not Available**         **Low Price: $476.64**

**Frigidaire FPCI-206T-8** is a 20.6-cubic-foot model with automatic defrost that consumes 146 kilowatt-hours of electricity per month. The unit contains 5.94 cubic feet of freezer space. The freezer features one interior shelf, removable ice bin, and two door shelves. The fresh food section has three adjustable cantilever shelves, three door shelves, two removable egg servers, a meat keeper, twin crispers, butter compartment, cheese compartment, and interior woodgrain trim. This model also has rollers, and the doors are reversible.
**SPECIFICATIONS: Height,** 65-7/8''; **Width,** 33-3/4''; **Depth,** 29-3/4''; **Shelf Capacity** (square feet), 31.9; **Warranty,** one year on parts and labor, with an additional four years on the compressor system (parts).
**Approximate Retail Price: $619.95**         **Low Price: $540.00**

**General Electric TBF-21DV,** a 20.8-cubic-foot model with automatic defrost, consumes 116 kilowatt-hours of electricity per month

*Prices are accurate at time of printing; subject to manufacturer's change.*

with the door heater switch set on low. The freezer section offers 6.96 cubic feet of space and contains an adjustable shelf, two door shelves and an ice bin. In the fresh food section, you will find three adjustable cantilever shelves, twin crispers, a meat keeper, two full-width door shelves, a cheese compartment, a butter compartment and an egg serving bin.
**SPECIFICATIONS: Height,** 66''; **Width,** 30-1/2''; **Depth,** 30-15/16''; **Shelf Capacity** (square feet), 30.0; **Warranty,** one year on parts and labor, with an additional four years on the compressor system (parts).
**Approximate Retail Price: $599.95**            **Low Price: $532.20**

**Whirlpool EET-221PK** is a 22.4-cubic-foot model with automatic defrost that consumes 140 kilowatt-hours of electricity per month with the door heater switch set on low. The model has 7.63 cubic feet of freezer space. The freezer also has one full-width interior shelf and two door shelves. The fresh food section contains four half-width adjustable cantilever shelves, an egg bin, twin crispers, a meat keeper, and three adjustable door shelves. You will find a butter compartment and utility compartment in the door. This model has dual controls, rollers, porcelain liners and a textured steel door.
**SPECIFICATIONS: Height,** 65-7/8''; **Width,** 32-3/4''; **Depth,** 32''; **Shelf Capacity** (square feet), 29.9; **Warranty,** one year on parts and labor, with an additional four years on the compressor system (parts).
**Approximate Retail Price: $589.00**            **Low Price: $554.40**

## SIDE-BY-SIDE REFRIGERATORS

**Admiral NS-2077,** a 20.1-cubic-foot unit that has automatic defrost, consumes 136 kilowatt-hours of electricity per month. The freezer side contains 6.57 cubic feet of space and includes four interior shelves, six door shelves, and a glide-out basket. The fresh food side has four shelves (three are adjustable cantilever types), a meat keeper, crisper, five door shelves, a butter keeper, an egg bucket, and a cheese compartment. The unit comes with rollers, dual controls, and uses the post-condenser loop to save energy.
**SPECIFICATIONS: Height,** 66-3/8''; **Width,** 31''; **Depth,** 29''; **Shelf Capacity** (square feet), 22.3; **Warranty,** one year on parts and labor, with an additional four years on the compressor system (parts).
**Approximate Retail Price: Not Available**        **Low Price: $479.00**

**Frigidaire FCI-20V3** is a 20.3-cubic-foot model with automatic defrost that consumes 159 kilowatt-hours of electricity per month. The freezer side has double doors and offers 6.97 cubic feet of space. The small freezer door allows access to frequently used items. The fresh food section contains four adjustable cantilever shelves, a meat keeper, crisper, three door shelves, two removable

*Prices are accurate at time of printing; subject to manufacturer's change.*

egg bins, plus butter and cheese compartments. The model also has rollers and dual controls.
**SPECIFICATIONS: Height,** 65-7/8"; **Width,** 33-3/4"; **Depth,** 29-3/16"; **Shelf Capacity** (square feet), 28.5; **Warranty,** one year on parts and labor, with an additional four years on the compressor system (parts).
**Approximate Retail Price: $799.95**         **Low Price: $694.80**

**White-Westinghouse RS216T** is a 21-cubic-foot three-door model with automatic defrost. The unit consumes 154 kilowatt-hours of electricity per month with the door heater switch set on low. The freezer side offers 8.23 cubic feet of space, five freezer shelves, a freezer basket, ice cube server, and juice-can dispenser. You will find a meat keeper, four tempered glass shelves and twin crispers in the fresh food section. This model also has rollers, door stops and door closers. The refrigerator door has four shelves, while the big freezer door has three.
**SPECIFICATIONS: Height,** 64-1/2"; **Width,** 33"; **Depth,** 27-3/4"; **Shelf Capacity** (square feet), 28.6; **Warranty,** one year on parts and labor with an additional four years on the compressor system (parts).
**Approximate Retail Price: Not Available**     **Low Price: $731.64**

**Admiral NS-2277** is a 21.8-cubic-foot model with automatic defrost that consumes 151 kilowatt-hours per month. The unit uses a post-condenser loop for energy conservation. Offering 6.57 cubic feet of freezer space, the freezer also has an ice bucket, four interior shelves, a glide-out basket and six door shelves. The fresh food section has four interior shelves, three of them adjustable, a meat keeper, crisper, butter and cheese compartments, an egg basket, and five door shelves. The unit comes with rollers and dual controls.
**SPECIFICATIONS: Height,** 66-3/8"; **Width,** 33"; **Depth,** 29"; **Shelf Capacity** (square feet), 24.0; **Warranty,** one year on parts and labor, with an additional four years on the compressor system (parts).
**Approximate Retail Price: Not Available**     **Low Price: $535.00**

**Whirlpool EED-221PK,** a 22.2-cubic-foot model with automatic defrost, consumes 146 kilowatt-hours of electricity per month with the door heater switch set on low. The freezer side contains 7.5 cubic feet of space and features five freezer shelves, a light, and a freezer bin. The freezer door has five shelves. You will find four adjustable cantilever shelves in the fresh food section, plus a crisper and removable meat pan with its own temperature control. The refrigerator door contains five shelves. This model features porcelain liners and a textured steel door.
**SPECIFICATIONS: Height,** 65-7/8"; **Width,** 32-3/4"; **Depth,** 32"; **Shelf Capacity** (square feet), 27.8; **Warranty,** one year on parts and

*Prices are accurate at time of printing; subject to manufacturer's change.*

labor, with an additional four years on the compressor system (parts).
**Approximate Retail Price: $729.95**  **Low Price: $675.60**

**General Electric TFF-24DV** is a 23.6-cubic-foot unit with automatic defrost that consumes 137 kilowatt-hours of electricity per month with the door heater switch set on low. The freezer section contains 8.68 cubic feet of space, four interior shelves, five door shelves and a slide-out basket. In the fresh food section, you will find four adjustable cantilever shelves, four plastic pans for meats or fruits and vegetables, and five door shelves. The model also has rollers and dual controls. This model is a superb energy performer for its size.
**SPECIFICATIONS: Height,** 66-1/4"; **Width,** 35-3/4"; **Depth,** 30-1/2"; **Shelf Capacity** (square feet), 27.9; **Warranty,** one year on parts and labor, with an additional four years on the compressor system (parts).
**Approximate Retail Price: $939.95**  **Low Price: $842.10**

*Prices are accurate at time of printing; subject to manufacturer's change.*

---

# SPECIAL INFORMATION SERVICE

### A Bonus for Readers of this CONSUMER GUIDE®

CONSUMER GUIDE® offers a special bonus to its readers who are interested in obtaining information as to where they can find the low prices on specific products listed in this guide. Simply fill out the form and mail. Include 25 cents for postage and handling.

**Please send me information on:**

Product _____ Model Number_____

Manufacturer_____

Product _____ Model Number_____

Manufacturer_____

Product _____ Model Number_____

Manufacturer_____

Your Name_____

Address_____

City_____ State _____ Zip Code_____

**CONSUMER GUIDE Magazine**
**3841 West Oakton, Skokie, Illinois 60076**

# Refrigerator Prices

## Amana

| | | Retail Price | Low Price |
|---|---|---|---|
| **BOTTOM MOUNT MODEL** | | | |
| BC20W | 20.1 Cu. Ft. | $799.95 | $657.80 |
| **TOP MOUNT MODELS** | | | |
| ESR-16W | 15.6 Cu. Ft. | $609.95 | $515.20 |
| ESRF-16W | 16.0 Cu. Ft. | 669.95 | 561.20 |
| TM18W | 18.2 Cu. Ft. | 549.95 | 483.00 |
| TC18W | 18.2 Cu. Ft. | 599.95 | 520.95 |
| TR20W | 20.0 Cu. Ft. | 649.95 | 563.50 |
| TD23W | 22.9 Cu. Ft. | 729.95 | 635.95 |
| **2 PLUS 2½ ENERGY SAVING TOP MOUNT MODELS** | | | |
| ESR-12A | 12.2 Cu. Ft. | $399.95 | $368.00 |
| ESR-14A | 14.1 Cu. Ft. | 449.95 | 405.95 |
| ESRF-14A | 14.2 Cu. Ft. | 499.95 | 441.60 |
| ESRFC-14A | 14.2 Cu. Ft. | 529.95 | 462.30 |
| ESRFC-16A | 16.2 Cu. Ft. | 579.95 | 507.15 |
| **SIDE-BY-SIDE MODELS** | | | |
| SR-19W | 19.4 Cu. Ft. | $869.95 | $739.45 |
| SR-22W | 22.3 Cu. Ft. | 949.95 | 806.15 |
| SR-25W | 25.4 Cu. Ft. | 1009.95 | 849.85 |
| SRI-19W | 18.8 Cu. Ft. | 1109.95 | 939.55 |
| SDI-22W | 21.8 Cu. Ft. | 1229.95 | 1033.85 |
| SDI-25W | 24.6 Cu. Ft. | 1279.95 | 1075.25 |

## Frigidaire

| | | | |
|---|---|---|---|
| **COMPACT CONVENTIONAL MODEL** | | | |
| I-43 | 4.3 Cu. Ft. | $249.95 | $225.60 |

*Prices are accurate at time of printing; subject to manufacturer's change.*

|  | Retail Price | Low Price |
|---|---|---|
| **CONVENTIONAL REFRIGERATORS** | | |
| D-10    10.0 Cu. Ft. | $339.95 | $306.00 |
| D-12    11.6 Cu. Ft. | 369.95 | 326.40 |
| **COMBINATION REFRIGERATORS & FREEZERS** | | |
| FD-12T    12.3 Cu. Ft. | $409.95 | $360.00 |
| FCD-150T    15.0 Cu. Ft. | 469.95 | 411.60 |
| FCD-170T    17.0 Cu. Ft. | 499.95 | 438.00 |
| **FROST-PROOF TOP FREEZER REFRIGERATORS & FREEZERS** | | |
| FPI-152T    15.2 Cu. Ft. | $489.95 | $430.80 |
| FPCI-152T-7    15.2 Cu. Ft. | 529.95 | 462.00 |
| FPI-170T    17.0 Cu. Ft. | 519.95 | 458.40 |
| FPCI-170T-7    17.0 Cu. Ft. | 559.95 | 482.40 |
| FPCI-206T-8    20.6 Cu. Ft. | 619.95 | 540.00 |
| FPF-200TI    20.0 Cu. Ft. | 919.95 | 801.60 |
| **FROST-PROOF SIDE-BY-SIDE REFRIGERATORS** | | |
| FCI-16V    16.5 Cu. Ft. | $659.95 | $589.20 |
| FCI-20V    20.3 Cu. Ft. | 769.95 | 668.40 |
| FCI-20V3    20.3 Cu. Ft. | 799.95 | 694.80 |
| FCI-22V    22.0 Cu. Ft. | 879.95 | 753.60 |

# General Electric

|  | Retail Price | Low Price |
|---|---|---|
| **DIAL DEFROST MODEL** | | |
| TA12SV | $329.95 | $291.90 |
| **COMBINATION/TOP FREEZER MODELS** | | |
| TB12SV | $389.95 | $334.80 |
| TB14SV | 419.95 | 363.00 |
| **NO FROST/TOP FREEZER MODELS** | | |
| TBF14DV | $479.95 | $426.60 |
| TBF16DV | 519.95 | 448.80 |
| TBF16CV | 539.95 | 474.60 |
| TBF16AV | 569.95 | 488.10 |
| TBF18EV | — | 393.60 |
| TBF18DV | 539.95 | 474.60 |
| TBF18CV | 589.95 | 510.00 |
| TBF21DV | 599.95 | 532.20 |
| **SIDE-BY-SIDE MODELS** | | |
| TFF18EV | $ — | $535.80 |
| TFF19DV | 679.96 | 611.70 |
| TFF22DV | 839.95 | 723.30 |
| TFF24DV | 939.95 | 842.10 |

*Prices are accurate at time of printing; subject to manufacturer's change.*

| CUSTOM DISPENSER MODELS | Retail Price | Low Price |
|---|---|---|
| TBF21RV | $799.95 | $707.40 |
| TFF22RV | 1089.95 | 963.60 |
| TFF24RV | 1189.95 | 1053.00 |

# KitchenAid

**MODELS**

| Model | Description | Retail | Low |
|---|---|---|---|
| FA056W2 | 4.2 Cu. Ft. Push Button Defrost | $— | $161.16 |
| FA056Z2 | 4.2 Cu. Ft. Push Button Defrost | — | 161.16 |
| FA116W1 | 11 Cu. Ft. Push Button Defrost | — | 225.40 |
| FA146W1 | 13.7 Cu. Ft. Manual Defrost | — | 270.84 |
| FB166W2 | 15.6 Cu. Ft. No Frost | — | 420.32 |
| FB196W3 | 18.9 Cu. Ft. No Frost | — | 537.05 |
| FC196W3 | 18.5 Cu. Ft. Side-by-Side | — | 598.00 |
| FC216W3 | 20.7 Cu. Ft. Side-by-Side | — | 664.70 |
| FKC | Icemaker Kit | — | 41.40 |

# Magic Chef

**MODELS**

| Model | Description | Retail | Low |
|---|---|---|---|
| FA056W2/Z2 | 4.2 Cu. Ft. Push Button Defrost | $— | $168.60 |
| FA116W1 | 11 Cu. Ft. Push Button Defrost | — | 235.20 |
| FA146W1 | 13.7 Cu. Ft. Manual Defrost | — | 282.60 |
| FB166W2 | 15.6 Cu. Ft. No Frost | — | 438.60 |
| FB196W3 | 18.9 Cu. Ft. No Frost | — | 560.40 |
| FC196W3 | 18.5 Cu. Ft. Side-by-Side | — | 624.00 |
| FC216W3 | 20.7 Cu. Ft. Side-by-Side | — | 693.60 |
| FKC | Icemaker Kit | — | 43.20 |

# Sanyo

**MODELS**

| Model | Description | Retail | Low |
|---|---|---|---|
| SR-4801-1W | Sanyo "Cube" Refrigerator | $109.95 | $92.96 |
| SR-4801-1X | Sanyo "Cube" Refrigerator | 119.95 | 95.20 |
| SR-4901-1W | Deluxe "Cube" Refrigerator | 119.95 | 95.20 |
| SR-4901-1X | Deluxe "Cube" Refrigerator | 124.95 | 97.44 |
| SR-6800-1X | 3 Cu. Ft. Refrigerator | 149.95 | 125.44 |
| SR-1275-1W /1C | Counter High Refrigerator | 159.95 | 133.28 |

*Prices are accurate at time of printing; subject to manufacturer's change.*

|  |  | Retail Price | Low Price |
|---|---|---|---|
| SR-1280-2W | Deluxe Counter High Refrigerator | $169.95 | $145.60 |
| SR-1280-2X | Deluxe Counter High Refrig. | 179.95 | 151.80 |
| SR-9000W | 9 Cu. Ft. Refrigerator | 239.95 | 184.80 |

**FREEZER/REFRIGERATOR**

| SR-1100 W | 2-Door, 11 Cu. Ft. | $289.95 | $221.76 |
|---|---|---|---|

# Tappan

**MODELS**

| | | | |
|---|---|---|---|
| 95-1204-00 | 12.2 Cu. Ft., Right Hand | $— | $304.80 |
| 95-1204-26 | 12.2 Cu. Ft., Right Hand | — | 310.80 |
| 95-1214-00 | 12.2 Cu. Ft., Left Hand | — | 304.80 |
| 95-1214-26 | 12.2 Cu. Ft., Left Hand | — | 310.80 |
| 95-1424-00 | 14.3 Cu. Ft., Right Hand | — | 404.40 |
| 95-1424-26 | 14.3 Cu. Ft., Right Hand | — | 410.40 |
| 95-1434-00 | 14.3 Cu. Ft., Left Hand | — | 404.40 |
| 95-1434-26 | 14.3 Cu. Ft., Left Hand | — | 410.40 |
| 95-1547-00 | 15.0 Cu. Ft., No Frost | — | 462.00 |
| 95-1547-17-26-23 | 15.0 Cu. Ft., No Frost | — | 468.00 |
| 95-1847-00 | 17.9 Cu. Ft., No Frost | — | 480.60 |
| 95-1847-26-23 | 17.9 Cu. Ft., No Frost | — | 486.60 |
| 95-1867-00 | 18.0 Cu. Ft., No Frost | — | 516.60 |
| 95-1867-05-17-26 | 18.0 Cu. Ft., No Frost | — | 522.60 |
| 95-2164-00 | 21.4 Cu. Ft., No Frost | — | 595.20 |
| 95-2164-17-16-23 | 21.4 Cu. Ft., No Frost | — | 601.20 |
| 95-2067-00 | Side-by-Side, No Frost | — | 633.60 |
| 95-2067-26 | Side-by-Side, No Frost | — | 639.60 |
| 95-2287-00 | 21.8 Cu. Ft. Side-by-Side, No Frost | — | 720.00 |
| 95-2287-17-26 | 21.8 Cu. Ft., Side-by-Side, No Frost | — | 726.00 |
| 95-2494-00 | 23.6 Cu. Ft., Side-by-Side, No Frost | — | 990.00 |
| 95-2494-05-17-26 | 23.6 Cu. Ft., Side-by-Side, No Frost | — | 996.00 |
| 95-1544-00 | 15.0 Cu. Ft., No Frost | — | 462.00 |
| 95-1544-17-26 | 15.0 Cu. Ft., No Frost | — | 468.00 |
| 95-1844-00 | 17.9 Cu. Ft., No Frost | — | 480.60 |
| 95-1844-17-26 | 17.9 Cu. Ft., No Frost | — | 486.60 |
| 95-1864-00 | 18.0 Cu. Ft., No Frost | — | 516.60 |

*Prices are accurate at time of printing; subject to manufacturer's change.*

|  |  | Retail Price | Low Price |
|---|---|---|---|
| 95-1864-05-17-26 | 18.0 Cu. Ft., No Frost | $— | $522.60 |
| 95-2084-00 | 20.1 Cu. Ft., No Frost | — | 693.60 |
| 95-2084-17-26 | 20.1 Cu. Ft., No Frost | — | 699.60 |
| 95-2284-00 | 21.8 Cu. Ft., No Frost | — | 770.40 |
| 95-2284-05-17-26 | 21.8 Cu. Ft., No Frost | — | 776.40 |

# Whirlpool

**SIDE-BY-SIDE MODELS**

| | | | |
|---|---|---|---|
| EED191PK | 19.1 Cu. Ft. Princess No Frost | $619.00 | $577.20 |
| EED191MM | 19.1 Cu. Ft. Mark w/Ice Maker | 729.00 | 673.20 |
| EED221PK | 22.2 Cu. Ft. Princess No Frost | 729.95 | 675.60 |
| EED221MM | 22.2 Cu. Ft. Mark w/Ice Maker | 829.00 | 769.20 |
| EAD251MM | 24.5 Cu. Ft. Mark w/Ice Maker | 1199.00 | 1084.80 |

**BOTTOM MOUNT FREEZER**

| | | | |
|---|---|---|---|
| EEB191PK | 19.1 Cu. Ft. Princess No Frost | $569.00 | $552.00 |

**TOP MOUNT FREEZER**

| | | | |
|---|---|---|---|
| EET151PK | 15.0 Cu. Ft. Princess No Frost | $459.00 | $433.20 |
| EET171PK | 17.2 Cu. Ft. Princess No Frost | 469.00 | 436.80 |
| EET171HK | 17.2 Cu. Ft. Hi-Efficiency No Frost | 519.00 | 482.40 |
| EET171MK | 17.2 Cu. Ft. Mark No Frost | 509.00 | 471.60 |
| EET171MM | 17.2 Cu. Ft. Mark w/Ice Maker | 569.00 | 525.60 |
| EET201PK | 19.6 Cu. Ft. Princess No Frost | 519.00 | 483.60 |
| EET201MK | 19.6 Cu. Ft. Mark No Frost | 559.00 | 517.20 |
| EET201MM | 19.6 Cu. Ft. Mark w/Ice Maker | 619.00 | 571.20 |
| EET221PK | 22.4 Cu. Ft. Princess | 589.00 | 554.40 |
| EET221MM | 22.3 Cu. Ft. Mark w/Ice Maker | 689.00 | 637.20 |

# White-Westinghouse

**MODELS**

| | | | |
|---|---|---|---|
| RC131T | 12.5 Cu. Ft. | $— | $300.84 |
| RT121T | 12.0 Cu. Ft. | — | 347.76 |
| RT142T | 14.0 Cu. Ft. | — | 390.00 |
| RT145T | 14.0 Cu. Ft. | — | 394.20 |
| RT146T | 14.0 Cu. Ft. | — | 430.68 |

*Prices are accurate at time of printing; subject to manufacturer's change.*

|        |              | Retail Price | Low Price |
|--------|--------------|--------------|-----------|
| RT183T | 17.9 Cu. Ft. | $ —          | $ 448.08  |
| RT184T | 18.2 Cu. Ft. | —            | 476.64    |
| RT188T | 18.2 Cu. Ft. | —            | 522.24    |
| RT214T | 20.8 Cu. Ft. | —            | 513.36    |
| RT218T | 20.8 Cu. Ft. | —            | 558.60    |
| RS193T | 19.1 Cu. Ft. | —            | 604.80    |
| RS196T | 19.0 Cu. Ft. | —            | 672.84    |
| RS214T | 21.1 Cu. Ft. | —            | 667.32    |
| RS216T | 21.0 Cu. Ft. | —            | 731.64    |
| RS219T | 21.0 Cu. Ft. | —            | 825.00    |

*Prices are accurate at time of printing; subject to manufacturer's change.*

---

# SPECIAL INFORMATION SERVICE

**A Bonus for Readers of this CONSUMER GUIDE®**

CONSUMER GUIDE® offers a special bonus to its readers who are interested in obtaining information as to where they can find the low prices on specific products listed in this guide. Simply fill out the form and mail. Include 25 cents for postage and handling.

**Please send me information on:**

Product _____ Model Number _____

Manufacturer _____

Product _____ Model Number _____

Manufacturer _____

Product _____ Model Number _____

Manufacturer _____

Product _____ Model Number _____

Manufacturer _____

Your Name _____

Address _____

City _____ State _____ Zip Code _____

**CONSUMER GUIDE Magazine**
**3841 West Oakton, Skokie, Illinois 60076**

# 1978 Freezers

**D**O YOU NEED a freezer? Undoubtedly, a properly used freezer is a convenient appliance. However, because of today's high cost of energy, there are serious questions about saving money with a freezer. An average freezer of say 14 cubic feet may cost around $350. Prorated over the average lifespan of 20 years, the monthly cost of the freezer would be about $1.50. If it is an average energy user, it may cost around $4 a month just to operate. Add the $1.50 for the basic cost of the freezer to the operating cost and you will see that you have to save about $5.50 a month—for the life of the unit—to pay for the freezer and the energy it consumes. Many consumers can save this much or more. For them, a freezer may represent a way to hold the line on food price increases. But, for many consumers, saving more than $60 a year by making timely or large purchases may not be possible. Convenience then becomes a major factor in deciding to buy a freezer.

You will make a sounder decision if you balance the life-cycle cost with the convenience a freezer offers. The life-cycle costs include purchase price, potential repair costs and expected energy costs. Savings obviously can be figured in, especially if there are practical reasons, such as freezing fruits or vegetables from a garden. However, the major benefit from owning a freezer remains convenience.

With today's larger capacity refrigerator/freezers you may have another option open to you. Assuming that your refrigerator is ten or more years old, you might want to consider replacing it with a new unit that offers an extra-large freezer section, thereby getting both added freezer space and a new refrigerator.

## Energy and the Freezer

FREEZERS, like other major appliances, are part of a government program to improve energy efficiency. Currently, a voluntary program seeks to improve efficiencies by about 45 percent by 1980. But there is a new bill in Congress that would require minimum standards on energy. This bill was expected to become law during late 1977 (as this material was being prepared).

Freezer manufacturers are expected to make improvements such as adding anti-sweat door heater switches that turn off the heaters during dry periods; some manufacturers are adding a post-condenser loop to eliminate sweating. Also expected are better compressor motors, better and thicker insulation, and better door gaskets.

Some of these improvements already have been made. Anti-sweat door heater switches are available, as are designs that use the post-condenser loop. Thicker insulation is available on some models. And better compressor motors are being used by some manufacturers.

The result of such efforts is improved energy efficiency. Higher prices also come with these improvements, but the added costs can be retrieved through lower electric bills.

CONSUMER GUIDE Magazine strongly recommends paying a little more to get an efficient freezer. Consider the cost in terms of the freezer's life cycle. An energy-efficient freezer can mean significant dollar savings. And, since freezers have an average lifetime of about 20 years, an efficient model will save you money for a long time to come.

CONSUMER GUIDE Magazine does not recommend a freezer with automatic defrost. Frankly, it adds cost to the unit without adding a great deal in terms of convenience. Generally, freezers only require defrosting two or three times a year since the door is not opened as often as it would be on a refrigerator. Automatic defrost will add to your purchase price and will consume energy monthly without saving a great deal of work. The Recommended Buys for freezers have been chosen with energy improvement uppermost in mind.

## Size It Right and Save

A FREEZER that stands empty a considerable amount of the time wastes money. Therefore, you should think carefully about the size unit you want. In addition to paying for unused "cool" space with a freezer that is too big, there is the matter of efficiency. A freezer operates more efficiently when kept full or nearly full.

CONSUMER GUIDE Magazine offers these guidelines to finding the appropriate freezer size: three to four cubic feet per family member; a couple of extra cubic feet added if you freeze garden products, prepare meals in advance, or entertain extensively.

**The Types of Freezers**

THERE ARE two basic types of freezers: chests and uprights. Uprights are the most expensive to buy (in similar sizes), but this is offset by the fact that they are a little more convenient to load. They require about the same amount of space as a refrigerator.

Chests are the most economical to buy. They are wide, low units with rear-hinged doors on top. While they require a lot of floor space, they also will go into "odd" spaces, like under basement stairs. Chests hold more food than uprights of the same size, but it can be hard to reach items at the bottom.

Uprights come in both manual and automatic defrost models; we do not recommend automatic defrost on a freezer. Chests are available only with manual defrost.

**Features Found on Freezers**

HERE ARE SOME of the features that commonly appear on chest or upright freezers:

**Baskets.** They hold bulk items. Chests usually have one or more baskets that slide. Uprights normally have one large one at the bottom of the unit.

**Controls.** Some models have controls that allow you to set different temperatures. Frankly, they are unnecessary in a well-designed freezer. The purpose of a freezer is to freeze and preserve foods for a given period of time. This is best accomplished at or slightly below zero.

**Defrost Systems.** Manual defrost is most common, mainly because chests only come with manual defrost. Automatic defrost is available on a few upright models; it adds expense to the cost of the unit and to its operation.

**Door Features.** Chests do not have door features. On uprights, door shelves may be shallow or deep. Many models include shelves that will accommodate different sizes of items: juice can racks are fairly standard.

**Drain.** A drain located at the bottom of the unit, which feeds into a drain pan or, better yet, has a hose that connects for easy removal of water is a recommended feature for units with manual defrost.

**Indicator Light.** A recommended feature, a small exterior light, usually red or orange, tells you that power is being supplied to the unit and it is functioning. It could save you the cost of the freezer's contents, especially if the unit is not checked frequently.

**Interior Light.** While not necessary, a small inside light, similar to the one in your refrigerator, can help you locate items.

**Locks.** A recommended feature, a key lock, usually one that "pops" out when unlocked, can protect your unit from unwanted entry. A lock is a good idea if the unit is in an area where children play or in a highly accessible area, such as a garage. The lock also may keep the door from being accidentally left open.

CONSUMER GUIDE Magazine recommends the following features: baskets, manual defrost, drains, indicator lights, and locks.

This table gives you the energy cost range for a specific size class of freezer. Knowing the monthly energy consumption of a model, you can compare its energy performance with what is available across the board. Information is from the Association of Home Appliance Manufacturers and is based on their freezer certification data.

## Energy Cost Ranges for Freezers

| Rated Total Refrigerated Volume In Cubic Feet | Ranges of Cost of Energy In Dollars Per Month At a Rate of 4 Cents Per Kilowatt-Hour For Models With | | | |
|---|---|---|---|---|
| | Manual Defrost | | Automatic Defrost | |
| | Min. | Max. | Min. | Max. |
| Less than 5.5 | 1.50 | 2.80 | — | — |
| 5.5 to less than 6.5 | 1.50 | 2.80 | — | — |
| 6.5 to less than 7.5 | 1.50 | 2.80 | — | — |
| 7.5 to less than 8.5 | 1.50 | 3.10 | — | — |
| 8.5 to less than 9.5 | 2.60 | 3.10 | — | — |
| 9.5 to less than 10.5 | 2.80 | 3.10 | — | — |
| 10.5 to less than 11.5 | 2.80 | 4.40 | 7.60 | 7.60 |
| 11.5 to less than 12.5 | 3.00 | 4.40 | 5.60 | 7.60 |
| 12.5 to less than 13.5 | 3.20 | 4.40 | 5.60 | 7.60 |
| 13.5 to less than 14.5 | 3.20 | 4.30 | 5.60 | 6.40 |
| 14.5 to less than 15.5 | 3.20 | 5.40 | 5.40 | 7.50 |
| 15.5 to less than 16.5 | 3.30 | 5.40 | 4.60 | 7.50 |
| 16.5 to less than 17.5 | 3.50 | 5.40 | 4.60 | 7.50 |
| 17.5 to less than 18.5 | 3.20 | 5.00 | 4.60 | 6.80 |
| 18.5 to less than 19.5 | 3.20 | 5.00 | 5.70 | 7.10 |
| 19.5 to less than 20.5 | 3.20 | 5.00 | 5.70 | 7.10 |
| 20.5 to less than 21.5 | 3.30 | 4.90 | 6.00 | 8.00 |
| 21.5 to less than 22.5 | 3.30 | 5.50 | 8.00 | 8.00 |
| 22.5 to less than 23.5 | 4.20 | 5.50 | 8.00 | 8.00 |
| 23.5 to less than 24.5 | 4.20 | 5.60 | — | — |
| 24.5 to less than 25.5 | 4.60 | 5.60 | — | — |
| 25.5 to less than 26.5 | 4.60 | 5.60 | — | — |
| 26.5 to less than 27.5 | 4.60 | 6.40 | — | — |
| 27.5 to less than 28.5 | 4.80 | 6.40 | — | — |
| 28.5 to less than 29.5 | 6.40 | 6.40 | 9.80 | 9.80 |
| 29.5 and over | 6.80 | 6.80 | 9.80 | 9.80 |

# 1978 Best Buys: Freezers

CONSUMER GUIDE Magazine evaluated both upright and chest freezers on the basis of price, energy efficiency, features and reliability. The models that offer a good balance of these elements are our Recommended Buys.

## CHESTS

**Kenmore (Sears) 47G 1709N** is a 9-cubic-foot unit that consumes 72 kilowatt-hours of electricity per month. An economy model, it lacks several features found on more expensive models. However, it does have a basket and a vinyl-clad counterbalanced lid. Its one disadvantage is its lack of a drain.
**SPECIFICATIONS: Height** (lid open), 60-1/2''; **Width,** 35''; **Depth,** 27-3/4''; **Capacity** (pounds), 315; **Warranty,** one year on parts and labor, with an additional four years on the compressor system (parts).
**Approximate Retail Price: $229.95    Low Price: Not Available**

**Gibson FH-10M4** is a 10.07-cubic-foot model that consumes 70 kilowatt-hours of electricity per month, which rates it as one of the best in the industry. It has a sliding basket and a lock, but no drain or indicator light. A roller kit is available as an option.
**SPECIFICATIONS: Height** (lid open), 56-3/8''; **Width,** 41''; **Depth,** 23-3/4''; **Capacity** (pounds), 350; **Warranty,** one year on parts and labor, with an additional four years on the compressor system (parts).
**Approximate Retail Price: Not Available    Low Price: $279.00**

**Amana C-15,** a 15-cubic-foot model, consumes 92 kilowatt-hours of electricity per month. The unit has a basket and a divider that can be used to make a special compartment. Its features include a self-aligning counterbalanced lid, temperature control, lock, signal light, and defrost drain. Unfortunately, Amana's service policies

*Prices are accurate at time of printing; subject to manufacturer's change.*

and maintenance are not very good.
**SPECIFICATIONS: Height** (lid open), 60-5/8''; **Width,** 41-1/2''; **Depth,** 30-5/8''; **Capacity** (pounds), 525; **Warranty,** five years on parts and labor—compressor; one year parts and labor on other components, with added four years (parts only).
**Approximate Retail Price: Not Available     Low Price: $346.80**

**Frigidaire F-203C** is a 20.3-cubic-foot model that consumes 118 kilowatt-hours of electricity per month. The unit has two baskets and a movable divider. Its other features include a lock, interior light, signal light, counterbalanced lid, and a drain. Chests of this particular size are not as efficient as other sizes. However, this model compares well within its size category.
**SPECIFICATIONS: Height** (lid open), 60-7/8''; **Width,** 57''; **Depth,** 29-1/2''; **Capacity** (pounds), 710; **Warranty,** one year on parts and labor, with an additional four years on the compressor system (parts).
**Approximate Retail Price: $479.95     Low Price: $415.20**

**Whirlpool EEH-232FW,** a 23.2-cubic-foot unit, consumes 122 kilowatt-hours of electricity per month. This large model has three sliding baskets and a divider. It also has a defrost drain, interior light, lock, and a temperature control.
**SPECIFICATIONS: Height** (lid open), 62-1/4''; **Width,** 62''; **Depth,** 28''; **Capacity** (pounds), 810; **Warranty,** one year on parts and labor, with an additional four years on the compressor system (parts).
**Approximate Retail Price: Not Available     Low Price: $421.20**

**White-Westinghouse FC258T** is a big 25.3-cubic-foot chest that consumes 114 kilowatt-hours of electricity, which makes it an excellent performer despite its huge size. It has a built-in lock, exterior defrost drain, and an interior light. This model also features a counterbalanced lid, two lift-out baskets and compartment dividers.
**SPECIFICATIONS: Height** (lid open), 60-1/2''; **Width,** 69-1/2''; **Depth,** 29-5/8''; **Capacity** (pounds), 885; **Warranty,** one year on parts and labor, with an additional four years on the compressor system (parts).
**Approximate Retail Price: Not Available     Low Price: $433.92**

## UPRIGHTS

**General Electric CA-12DV** is an 11.6-cubic-foot model that consumes 98 kilowatt-hours of electricity per month. With manual defrost, the unit has a total shelf area of 11.6 square feet. It has three fast-freeze interior shelves and four deep door shelves. An economy model, it lacks an indicator light, interior light and a defrost drain. This model does have porcelain-on-steel liners, and lock and door stops.
*Prices are accurate at time of printing; subject to manufacturer's change.*

**SPECIFICATIONS: Height,** 61"; **Width,** 28"; **Depth,** 29"; **Capacity** (pounds), 400; **Warranty,** one year on parts and labor, with an additional four years on the compressor system (parts).
**Approximate Retail Price: $329.95**　　　　**Low Price: $290.70**

**Frigidaire F-128U,** a 12.8-cubic-foot model, consumes 85 kilowatt-hours of electricity per month. It has a manual defrost system and a drain with stowaway drain hose. Its four interior shelves (three are the fast-freezing type) offer 13.2 square feet of area. The door has three shelves and one juice-can shelf. The unit also has a lock.
**SPECIFICATIONS: Height,** 59-1/8"; **Width,** 28"; **Depth,** 29-5/8"; **Capacity** (pounds), 440; **Warranty,** one year on parts and labor, with an additional four years on the compressor system (parts).
**Approximate Retail Price: $369.95**　　　　**Low Price: $325.20**

**Kelvinator UDM-144K** is a 14.4-cubic-foot model with the best energy performance in its class: 81 kilowatt-hours of electricity per month. It has four interior fast-freezing shelves and four deep-door shelves. Total shelf area is 14.8 square feet. It has a basket for bulk items, a temperature control, a lock and a defrost drain. This manual defrost model does not have an interior or indicator light.
**SPECIFICATIONS: Height,** 63"; **Width,** 28"; **Depth,** 28-3/4"; **Capacity** (pounds), 500; **Warranty,** one year on parts and labor, with an additional four years on the compressor system (parts).
**Approximate Retail Price: Not Available**　　**Low Price: $299.00**

**Amana ESU-15,** a 15.1-cubic-foot upright, is one of Amana's new line of energy-saving manual defrost freezers. Extra insulation and overall energy efficiency improvements create a unit that consumes only 68 kilowatt-hours of electricity per month. The unit has a recessed interior light, a temperature control, lock, five door shelves, four interior shelves, a glide-out basket, and a defrost drain. The design uses a radiant-shell condenser that eliminates the need for an energy-consuming condenser fan motor. Unfortunately, Amana's service policies and maintenance are not very good.
**SPECIFICATIONS: Height,** 62-27/32"; **Width,** 28"; **Depth,** 28-13/16"; **Capacity** (pounds), 530; **Warranty,** five years on parts and labor for the compressor system; one year (parts and labor) on other components, with an additional four years (parts only).
**Approximate Retail Price: Not Available**　　**Low Price: $393.60**

**Admiral F-1676,** a 15.8-cubic-foot manual defrost unit, consumes 108 kilowatt-hours of electricity per month. It has a drain, an interior light and a lock. Its total shelf capacity is 17.9 square feet with four interior shelves, glide-out drawer, four deep-door shelves, and two juice-can racks. It also has a textured steel door.
**SPECIFICATIONS: Height,** 66-1/2"; **Width,** 30"; **Depth,** 29-1/4"; **Capacity** (pounds), 550; **Warranty,** one year on parts and labor,
*Prices are accurate at time of printing; subject to manufacturer's change.*

with an additional four years on the compressor system (parts).
**Approximate Retail Price: $369.00**     **Low Price: $294.40**

**Whirlpool EEV-161F** is a 15.9-cubic-foot manual defrost model that consumes 94 kilowatt-hours of electricity per month when the door heater switch is set on low. It has a temperature control, porcelain-on-steel interior, a basket, defrost drain system, four interior shelves, five deep-door shelves plus two juice-can shelves, an indicator light, and an interior light. The unit also has a textured steel door and a key-eject lock.
**SPECIFICATIONS: Height,** 66"; **Width,** 29-3/4"; **Depth,** 31-5/8"; **Capacity** (pounds), 550; **Warranty,** one year on parts and labor, with an additional four years on the compressor system (parts).
**Approximate Retail Price: Not Available**     **Low Price: $344.40**

**Amana ESU-17,** a 17.1-cubic-foot manual defrost unit, is another model in Amana's new energy-saving freezer line. It consumes only 75 kilowatt-hours of electricity per month. It has all the same features as the Amana ESU-15 except that it has six door shelves where the model ESU-15 has five. Unfortunately, Amana's service policies and maintenance are not very good.
**SPECIFICATIONS: Height,** 65-27/32"; **Width,** 28"; **Depth,** 30-7/16"; **Capacity** (pounds), 600; **Warranty,** five years on parts and labor for the compressor; one year parts and labor on other components, with an additional four years (parts only).
**Approximate Retail Price: Not Available**     **Low Price: $428.40**

**White-Westinghouse FU188R** is an 18-cubic-foot unit that consumes 88 kilowatt-hours of electricity per month. It has five full-width deep-door shelves and four interior fast-freeze shelves with a total shelf area of 18.6 square feet. This model features an interior light, an indicator light, a lock, and a bulk-item basket. The basket could be a slight bit bigger. The unit is a manual defrost type and has a drain.
**SPECIFICATIONS: Height,** 64-9/16"; **Width,** 30"; **Depth,** 30-3/4"; **Capacity** (pounds), 630; **Warranty,** one year on parts and labor, with an additional four years on the compressor system (parts).
**Approximate Retail Price: Not Available**     **Low Price: $373.20**

**General Electric CA-21DV,** a 21.1-cubic-foot model with manual defrost, consumes 94 kilowatt-hours of electricity per month. It is an excellent energy performer considering its size. This model includes a temperature control, interior light, drain, lock, and a bulk-item basket. Five interior shelves offer 23.8 square feet of space. The door has four shelves and two juice-can shelves. The unit also has one adjustable interior shelf.
**SPECIFICATIONS: Height,** 70-1/8"; **Width,** 32"; **Depth,** 28-7/8"; **Capacity** (pounds), 740; **Warranty,** one year on parts and labor, with an additional four years on the compressor system (parts).
**Approximate Retail Price: $499.95**     **Low Price: $444.00**

*Prices are accurate at time of printing; subject to manufacturer's change.*

# Freezer Prices

## Amana

| "DEEPFREEZE" CHEST FREEZERS | | Retail Price | Low Price |
|---|---|---|---|
| C-7 | 7.2 Cu. Ft. | $— | $236.40 |
| C-9 | 9.1 Cu. Ft. | — | 255.60 |
| C-11 | 11.0 Cu. Ft. | — | 306.00 |
| C-15 | 15.0 Cu. Ft. | — | 346.80 |
| C-19 | 19.0 Cu. Ft. | — | 390.00 |
| C-23 | 23.0 Cu. Ft. | — | 430.80 |
| C-28 | 28.0 Cu. Ft. | — | 466.80 |
| **UPRIGHT FREEZERS** | | | |
| ESU-13 | 13.1 Cu. Ft. | $— | $358.80 |
| ESU-15 | 15.1 Cu. Ft. | — | 393.60 |
| ESU-17 | 17.1 Cu. Ft. | — | 428.40 |
| U-23 | 23.2 Cu. Ft. | — | 489.60 |
| ESUF-14 | 14.1 Cu. Ft. | — | 430.80 |
| ESUF-16 | 16.1 Cu. Ft. | — | 484.80 |
| UF-22 | 21.9 Cu. Ft. | — | 565.20 |

## Frigidaire

| CHEST FREEZERS | | | |
|---|---|---|---|
| F-053C | 5.3 Cu. Ft. | $289.95 | $255.60 |
| F-083C | 8.3 Cu. Ft. | 334.95 | 292.80 |
| F-101C | 10.1 Cu. Ft. | 369.95 | 321.60 |
| F-153C | 15.3 Cu. Ft. | 414.95 | 356.40 |
| F-203C | 20.3 Cu. Ft. | 479.95 | 415.20 |
| F-253C | 25.3 Cu. Ft. | 539.95 | 464.40 |

*Prices are accurate at time of printing; subject to manufacturer's change.*

|  |  | Retail Price | Low Price |
|---|---|---|---|
| **UPRIGHT FREEZERS** | | | |
| F-128U | 12.8 Cu. Ft. | $369.95 | $325.20 |
| F-160U | 16.0 Cu. Ft. | 429.95 | 375.60 |
| F-191U | 19.1 Cu. Ft. | 499.95 | 440.40 |
| F-211U | 21.1 Cu. Ft. | 529.95 | 468.00 |
| **UPRIGHT FROST-PROOF FREEZERS** | | | |
| FP-156U | 15.6 Cu. Ft. | $499.95 | $435.60 |
| FP-174U | 17.4 Cu. Ft. | 529.95 | 459.60 |

# General Electric

| **CHEST MODELS** | | | |
|---|---|---|---|
| CB5DV | Manual Defrost | $259.95 | $236.70 |
| CB8DV | Manual Defrost | 299.95 | 268.50 |
| CB15DV | Manual Defrost | 389.95 | 343.20 |
| CB20DV | Manual Defrost | 439.95 | 390.00 |
| CB25DV | Manual Defrost | 489.95 | 435.30 |
| **UPRIGHT MODELS** | | | |
| CA12DV | Manual Defrost | $329.95 | $290.70 |
| CA15DV | Manual Defrost | 379.95 | 336.00 |
| CA21DV | Manual Defrost | 499.95 | 444.00 |
| CAF16CV | No Frost | 459.95 | 405.90 |

# Sanyo

| **CHEST MODEL** | | | |
|---|---|---|---|
| HF-4950-1X | Sanyo "Cube" | $129.95 | $107.52 |
| **UPRIGHT MODELS** | | | |
| HF-1350-1W | Counter High Upright | 179.95 | 147.84 |
| HF-1350-1X | Counter High Upright | 189.95 | 150.08 |

# Whirlpool

| **CHEST MODELS** | | | |
|---|---|---|---|
| EEH061FW | 6.0 Cu. Ft. Compact | $— | $240.00 |
| EEH091FW | 9.0 Cu. Ft. Compact | — | 270.00 |
| EEH153FW | 15.0 Cu. Ft. Custom | — | 340.80 |
| EEH182FW | 18.0 Cu. Ft. Supreme | — | 376.80 |
| EEH232FW | 23.0 Cu. Ft. Supreme | — | 421.20 |
| EEH272FW | 27.0 Cu. Ft. Supreme | — | 462.00 |

*Prices are accurate at time of printing; subject to manufacturer's change.*

| **UPRIGHT MODELS** | | Retail Price | Low Price |
|---|---|---|---|
| EEV120FW | 12.1 Cu. Ft. Deluxe | $— | $298.80 |
| EEV161FW | 16.0 Cu. Ft. Custom, Textured Door | — | 344.40 |
| EEV202XW | 20.0 Cu. Ft. Textured Steel Door | — | 429.60 |
| EEV271FW | 27.3 Cu. Ft. | — | 555.60 |
| EEV151NW | 15.0 Cu. Ft. Custom, No Frost | — | 397.20 |
| EEV200NW | 19.6 Cu. Ft. Custom, No Frost | — | 462.00 |

# White-Westinghouse

| **CHEST MODELS** | | | |
|---|---|---|---|
| FC153T | 15.3 Cu. Ft. | $— | $298.20 |
| FC158T | 15.3 Cu. Ft. | — | 338.76 |
| FC200T | 20.3 Cu. Ft. | — | 334.44 |
| FC208T | 20.3 Cu. Ft. | — | 394.08 |
| FC258T | 25.3 Cu. Ft. | — | 433.92 |

| **COMPACT CHEST MODELS** | | | |
|---|---|---|---|
| FC053T | 5.3 Cu. Ft. | $— | $229.68 |
| FC105T | 10.1 Cu. Ft. | — | 275.52 |

| **UPRIGHT MODELS** | | | |
|---|---|---|---|
| FU133T | 13.1 Cu. Ft. | $— | $298.68 |
| FU164T | 16.1 Cu. Ft. | — | 344.16 |
| FU182R | 18.0 Cu. Ft. | — | 342.72 |
| FU188R | 18.0 Cu. Ft. | — | 373.70 |
| FU196T | 18.6 Cu. Ft. | — | 376.44 |
| FU208R | 20.1 Cu. Ft. | — | 397.56 |

*Prices are accurate at time of printing; subject to manufacturer's change.*

# Washers/ Dryers

THERE WAS a day when only home owners could reasonably afford the space necessary for a laundry center. Today, there are models and styles that will fit just about any home environment—from summer cottage to apartment building, from large rambling single family homes to townhouses and duplexes. There is a laundry pair that will suit both your wants and needs, if you take the time to search out the right solution.

Typically, automatic washers now average about 11 years of life. Dryers fare a little better; gas models last an average 13 years and electrics about 14 years. There are differences between bottom-of-the-line and more expensive units. Design and construction can vary by a fair margin, with the better and more solid units existing at the middle and top of the model line. As with many appliances, CONSUMER GUIDE Magazine finds that the best overall values tend to be found in middle-of-the-line units. These models generally have the design and construction qualities of their more expensive counterparts without some of the features that are nice, but not always necessary.

Safety has become an expected part of today's laundry appliances. Unlike the wringer-type washer, today's automatic washer does its work without the potential for trouble. Most washers have an interlock switch that stops the agitator or spin action if the lid is opened. And some washers have a lid locking mechanism that prevents opening the lid during the spin cycle. Dryers normally will be found with the interlock door switch that stops drum rotation when the door is opened.

On washers, look for the Underwriters Laboratories certification seal. The UL seal means that the machine meets established electrical safety standards. Electric dryers that are UL listed must meet electrical and safety standards of their own. On gas dryers, look for the American Gas Association blue flame seal. The A.G.A. seal assures you that the unit meets existing industry safety standards established for gas dryers.

**Washer and Dryer Energy Efficiency**

WASHERS AND dryers are involved in a government/industry program to reduce energy consumption. Currently, target goal improvements have been proposed for these appliances by the Federal Energy Administration. For automatic washers, the goal is to reduce energy by 47 percent by 1980. For electric dryers, the goal is an eight-percent energy reduction, while for gas dryers the goal is an 18-percent reduction. While this program is moving ahead, there is legislation pending in Congress that would replace the target goal program with minimum energy standards for both washers and dryers. The legislation, still in Congress as this report was prepared, was expected to pass.

While the setting of minimum standards on energy would change the manner in which the appliance industry is approaching the energy question, there are some things that can be discussed in terms of what manufacturers are likely to do to reduce energy consumption.

Little probably will be done to change the mechanical nature of washers, since about 95 percent of the energy required to wash a typical load of clothes goes to heat the water consumed. Hot water use has been declining, principally because of fabrics that require warm or cold washing. Cold rinsing is one major step that consumers can take to reduce energy use. Rinsing does not require hot water, since it is a mechanical function. Washer manufacturers are making cold rinse standard and restricting warm rinses to certain models and specific cycle options. Cold rinsing could save an estimated eight percent of the energy required to do a typical load (in place of warm rinsing).

Hot water may also be saved by reducing the amount of water used in specific cycles. Manufacturers can only go so far on this point. Most better machines already offer water level selection. However, consumers must use this feature to save energy.

On dryers, energy savings will come from two principal areas: replacing standard pilots with electric ignition systems and in automatically terminating the drying cycle.

Most gas dryers already have pilotless ignition systems. However, those that still have standing pilots will make the switch. Overdrying probably is the biggest waster of energy. Thus, manufacturers probably will offer automatic termination systems on more dryers (perhaps on all models, depending on where minimum energy standards are set). Models with such automatic controls would have cycles set by moisture sensing rather than by time. The dryer would be shut off when clothes reached a certain moisture content point rather than allowing the cycle to continue for the set time. Other design changes, such as better airflow designs, door seals, and increased insulation could add a few percent to energy improvement goals.

As you may have guessed by now, much of the potential for saving energy with washers and dryers depends on you. Your habits and washing/drying selections can make a difference. CONSUMER GUIDE Magazine recommends that you use cold rinse for all wash loads. And always match the water level to the size of your load. With your dryer, use the automatic dryness control, if your unit has one. This will eliminate wasted energy used in overdrying the load. In buying new laundry appliances, make sure that these options are available to you. CONSUMER GUIDE Magazine has taken such factors into account in selection of the Recommended Buys. Obviously, some of these energy-saving features add cost to the unit. Over time, you will get back this added cost and more by paying less to operate the unit.

**Other Washer and Dryer Trends**

WITH THE TREND toward smaller homes, townhouses, condominiums, and space-limited apartments, there has come a move toward compact washers and dryers. In this context, a distinction should be made between compact and portable units. Portables are small, limited-feature machines that do a fair job at washing and spin-drying clothes. Compacts, in essence, are smaller versions of full-size machines with the same or similar features. The major difference has to do with size and capacity. The compact units are designed to fit in limited space—they may be stacked one on top of the other in some cases, or installed under a counter in other cases.

While compact units have been gaining in popularity, units at the other end of the scale, 18 to 20 pound capacity, also have become more popular. Thus, the marketplace seems to be going in two directions at once, toward smaller units and toward larger models.

Large-capacity machines are more in demand among some consumers because more women work outside of the home today. These homemakers do not have the time or the desire to spend a lot of time doing the family's laundry. Compact machines, on the other hand, bring in-home laundry facilities to many consumers that would otherwise have to use outside facilities. Also, women that work in the home may find these smaller units more efficient for frequent washing needs. If laundry is being done each day or every other day, a smaller capacity machine may fit the bill.

### Types of Washers

WASHERS CAN BE divided into four basic types and styles: top-loading full size machines, front-loading full size machines, compacts and portables.

**Full-Size Top-Loading, Agitator.** The most popular type has a lid on the top of the machine that opens to the back or side. An agitator forces water through the clothes. Capacity ranges from 14 to 20 pounds.

**Full-Size Front-Loading, Tumbler.** White-Westinghouse currently markets the only units of this type. Units have a door in the front and a tumbler system that forces clothes through the water. Capacity is limited to 16 or 18 pounds.

**Compacts.** Smaller in physical size, the compact usually has a capacity of eight to 12 pounds. Models have many of the same features found on larger units. Both top-loading and front-loading types are available.

**Portables.** Very small units, usually from five to eight pounds capacity. While some compacts are "portable," the true portable connects to a water faucet and normally requires transfer of clothes from a wash chamber to a spin drum.

### Types of Dryers

DRYERS COME in both gas and electric models. In addition, there are full-size models, compacts and portables. Gas dryers, in standard and compact sizes, require a gas line and venting. They are usually more expensive to buy than electrics and generally less expensive to operate. Heat is generated by a gas burner that is usually ignited by an electric ignitor. Electric dryers, in both standard and compact sizes, require a 220/240 volt grounded circuit and generally should be vented to remove steam. Heat is generated by an electric element.

Full-size and compact models in both gas and electric have the capacity and features to match their companion washers. All full-size models are front-loading. While so-called portables exist, the line between compacts and portables is indistinct. Portables obviously can be moved about. Perhaps the best way to distinguish between a portable and a compact dryer is that true portables have very small capacity and are electric. Most of the true portable dryers plug into ordinary 115-volt household circuits.

### Washer and Dryer Features

AUTOMATIC WASHERS offer a choice of wash and spin speeds. This choice may include normal agitation/normal spin, normal agitation/slow spin, and slow (gentle) agitation/slow spin. CONSUMER GUIDE Magazine recommends models with two speeds: normal agitation/normal spin and slow agitation/slow spin.

We also recommend models that offer at least three wash/rinse temperatures: cold/cold, warm/cold, and hot/cold. Some units offer an additional two choices, warm/warm and hot/warm. Because rinsing does not require warm or hot water, pick a unit with only cold rinsing and you will save energy without worrying to remember to set the machine for a cold rinse.

Better washers come with controls that are preset for complete wash cycles. The user may have to set wash/rinse water temperatures and speed, but the unit controls such factors as agitation time, the number of rinses, and spin cycle lengths. Preset controls often are available for normal loads, heavy-duty loads, permanent press, knits, and delicate items.

Top-of-the-line models may have fully programmed controls. Such controls take care of all settings at the push of a button. CONSUMER GUIDE Magazine admits this makes for convenience, but finds the added cost hard to justify.

Clothes that have been through the spin cycle of an automatic washer must be dried in an automatic dryer to remove wrinkles. Normal loads require drying times of about 40 minutes. Some dryers function by setting a timer for the number of minutes desired. CONSUMER GUIDE Magazine recommends units with dryness-sensing controls. These units run until the load is dry by sensing the moisture content of the clothes or vented air. They eliminate overdrying that can occur with strictly timed drying.

Dryers, both gas and electric, should be vented to the outside to remove hot air and steam. Concerns over energy have raised questions about venting this waste heat in winter. Heat-transfer devices that collect and transfer this heat can be installed. One such device is the In-O-Vent. For safety, gas dryers always should be vented to the outside.

## Washer Feature Checklist

| Feature | CG Rating/Opinion |
|---|---|
| **Cycles:** | |
| 1. Preset — Semiprogrammed units, pushing button sets the wash action. You may have to set wash/rinse temperatures and you may have to set wash water level. | Recommended. |
| 2. Programmed — Fully programmed, button sets the wash action and wash-rinse temperature. You may be able to set water level. Buttons for all types of loads. | Nice, but not necessary. |

| Feature | CG Rating/Opinion |
|---|---|
| **Dispensers:** | |
| 1. Bleach — Releases bleach at right stage, also dilutes it. | Recommended. |
| 2. Fabric softener. | Recommended. |
| **Lint Filters:** | |
| Keep lint from redepositing on clothes, many are self-cleaning. | Standard on most models. |
| **Safety Features:** | |
| 1. Lid lock — Locks lid during spin cycle, units also have lid switch. | Recommended. |
| 2. Lid switch — Opening lid stops agitator or spin action, some units require restart after opening. | Recommended. |
| **Speeds:** | |
| 1. Normal — Agitator and spin speed at normal. | Recommended. |
| 2. Normal/slow — Agitator at normal, spin at slow. | Nice, but not necessary. |
| 3. Slow — Agitator and spin at slow. | Recommended. |
| 4. Slow/normal — Agitator at slow, spin at normal (or even fast). | Nice, but not necessary. |
| **Tub Materials:** | |
| 1. Coated steel — Zinc or other coating to keep tub from rusting. | Good. |
| 2. Porcelain — Excellent corrosion resistance, smooth finish. | Better. |
| 3. Stainless steel — Excellent corrosion protection, smooth surface, more expensive. | Better. |
| **Unbalanced Load:** | |
| 1. Buzzer/stop — Washer shuts off and a buzzer sounds if load becomes too unbalanced during spin (nuisance if touchy). | Good. |
| 2. Compensating — Unit compensates for unbalanced load and does not shut off (spin performance can be reduced if load is badly unbalanced). | Better. |

| Feature | CG Rating/Opinion |
|---|---|
| **Water Level:** | |
| 1. Fixed — Two, three or four settings between full and lesser amounts. | Good. |
| 2. Variable — Infinite control of level from low to full. | Better. |
| **Water Temperature:** | |
| Wash/rinse combinations | |
| 1. Cold/cold. | Recommended. |
| 2. Warm/cold. | Recommended. |
| 3. Hot/cold. | Recommended. |
| 4. Warm/warm. | Not necessary. |
| 5. Hot/warm. | Not necessary. |
| **Others:** | |
| 1. Hand wash — Small basket or hand-size agitator for delicate items. | Recommended. |
| 2. Lighting — A light on work surface (top) or control panel. | Recommended. |
| 3. Scale — Lid scale for weighing loads. | Nice. |
| 4. Suds-saver — Saves detergent water for more than one load. | Questionable performance. |

### Dryer Feature Checklist

| Feature | CG Rating/Opinion |
|---|---|
| **Cycles:** | |
| 1. Preset — Specific temperature cycles for some fabrics, you can set temperatures for others. | Recommended. |
| 2. Programmed — Set cycles for all types of fabrics/loads. | Nice, but not necessary. |
| **Drying Control:** | |
| 1. Time — You set the time (and fabric/load type or temperature), unit runs for that amount of time and shuts off. | Good. |

| Feature | CG Rating/Opinion |
|---|---|
| 2. Automatic — Sensor "feels" moisture in clothes or measures exhaust air temperature and shuts off unit when clothes are dry. | Recommended. |
| **Temperature Selection:** Some models offer choices of temperatures to better suit different fabrics. | Recommended. |
| **Speeds:** More than one drum speed to match loads and/or fabrics. | Nice, but not necessary. |
| **Lint Filter:** Important to performance. Should be easy to get at and remove. | Standard. |
| **Air Fluff:** No-heat setting to remove wrinkles or to freshen clothes. | Nice, if you need it. |
| **End-Of-Cycle Signal:** Buzzes when drying is done. | Recommended. |
| **Wrinkle Prevention:** Feature that turns drum on and off without heat after drying to prevent wrinkles. | Nice, if you're in the habit of leaving machine for long periods. |
| **Drum Materials:** Similar to those available on washers: | |
| 1. Coatings | Good. |
| 2. Porcelain | Better. |
| 3. Stainless steel | Better. |
| **Others:** | |
| 1. Pedal — Opens door with touch of foot. | Nice, but not necessary. |
| 2. Drum light — Goes on when door is opened. | Recommended. |
| 3. Panel light — Worktop or control panel. | Recommended. |
| 4. Door switch — Stops tumbling when door is opened, may require re-start. | Recommended. |

# 1978 Best Buys: Washers/Dryers

CONSUMER GUIDE Magazine rated washers and dryers—after studying the leading models—on the basis of design, performance, construction and reliability. We felt that washers should have at least two speeds, cycles capable of handling today's needs, at least three choices of wash/rinse temperatures and some degree of water-level selection. When judging dryers, we looked for units that could handle modern fabrics and the types of loads found in the average household.

## FULL-SIZED WASHERS

**Frigidaire WC** is an 18-pound, large-capacity automatic washer built for heavy-duty use. The two-speed unit allows infinite water level selection, has four wash/rinse temperature options, a detergent dispenser and a bleach dispenser. Cycles include knits, three permanent press, and two regular. A fabric softener dispenser is available as an extra option.
**SPECIFICATIONS: Height,** 44-1/4"; **Width,** 27"; **Depth,** 28-1/4"; **Volts/amps,** 120/15; **Speeds,** normal/normal and slow/slow; **Capacity** (pounds of dry clothes), 18; **Warranty,** one year on parts and labor; second year (parts), with three additional years on the transmission (parts).
**Approximate Retail Price: $379.95**　　　　　**Low Price: $328.80**

**General Electric WWA-5800V** is a standard-sized washer with 16-pound capacity. It has one speed, three wash/rinse temperature options and four water level selections. It also has a bleach dispenser and a fabric softener dispenser. Cycles include regular, delicates, permanent press, and activated soak. The unit offers GE's Mini-Basket for small and delicate loads.
**SPECIFICATIONS: Height,** 42-1/2"; **Width,** 27"; **Depth,** 25"; **Volts/amps,** 115/15; **Speeds,** normal and slow; **Capacity** (pounds of dry clothes), 16; **Warranty,** one year on parts and labor.
**Approximate Retail Price: $319.95**　　　　　**Low Price: $276.00**

*Prices are accurate at time of printing; subject to manufacturer's change.*

**Hotpoint WLW-2700T,** a standard-size 16-pound washer, has two speeds and a handwash feature. The handwash feature includes a special second agitator under the main agitator. It is used for small loads and lightly soiled clothes. An advantage of this feature is that you can wash a few items without wasting water. Cycles include handwash, permanent press and regular. The regular cycle can be set for heavy, normal or lightly soiled clothes. This model also has infinite water level selection and three wash temperature selections. Both a bleach and fabric softener dispenser are features on the unit.
**SPECIFICATIONS: Height,** 42-1/2"; **Width,** 27"; **Depth,** 25"; **Volts/amps,** 120/15; **Speeds,** normal and slow; **Capacity** (pounds of dry clothes), 16; **Warranty,** one year on parts and labor.
**Approximate Retail Price: $318.95            Low Price: $245.00**

**Kenmore (Sears) 26 G-2791,** a large-capacity washer, features a Dual-Action agitator. The two-speed unit has cycles for normal soil, permanent press and knit-delicate, prewash and presoak. Built for heavy-duty use, it also has five wash/rinse temperature selections, four water-level settings (including an extra-low setting), a fabric softener dispenser, and a bleach dispenser.
**SPECIFICATIONS: Height,** 43"; **Width,** 29"; **Depth,** 25-1/2"; **Volts/amps,** 120/9.8; **Speeds,** normal and slow; **Capacity** (pounds of dry clothes), 18; **Warranty,** one year on parts and labor, with four additional years on the gear case (parts).
**Approximate Retail Price: $319.95      Low Price: Not Available**

**Maytag A608** is a large-capacity unit with two wash-action speeds. It has cycles for permanent press, regular, delicate, and soak. Offering four water level selections and four wash/rinse temperature combinations, it also has a bleach dispenser and a fabric softener dispenser. A quiet unit, this Maytag has one of the best reliability records in the industry. It is slightly more expensive than some other models.
**SPECIFICATIONS: Height,** 43-1/8"; **Width,** 25-1/2"; **Depth,** 27"; **Volts/amps,** 115/15; **Speeds,** normal and slow; **Capacity** (pounds of dry clothes), 18; **Warranty,** one year on parts and labor, second year on parts, third to fifth year on cabinet parts (against rust).
**Approximate Retail Price: Not Available      Low Price: $389.70**

**Maytag A208,** a standard-size 16-pound machine, has many of the same features found on model A608. The 208 does not have a soak cycle and it offers three water level selections instead of four. It is a dependable and economical unit.
**SPECIFICATIONS: Height,** 43-1/8"; **Width,** 25-1/2"; **Depth,** 27"; **Volts/amps,** 115/15; **Speeds,** normal and slow; **Capacity** (pounds of dry clothes), 16; **Warranty,** one year on parts and labor, second year on parts, third to fifth year on cabinet parts (against rust).
**Approximate Retail Price: Not Available      Low Price: $342.90**
*Prices are accurate at time of printing; subject to manufacturer's change.*

**Speed Queen FA-3591** is a 16-pound standard-capacity washer with a stainless steel tub that should last a long time. It has five wash/rinse temperature selections and four speed options. Water level selections give you four choices. Cycles include normal, permanent press/knit, and a prewash soak. The model has removable front and top panels for quick service access.
**SPECIFICATIONS: Height,** 43-1/2"; **Width,** 25-5/8"; **Depth,** 28-1/8"; **Volts/amps,** 120/15; **Speeds,** four; **Capacity** (pounds of dry clothes), 16; **Warranty,** one year on parts and labor, with an additional nine years on the transmission (parts).
**Approximate Retail Price: $398.00****Low Price: $368.00**

**Whirlpool LFA-7800,** a large-capacity unit, will wash 18 pounds of clothes. This five cycle machine has a self-cleaning filter, bleach dispenser, fabric softener dispenser, four water level selections, and five wash/rinse temperature combinations, plus two-speed operation. It is an excellent permanent press machine. A suds-saver system is available as an option.
**SPECIFICATIONS: Height,** 43-1/8"; **Width,** 29"; **Depth,** 25-1/2"; **Volts/amps,** 120/15; **Speeds,** normal and slow; **Capacity** (pounds of dry clothes), 18; **Warranty,** one year on parts and labor.
**Approximate Retail Price: $379.00****Low Price: $344.40**

**White-Westinghouse LA-501P** is an 18-pound machine for heavy-duty use. Cycles include normal, soak and knits. It also can handle permanent press items. Featuring five water level choices and five wash/rinse temperature combinations, this washer has a porcelain tub and a bleach dispenser. A fabric softener dispenser is available as an option. The lid on this model, which serves as a scale, locks during the spin cycle.
**SPECIFICATIONS: Height,** 43"; **Width,** 26-7/8'; **Depth,** 27"; **Volts/amps,** 120/15; **Speeds,** three combinations; **Capacity** (pounds of dry clothes), 18; **Warranty,** one year on parts and labor, with an additional four years on the transmission (parts).
**Approximate Retail Price: Not Available****Low Price: $330.60**

## COMPACT WASHERS

**General Electric WWP-1150V** is a compact washer that measures only 21 inches wide. It has three wash cycles, including permanent press. In addition, you can select three water levels and three wash/rinse temperature combinations. It comes with casters, but can be permanently installed.
**SPECIFICATIONS: Height,** 35-3/8"; **Width,** 21"; **Depth,** 21"; **Volts/amps,** 115/3.6; **Speeds,** Normal (one); **Capacity** (pounds of dry clothes), 8; **Warranty,** one year on parts and labor.
**Approximate Retail Price: $299.95****Low Price: $267.30**

**Whirlpool LFC-4900,** another compact unit, has many of the same features found on its larger counterparts. It has five cycles, two
*Prices are accurate at time of printing; subject to manufacturer's change.*

speeds, four water level selections, and is only 24 inches wide. It can be rolled about on casters or permanently installed. When installed, there are five wash/rinse temperature combinations. This Whirlpool model is a top-loading agitator type of washer.
**SPECIFICATIONS: Height,** 32-1/2"; **Width,** 23-7/8"; **Depth,** 20-1/2"; **Volts/amps,** 120/15; **Speeds,** normal and slow; **Capacity** (pounds of dry clothes), 8 to 10; **Warranty,** one year on parts and labor.
**Approximate Retail Price: $349.00　　　　　Low Price: $316.80**

**White-Westinghouse LT-170** is a Space Mate compact washer featuring front-loading design. It can be stacked, built into or through a wall, or built in under a counter. It is 27 inches wide, but not as tall as full-sized models. The features include five water level selections, three wash temperature selections, and two rinse temperature selections. You can wash normal loads, as well as permanent press, knits, and delicates in this machine. The door doubles as a scale and the lid locks during the spin cycle.
**SPECIFICATIONS: Height,** 34-5/8"; **Width,** 27"; **Depth,** 25-1/2"; **Volts/amps,** 120/15; **Speeds,** normal (one); **Capacity** (pounds of dry clothes), 12; **Warranty,** one year on parts and labor.
**Approximate Retail Price: Not Available　　　Low Price: $399.24**

## FULL-SIZED DRYERS

**Frigidaire DEI** is an electric dryer that matches their Model WC washer. Cycles include regular, delicate, automatic drying (senses dryness and turns unit off when clothes are dry), and no-heat. It has an end-of-cycle signal and a fabric selector for delicate, regular, and knits/permanent press. The gas version of the same dryer is model DGI.
**SPECIFICATIONS: Height,** 44-1/4"; **Width,** 27"; **Depth,** 26-13/16"; **Volts/amps,** 120-240/30; **Venting,** 4-way; **Lint Trap Location,** up front, bottom of access; **Warranty,** one year on parts and labor, second year on parts.
**Approximate Retail Price: $289.95　　　　　Low Price: $252.00**

**General Electric DDE-5900V** is an electric dryer (DDG-5980V is the gas version) that matches GE's WWA-5800V washer. It features automatic drying control. The settings include permanent press, knits, regular, delicate; it also has an air fluff setting. This dryer has an end-of-cycle signal and a porcelain drum.
**SPECIFICATIONS: Height,** 43-1/2"; **Width,** 27"; **Depth,** 25"; **Volts/amps,** 120-240/30; **Venting,** 4-way; **Lint Trap Location,** up front, bottom of access; **Warranty,** one year on parts and labor.
**Approximate Retail Price: $239.95　　　　　Low Price: $214.50**

**Hotpoint DLL-2550P** is a gas dryer (DLB-2550P is the same in electric) with cycles for normal, permanent press/knits, and deli-
*Prices are accurate at time of printing; subject to manufacturer's change.*

cate. It also has an air fluff setting. Featuring automatic dryness sensing control, it has an up-front filter, porcelain enamel drum, and an end-of-cycle signal. This unit matches Hotpoint washer WLW-2700T.
**SPECIFICATIONS: Height,** 42-1/2"; **Width,** 27"; **Depth,** 25"; **Volts/amps,** 115/15; **Venting,** 3-way; **Lint Trap Location,** up front, bottom of access; **Warranty,** one year on parts and labor.

**Approximate Retail Price: $279.95**          **Low Price: $220.00**

**Kenmore (Sears) 26 G-7691,** a gas dryer, features an automatic dryness control. It has a full-width door, an extra-large drum, a two-position fabric selector, and a wrinkle-prevention feature. Cycles include automatic (all-fabric), timed and air fluff. This model matches Kenmore 26 G-2791 washer. Model 26 G-6691 is a similar unit in electric.
**SPECIFICATIONS: Height,** 43"; **Width,** 29"; **Depth,** 27-1/2"; **Volts/amps,** 120/6; **Venting,** 3-way; **Lint Trap Location,** top, rear; **Warranty,** one year on parts and labor.

**Approximate Retail Price: $274.95**      **Low Price: Not Available**

**Maytag D608** is Maytag's second best big-load dryer. Cycles include permanent press, regular, damp dry, air fluff, plus regular and low-temperature selections. It has an end-of-cycle signal and an end-of-cycle conditioning period. A special feature is its electronic control drying system, which senses moisture in clothes and shuts the dryer off when clothes are dry. This can eliminate energy wasted in overdrying. The model is available in electric or pilotless ignition gas. It is a good companion to their A608 washer.
**SPECIFICATIONS: Height,** 43-1/8"; **Width,** 28-1/2"; **Depth,** 27"; **Volts/amps,** (electric) 240/30, (gas) 115/15; **Venting,** 3-way; **Lint Trap Location,** up front, bottom of access; **Warranty,** one year on parts and labor, second year on parts, third to fifth year on cabinet parts (against rust).

**Approximate Retail Prices:**      **Low Price (Electric): $304.80**
**Not Available**      **Low Price (Gas): $340.08**

**Maytag D408,** in either gas or electric, is a companion to either the A608 or A208 Maytag washer. This model has Auto-Dry control, which uses a thermostat in the exhaust air to judge the dryness of clothes. It also has an end-of-cycle signal, regular and low-temperature settings, and a wrinkle-preventing feature. Cycles include permanent press, regular, damp dry, and air fluff. The gas model has pilotless ignition.
**SPECIFICATIONS: Height,** 43-1/8"; **Width,** 28-1/2"; **Depth,** 27"; **Volts/amps,** (electric) 240/30, (gas) 115/15; **Venting,** 3-way; **Lint Trap Location,** up front, bottom of access; **Warranty,** one year on parts and labor, second year on parts, third to fifth year on cabinet parts (against rust).

**Approximate Retail Prices:**      **Low Price (Gas): $309.60**
**Not Available**      **Low Price (Electric): $273.60**

*Prices are accurate at time of printing; subject to manufacturer's change.*

**Speed Queen FE-6031** is an electric dryer with a stainless steel dryer drum. Features include an in-the-door filter, end-of-cycle signal, and temperature selections for heavy, normal, permanent press/knits and delicates. It also has an air fluff setting. The unit does not have an automatic dryness control, but does have set cycles as well as allowing for timer-controlled drying. It matches up with Speed Queen Model FA-3591 washer. The same unit in gas is model FG-6041.
**SPECIFICATIONS: Height,** 43"; **Width,** 30"; **Depth,** 28-1/8"; **Volts/amps,** 120-240/30; **Venting,** 4-way; **Lint Trap Location,** in the door; **Warranty,** one year on parts and labor, added lifetime on drum (parts).
**Approximate Retail Price: $298.00**          **Low Price: $268.00**

**Whirlpool LFE-7800,** an electric dryer, matches Whirlpool's LFA-7800 washer. It allows you to set five drying temperatures and has a special knit cycle and a cool-down period for permanent press. The features include a full-width door, automatic dryness sensing control, and a porcelain enamel drum. It also has a drying rack for bulky or special items. Similar features can be found on gas Model LFI-7801.
**SPECIFICATIONS: Height,** 43"; **Width,** 29"; **Depth,** 25-1/2"; **Volts/amps,** 120-240/30; **Venting,** 1-way; **Lint Trap Location,** top right, rear; **Warranty,** one year on parts and labor.
**Approximate Retail Price: $279.00**          **Low Price: $252.00**

**White-Westinghouse DG-500P** is a gas dryer (electric equivalent is Model DE-500) to match the W-W Model LA-501 washer. A heavy-duty unit with a large access door and up-front filter, it has temperature selections for automatic drying, regular, and delicates. It also has an air fluff feature. Timer cycle options include damp dry, time dry or automatic drying.
**SPECIFICATIONS: Height,** 43"; **Width,** 26-7/8"; **Depth,** 25-1/2"; **Volts/amps,** 120/15; **Venting,** 3-way; **Lint Trap Location,** up front, bottom of access; **Warranty,** one year on parts and labor.
**Approximate Retail Price: Not Available**      **Low Price: $266.04**

## COMPACT DRYERS

**General Electric DDP-1200V** is a compact electric dryer to match GE Model WWP-1150V compact washer. It has three cycles including permanent press. This dryer operates on standard household current and does not require outside venting.
**SPECIFICATIONS: Height,** 28-1/2"; **Width,** 21"; **Depth,** 19"; **Volts/amps,** 115/12; **Venting,** none; **Lint Trap Location,** up front; **Warranty,** one year on parts and labor.
**Approximate Retail Price: $199.95**          **Low Price: $174.30**

**Whirlpool LFE-4930,** a compact electric dryer, matches the Whirlpool LFC-4900 compact washer. Featuring four cycles, including

*Prices are accurate at time of printing; subject to manufacturer's change.*

an air fluff cycle, this dryer can be wall-mounted, racked or stacked. You have a choice of three temperature settings. This model requires a 240-volt circuit.

**SPECIFICATIONS: Height,** 30-1/4"; **Width,** 23-7/8"; **Depth,** 20-1/2"; **Volts/amps,** 120-240/30; **Venting,** 2-way; **Lint Trap Location,** inside, at back of drum; **Warranty,** one year on parts and labor.

**Approximate Retail Price: $239.00**            **Low Price: $217.20**

**White-Westinghouse DE-170** is a matching Space Mate electric dryer (a gas Space Mate is Model DG-170) to washer LT-170. The unit offers drying temperature selections for regular, low and automatic dry. It also features an air fluff setting, an adjustable end-of-cycle signal and an interior drum light.

**SPECIFICATIONS: Height,** 34-5/8"; **Width,** 27"; **Depth,** 25-1/2"; **Volts/amps,** 120-240/30; **Venting,** 3-way; **Lint Trap Location,** up front, bottom of access; **Warranty,** one year on parts and labor.

**Approximate Retail Price: Not Available**      **Low Price: $270.84**

## LAUNDRY CENTER

**Frigidaire LC-3** is a washer and dryer in one unit. The dryer is mounted at eye-level above the top-loading washer. The two-speed washer has cycles that include regular and delicate. You have a choice of four water temperature selections. The dryer has an automatic dry feature that eliminates overdrying. The dryer also offers time drying and fabric selection that includes regular, delicate and no-heat. A space saver, this two-units-in-one-cabinet is only 24 inches wide.

**SPECIFICATIONS: Height,** 65-3/4"; **Width,** 24"; **Depth,** 27-1/8"; **Volts/amps,** 120-240/30; **Speeds,** normal and slow; **Venting,** rear or right side; **Capacity** (pounds of dry clothes), 12; **Warranty,** one year on parts and labor, second year on parts, three more years on transmission (parts).

**Approximate Retail Price: $559.95**           **Low Price: $487.20**

*Prices are accurate at time of printing; subject to manufacturer's change.*

# Washer/Dryer Prices

## Frigidaire

| | | Retail Price | Low Price |
|---|---|---|---|
| **ELECTRIC DRYERS** | | | |
| DE | Timed Dry, 18 Lbs. | $249.95 | $218.40 |
| DEC | Timed Dry, 18 Lbs. | 269.95 | 232.80 |
| DEI | Auto. Dry, 18 Lbs. | 289.95 | 252.00 |
| DECI | Auto. Dry, 18 Lbs. | 339.95 | 296.40 |
| **GAS DRYERS** | | | |
| DG | Timed Dry, 18 Lbs. | $289.95 | $254.40 |
| DGC | Timed Dry, 18 Lbs. | 309.95 | 268.80 |
| DGI | Auto. Dry, 18 Lbs. | 329.95 | 288.00 |
| DGCI | Auto. Dry, 18 Lbs. | 379.95 | 332.40 |
| **HEAVY-DUTY WASHERS** | | | |
| WD-A | 2-Speed, 16 Lbs. | $349.95 | $313.20 |
| WC | 2-Speed, 18 Lbs. | 379.95 | 328.80 |
| WID | 2-Speed, 18 Lbs. | 399.95 | 342.00 |
| WIC-A | 2-Speed, 18 Lbs. | 469.95 | 409.20 |
| **LAUNDRY CENTERS** | | | |
| LC-3 | 2-Speed, 240 Volts. | $559.95 | $487.20 |
| LC-115 | 2-Speed, 120 Volts. | 559.95 | 487.20 |
| LC-3WG | Woodgrain, 240 Volts. | 579.95 | 499.20 |
| LC-115WG | Woodgrain, 120 Volts. | 579.95 | 499.20 |

## General Electric

| | | Retail Price | Low Price |
|---|---|---|---|
| **ELECTRIC DRYERS** | | | |
| DDE4000V | Timed Control, 1-Cycle. | $— | $171.60 |

*Prices are accurate at time of printing; subject to manufacturer's change.*

|  |  | Retail Price | Low Price |
|---|---|---|---|
| DDE5300V | Timed Control, 2-Cycle. | $219.95 | $197.52 |
| DDE5900V | Auto. Control, 3-Cycle | 239.95 | 214.50 |
| DDE7500V | Auto. Control, 3-Cycle | 259.95 | 226.80 |
| DDE8200V | Auto. Control, 3-Cycle, Large Capacity | 279.95 | 244.20 |
| DDE9200V | Elec. Control, 3-Cycle, Large Capacity | 299.95 | 261.30 |
| DDP1200V | Compact Dryer | 199.95 | 174.30 |

**GAS DRYERS**

|  |  |  |  |
|---|---|---|---|
| DDG5380V | Timed Control, 2-Cycle. | $259.95 | $234.30 |
| DDG5980V | Auto. Control, 3-Cycle | 279.95 | 251.40 |
| DDG7580V | Auto. Control, 3-Cycle | 299.95 | 263.70 |
| DDG8280V | Auto. Control, 3-Cycle, Large Capacity | 319.95 | 280.80 |
| DDG9280V | Elec. Control, 3-Cycle, Large Capacity | 339.95 | 297.90 |

**COMMERCIAL DRYERS**

|  |  |  |  |
|---|---|---|---|
| DDC0580V | Timed, 2-Cycle | $209.90 | $189.00 |
| DDC4580V | Timed, 2-Cycle | 249.95 | 225.60 |

**WASHERS**

|  |  |  |  |
|---|---|---|---|
| WWA3100V | 1-Speed, 1 Cycle, Lge. Capacity | $— | $224.40 |
| WWA3200V | 2T-Speed, 2-Cycle, Lge. Capacity | — | 241.50 |
| WWA5500V | 1-Speed, 2-Cycle | 299.95 | 263.70 |
| WWA5800V | 1-Speed, 2-Cycle | 319.95 | 276.00 |
| WWA7050V | 2T-Speed, 2-Cycle | 319.95 | 276.00 |
| WWA7070V | 3-Speed, 2-Cycle | 339.95 | 293.10 |
| WWA8300V | 1-Speed, 2-Cycle, Lge. Capacity | 319.95 | 276.00 |
| WWA8320V | 2-Speed, 2-Cycle, Lge. Capacity | 339.95 | 293.10 |
| WWA8350V | 2-Speed, 4-Cycle, Lge. Capacity | 369.95 | 318.90 |
| WWA8450V | 4-Speed, 4-Cycle, Lge. Capacity | 399.95 | 343.20 |
| WWA8500V | 4-Speed, 3-Cycle, Lge. Capacity | 439.95 | 375.30 |
| VWA7345V | Suds Saver Model | 349.95 | 301.80 |
| WWA8355V | Suds Saver Model, Lge. Capacity | 389.95 | 336.00 |
| WWP1150V | Compact Model | 299.95 | 267.30 |

# Maytag

**AUTOMATIC WASHERS**

|  |  |  |  |
|---|---|---|---|
| A806 | 4-Cycle, 4-Speed Comb., Big Tub | $— | $427.50 |
| A608 | 3-Cycle, 2-Speed, Big Tub | — | 389.70 |
| A608S | Suds Return System | — | 406.50 |
| A408 | Fabric-matic, 4-Cycle, Big Tub | — | 371.70 |
| A408S | Suds Return System | — | 388.50 |
| A208 | 2-Cycle, 2-Speed, Standard Tub | — | 342.90 |
| A208S | Suds Return System | — | 359.70 |
| A108 | Fabric-matic, 3-Cycle, Standard Tub | — | 326.70 |

*Prices are accurate at time of printing; subject to manufacturer's change.*

|  |  | Retail Price | Low Price |
|---|---|---|---|
| A108S | Suds Return System | $— | $343.50 |
| A106F | Special Order | — | 307.50 |
| A106 | 2-Cycle, 1-Speed, Standard Tub | — | 302.70 |

## ELECTRIC DRYERS

|  |  |  |  |
|---|---|---|---|
| DE808 | Electronic Control, 4-Cycle | $— | $325.20 |
| DE608 | Electronic Control, 4-Cycle | — | 304.80 |
| DE408 | Auto-Dry, 4-Cycle | — | 273.60 |
| DE308 | Timed-Dry, 3-Cycle | — | 244.20 |
| DE106 | Timed-Dry, 3-Cycle | — | 237.00 |
| DE91 | Special Order | — | 224.40 |

## GAS DRYERS

|  |  |  |  |
|---|---|---|---|
| DG808 | Electronic Control, 4-Cycle | $— | $361.20 |
| DG608 | Electronic Control, 4-Cycle | — | 340.08 |
| DG408 | Auto-Dry, 4-Cycle | — | 309.60 |
| DG308 | Timed-Dry, 3-Cycle | — | 280.20 |
| DG106 | Timed-Dry, 3-Cycle | — | 273.00 |

## PORTA-WASHER & PORTA-DRYER

|  |  |  |  |
|---|---|---|---|
| A50 | Porta-Washer | $— | $230.70 |
| DE50 | Porta-Dryer | — | 154.80 |

## WRINGER WASHERS

|  |  |  |  |
|---|---|---|---|
| E2L | Square Aluminum Tub | $— | $274.20 |
| E2LP | With Pump | — | 283.80 |
| N2L | Round Porcelain Tub | — | 241.20 |
| N2LP | With Pump | — | 250.80 |
| N2M | With Gas Engine | — | 307.20 |

# Whirlpool

## AUTOMATIC WASHERS

| LFC4500 | Compact 3 Cycle, 1 Speed | $309.00 | $284.40 |
|---|---|---|---|
| LFC4900 | Convertible Portable, 5 Cycle | 349.00 | 316.80 |
| LFB5300 | 24" Automatic 3 Cycle | 299.00 | 277.20 |
| LFB7750 | 24" Automatic 5 Cycle | 339.00 | 310.80 |
| LFA5300 | Extra Large Capacity, 3 Cycle | 299.00 | 282.00 |
| LFA5380 | Extra Large Capacity, 3 Cycle | 319.00 | 296.40 |
| LFA5700 | Extra Large Capacity, 4 Cycle | 319.00 | 289.20 |
| LFA5705 | Extra Large Capacity w/Suds Miser | 339.00 | 307.20 |
| LFA5800 | Extra Large Capacity, 4 Cycle | 349.00 | 319.20 |
| LFA5805 | Extra Large Capacity w/Suds Miser | 369.00 | 337.20 |
| LFA7700 | Extra Large Capacity, 5 Cycle | 349.00 | 319.20 |
| LFA7705 | Extra Large Capacity w/Suds Miser | 369.00 | 337.20 |

*Prices are accurate at time of printing; subject to manufacturer's change.*

|         |                                      | Retail Price | Low Price |
|---------|--------------------------------------|--------------|-----------|
| LFA7800 | Extra Large Capacity, 5 Cycle        | $379.00      | $344.40   |
| LFA7805 | Extra Large Capacity w/Suds Miser    | 399.00       | 362.40    |
| LFA9800 | Extra Large Capacity, Elec. Cycle    | 429.00       | 398.40    |
| LDA5520 | 2 Speed Auto., 3 Cycle               | —            | 259.20    |
| LDA7000 | 2 Speed Auto., 4 Cycle               | —            | 295.20    |
| LDA7005 | 2 Speed Auto., 4 Cycle, Suds Miser   | —            | 312.00    |
| LDA7500 | 2 Speed Auto., Large Capacity        | —            | 314.40    |
| LDA7505 | 2 Speed Auto., Large Capacity        | —            | 333.60    |
| LDA5600 | 2 Speed Auto., Knit Setting          | —            | 261.60    |
| LDA5605 | 2 Speed Auto. w/Suds Miser           | —            | 278.40    |
| LDA6800 | 2 Speed, Extra Large Capacity        | —            | 302.40    |
| LDA6805 | 2 Speed, Extra Large w/Suds Miser    | —            | 319.20    |

### ELECTRIC DRYERS
|         |                                      | Retail Price | Low Price |
|---------|--------------------------------------|--------------|-----------|
| LFE4900 | Portable, 1 Speed, 2 Temp.           | $219.00      | $196.80   |
| LEF4930 | Portable, 1 Speed, 2 Temp.           | 239.00       | 217.20    |
| LFE5700 | 1 Speed, 3 Temperatures              | 229.00       | 213.60    |
| LFE5800 | 1 Speed, 5 Temperatures              | 249.00       | 230.40    |
| LFE7800 | Large Capacity, 1 Speed, 5 Temp.     | 279.00       | 252.00    |
| LFE9800 | Large Capacity Electronic Cycle      | 339.00       | 312.00    |
| LDE5520 | 1 Speed, 3 Temp. 5 Cycle             | —            | 187.20    |
| LDE7500 | 5 Auto. Cycles, Large Capacity       | —            | 213.60    |
| LDE5920 | 3 Temperatures, Knit Cycle           | —            | 204.00    |

### GAS DRYERS
|         |                                      | Retail Price | Low Price |
|---------|--------------------------------------|--------------|-----------|
| LFI5701 | 1 Speed, 3 Temperatures              | $269.00      | $249.60   |
| LFI5801 | 1 Speed, 5 Temperatures              | 289.00       | 266.40    |
| LFI7801 | 1 Speed, 5 Temp., Large Capacity     | 319.00       | 288.00    |
| LFI9801 | Selector Control, Large Capacity     | 379.00       | 348.00    |
| LDI5521 | 1 Speed, 3 Temp., 5 Cycle            | —            | 222.00    |
| LDI7501 | 5 Auto. Cycles, Large Capacity       | —            | 248.40    |
| LDI5921 | 3 Temperatures, Knit Cycle           | —            | 238.80    |

# White-Westinghouse

### ELECTRIC DRYERS
|        |     |          |
|--------|-----|----------|
| DE270P | $—  | $190.68  |
| DE450P | —   | 201.36   |
| DE495P | —   | 219.00   |
| DE500P | —   | 228.36   |
| DE503P | —   | 218.16   |
| DE570P | —   | 246.00   |
| DE870P | —   | 270.48   |

### GAS DRYERS
|        |     |          |
|--------|-----|----------|
| DG450P | $—  | $238.68  |
| DG495P | —   | 255.96   |

*Prices are accurate at time of printing; subject to manufacturer's change.*

|  |  | Retail Price | Low Price |
|---|---|---|---|
| DG500P | .................................. | $— | $266.04 |
| DG570P |  | — | 283.20 |
| DG870P |  | — | 308.16 |

## SPACE MATE MODELS

| | | | |
|---|---|---|---|
| LT100P | Washer | $— | $381.12 |
| DE100P | Electric Dryer | — | 220.92 |
| LT170P | Washer | — | 399.24 |
| DE170P | Electric Dryer | — | 270.84 |
| DG170P | Gas Dryer | — | 308.16 |

## WASHERS

| | | | |
|---|---|---|---|
| LA270P | Agitator Model | $— | $282.48 |
| LA395P | Agitator Model | — | 276.72 |
| LA410P | Agitator Model | — | 290.64 |
| LA495P | Agitator Model | — | 314.40 |
| LA501P | Agitator Model | — | 330.60 |
| LA503P | Agitator Model | — | 299.40 |
| LA570P | Agitator Model | — | 346.92 |
| LA870P | Agitator Model | — | 377.04 |
| LT503P | Tumbler Model | — | 374.04 |
| LT570P | Tumbler Model | — | 416.76 |
| LT870P | Tumbler Model | — | 446.64 |

*Prices are accurate at time of printing; subject to manufacturer's change.*

# 1978 Dishwashers

USING A MECHANICAL dishwasher in place of a human one appeals to many people. This year as last, about three million households will buy a new one or replace an old one. About 35 different brands of dishwashers are available. Typically, a dishwasher lasts about 11 years. You can expect to pay from about $200 to $500.

**Where Dishwashers Fit in the Energy Picture**

DISHWASHERS currently are part of a government program to reduce energy consumption. This voluntary program seeks to improve the efficiency of dishwashers by 25 percent by 1980 (compared to 1972). The program, administered by the Federal Energy Administration (FEA), has been underway for about two years. While the program continues, expectations are that new legislation will replace it.

Congress is working on a new energy bill that would replace the voluntary energy program with minimum energy efficiency standards. Dishwashers are included in the bill.

When you begin to analyze the energy consumed by dishwashers, you very quickly learn that the vast majority of it goes into heating the water used for cleaning the dishes. In fact, about 80 percent of the energy required to wash a load of dishes goes into the hot water. Another ten percent is required to operate the unit; the remaining ten percent goes to the heated (or powered) drying cycle.

At first glance, it looks like the best place to start conserving energy is by reducing the hot water needed in a dishwasher. This, it seems, might be approached by reducing the amount and/or by reducing the temperature of the water, or both. The industry is working on reduced rinse cycles, changes in dishwasher tub geometry, as well as better water level control, to reduce the amount of hot water consumed. Eventually changes may produce about a 15 percent energy improvement. The temperature of hot water poses a different problem. Manufacturers say there is no detergent available that can clean dishes adequately below 140°F. And, of course, the water's temperature primarily is controlled by the consumer's setting of the hot water heater.

There probably is not much that can be done to vastly improve the mechanical operation of dishwashers. Some gains may come from better controls. Elimination of the powered drying cycle would save up to ten percent of the energy required by a typical load. Currently, most manufacturers have a power saver switch on one or more models that turns off the heating cycle and allows dishes to air dry.

As this report was being written, it looked as if legislation to set minimum energy standards would be passed by Congress. While no one was sure about just where the minimums would be set, most experts felt it would eventually mean higher dishwasher prices. The cost of energy improvements may range from $15 to about $50, depending on how far manufacturers will have to change their models to meet minimum standards. Changes that involve new cavity designs probably would be the most expensive.

### Use Patterns Can Save Energy

SWITCHES THAT eliminate the drying cycle will save energy only if they are used. Similarly, other use factors can help you get the best performance from your dishwasher at the lowest energy cost.

Most dishwashers today do a far superior cleaning job compared to models of five or ten years ago. You should scrape heavy food residues from plates before loading, but you do not have to pre-wash them; prewashing uses energy in the form of hot water. Running the unit only with full loads also will keep energy costs down. And, using the short wash cycle (on units that have this feature) when dishes are only moderately soiled will help, too. (This cycle may be appropriate for up to 75 percent of a household's typical loads.)

### Types of Dishwashers

YOU WILL FIND dishwashers in two basic types—built-in and portable. In portables, there are units that can be built in later, the convertible/portables, and models that will always require manual hook-up to water and power (they cannot be built in). Of the two, convertibles are far and away the more popular.

For most homeowners, the built-in or undercounter model is more convenient. It is fixed in place, loads from the front, and does not require any further attention other than loading and unloading. There is one penalty: you give up cabinet space to build in a unit. However, CONSUMER GUIDE Magazine believes that you will find this approach more beneficial in terms of both use and kitchen decor.

Convertible portables are basically the same as built-ins. Used as portables, these models have a hose that connects to the faucet and a power cord that should be connected to a grounded outlet. They load from the front and have casters (that can be removed) for easy movement. Hoses and electrical cords can be removed if they are built in. This dual capability—portable or built-in—does add a few dollars to the cost of the units.

Portables, as already mentioned, cannot be built in. You will find a limited choice available. There are models that load from the front and those that load from the top. Front-loaders are virtually identical to convertibles, which is why most manufacturers do not offer a strictly portable unit. Top-loading models are a little cheaper and require less floor space, but they have less capacity and are a little harder to load.

There also are several "specialty" dishwashers on the market. These units include combination range/dishwashers (Modern Maid), under-the-sink dishwashers (General Electric), and combination sink/dishwashers (KitchenAid).

**Features Found on Dishwashers**

FEATURES VARY from brand to brand and even from model to model within a brand line. As with all such things, cost, personal preference and need should be the major factors in your buying decisions.

**Cycles.** Models are available with as few as two cycles, or as many as eight. Generally, the more cycles, the higher the price. Cycles may be set by pushbuttons or with a timer/dial, or a combination of both. The minimum cycles include a normal wash cycle and a short wash cycle. A common extra, a soak cycle or pots-and-pans cycle will handle very heavily soiled cookware and dishes. A rinse-and-hold cycle allows you to accumulate dishes for a full load and can be very convenient if you have a small family or if the members of your family tend to eat at different times. Other cycles sometimes included in a dishwasher are a china and crystal cycle, a sanitizer cycle (the heating element heats the water to higher temperatures), and a plate warmer. All of these serve some function, but they are not critical to a good machine. Your best bet lies in the basic cycles and those others that will serve your day-to-day needs. Perhaps the most important feature associated with cycles is the power saver setting. This eliminates the drying cycle and allows dishes to air dry. CONSUMER GUIDE Magazine recommends this feature and recommends consumers make use of it as frequently as possible.

**Drying Systems.** Two different systems exist. The most common is the convection drying system that uses a heating element and the natural rising action of hot air. Forced-air drying systems are less common. In forced-air systems, a fan blows air over a heating element and around dishes. Forced-air systems do a better job, but are more expensive. Again, models that allow the heating cycle to be shut off are a smart buy.

**Spray Action.** Spray action may involve one, two or three wash levels. The best action comes from units with spray arms at the top and bottom and a turret to help spray the upper rack. Units with arms at the top and bottom do a good job. Another two-level wash action uses a turret and a bottom spray arm. And, units with only one rotating arm at the bottom do a fair job.

**Racks.** Roll-out, adjustable racks are the best for overall convenience on front-loaders, but are usually available only on top-of-the-line models. Nonadjustable roll-out racks function well. On top-loading portables, racks that lift up when the door opens are best. Removable silverware baskets are convenient.

**Dispensers.** Detergent dispensers release the detergent at the right point in the wash. Rinse dispensers release agents that prevent spotting during the rinse cycle.

**Interiors.** Porcelain enamel on steel remains the best overall material for dishwasher interiors. Stainless steel, though not commonly used, is a good second. Plastic and epoxy-coated interiors also are adequate.

**Styling.** Most manufacturers are using the front "panel" pack of colors. This allows you a choice of any one of four colors and the option of changing the color at a later date. Some manufacturers are offering the new almond (beige) color. In addition, a variety of special looks can be created with decorator or black-glass front kits. Cutting-board or decorative wood tops are available on some convertibles and portables.

**Others.** Standard features on most of the good and better dishwashers are soft-food disposers that pulverize food wastes and screens that prevent large scraps from entering and blocking the pump assembly.

CONSUMER GUIDE Magazine recommends two- or three-level spray action, either drying system, adjustable racks and removable silverware baskets, porcelain enamel on steel interiors, detergent and rinse aid dispensers, as well as screens and soft-food disposers. As far as cycles go, we recommend at least two—preferably normal and a short wash. The rinse-and-hold cycle adds convenience. And, if you do a lot of baking, roasting, and heavy cooking, look seriously at a soak or pots-and-pans cycle. Add other cycles to fit special needs, but remember, the more cycles, the higher the price tag and the more energy used, as a general rule.

# 1978 Best Buys: Dishwashers

Energy economy, features and overall performance in relation to price were the basis for these Recommended Buy ratings. CONSUMER GUIDE Magazine also took into account the manufacturers' reputations for reliability and service.

## BUILT-IN DISHWASHERS

**The General Electric GSD-463** has a Tuff-Tub epoxy-coated interior, which is good (although we do not rate it as high as porcelain enamel). The model has a power saver to eliminate heated drying. It also has three-level washing action, a turret and two spray arms. Reversible front panels give you color choices. This model has a rinse-aid dispenser and a soft-food disposer. Cycles include pots-and-pans, normal wash, short wash (on dial), and rinse-and-hold.
**SPECIFICATIONS: Height,** 36''; **Width,** 24-5/8''; **Depth,** 25-1/2''; **Heating Element Wattage,** 700; **Volts,** 115; **Regular Wash** (gallons), 16.5; **Warranty,** one year on parts and labor.
**Approximate Retail Price: $359.95**　　　　**Low Price: $306.60**

**KitchenAid KDC-18** is a dishwasher with a strong reliability record and better-than-average lifetime performance. The unit has a porcelain-on-steel interior, removable silverware basket, an energy saver button to eliminate the heating element during drying, a forced-air drying system, three-level washing action, and a heavy-duty 1/2 horsepower motor. The unit has a normal wash cycle and a rinse-and-hold cycle. A rinse-aid dispenser is optional.
**SPECIFICATIONS: Height,** 34-1/2''; **Width,** 24''; **Depth,** 25-13/16''; **Heating Element Wattage,** 800; **Volts,** 115; **Regular Wash** (gallons), 11.8; **Warranty,** one year on parts and labor, four additional years on motor (parts).
**Approximate Retail Price: $419.00**　　　　**Low Price: $387.50**

*Prices are accurate at time of printing; subject to manufacturer's change.*

**Magic Chef MD-357,** a six-cycle dishwasher with reversible color panels, has an energy saver option to cut off the drying cycle. The unit features two full-size spray arms and will hold a 16-place setting of dishes. Detergent and rinse-aid dispensers are included. The interior is porcelain on steel. This model has a soft-food disposer.
**SPECIFICATIONS: Height,** 36"; **Width,** 24"; **Depth,** 26"; **Heating Element Wattage,** 750; **Volts,** 115; **Regular Wash** (gallons), 13.2; **Warranty,** one year on parts and labor.
**Approximate Retail Price: Not Available**     **Low Price: $224.95**

**Maytag's Model WU-401** includes an energy-saver button to allow washing without the heated drying cycle. Cycles include heavy, regular, and rinse-and-hold (a plate warmer and rinse-and-dry setting are on the dial). The model has a porcelain-on-steel tub and three levels of wash action. Moderately priced, the unit represents solid value. A rinse dispenser is optional.
**SPECIFICATIONS: Height,** 35"; **Width,** 24"; **Depth,** 24"-1/16"; **Heating Element Wattage,** 750; **Volts,** 115; **Regular Wash** (gallons), 13.75; **Warranty,** one year on parts and labor, an additional year on all parts, plus another three years on cabinet and exterior front panel against rust (parts only).
**Approximate Retail Price: Not Available**     **Low Price: $367.80**

**Whirlpool SDU-5000** has three automatic cycles and an energy saving option. The unit has a porcelain-enameled tub, filter, in-the-door silverware basket, reversible front color panels, convection drying, and a concealed door latch. Cycles include a short wash, super wash, and a super scour. Washing action comes from two spray arms and a center turret.
**SPECIFICATIONS: Height,** 34-5/32"; **Width,** 23-7/8"; **Depth,** 25-15/16"; **Heating Element Wattage,** 800; **Volts,** 120; **Regular Wash** (gallons), 13.9; **Warranty,** one year on parts and labor.
**Approximate Retail Price: $319.00**     **Low Price: $298.80**

## CONVERTIBLE DISHWASHERS

**Frigidaire DWM-33** offers an energy saving option and four-level washing action. Cycles include pots-and-pans, normal soil, quick wash, rinse-and-dry, and rinse-and-hold. A plate warmer is on the dial. The unit features both a detergent and a rinse-aid dispenser. It also has a removable silverware basket. The melamine laminate top is in a butcher-block pattern. This model has a snap-on, snap-off water connection.
**SPECIFICATIONS: Height,** 37-5/8"; **Width,** 24-1/4"; **Depth,** 28-1/2"; **Heating Element Wattage,** 900; **Volts,** 115; **Regular Wash** (gallons), 14.7; **Warranty,** one year on parts and labor.
**Approximate Retail Price: $349.95**     **Low Price: $300.00**

*Prices are accurate at time of printing; subject to manufacturer's change.*

**Hotpoint HDB-776** has an energy saving option that eliminates the drying cycle. Cycle choices include power scrub (pots-and-pans), normal wash, normal wash without heated dry, rinse-and-hold, and short wash. Featuring a soft-food disposer, detergent dispenser, rinse-aid dispenser, a decorator wood work top, three-level washing action, and a removable silverware basket, the model can be connected with an easy-to-use unicouple faucet connector.
**SPECIFICATIONS: Height,** 36-3/4"; **Width,** 24-3/8"; **Depth,** 25"; **Heating Element Wattage,** 700; **Volts,** 115; **Regular Wash** (gallons), 16.5; **Warranty,** one year on parts and labor.
**Approximate Retail Price: $329.95**        **Low Price: $250.00**

**KitchenAid KDC-58** is the convertible/portable equivalent to the built-in custom model KDC-18. It has all the same features plus an easy-use faucet adapter and casters. No conversion kit is needed to build in the unit later. This model comes with a butcher-block top.
**SPECIFICATIONS: Height,** 36"; **Width,** 24"; **Depth,** 23-3/16"; **Heating Element Wattage,** 800; **Volts,** 115; **Regular Wash,** (gallons), 11.8; **Warranty,** one year on parts and labor, four additional years on motor (parts).
**Approximate Retail Price: $459.00**        **Low Price: $424.35**

**Kenmore (Sears) 65 G-76051N,** with two-level wash action and forced-air drying, has an energy saver to eliminate the heating element during drying. Cycles include rinse-and-hold, normal wash, and pots-and-pans. The model has a porcelain enameled interior and door liner. Besides a detergent dispenser and rinse-aid dispenser and silverware basket, this model has another useful feature: a long utensil basket with a hinged-lid compartment for small items.
**SPECIFICATIONS: Height,** 36"; **Width,** 24-1/8"; **Depth,** 26-1/4"; **Heating Element Wattage,** 750; **Volts,** 115; **Regular Wash** (gallons), 13.8; **Warranty,** one year on parts and labor, four additional years on parts and labor for tub and interior door panel.
**Approximate Retail Price: $289.95**        **Low Price: Not Available**

**Whirlpool SDF-3700** has three automatic cycles—super wash, rinse-and-hold, and short wash—plus an energy saving dry selector switch, which allows you to either air dry or use heat during drying. The model has three-level washing action, dual detergent dispensers, hideaway electric cord and fill/drain hoses, silverware basket, and a vinyl-clad steel top. This model also has a porcelain-on-steel tub. To build-in the unit later, a conversion kit is required.
**SPECIFICATIONS: Height,** 36-3/8"; **Width,** 24-1/8"; **Depth,** 26-1/4"; **Heating Element Wattage,** 635; **Volts,** 120; **Regular Wash** (gallons), 13.9; **Warranty,** one year on parts and labor.
**Approximate Retail Price: $279.95**        **Low Price: Not Available**

*Prices are accurate at time of printing; subject to manufacturer's change.*

**White-Westinghouse SC450W** comes with an energy-saver control that reduces electricity consumption by about 30 percent when used to eliminate heated drying. The model has two-level wash action. Cycles include pots-and-pans, normal, rinse-and-hold, and rinse-and-dry. It also has a soft food disposer and a porcelain enameled interior. The unit comes with a butcher block pattern Micarta® top, but a hardwood cutting board top is available as an option. It has both detergent and rinse-aid dispensers.
**SPECIFICATIONS: Height,** 36-1/2''; **Width,** 24-7/8''; **Depth,** 27-3/8''; **Heating Element Wattage,** 800; **Volts,** 120; **Regular Wash** (gallons), 14.3; **Warranty,** one year on parts and labor.
**Approximate Retail Price: Not Available**   **Low Price: $292.20**

## PORTABLE DISHWASHERS

**KitchenAid KDW-7** is a top-loading portable with three automatic cycles: full cycle, rinse-and-hold, and a soak cycle. The unit has many of the features found on built-in and convertible/portable models from KitchenAid, including porcelain interior, forced-air drying, 1/2-horsepower motor, detergent dispenser, and silverware basket. A rinse-aid dispenser is standard on this model. The top comes as either a one-inch hardwood cutting board or a heat resistant laminate. The top rack automatically lifts up when the lid is opened. This model also features an automatic cord reel and faucet adapter with aerator.
**SPECIFICATIONS: Height,** 36-1/4''; **Width,** 22-1/2''; **Depth,** 26-3/4''; **Heating Element Wattage,** 700; **Volts,** 120; **Regular Wash** (gallons), 12; **Warranty,** one year on parts and labor, four additional years on motor (parts).
**Approximate Retail Price: $369.00**   **Low Price: $343.85**
*Prices are accurate at time of printing; subject to manufacturer's change.*

# 1978 Garbage Disposers

BETTER FOOD waste disposers can handle almost any type of food waste, disposing of soft foods, bones, stringy foods, rinds and even corn cobs. You can find disposers ranging in cost from about $50 to $175.

Energy is not a major factor in the operation of in-the-sink disposers. In a month's time, energy cost can probably be measured in cents. For the small investment, much of the messy part of kitchen clean-up is greatly simplified. Disposers, by grinding and removing food wastes, also eliminate odors, a major benefit in hot weather.

While the old saw about "you get what you pay for" may have lost some of its meaning in these inflation-plagued times, it generally still does hold true for disposers. Unlike some other products, top-of-the-line disposers, as well as some middle-of-the-line models, are better than the bottom-of-the-line models. It is not just features that separate the bottom from the top.

Better disposers normally have heavy-duty motors (1/2 horsepower) and more components made from better, corrosion-resistant materials, such as stainless steel. These factors make the top-of-the-line disposers the best values.

CONSUMER GUIDE Magazine, therefore, recommends middle and top-of-the-line disposers. Reliability, expected lifetime, and performance (especially with hard-to-grind items) are primary reasons. Inexpensive units may not stand up well to the kinds of food waste many people expect disposers to take. Overloading or jamming can be more troublesome with some inexpensive models.

There also is the matter of safety. Heavy-duty units usually have anti-jam systems. These features reverse the grinding direction to clear obstructions. Such systems virtually eliminate the need to insert anything into the disposer, such as your hand, to clear it.

In general, most homes with a standard kitchen sink will accommodate a disposer. However, a word of caution for homeowners with septic tanks: check with a local expert before you install a disposer. If you are building a home with a septic system, ask your contractor about a disposer. All homeowners should check local codes before installing a disposer or having one installed.

**Disposer Features**

MANY FEATURES on a disposer will help it do a more effective job of grinding and removing wastes. Other features, such as fancy housing and attractive styling, are more to entice buyers. After all, the disposer, once installed, will be out of sight.

**Anti-jam Systems.** Features that reverse or apply power jolts to free obstructions are recommended.

**Corrosion Resistance.** Better models have stainless steel grind-impeller assemblies, sink flanges and drain housings. Corrosion resistance features assure a long life for the unit.

**Motor.** Generally, the better units have 1/2-horsepower motors; less expensive units have 1/3-horsepower motors. The heftier motors are more efficient.

**Mounting Systems.** A variety of mounting systems exist, but many of the better models have what manufacturers refer to as "quick" mounting systems. In essence, this means that they can be installed easily, normally without the use of special tools.

**Sound Insulation.** This is another principle difference between inexpensive and better units; the better models have rubber, plastic foam, or other sound insulation.

**Dishwasher Drain.** A connection into which a dishwasher drain hose can be installed, usually in the side of the disposer body, greatly simplifies plumbing work for consumers who have or are planning to add a dishwasher.

**Two Basic Types of Disposers**

DISPOSERS COME in batch-feed and continuous-feed models. Each has certain advantages, as well as their own manner of operation.

Batch-feed units are a slight bit more expensive to purchase, principally because the "wiring" is already done on these models. Thus, they are slightly less expensive to have installed (you probably should figure on spending $25 to $35 for installation). Batch-feed units have the on-off switch control in the cover. You load the unit, put on the cover, and turn it to the "on" position to activate the disposer. You cannot add additional wastes without stopping the unit.

Continuous-feed units are wired to a wall switch. These units require an additional cost to install (figure on about $50 to $60) because of the need for an electric line. However, the units are less expensive to buy. You load continuous-feed models, put on a cover that prevents things from flying out while allowing water into the unit, and turn on the wall switch. Additional wastes can be added while the unit is running, hence the name continuous-feed. Please note that this particular element of these models can make them hazardous if you are careless. With the safety cover removed, items can fall into the disposer; many consumers have lost more than one piece of silverware in this type of slip-up. The units are safe — as long as you use them as intended.

For consumers replacing a disposer, you are probably best off putting in the type you had. This will keep your installation costs to a minimum.

Most manufacturers offer one or more models with ground power cords that simply plug into a below-the-sink outlet. These models may carry different model numbers to distinguish this feature. They are usually identical to other models with this one exception.

---

## SPECIAL INFORMATION SERVICE

**A Bonus for Readers of this CONSUMER GUIDE®**

CONSUMER GUIDE® offers a special bonus to its readers who are interested in obtaining information as to where they can find the low prices on specific products listed in this guide. Simply fill out the form and mail. Include 25 cents for postage and handling.

**Please send me information on:**

Product _____ Model Number _____

Manufacturer _____

Product _____ Model Number _____

Manufacturer _____

Your Name _____

Address _____

City _____ State _____ Zip Code _____

**CONSUMER GUIDE Magazine**
**3841 West Oakton, Skokie, Illinois 60076**

# 1978 Best Buys Garbage Disposers

When reviewing the various garbage disposers now available, CONSUMER GUIDE Magazine emphasized sturdy construction and corrosion-resistant parts. Disposers from manufacturers that offer a full range of models received special attention. Those models that combine good features and reasonable prices are our Recommended Buys.

## BATCH-FEED DISPOSERS

**General Electric GFB-910** is a sound-insulated, batch-feed disposer with a Carboloy cutter, polyester drain housing, and automatically resetting overload protection. The motor is 1/2-horsepower. The unit also has a stainless steel sink flange, hopper, flywheel, impellers and shredder. It also has a dishwasher drain. This is GE's best batch-feed type of disposer.
**SPECIFICATIONS: Drain Diameter,** standard; **Volts,** 115; **Mounting,** Keyhole, quick mount; **Warranty,** one year on parts and labor.
**Approximate Retail Price: $149.95**  **Low Price: $119.95**

**In-Sink-Erator 17,** a stainless steel, batch-feed unit, has polystyrene sound insulation. Its automatic reversing feature is an advantage. It has a 1/2-horsepower motor, cast-in crusher lugs in place of swinging impellers (longer lasting when cast in), and a special self-service wrench to free jams not cleared by the reversing action.
**SPECIFICATIONS: Drain Diameter,** standard; **Volts,** 115; **Mounting,** Quick-lock; **Warranty,** one year on parts and labor, with four additional years on specified parts (parts only).
**Approximate Retail Price: $120.00**  **Low Price: Not Available**

**KitchenAid KWS-200** has a patented Magnestart cover; the unit automatically starts when the cover-control is in position. The unit also has full sound insulation, a 1/2-horsepower motor, chrome

*Prices are accurate at time of printing; subject to manufacturer's change.*

shredder ring, cast stainless steel alloy grind wheel, and a stainless steel grind chamber. The unit comes with a special Wham Jam Breaker. Pressing the breaker button delivers 120 jolts per second to break any jam not cleared by an electronic reversing feature. KitchenAid has maintained an excellent durability record. Their units are expensive, but the price reflects their quality.

**SPECIFICATIONS: Drain Diameter,** standard; **Volts,** 115; **Mounting,** Quick-click; **Warranty,** one year on parts and labor, with four additional years on specified parts (parts only).

**Approximate Retail Price: $179.00**         **Low Price: $143.20**

**Maytag FB-20** features complete sound insulation and an automatic-start lid that turns the unit on and off. This unit features a stainless steel grind chamber, shredder ring, impeller arms, a rind positioner, and two fibrous waste cutting blades. It has a corrosion-resistant glass-filled polypropylene drain chamber, as well as a 1/2-horsepower motor and a dishwasher drain.

**SPECIFICATIONS: Drain Diameter,** standard; **Volts,** 115; **Mounting,** QuikConnect; **Warranty,** one year parts and labor, with a second year on parts, plus another three years against part failure due to rust or corrosion.

**Approximate Retail Price: Not Available**         **Low Price: $145.00**

**Whirlpool SYD-80** has a 1/2-horsepower motor with automatically reset overload protection. The unit has a stainless steel sink flange, shredding ring and impeller. It also has an insulated sound shield. There is an automatic reversing feature to clear any jam that might occur. The entire power pack of the unit (the motor assembly) can be removed without disturbing plumbing or tying up the sink.

**SPECIFICATIONS: Drain Diameter,** standard; **Volts,** 120; **Mounting,** Easy type; **Warranty,** one year on parts and labor.

**Approximate Retail Price: $109.95**         **Low Price: $87.95**

## CONTINUOUS-FEED DISPOSERS

**General Electric GFC-810** has all the same features of batch-feed Model GFB-910. The only difference is that this model is turned on and off via a wall switch.

**SPECIFICATIONS: Drain Diameter,** standard; **Volts,** 115; **Mounting,** Keyhole, quick mount; **Warranty,** one year on parts and labor.

**Approximate Retail Price: $129.95**         **Low Price: $103.95**

**In-Sink-Erator 707** is In-Sink-Erator's best continuous-feed disposer. It has a double stainless steel inner and outer shell, which should give it extended life. The unit has a 1/2-horsepower motor and the other features found on batch-feed Model 17. This model holds more than eight cups of waste.

**SPECIFICATIONS: Drain Diameter,** standard; **Volts,** 115; **Mounting,** Quick-lock; **Warranty,** one year on parts and labor, with an

*Prices are accurate at time of printing; subject to manufacturer's change.*

additional four years on specified parts (parts only).
**Approximate Retail Price: $121.75    Low Price: Not Available**

**KitchenAid KWI-200** is the continuous-feed counterpart to batch-feed Model KWS-200. It has all the same features except the Magnestart cover. This unit operates via a wall switch. Otherwise, the same performance and lifetime characteristics can be expected from the batch-feed model.
**SPECIFICATIONS: Drain Diameter,** standard; **Volts,** 115; **Mounting,** Quick-click; **Warranty,** one year on parts and labor, with an additional four years on specified parts (parts only).
**Approximate Retail Price: $159.00    Low Price: $127.20**

**Maytag FC-20** is the continuous-feed unit comparable to the batch-feed Model FB-20. It has all the same features of the FB-20, including a 1/2-horsepower motor.
**SPECIFICATIONS: Drain Diameter,** standard; **Volts,** 115; **Mounting,** QuikConnect; **Warranty,** one year on parts and labor, with a second year on parts, plus another three years against part failure due to rust or corrosion.
**Approximate Retail Price: Not Available    Low Price: $125.00**

**Tappan 51-1086** is a brute of a unit with its 3/4-horsepower motor. An excellent value for its features, the model offers a three-bolt mounting system for quick installation, a dishwasher drain, sound insulation, and an automatic reversing feature to keep it running free of jams.
**SPECIFICATIONS: Drain Diameter,** standard; **Volts,** 115; **Mounting,** three-bolt (quick); **Warranty,** one year on parts and labor.
**Approximate Retail Price: $119.95    Low Price: $95.95**

**Waste-King Universal SS-8000** is a continuous-feed, heavy-duty model with a 1/2-horsepower motor. It also has sound insulation for quiet operation. A large number of the unit's parts are made from stainless steel. There is no reversing feature. Waste-King disposers have maintained a better-than-average repair and lifetime history.
**SPECIFICATIONS: Drain Diameter,** standard; **Volts,** 120; **Mounting,** Fast-mount; **Warranty,** one year on parts and labor, with an additional four years on specified parts (parts only).
**Approximate Retail Price: $159.95    Low Price: $124.95**
*Prices are accurate at time of printing; subject to manufacturer's change.*

# 1978 Trash Compactors

TRASH COMPACTORS can make getting trash together and bagging it a little more tolerable. They reduce typical solid wastes to one-fourth of their original bulk (about 75 percent of refuse is "air"). They don't consume a lot of energy, since they are used infrequently. In other words, if you put out four bags of trash in a week, you probably would put out one bag of compacted trash. This is about the amount of refuse generated by a family of four. A compacted trash bag weighs in at between 25 to 30 pounds, although they can go as high as 40 pounds if a lot of bottles and cans make up wastes. Ranging in price from about $150 to around $350, compactors are a convenience item that can help keep the trash can area neat.

**Compactors Differ in Design and Type**

WASTE BUCKETS or containers in compactors may be either round or rectangular. Many consumers find the round bucket more convenient.

There are other basic differences in compactor designs, but these are hidden by outward appearance. The real difference between various units is in the method of compaction—ram screw, or combination scissor jack and ram screw. Both types do an effective job of compacting wastes, with the scissor-screw being a slight bit more powerful.

In addition to these design differences, there are models that can be built in, as well as models that stand by themselves. A few manufacturers offer convertible units—models that can be either free-standing or built in under a counter.

The type you want is probably best determined on the basis of where you expect to put the unit. For many consumers, the kitchen is the logical place, since this is where most of the waste is generated. However, you will have to give up about 15 inches of cabinet space to build in a compactor. Or, you will have to give up floor space for a free-standing unit. CONSUMER GUIDE Magazine believes the built-in unit will present a more pleasing appearance in the kitchen, if you can give up the cabinet space.

While the kitchen is the ordinary place, it is by no means the only location. Many consumers have found a basement, utility room or garage installation to be quite handy. For these locations, a free-standing model is recommended.

### The Features of Compactors

FEATURES DO NOT differ widely from one brand to another. Basic differences deal more with design and use. About the only major feature that some models have and others lack is an automatic deodorizing system.

**Containers.** All trash compactors have a rectangular or round bucket in which trash is compacted. The round container is somewhat more convenient to handle, especially when heavy.

**Deodorizer System.** Though most trash compactors have either automatic or manual deodorizing systems, nothing will truly "deodorize" a large amount of trash. That is especially true in warm weather if "wet" garbage and spoiling waste is involved. Some models do not have a built-in system.

**Locks.** Locks, used primarily to turn on the unit, are a good idea to prevent children from playing with the compactor. Types of locks include key-locks and an on/off knob that can be removed. The removable knob is a little better.

**Styling.** Color choices are available from some manufacturers who offer sets of front panels (two panels), each side having a different color. Decorator kits also are available from some manufacturers to customize the front.

**Trash Doors/Access.** Access to the container depends on the design of the specific model. There are automatic slide-out drawers, pull-out drawers, automatic swing-out buckets, side-opening doors, and doors that tilt from the top. The most convenient of these are the automatic slide-out drawer, which slides out when a toe bar is depressed, and the automatic swing-out bucket (the automatic feature does add a slight extra cost to the unit).

# 1978 Best Buys: Trash Compactors

CONSUMER GUIDE Magazine reviewed trash compactor models on the basis of price, features, the general reputation of the product and the manufacturer's standing in the field. Our Recommended Buys are the compactors that give you the most value for your money.

## CONVERTIBLE COMPACTOR

**General Electric GCG-661** can be used as a free-standing unit or it can be built-in under a counter. The model has many convenient features, including a swing-out bucket with a handle, a touch-latch system for easy opening, a reversible-swing door, and reversible front color panels. The unit has a key-knob that can be removed to keep children from cycling the unit. This model includes an automatic deodorizer system. It operates on a combination scissor-screw principle and develops about 3000 pounds of force.
**SPECIFICATIONS: Height,** 34-1/2"; **Width,** 14-7/8"; **Depth,** 18"; **Basket,** Round; **Loading,** Automatic, Swing-out bucket; **Warranty,** one year on parts and labor.
**Approximate Retail Price: $299.95**      **Low Price: $260.10**

## BUILT-IN COMPACTORS

**Hotpoint HCH-411** is designed to be built-in under a counter. It has most of the same features found on GE model GCG-661, including a swing-out basket, touch-latch system and key-knob lock. It fits in a 15-inch base cabinet space. This model has a manual deodorizer system, which is released by pressing a button on the control panel.
**SPECIFICATIONS: Height,** 34-1/2"; **Width,** 14-7/8"; **Depth,** 18"; **Basket,** Round; **Loading,** Swing-out bucket; **Warranty,** one year on parts and labor.
**Approximate Retail Price: $220.00**      **Low Price: $207.00**
*Prices are accurate at time of printing; subject to manufacturer's change.*

**Tappan 52-2335** is another unit for under-the-counter installation. It operates on the ram-screw principle, developing about 3000 pounds of compaction force. It has a key-lock operation, reversible front color panels, and a pull-out drawer (with a round trash container). It does not feature an easy-open system, nor does it have a deodorizer system. This model requires special bags.
**SPECIFICATIONS: Height,** 34-1/4"; **Width,** 14-7/8"; **Depth,** 18"; **Basket,** Round; **Loading,** Pull-out drawer; **Warranty,** one year on parts and labor.
**Approximate Retail Price: $289.95**　　　　　**Low Price: $247.75**

**Whirlpool SDC-8000** is also for built-in use. It has a touch-toe drawer opener, which allows you to open the drawer by pressing a bar with your foot. The features on this model include an automatic deodorizer system, reversible front color panels and a removable key knob. The unit's twin ram-screws develop about 2300 pounds of force. The drawer has a removable drop-down side for easy bag removal. A special bag carrier also makes removing and carrying full bags easier.
**SPECIFICATIONS: Height,** 34-1/4"; **Width,** 15"; **Depth,** 24"; **Basket,** rectangular; **Loading,** Automatic slide-out drawer; **Warranty,** one year on parts and labor.
**Approximate Retail Price: $259.95**　　　　　**Low Price: $240.00**

## FREE-STANDING COMPACTORS

**Frigidaire TC-3,** a free-standing unit with a walnut veneer wood top, gives you extra work space. Reversible front color panels are included. The model has a round bucket in its pull-out drawer. It also features a manual deodorizer system. The model has a key-lock system of operation. Ram force is about 3000 pounds in this unit.
**SPECIFICATIONS: Height,** 36"; **Width,** 15"; **Depth,** 18-1/4"; **Basket,** Round; **Loading,** Pull-out drawer; **Warranty,** one year on parts and labor.
**Approximate Retail Price: $309.95**　　　　　**Low Price: $273.60**

**Whirlpool SDC-4500** is a free-standing compactor with reversible front color panels. The unique feature on this unit is a special compartment for solid air freshener. The model has a key-knob operation and the knob can be removed. The unit also has a drop-down panel on the drawer to aid removal of compacted waste. The top exterior of the unit is made of textured steel, which hides fingerprints and scratches, as well as improving its overall appearance.
**SPECIFICATIONS: Height,** 34-1/4"; **Width,** 15"; **Depth,** 24"; **Basket,** rectangular; **Loading,** Pull-out drawer; **Warranty,** one year on parts and labor.
**Approximate Retail Price: $269.95**　　　　　**Low Price: $221.35**

*Prices are accurate at time of printing; subject to manufacturer's change.*

# 1978 Ranges

THE ASSORTMENT of range models, in gas or electric, can be confusing. Just about anything you can imagine is available: from two types of oven cleaning systems to a number of size options; from built-ins to free standers; from combination microwave ranges to smoothtops. With all of these possibilities, it is no wonder that prices today run from about $200 to more than $1000.

Ranges last a long time. Gas models last an average of 13.5 years, while electrics average just over 12 years. About three-fourths of the electrics sold are free-standing models. Just over 80 percent of all gas ranges are free-standing types.

Overall, electrics now out-sell gas ranges. Personal preference remains a major reason for choosing one over the other. However, in some parts of the country you may not have a choice because natural gas is not available for new homes or increased loading (replacing an electric range with a gas model) is not permitted in existing homes.

Which is best?

Both gas and electric ranges do a good job and come in many types. If you have a preference, it probably stems from the fact that you are more familiar with one compared to the other. Most users that make a switch find they can use the other type without difficulty after a learning period.

Gas surface burners are easier to control, allowing more precise and instantaneous adjustment. That is not to say that electric elements do not work well. It also is true that electric ovens do not dry foods out as much as gas ovens, but that does not mean that gas ovens do a poor job. The pros and cons boil down more to personal preference than serious differences.

### How Energy Affects Ranges

RANGES ARE part of a goverment energy program that seeks to improve efficiency overall by 64 percent by 1980—104 percent improvement in gas ranges, three percent for electric ranges, and five percent for microwave ovens. The largest improvement is slated for gas ranges because that is where the government sees the most need for upgrading efficiency.

As this report was being compiled, Congress was expected to pass legislation that would replace the current target goal program with minimum efficiency standards. In other words, the government, through the Federal Energy Administration, is expected to set a limit on how much energy a specific type of range can consume in a given period of time.

For both gas and electric range manufacturers, energy improvements may be found in increased and improved oven insulation. Better oven door seals might add some savings. Convection ovens, ovens that cook via forced heated air, may provide some additional savings.

Manufacturers are working on these and other energy-saving improvements. Some examples already are on the market. More insulation can be found in units with self-cleaning ovens. Prospects are that similar insulation packages will show up on ovens without the self-cleaning feature. Convection ovens are available in both gas and electric. Tappan has two gas models and recently introduced an electric unit. Jenn-Air brought the first electric convection range to the consumer market and remains the major part of this movement.

Gas range manufacturers can be expected to continue to replace standing pilots, in both ovens and on surface burners, with pilotless ignition systems. Pilotless ignition involves an electric or electronic ignition; the igniter sparks or glows to light the gas when turned on. The move in this direction is already well underway. CONSUMER GUIDE Magazine recommends the extra cost for pilotless ignition models because there is a payback in terms of cost savings on natural gas.

Electric range manufacturers should be able to achieve whatever standards are set by fine tuning their models, by upgrading the oven door seal and improving insulation. Manufacturers of microwave ovens should be able to meet goals by relatively minor changes (some have already made these "fixes"), assuming standards are set that would reflect about the same percentage improvements as proposed goals (five percent improvement).

Ironically, some recent industry moves to build better, safer products have been counter-effective in terms of energy. The range industry recently went through major redesigns to reduce exterior surface temperatures, thereby reducing burn potential. In making these changes, manufacturers had to give up a slight bit of energy efficiency.

Another product trend runs counter to the current energy situation: smoothtop electric ranges. Here is a range that consumers are choosing in ever-increasing numbers. Yet, they are not as energy efficient as the standard electric range with sheath-type surface elements. Consumers are choosing styling over energy efficiency.

Prices are going to rise as manufacturers put energy improvements into place. Pilotless ignition can raise the price of a gas range from between $20 to $30. Other improvements on ranges, both gas and electric, could add $15 or more. Ranges that use new principles, such as convection cooking, may cost $50 or $60 more than conventional units. However, energy efficiency improvements are unlike simply dressing a model up with features; there is a real return buying a range with such improvements. For the extra price, you get a range that will cost you less to operate.

**Types and Styles of Ranges**

RANGES COME in a variety of types. Built-in models have a separate oven built into a wall and a separate cooktop that usually is set into a counter above cabinets. Drop-in ranges are designed to be installed on a sidewall, in an island, counter or peninsula. If you do not like the built-in approach, there is the ever-popular and flexible free-standing style. Free-standing ranges come in different widths, have an oven below the cooking surface, and have sides and a back.

Another popular style is the over-and-under unit that has two ovens, one above the other with the cooking surface in between. These tall units are often called eye-level or double-decker ranges. If you want to install a range between two cabinets, there are slide-in models. Slide-in models look like free-standing ranges, but they normally have frame sides and back. They look built-in because they fit snugly, usually with a top that overlaps the counter on each side.

Combination ranges offer conventional cooking with microwave convenience. The units are gaining popularity and more of these models will be appearing on the market. Gas and electric models are available. One type is the free-standing electric that has two ovens in one: a conventional electric oven and a microwave. You can cook with a combination of conventional heat and microwave speed, or with microwave energy alone, or with conventional heat only. Also available are both gas and electric eye-level models. In these types, the lower oven usually is a conventional type and the upper oven is a microwave. Combination ranges, also called cooking centers, are expensive. Most are in the $750 to $1000 and over class. If you consider the fact that they represent two complete products (with a high degree of cooking flexibility) in one appliance, you can see the reason for their high cost.

The smoothtop is a variation of the electric range. It has a smooth ceramic surface, usually in one piece, with the electric elements hidden under marked areas. They are gaining widespread appreciation from consumers. Smoothtops are slightly less efficient than standard electric ranges.

Convection ranges, widely used in restaurant and institutional cooking, are available on the consumer market. A convection oven uses a fan and heated-air movement to cook foods faster and at lower temperatures. The concept has two benefits going for it: fast cooking and the need to save energy. Gas and electric models are available.

### Range/Oven Features

NOT ONLY do styles and types of ranges abound, but the same thing applies to features. Many features add convenience, like lift-up tops to aid cleaning. Others can save energy, like pilotless ignition on gas ranges.

**Broilers.** Most units have the broiler in the oven cavity or under the oven in a separate compartment. Waist-high broilers are at the top of the oven cavity or in their own compartment above the oven. Both types are good; waist-high broilers are a little more convenient because you do not have to stoop down to use them.

**Burners/Elements.** Most electric ranges have two six-inch elements and two eight-inch elements. Gas ranges usually have four surface burners of the same size. They may have standing pilots or pilotless ignition (either glow-type or spark-type). Some models also offer thermostatically controlled or automatic burners, which most people can do without (they are subject to failure and add extra dollars to the unit). Infinite heat controls on electrics are extremely convenient. A fast-heating feature on electric elements is recommended.

**Cooktops.** Removable pans or bowls under burners/elements are a plus when it comes to clean-up. Lift and locking tops also help cleaning chores.

**Oven Cleaning Systems.** Two such systems exist: self-cleaning and continuous-cleaning. Self-cleaning ovens use a pyrolytic, or high heat, system to incinerate oven grime to a powdery ash you can wipe up with a damp cloth. An expensive feature, it actually will remove heavy splatters and baked-on foods. Units with this feature can be identified by a locking handle or latch at the top of the oven door. The cycle begins when the oven door is locked and you push the cleaning button. The temperature will rise 800 to 1000 degrees. When the oven hits about 500 degrees, a second internal lock engages to prevent you from opening the door. The cleaning takes anywhere from two to four hours, depending on the model and brand. When the cycle has been completed, the oven begins to cool. When it cools to about 500 degrees, the safety lock disengages.

If used frequently, this feature can add to your energy costs. However, manufacturers maintain that the heavier insulation used in self-cleaners offsets periodic use because it saves energy.

Continuous-cleaning or catalytic systems are in fact a special porous finish on oven interior liners. The finish tends to absorb and spread oven soils in a way that promotes oxidation at normal oven temperatures. The continuous-clean system will handle small splatters, but large spills should be wiped up. You should not count on this type of oven to thoroughly "clean" itself. Oxidation takes place over a period of time and leads to what is best described as a "presentably clean" oven. If you must clean it, be careful not to use abrasive cleaners that would spoil the special finish.

CONSUMER GUIDE Magazine suggest considering a self-cleaning oven only if such a feature is very important to you and you use your oven a great deal. A continuous-clean oven is recommended if you wish to avoid some oven clean-up.

**Programmed Ovens.** All programmed systems are expensive features; do not bother buying them if you will not use them frequently. The best such system is one that delays the start of cooking to a preset time, cooks for the set period, then drops to a keep-warm temperature until you terminate the cycle. The next best system is the cook-and-hold system. Two other systems are available: delay-and-cook which turns the oven on at a preset time, cooks, then turns the oven off; and a start-and-stop type that turns the oven off at a given period of time after you start it. The latter two systems are both good, but cook-and-hold and delay-cook-and-hold are better.

**Range Hood.** An optional item, a range hood is a recommended product. Two types are available—vented and unvented. Unvented units trap and hold grease and odors; vented types remove them.

**Removable Oven Door.** A lift-off oven door makes cleaning easier on standard oven models.

**Storage.** Sizes of storage and locations differ from unit to unit. If you have special needs, explain these to the dealer when you shop.

**Warming Shelf.** A shelf located above the cooktop to keep foods warm is available; it is not a necessary feature.

**Windows and Oven Lights.** Many models come with oven door windows or black glass doors with windows. A window combined with an interior oven light is recommended because it allows you to check cooking progress without opening the oven door. Opening the door means lost heat and higher energy consumption.

**Other Features.** Clocks, timers, control panel and cooktop lighting are nice features, but they are not necessary to the function of the range. Other nice, but not necessary features you may find include: griddles that plug in or fit over two burners; meat thermometers that automatically signal and turn off the oven when meat is done; rotisseries to turn food during oven cooking.

# 1978 Best Buys: Ranges

CONSUMER GUIDE Magazine has judged electric and gas ranges on the basis of ease and efficiency of operation, special features, safety, performance and price. The following models were found to be superior.

## FREE-STANDING ELECTRIC RANGES

**Frigidaire REG-38**, a 30-inch model with a self-cleaning oven, features a timer, oven light, signal light, digital clock, programmed oven, infinite element controls, black-glass oven door with a window, surface lighting, and a storage drawer. The unit has two six-inch elements and two eight-inch elements. It also has one element with an automatic control, which is not absolutely necessary. The model has a fairly high retail price because of the self-cleaning feature.
**SPECIFICATIONS: Height,** 50''; **Width,** 30''; **Depth,** 29-1/4''; **Warranty,** one year on parts and labor.
**Approximate Retail Price: $609.95**　　　　**Low Price: $531.60**

**General Electric JBP-26V** is another 30-inch unit that has a self-cleaning oven. This model has two six-inch elements and two eight-inch elements that plug in. One element also has an automatic control. Other features include an oven window, oven light, surface light, clock and timer, automatic oven control, and infinite heat element controls. The unit is well priced for the features it carries.
**SPECIFICATIONS: Height,** 44-5/8''; **Width,** 29-7/8''; **Depth,** 26-1/2''; **Warranty,** one year on parts and labor.
**Approximate Retail Price: $529.95**　　　　**Low Price: $410.70**

**Hotpoint RC-548T** is a 40-inch model with a standard oven. The unit has a lift-off oven door with a window. Other features include a cooktop light, dial clock and timer, automatic oven, oven light, and

*Prices are accurate at time of printing; subject to manufacturer's change.*

two six-inch and two eight-inch elements. The unit's big plus (in this big size) is the amount of storage space that it has.
**SPECIFICATIONS: Height,** 45-3/4"; **Width,** 40"; **Depth,** 27-1/2"; **Warranty,** one year on parts and labor.
**Approximate Retail Price: $419.95**　　　　**Low Price: $320.00**

**Kelvinator REC-305M** is a 30-inch electric with a continuous-clean oven. The model has high-speed plug-in elements—two six-inch and two eight-inch ones. It also has chrome drip pans, a lift-off oven door, an oven window, a lift-up cooktop, dial clock and timer, oven light, and a storage drawer. The unit has "toe space" at the bottom as an added convenience.
**SPECIFICATIONS: Height,** 44-3/4"; **Width,** 30"; **Depth,** 26-7/8"; **Warranty,** one year on parts and labor.
**Approximate Retail Price: $349.95**　　　　**Low Price: $324.00**

**Whirlpool RDE-3300** is a 30-inch unit with a continuous-cleaning oven. One of the four infinite heat elements is eight inches, the others are six inches. The model has an oven window, oven light, clock and timer, lift-up cooktop, and a storage drawer. It also has a recessed top to hold spills.
**SPECIFICATIONS: Height,** 44-1/4"; **Width,** 30"; **Depth,** 25"; **Warranty,** one year on parts and labor.
**Approximate Retail Price: $349.95**　　　　**Low Price: $324.00**

**White-Westinghouse KF-332,** a 30-inch model with a continuous-clean oven, features an automatic timing center, a black-glass oven door, oven window, oven light, signal lights, and a storage drawer. This model has one eight-inch and three six-inch elements. The elements have an infinite number of heat settings between low and high and are the plug-in type.
**SPECIFICATIONS: Height,** 45-7/8"; **Width,** 30", **Depth,** 25-13/16"; **Warranty,** one year on parts and labor.
**Approximate Retail Price: Not Available**　　　**Low Price: $336.60**

## FREE-STANDING GAS RANGES

**Caloric RSP-366,** a 30-inch unit with a self-cleaning oven, has pilotless ignition, which saves energy. Features include clock and timer, automatic oven control, oven light, cooktop light, and a lift-up/lock cooktop. The unit does not have pans under the burners.
**SPECIFICATIONS: Height,** 44-3/8"; **Width,** 30"; **Depth,** 26-1/2"; **Warranty,** one year on parts and labor.
**Approximate Retail Price: $649.95**　　　　**Low Price: $565.80**

**Kenmore (Sears) 22 G-72871N** is a 30-inch model with pilotless ignition, which may reduce gas consumption by more than 35 percent. The unit has a continuous-cleaning oven, black-glass

*Prices are accurate at time of printing; subject to manufacturer's change.*

oven door with window, digital clock, timer, lift-off cooktop, fully automatic oven, and panel light. Burner and oven controls are at the front of the unit.
**SPECIFICATIONS: Height,** 47-3/8"; **Width,** 29-15/16"; **Depth,** 28"; **Warranty,** one year on parts and labor.
**Approximate Retail Price: $439.95**      **Low Price: Not Available**

**Magic Chef 336W-6KLPX** is a 30-inch model with continuous-cleaning oven and energy-saving pilotless ignition. This model has a digital clock and timer, tempered-glass backguard with light, a black-glass door with window, oven light, and controls at the front. The unit does not have drip pans, but the burner areas are recessed to hold any spills.
**SPECIFICATIONS: Height,** 46"; **Width,** 30"; **Depth,** 26-5/8"; **Warranty,** one year on parts and labor.
**Approximate Retail Price: Not Available**      **Low Price: $417.00**

**Roper 1636,** a 36-inch gas model with gas-saving pilotless ignition and a continuous-clean oven, has a lift-up/lock cooktop, removable oven door, and patterned black-glass window. Other features include a clock, timer, cooktop light, and large storage compartment.
**SPECIFICATIONS: Height,** 47"; **Width,** 35-15/16"; **Depth,** 27"; **Warranty,** one year on parts and labor.
**Approximate Retail Price: $369.95**      **Low Price: $357.60**

**Tappan 30-3457** is a 30-inch model with pilotless ignition and continuous-cleaning oven interior. It has a roll-out broiler, lift-off oven door, chrome bowls under burners, digital clock, timer, and automatic oven controls. The model also has a lift-and-lock top that is recessed to catch spills. The unit has a black-glass oven door with window. The model is available in five colors, including almond (beige).
**SPECIFICATIONS: Height,** 46-5/8"; **Width,** 30"; **Depth,** 25"; **Warranty,** one year on parts and labor.
**Approximate Retail Price: $499.95**      **Low Price: $451.20**

**Tappan 30-3847** is a 30-inch Convectionaire model. The unit saves energy two ways, through its forced air cooking principle and also with its pilotless ignition. The unit also has a self-cleaning oven. Other features include a clock and timer, lift-and-lock cooktop, chrome burner bowls, waist-high broiling, lift-off door, and a cooktop light. This is Tappan's second convection gas model and it's priced to sell competitively with other models having similar features, but lacking the convection feature.
**SPECIFICATIONS: Height,** 46-5/8"; **Width,** 30"; **Depth,** 25"; **Warranty,** one year on parts and labor.
**Approximate Retail Price: $609.95**      **Low Price: $542.40**

*Prices are accurate at time of printing; subject to manufacturer's change.*

## OVER AND UNDER RANGES

**Caloric EJP-395,** a 30-inch wide, double-decker electric range with continuous-cleaning ovens, has black-glass oven doors, high-speed elements that plug-in, automatic oven controls, digital clock, timer, and an oven light in both ovens. The model also has a surface light, infinite heat controls on elements, and a storage drawer. The unit has two six-inch and two eight-inch elements. An optional hood is available.
**SPECIFICATIONS: Height,** 66''; **Width,** 30''; **Depth,** 25-1/4''; **Warranty,** one year on parts and labor.
**Approximate Retail Price: $549.95**          **Low Price: $478.40**

**Magic Chef 226C-6BKLZ** is an over-and-under double oven gas range with an energy-saving pilotless ignition and two continuous-cleaning ovens. The unit has woodtone glass doors, which make it an attractive unit. Other features include a digital clock, timer, lighted backsplash, oven windows and lights, a removable oven door, a lift-up cooktop, and recessed burner areas.
**SPECIFICATIONS: Height,** 65-5/8''; **Width,** 30''; **Depth,** 26-5/8''; **Warranty,** one year on parts and labor.
**Approximate Retail Price: $699.95**          **Low Price: $468.50**

**Magic Chef 267W-6CLXM4,** an over-and-under electric combination range, has an eye-level microwave oven and lower electric oven with continuous-cleaning interior. Features include digital clock, timer, lift-up and lock cooktop, black-glass oven doors, infinite heat controls on the two six-inch and two eight-inch elements, surface light, and oven light.
**SPECIFICATIONS: Height,** 65-5/8''; **Width,** 30''; **Depth,** 26-5/8''; **Warranty,** one year on parts and labor, with four additional years on the magnetron tube (parts).
**Approximate Retail Price: Not Available**      **Low Price: $844.80**

## COMBINATION RANGES

**Caloric RKP-397** is an over-and-under gas combination range with pilotless ignition and a self-cleaning lower oven. The microwave oven is located at the top at eye-level. The unit has black-glass oven doors, oven lights, a surface light, lift-off lower oven door, an automatic oven control for lower oven, plus a five-minute and 30-minute timer for the microwave oven. The unit is available in standard colors, plus almond (beige).
**SPECIFICATIONS: Height,** 65-3/4''; **Width,** 30''; **Depth,** 26-1/2''; **Warranty,** one year on parts nd labor, plus four additional years on the magnetron tube (parts).
**Approximate Retail Price: $1225.00**        **Low Price: $1028.10**

*Prices are accurate at time of printing; subject to manufacturer's change.*

**Litton 610** is a free-standing, electric combination range with a continuous-cleaning oven. It combines the microwave oven and the conventional oven into one oven. Features include a microwave oven timer, conventional oven timer, black-glass door, clock, infinite heat control on the two six-inch and two eight-inch elements, mini-food shelf, oven light, surface light, and an automatic oven control. The oven can be used as a microwave only, conventional only, or by combining both types of cooking.
**SPECIFICATIONS: Height,** 47-3/4"; **Width,** 29-7/8"; **Depth,** 25-1/4"; **Warranty,** one year on parts and labor, with four additional years on the magnetron tube (parts).
**Approximate Retail Price: $699.00**        **Low Price: $656.00**

**Tappan 77-4966** combines an eye-level microwave oven with a self-cleaning lower electric oven. Both ovens have black-glass doors. The microwave oven has an interior light and a swing-open door. The lower electric oven features a waist-high broiler and a lift-off oven door. The surface elements plug in and are of the infinite heat setting type. There are two six-inch elements and two eight-inch elements. This unit features timers for both ovens plus a digital clock. The model also has a full-width storage drawer at the bottom.
**SPECIFICATIONS: Height,** 66-5/16"; **Width,** 30"; **Depth,** 25"; **Warranty,** one year on parts and labor, with four additional years on the magnetron tube (parts).
**Approximate Retail Price: $1050.00**        **Low Price: $971.40**

## SMOOTHTOP RANGES

**Frigidaire REG-38C** has two six-inch and two eight-inch elements under its smooth ceramic top. This 30-inch, free-standing unit has a self-cleaning oven, automatic oven control, digital clock, console light, oven light, and a black-glass oven door with a window. Its elements are infinitely adjustable. The unit also has a "hot surface" signal light. It comes in standard colors, plus almond and poppy red.
**SPECIFICATIONS: Height,** 50"; **Width,** 30"; **Depth,** 29-1/4"; **Warranty,** one year on parts and labor.
**Approximate Retail Price: $819.95**        **Low Price: $714.00**

**General Electric JBP-87G,** a 30-inch smoothtop, free-stander with a self-cleaning oven, features a black-glass door, infinite element controls, digital clock, timer, automatic oven control, surface and oven cleaning cycle indicator lights, as well as an oven window. Below the one-piece ceramic top are two six-inch elements and two eight-inch elements. The two features, smooth top and self-cleaning oven, make this an expensive unit.

*Prices are accurate at time of printing; subject to manufacturer's change.*

**SPECIFICATIONS: Height,** 47-3/4"; **Width,** 29-7/8"; **Depth,** 25'1/8"; **Warranty,** one year on parts and labor.
**Approximate Retail Price: $789.95**       **Low Price: $692.70**

**Kenmore 22 G-91871N** is an economical 30-inch, free-standing smoothtop. The ceramic cooktop has two six-inch elements and two eight-inch heating elements. This model has an automatic oven control, continuous-cleaning oven interior, oven window and light, panel light, dial clock, timer, and a storage drawer. This model represents an excellent value for its features.
**SPECIFICATIONS: Height,** 44-15/16"; **Width,** 30"; **Depth,** 27-7/16"; **Warranty,** one year on parts and labor.
**Approximate Retail Price: $399.95**     **Low Price: Not Available**

**Whirlpool RDE-395PP** is a 30-inch free stander with a self-cleaning oven. The unit is loaded with features: black-glass oven door with window, oven light, digital clock and timer, surface signal lights, top panel light, removable oven door, removable storage drawer, and infinite heat controls on elements. Under the smooth ceramic surface are two six-inch and two eight-inch elements.
**SPECIFICATIONS: Height,** 46-9/16"; **Width,** 30"; **Depth,** 25"; **Warranty,** one year on parts and labor.
**Approximate Retail Price: $729.95**       **Low Price: $686.40**

## BUILT-IN RANGES

**Caloric RTP-307,** a 30-inch built-in cooktop with pilotless ignition, has tri-set (low, medium, or high) burners that allow positive "click" positions as well as infinite adjustment. The cooktop is hinged for easy cleaning.
**SPECIFICATIONS: Height,** 3"; **Width,** 29-1/2"; **Depth,** 21"; **Warranty,** one year on parts and labor.
**Approximate Retail Price: $169.95**       **Low Price: $141.45**

**Hardwick 7224-800R,** a gas built-in wall oven with pilotless ignition, is an energy-saving economical unit with good features. A companion cooktop, Model 423, also has pilotless ignition and gives you four built-in burners. The cooktop is shallow and has a lift-up feature for cleaning.
**SPECIFICATIONS FOR OVEN: Height,** 44-25/32"; **Width,** 23-5/8"; **Depth,** 23"; **Warranty,** one year on parts and labor.
**Approximate Retail Price: $369.00**     **Low Price: Not Available**

**SPECIFICATIONS FOR COOKTOP: Height,** 2-7/8"; **Width,** 30"; **Depth,** 21-13/16; **Warranty,**
**Approximate Retail Price: $138.00**     **Low Price: Not Available**

*Prices are accurate at time of printing; subject to manufacturer's change.*

**Modern Maid QCO-480** is an electric double oven for wall installation. It has continuous cleaning, lift-off doors, automatic oven controls, and a clock/timer. WET-350 is a companion cooktop with four elements. The cooktop has two six-inch elements and two eight-inch elements with infinite heat controls. It also has a drip-proof outer edge.
**SPECIFICATIONS FOR OVEN: Height,** 45-3/4"; **Width,** 23-3/4"; **Depth,** 22-1/2"; **Warranty,** one year on parts and labor.
**Approximate Retail Price: Not Available    Low Price: $341.40**

**SPECIFICATIONS FOR COOKTOP: Height,** 3"; **Width,** 28-3/4"; **Depth,** 21"; **Warranty,** one year on parts and labor.
**Approximate Retail Price: Not Available    Low Price: $142.85**

**Roper 1087** is a gas double-oven for wall installation. It features pilotless ignition and two continuous-cleaning ovens. The unit has black-glass doors, a broiler in the upper oven, digital clock, automatic upper oven, two oven lights, and a fluorescent light at the top. A companion lift-up cooktop, model 1176, is a four-burner model with chrome spill trays.
**SPECIFICATIONS FOR OVEN: Height,** 50-7/16"; **Width,** 22"; **Depth,** 23-3/4"; **Warranty,** one year on parts and labor.
**Approximate Retail Price: $629.95    Low Price: $573.55**
**SPECIFICATIONS FOR COOKTOP: Height,** 3"; **Width,** 35-1/2"; **Depth,** 20-1/2"; **Warranty,** one year on parts and labor.
**Approximate Retail Price: $149.95    Low Price: $135.55**

**White-Westinghouse KB-451** is a built-in electric double oven. It has black-glass doors, continuous-cleaning in both ovens and many standard features. A companion cooktop, Model KP-830, is a built-in, smoothtop, ceramic cooking surface with infinite heat controls. The control slide knob can be removed for added safety.
**SPECIFICATIONS FOR OVEN: Height,** 48-5/8"; **Width,** 25"; **Depth,** 23"; **Warranty,** one year on parts and labor.
**Approximate Retail Price: Not Available    Low price: $410.16**
**SPECIFICATIONS FOR COOKTOP: Height,** 5-3/8"; **Width,** 34-13/32"; **Depth,** 21-3/8"; **Warranty,** one year on parts and labor.
**Approximate Retail Price: Not Available    Low Price: $380.28**

## DROP-IN RANGES

**Modern Maid ACU-526,** a 30-inch electric model, contains a continuous-cleaning oven. This model has a lift-up top, two six-inch elements and two eight-inch elements, infinite heat controls, a clock, and a timer. The range's edge overlaps the counter to prevent spills from running down the range's sides.
**SPECIFICATIONS: Height,** 40-5/16"; **Width,** 29-7/8"; **Depth,** 25-5/16"; **Warranty,** one year on parts and labor.
**Approximate Retail Price: Not Available    Low Price: $335.80**
*Prices are accurate at time of printing; subject to manufacturer's change.*

**Roper 1546** is a 30-inch gas model with a continuous-cleaning oven. It also features a lift-up chrome cooktop, automatic oven controls, timer, clock, oven light, and a black-glass oven door.
**SPECIFICATIONS: Height,** 28"; **Width,** 29-1/4"; **Depth,** 23-1/8"; **Warranty,** one year on parts and labor.
**Approximate Retail Price: $459.95**          **Low Price: $433.50**

## SLIDE-IN RANGES

**Roper 1426,** a 30-inch gas model, has a continuous-cleaning oven. This model includes a lift-up-and-lock cooktop, roll-out broiler, black-glass oven window, oven light, and full-width oven door handles.
**SPECIFICATIONS: Height,** 40-1/8"; **Width,** 29-7/8"; **Depth,** 27-3/4"; **Warranty,** one year on parts and labor.
**Approximate Retail Price: $274.95**          **Low Price: $264.30**

**White-Westinghouse KS-735** is a 30-inch electric model with a self-cleaning oven. It has one eight-inch and three six-inch elements, a black-glass window, automatic oven control, and controls on one side.
**SPECIFICATIONS: Height,** 35-1/4"; **Width,** 30-1/8"; **Depth,** 25"; **Warranty,** one year on parts and labor.
**Approximate Retail Price: Not Available**          **Low Price: $533.16**
*Prices are accurate at time of printing; subject to manufacturer's change.*

# 1978 Microwave Ovens

UNTIL FAIRLY recently, microwave ovens were used primarily in commercial establishments. The first microwave oven was developed in 1945, but it was not until the introduction of counter-top models for the home in 1967 that these appliances became really popular. Microwave ovens now outsell conventional gas and electric ranges, and the industry estimates that 50 percent of American homes will contain a microwave oven by 1985.

**How Microwaves Work**

THE MICROWAVE oven converts electric power to microwaves. This is done by a magnetron inside the oven. This magnetron consists of two basic elements—a cathode which emits electrons and an anode which collects them. Together they form an electron tube that creates a magnetic field.

The microwaves from the magnetron are transmitted through a wave guide to a feedbox. A wave stirrer helps scatter the microwaves around the oven cavity to produce an even heating pattern. When these waves enter food, the liquid molecules within the food begin to vibrate at a terrific rate. The friction created by this rapid vibration produces heat (much like the heat you can produce by rubbing your hands together quickly). This heat is conducted through the food, cooking it from the outside in. This method of cooking offers several distinct advantages.

### Energy Conservation

MICROWAVE OVENS are energy-efficient because cooking is so much faster than conventional cooking. All the energy produced is absorbed by the food rather than being partially dissipated into the air. This has the added advantage of keeping the kitchen cool, an attractive feature during the summer months when conventional ovens emit an uncomfortable amount of heat. Since conventional ovens raise the temperature of room air, they often waste energy indirectly, as well as directly, by making an air conditioner work overtime.

### Speed and Convenience

BECAUSE MICROWAVE ovens defrost and cook so quickly, they are tremendous time-savers for the busy cook. Although a few foods, such as noodles and other forms of pasta, take almost as much time as they would on a conventional stove, most foods require only one fourth to one half as much cooking time in the microwave oven.

One of the most attractive features of microwave cooking is its great convenience. The microwave oven lets you cook right in the serving dish or on dinner plates. This eliminates most dirty pots and pans. Microwave cooking is clean cooking, because oven walls do not heat up. Spills and spatters can be wiped up with a damp cloth. The baked-on spills so common in conventional ovens simply do not happen.

Since foods reheat so rapidly in a microwave oven, leftovers taste fresh. In addition, the busy cook can prepare time-consuming meals in advance, reheating them just before serving.

### Disadvantages

MICROWAVE COOKING, despite all it has to offer, does have some drawbacks. Perhaps the most important of these is the "multiplier effect." One strip of bacon, for example, is usually ready in about one minute, while four strips require four minutes or more of cooking time. Large amounts of food will probably need almost as much cooking time in a microwave oven as they do in a conventional oven.

Other disadvantages often mentioned by consumers are unsatisfactory texture and browning and the fact that some foods, such as eggs in the shell and popovers, are better prepared in a conventional oven. Unsatisfactory texture is usually the result of overcooking, and experience with the oven will solve this problem easily. You can compensate for the lack of browning by using sauces or by placing the food in the broiler of your conventional oven for a few minutes. Some manufacturers have tried to overcome this problem by including built-in browning elements in their units. Others offer optional browning trays.

## Safety

ANY NEW technological development raises safety questions. Microwave manufacturers claim that their ovens are the safest of all home appliances. Although some researchers feel that the long-range, cumulative effect of microwaves are still unknown, no safety hazards have been documented, and the federal government regards the ovens as safe. The only reported case of injury was that of a man who attempted to tamper with the built-in safety mechanisms in his unit.

The most important of these safety features is the door seal, the mechanism that defends against microwave leakage. The doors and their seals are required to meet strict Federal standards. In addition, all ovens must shut off automatically when the oven doors are opened, making it impossible for microwaves to pour out into the room.

Some consumers have worried about the presence of microwaves in the cooked food, but this fear is groundless. Microwaves are not a substance which remains inside the food, but a form of energy which ceases to exist as soon as the power is turned off. When you switch off an electric light, for example, the light rays immediately disappear. Microwaves work the same way.

As long as the user follows the directions supplied by the manufacturer, microwave ovens are considered safe.

## The Owner's Manual

EVERY MICROWAVE oven is accompanied by an owner's manual containing instructions for installation and use. Since microwave ovens vary from model to model, it is essential that you read through the manual for your particular model with great care.

Make sure your oven is properly grounded and that the power source matches the oven's requirements. The three-pronged plug is an excellent safety feature that grounds the power effectively. If you do not have a three-hole outlet, some rewiring may be needed.

## Safety Precautions

A FEW SIMPLE precautions will keep your oven in good repair and prevent accidental damage.

1. Never tamper with the wiring or door seal of your oven. All repairs should be made by qualified servicemen who have received special training. Your owner's manual will tell you where to find authorized service centers.

2. Never place metal objects inside the oven unless your manual specifically states that small amounts of metal (such as skewers or pieces of aluminum foil) may be used. Metal conducts electricity and may result in arcing of the current.

3. If your oven door opens from the top, never set dishes or

utensils down on the open door. This could damage the protective seal.

4. Always keep a glass of water inside the oven when it is not in use. If the oven is accidentally turned on while empty, the microwaves may damage the magnetron. The glass of water will prevent this because the water will absorb the energy.

## Microwave Features

ALMOST ANY model now on the market is adequate for small tasks such as heating water, melting butter and quick-cooking small amounts of food. If you plan to take real advantage of the possibilities of microwave cooking, however, you must consider several factors before deciding which model best suits your needs. There are a number of special features available—for a price. Some are important to the serious microwave cook and others are optionals that you may not consider worth the extra money.

**Wattage.** Although the power outputs of the different models vary between 400 and 1000 watts, most ovens designed for home use are in the 600- to 675-watt range. Wattage determines how fast the oven cooks. The low-power models cook just as well, but they do take a bit longer. Even the higher-wattage ovens may need more time if you cook during peak power consumption periods because the heavy power demand will prevent the oven from working at full capacity. Cooking times will need to be adjusted to the oven's output.

**Controls.** When you select a microwave oven, you can choose among a wide variety of control systems. They range from push-button simplicity to electronic programming.

The bottom-of-the-line models usually cook on full power only. Slightly more expensive models have a separate defrost dial. These models are certainly the easiest to use because the cook has little to do except set the cooking time. The middle-range ovens have dial or lever settings that provide more flexibility. The sophisticated touchpad models allow the cook the greatest variety of programs. More types of programming mean greater control over different types of cooking. Ovens with a "memory" feature permit two or more stages of programming for convenience. Although these controls can be somewhat bewildering at first, a little practice and experimentation will teach you how to use them successfully.

**Settings.** The most inexpensive models have only one, full-power setting. Better models add a defrost or partial-power setting. The advanced microwave ovens offer up to ten different settings.

If you plan to use your oven only for simple tasks such as reheating, a one-setting model may satisfy your needs. CONSUMER GUIDE Magazine recommends, however, that you purchase a model with at least a second, partial-power (defrost) setting. In order to use microwave cooking efficiently, you need this second setting. It enables you to defrost and to cook more delicate foods with good results. The variable cooking models, as the multisetting ovens are called, do offer more flexibility. Even the cheapest models are not cheap, of course.

Different settings turn the power on and off at different intervals. Whenever the power is on, it works at full strength. The various settings simply determine the percentage of time the oven is actually working during the cooking cycle. If you have a one-speed oven, you can cycle it yourself by cooking in short bursts, manually turning it off and on. A partial-power setting switches the oven on and off automatically which means you will not have to manually stop and start the oven every few seconds. During the "off" periods, the food continues to cook by conduction.

Unfortunately, many settings have vague names such as "Roast" or "Simmer." Percentage designations would be far more helpful. The ten-speed ovens are easy to figure out because each setting is ten percent higher than the preceding one, but other models are not so simple. The problem is complicated by a lack of standardization from brand to brand. Some manufacturers have adopted setting names similar to those on electric ranges, while others have settled on arbitrary designations. The same setting name may mean different things on different models. "Defrost," for example, may indicate 50 percent power on one oven and 33 percent power on another. This makes it difficult to use recipes intended for one model in another oven.

**Timers.** Since microwave cooking instructions, for the most part, are based on time rather than on temperature, the built-in timer is an important element of oven efficiency. The time computed is based on the temperature needs of food to be cooked.

The more inexpensive ovens have dial settings for minutes and seconds. Before buying, check to see how fine the time divisions are. The more accurately you can set the time, the more successful you will be. At least the first three or four minutes should be divided into 15-second intervals. You should be able to set the minute timer for at least 30 minutes. Some of the shorter timers require resetting for most recipes, a nuisance to avoid whenever possible.

The computerized timers found in higher-priced models can be set for longer periods (usually more than 90 minutes) and are much more precise. The digital-control ovens also have "countdown" clocks that show the exact amount of cooking time left. These usually double as regular clocks, showing the time of day when the oven is not in use.

**External Features.** The outer appearance of the oven is a minor factor because there is so little variation in styling among the different models. A few are covered in leatherette or chrome, but most have a wood-grain finish rather like that on a portable television set which is easy to maintain and will not show scratches. The majority have doors that are hinged at the side, but some drop forward. This may make a difference if positioning the model in your kitchen presents difficulties.

**Oven Window.** A more important consideration is the oven window. The window is made up of a piece of metal placed between sheets of clear glass. The metal is punctured so that you can see through it, but the holes are too small for microwaves to pass through. Since the "look" of food is one way of judging doneness in microwave cooking, good visibility is a great advantage. Generally, the inside of the window is covered with a sheet of clear plastic to protect the screening from becoming soiled and should not be removed.

There are a number of factors to consider when evaluating the oven interior. What happens inside the oven is, after all, your main reason for buying one. Although all microwave appliances work on the same general principle, modifications and special features distinguish one model from another.

**Oven Size.** The actual size of the oven cavity varies substantially. One interior may be twice the size of another even though the exterior dimensions are very similar. The smaller ovens are adequate for single- or two-serving meals, but a larger family may need an oven with a greater capacity. As a rule of thumb, any oven that holds a 13 x 9 x 2-inch baking dish is probably large enough for most families.

**Oven Finish.** There is some debate over the merits of acrylic versus stainless steel finishes. Those who favor the acrylic coating say that this surface provides more even heating and is easier to clean. The advocates of stainless steel, on the other hand, maintain that the stainless finish is less likely to become scratched. Both sides make some good points, but CONSUMER GUIDE Magazine prefers the matte-finish acrylic surface because it is easier to keep clean.

**Shelves.** Some of the microwave ovens have built-in shelves and others have removable ones. If the shelf is made of glass, the removable type is the better bet. If a built-in glass shelf is broken, the entire oven must be returned to the manufacturer for replacement. CONSUMER GUIDE Magazine recommends built-in ceramic shelves, which are the least likely to be damaged and the easiest to keep clean.

**Turntables.** Because there are "hot spots" inside the oven —areas in which cooking takes place faster—most recipes call for rotating the food at intervals. Rotation equalizes exposure to the microwaves and ensures even cooking. Some ovens contain a turntable that automatically rotates the food for you. Turntables were developed before stirrer fans, which distribute microwaves more evenly. Turntables tend to have a cold spot in the center and limit the size of utensils you can use. Turntables can be difficult to clean.

**Browning Elements.** Many manufacturers now include built-in browning elements in their units and others offer optional browning trays. These are intended to overcome the lack of visual appeal sometimes found in microwave-cooked foods. The browning element is really a broiler that begins to operate when the regular cooking cycle ends. Since most kitchens already possess a more effective and energy efficient broiler in the conventional stove, this seems to be an unnecessary feature. In addition, the browning element consumes much of the power saved by using the microwave oven and eliminates the easy cleaning that is such an advantage.

**Temperature Probe.** Some ovens come with a temperature probe attached through the oven wall. This sensor works in the same way as a meat thermometer. It is inserted into the food before cooking and the oven is set for a specific temperature (usually about 20 degrees cooler than the desired finished temperature since food continues to cook by conduction after leaving the oven). In most ovens, when the predetermined temperature is reached on the probe, the oven shuts off automatically. The probe is useful for large cuts of meat and dense, solid foods, but is not so helpful in preparing liquid or soft foods.

---

## SPECIAL INFORMATION SERVICE

**A Bonus for Readers of this CONSUMER GUIDE®**

CONSUMER GUIDE® offers a special bonus to its readers who are interested in obtaining information as to where they can find the low prices on specific products listed in this guide. Simply fill out the form and mail. Include 25 cents for postage and handling.

**Please send me information on:**

Product _____ Model Number _____

Manufacturer _____

Product _____ Model Number _____

Manufacturer _____

Product _____ Model Number _____

Manufacturer _____

Product _____ Model Number _____

Manufacturer _____

**CONSUMER GUIDE Magazine**
**3841 West Oakton, Skokie, Illinois 60076**

# 1978 Best Buys: Microwave Ovens

CONSUMER GUIDE Magazine evaluated the leading microwave oven models on the basis of ease of operation, sturdiness of construction, efficiency, performance, reliability, special-features and price. The following models were selected by our staff of experts as offering the greatest value.

**Kenmore (Sears) 22G 99872N** features variable cooking and a temperature probe. There are ten power settings that show the percentage of full power being used. The temperature probe, which can be used in a variety of ways, is a helpful tool, particularly when preparing roasts. Clear instructions accompany the oven. The oven finish is acrylic and there is a nonremovable glass shelf. Door visibility is good.

This oven is manufactured by Litton. Although its power is reported as "slightly less" than the models bearing the Litton name, it can be expected to deliver the quality associated with Litton.

**Approximate Retail Price: $419.95****Low Price: Not Available**

**Magic Chef MW3172-6P** is a space-age appliance that offers electronic touchpad operation, variable cooking and a three-stage memory programming system. While this sounds overwhelming to the cook who is not technologically inclined, the owner's manual contains numerous illustrations that show exactly how to run the machine. The power settings progress in increments of 10 percent of full power, a good system that enables the cook to know precisely how much power is being used at each setting and one that offers great flexibility. The three-stage memory permits the cook to program delayed starting and automatic shut-off. The oven finish is acrylic and door visibility is excellent. A good cookbook accompanies the Magic Chef models.

**Approximate Retail Price: Not Available****Low Price: $475.20**

*Prices are accurate at time of printing; subject to manufacturer's change.*

## ALSO RECOMMENDED

**Litton 460** features a touchpad-operated electronic display. The variable cooking settings are divided into ten, permitting the cook to know the exact percentage of full power being used. The memory element allows programmed two-stage cooking without resetting. The timer goes up to 99.99 and functions on the countdown principle. The oven finish is acrylic and door visibility is excellent. An unobtrusive buzzer sounds twice to signal the end of cooking. The accompanying cookbook is excellent. Although this computer-age appliance seems complicated to operate at first, the clear instructions provided and the elegant design of the model ensure that a little practice will make perfect.
**Approximate Retail Price: $569.00**            **Low Price: $455.95**

**Panasonic NE 7800**, a 700-watt oven with variable cooking power, is Panasonic's top-of-the-line model. A 60-minute timer controls the settings. One unusual setting is the "flash defrost" which offers extra-quick defrosting of small frozen items. The oven includes a temperature probe that automatically ends cooking when a preset temperature is reached. The oven interior is acrylic and has a removable glass shelf. Visibility is very good since the screen over the door has an extremely fine mesh. A gentle bell signals the end of cooking. The recipe book that accompanies the oven is sketchy but adequate. The oven did an excellent job on most foods, including custards and other egg recipes, but the souffle recipe found in the cookbook produced unsatisfactory results. Unfortunately, the dials that control the time setting were hard to use. Nevertheless, the standard boiling water test did show that this model was faster than most.
**Approximate Retail Price: $499.95**        **Low Price: Not Available**

**Whirlpool REM7600** has unusually named power settings (high, medium high, medium, medium low, and low) based on those of electric ranges. Whirlpool felt that these terms would be more familiar to the cook. A special knob sets seconds in five-second increments, permitting more accurate timing than is possible on many models. Another feature is a temperature probe that is helpful for large, uniformly shaped pieces of food. The probe automatically cuts down power as food reaches the predetermined temperature setting. While the oven window is easy to see through, it tended to fog. The only major negative factor is the door handle, which can be twisted off. The large accompanying cookbook, prepared by *Better Homes and Gardens,* has many good recipes.
**Approximate Retail Price: $469.95**        **Low Price: Not Available**
*Prices are accurate at time of printing; subject to manufacturer's change.*

# 1978 Air Conditioners

YOU CAN find room air conditioners on the market today that will cool anything from a small room to nearly an entire house. In other words, the consumer has a great deal of choice in the size and type of units available. And today's room units do a great deal more than simply cool the air—i.e., they circulate it; they can clean it and remove odors; and they remove moisture to provide true comfort in hot humid weather.

Once considered a luxury, the air conditioner is now in widespread use. Air conditioning in businesses, restaurants, and other commercial establishments has led more and more individuals to put such comfort units into their homes. Surprisingly, room air conditioners today sell at lower prices than their predecessors did. Twenty-five years ago, a typical room air conditioner cost $335. Today, a typical unit costs about $250. Of course, prices vary according to capacity, features, and efficiency. Very small units start at about $125 and go up to about $500 for big-capacity models.

One of the most important factors to consider when buying a room air conditioner is the unit's capacity. Once you decide what room (or rooms) you wish to cool, then you need to determine the correct size air conditioner for that job. The proper size unit will cool and dehumidify the area adequately. Too small a unit will not cool sufficiently, while too large a unit will not dehumidify properly—cycling on and off too frequently—leaving you with a cool but clammy and uncomfortable room.

**Room Air Conditioner Worksheet**

CONSUMER GUIDE Magazine has included a step-by-step Room Air Conditioner Worksheet with this report to aid you in determining the proper capacity of the unit you need. Complete the worksheet prior to shopping, and then if you have any doubts about capacity, you can discuss your needs with the dealer.

I. Estimate the cooling capacity you will need.
1. Determine the floor area of the room to be cooled (multiplying length by width):
   \_\_\_\_ Feet long X \_\_\_\_ feet wide = _____ square feet
2. Find the corresponding square footage on the left side of the Cooling Load Chart. Move horizontally to the right until you intersect the center of Band A, B, or C, depending on what kind of space is above the room (circle appropriate one):
   Band A—Occupied room above room to be cooled.
   Band B—Insulated ceiling and unoccupied attic above room to be cooled.
   Band C—Uninsulated ceiling and unoccupied attic above room to be cooled.
3. Within the band, move to the left for a northern or shady exposure, or to the right for a sunny exposure (check one):
   \_\_\_\_ Left for northern or shady exposure.
   \_\_\_\_ Right for sunny exposure.

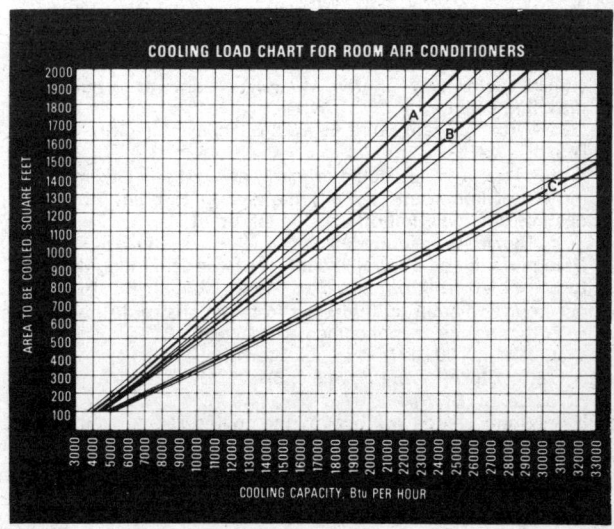

Step 2 and 3

CONSUMER GUIDE 349

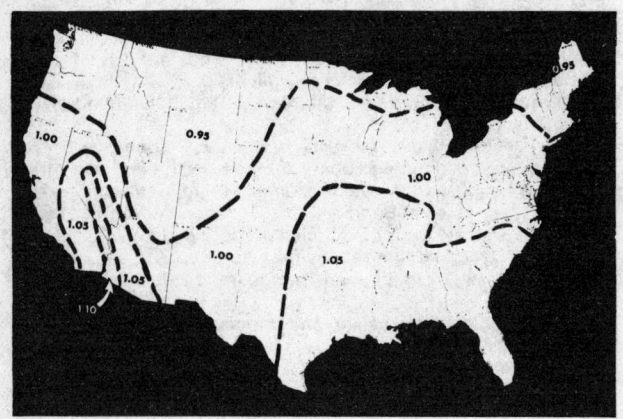

Step 5

4. From this point, move straight down to the bottom of the chart to determine the unadjusted cooling capacity in Btu per hour: Unadjusted cooling capacity from chart: _____ Btu/hr.
5. Find your geographical area on the map which shows the climate factor for your area. Multiply the answer to point 4 by the climate factor:
_____ Btu/hr. (from point 4) X _____ (climate factor) = _____ Btu/hr.
6. If the room is to be cooled primarily at night and daytime cooling is not important, multiply the answer to point 5 by 0.7. If daytime cooling is important, skip this point.
_____ Btu/hr. (from point 5) X 0.7 = _____ Btu/hr.
7. Determine the number of linear feet of wall separating the room to be cooled from other cooled rooms. Multiply this by 30 Btu per hour and subtract the result from the answer to point 5 or 6. If other rooms are not cooled, skip this point.
a. _____ feet X 30 Btu/hr. = _____ Btu/hr.
b. _____ Btu/hr. (from point 5 or 6) - _____ Btu/hr. (from a) = _____ Btu/hr.
8. If only one person will occupy the cooled room, subtract 600 Btu per hour from the answer to point 7, 6 or 5. If three or more people will occupy the room, add 600 Btu per hour for each person over two:
a. One person: _____ Btu/hr. (from point 7, 6 or 5) -600 Btu/hr. = _____ Btu/hr.
b. Two people: _____ Btu/hr. (from point 7, 6 or 5)

c. Three or more people: _____ Btu/hr. (from point 7, 6 or 5)
± _____ Btu/hr. (600 for each person over two) = _____ Btu/hr.
9. Add 4000 Btu per hour to the answer from point 8 if the area to be cooled includes a kitchen. If it does not, point 8 is your final answer:
_____ Btu/hr. (from point 8) + 4000 Btu/hr. (if area includes a kitchen) = _____ Btu/hr.

The answer to point 8 or point 9 is the approximate cooling capacity you will need. Enter that figure below:
_____ Btu/hr. = Estimated Cooling Capacity.

II. Type of installation (check appropriate one):
_____ Double-hung window
_____ Casement window
_____ Sliding window
_____ Through-the-wall space

III. Dimensions of window or space:
_____ inches high by _____ inches wide

IV. Type of circuit available (check appropriate one):
_____ 115-volt, 15-amp branch circuit (might have other electrical product on this circuit).
_____ 115-volt, 15-amp isolated circuit (nothing else on circuit).
_____ Other. Fill in: _____ -volt, _____ -amp.

## The Energy Question

A FEW STATES and cities have already set energy standards for room air conditioners, and the federal government is in the process of doing the same on a national basis. Currently, the industry is working toward 1980 target goals that seek to improve energy efficiency by 30 percent, but a bill pending in Congress would change this approach. President Carter's National Energy Policy legislation contains a provision that would replace target goals with minimum energy efficiency standards. This provision—which would set standards for other major appliances as well as room air conditioners—has been approved by the House-Senate conference committee trying to work out differences between a House-passed and Senate-passed version of the energy legislation. As this report was being compiled, Washington experts were expecting the legislation to pass "within a few weeks."

The changes that room air conditioner manufacturers are making to improve energy efficiency include more efficient motors, improved designs, and cycling the fan with the compressor (already present on many models). The challenge of improving air conditioner efficiency is more of an economic one than a technological one. High-efficiency units involve more materials, and thus cost more than low-efficiency models. In fact, the cost of high-efficiency units is often substantially higher than the prices for low-efficiency units.

Nevertheless, CONSUMER GUIDE Magazine recommends the purchase of high-efficiency units. Lower energy bills compensate for the additional cost of high-efficiency room air conditioners. People who run their air conditioners a good many hours during the cooling season (say, more than 500 hours) could wind up saving a substantial amount of money with a high-efficiency unit.

You will find a growing number of high-efficiency models from which to choose. Since increased efficiency requires larger coil surfaces, however, your choice of the small and highly portable units may be somewhat limited—especially in terms of units for special types of window installation.

To understand how high-efficiency units can help hold the line on energy bills, consider two hypothetical room air conditioners —one a moderately efficient unit with an EER (Energy Efficiency Ratio) of 7.5, the other an extremely efficient unit with an EER of 11.6

If you live in an area of the country where you would operate the unit 400 hours a season (Chicago would be a good example), the unit with the higher EER would save you almost $8 a year on the basis of electricity costing 4¢ per kilowatt-hour. On the same cost basis, your savings would be about $19 if you ran the unit 1000 hours a season (a good estimate for St. Louis). It is important to note, moreover, that power costs are higher than 4¢ per kilowatt-hour in many parts of the country. In the East power rates have hit 8¢ or more per kWh, and obviously as electricity costs rise so do the savings associated with the high-efficiency room air conditioners.

CONSUMER GUIDE Magazine has used the EER measurement as a prime criterion in rating the various room air conditioning units currently available. All "Best Buy" selections belong in the high-efficiency category—i.e., possessing EERs above 7.5.

**Other Factors To Consider**

MOST ROOM air conditioners carry a full one-year warranty that covers both labor and parts. In addition, most manufacturers also provide an additional four years of warranty coverage on the compressor system.

Many room air conditioners need only to be plugged directly into a normal grounded household outlet—one not heavily loaded with other electrical appliances. These are the units that draw 7.5 amps and operate on 115 volts. Units that operate on 115 volts but draw 12 amps should be plugged into their own outlet on which no other electrical devices draw. The large-capacity models generally require special circuits of 208/230 volts.

Different types and styles of air conditioner units are available to meet individual installation needs. The most common types fit double-hung windows, but there are models for sliding windows, casement windows, or through-the-wall mounting.

**Feature Checklist**

TO SIMPLIFY your purchasing decision, CONSUMER GUIDE Magazine has prepared the following list of important features.

**Air Movement.** Louvers and vents that can adjust air movement in different directions are important; the most convenient types are generally those that are fully adjustable. Motor-driven louvers or vents that consume additional electricity cannot be recommended on a cost-savings basis.

**Fan Speeds.** Inexpensive models usually have a one-speed fan. Better models may have two or more speeds—a high speed for fast cooling and a low one to maintain cooling at a relatively quiet level. Deluxe models sometimes offer solid-state infinite speed control, which allows you to dial a complete range of speeds. Many models now include a setting so that the fan cycles on and off with the compressor. Previously, the fan ran continuously, circulating the air at all times. The cycling feature represents one of the approaches being taken to improve air conditioner energy efficiency.

**Filters.** All room air conditioners possess some type of filter to clean the air. All types of filters require periodic cleaning or replacement. Therefore, the most important consideration in regard to the filter is the ease with which you can reach and clean it.

**Noise.** Noise is a difficult factor to judge in the showroom, although an actual demonstration of the unit you intend to buy is helpful. Air conditioners sound different in different environments. For example, the same unit may sound louder in a kitchen where hard surfaces tend to reflect noise than in a carpeted bedroom. Look for and ask about construction methods—isolation of noise-making components, noise-absorbing rubber bushings, and other forms of sound insulation—used to make the unit quieter.

**Styling.** Most units come with one form or another of simulated woodgrain fronts, although other finishes also are available. Air conditioners with hidden controls (i.e., controls behind an access panel) are not only pleasing to look at, but also tend to prevent small children from playing with the unit.

**Thermostatic Controls.** Usually, this control takes the form of a dial with numbered settings, frequently from one to ten. The compressor turns on and off in relation to the thermostat setting. Some models also provide a fan-only setting that allows the fan to circulate air in a room without activating the compressor.

**Ventilation.** An exhaust setting, which vents air to the outside, is helpful in removing odors or smoke. A fresh-air setting, which brings in a small amount of fresh air as it cools the existing room air, is helpful in preventing staleness or mustiness. A fresh-air setting combined with the fan-only feature allows you to circulate outside air on days when air movement by itself is sufficient to make the room comfortable. Many room air conditioners offer both an exhaust and a fresh-air setting.

# 1978 Best Buys Air Conditioners

CONSUMER GUIDE Magazine has examined room air conditioners from all the principal manufacturers. Such elements as frequency of repair histories, design, and general features were weighed carefully.

In selecting the recommended models, energy efficiency was given serious consideration. The models we chose are the ones that we believe offer the best balance of efficiency, features, reliability, and a history of good, overall performance. While efficiency was the major factor, there were other criteria, including the total value-for-price per unit.

## 5000 BTU/HR. TO 6000 BTU/HR.

**Fedders ALRO5F2HB** is a 5000-Btu/hr. portable model with an Energy Efficiency Ratio (EER) of 8.8, among the highest available in a small air conditioner. The unit allows variable airflow left and right; has a simulated woodgrain front, hidden controls, and three cooling speeds; and also has pull-out side panels that make for easy installation.
**SPECIFICATIONS: Height,** 12-1/2''; **Width,** 20''; **Depth,** 19-9/32''; **Weight,** 73 lbs.; **Maximum Window Width,** 39''; **Watts,** 570; **Volts,** 115; **Amps,** 5.0; **Moisture Removal Rate** (pints per hour), 1.2; **Fan Speeds,** 3; **Air Delivery** (cubic feet per minute), Not Available; **Warranty,** one year on parts and labor, additional four years on the compressor system (parts and labor).
**Approximate Retail Price: $259.95**          **Low Price: $215.75**

**Kenmore (Sears) 770590** is a 5000-Btu/hr. model with an EER of 8.0 designed for double-hung window installation. Though not as quiet as other models in its high-speed fan position, it does have an automatic setting that allows the fan to cycle with the compressor to save energy. It also has hidden controls and good air directional control.

*Prices are accurate at time of printing; subject to manufacturer's change.*

**SPECIFICATIONS: Height,** 14-1/2''; **Width,** 20-1/2''; **Depth,** 13-7/8''; **Weight,** 55 lbs.; **Maximum Window Width,** 36''; **Watts,** 625; **Volts,** 110-120; **Amps,** 6.0; **Moisture Removal Rate** (pints per hour), 1.4; **Fan Speeds,** 2; **Air Delivery** (cubic feet per minute), Not Available; **Warranty,** one year on parts and labor, additional four years on the compressor system (parts and labor), ten years on the outdoor portion of the case (parts).
**Approximate Retail Price: $229.95**     **Low Price: Not Available**

**White-Westinghouse AC057T8D** is another 5000-Btu/hr. unit for double-hung window installation. This model has an EER of 8.0 and draws 5.5 amps. It has a three-speed fan, an 11-position thermostat, and a vent but no fan-only setting. It allows the fan to cycle on and off with the compressor via a special setting and it has hidden controls.
**SPECIFICATIONS: Height,** 12-7/16''; **Width,** 19-1/4''; **Depth,** 17-1/4''; **Weight,** 69 lbs.; **Maximum Window Width,** Not Available; **Watts,** 625; **Volts,** 115; **Amps,** 5.5; **Moisture Removal Rate** (pints per hour), 1.6; **Fan Speeds,** 3; **Air Delivery** (cubic feet per minute), 150; **Warranty,** one year on parts and labor, additional four years on the compressor system (parts and labor).
**Approximate Retail Price: Not Available**     **Low Price: $204.60**

**Friedrich SP05D10** is a 5200-Btu/hr. model with a very high EER of 9.1. It has a setting to allow the fan and compressor to cycle on and off together, a two-speed fan, a fan-only setting, an air exhaust control, six-way airflow control, and a slide-out chassis. The unit is quiet compared to many other models.
**SPECIFICATIONS: Height,** 13-13/16''; **Width,** 25''; **Depth,** 26''; **Weight,** Not Available; **Maximum Window Width,** 42''; **Watts,** 570; **Volts,** 115; **Amps,** 5.0; **Moisture Removal Rate** (pints per hour), 1.0; **Fan Speeds,** 2; **Air Delivery** (cubic feet per minute), Not Available; **Warranty,** one year on parts and labor, additional four years on the compressor system (parts and labor).
**Approximate Retail Price: $289.95**     **Low Price: Not Available**

**General Electric AGJE906LB** is a 6000-Btu/hr. model with an EER of 8.8. The ten-position thermostat and three fan-speed operation, including three fan-only speeds, make for a versatile unit. It has a power saver that cycles the fan off and on with the compressor and an air exchange feature, but it does not have hidden controls. The distribution control is good. With a kit, the unit can be installed through the wall.
**SPECIFICATIONS: Height,** 15-5/8''; **Width,** 26''; **Depth,** 19-1/4''; **Weight,** 97 lbs.; **Maximum Window Width,** 42''; **Watts,** 680; **Volts,** 115; **Amps,** 6.0; **Moisture Removal Rate** (pints per hour), 1.3; **Fan Speeds,** 3; **Air Delivery** (cubic feet per minute), 260; **Warranty,** one year on parts and labor, additional four years on the compressor system (parts and labor).
**Approximate Retail Price: $339.95**     **Low Price: $289.50**

*Prices are accurate at time of printing; subject to manufacturer's change.*

**Gibson ASO6B6SEB** is a 6000-Btu/hr. model designed to fit sliding and casement windows. It has a rather low EER of 7.1, but high efficiency is hard to find in this type of unit. It features Gibson's powered air sweep, which distributes air well but requires energy to do so. Louvers at the top allow for up and down air control. It has an exhaust control, a humidity control, three fan speeds, but does not have hidden controls.
**SPECIFICATIONS: Height,** 20-17/32"; **Width,** 14-1/2"; **Depth,** 25-1/16"; **Weight,** 105 lbs.; **Maximum Window Width,** 41-3/8"; **Watts,** 850; **Volts,** 115; **Amps,** 7.5; **Moisture Removal Rate** (pints per hour), 2.3; **Fan Speeds,** 3; **Air Delivery** (cubic feet per minute), 210; **Warranty,** one year on parts and labor, additional four years on the compressor system (parts).
**Approximate Retail Price: Not Available**      **Low Price: $276.00**

## 7000 BTU/HR. TO 9000 BTU/HR.

**Carrier 51EHOO71B** is a 7000-Btu/hr. unit designed for installation in double-hung windows. Its EER is 8.1. Air direction control is fair; one cannot direct the air up and down. It has two fan speeds, an exhaust system to remove odors and smoke, and an adjustable thermostat, but it does not have hidden controls.
**SPECIFICATIONS: Height,** 15-5/8"; **Width,** 23-1/2"; **Depth,** 22-1/4"; **Weight,** 105 lbs.; **Maximum Window Width,** Not Available; **Watts,** 860; **Volts,** 115; **Amps,** 7.5; **Moisture Removal Rate** (pints per hour), 1.2; **Fan Speeds,** 2; **Air Delivery** (cubic feet per minute), 260; **Warranty,** one year on parts and labor, additional four years on the compressor system (parts).
**Approximate Retail Price: Not Available**      **Low Price: $264.00**

**Friedrich SSO7D10** is another 7000-Btu/hr. unit for installation in double-hung windows. With an impressive EER of 10.7, it ranks among the most efficient units available. It has a five-speed blower/fan, fresh air intake and exhaust, a fan-only setting, excellent air direction control, and a setting to cycle the fan and compressor on and off together. Moisture removal, because of the high efficiency, leaves a little to be desired.
**SPECIFICATIONS: Height,** 15-11/16"; **Width,** 25-15/16"; **Depth,** 26-1/2"; **Weight,** 153 lbs.; **Maximum Window Width,** 42"; **Watts,** 655; **Volts,** 115; **Amps,** 6.0; **Moisture Removal Rate** (pints per hour), 0.6; **Fan Speeds,** 5; **Air Delivery** (cubic feet per minute), Not Available; **Warranty,** one year on parts and labor, additional four years on the compressor system (parts and labor).
**Approximate Retail Price: $369.95**      **Low Price: Not Available**

**Frigidaire A8-LE-HE** is a 7500-Btu/hr. unit with an EER of 8.7 and with a control that turns the fan off with the compressor. Designed for double-hung window installation, the unit has two cooling settings, two conventional fan-cooling speeds, two fan-only
*Prices are accurate at time of printing; subject to manufacturer's change.*

speeds, and an exhaust. Moisture removal is good, and controls are hidden by a sliding panel.
**SPECIFICATIONS: Height,** 14-7/16"; **Width,** 24-1/4"; **Depth,** 25-1/2"; **Weight,** 145 lbs.; **Maximum Window Width,** 40"; **Watts,** 860; **Volts,** 115; **Amps,** 7.5; **Moisture Removal Rate** (pints per hour), 2.0; **Fan Speeds,** 2; **Air Delivery** (cubic feet per minute), 290; **Warranty,** one year on parts and labor, additional four years on the compressor system (parts).
**Approximate Retail Price: $379.95**　　　　**Low Price: $330.00**

**Gibson AMO8B6EGBA** is an 8000-Btu/hr. model with an EER of 9.4. The unit has a powered air sweep, three fan speeds, good air direction control, and an energy saver to cycle the fan and compressor together. It also has a humidity control, an exhaust feature and hidden controls. It was judged very good in terms of quiet operation.
**SPECIFICATIONS: Height,** 15-19/32"; **Width,** 23"; **Depth,** 18-15/16"; **Weight,** 106 lbs.; **Maximum Window Width,** 40"; **Watts,** 855; **Volts,** 115; **Amps,** 7.5; **Moisture Removal Rate** (pints per hour), 2.6; **Fan Speeds,** 3; **Air Delivery** (cubic feet per minute), 280; **Warranty,** one year on parts and labor, additional four years on the compressor system (parts).
**Approximate Retail Price: Not Available**　　　　**Low Price: $294.00**

**Kelvinator CX308M1QA** is an 8000-Btu/hr. model with an EER of 9.4. The model is virtually identical in features to the Gibson model of the same size.
**SPECIFICATIONS: Height,** 15-19/32"; **Width,** 23"; **Depth,** 18-15/16"; **Weight,** 106 lbs.; **Maximum Window Width,** 40"; **Watts,** 855; **Volts,** 115; **Amps,** 7.5; **Moisture Removal Rate** (pints per hour), 2.6; **Fan Speeds,** 3; **Air Delivery** (cubic feet per minute), 280; **Warranty,** one year on parts and labor, additional four years on the compressor system (parts).
**Approximate Retail Price: $299.00**　　　　**Low Price: Not Available**

**Kenmore (Sears) 770890** is an 8000-Btu/hr. model with an EER of 9.4. The unit has three-speed fan operation, an exhaust, quick-mount installation, simulated woodgrain front, hidden controls, four-way air control (judged good), and a power-saving setting to cycle fan and compressor on and off together.
**SPECIFICATIONS: Height,** 15-19/32"; **Width,** 23"; **Depth,** 19-7/8"; **Weight,** 106 lbs.; **Maximum Window Width,** 40"; **Watts,** 855; **Volts,** 115; **Amps,** 7.5; **Moisture Removal Rate** (pints per hour), 2.6; **Fan Speeds,** 3; **Air Delivery** (cubic feet per minute), 280; **Warranty,** one year on parts and labor, additional four years on the compressor system (parts and labor), ten years on the outside portion of case (parts).
**Approximate Retail Price: $319.95**　　　　**Low Price: Not Available**

*Prices are accurate at time of printing; subject to manufacturer's change.*

**Whirlpool ADF-P80-20** is an 8000-Btu/hr. unit with an EER of 9.3. The unit has an energy saving feature to cycle the fan on and off with the compressor, an exhaust and fresh air intake, hidden controls, and three fan speeds. Its two-way air direction, though, could be better.
**SPECIFICATIONS: Height,** 15"; **Width,** 22-11/16"; **Depth,** 22-3/4"; **Weight,** 111 lbs.; **Maximum Window Width,** 38"; **Watts,** 860; **Volts,** 115; **Amps,** 7.5; **Moisture Removal Rate** (pints per hour), 2.5; **Fan Speeds,** 3; **Air Delivery** (cubic feet per minute), Not Available; **Warranty,** one year on parts and labor, additional four years on the compressor system (parts and labor).
**Approximate Retail Price: $349.00**        **Low Price: $305.90**

**Amana's ES9-2MR** is an 8500-Btu/hr. model with a very high EER of 9.9. The unit has a good air direction control, good sound insulation, two fan speeds, fresh air and exhaust, two fan-only settings, and a simulated woodgrain front. It does not have hidden controls, however.
**SPECIFICATIONS: Height,** 15-3/8"; **Width,** 24"; **Depth,** 23"; **Weight,** 140 lbs.; **Maximum Window Width,** 40"; **Watts,** 860; **Volts,** 115; **Amps,** 7.5; **Moisture Removal Rate** (pints per hour), 1.9; **Fan Speeds,** 2; **Air Delivery** (cubic feet per minute), 265; **Warranty,** one year on parts and labor, additional four years on the compressor system (parts and labor) and on all other parts (parts only).
**Approximate Retail Price: Not Available**        **Low Price: $345.00**

**White-Westinghouse AHO97T7D** is an 8500-Btu/hr. unit with a high EER of 10.0. This unit represents top value for heavy users of room units. It has an 11-position thermostat including a power-saving feature to cycle the fan on and off with the compressor and three fan speeds for both cooling and fan-only air circulation.
**SPECIFICATIONS: Height,** 14-7/16"; **Width,** 24-1/4"; **Depth,** 23-5/8"; **Weight,** 124 lbs.; **Maximum Window Width,** 41"; **Watts,** 850; **Volts,** 115; **Amps,** 7.5; **Moisture Removal Rate** (pints per hour), 2.9; **Fan Speeds,** 3; **Air Delivery** (cubic feet per minute), 250; **Warranty,** one year on parts and labor, additional four years on the compressor system (parts and labor).
**Approximate Retail Price: Not Available**        **Low Price: $355.00**

### 10,000 BTU/HR. TO 12,600 BTU/HR.

**Fedders ASL10E2HB** is a 10,000-Btu/hr. model designed for installation in double-hung windows. It has an EER rating of 11.6, which puts it at the top of high-efficiency units. It offers three-speed cooling, an adjustable thermostat, an exhaust feature, a good air direction control, and hidden controls.
**SPECIFICATIONS: Height,** 18-1/4"; **Width,** 26"; **Depth,** 27-5/8"; **Weight,** 152 lbs.; **Maximum Window Width,** 39"; **Watts,** 860; **Volts,** 115; **Amps,** 7.5; **Moisture Removal Rate** (pints per hour), 3; **Fan**

*Prices are accurate at time of printing; subject to manufacturer's change.*

**Speeds,** 3; **Air Delivery** (cubic feet per minute), Not Available; **Warranty,** one year on parts and labor, additional four years on the compressor system (parts and labor).
**Approximate Retail Price: $499.95**          **Low Price: $414.95**

**Whirlpool ADF-S10-20** is a 10,000-Btu/hr. model designed for installation in sliding windows. The EER is just a fair 7.3, but high-efficiency models are not readily available in sliding-window units. This unit has two fan speeds, air changer control, and an energy-saving feature that cycles the fan and compressor on and off together. It does not have hidden controls, and since it draws 12 amps, it should be put on a separate circuit.
**SPECIFICATIONS: Height,** 20-1/4"; **Width,** 14-1/2"; **Depth,** 22-5/8"; **Weight,** 103 lbs.; **Maximum Window Height,** 38"; **Watts,** 1375; **Volts,** 115; **Amps,** 12; **Moisture Removal Rate** (pints per hour), 2.8; **Fan Speeds,** 2; **Air Delivery** (cubic feet per minute), Not Available; **Warranty,** one year on parts and labor, additional four years on the compressor system (parts and labor).
**Approximate Retail Price: $369.00**          **Low Price: $320.00**

**Frigidaire A13-MEA-HE** is a 12,600-Btu/hr. unit with a high EER of 9.6. The model has three cooling speeds, two fan-only speeds, and an Electri-Saver feature that cycles the fan off and on with the compressor. It also has hidden controls, fresh air intake and exhaust, and an air-powered air sweeping action. This model is a heavyweight and draws 12 amps, which means that it should be put on a separate circuit.
**SPECIFICATIONS: Height,** 18"; **Width,** 26"; **Depth,** 33-1/8"; **Weight,** 201 lbs.; **Maximum Window Width,** 40"; **Watts,** 1315; **Volts,** 115; **Amps,** 12; **Moisture Removal Rate** (pints per hour), 3.8; **Fan Speeds,** 3; **Air Delivery** (cubic feet per minute), 450; **Warranty,** one year on parts and labor, additional four years on the compressor system (parts).
**Approximate Retail Price: $499.95**          **Low Price: $448.50**

## 13,500 BTU/HR. TO 18,500 BTU/HR.

**Friedrich SM13D10** is a 13,500-Btu/hr. model with an EER of 9.8, which represents high efficiency in this size class. It has five fan speeds, a fan-only setting, vent control that allows exhaust or fresh air intake, and an energy-saving setting to cycle the fan and compressor together. Moisture removal is good, and air direction control is excellent.
**SPECIFICATIONS: Height,** 17-11/16"; **Width,** 25-15/16"; **Depth,** 26-1/2"; **Weight,** 162 lbs.; **Maximum Window Width,** 42"; **Watts,** 1380; **Volts,** 115; **Amps,** 12; **Moisture Removal Rate** (pints per hour), 2.9; **Fan Speeds,** 5; **Air Delivery** (cubic feet per minute), 390; **Warranty,** one year on parts and labor, additional four years on the compressor system (parts and labor).
**Approximate Retail Price: $499.95**          **Low Price: Not Available**

*Prices are accurate at time of printing; subject to manufacturer's change.*

**Kenmore (Sears) 771490** is a 14,000-Btu/hr. unit with an EER of 10.1. The model has three fan speeds, four-way air direction control, exhaust and fresh air intake, and a power-saver switch that allows the fan to cycle on and off with the compressor. It also has a slide-out chassis that can be installed in a window or through-the-wall, a simulated woodgrain front, and hidden controls.
**SPECIFICATIONS: Height,** 18-3/4"; **Width,** 25-7/8"; **Depth,** 28-13/16"; **Weight,** 165 lbs.; **Maximum Window Width,** 40"; **Watts,** 1380; **Volts,** 115; **Amps,** 12; **Moisture Removal Rate** (pints per hour), 4; **Fan Speeds,** 3; **Air Delivery** (cubic feet per minute), Not Available; **Warranty,** one year on parts and labor, additional four years on the compressor system (parts and labor); ten years on the outdoor portion of the case (parts).
**Approximate Retail Price: $449.95**　　　**Low Price: Not Available**


**Whirlpool ADF-170-42** is a 17,000-Btu/hr. model that requires 230 volts and has an EER of 8.6, which is very good for this large size. (The unit capacity is 16,500 Btu/hr. at 208 volts with an EER of 8.4.) In addition to an energy-saving option to cycle fan and compressor together, the unit has three fan speeds, a good four-way air direction control, exhaust and fresh air intake, and a slide-out chassis that can be installed through the wall. It does not have hidden controls, however.
**SPECIFICATIONS: Height,** 18-3/4"; **Width,** 25-7/8"; **Depth,** 28-1/4"; **Weight,** 173 lbs.; **Maximum Window Width,** 40"; **Watts,** 1985/1975; **Volts,** 230/208; **Amps,** 9.0/10.0; **Moisture Removal Rate** (pints per hour), 4.7; **Fan Speeds,** 3; **Air Delivery** (cubic feet per minute), Not Available; **Warranty,** one year on parts and labor, additional four years on the compressor system (parts and labor).
**Approximate Retail Price: $489.00**　　　**Low Price: $430.00**


**Amana ES619-3R** is an 18,500-Btu/hr. model that requires 230 volts and has an EER of 9.3; the unit has a capacity of 18,100 Btu/hr. at 208 volts. It has an exhaust and fresh air intake feature, a three-speed fan, and a fan-only setting. Its air distribution control is excellent. The unit can be installed in a window or through the wall.
**SPECIFICATIONS: Height,** 19-1/2"; **Width,** 27"; **Depth,** 29-3/8"; **Weight,** 210 lbs.; **Maximum Window Width,** 48"; **Watts,** 2000/1950; **Volts,** 230/208; **Amps,** 9.0/9.6; **Moisture Removal Rate** (pints per hour), 6; **Fan Speeds,** 3; **Air Delivery** (cubic feet per minute), 550; **Warranty,** one year on parts and labor, additional four years on the compressor system (parts and labor) and all other parts (parts only).
**Approximate Retail Price: Not Available**　　　**Low Price: $549.60**
*Prices are accurate at time of printing; subject to manufacturer's change.*

## OVER 20,000 BTU/HR.

**General Electric AGGS627DD** is a 27,000-Btu/hr. unit that requires 230 volts (capacity is 26,600 at 208 volts). It has an EER of 8.0, and it is a big, heavy unit at 254 pounds. This model has dual blowers, dual air discharge, a slide-out chassis that can be removed from inside or outside, a ten-position thermostat, and air exhaust. It has three cooling speeds and three fan-only settings, but it does not have hidden controls. It can be installed in a window or through the wall.

**SPECIFICATIONS: Height,** 21-7/8"; **Width,** 27-3/8"; **Depth,** 37-1/2"; **Weight,** 254 lbs.; **Maximum Window Width,** Not Available; **Watts,** 3370/3320; **Volts,** 230/208; **Amps,** 15.3/16.0; **Moisture Removal Rate** (pints per hour), 5.8; **Fan Speeds,** 3; **Air Delivery** (cubic feet per minute), 1050; **Warranty,** one year on parts and labor, additional four years on the compressor system (parts and labor).

**Approximate Retail Price: $749.95**      **Low Price: $639.95**
*Prices are accurate at time of printing; subject to manufacturer's change.*

---

# SPECIAL INFORMATION SERVICE

**A Bonus for Readers of this CONSUMER GUIDE®**

CONSUMER GUIDE® offers a special bonus to its readers who are interested in obtaining information as to where they can find the low prices on specific products listed in this guide. Simply fill out the form and mail. Include 25 cents for postage and handling.
**Please send me information on:**

Product _____ Model Number _____

Manufacturer _____

Product _____ Model Number _____

Manufacturer _____

Product _____ Model Number _____

Manufacturer _____

Your Name _____

Address _____

City _____ State _____ Zip Code _____

**CONSUMER GUIDE Magazine**
**3841 West Oakton, Skokie, Illinois 60076**

# 1978 Smoke Detectors

SMOKE DETECTORS are deceptively simple devices that provide the least expensive fire insurance policy a family can have. Single-station detectors, ranging in price from $25 to $80, can alert you to danger in time for you to escape from a burning house.

There are two basic designs. Ionization models respond rapidly to the small smoke particles characteristic of an open-flame fire, while photoelectric models are sensitive to the large smoke particles of a smoldering fire.

CONSUMER GUIDE Magazine would like to see a device that combines the best features of these two designs. Unfortunately, no such detector is now on the market. You will have to decide which model—ionization or photoelectric—is best suited for the area you want to protect. A complete fire detection system in your home might include several units linked together so that every unit goes off when one does. A combination of ionization and photoelectric models will provide the most protection.

**How They Work**

THE HEART of both the ionization and the photoelectric detector is a small chamber which responds to smoke by triggering a built-in buzzer. The main differences are also within the chambers. In an ionization system, radioactive particles are forced into the chamber. An infinitesimal electric current of less than one millionth of an ampere is pumped through. The radioactive particles, actually harmless alpha particles, act as a conductor to complete the circuit. When smoke enters the ion chamber, the electrical flow is disrupted. A sensing device is preset to measure a drop in conductivity and, when that point is reached, the alarm automatically sounds.

The fact that ionization detectors contain radioactive materials should not cause you any concern—so do many watches. There is no potential hazard to family members from these devices. Photoelectric detector makers frequently allude to the "radioactive" material in ion chambers, and a couple even have "Non-Radioactive" printed on their display boxes. These are great scare tactics, but they are totally unfounded. The ionization detectors use alpha radiation that is not detectable outside of the casing.

A photoelectric detector has a light-sensitive photo cell within its smoke chamber. When light strikes the cell, the alarm is automatically triggered. A small light beam is directed through the chamber in such a way that it does not shine on the photo cell. When smoke enters the chamber, however, the light is diffused. The photo cell is stimulated by the smoke-reflected light, and the alarm sounds.

**Ionization Versus Photoelectric Models**

IN OUR tests, the two types performed fairly consistently by class, but we found vast differences in the sensitivities of the two classes. While photoelectric manufacturers deny it, our tests showed conclusively that these models were insensitive to clean-burning (paper, wood and cloth) fires. None of the photoelectrics responded during the first round of tests at 5 percent smoke obscuration. Many failed to respond even at 10 percent or 12 percent smoke obscuration.

Ionization detectors responded immediately—often within less than one minute—to our paper, wood and cloth fires in an 8 x 6-foot unventilated room. Using a smoke level measuring device comparable to those used by Underwriters Laboratories and the U.S. Environmental Protection Agency, we conducted repeated tests with materials producing black smoke and low-visibility smoke. Our results consistently favored the ionization detectors.

But the vast majority of deaths by fire are not the result of clean fires easily detected by an ionization detector. According to studies by the National Fire Protection Association, household deaths are most often caused by heavy smoke and gas inhalation. These are produced by slow-burning smoldering fires.

CONSUMER GUIDE Magazine, therefore, spent a great deal of time attempting to produce consistent test results for smoldering fires. To duplicate this situation we used upholstery material (both cotton and foam). We inserted an electric charcoal starter (a heating element which looks like a racketball racket without strings) into the materials and timed the slow, smoke-producing process.

Here the tables were turned. The photoelectric devices typically responded from three to five minutes earlier to the smoke fires than did the ionization detectors. Interestingly enough, when we included a wool blanket over the test material for one test, a flame-type fire resulted, and the ionization detector immediately responded, while the photoelectric did not. The photoelectrics we tested, with few exceptions, appeared to have a narrow range of smoke interest. They responded almost exclusively to smoldering fires.

Which type of detector should you have in your home? CONSUMER GUIDE Magazine suggests at least one of each. Ionization detectors are clearly superior in responding to most types of flaming fires. And ionization detectors were the only ones that responded to all kinds of fires. Yet, photoelectric devices give household occupants an extra few minutes of warning of the smoldering fires which overcome most people while they are asleep. Every second is critical when concentrations of smoke become high.

### Battery Versus Plug-In Models

BATTERIES HAVE a number of significant shortcomings. The most obvious is that they wear out. A smoke detector battery must be replaced annually. Luckily, all the units we tested had a fail-safe system built in. When the battery is weak, the smoke detector begins to sound in a low, intermittent pattern which tells you it is replacement time.

Buying these replacements is not always easy, however. Some of the battery-powered models require exotically sized batteries that are nearly impossible to find in local stores.

Other disadvantages include the inconsistency in power from one battery to another of the same make and the battery's reaction to variations in temperature. They lose power when cold, a factor that might prove crucial in the middle of a winter night.

On the positive side, battery-operated units will function when fire interrupts the normal house current operation. They also provide a greater versatility of location. Electrical cords, in addition to being unattractive, limit the number of places where you can install your detector. CONSUMER GUIDE Magazine found that the ideal location for a detector was not always possible with the restrictions caused by an electric cord.

### Other Factors To Consider

THERE ARE other, secondary considerations that should influence your buying decision. Ionization detectors, for instance, are far more sensitive to a vast array of environmental factors. Air flows typical of an air-conditioned house will confuse the ionization detector, rendering it less sensitive in some positions and more sensitive in others. Also, normal cigarette smoke and airborne particles from cooking can set off the ionization detectors. Most ionization detectors will also sound false alarms if they are stationed within reach of steam from a bathroom or auto exhaust in a garage. Some manufacturers won't even recommend them for attics, since high temperatures and humidity will set them off on summer days.

Ionization detectors are also highly sensitive to changes in humidity and to dust and other accumulations of foreign matter entering the smoke chamber. This can greatly impede the flow of air and the effectiveness of an ionization model. Several of the units tested have resolved this problem to some extent with a dual-chamber approach. The second chamber is a reference unit. It is enclosed, except for openings to allow for changes in temperature, pressure, and humidity. The reference chamber thus provides a constant standard which automatically recalibrates the smoke sensor for maximum sensitivity to fire detection.

Sensitivity, moreover, is not a blessing when it results in numerous false alarms. In an in-depth British study published in 1970, smoke detectors as a group were shown to have a false alarm to real fire ratio of 14:1. Because the photoelectrics are far less sensitive to these normal household concentrations of smoke, there is considerably less chance of these false alarms occurring.

Frequent false alarms are an annoyance. After a dozen or so frightening false alarms, the average family is apt to unplug or disconnect the smoke detector for peace of mind. The result is no protection at all.

One major consideration is the noise level of a smoke alarm. No matter how sensitive a unit is, if it doesn't wake you up when it goes off, it is useless. We strongly recommend tandem hookups. If you cannot afford this more expensive system, install a single-station unit in each bedroom. If you have only one detector located in a hallway near the bedrooms, sleep with the bedroom doors open. Most units are loud enough to wake normal sleepers if the siren doesn't have to pass through sound barriers.

**Effective Placement**

SMOKE DETECTORS should be placed to give maximum warning to a sleeping family. The minimum protection you should have is a detector on the ceiling of the hallway outside your bedroom doors. If you have a sprawling house with bedrooms far apart, you need detectors by each bedroom. If anyone in the family smokes in bed, an additional detector located over the bed is a good idea.

CONSUMER GUIDE Magazine recommends that you choose an ionization detector as the first line of defense in bedroom hallways. A photoelectric detector is probably better over the bed, since mattress fires are usually the smoldering variety that they respond to best.

If you can afford additional units, place them in the basement, living room and family rooms. Be sure to test the sound levels of these more distant detectors.

In rating the numerous smoke detectors, CONSUMER GUIDE Magazine felt that a multiple rating system was the only way to establish an equitable standard. Sensitivity to smoke of all kinds and the noise and frequency of the siren were given the greatest weight, but many other features, such as the design's simplicity, ease of installation, flexibility of location, power supply, warranty, owner instructions, and price, had to be considered. We did not feel photoelectrics should be rated in the same manner as ionization detectors because they were not designed to respond in the same manner to the same fire patterns. Also, battery-powered models were generally compared to others of their kind. This was done because CONSUMER GUIDE Magazine feels strongly that the homeowner should select one house-current model and one battery-powered model. One of these should be an ionization model and one a photoelectric model.

Our tests could not lead us to recommend a photoelectric unit as the only smoke detector in an apartment or small house. They were simply impervious to flaming fires. The ionization detectors recommended did not react to smoldering fires as rapidly as photoelectrics, but they did react, which was more than we could say of photoelectrics when faced with flaming wood or paper fires.

Most homes, however, should have two or more smoke detectors, and the second detector purchased definitely should be a photoelectric model.

---

# SPECIAL INFORMATION SERVICE

**A Bonus for Readers of this CONSUMER GUIDE®**

CONSUMER GUIDE® offers a special bonus to its readers who are interested in obtaining information as to where they can find the low prices on specific products listed in this guide. Simply fill out the form and mail. Include 25 cents for postage and handling.

**Please send me information on:**

Product _____ Model Number _____

Manufacturer _____

Your Name _____

Address _____

City _____ State _____ Zip Code _____

**CONSUMER GUIDE Magazine**
**3841 West Oakton, Skokie, Illinois 60076**

# 1978 Best Buys: Smoke Detectors

BECAUSE THEY are designed on different principles, photoelectric and ionization detectors were rated separately. Emphasis was placed on quickness to respond, sound level, reliability and ease of testing and maintenance. Since smoke detectors are intended to save lives, price was a minor consideration when our "Best Buys" were selected.

## IONIZATION MODELS
### Best Buy

**Guardion FB-1** was a prime contender for top ratings in several categories. Even though it is an ionization detector, the Guardion responded very well to smoldering fires — as well as at least one of the photoelectric units. On flaming fires, the Guardion was more responsive in every category. But, we were disappointed in the Guardion's sound level. It was the quietest ionization detector tested at ten feet, and yet, because of its low-frequency sound, did very well in penetrating a door. The Guardion is a bit difficult for the homeowner to test.

**Approximate Retail Price: $50**                  **Low Price: $35**

### Also Recommended

**BRK First Alert** (also sold as Sears Early One) comes in both plug-in and battery models. We tested the battery model and were favorably impressed. The units responded rapidly to flame fires and were fairly responsive to the smoldering fires, too. The sirens were loud, surprisingly so, considering that they were battery-powered. They also are available with a built-in heat detector that complements the basic sensor system. The BRK First Alert and Sears Early One are easy to test and virtually trouble-free. The battery models use a commonplace 9-volt power source. The dual ioniza-

*Prices are accurate at time of printing; subject to manufacturer's change.*

tion chambers are less apt to cause false alarms in humid weather or because of smoking or cooking nearby.
**Approximate Retail Price: $49**                          **Low Price: $27**

## PHOTOELECTRIC MODELS
Best Buys

**Gard-Site 081-600** responded fastest to smoldering fires when mounted on a wall or on the ceiling. The Gard-Site had a very loud, strong sound. It was enough to wake a heavy sleeper, even through a door at 18 feet. Also, the Gard-Site is among the least expensive units on the market. It typically retails for under $30. The device comes with a five-year guarantee, and, judging by the overall sturdiness of construction, the company isn't taking much of a chance with its long-term support. The Casady Gard-Site could have been improved, we think, by adding an LED instead of the old-style bulb it is equipped with. But even with some drawbacks, this plug-in model is a fine investment.
**Approximate Retail Price: $25**              **Low Price: Not Available**

**Gillette Captain Kelly 9410** has several outstanding features. It responded extremely well to smoldering fires and eventually to paper and wood fires. The unit is designed for wall mounting. Because it is square, it looks more like an intercom than other smoke detectors which are usually round. The wall-mounted position is preferred for photoelectric detectors. Smoke from a smoldering fire is heavy. It rises by piling up in layers, and the wall-mounted model will thus respond more rapidly. The Captain Kelly has the loudest alarm of its class, both for close ranges and through a door at 18 feet. It was most easily tested and came with a longer-than-average cord for better placement, yet actually needed less cord because it is wall mounted. Please note that our recommendation pertains strictly to the 9410 plug-in model. The battery-operated Captain Kelly is not preferred because of the weak sound of its alarm and its exotic battery.
**Approximate Retail Price: $40**                          **Low Price: $27**

*Prices are accurate at time of printing; subject to manufacturer's change.*

# 1978 Personal Care Appliances

A WIT ONCE remarked, "Beauty is only skin deep, but it's the part that shows!" Taking the comment to heart, manufacturers of personal care appliances have created hundreds of products that promise to do their best for every part of the body that shows—and even some that don't. As a result, finding one's way through the personal care appliance maze has become a challenge of the first order. It isn't enough to know that you need a hair dryer. Today's buyer must be aware of all the infinite variations in design and function currently on the market and then decide among them. CONSUMER GUIDE Magazine can help make that decision easier. Our product evaluations are based on three criteria: the needs of the buyer; how products perform in meeting those needs; and whether or not price is in line with performance.

## Versatility

AN APPLIANCE with more than one use isn't necessarily a better buy. A versatile appliance should perform each of its functions well, or it really isn't versatile. All the attachments that come with a styler/dryer, for example, may look impressive in the store, but if they are difficult to use, ineffective or unsafe, they aren't worth the extra money. And, speaking of money, attachments always add to the cost of the appliance, so make sure you're going to use them. If all you want to do is blow dry your hair, don't purchase a more expensive styler/dryer with comb and brush attachments.

## Safety

IT IS DIFFICULT to judge exactly how safe an appliance is just by looking at it in the store. The best clue to product safety is the seal of the Underwriters Laboratories. Before you buy, look for the letters "UL" printed or molded right onto the product near the model number. Manufacturers voluntarily have their products checked by Underwriters Laboratories which tests the products to see if they meet certain safety standards. If they do, they are added to the UL's product listing.

Naturally, this only covers safety under normal conditions. Safe performance depends on how you handle the product at home. Read the use-and-care instructions that are packed with the unit or printed on the package before you operate the appliance. Keep the booklet in a convenient place so you can refer to it when questions arise later on.

Most instruction booklets advise against using a unit that has been dropped or broken and they discourage home repairs. Some manufacturers will not honor a guarantee if a handyman has tried to fix an appliance before taking it to the authorized repair service. Never operate an appliance with a worn or frayed cord. CONSUMER GUIDE Magazine must advise against children using personal care products without adult supervision. This is especially true of high-wattage hair dryers which produce heat too intense for the delicate hair and scalps of young children. We recommend that no hair dryers be used *by* children, and, if used *on* children, that they are set on the lowest heat and speed settings.

## Cost

WHERE YOU BUY will influence cost, as will the variety of functions an appliance is supposed to perform, the number and quality of attachments and packaging. Department stores usually have the biggest selection and better services, but discount stores offer lower prices in exchange for less service. You can get a real deal by watching for advertised specials during the off-season.

The more sophisticated the appliance, the more costly it is likely to be. Be sure you know exactly what you expect an appliance to do for you before you buy. Fancy attachments and elaborate packaging may add substantially to the cost without providing any real performance benefits. But, don't sacrifice quality for a bargain. You usually get what you pay for, so be sure the appliance is well-made, durable, easy to operate and safe. Cost of operation is an important factor, too, especially among products that tout high wattage as an advantage. Hair dryer manufacturers may brag about "1000 watts" or even "1400 watts," but often the higher-wattage models don't dry hair any better even though they cost more to operate. With many, you actually get too much power and heat for controlled, comfortable drying. Remember, the cost of operating an appliance depends on its wattage, the number of hours you use it and the cost of electricity per kilowatt-hour in your community.

## Guarantee and Warranty

THE WORDS "guarantee" and "warranty" are interchangeable. The guarantee is a printed statement, often found on the last page of the instruction booklet that comes with the appliance. The time to read it is before you buy. Understand what parts and service are covered and how long the guarantee lasts. If service is needed, the appliance may need to go to a special repair center. If it must be shipped, find out who pays.

## Usability

CAN YOU REALLY style your own hair the way they do in the beauty parlor with your new dryer? Chances are it will take practice. Read the use booklet before you buy and examine the appliance to see if it seems within your skill. It may take a good bit of determination to get the knack of a new appliance; be sure it is worth the effort.

Try out the appliance in the store whenever possible. With shavers and hair dryers, of course, this is hardly feasible, but do at least get the feel of the unit. It takes quite a while to dry hair, for example, and your arm may tire if you are using a dryer that is not well-balanced or one that is too heavy. Also check to see if it can be held comfortably. Some hand-held appliances are too bulky and too long. If you're left-handed, also try the controls in the store. Most personal care appliances are made for right-handed persons and adjusting the controls during use can be awkward for lefties.

## Storage

IF SPACE IS at a premium in your home, one new appliance may be one too many. You may want to consider buying personal care appliances designed for travel. The scaled down Sunbeam Swing-Aire 1000 blow dryer, for example, features a foldaway pistol grip, so it only takes up a minimum of space when not in use. With roller hairsetters, consider what storage problems or inconveniences may be encountered if the unit doesn't provide compartments for storing roller pins and pads. Some personal care products have built-in rings for hanging. Others have stands or cases that can be used for storage. While shopping, try to visualize where your electrical outlets are located and where you will be able to store the appliance.

## Curlers (Curling Irons)

DESIGNED FOR spot curling, curling irons offer dry or steam heat. Some models can convert from dry to steam. Dry heat does the job, but some people prefer the mist method. When steam is used, it may help to pin the curl after the iron is removed until the hair is completely dry. Otherwise, a slightly damp curl may droop.

Features to look for on curling irons include a heat-resistant tip that you can touch without burning your fingers and a nonstick finish. Additionally, try to find a unit that has a signal dot to show that the iron is properly heated and a warning light. Without this safety feature, it's possible to forget that the unit is plugged in and serious burns or fire hazards may result.

Also consider the total length of the curling iron. Clairol's new Crazy Baby is marketed as a portable/travel curling iron, but its unique shorter length makes it much easier to use and control than most styling wands available. It also features an innovative "heat shield" that can be slipped on over the iron immediately after use. This prevents burning and alleviates the need for waiting before storing the appliance. This unit performed as efficiently and effectively as the longer ones on the market.

CONSUMER GUIDE Magazine prefers a curling iron with a stand. Some have a stand built onto the handle, but a separate stand is a further safeguard and more sturdy. A swivel cord is another advantage because the cord tends to twist during use.

**Curlers (Electric Rollers)**

ROLLER HAIRSETTERS, designed to provide a quick set, come in both dry and mist versions. Each type has its supporters and the version you choose is largely a matter of personal preference. You must consider the length and style of your hair; these factors determine the number and size of the rollers most advantageous for you. Roller teeth should be smooth to prevent tangling and the pins used to hold them should be easy to insert and remove when hot. If any rollers will touch your cheek or neck, be sure that pads to protect these sensitive areas are included. The unit should also have a ready indicator.

Here again, a warning light is a good safety feature to look for. Most units turn on automatically when plugged in. Without a visual device to alert the user that the unit is hot, burns, fire hazards and product damage can result from neglecting to unplug the unit. The most ideal roller hairsetter has an independent on/off switch as well. Look for curlers that have gripping edges that do not become as hot as the main part of the roller.

**Hair Dryers (Blow Dryers)**

THIS CATEGORY includes all hand-held appliances that are designed to perform a single function—drying hair. They are not intended for use as stylers, per se, so most feature no attachments other than a concentrator nozzle to strengthen and direct air flow.

As with all hand-held appliances, CONSUMER GUIDE Magazine

considers weight, balance and length to be the top considerations when choosing a suitable blow dryer. Weight and balance will affect how long you can hold the dryer at arm's length comfortably. The length will determine how effective the dryer will be for drying hair in hard-to-reach places, like the back of the head, and how well the dryer can be maneuvered. If the unit features a concentrator nozzle attachment, this can add as much as three inches to its overall length. Try to get the feel of the dryer before you buy.

Judging by the promotion of most blow dryers, manufacturers think the consumer is concerned about wattage. Testing showed that 500 to 700 watts is sufficient for good drying. You should also know that wattage and drying power are not directly proportional. Drying depends on both heat and air flow. Look for a dryer with at least two heat settings and two speed settings. Separate switches for heat and air speed are best. You may find that you are extra-sensitive to heat and will appreciate being able to reduce it while letting the air blow full force.

## Hair Dryers (Comb-Brush Dryers)

THESE HAIR care appliances are multipurpose and usually feature at least two separate airflow and heat settings, plus a variety of styling attachments. Optimally, these units offer a higher temperature and airflow for drying and reduced power and heat for styling. The more versatile and efficient ones provide a considerable range of selections for both—on separate switches. Some profess to have different settings, but the variation is so slight it's difficult to detect a difference from one setting to the next.

The wattage game is played with styler/dryers, too. But, as with blow dryers, the models with the highest wattage do not always perform the best. Since they are hand-held, the weight of styler/dryers should concern the buyer, as should the balance and length, especially when using attachments.

Attachments for these models may include an air-concentrating adaptor, a curler, comb and brush. Before you buy, be sure you are likely to use all of the attachments provided or look for a unit that only includes the ones you want.

## Hot Lather Dispensers

CONSUMERS WHO prefer the blade razor are still considered fair game by appliance manufacturers. For this market, gadgets have been designed to heat shave cream as it leaves the aerosol can.

Cordless hot lather dispensers are plugged directly into an electrical outlet. All tested models were ready to use in under two minutes. Wattage of the models tested varied; but none used a significant amount of power. Most had a signal light that glowed while heating, and went off when the unit was ready. When buying, CONSUMER GUIDE Magazine recommends a model that will accept various sizes of aerosol shave cream cans.

## Irons

THE OPTIONS available on irons range from the simplest steam setting to spray, "burst of steam," self-cleaning and nonstick coatings on the soleplate. Some irons also offer indicator lights and a water-level indicator.

The features you need in an iron, of course, depend upon your attitude toward ironing. While CONSUMER GUIDE Magazine cautions against buying more features than you need, you should buy the features necessary for your clothing care routine. For some people, ironing is an occasional but odious task, limited to setting creases in permanent press garments; the luxury burst of steam feature may be important to such individuals, justifying its additional cost. Home seamstresses may also need some of the more exotic features for pressing during garment construction. If you never use more than the steam setting, you would be wasting money on a deluxe iron.

Once again, weight and maneuverability are important factors. If you do a considerable amount of ironing, you need a unit that you can manage comfortably. Most of the newer models have reversible cords so that left-handed people can handle them easily.

## Shavers

BOTH MEN and women use electric shavers, but most manufacturers aim their advertising at men. Manufacturers claim that their products will give even the toughest-bearded hombre a cleaner and closer shave. And, if the comparison is made with electric shavers as they were only a few years ago, the claim is well grounded. But measured against electric shavers, the blades have it.

Loyal electric fans stick by their shavers anyway, on grounds of comfort and convenience. Shavers come in cord and cordless styles: some shavers are convertible. A shaver in the desk drawer or glove compartment makes quick touchups possible throughout the day. And they do not require shave creams, water, towels or mess.

Campers, travelers or others who shave in places where electrical outlets are not readily available prefer the cordless electric shaver. The obvious disadvantages of the cordless models are that they must be recharged fairly frequently and the proper voltage must be available. This year the first cordless women's shaver, the Remington WER 6000, was introduced.

# 1978 Best Buys: Personal Care Appliances

Every year brings a large number of new personal care appliances onto the market. Because it would be impossible for the individual shopper to try all these appliances, CONSUMER GUIDE Magazine has tested and evaluated many kinds of personal care products. The products were judged on the basis of performance, convenience, safety and price. Those products with the best scores were selected as our "Best Buys."

## CURLERS (Curling Irons)
### Best Buy

**Clairol Crazy Baby** steam styler is a smaller version of Clairol's Crazy Curl steam styling wand, measuring only about 8-1/2 inches from tip to tip. During testing, we found this shorter length to be an important asset. The Crazy Baby is lighter and much easier to handle and control than the longer appliance. It performed with the same efficiency and produced the same results as the regular Crazy Curl wand, using both dry and mist methods. Like its larger counterpart, it has a signal light—an important safety feature—as well as a red signal dot and nonstick coating. The Crazy Baby has two other distinguishing characteristics. It comes with a voltage adaptor for overseas travel and a heat shield. The shield is a long plastic tube that can be slipped over the iron while it is still hot for immediate storage. We feel this feature is an excellent one that makes this appliance much more convenient and safe.

**Approximate Retail Price: $25.99**          **Low Price: $16.09**

### Also Tested

**Clairol Crazy Curl C-200** steam styling wand is Clairol's standard curling iron appliance. It features steam/dry options, as well as a convenient red signal dot, nonstick coating, a stand attachment, and a warning light (a definite safety plus). When tested, it per-

*Prices are accurate at time of printing; subject to manufacturer's change.*

formed efficiently and effectively. The enclosed instruction booklet was very informative, with easy-to-follow styling suggestions. There is little to distinguish this appliance from others on the market in terms of performance, but the stand attachment and warning light are important extras that set it apart from the rest.
**Approximate Retail Price: $19.99**            **Low Price: $12.64**

**General Electric Touch 'N Curl V** proved to be a very efficient, versatile and effective curling iron/styler when tested under home conditions. It is designed to be used as both a "dry" curling iron, relying on heat alone to set the curl, and as a "mist" curler for curling with less drying of the hair. Both methods were equally effective. In general, we found the Touch 'N Curl to be a good appliance for home use in terms of performance and design. Many features of value to the consumer were noted during testing. The curling barrel has a nonstick coating for easy cleaning. A convenient signal light serves as a warning that the unit is on. This is especially important for safety and the prevention of injury. In addition, the unit features a red signal dot that changes color when the curling iron is ready to use. This unit also comes with a large roller/comb attachment that slides on over the barrel. It provides larger, fuller curls. The instruction booklet is easy to follow, with good styling tips and safety information.
**Approximate Retail Price: $20.98**            **Low Price: $15.59**

**Norelco Curly Q Model HB1600** is a simply designed, easy-to-use iron. It has a ready dot that turns black after a preheating period of about three minutes and features an eight-foot swivel cord. You can use it as a dry setter or as a mist setter. Either way, our testers found it a satisfactory model that makes medium-size curls without difficulty.
**Approximate Retail Price: $14.95**            **Low Price: $10.33**

## CURLERS (Electric Rollers)
### Best Buys

**Clairol C-20S** is recommended because of its ease of operation, fast warm-up time and economical price. The newest Clairol 20 features improved rollers with ribs that reduce tangling and rims that prevent the hair from sliding off. Clairol's rollers are also the best for heat retention. The Clairol C-20S is a dry-only model.
**Approximate Retail Price: $25.99**            **Low Price: $16.09**

**Clairol Kindness Deluxe 3-Way Hairsetter K-400S** is, in our opinion, the definitive electric hair curler set. It features three settings—dry, mist, and conditioning—for versatility and less hair damage. Even the conditioner is provided in the package. Several design assets were noted during testing, including built-in storage slots for storing roller pins, protective foam pads, and convenient

*Prices are accurate at time of printing; subject to manufacturer's change.*

detachable cord. Unlike most sets, the Kindness Deluxe offers an on/off switch as well as a signal light to alert the user when curlers are properly heated. After testing this unit under home handling conditions, we found it to be one of the most versatile, efficient, safe, and convenient electric hairsetters on the market. It comes with six jumbo, ten medium, and four small rollers, with color-coded pins for each size.

**Approximate Retail Price: $39.99**  **Low Price: $25.29**

## Also Tested

**Lady Schick Lasting Curls Moist Hairsetter Model 71-C** is a typical electric curler set, relying on steam to heat the rollers and provide the curling action. It comes with 20 rollers in three sizes, pins and clips, and four foam pads to protect sensitive skin from the hot rollers. In general, this unit performed well when tested under home handling conditions. The instructions were easy to follow and safety considerations were emphasized in the accompanying booklet. A red dot turns maroon to signal when the curlers are ready for use, but there is no independent on/off switch or warning light to remind the user that the unit is plugged in. The set begins to heat as soon as it is plugged in and the rollers are ready for use in a reasonable amount of time.

**Approximate Retail Price: $27.95**  **Low Price: $19.26**

## HAIR DRYERS (Blow Dryers)
## Best Buys

**Conair Vagabond 063** is a 22-ounce, 1000-watt hair dryer. It is distinguished by a dual voltage switch, which makes it suitable for use in foreign countries. All controls are located on the front of the comfortable pistol grip. Two separate rocker switches turn the unit on and off and select either a high speed/high heat or low speed/low heat setting. A heat concentrator is included. The Vagabond 063 is a sturdy, simple unit that would be a good value for travelers.

**Approximate Retail Price: $28.99**  **Low Price: $17.25**

**Gillette Promax Compact** is a child of the jet age; its "Turbo-Flo" design brings to mind fan jets geared for high speed travel. This dryer is suitable for travel, too, being only 6 x 6-1/2 inches long and light in weight. A very easy-to-read use-and-care booklet accompanies the Promax Compact. Its illustrations and directions are well done; they should be helpful to anyone just learning to style hair. One switch on the handle of the Promax permits three heat levels and three airflow settings.

**Approximate Retail Price: $21.99**  **Low Price: $14.72**

*Prices are accurate at time of printing; subject to manufacturer's change.*

**Schick 1000 Drying Stick** represents a new concept in blow dryers. It's shaped like a long, tapered tube with one end functioning as the air vent and the wider end serving as a rotating control device for adjusting the dryer to four temperature and two heat settings. During testing we noted several outstanding advantages to this unique dryer. First, the controls offer two "off" settings, one at each end of the control device. This is a great feature for left-handed people—people who are often forgotten by designers of personal care appliances. The Schick Drying Stick also boasts what we feel is an important safety feature. The air intake system is a series of slanted notches around the entire handle end of the tube. This makes it impossible for hair to become tangled in the intake mechanism and equally impossible for the air intake to become totally blocked, causing overheating. From a performance standpoint, it is exceptionally lightweight and easy to maneuver. The slim tube is held comfortably at all points. The various settings provide adequate heat and power options for all drying applications and needs. The wattage varies from 100 to 400 to 750 to 1000.

**Approximate Retail Price: $22.99**     **Low Price: $15.53**

## Also Tested

**American Electric American Star 1400** pistol-grip hair dryer performed adequately when tested under home conditions. It was lightweight and well-sized for control and easy drying. Several drawbacks were noted however. Controls for three heat and two air settings are located on a rotating wheel switch placed on the back spine of the pistol grip. The wheel is hard to move, especially during use, and it is difficult to tell which setting it is on. The style setting was much too strong and too hot for optimum styling; even the medium setting was excessive in both heat and airflow. The unit we tested included no instruction booklet, just safety and warranty (one-year) information. A concentrator nozzle was the only attachment.

**Approximate Retail Price: $14.95**     **Low Price: $8.17**

**Conair Pro Baby 088** hair dryer is one of the most unusual models to come out in recent years. Shaped like a curved, tapered tube, it can be hand-held for blow drying or set on the table in an upright position for two-handed styling. The round base of the unit doubles as the control device. By rotating the base, the unit can be turned on and off and two speed-temperature settings (600 and 1200 watts) selected. The Pro Baby performed well under testing, drying hair rapidly. The curled shape made it easy to direct the airflow around the back of the head and in hard-to-reach places. Several problems were noted, however. The base does not appear to be very sturdy, especially considering that it has to double as the control. With frequent use, this feature could be a weak point.

*Prices are accurate at time of printing; subject to manufacturer's change.*

When the unit is placed upright as a table model, the motor is exposed and there is a danger of burning oneself or of dropping something into the motor. Also, the tapered tube-shape forces people with small hands to hold the unit close to the top when using it as a blow dryer. Two screws located on the sides of the top part of the unit became very hot in a matter of seconds. If the user were holding the dryer at that particular location, he or she would be burned.

**Approximate Retail Price: $23.99**  **Low Price: $14.93**

**Conair Pro 1000** is a pistol-grip blow dryer that is distinguished by its rugged construction and durability. Made to last, it is sturdier than most dryers on the market, but not overly heavy or hard to handle. When tested, it dried hair with a powerful airflow, in two temperatures. We found it to be a bit too powerful (1000 watts) for careful styling, but very effective for drying purposes. The controls — one switch for temperature and an on/off switch — are located on the side of the handle. The contoured handle fits the hand well for comfort. Additional features include a hanger clip for storage and a concentrator nozzle attachment.

**Approximate Retail Price: $19.99**  **Low Price: $11.67**

**Conair Pro Style 065** blow dryer is marketed as a professional appliance. It has two heat switches that when adjusted in various combinations, produce four different temperatures and two speeds. In addition, there is an on/off switch. These complicated controls are located on the side of the contoured pistol grip. There are no markings in close proximity to the switches to tell the user which combinations produce which temperatures and speeds. These instructions are not included in the use-and-care booklet either. During testing, it was eventually discovered that the instructions are embossed on the reverse side of the handle. We found this to be especially confusing to the user. This model is exceptionally durable and well built, but it is also heavier and longer than most pistols and harder to control. The powerful motor (1200 watts) makes it top-heavy. Under home conditions, this dryer appeared to be overly powerful for regular use, especially for styling. The result is fast drying, with a "wind tunnel" effect. A concentrator nozzle is included.

**Approximate Retail Price: $29.99**  **Low Price: $17.86**

**General Electric Power-Turbo Pistol Dryer PRO 10** is touted for its "turbo" motor, but we could find no basic difference in performance from other models. It was very light and easy to use, though the sculptured handle was a bit awkward. The slide switch controls provide high (1200 watts), medium and low settings, with high and medium having the same air flow but different degrees of heat. One advantage was noted: the air inlet for the unit is located at the extreme end of the pistol barrel. From a safety standpoint, this

*Prices are accurate at time of printing; subject to manufacturer's change.*

makes it more unlikely that hair will get caught or tangled in the intake mechanism. Overall, the Power-Turbo is a very effective hair dryer. It includes a concentrator nozzle attachment and a one year warranty.

**Approximate Retail Price: $20.98**                  **Low Price: $15.59**

**Gillette Promax Compact 1200** is a streamlined pistol-grip hair dryer. It allows for four combination settings of heat and air flow for both drying and styling applications. We found the controls adequate but a bit difficult to operate. Very effective and powerful for drying, this unit also adjusts air flow and temperature for styling, using only 250 watts on the low/cool setting. It is small, lightweight and easy to control. In general, it is a very satisfactory dryer, but not outstanding. The enclosed instruction booklet is very easy to read and understand, with helpful hints on how to style. Gillette also provides a one-year warranty and a toll-free number for consumer questions. The only attachment is a concentrator nozzle.

**Approximate Retail Price: $24.99**                  **Low Price: $17.25**

**Merit Stylist Dryer** is marketed as a professional pistol-grip dryer and, at 1200 watts, it is extremely powerful. As an added feature, it comes with a stand so that it can also be used as a table model, freeing the hands for styling. We noted several problems with this unit. Three slide switches, including a separate on/off switch, on the pistol grip serve as the controls; combinations of various switch positions provide two speeds and four temperatures. But information about "what's what" is only included in the instruction booklet. It is impossible to determine exactly how to achieve the various settings without having the book in front of you. It was also noted during testing that these complicated settings really don't offer much differentiation in heat and airflow except for the extremes. This model was very heavy and hard to hold and overly long for good control—especially when the concentrator nozzle was attached. The stand attachment is a great idea, but it was of poor quality. We feel it should be sturdier and that a system of notches should be incorporated in the design so that the dryer can be held securely in a variety of positions. The enclosed instruction booklet was sketchy and overly simplified.

**Approximate Retail Price: $19.95**                  **Low Price: Not Available**

**Norelco Shape 'N Dry 750** performed well when tested under home handling conditions. Though the wattage (750) is somewhat lower than many dryers on the market, the unit dried hair quickly without excessive force. The controls are conveniently placed along the back of the handle, allowing the user to switch settings during use. In addition to the "dry" setting, this model features a separate setting for styling. This setting operates on 360 watts, for less airflow and a slightly cooler temperature. Five styling attachments, including a brush, three types of combs and a spot dryer, are

*Prices are accurate at time of printing; subject to manufacturer's change.*

included. From a design standpoint, this dryer was judged to be very maneuverable, due to its light weight and slim, easy-to-hold handle. One potential problem was noted during testing: the spot dryer attachment should never be placed directly over a curler. This blocks the heating unit and causes overheating. But, like most dryers on the market, this unit has a built-in safety thermostat that automatically shuts it off when overheating occurs. The instruction booklet features easy-to-follow diagrams showing how attachments are used. Safety information is provided in a separate brochure.

**Approximate Retail Price: $22.95**     **Low Price: $17.97**

**Schick Pro Jet 1000** is a pistol dryer/styler that performed well when tested under home handling conditions. It is extremely lightweight and short enough to provide maximum control. The airflow vent is larger than most, providing faster drying. In addition, the air intake mechanism is located at the end of the pistol barrel for optimum safety. A slide switch located on the side of the pistol grip offers off/style/dry settings. On each setting, the temperature and power are ideal for both applications. A concentrator nozzle is the only attachment. Again, the packaging is more elaborate than necessary and may affect price. Overall, we found this unit to be a very practical home dryer/styler.

**Approximate Retail Price: $21.99**     **Low Price: $15.24**

**Sunbeam Odyssey 1200 Blower/Styler** is a lightweight easy-to-maneuver pistol-grip blow dryer with two speeds and three heat settings. The controls are located along the pistol-grip on a single slide-switch. This is a good appliance for all drying and styling uses. The wattage, and therefore the strength of the air flow, is altered to correspond with each temperature setting. The range is from 300 watts for "cool" to 625 watts for "low" and 1200 watts for "high." This versatility allows maximum control for styling. Its elongated design and slanted handle allow the user to direct the air flow easily, even to hard-to-reach places. A slanted concentrator nozzle is included for additional control.

**Approximate Retail Price: $28.50**     **Low Price: $21.26**

**Sunbeam Swing-Aire 1000** is marketed as a portable blow dryer, due to its light weight and compactability. A modified pistol-grip dryer in design, the handle folds up when not in use, so the unit takes up only a few cubic inches. During testing, it proved to be very powerful, in spite of its small size. Operating on 1000 watts with high and low heat settings, it has an exceptionally large air vent for fast drying. However, this unit is not a "styler" per se. Air output is equally strong on both settings. Since it weighs well under one pound, it also had good maneuverability and control. Extra features include a hanger clip for storage and a nozzle attachment for concentrating the air flow.

**Approximate Retail Price: $24.95**     **Low Price: $18.83**

*Prices are accurate at time of printing; subject to manufacturer's change.*

## HAIR DRYERS (Comb-Brush Dryers)
## Best Buys

**Clairol Air Brush AB-3** includes a detangler, heat concentrator, styling comb and nylon bristle styling brush, all of which attach and detach smoothly. A release button eliminates the need to touch hot attachments.

Although rated at only 500 watts, the Air Brush performs better and faster than many models rated at higher wattage. In addition, it is compact, easy to hold and ideal for traveling—converting from 110 to 220 volts. There are two heat and air flow settings: moderate heat and air flow for styling; and high heat and stronger air flow for drying. The controls are conveniently located within easy reach of the user's thumb.

**Approximate Retail Price: $27.99**   **Low Price: $19.60**

**Conair The Wiz AW-1** is a 1000 watt wand-style dryer that is ten inches long. It has five attachments that fit onto its nose; with its brush in place, it is 16 inches long and resembles an oversized electric toothbrush. Besides the 360-degree circular brush, which seems to be favored by hair stylists for wedge-type haircuts, there are three combs of varying fineness (one large one to "pick and lift" natural hair styles), and an air concentrator to dry small sections of hair. The concentrator is designed to fit over roller curlers. The control for the Wiz is located on the handle and has a "dry" and "style" setting, in addition to the "off" setting. In testing, it proved to be easy to handle and well balanced. CONSUMER GUIDE Magazine particularly approves of the swivel cord feature that prevents the cord from twisting during use.

**Approximate Retail Price: $31.99**   **Low Price: $18.96**

**Sunbeam 1000 Vari-A-Matic** is a 1000-watt dryer/styler with two distinguishing characteristics. This unit appears to be more well-built than the average, made of a tough, durable plastic that should stand up well to repeated use. It is heavier than most dryers of this type, but not unwieldy. Durability is probably preferable to lightness. In addition, the Sunbeam Vari-A-Matic offers a continuous range of temperature/power settings—starting at low/cool and progressing to high/hot. There are no specific settings, per se, so there is more subtle control and more versatility. The heat and airflow are controlled by a rotary switch on the side of the handle. The switch provides both directional arrows and color-coding (blue for cool, progressing to orange for hot). All settings within the range provide a good amount—not too much—of both heat and power. This unit comes with five attachments: a concentrator, wide-toothed comb, fine-toothed comb, double-row brush, and a separate attachment handle.

**Approximate Retail Price: $33.50**   **Low Price: $25.02**

*Prices are accurate at time of printing; subject to manufacturer's change.*

## Also Tested

**Clairol Hot Stuff 1000 Multi-Dryer** is a cross between the newer tube-like drying sticks and regular hand-held dryers. The basic unit is shaped like a modified tube, with the motor encased in a "bulge" just above the cord. A slide switch on the side of the tube offers two heat and two airflow settings, marked "dry" and "style." Due to the tube shape, the controls are equally accessible to left- and right-handed persons. For drying, two attachments can be connected to the top of the tube. One, a unique elbow directional nozzle, offers good control for hard-to-reach places and spot drying. The other is a wide-angle concentrator that can be used alone for drying or in conjunction with the fine-toothed and detangling comb attachments for styling. A round styling brush that snaps onto the end of the tube is also included. When tested, this unit performed well, drying and styling with ease and efficiency. It is lightweight and can be held comfortably.

**Approximate Retail Price: $31.49**　　　　**Low Price: $19.54**

**Northern Lifestyler/Styler-Dryers 1861 and 1833** performed well under testing. Operating at a maximum of 850 watts, Model 1861 was effective for drying and the style setting provided optimum heat and airflow. The wide air outlet on this unit helped it dry faster than regular pistol dryers. It comes with comb and brush attachments that are simple to attach and remove. In general, we found this unit to be very satisfactory in all areas. Model 1833 gave the same performance with a little less wattage. The same attachments were included with this model. One distinguishing characteristic of the lower-wattage model was its slightly curved handle. This made the unit exceptionally easy to control, especially in hard-to-reach places.

**Approximate Retail Prices:**　　　　**Low Prices:**
**Model 1861: $19.95**　　　　　　　　**Model 1861: $13.70**
**Model 1833: $17.95**　　　　　　　　**Model 1833: $12.35**

**Schick Adjustable Power Styler 1000** offers several nice options to users. It features two control switches: one, a slide switch on the back of the handle, regulates airflow for drying and styling; the second is a rotary switch to regulate four heat settings. The rotary switch is on both sides of the handle, offering equal accessibility for right- and left-handed persons. And, the range of heat settings offered is wide enough for all styling and drying applications. During testing, this unit performed well, with exceptional maneuverability. Its attachments include a concentrator, wide- and fine-toothed combs, brush, and separate attachment handle. As noted on other Schick products, the elaborate packaging may affect price:

**Approximate Retail Price: $31.99**　　　　**Low Price: $21.28**

*Prices are accurate at time of printing; subject to manufacturer's change.*

**Schick Grooming Stick and Styling Stick** are identical except for attachments. The settings (off/dry/style) are controlled by a slide switch located on the side of the handle end of the tube. The tube is more tapered than the Drying Stick, but wider and harder to hold. For maneuverability, it must be held midway up the tube, away from the switch. The tube is also longer and, with the attachments, it is more difficult to operate. The air intake system on these two appliances is similar to the Drying Stick, but not quite as protected.

The Schick Styling Stick package is a sophisticated one. It includes four regular attachments—a comb, brush, round styling brush, and a large metal roller that slips on over the round brush and heats up so it can be used like a curling iron. Also included is a separate attachment holder for two-handed styling.

The Schick Grooming Stick provides fewer styling options. It comes with a comb, brush, and attachment holder, plus a canvas tote bag for traveling. This feature alone probably adds to the price considerably and is not worth the difference in value.

Both the Styling Stick and Grooming Stick run on 900 watts, and they both performed well under testing, drying and styling with efficiency. There is one other thing to note: Schick's packaging for its personal hair care appliances (with the exception of the electric curler set we tested) is very elaborate. This could affect price in a negative way without benefiting the consumer.

**Approximate Retail Prices:** **Low Prices:**
**Grooming Stick: $28.99** **Grooming Stick: $19.55**
**Styling Stick: $28.99** **Styling Stick: $19.55**

**Schick Power Styler 800** proved to be a very adequate and efficient dryer/styler. The slide switch on the side of the handle provides both dry and style settings, with appropriate temperature and airflow. Light in weight, it is simple to control with a slim, easy-to-hold handle. This dryer has few distinguishing characteristics, but it is very practical for home use. In addition to the main unit, it features a concentrator, fine-toothed comb, detangling comb, brush, and separate attachment handle for two-handed styling. As with other Schick products, the fancy packaging should be considered when judging value.

**Approximate Retail Price: $26.99** **Low Price: $18.34**

**Sunbeam Power Plus 900 Hair Dryer/Styler** is one of Sunbeam's top-of-the-line dryer models, marketed as a "jack of all trades" for home hair care. Included with the dryer are both wide-toothed and fine-toothed comb attachments, a brush attachment and a handle to which each attachment can be secured for two-handed styling. When tested for performance, the unit dried hair quickly without excessive force. Sculptured, one-piece design makes it light in weight and easy to hold, with the controls conveniently placed on the inside of the slim handle. It features two settings, "dry" and "style." The style setting operates with less airflow and lower heat.

*Prices are accurate at time of printing; subject to manufacturer's change.*

The enclosed instruction booklet gives styling suggestions for both men and women.
**Approximate Retail Price: $24.95**                 **Low Price: $18.48**

## HOT LATHER DISPENSERS
**Best Buy**

**Clairol Hot Shave Capsule** plugs into a wall outlet to heat, then fits onto a can of aerosol shave cream to produce hot lather. It is a little larger than other cordless models tested. It is completely immersible. The Hot Shave Capsule fits any size standard aerosol shave cream can. Lather felt warm when the unit was tested right after the signal light indicated the unit was ready—95 seconds after it was plugged in. However, for more heat, the user can leave it plugged in for an extra 30 to 60 seconds. The cordless unit has a removable plastic cover that fits over the prongs, and a travel pouch to accommodate the Capsule, razor, and blades.
**Approximate Retail Price: $15.99**            **Low Price: $10.34**

### Also Tested

**General Electric Shavers Choice Model SCD-3,** a sturdy plastic unit, holds 4- to 11-ounce cans of shaving cream and gels. A heat-control dial, adjustable from low to high, indicates ranges for both creams and gels. The highest temperature setting produces lather almost too hot to hold.

Model SCD-3 offers a luxury feature in its dispenser for after-shave lotion. While convenient, this feature does not justify the unit's additional cost. The Shavers Choice SCD-3 provides cord storage and a wall-mount.
**Approximate Retail Price: $14.98**           **Low Price: $12.98**

**Northern Electric Little Lather Model 8355** is a simple little unit, but it does the job in short order. It plugs directly into a wall outlet and heats in one minute. This was about 30 seconds faster than most other models tested, and for those people who operate on split-second timing in the morning, that might be a plus. The Little Lather's soapy tip can be rinsed under water after use, but the unit is not completely immersible. It has an indicator light that glows red while heating and goes out when ready. It fits all sizes of aerosol cans. A use-and-care booklet is packed with the unit.
**Approximate Retail Price: $7.95**              **Low Price: $5.45**

## IRONS
**Best Buys**

**Hamilton Beach Smart Iron Model 890** is designed to take most of the guesswork out of ironing. A ready light signals when the

*Prices are accurate at time of printing; subject to manufacturer's change.*

soleplate has reached the proper temperature. A self-cleaning feature sweeps lint and mineral deposits out with the steam. Both the spray and the "burst of steam" work well and the large number of steam vents (65) provides good coverage. We like two special safety features: the extra-wide resting heel and the power light that stays on as long as the iron is plugged in. The reversible cord is particularly nice for lefties. The iron comes with a 16-page use-and-care booklet that includes a useful fabric guide chart.

**Approximate Retail Price: $39.95**                  **Low Price: $19.55**

**Sunbeam Shot of Steam Today Iron Model 10-23** is lightweight and easy to handle. It provides plenty of steam despite the fact that it has only nine steam vents. Because it can also be used as a hand steamer, it makes a good travel iron, combining versatility with lightness. The low wattage (600 watts) makes it economical to use. The one major disadvantage of this model is that it has no resting heel and must be on its side when not in use. Another Today model, the 10-14, is identical except that it lacks variable steam control.

| Approximate Retail Prices: | Low Prices: |
|---|---|
| Model 10-23: $24.75 | Model 10-23: $19.93 |
| Model 10-14: $22.50 | Model 10-14: $18.11 |

## Also Tested

**General Electric Light 'N Easy Instant Spray Model F201** is too lightweight (1.6 pounds) to be really useful, but you might consider it if you need a small travel iron. The iron tends to drag on the fabric and is awkward to handle because the cord is too heavy for the iron. It has only 25 steam vents; not enough for heavier tasks. The spray features work well and the cord is reversible. The small soleplate, however, means that you spend more time ironing.

**Approximate Retail Price: $22.98**                  **Low Price: $17.59**

**General Electric Light 'N Easy Surge of Steam Model F200** weighs no more than its Instant Steam companion model (1.6 pounds), but works a bit better because of the extra steam. Like the Instant Steam, it is rather awkward to handle because the reversible cord is too heavy for the iron. The small soleplate adds appreciably to ironing time.

**Approximate Retail Price: $21.98**                  **Low Price: $16.75**

**Proctor-Silex Spray/Steam/Dry Iron Model I635H** has only 29 steam vents, but the spray works well. Like the Super Steam model, it has a large (ten-ounce) "See-Thru" tank that uses tap water and that doesn't have to be emptied. The cord is reversible.

**Approximate Retail Price: $27.95**                  **Low Price: $16.10**

**Proctor-Silex Super Steam/Dry Iron Model I525H** has a number of attractive features. It is self-cleaning and the large "See-Thru"

*Prices are accurate at time of printing; subject to manufacturer's change.*

water tank doesn't have to be emptied. It uses tap water and has a large opening for easy filling. The extra steam feature works well and the 71 steam vents give excellent coverage. The cord is reversible.

**Approximate Retail Price: $31.95**            **Low Price: $17.60**

## SHAVERS
### Best Buys

**Ronson 1000XL Model 22602,** a quiet comfortable shaver, has 36 cutter blades beneath a thin, flexible, stainless steel shaving screen. The shaver's deep, hollow cap provides storage for the coil cord and cleaning brush plus a mirror. The case is convenient for travel; a wall-bracket eases at-home storage. Separate switches control the shaver and trim features. Replacement cutting systems and cords are available.

**Approximate Retail Price: $39.95**            **Low Price: $28.35**

**Ronson Spiromatic XL Model 24601** offers a close and fairly fast shave. The angled head is comfortable, and the unusual circular blades can be rotated to present fresh cutting surfaces. The snap-on blades are replaceable, and the screen is easily detached for cleaning or replacement. A retractable trimmer for sideburns, moustaches and beards is operated by a separate slide control. Model 24701 is identical in most respects, but is cordless and rechargeable.

**Approximate Retail Prices:**          **Low Prices:**
**Model 24601: $39.95**                    **Model 24601: $28.35**
**Model 24701: $54.95**                    **Model 24701: $39.00**

**Schick Flexamatic 400** shavers feature a super-thin flexible head that allows the blades to provide an exceptionally close shave. A drawback, however, is that special care must be taken to prevent damage to the thin screen. The 400 model is an economical cord shaver with dual voltage and an extra-wide trimmer for shaving long hairs on the neck, sideburns and moustache.

**Approximate Retail Price: $54.98**            **Low Price: $33.29**

### Also Tested

**Lady Schick Electric Shaver** is a very traditional women's shaver model, with standard features and design and giving about the same results as others on the market. There have been few technical advances recently in the area of women's electric shavers. Most, including this model, are adequate for defuzzing applications, but not outstanding. As with other appliances of this type, the unit turns on automatically when plugged in and it can be stopped only by unplugging. This is often inconvenient.

**Approximate Retail Price: $16.98**            **Low Price: $10.06**

*Prices are accurate at time of printing; subject to manufacturer's change.*

**Remington Smooth & Silky Women's Electrics** come in three models—WER 4000, WER 5000 and WER 6000. Each model has its own color system and travel case design. The higher-priced models, of course, have the more elaborate cases. The WER 5000 and WER 6000 have on/off switches while the WER 4000 turns on automatically when plugged in. The WER 6000 is rechargeable, adding to its convenience and portability. The basic shaving unit common to all three models performed well under testing. It shaved both long and short hair smoothly and easily. The slim, tapered design made it easy to control, especially under the arms. Two problems, however, were noted during testing. The detachable coil cord was quite short, limiting the area in which it can be used, and it was difficult to attach and remove. The enclosed use-and-care booklet was sketchy and not very informative, particularly for those using an electric razor for the first time.

**Approximate Retail Prices:**
**Model WER 4000: Not Available**
**Model WER 5000: Not Available**
**Model WER 6000: Not Available**

**Low Prices:**
**Model WER 4000: $17.65**
**Model WER 5000: $22.15**
**Model WER 6000: $28.00**

**Remington XLR Electrics** give fairly close shaves, but razor burn makes them uncomfortable to use. In addition, the trimmer switch is awkwardly placed. There are three XLR models: the XLR-3000 is the deluxe rechargeable version, while the XLR-2000 and the economy XLR-1000 are cord operated. All three models have Remington's removable "triple-shaving" head assemblies.

**Approximate Retail Prices:**
**Model XLR-1000: Not Available**
**Model XLR-2000: Not Available**
**Model XLR-3000: Not Available**

**Low Prices:**
**Model XLR-1000: $39.20**
**Model XLR-2000: $45.65**
**Model XLR-3000: $52.35**

**Sunbeam Groomer Razor 8000** is definitely inferior to the others tested. The Remington and Ronson models gave closer, more comfortable shaves. There was an unacceptable amount of razor burn, and it is too big and bulky for comfortable handling. The trimmer, which has fine settings, is its best feature.

**Approximate Retail Price: $49.95** **Low Price: $40.93**

*Prices are accurate at time of printing; subject to manufacturer's change.*

# Personal Care Appliance Prices

## American

| | | Retail Price | Low Price |
|---|---|---|---|
| **HAIR DRYERS** | | | |
| 1400 | American "Star" Pro Hair Dryer | $14.95 | $8.17 |
| 1500 | American "Free 'N Easy" Pro Hair Dryer | 15.95 | 8.63 |
| 1600 | American "1600" Pro Dryer | 16.95 | 9.94 |

## Clairol

| | | | |
|---|---|---|---|
| **HAIRSETTERS** | | | |
| C20S | Clairol 20 Instant Hairsetter | $25.99 | $16.09 |
| K400 | Kindness Deluxe 3-Way Hairsetter | 39.99 | 25.29 |
| K420 | Kindness 3-Way Hairsetter | 34.99 | 21.84 |
| K500 | Carmen Hairsetter | 45.99 | 28.74 |
| 200 | Crazy Curl Steam Styling Wand | 19.99 | 12.64 |
| C100 | Crazy Baby Steam Styling Wand | 25.99 | 16.09 |
| **HOT SHAVE SYSTEM** | | | |
| CAP3 | Hot Shave Capsule Kit | $15.99 | $10.34 |
| **MAKE-UP MIRRORS** | | | |
| LM3 | True-To-Light III Make-Up Mirror | $39.99 | $25.29 |
| RM1 | Mirror Mirror | 20.99 | 12.64 |
| LM20 | Lighted Make-Up Mirror | 27.99 | 17.24 |
| **MOISTURIZER & MASSAGER** | | | |
| MMS | Moisture Lover | $16.49 | $10.34 |
| SM1 | Skin Machine | $16.49 | $10.34 |

*Prices are accurate at time of printing; subject to manufacturer's change.*

|  |  | Retail Price | Low Price |
|---|---|---|---|
| **NAIL CARE** | | | |
| NM1 | Nail Works | $16.49 | $10.34 |
| **STYLER/DRYERS** | | | |
| TD1 | Son of a Gun 1200 | $28.99 | $17.81 |
| RBD1000 | Hot Stuff Multidryer | 31.49 | 19.54 |
| AB-3 | Air Brush Styling Dryer | 27.99 | 19.60 |
| **WHIRLPOOL** | | | |
| FF1 | The Foot Fixer | $43.99 | $27.59 |

# General Electric

|  |  | Retail Price | Low Price |
|---|---|---|---|
| **CURLER/STYLERS** | | | |
| CS-1 | GE Touch 'N Curl | $13.98 | $10.19 |
| CS-5 | Touch 'N Curl V | 20.98 | 15.59 |
| CS-4 | GE Touch 'N Curl IV | 26.98 | 20.39 |
| **FACIAL CLEANER** | | | |
| FCM-1 | The Clean Scene | $12.98 | $9.59 |
| **HAIRDRYERS** | | | |
| PRO-10 | Power Turbo Pro Pistol Dryer | $20.98 | $15.59 |
| PRO-11 | Super Turbo Pro Pistol Dryer | 27.98 | 20.99 |
| PRO-5 | Power Pro Pistol Dryer | 22.98 | 16.79 |
| PRO-6 | Super Pro Pistol Dryer | 29.98 | 22.79 |
| HD-21 | Soft Bonnet Hair Dryer | 25.98 | 19.79 |
| HD-18 | Soft Bonnet Hair Dryer | 29.98 | 22.79 |
| HD-61SS | Salon Hair Dryer | 35.98 | 27.59 |
| HD-63SS | Salon Hair Dryer | 39.98 | 29.99 |
| **HAIRSETTER** | | | |
| HCD-4 | 3-Way Speedsetters | $26.98 | $20.39 |
| **IRONS** | | | |
| F240WH | Spray, Extra Steam Iron | $37.50 | $27.89 |
| F92 | Spray Iron | 20.98 | 15.59 |
| F95AV | Spray Iron | 22.98 | 17.20 |
| F95AVT | Spray Iron | 23.98 | 17.99 |
| F210WH | Spray Iron | 33.50 | 26.08 |
| F210WHT | Spray Iron | 34.98 | 26.98 |
| F63T | Steam Iron | 15.98 | 11.88 |
| F79WH | Steam Iron | 20.98 | 15.29 |
| F218HRT | Steam Iron | 30.98 | 23.39 |

*Prices are accurate at time of printing; subject to manufacturer's change.*

|  |  | Retail Price | Low Price |
|---|---|---|---|
| F116BL | Extra Steam Iron | $24.98 | $18.89 |
| F220HR | Extra Steam Iron | 31.98 | 23.99 |
| F200HR | Light 'N Easy Iron | 21.98 | 16.75 |
| F201WH | Light 'N Easy Iron | 22.98 | 17.59 |
| F54 | Dry Iron | 16.98 | 12.59 |
| F54AV | Dry Iron | 16.98 | 12.59 |
| F49 | Travel Iron | 24.98 | 18.89 |

### MAKE-UP MIRRORS
| IM-4 | Lighted Make-Up Mirror | $17.98 | $13.79 |
|---|---|---|---|
| IM-5 | Lighted Make-Up Mirror | 20.98 | 15.59 |
| IM-1 | Lighted Make-Up Mirror | 26.98 | 20.39 |

### MANICURE SET
| MS-3 | La Manicure | $16.98 | $13.19 |
|---|---|---|---|

### SHAVE CREAM DISPENSERS
| SCD-1 | Your Choice | $12.98 | $9.59 |
|---|---|---|---|
| SCD-3 | Shavers Choice | 14.98 | 12.98 |

### MASSAGERS
| MR-1 | Massager | $15.98 | $11.99 |
|---|---|---|---|
| MR-2 | Massager | 20.98 | 15.59 |

### HEATING PADS
| P-55 | Heating Pad | $9.98 | $6.89 |
|---|---|---|---|
| P-66 | The "Back Pad" | 11.98 | 8.39 |
| P-68 | The "Moist Pad" | 14.50 | 10.19 |

### STYLING DRYERS
| PB-1 | Power Brush | $26.98 | $20.39 |
|---|---|---|---|
| SD-5 | Zoom 1000 Styling Dryer | 24.98 | 19.19 |
| SD-8 | Vari-Power Styling Dryer | 31.98 | 23.99 |
| SB-1 | Superblow The Hair Care Center | 41.98 | 31.79 |

### TOOTHBRUSHES
| TB-5 | Toothbrushes | $18.98 | $14.39 |
|---|---|---|---|
| TB-9 | Toothbrushes | 24.98 | 18.59 |
| TBC-20 | Toothbrushes | 11.98 | 8.99 |

# Gillette

### CURLER
| 9330 | Supercurl Compact | $15.99 | $11.04 |
|---|---|---|---|

*Prices are accurate at time of printing; subject to manufacturer's change.*

|  |  | Retail Price | Low Price |
|---|---|---|---|
| **STYLING DRYERS** | | | |
| 9010 | Promax Compact Dryer | $21.99 | $14.72 |
| 9160 | Supermax 2 Adjustable Styler/Dryer | 28.99 | 20.01 |
| 9180 | Supermax 2 Styler/Dryer | 24.99 | 17.54 |
| 9210 | Promax Compact 1200 Dryer | 24.99 | 17.25 |

# Hamilton Beach

| **IRONS** | | | |
|---|---|---|---|
| 833W | Burst of Steam Iron | $32.95 | $16.09 |
| 866B | Burst of Steam Iron | 31.95 | 13.79 |
| 890 | Smart Iron | 39.95 | 19.55 |
| **ELECTRIC SCISSORS** | | | |
| 348G | Electric Scissors | $12.95 | $7.46 |
| **HAIR DRYER** | | | |
| 1845 | Hard Hat Hair Dryer | $34.95 | $17.81 |

# Norelco

| **COMPLEXION CARE** | | | |
|---|---|---|---|
| HB9500 | Complexion Plus | $14.95 | $10.33 |
| **SHAVERS** | | | |
| HP1121 | Tripleheader Rotary Razor | $39.95 | $35.63 |
| HP1134 | Budget Speed Shaver 20 | 24.95 | 19.49 |
| HP1308 | Rechargeable Tripleheader | 48.95 | 42.53 |
| HP2115 | Ladybug Deluxe Shaver | 21.95 | 17.80 |
| **STYLER/DRYERS** | | | |
| HB1600 | Curly Q Wand | $14.95 | $10.33 |
| HB1707 | Gotch Gun-Red | 22.95 | 14.35 |
| HB 6600 | Shape 'n Dry 750 | 22.95 | 17.97 |
| **SUNLAMP** | | | |
| HB5000 | Deluxe Sunlamp | $62.95 | $41.38 |

# Oster

| **HAIR TRIM SETS** | | | |
|---|---|---|---|
| 60610 | 10-Piece Home Hair Trim Set | $26.95 | $16.68 |

*Prices are accurate at time of printing; subject to manufacturer's change.*

|  |  | Retail Price | Low Price |
|---|---|---|---|
| 28416 | Raycine 16-Piece Home Hair Trim Set | $15.95 | $10.12 |

# Remington

**SHAVERS**

| | | | |
|---|---|---|---|
| XLR-3000 | 3000 World-Wide® Rechargeable Electric | — | $52.35 |
| XLR-2000 | 2000 Electric | — | 45.65 |
| XLR-1000 | 1000 Electric | — | 39.20 |
| RR—1 | Radial® Rechargeable World-Wide® | — | 50.40 |
| RC-5 | Radial® Cord | — | 41.45 |
| ST-1 | Soft Touch® Cord | — | 38.10 |
| CH-1 | Challenger® Cord | — | 22.15 |
| WER-6000 | Smooth & Silky® Rechargeable Woman's Electric | — | 28.00 |
| WER-5000 | Smooth & Silky® Woman's Electric | — | 22.15 |
| WER-4000 | Smooth & Silky® Woman's Electric | — | 17.65 |

# Ronson

**SHAVERS**

| | | | |
|---|---|---|---|
| 24601 | Spiromatic XL Electric | $39.95 | $28.35 |
| 24701 | Spiromatic Cordless Dual Volt | 54.95 | 39.00 |
| 22602 | 1000XL Electric | 39.95 | 28.35 |
| 22601 | 1000 Electric | 33.95 | 24.10 |

# Schick

**FACIAL SAUNA**

| | | | |
|---|---|---|---|
| 60-C | Lady Schick Facial Sauna | $37.95 | $26.39 |

**HAIR DRYERS**

| | | | |
|---|---|---|---|
| 2001-C | Lady Schick Custom Salon | $46.95 | $32.14 |

**HAIRSETTERS**

| | | | |
|---|---|---|---|
| 71-C | Lady Schick Lasting Curls | $27.95 | $19.26 |
| 75-C | Lady Schick Lasting Curls | 32.95 | 22.43 |

*Prices are accurate at time of printing; subject to manufacturer's change.*

|  |  | Retail Price | Low Price |
|---|---|---|---|
| **STYLERS/DRYERS** | | | |
| CI-5 | Lady Schick Quick Curl | $12.99 | $9.14 |
| CI-6 | Lady Schick Quick Curl Compact | 17.99 | 12.54 |
| ST-2 | Schick Styling Stick | 28.99 | 19.55 |
| ST-3 | Schick Grooming Stick | 28.99 | 19.55 |
| ST-4 | Lady Schick Styling Stick | 35.99 | 24.72 |
| ST-5 | Schick Grooming Stick | 33.99 | 23.58 |
| PJ 1000 | Schick Pro Jet 1000 | 21.99 | 15.24 |
| PJ 1200 | Schick Pro Jet 1200 | 24.99 | 17.25 |
| PJ 1500 | Schick Pro Jet 1500 | 30.99 | 20.13 |
| DS-10 | Schick Drying Stick 1000 | 22.99 | 15.53 |
| DS-12 | Schick Drying Stick 1200 | 28.99 | 18.13 |
| DS-15 | Schick Drying Stick 1500 | 31.99 | 21.85 |
| PS 800 | Schick Power Styler 800 | 26.99 | 18.34 |
| APS 1000 | Schick Adjustable Power Styler 1000 | 31.99 | 21.28 |
| **SHAVERS** | | | |
| 400 | Schick Deluxe Flexamatic Cord | $54.98 | $33.29 |
| 209 | Schick Custom | 23.98 | 14.38 |
| 109 | Lady Schick Jewel Shaver | 16.98 | 10.06 |

# Sunbeam

|  |  | Retail Price | Low Price |
|---|---|---|---|
| **BODY BRUSH** | | | |
| 60-11 | Bod-Machine Body Brush, 2 Speeds | $17.95 | $13.60 |
| **CURLER/STYLERS** | | | |
| 54-74 | Dial-A-Style Mist-Stick | $25.95 | $21.03 |
| 54-124 | Mistee Mist-Stick II | 16.95 | 14.79 |
| **HAIR DRYERS** | | | |
| 50-18 | Jet Set Flair Hair Dryer | $23.50 | $17.61 |
| 51-14 | Portable Professional Hard Hat | 29.50 | 18.81 |
| 52-61 | Power Breeze "700" Deluxe | 20.95 | 15.67 |
| 52-87 | Power Plus "900" Dryer/Styler | 24.95 | 18.48 |
| 52-191 | Vari-A-Matic Dryer/Styler | 33.50 | 25.02 |
| 52-167 | Odyssey Blower/Dryer | 28.50 | 21.26 |
| 52-188 | Swing-Aire Blower/Dryer | 24.95 | 18.83 |
| **HAIR TRIMMERS/CLIPPERS** | | | |
| 77-19 | Mister Touch-Up Cutter Comb | $22.50 | $18.11 |
| 63-18 | 10-Piece Clipmaster Hair Clippers | 10.95 | 6.92 |
| 63-28 | 17-Piece Clipmaster Hair Clippers | 13.95 | 11.04 |

*Prices are accurate at time of printing; subject to manufacturer's change.*

## IRONS

| | | Retail Price | Low Price |
|---|---|---|---|
| 11-193 | Jewel Self-Cleaning "Shot of Steam" | $32.99 | $26.55 |
| 12-21 | Spray Mist Steam or Dry | 24.99 | 20.11 |
| 12-71 | Jewel Spray Mist Self-Cleaning | 37.99 | 30.58 |
| 13-10 | Ironmaster Dry Iron | 17.50 | 14.09 |
| 10-14 | Shot of Steam Today Iron | 22.50 | 18.11 |
| 10-23 | Variable Control Shot of Steam | 24.75 | 19.93 |
| 11-51 | Steam or Dry Iron | 22.99 | 18.50 |

## LATHER DISPENSER

| | | | |
|---|---|---|---|
| 74-39 | Lather Man Hot Shave | $6.95 | $5.99 |

## SHAVERS

| | | | |
|---|---|---|---|
| 75-249 | Groomer Razor 8000 | $49.95 | $40.93 |
| 75-269 | Cord/Cordless Groomer Razor 8000 | 59.95 | 48.86 |
| 75-19 | Shavemaster Shaver & Groomer | 46.95 | 37.81 |
| 75-29 | Multi-Volt Shavemaster & Groomer | 48.95 | 39.61 |
| 75-39 | Cord-Cordless Shavemaster & Groomer | 57.95 | 46.61 |
| 75-128 | Shavemaster Shaver | 21.95 | 16.91 |
| 76-14 | Lady Sunbeam Twin Head Shaver | 23.95 | 18.87 |
| 76-27 | Lady Sunbeam Twin Head Shaver | 23.95 | 18.87 |
| 76-194 | Lady Sunbeam Dual-Head Shaver | 19.95 | 15.80 |
| 76-207 | Lady Sunbeam Dual-Head Shaver | 19.95 | 15.80 |
| 76-171 | Lady Sunbeam Micro-Twin Shaver | 12.95 | 8.63 |
| 76-67 | Lady Sunbeam Twin-Head Shaver | 12.95 | 8.63 |

## TOOTHBRUSH

| | | | |
|---|---|---|---|
| 65-78 | Cordless Electric Toothbrush | $24.95 | $20.09 |

---

# Teledyne

## WATER PIKS

| | | | |
|---|---|---|---|
| 37 | Deluxe Water Pik | $36.95 | $23.60 |
| 49 | Standard Water Pik | 31.95 | 20.40 |
| 76 | Water Pik Slimline Oral | 41.95 | 26.80 |
| SM2 | Wall-Mount Shower Massage | 24.95 | 15.49 |
| SM3 | Hand-Held Shower Massage | 39.95 | 24.81 |
| BJ75 | Oral Hygiene Center | 44.95 | 28.72 |
| SVR22 | Super Saver Shower Massage | 29.95 | 18.60 |
| SVR32 | Hand-Held Super Saver Shower Mass. | 44.95 | 27.91 |

*Prices are accurate at time of printing; subject to manufacturer's change.*

# 1978 Photo Equipment

**T**HERE ARE MANY people who are happy with simple little "box" cameras and who say, "I'm no big photographer—I just take snapshots." There are others who never seem to go anywhere without several sophisticated cameras slung over their shoulders and gadget bags filled to overflowing with lenses, filters and film. Whether the goal is to make one-of-a-kind souvenirs of special occasions or to earn a living as a professional photographer, there are cameras available to suit your needs. CONSUMER GUIDE Magazine's staff of photographic experts has tested dozens of photography products from the simplest models to the most highly advanced.

The type of camera and accessories you buy, whether you are interested in still photography or in movies, depends upon your ambitions. Many experts would advise beginners to buy a camera that is more versatile than they need at present so that it does not become restrictive too quickly. Yet it might be possible to obtain everything you want from the least expensive camera available. If you should buy a camera and find later that you have progressed beyond its abilities, you can trade it in, or—as many professionals and advanced amateurs do—hang onto it as a second "reserve" camera.

There are some questions about photographic equipment that only the individual buyer can answer. Are you looking for a "grab and shoot" camera that will never miss a shot, or do you want a camera that requires enough effort on your part so that every picture becomes a learning experience? Will you be content with snapshots, or will you become intent on creating works of art? Is the ability to carry your camera with you everywhere in your pocket or purse more important than the opportunity to experiment with a much more complex piece of equipment? How much money do you want to spend?

With so many types and brands of photography products available in so many price ranges, your selection must be based on your goals and budget. However, we can help you determine which cameras and other equipment have the features you desire. The following reviews of the various film formats and accessories are intended to provide an overview of what is available.

### SLR Cameras

THE STANDARD 35mm single-lens reflex camera is just that—a standard piece of equipment for professional and amateur photographers all around the world.

One reason for the SLR's wide acceptance is its viewing and metering system. As its name suggests, the single-lens reflex allows the user to make light readings and view the scene through the same lens system that takes the picture. Lens interchangeability adds to the SLR's versatility. A photographer can quickly switch to a telephoto lens to bring distant objects into view, or use a wide-angle lens to stretch perspective and exaggerate the depth of the scene.

New advances in camera design have resulted in lighter, smaller SLRs that are easier to hold and carry. Computer technology has allowed camera manufacturers to add automation to their SLRs. The result is that some cameras can set their own shutter speeds, and others can adjust their own lens openings. A quick twist of the focusing ring and a push on the shutter button is usually all that is necessary to get an acceptable photograph with one of these automatics. Furthermore, automatic focusing is just around the corner.

SLRs vary greatly in ability, size, weight and price. Some are complex machines with an astounding array of sophisticated features; others are simpler and much less expensive.

### Compact 35mm Cameras

THE TERM "compact" is used to describe the wide range of cameras that use the 35mm film format but that do not have a single-lens reflex system. The classification includes rangefinders as well as other small 35mm cameras that are neither rangefinders nor SLRs.

A rangefinder does not allow the user to view the scene through the lens that takes the picture, but it does enable the photographer to focus the picture-taking lens accurately. Such cameras incorporate a viewing system with a visible means of determining precise focus. The user adjusts the focus ring on the lens until the image in the viewfinder looks sharp.

A non-rangefinder camera forces the photographer to guess the distance between the subject and the camera. Many of these cameras have distance markings on the focusing ring. The user merely turns the ring and estimates the correct setting. This is called zone focusing.

Compact 35mm cameras have several advantages over the SLRs. They are often lighter and smaller than any SLR could be. Their viewing screens often are brighter. These cameras have fewer moving parts and are often less expensive than SLRs.

**Larger-Format Cameras**

GIVEN THAT THE 35mm film format and the cameras that use it are so versatile, technically advanced and readily available, why would any photographer want to be burdened with a larger camera that uses a larger film? The answer is that larger film sizes mean larger negatives and slides. The larger the film image, the less magnification necessary to enlarge it for printing or projection. Some photographers are willing to spend extra money for cameras that are bulky and less convenient to use than 35mm machines in order to get the added enlargement detail provided by bigger film formats.

The category of larger-format cameras includes everything from the popular 2-1/4 by 2-1/4 inch film size to cameras that use sheet film almost as big as a piece of typing paper. The medium-format category includes cameras that use film that is 2-1/4 inches tall; some take square pictures, while others take photographs that are narrower or wider.

The medium-format camera is an important tool for the protessional photographer who often must make very large enlargements or photographs with extremely fine detail. However, camera manufacturers have also been working to develop medium-format machines that will be accepted by amateurs. The result is that several of these cameras are almost as easy to use as are 35mm SLRs.

**Cartridge Cameras**

MANY INTRIGUING little cameras often can be seen in shops that sell used photographic equipment. These cameras probably would take good pictures if film to fit them could be found. Instead, they collect dust because their formats are extinct.

Film formats have come and gone. One of the survivors is a system that some observers of the photographic industry once thought would never amount to much more than a toy. It is the 110 cartridge. Several years ago, when 110-format cameras already were packed with enough features to take them out of toyland and put them in the hands of admiring professional photographers, many people assumed the 110s had reached their upper limits.

Yet they continued to evolve. Now there are new 110 cameras with zoom lenses, through-the-lens metering and varying degrees of automation. The small proportions of the 110 cameras continue to be a strong selling point, but some new models approach the weight of 35mm compacts. The small size can be a handicap: the negatives and slides 110s produce require great magnification and therefore are not as effective as larger film formats when maximum detail is the goal.

**Instant-Picture Cameras**

SUDDENLY, THERE IS great interest in instant photography and new competition for the leading company in the field. This format is growing in complexity to satisfy the casual snapshooter and the professional alike.

Basically, there are three types of instant film. One is the peel-apart-and-time format for black-and-white pictures. This type requires the user to time the development of the picture and then peel away and discard a gooey piece of paper. The second type is a color version of the peel-apart system. The third, and the type that is receiving the greatest amount of attention from the companies in the business, is the dry color system. This kind of film requires no timing, no gooey paper and no litter. The photograph comes out of the camera dry but with no visible image. After a few minutes, the full color comes up to produce a photograph that is often strikingly sharp and true.

The cameras using the dry system differ primarily in shape and weight. Some use tiny motors to roll out the photograph, while others require the user to turn a crank. The most highly advanced of these cameras are nearly as expensive as lower-priced SLRs, while the least expensive instant cameras are priced about the same as some of the medium-priced 110 "pocket" cameras.

**Electronic Flash Units**

FLASH UNITS, like the cameras with which they are used, vary greatly in complexity, ability and size. There are units that do nothing more than light up like flashcubes when the camera's shutter button is pressed. They may be weak, but they are easy to carry. Other units can see and interpret the light they throw and make instantaneous adjustments to suit the photographer's requirements. These units, for the most part, are larger and heavier than the non-automatic ones.

Factors to be considered when shopping for an electronic flash, then, are the size and power output. There is a choice of heavy flashes that are often unwieldy but very powerful, smaller ones suitable for snapshots, and a vast assortment of units in between.

**Darkroom Equipment**

AS AMATEUR photographers progress through the hobby, they

often decide to carry the picture-making process through to the end. That is, they want to snap the shutter and then develop and print the picture. For that reason, makers of darkroom equipment have been designing enlargers and other products especially suited to the home darkroom.

The appearance and function of the enlarger has not changed dramatically in many years. In fact, one leading model today looks almost exactly the way it did when it was introduced more than 20 years ago. Enlargers do vary, however, in their convenience of operation, their ability to accept various film formats and their price.

**Super 8 Cameras and Projectors**

WHETHER THE GOAL is to make simple home movies of children's birthday parties and other family activities or to produce film productions that rival those of Hollywood, Super 8 cameras are available to suit the filmer's tastes and talents.

There are simplistic little machines that are the motion-picture equivalent of the pocket snapshot camera, and there are Super 8 cameras capable of making films of professional quality. Special lenses for special effects, the ability to film in low-light conditions and improvements in sound-recording devices have greatly enlarged the realm of the Super 8 enthusiast.

As could be expected, the machines used to display these advanced films have also reached a new level of sophistication. There are projectors that feature high-fidelity sound reproduction, superb clarity of the projected image and great convenience of operation.

# 1978 Best Buys Photo Equipment

CONSUMER GUIDE Magazine's photographic test staff has evaluated dozens of cameras and movie projectors and has rated them according to overall quality, convenience, capabilities and price. Within each of the categories below, the products are listed in order of dollar-for-dollar value.

## SINGLE-LENS REFLEX CAMERAS

**The Olympus OM-2** is the automatic version of the camera that started the SLR downsizing trend. At a weight of much less than two pounds, the OM-2 truly is an impressive little handful. We found it easy and fun to use. The meter of the OM-2 is almost unbelievably versatile. Our only criticism of the automatic Olympus is that its viewfinder does not display as much information as we would find helpful.
**(Chrome w/50mm f/1.4 lens)**
**Approximate Retail Price: $574.95**          **Low Price: $379.50**

**The Konica Autoreflex N-T3,** a shutter-priority automatic, has a comfortable shutter button. The T3 performed well in our tests, although one deficiency is the lack of a ratchet on the rapid-advance lever. Its price is rather high, but we can still rate the Konica as a very good value if shutter-priority automation is your top priority. The N-T3 is in most ways identical to the T3, but includes a fixed hot shoe and eyepiece shutter.
**(Microdiaprism focusing screen and 50mm f/1.7 lens)**
**Approximate Retail Price: $509.95**          **Low Price: $374.65**

**The Yashica FX-1** is an interesting aperture-priority automatic in its own right, but one of its best features is its ability to mount the full line of Yashica lenses as well as all Zeiss lenses designed for the Contax RTS. The viewfinder is dim and restricted, but the metering system is accurate and has a wide range.
**(50mm f/1.4 lens)**
**Approximate Retail Price: $545.00**          **Low Price: $385.50**

*Prices are accurate at time of printing; subject to manufacturer's change.*

**The Contax RTS** is easy to operate in both its aperture-priority automatic mode and manually. It has one of the brightest viewfinders we have ever tested. However, the finder showed us only 84 percent of the image recorded on film. We judge that poor for a camera that carries so high a list price.
**(50mm f/1.4 lens)**
**Approximate Retail Price: $765.00**         **Low Price: $540.85**

**The Olympus OM-1,** nonautomatic companion to the OM-2, has received high ratings from CONSUMER GUIDE Magazine's photographic equipment testers because of its trend-setting dimensions and ease of operation. It does not have a battery checker, its viewfinder does not display aperture or shutter-speed data, and it is relatively expensive. However, in terms of overall quality and convenience, it is a very good value.
**(Chrome w/50mm f/1.4 lens)**
**Approximate Retail Price: $419.95**         **Low Price: $277.15**

**The Fujica ST-801** uses light-emitting diodes to indicate exposure, and we found them to be accurate in our tests. The view through the finder is bright. Accurate focusing aids make sharp pictures easy to obtain. The only criticism we have of the 801 concerns its lens-mount system: this camera uses the Praktica thread mount, which can be both an advantage and a disadvantage. Nevertheless, we believe the Fujica 801 offers good value for the price.
**(Chrome w/55mm f/1.8 lens)**
**Approximate Retail Price: $380.00**         **Low Price: $285.00**

**The Yashica FR** does not have the sleek, rounded styling of the Contax RTS or its automation, but the cameras are nearly identical in most other ways. Like the Contax, the Yashica has a bright viewfinder. Its meter is accurate, easy to understand and efficient. A feather-touch shutter button helps assure sharp pictures. The FR accepts the full line of Zeiss lenses designed for the Contax, plus Yashica optics.
**(50mm f/1.7 lens)**
**Approximate Retail Price: $412.50**         **Low Price: $292.85**

**The Nikon FM** is one member of Nikon's new generation of cameras. It is smaller and lighter than Nikons of old, is easy to handle and does not cost as much as some of the company's bigger models. It has a bright viewfinder that displays f-stop and shutter speed data. Its photodiode metering system responds quickly to changes in light, but the range between several of the little lights is sometimes too great to ensure precise measurements.
**(50mm f/2 lens)**
**Approximate Retail Price: $487.50**         **Low Price: $348.55**

**The Konica Autoreflex TC** is moderately priced, light and compact. We found it fast to operate in its automatic mode, slow in the

*Prices are accurate at time of printing; subject to manufacturer's change.*

manual mode. Tests of shutter speeds from 1/8 to 1/1000 second (the only ones available) showed them to be accurate. The viewfinder provides a restricted view and is somewhat dim and flat, but focusing is easy in dim light because of the effective focusing aids.

**(50mm f/1.7 lens)**
**Approximate Retail Price: $298.45**            **Low Price: $219.20**

## 35mm RANGEFINDERS

**The Konica C35 EF** is no larger and not significantly heavier than some of the popular 110 cartridge cameras, but the larger image size of the 35mm format provides the Konica's users with greater clarity than is possible with 110 film. The C35's pop-up flash is convenient, powerful enough for most snapshot uses and as economical as throw-away systems used by 110 cameras. We rate the Konica a good value for the snapshooter or for the advanced amateur who wants a second camera.
**Approximate Retail Price: $165.00**            **Low Price: $121.25**

**The Minox 35EL** is the smallest, lightest, most compact full-frame 35mm camera available. It features aperture-preferred automatic exposure control, but it has no rangefinder. Focusing is of the zone type. The basic appeal of the Minox is its small size; the biggest drawback is the same thing. We found it so small as to be inhibiting, and its light weight works against it. However, in terms of a true pocketable 35mm camera, there is nothing like it.
**Approximate Retail Price: $183.00**            **Low Price: $140.90**

## 110 CARTRIDGE CAMERAS

**The Minox 110S** includes more sophisticated features than almost all of its competitors. It features aperture-preferred exposure automation, an electronic shutter, an f/2.8 lens, a rangefinder that proved to be very accurate and easy to use, and a weight of only five ounces. As could be expected for a camera that does all of this, the Minox 110S is expensive. However, we rate it a good value for the advanced 110 photographer.
**Approximate Retail Price: $219.60**            **Low Price: $164.70**

**The Rollei A110** is unquestionably a pocket camera: it is small enough to be carried in a vest pocket. Construction is excellent and practical, but the Rollei has no rangefinder and lacks fast shutter speeds. Even so, if you are looking for a very small camera that is capable of making high-quality 110 prints, the Rollei A110 is in a class almost by itself.
**Approximate Retail Price: $290.00**            **Low Price: $211.70**

**The Minolta 110 Zoom** is actually a 110 SLR; that is, the scene is viewed through the same lens that takes the picture. The zoom lens

*Prices are accurate at time of printing; subject to manufacturer's change.*

is versatile and works effectively. Aperture-priority automation increases the camera's effectiveness for grab-and-shoot photography. To get all of these abilities, however, you must settle for greater bulk. The Minolta cannot really be considered a pocket 110.
**Approximate Retail Price: $265.00**  **Low Price: $174.90**

**Fujica's 350 Zoom** sacrifices the convenience of an adjustable shutter for the convenience of adjustable focal length. In other words, the 350 has a zoom lens that works well, but the camera offers only one shutter speed. That speed, 1/125 second, is fast enough to prevent blurred pictures. There is no rangefinder: focusing is done by zone. The 350 does not do everything that the Minolta 110 Zoom does, but what it does, it does well.
**Approximate Retail Price: $119.50**  **Low Price: $89.65**

**The Hanimex VEF Zoom** is another 110 with a zoom lens. Like the Fujica zoom 110, the Hanimex has only one shutter speed — 1/125 second. Unlike the Fujica, however, the Hanimex has a vertical layout. That means it is held more like a small SLR than a pair of binoculars. This helps to reduce camera shake. The camera lacks a rangefinder, so focusing must be done by using the zone system. Despite its superior handling characteristics, the Hanimex is a simple box camera designed for casual snapshooters.
**Approximate Retail Price: $66.95**  **Low Price: $43.50**

## INSTANT CAMERAS

**Polaroid's Pronto** is CONSUMER GUIDE Magazine's choice as the best low-price camera for the instant-picture photographer. It is easy to hold and to use and turns out a sharp photograph using the SX-70 "dry" color system.
**Approximate Retail Price: $66.00**  **Low Price: $47.20**

**Polaroid's Reporter** seems to be the exception to the rule of planned obsolescence in the photographic industry. Rather than creating a camera that makes a whole range of products obsolete, Polaroid has developed one that uses several different types of Polaroid film that have been available for many years.
**Approximate Retail Price: $57.00**  **Low Price: $40.75**

**The Polaroid OneStep,** compared to the instant cameras from Kodak, is easier to handle and more pleasant to use.
**Approximate Retail Price: $39.95**  **Low Price: $28.55**

## ENLARGERS

**The Beseler 23C enlarger** is still a good value, 20 years after its introduction. In the past two decades, it has changed little. We like it just as it is. It may look old-fashioned, but it is rugged and
*Prices are accurate at time of printing; subject to manufacturer's change.*

stable. A vast assortment of lens boards, a color head and other accessories are available. The list price is high, but the Beseler is often sold at a big discount. At the discounted price, the 23C is clearly a "Best Buy."

**Approximate Retail Price: $269.96**      **Low Price: $193.00**

**The Durst M601** is a well-made, versatile and functional enlarger. From the standpoint of mechanical engineering, it is one of the most sophisticated and well-built enlargers we have tested. It is rugged enough to withstand frequent use and has an excellent film carrier system. The color head available for the M601 is also well designed.

**Approximate Retail Price: $264.95**      **Low Price: $212.00**

## SUPER 8 CAMERAS

**The Elmo 350 SL** sound camera offers the user an uncomplicated control layout, a lens that produces good image quality, a zoom system that makes both manual and power zooming smooth, and an effective rangefinder. We at first had reservations about the camera's on-camera boom microphone, but we found the 350 to be quiet and capable of good sound recording.

**Approximate Retail Price: $419.95**      **Low Price: $300.25**

**The Elmo 612R** is an advanced, efficient, accurate camera that combines sophisticated features with the ability to film in low light. It is a well-made instrument that gives every indication of being a precision performer.

**Approximate Retail Price: $1100.00**      **Low Price: $793.65**

**The Fujica ZC 1000,** with its interchangeable lenses, variable shutter, forward and reverse run and frame counter, is a camera with full professional capability. The mirror-shutter viewing system is perhaps the most efficient ever to appear in an 8mm camera. Coupled with a double-system sound capability and a wide variety of accessories, the ZC 1000 is one of the best 8mm cameras for people engaged in serious film work.

**Approximate Retail Price: $1249.95**      **Low Price: $937.45**

**The Chinon 506 SM XL** may be the most fully equipped XL sound camera on the market today, combining a 5:1 f/1.2 zoom with fully automatic and manual exposure and recording control. Although the rangefinder and VU meter were rather difficult to use in low light levels, the camera earned a good rating for its versatility and the full user control it permits.

**Approximate Retail Price: $520.00**      **Low Price: $369.20**

**The Canon AZ 1014** is a solid, sophisticated silent Super 8 camera with many features and provocative creative potential. However,

*Prices are accurate at time of printing; subject to manufacturer's change.*

our staff had some difficulty in operating more than one feature at a time while holding it in the hand.
**Approximate Retail Price: $875.00**   **Low Price: $621.25**

**The Minolta Autopak 8 D12** is an advanced silent camera with several features that allow precise control over pictorial content including adjustable backlight/spotlight compensation and a variable shutter. Those features, in combination with the D12's solid construction and high quality of its 12:1 macro powerzoom lens, make it a worthy contender for the attention of film makers interested in sophisticated Super 8 cameras.
**Approximate Retail Price: $950.00**   **Low Price: $627.00**

**The Kodak Ektasound 240** has a zoom Ektar lens that is one of the top lenses manufactured anywhere in the world today. The camera is light and easy to operate, and its sound quality is much better than that of the earlier 150 and 160 models. The 240 does not have a rangefinder or any form of manual exposure control, but CONSUMER GUIDE Magazine rates the Kodak 240 as good as any other camera in its price range and as good as some priced higher.
**Approximate Retail Price: $399.50**   **Low Price: $307.60**

## SUPER 8 PROJECTORS

**The Eumig R 2000,** with its built-in rear-projection screen, makes the viewing of movies simple and swift. It also can be used for conventional front projection. In either case, it produces a bright, sharp image. Its large variety of slow-motion speeds have a practical as well as an amusement value, and its quiet operation is an asset. The difficulty of reaching its film path for cleaning is the one important deficiency in an otherwise excellent design.
**Approximate Retail Price: $390.00**   **Low Price: $272.60**

**The Kodak Moviedeck 285** is a sound projector with playback and sound-on-sound recording features that is easy to operate and is well suited for quality home movie purposes. Its emphasis on styling, however, complicates the process of keeping the internal mechanism clean. The 285 offers good lens quality, compactness, good tone, and the option of projecting on a conventional screen or its own built-in screen.
**Approximate Retail Price: $434.50**   **Low Price: $317.20**

*Prices are accurate at time of printing; subject to manufacturer's change.*

# 1978 Video Games

THE LOW COST of duplicating integrated circuits and the economic advantages of high-volume production drive down the price of electronic equipment. Digital electronic watches and electronic calculators are examples of this rule. "Ball-and-paddle" video games that sold for $65 last year are now priced at less than $20 in some parts of the country.

This year, video games can be divided into the following categories, in ascending cost: (1) Basic "ball-and-paddle" games; (2) new games such as tank battle or pinball games; and (3) programmable microprocessor games with game cartridges.

## Ball - and Paddle - Games

THE VIDEO ball-and-paddle game, first introduced in 1972 by Magnavox and brought into prominence by Atari a few years later with on-screen digital scoring, is quite inexpensive today.

Tennis is a basic game of this design. All the other basic ball games operate similarly, although the field varies. For example, there is a net—a vertical center line—depicted on the TV screen, horizontal lines to mark off the court, tennis rackets represented by small vertical lines controlled by the players, and a small square to simulate the tennis ball.

In the most elementary form of this game, the ball is served randomly at an angle from one side of the net. If the ball hits the top or bottom field boundary, it will be reflected at the same angle. The player on the ball's side of the net must intercept the ball before it passes him. If the ball gets by him, a point is registered on screen

*Prices are accurate at time of printing; subject to manufacturer's change.*

for the opponent. If the ball is hit, it rebounds off the racket toward the opponent. Play continues until one player reaches maximum score, most often 15 points. Any hits or misses made after a winning score is reached will not cause the score to change. To play again, a reset button must be pressed, setting the score to zero for each competitor. There are generally a few different audio sounds emitted, one for side boundary ball reflections, racket hits and a score.

There are a host of options that manufacturers may offer to upgrade the game, each one adding to its cost. Here are some examples: (1) ball served directly from the server's racket, permitting him to place it in a particular spot on his opponent's side of the court; (2) a variety of angles at which the ball rebounds from a player's racket; (3) automatic speedup of ball travel after a short rally; (4) selective ball speeds, sometimes called "difficulty switch"; (5) selective paddle size, sometimes combined with number 4; (6) remote controls; (7) four-player option; (8) color display if played on a color TV set; (9) horizontal movement of a racket in addition to vertical movement, generally controlled by a "joystick"; (10) "time out" switch to maintain score but stop play; (11) player-controlled ball serve speed or ball "English."

Most often, many games are incorporated into a single ball-and-paddle machine, all based on the same principle. For example, some provide a handball or squash game, in which the tennis net line is positioned at one end of the screen to simulate a wall. In this case, the paddles are most often fixed slightly apart so that they may be moved up and down on the screen without bumping into each other.

Whatever upgrading options are incorporated into the tennis game would be applicable to any other game integrated into a model, of course. In general, if a player hits a squash ball when it is not his turn, the ball will pass right through the racket as if it were not there. In more sophisticated games, the ball will change to a specific color—blue, for instance—to match the color of the racket used by the appropriate player.

Hockey is another common game that is selectable for a standard ball-and-paddle machine. This game differs according to the manufacturer's design. For example, there might be a choice of the size of a goal opening. A smaller opening would be more challenging for adults; perhaps frustrating for youngsters. The goalie stick is always movable, but sometimes a forward's stick is not. One game has a number of forwards, simulated by small vertical lines, that are machine controlled to move slightly up and down. Here, the puck runs an automated obstacle course. Also, a forward might be fixed in position on the opponent's side of the court or might be in the player's court side.

A significant hockey modification for 1978 places the hockey goal on the field with a wall behind it so that it more closely resembles the real game. Here, the puck can rebound off the wall behind the goal.

*Prices are accurate at time of printing; subject to manufacturer's change.*

## Selecting a Ball-and-Paddle Game

BALL-AND-PADDLE games today range from about $14 to $65. In most cases, but not all, you get what you pay for. You should compare features and weigh them against price. This is especially true in some urban areas, where heavy discounting is the rule rather than the exception. As an example of how tricky this can be, Radio Shack, which often offers great value in its products, offers basic ball-and-paddle video games this year that are grossly overpriced.

The least expensive video games generally will provide three to five selectable games, black-and-white display on either a black-and-white TV or color TV, three audio beeps to accent play, on-screen digital scoring and skill positions for beginner or pro. The choice of games might be tennis, hockey, handball and catch. Except for packaging, a particular game among the selections that you like, or remotes instead of console knobs, these games are essentially the same. If the unit is intended only for use by a young child or if price is a major concern, buy the least expensive one in this category from a reliable dealer. The most you should spend in this category is about $20.

The next step up in this class of games adds a photoelectric gun. This type of video game adds two games to the basic game selection group: target shooting and a second version called skeet shooting. This will likely double the cost of the game. Coleco's Telstar Ranger, which has a "Colt 45" pistol, is typical of games in this class. Its suggested retail price is $75, but is discounted in large cities to about $40.

Other ball-and-paddle games feature blazing color (on a color TV set, of course). Prices, however, are only about $6 to $20 higher than those of the latter category, trading off color for a pistol. But you generally gain some additional extras. For example, the Magnavox Odyssey 4000 video game, with a catalog price of $70 and a discounted price as low as $45, offers eight games in color; includes a built-in AC adapter (an adapter usually must be purchased separately in order to use house current); and joystick remote controls that provide vertical, horizontal and diagonal movement of a racket. In addition to the standard games such as tennis and hockey, it has basketball and gridball games. Atari's new Ultra Pong, replacing its former Super Pong, also offers full color plus 16 game variations that include Barrier Hockey and Barrier Pong. The Barrier games issue a variety of field changes with different barriers to give each game a new twist. It is priced at about $43.

## Specialized Non-Paddle Video Games

FROM $50 TO $80 is a new type of entry this year: specialized non-paddle video games. Atari's specialized line is a prime ex-

*Prices are accurate at time of printing; subject to manufacturer's change.*

ample of what is being offered. The company has introduced three different types of "dedicated" circuit games called Tank II, Video Pinball and Stunt Cycle.

Tank II is based on the company's coin-operated Tank game. There are remote joysticks for maneuvering tanks around the screen, a red firing button, tank sound effects, land mines and bunkers. Suggested retail price is about $65. Coleco has a similar dedicated game called Telstar Combat I. Its retail price is $90, although we have seen it discounted to as low as $50. It has a tank-style console and dual tank controls with built-in firing buttons, and realistic booming battle sound effects. Both have on-screen digital scoring.

According to Atari, its Video Pinball is expected to be the most popular of its dedicated games. It offers seven games: four pinball sequencers with flippers, bumpers and targets; two dribbling and shooting basketball games; and a game called Breakout, where the player tries to remove a wall of bricks one at a time so that he can escape. There is a handicap switch for four levels of play difficulty. A large, round knob is the control mechanism, and a rectangular pushbutton is depressed to serve the ball. Price is about $80.

Atari's third dedicated game, Stunt Cycle, is a version of the company's commercial game. Here, a player holds onto simulated motorcycle handlebars and tries to jump over as many buses as possible, starting with eight and working up to 32. Realistic motor noises and crash sounds add to the fun. Three other selectable games are provided. They are based on timed obstacle runs and variations of bus jumping. Stunt Cycle is in color and has a professional/amateur switch. Price is about $75.

**Programmable Video Games**

A NEW BREED of video games is the programmable type. As its name implies, the user can change the game format whenever he wishes by inserting a new computer program into the machine.

The programs are contained in packages that resemble eight-track tape cartridges. When inserted into a slot in a programmable console, the electronics within the cartridge feed a certain program to a built-in microprocessor. Each new cartridge contains a group of new games or other presentations. These programmable machines are not inexpensive and cartridges are typically priced at $20 each.

There are a number of companies in the programmable video game field, but only a handful produce enough machines so that they are available across the country, and sufficient game cartridges to keep owners happy.

Fairchild Camera and Instruments was the first to introduce such a game with its Video Entertainment Center last year. It is built around the manufacturer's own F-8 microprocessor. List price is $170. Like many programmables, it does not seem to be widely discounted. The company's Videocart cartridges cost $20 each.

*Prices are accurate at time of printing; subject to manufacturer's change.*

Games are reproduced in full color on a color TV screen. With more than a score of game cartridges and a year's head start, Fairchild must be considered the leader in this field.

The game's attractive console is connected to television receiver antenna terminals at the back of the set. There are four control keys on the console, plus a reset score key. A game cartridge slot, similar to one on an eight-track tape player, is at the right side.

The console controls include adjustable ball speed, variable game time limits, and a game freeze so that a player or players can take a break and resume action later. There are two games, Tennis and Hockey, built in so the buyer can play immediately without purchasing separate game cartridges.

The two controls are remotes and can be placed anywhere up to eight feet from the game console. Atop each of them is a triangular player control that can be rotated, pushed left and right, pushed in and pulled out. A small engraved guide indicates which side should face the TV set so that right and left movements will be natural for the user. It does take some practice before the user is totally familiar with these controls, but once mastered they are easy to use. They are the most susceptible to damage of any part of the machine, though, because of the abuse they take from players.

Among the many game cartridges available for sale now are the following: Desert Fox, a tank game; Blackjack, a card game; Maze, a cat-and-mouse game where a cat tries to devour a mouse before it can get out of the maze; Math Quiz; Baseball; and Spitfire, a fighter-plane game.

The color displayed on the TV screen ranges from very good to excellent, depending upon the game. The game is set at the factory to play on Channel 3. If Channel 3 is used for regular television broadcasting in your area, be sure to ask your dealer to set it to Channel 4 before you take it home. The Fairchild is powered directly from house current. Simply plug in a large adapter that comes as part of the unit.

RCA followed Fairchild with its STUDIO II Home TV Programmer, at a suggested retail price of $150. The rectangular Studio II console features two digital keyboards (like calculator keyboards) with ten keys each. Many game cartridges are available, priced from $15 to $20. The game's most serious drawback is that it does not display games in color.

Atari, the Pong manufacturer, has not ignored the programmable games area either. Its Video Computer System, with a suggested retail price of about $190, is really the only direct competitor that Fairchild has. It comes complete with a 27-game program cartridge, which is a combat package of Tank Pong, Bi-Plane and Jet Fighter. Its TV display is in color. The main console has a difficulty switch, while players utilize remote controls for the action. Sound effects inspire the participants, and scores are displayed on the screen. The VCS comes with two joysticks and four detachable paddle controls.

*Prices are accurate at time of printing; subject to manufacturer's change.*

The joysticks are easier to get used to than Fairchild's triangular remotes. The main difference between the Atari and the Fairchild game is that Fairchild already has a large library of cartridges and Atari does not. As a major force in this industry, though, Atari is expected to catch up soon. Atari's game philosophy is different from Fairchild's. Atari believes in packing a great number of game variations into a cartridge—Video Olympics has 50 game variations; Space Mission has 17 game variations. Atari's and Fairchild's cartridges are not interchangeable.

Sears' new Video Arcade programmable game at $180 appears to be very similar to Atari's, as do its cartridges. Coleco's "Telstar Arcade" is the final reprogrammable, microprocessor-based video game we recommend at this time. At a price of $130 that includes three color game cartridges, and a discounted price as low as $87, it is an interesting buy. It features a tri-dimensional console with a steering wheel and shift lever for its Road Race game, and a light-activated pistol that sits in a holster on the console for its Quick Draw game. The third side of the console contains the basic main console controls, and the cartridges plug into the top. An AC adapter is included. The machine also includes Tennis, with slam control and fast-serve changes. Many other cartridges are promised. Again, as one of the leaders in the video game industry, we expect Coleco to produce more game cartridges.

The Telstar Arcade is different in that the user steers, shifts and accelerates over an obstacle course in a race against time. The action is accompanied by crash sounds. A pistol can be removed from the console's holster and fired at a moving target. This game is more suited to youngsters than adults. The package is more cheaply made in comparison to the other programmables, but its cost is lower.

Fairchild's game is a slick-looking, cleverly designed unit with many game cartridges on the market right now. Each game cartridge contains a very few games but each is well presented. The cartridges offer a wide choice from combat to gambling to educational uses. Atari and Sears offer similar machines, each directly competitive to Fairchild's. Each cartridge has a great number of games, mostly of the action-sports or combat types. Only a handful of them are on the market right now. Coleco's is less costly, more cheaply packaged, but decidedly more appealing to young children. Very few Coleco cartridges are available at this time.

All the companies mentioned are important factors in the video game business. We recommend that you check out service facilities with your dealer. The electronics parts usually have a long life, but the mechanical parts are exposed to severe user abuse and could need service.

**Non-Video Electronic Games**

THERE ARE MANY non-video electronic games that can provide

*Prices are accurate at time of printing; subject to manufacturer's change.*

considerable fun. Though there is no real substitute for graphic action on a TV screen, the non-video games are quite challenging and almost as costly as the black-and-white video "ball" games. Leading the pack is Parker Brothers' Code Name: Sector. The game is a fine example of an electronics game without video. It uses a microprocessor, just as the programmable video games do. The game is a sort of battleship game with a twist: a microprocessor moves an invisible submarine to one of 4800 possible positions under the sea. Readouts give speed, depth and direction of the sub as players try to blow it up. Interestingly, the sub can fire back if the destroyers are close enough. It sells for about $40.

Mattel Electronics offers three hand-held games that are the size of calculators: Missile Attack, Football and Auto Race. They, too, use microprocessors. In Missile Attack, enemy missiles are launched against the player who must destroy them with his own missiles. If the enemy gets through, that is the end, signified by the machine playing "Taps." It is great fun for under $25.

Milton Bradley markets an electronic battleship game that is also controlled by computer circuitry. It is a board-type game with a hide-and-seek battle on the high seas. Sounds simulate live action. We have seen it priced at $25.

For those who take their fun more seriously, there are a host of electronic games on the market that allow users to match wits with a computer. The most successfully marketed one—and therefore the one that you are most likely to be able to buy—is Fidelity Electronics' Chess Challenger. Users play against a computer according to the rules of chess. An average chess player will beat the computer 25 percent to 70 percent of the time, according to the manufacturer. The self-contained unit has a chess board, electronic controls and readouts to display the new position that the player has chosen. A lamp lights up when the player is in check, and another lamp lights when the computer is checkmated. There is a 12-button keyboard for entering moves. It sells for about $180 to $200.

Even the calculator people have moved into the game area. Both Texas Instruments and Hewlett-Packard have many games that can be played on the programmable calculators they produce. TI uses plug-in modules for games like Mars Lander, Golf Handicapper, Bridge and Chess Rankings. H-P has a game pack with prerecorded magnetic cards for use with its HP-67 and HP-97 calculators. Games include Slot Machine, Submarine Hunt, Golf, Racetrack, and others.

*Prices are accurate at time of printing; subject to manufacturer's change.*

# Index

Air conditioners 348, 361
    best buys 354
    energy considerations 351
    features 353
    general information 348
    worksheet 348
American Motors (see, Autos)
Amplifiers,
    best buys 171
    general information 158
Appliances (see, individual appliances)
Autos,
    accessories price lists 25
    best buys,
        compact 22
        intermediate 23
        luxury 24
        medium standard 23
        personal luxury 24
        sports car, American 22, imported 22
        standard 23
        subcompact 21
    manufacturers review 9
    models,
        Accord (Honda) 19, 21
        AMX (American Motors) 9
        Arrow/Sapporo (Plymouth) 18
        Aspen (Dodge) 10
        Audi 5000 (Audi) 18
        Audi Fox (Audi) 18
        BMW 733i (BMW) 18
        Bobcat (Mercury) 13
        Bonneville (Pontiac) 17, 23
        BRAT (Subaru) 20
        Brougham (Cadillac) 15
        Camaro (Chevrolet) 15, 22
        Capri II (Ford) 18
        Caprice (Chevrolet) 15, 23
        Catalina (Pontiac) 17
        Celica (Toyota) 20
        Century (Buick) 14, 23
        Charger (Dodge) 10
        Chevette (Chevrolet) 15
        Civic (Honda) 19
        Colt (Dodge) 19
        Concord (American Motors) 9
        Continental (Lincoln) 12
        Continental Mark V (Lincoln) 13, 24
        Cordoba (Chrysler) 9, 24
        Corvette (Chevrolet) 15, 22
        Cougar (Mercury) 13
        Cutlass (Oldsmobile) 16, 23, 24
        Dasher (Volkswagen) 20
        Datsun 510 19
        Delta (Oldsmobile) 17, 23
        DeVille (Cadillac) 15
        Diplomat (Dodge) 10
        Eldorado (Cadillac) 15
        Electra (Buick) 14
        Fairmont (Ford) 11, 22
        Fiesta (Ford) 19, 22
        Firebird (Pontiac) 17, 22
        Fleetwood (Cadillac) 24
        GLC (Mazda) 19
        Granada (Ford) 11
        Grand Prix (Pontiac) 17, 24
        Gremlin (American Motors) 9
        Horizon (Plymouth) 11, 21
        Impala (Chevrolet) 15
        Jaguar (British Leyland) 18
        LeBaron (Chrysler) 10
        LeCar (Renault) 20
        LeMans (Pontiac) 18, 23
        LeSabre (Buick) 14, 23
        LTD (Ford) 12
        Magnum (Dodge) 10
        Malibu (Chevrolet) 16, 23
        Marquis (Mercury) 13
        Matador (American Motors) 9
        Mercedes-Benz 300D (Mercedes-Benz) 24
        MG (British Leyland) 18
        Monaco (Dodge) 10
        Monarch (Mercury) 13
        Monte Carlo (Chevrolet) 16, 24
        Monza (Chevrolet) 16
        Mustang II (Ford) 12
        Newport (Chrysler) 10
        New Yorker (Chrysler) 10
        Nova (Chevrolet) 16, 22

Oldsmobile 98
   (Oldsmobile) 23
Omega (Oldsmobile) 17
Omni (Dodge) 11, 21
Opel (British Leyland) 19
Pacer (American Motors) 9
Peugeot 604 (Peugeot) 19
Phoenix (Pontiac) 18
Pinto (Ford) 12
Rabbit (Volkswagen) 20, 21
Regal (Buick) 14, 24
Riviera (Buick) 14
Scirocco (Volkswagen) 20, 22
Saab 99 EMS (Saab) 20
Saab 99 GLE (Saab) 20
Sapporo (Plymouth) 18
Seville (Cadillac) 15
Skyhawk (Buick) 14
Skylark (Buick) 14
Spider Veloce (Alfa Romeo) 18
Starfire (Oldsmobile) 17
Sunbird (Pontiac) 18
Thunderbird (Ford) 12, 24
Toronado (Oldsmobile) 17, 24
Triumph (British Leyland) 18
Versailles (Lincoln) 13
Volare (Plymouth) 11, 22
Volvo 242 GT (Volvo) 20
Zephyr (Mercury) 13
price lists 25
tape decks 184

Bag sealers,
   best buys 211
   general information 201
Blenders,
   best buys 212
   general information 202
   price lists 224
Blow dryers (see, Hair dryers)
Brooms, electric (see, Vacuum cleaners)
Buick (see, Autos)
Burger makers,
   best buys 213
   general information 202

Cadillac (see, Autos)
Cameras (see also, Photo equipment),
   cartridge,
      best buys 403
   compact 35mm,
      best buys 403
   instant-picture,
      best buys 404
   movie,
      best buys 406
   single-lens reflex,
      best buys 401
Can openers,
   best buys 214
   general information 203
   price lists 224
Cartridges, record
   best buys 174
   general information 160
Cassettes, tape (see, Tape recorders)
CB radios 193-199,
   general information 193
   test reports 195
Chevrolet (see, Autos)
Chrysler (see, Autos)
Clothes dryers (see, Dryers)
Clothes washers (see, Washers)
Coffee makers,
   automatic drip,
      best buys 214
      price lists 224
   percolators,
      best buys 215
      price lists 224
Crepe makers,
   best buys 215
   price lists 224
Crock pots (see, Slow cookers)
Curlers,
   curling irons,
      best buys 375
   electric rollers,
      best buys 376
Darkroom equipment (see, Photo equipment)
Dishwashers 308-315
   best buys,
      built-in 312
      convertible 313
      portable 315
   energy considerations 308
   features 310
   general information 308
Dodge, (see, Autos)
Dryers 288-307
   best buys,
      compact 301
      full-sized 299
   energy considerations 289
   features 291
   general information 288
   price lists 303
Electric brooms (see, Vacuum cleaners)
Electric knives (see, Knives, electric)
Electric rollers (see, Curlers)
Electric shavers (see, Shaving equipment)
Electronic flash units (see, Photo equipment)

Electronic games (see, Games)
Energy considerations (see, individual product listings)
Enlargers (see, Photo equipment)
Floor care appliances (see also, individual appliances) 235-255
    best buys 239
    general information 235
    price lists 252
Food preparation appliances (see also, individual appliances) 200-234
Food processors,
    best buys 217
    general information 205
    price lists 224
Ford (see, Autos)
Freezers 277-287
    best buys,
        chests 281
        uprights 282
    energy considerations 278
    features 279
    general information 277
    price lists 285
Fryers,
    fry pans,
        best buys 217
    small deep fryers,
        best buys 218
Games, electronic,
    general information 412
    video 113, 407
Garbage disposers (see also, Trash compactors) 316-321
    best buys,
        batch-feed 319
        continuous-feed 320
    features 317
    general information 316
Hair Dryers,
    blow dryers,
        best buys 377
    comb-brush,
        best buys 382
Hamburger makers (see, Burger makers)
Headphones,
    best buys 176
    general information 162
Hi-fi components (see also, individual components) 154-178
    add-ons 156
    best buys 171
    best buy systems,
        budget 167
        mid-priced 167
        high-priced 168
        super "dream" 169
Hot lather dispensers (see, Shaving equipment)
Irons,
    best buys 385
Knives, electric
    best buys 216
Lather dispensers (see, Shaving equipment)
Lincoln (see, Autos)

Mercury (see, Autos)
Mixers,
    multipurpose,
        best buys 220
    portable,
        best buys 219
    stand,
        best buys 220
Microwave ovens (see also, Ovens) 339-347
    advantages of 340
    best buys 346
    disadvantages of 340
    energy considerations 340
    features 342
    general information 339
    principles of 339
    safety 341
Movie,
    cameras 400, 406
    projectors 396
Oldsmobile (see, Autos)
Ovens (see also, Microwave ovens),
    broilers,
        best buys 221
        general information 209
        price lists 224
    other countertop,
        best buys 222
        general information 209
        price lists 224
Personal care appliances (see also, individual appliances) 369-395
Photo equipment 396-406
    best buys 401
    cameras (see, Cameras)
    darkroom equipment 399, 404
    enlargers 399, 404
    flash units 399
    general information 396
    projectors 396
Plymouth (see, Autos)
Pontiac (see, Autos)
Projectors (see, Photo equipment)
Radios (see, CB radios)
Ranges (see also, Microwave ovens and Ovens) 326-338
    best buys,
        electric, built-in 337, combination 334, drop-in 337, free-standing 331, over-and-under 334, slide-in 338, smoothtop 335
        gas, built-in 337, combination 335, drop-in 338, free-standing 332, over-and-under 334, slide-in 338, smoothtop 335
    energy considerations 327
    features 329

general information 326
Receivers,
   best buys 172
   general information 157
Record players (see, Hi-fi components and Tape recorders)
Refrigerators 256-270
   best buys 264
   energy considerations 256
   features 261
   general information 256
   price lists 271
   types 259
Rollers, electric (see, Curlers)
Shaving equipment,
   electric shavers,
      best buys 387
   hot lather dispensers
      best buys 385
Slow cookers,
   best buys 222
   general information 209
   price lists 224
Smoke detectors 362-368
   best buys,
      ionization 367
      photoelectric 368
   general information 362
   placement 365
   power source 364
   principles of 362
   radiation 363
Speakers,
   best buys 177
   general information 160
Styler-dryers (see, Hair dryers)
Tape recorders 179-192
   best buys,
      cassettes 189
      open-reel 187
   general information 179
   tape decks,
      automobile 184
      care 185
      performance 182
      specifications 180
Televisions (see also, Video games) 109-153
   best buys,
      black-and-white portables 139
      color consoles 136
      color portables,
         large-screen 132,
         small-screen 129
   built-in games 113
   channel selection 111
   color tuning 110
   console vs. portable 116
   features, optional 117,
      recommended 114
   general information 109
   how to shop 120
   manufacturers review 121
   picture tubes 112, 115
   price lists 141
   pricing 118

Toasters,
   best buys 223
   general information 210
Trash compactors (see also, Garbage disposers) 322-325
   best buys,
      built-in 324
      convertible 324
      free-standing 325
   features 323
Tuners,
   best buys 171
   general information 158
Turntables,
   best buys,
      multiple-play 173
      single-play 174
   general information 159
Video games (see also, Televisions) 407-413
   ball-and-paddle 407
   built-in 113
   non-paddle 409
   programmed 410
Vacuum cleaners,
   brooms and portables,
      best buys 249
      general information 237
      price lists 252
      test reports 249
   canisters,
      best buys 241
      general information 236
      price lists 252
      test reports 242
   combinations,
      best buys 244
      general information 237
      price lists 252
      test reports 244
   heavy-duty,
      best buys 247
      general information 238
      price lists 252
      test reports 247
   uprights,
      best buys 239
      general information 236
      price lists 252
      test reports 240
   rating systems 236
Waffle bakers,
   best buys 223
   general information 210
   price lists 224
Washers 288-307
   best buys,
      compact 298
      full-sized 296
   energy considerations 389
   features 291
   general information 288
   price lists 303